Collins
ECONOMICS for CAPE

Dave Ramsingh

Collins

HarperCollins Publishers
1 London Bridge Street
London SE1 9GF

HarperCollins*Publishers*,
Macken House, 39/40 Mayor Street Upper,
Dublin 1, D01 C9W8 Ireland

First edition 2015

10 9 8 7 6 5

© HarperCollins *Publishers* Limited 2015

ISBN 978-0-00-811589-0

Collins ® is a registered trademark of HarperCollins Publishers Limited

www.collins.co.uk/caribbeanschools

A catalogue record for this book is available from the British Library

Typeset by QBS

Printed and bound in Great Britain by
Ashford Colour Ltd

All rights reserved. No part of this book may be reproduced, stored in a retrieval system, or transmitted in any form or by any means, electronic, mechanical, photocopying, recording or otherwise, without the prior permission in writing of the Publisher. This book is sold subject to the conditions that it shall not, by way of trade or otherwise, be lent, re-sold, hired out or otherwise circulated without the Publisher's prior consent in any form of binding or cover other than that in which it is published and without a similar condition including this condition being imposed on the subsequent purchaser.

Without limiting the exclusive rights of any author, contributor or the publisher of this publication, any unauthorised use of this publication to train generative artificial intelligence (AI) technologies is expressly prohibited. HarperCollins also exercise their rights under Article 4(3) of the Digital Single Market Directive 2019/790 and expressly reserve this publication from the text and data mining exception.

If any copyright holders have been omitted, please contact the Publisher who will make the necessary arrangements at the first opportunity.

Author: Dave Ramsingh
Illustrators: QBS
Publisher: Elaine Higgleton
Commissioning Editor: Tom Hardy
Project Manager: Sarah Dev-Sherman for QBS
Managing Editor: Sarah Thomas
Editor: Stephen York
Copy Editor: Sylvia Worth
Proofreader: Carol Osborne

This book contains FSC™ certified paper and other controlled sources to ensure responsible forest management.

For more information visit: www.harpercollins.co.uk/green

PHOTO CREDITS

The publisher would like to thank the following for their kind permission to reproduce their photographs:

Page 5, Andre Jenny/Alamy; Page 11, Darren Newbery/Alamy; Page 17, Cyril Hou/Shutterstock; Page 22, Greg Johnston/Danita Delimont/Alamy; Page 36, Mardis Coers/Contributor/Getty Images; Page 45, THEGIFT777/iStock; Page 51, ImageBROKER/Alamy; Page 58, Robert Fried/Alamy; Page 66, Blend Images/Jetta Productions/Alamy; Page 75, Charles Bowman/Alamy; Page 79, Bloomberg/Contributor/Getty Images; Page 92, Rj Lerich/Shutterstock; Page 100, RubberBall/Alamy; Pages 109, 142, 168, Art Directors & Trip/Alamy; Pages 118, 181, Robert Harding Picture Library Ltd/Alamy; Page 125, Chuck Savage/Corbis; Page 134, Denguy/Getty Images; Page 147, Stuwdamdorp/Alamy; Page 153, Bob Krist/Corbis; Page 156, Glowimages/Getty Images; Page 163, Atomazul/Shutterstock; Page 174, Hurst Photo/Shutterstock; Page 188, Ashley Allen/CON/Contributor/Getty Images; Page 198, Helene Rogers/Art Directors & TRIP/Alamy; Page 206, Andrea De Silva/Reuters; Page 212, Oleg_Mit/Shutterstock; Page 220, Image Source Plus/Alamy; Page 226, Angela Waye/Shutterstock; Page 236, Altrendo images/Getty Images; Page 251, Geography Photos/Contributor/Getty Images; Page 260, R. Gino Santa Maria/Shutterstock; Page 268, Dburke/Alamy; Page 273, Assalve/iStock; Page 279, Rolf Richardson/Robert Harding World Imagery/

Contents

Chapter 1	The economic problem	5
Chapter 2	Economic systems	11
Chapter 3	Tools of economic analysis	17
Chapter 4	Theory of demand	22
Chapter 5	Elasticity of demand	36
Chapter 6	How to produce: theory of supply I	45
Chapter 7	How to produce: theory of supply II	51
Chapter 8	Market equilibrium	58
Chapter 9	The cost of production	66
Chapter 10	Market structures	75
Chapter 11	Price, revenue and profit concepts	79
Chapter 12	Monopoly and monopolistic competition	92
Chapter 13	Oligopoly and contestable markets	100
Chapter 14	Market failure	109
Chapter 15	Role of government and market failures	118
Chapter 16	Theory of income distribution	125
Chapter 17	The interaction of labour markets and unions	134
Chapter 18	Interest, profit and rent	142
Chapter 19	The distribution of income	147
Chapter 20	Macroeconomics	153
Chapter 21	National income: the circular flow of income	156
Chapter 22	National income: determination	163
Chapter 23	Consumption and savings	168
Chapter 24	Investment	174
Chapter 25	National income equilibrium: Keynesian cross model	181
Chapter 26	Fiscal policy	188
Chapter 27	Money and banking	198
Chapter 28	Monetary policy	206
Chapter 29	Inflation	212

Chapter 30	Unemployment	220
Chapter 31	The main classical and Keynesian economic ideas	226
Chapter 32	International trade	236
Chapter 33	Exchange rates	251
Chapter 34	Balance of payments	260
Chapter 35	Foreign direct investment	268
Chapter 36	Economic growth	273
Chapter 37	Economic development	279
Chapter 38	Globalisation	284
Chapter 39	International financial institutions	287
Chapter 40	Guidelines for internal assessment project	292
Glossary		297
Index		300

Download your eBook at www.collins.co.uk/internationalresources

The economic problem

INTRODUCTORY ECONOMICS A TEXTBOOK FOR CAPE ECONOMICS STUDENTS

LEARNING OBJECTIVES

- Define scarcity.
- Identify three main choices: what, how and for whom to produce.
- Explain opportunity cost.
- Explain the production possibility frontier and diminishing, increasing and constant returns.
- Explain Pareto optimality.

REQUIRED KNOWLEDGE

- Introductory knowledge of scarcity
- Opportunity costs
- Economic systems
- Free and economic goods

TOPIC VALUE

Scarcity is the world's most pressing problem, especially for poorer nations.

Introduction

The subject 'economics' derives its name from the Greek word 'Oikonomia', which means household management. In effect, that is, deriving the best value and benefit from the limited resources of the household as it seeks to satisfy the wants and needs of its members.

To economise is simply the prudent use of resources. The word 'economy' refers to a system in which domestic producers, consumers and the government interact, each in their own interest. This is called a closed economy. A four-sector or open economy includes the government, domestic producers, consumers and the foreign sector.

Economics is usually explained as the study of how human wants are satisfied with resources that are not only scarce, but which can also be used in alternative ways.

An **economic problem** exists when society's unlimited wants and needs cannot be satisfied by the world's limited resources. There are several economic problems in society, such as poverty, unemployment and squatter settlements, to name a few. These all result from a problem of scarcity.

Scarcity in this sense does not mean something 'rare' but rather the inability to satisfy human wants. Table 1.1 below summarises the scarcity problem.

Table 1.1 The scarcity problem

Limited resources	Unlimited wants	Economic problem
Houses	Housing	Homelessness, squatting
Classroom, facilities, teachers	Education	Lack of skills, illiteracy
Arable land	Food	Labour, poverty, malnutrition

Limited resources refer to the means of production that are used to create goods and services. These resources are also called factor inputs or factors of production and consist of land, labour, capital and enterprise. These resources will be discussed in greater detail in a later chapter but, briefly, they are explained as:

> **Land:** anything above or below the ground that is provided by nature, e.g., air, sunshine, fish, minerals, trees, water; also called natural resources.
> **Labour:** human mental or physical effort of any kind, e.g., skilled, unskilled or a professional type of skilled labour such as a brain surgeon.
> **Capital:** producer goods that enable future production; this is also called manufactured resources, e.g., machines.
> **Enterprise:** This is also considered a human resource because it organises and coordinates the other factor inputs to produce goods and services.

Citizens living in very developed countries like the USA or Europe enjoy more than the basic comforts of life, yet they desire more luxuries.

Since scarcity is the inability to satisfy human wants, developed countries suffer from the scarcity problem just as developing countries do.

Key points

Scarce resources such as land, labour, capital and enterprise combine to produce goods and services to satisfy society's needs and wants. Scarcity exists in developing as well as developed countries.

When resources are limited in supply and wants and needs are unlimited, it is necessary to use limited resources prudently. A society cannot have everything all at once; choices therefore have to be made. The three most basic choices all societies must make are:

1. **What to produce?** The question relates to what goods and services are to be produced and in what combination. Should a society produce more consumer goods such as, for example, cell phones, cars, food, clothes, or capital goods such as factories and machines? What is clear is that producing more of one type of good means less of the other due to limited resources. What to produce then may simply be referred to as the *product combination* that a society chooses.

2. **How to produce?** The choice to be made in this case is the combination of factors of production that should be used. Should sugar cane production in Barbados use more labour than capital or vice versa? Less labour would mean releasing human labour and replacing it with machines, for example reaping sugar cane with a mechanical harvester. A mechanical harvester would do a more efficient job because producers would aim to get the greatest output (sugar) from the smallest input (harvester), so it becomes a choice of the factor combination that achieves the lowest cost of production.

3. **For whom to produce?** This question concerns the manner in which the goods and services produced are distributed. This is so since a limited quantity becomes available to individuals who may desire more than the quantity offered to them. Think of tickets for a limited overs cricket match or tickets for the World Cup. Lines are formed to distribute the available quantity because the capacity at the stadium is fixed.

Various means have also been used to distribute goods and services such as:

> Lotteries
> Rationing (especially during a shortage)
> Food stamps
> A system of merit or need
> A price system
> Queues.

The price system, however, works well for high-income earners, whose money may command a bigger claim to scarce goods and services than low-income earners. The 'for whom' issue, therefore, is considered very important, since it is people who own wealth that command the majority share of output. The reason for this is attributed to an unequal distribution of income.

Key point
The three basic choices all societies must make are what, how and for whom to produce, with the limited resources that are available at any given point in time. The 'for whom' question is important because it is linked to poverty and the standard of living.

Opportunity cost
Making a choice implies a sacrifice. For example, if you go to a cafeteria with limited pocket money you may choose one item and give up purchasing the others. You cannot choose everything you see because your money is limited.

The choice of a soft drink may mean giving up a chocolate bar. The sacrifice of giving up the chocolate bar is referred to as the opportunity cost of purchasing a soft drink. The real or opportunity cost of purchasing the soft drink is different from the money cost of the soft drink. Opportunity cost may therefore be defined as the sacrifice of the next best choice whenever economic decisions are made.

Common error
Be careful to distinguish between choice numbers 1 and 2, 3, 4, 5 or 6. The opportunity cost of choosing number 1 is choice number 2 given up, not the third, fourth, fifth or the sixth choice on sale in the cafeteria. There are other costs which will be explored in subsequent chapters.

Other examples of opportunity cost are given in table 1.2:

Table 1.2 Opportunity cost

Decision	Choice	Opportunity cost
Firm	Purchasing vehicles	Investing the money in the bank
Government	Building three schools	Building access roads for farmers
Community	Building a community centre	Buying a cricket ground
Family	Sending a student to university	Renovating the roof

A very simple explanation of opportunity cost is illustrated by a diagram called the production possibility frontier (PPF), also sometimes called a production possibility curve, production transformation curve or production possibility boundary.

A production possibility curve shows the different combinations of two types of goods that a country's resources can produce when all of the resources are fully employed. Be mindful that many goods are produced in a country but, to illustrate the point, only two are chosen to explain the concept of opportunity cost. Choosing only two goods therefore is a limiting assumption. Other assumptions that are made when drawing the production possibility curve are:

> **Technology is fixed.**
> **No foreign trade exists.**
> **Output is measured on a yearly basis.**
> **The level of resources is fixed.**
> **Output is measured in units.**
> **Resources are perfectly mobile.**

A production possibility curve can be plotted from table 1.3, showing different combinations of bananas and oil production in a Caribbean territory.

Table 1.3 Production possibility and opportunity cost

Combination	Bananas (000 kg)	Oil barrels (000 bpd)
A	8	0
B	7	3
C	6	5
D	5	6.3
E	4	7
F	3	7.5
G	2	8
H	1	8.5
I	0	9

If the data in table 1.3 is plotted on a graph, it would look like the production possibility curve shown in figure 1.1.

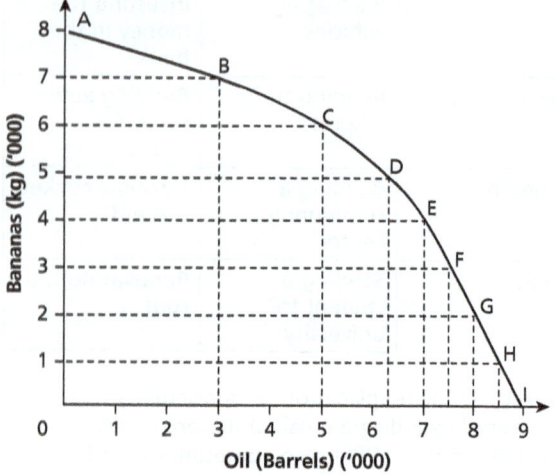

Figure 1.1 Combinations of a production possibility curve showing increasing opportunity cost

Observations
If only bananas are produced and no resources allocated to oil production, then 8,000 kg of bananas will be produced and zero barrels of oil. Similarly, if only oil is produced then 9,000 barrels per day (bpd) would be produced and 0 kg of bananas. Society, however, needs both goods; therefore, moving from combination A to B requires a shift of factor inputs from banana production to oil. When this happens, 1,000 kg of bananas are given up to produce 3,000 barrels of oil at a ratio of 1 kg of bananas to three barrels of oil. The gradient or slope of the curve at that point therefore is a loss of one to gain three. We conclude that the opportunity cost of choosing combination B over A is 1,000 kg of bananas. Note: because the curve is not a straight line it has a different slope at different points.

Key point
Choosing a different combination of two goods incurs an opportunity cost, which expresses what is sacrificed in order to produce another good.

Reason for the concave shape of the PPF
The PPF owes its 'bowed out' or concave shape to the law of increasing costs. Refer again to table 1.3 and figure 1.1.

Careful reading would reveal that moving from combination A to B sacrifices the resources producing 1,000 kg of bananas to achieve 3,000 barrels of oil. Moving down the PPF to combination C, D, E and F, the same 1,000 kg of bananas given up yield 2,000 barrels of oil for combination C but not for combination D, E and F. From combination B to C yields 2,000 bpd, C to D yields 1,300 and only 500 barrels of oil for combinations E to F.

This may be explained by the fact that the resources are more suited to banana production than oil production and adding these extra resources to oil production eventually leads to overcrowding of fixed oil resources, causing the rate of production to decrease. This is due to an important law in economics called the law of diminishing returns or the law of increasing costs.

Reason for the convex shape of the PPF
Table 1.4 and figure 1.2 illustrate a different PPF with a 'bowed in' or convex shape. On this occasion, moving down the curve from different combinations between A to F results in sacrificing resources producing 20 kg of bananas and applying these resources to achieve more and more barrels of oil.

Table 1.4 Combinations of a PPF decreasing opportunity cost

Combination	Bananas (000 kg)	Oil (000 bpd)
A	80	0
B	60	10
C	40	25
D	20	50
E	0	100

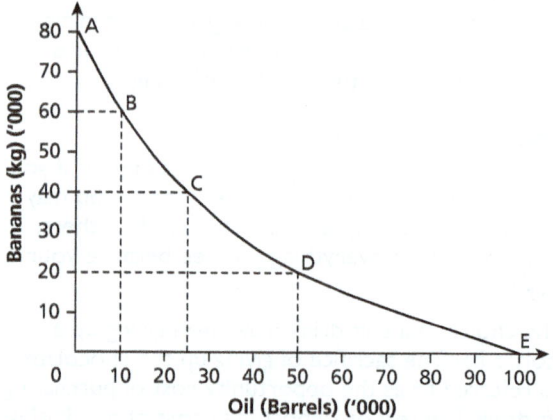

Figure 1.2 Combinations of a PPF showing decreasing opportunity cost

Moving from combination A to B on figure 1.2, 20 kg of bananas are given up to allow resources to transfer to oil where the gain in oil is 10 barrels.

Moving from point B to point C, 20 kg of bananas given up yield 15 barrels of oil. Note again that from combination C to D the gain in oil is 25 barrels and D to E, 50 barrels. In this case, the resources taken from bananas and redirected to oil is better suited to oil production than bananas. This is the law of decreasing opportunity cost in action. It is also called the law of increasing returns in production.

Summary
When the PPF is convex to the origin, moving down the curve from left to right results in **increasing returns or decreasing opportunity costs**.

The linear PPF
A close examination of the linear PPF in figure 1.3 shows that moving from combinations A through to F indicates a one-to-one ratio, that is, 1,000 kg of corn given up would yield 1,000 kg of peas. The conclusion to be drawn in this instance is that resources are equally productive when they are allocated to either good. We refer to this phenomenon as the **law of constant opportunity costs**.

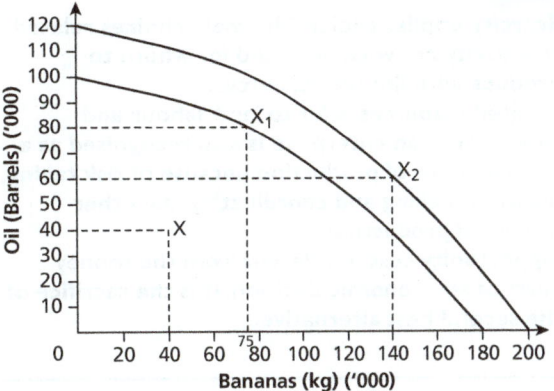

Figure 1.4 Combinations showing points within and outside the PPF

Summary
Points within the PPF denote underemployed resources or inefficiency in production, while points on the curve denote efficiency. Points beyond the PPF are unattainable in the present but may be attainable in the future, if productivity increases and other newly discovered resources shift the curve outward, as X_2.

Pareto optimality

Pareto optimality is achieved when goods and services are produced in the quantities desired by society (allocative efficiency) and at the lowest cost (productive efficiency). When this is achieved it is impossible to allocate resources in an economic system, improving the position of some without reducing the position of others.

If resources are employed and everyone benefits and no one loses, this is called a Pareto Improvement. Pareto efficiency is then said to be achieved when it is impossible to improve someone's position without reducing the position of others.

Pareto optimality then has to do with the allocation of all resources related to production, distribution and consumption. Pareto optimality exists on all points on the production possibility curve. This concept is analysed in greater detail in chapter 14.

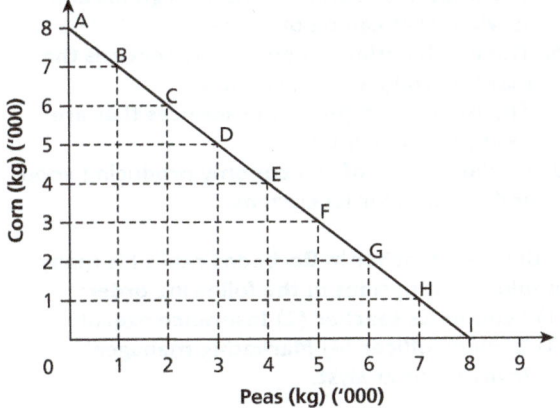

Figure 1.3 Combinations of the linear PPF showing constant opportunity cost

This curve is typical of production of similar goods, for example, corn and peas production.

Key point
A linear production possibility frontier illustrates an equal ratio of exchange when resources are shifted from the production of one good to the other.

Points within and outside the PPF
A combination of bananas and oil represented in figure 1.4 by point X, that is, 40,000 bananas and 40,000 bpd of oil means that resources are inefficiently employed or that there are unemployed resources yielding less output of both goods. Moving to point X_1 (75,000 bananas and 80 bpd of oil) and using idle resources yields more of both goods. This point illustrates efficiency in production.

Over a 10–20-year period, new technology, inventions resulting from research and development, innovation and investment that increase capacity, may shift the curve outward resulting in production of more of both goods as illustrated in point X_2. This is also referred to as long-term economic growth.

Chapter summary

> Economics is the study of how man satisfies his unlimited wants with his limited resources that have alternative uses.
> All economic problems such as unemployment, poverty, pollution, price level increases (inflation), foreign exchange shortages, food, housing, schooling, transport shortages are linked to the problem of scarcity.

- Scarcity implies choice. The main choices related to scarcity are what, how and for whom to produce with limited resources.
- Limited resources refer to land, labour and capital. Human enterprise is also recognised as a crucial factor of production because of risk taking, decision making and coordinating the other factors of production.
- Opportunity cost is different from the money costs of an economic decision. It is the sacrifice of the second best alternative.

Practice questions

1. A worker in a Jamaican factory is currently earning J$300.00 for a 30-hour working week. He is offered a 10 per cent wage increase or a basic wage of J$310.00 and reduced working hours of 28 hours. What is the opportunity cost if the worker chooses 28 hours of work?
   a. 2 hours
   b. 28 hours
   c. J$10.00
   d. J$20.00

2. Which of the following best defines the concept of 'scarcity'?
   a. Goods and services to consumers are in short supply.
   b. There are not enough resources available at present.
   c. The excess of human wants over the economy's resources.
   d. The wants of society are greater than the supply of goods.

3. A potter can make any combination of items using the following options below.

Cups	Saucers
94	13
70	16

   What is the opportunity cost of making one saucer?
   a. 1 cup
   b. 5 cups
   c. 7 cups
   d. 8 cups

4. Which of the following statements BEST defines a 'production possibility frontier'?
   a. The limit of the combinations of goods and services that can be produced
   b. The combinations of goods and services that may be produced in a country
   c. The mixture of goods and services that are desired by a country
   d. An illustration of an economy producing goods and services for its citizens.

5. A Business teacher in Barbados ranks his many employment options in the following order:
   (1) Economics teacher (2) Insurance executive, (3) Banking officer (4) Marketing manager (5) Investment analyst.

   What is the opportunity cost of choosing to be an Economics teacher?
   a. Investment analyst
   b. Marketing manager
   c. Bank officer
   d. Insurance executive.

2 Economic systems

LEARNING OBJECTIVES

- Describe the three main economic systems.
- Explain the what, how, for whom issues.
- Distinguish between the different systems.
- Identify the advantages and disadvantages of each system.

REQUIRED KNOWLEDGE

- Basic knowledge of economic systems.

TOPIC VALUE

What is the most efficient economic system? After analysing all systems in existence you should be able to answer this question.

Introduction

An economic system is one that is designed to solve the economic problem, that is, a solution to the choice of product combination (what to produce), factor input combination (how to produce) and the best way to distribute the resulting output (for whom to produce). The choice of any such system is determined by political factors. An economic system must make decisions with respect to:

› **Ownership of resources:** should there be private or public ownership of resources, e.g., land and raw materials.
› **Profit:** should private individuals earn and keep profit they earn or should the state collect profit for redistribution to the population?
› **Role of government:** how much government economic activity should exist?
› **Freedom to choose:** can producers sell to consumers freely, giving them freedom to choose how much they want, or is a quota, queuing up, or a merit/need system needed to share out goods and services?

Key point

Economic systems attempt to put mechanisms in place to solve the economic problem of what, how and for whom to produce and also to clearly identify the roles that the government and private enterprise will play. Systems are chosen by political arrangements, and are considered very important, since it is people who own wealth that command the majority share of output. The reason for this is attributed to an unequal distribution of income.

Economic system: success or failure?

How successfully an economic system operates may be an open debate but solving the economic problem will depend on choices to be made. Three basic choices that are common in any economy are:

› **What to produce:** necessities or luxuries?
› **How to produce:** more or less capital or labour?
› **For whom to produce:** how is output to be distributed?

These three choices are managed differently according to the economic system that a country chooses. There are four economic systems (see below) that try to achieve these three choices. Economic systems attempt to address the following issues:

› **Freedom for all participants in the chosen system with respect to choice**
› **The degree of competition and control of monopoly elements**
› **How much power is given to consumers or producers**
› **The quality, availability and affordability of goods and services**
› **Protection for consumers and producers**
› **The employment of all citizens**
› **The rate of growth of the economy**
› **Control of price level increases**
› **The general standard of living of the citizens**
› **Self-sufficiency and economic independence**
› **Preservation of the environment**
› **Quality and quantity of public and merit goods.**

These are only a few of the criteria by which an economic system is judged.

Key point

Economic systems are evaluated according to, for example, the degree of success in distributing income evenly, the standard of living of the citizens, the full employment of resources, slow and sustained growth of the economy, a stable price level and other basic criteria related to preservation of the environment.

Subsistence economy

Economic systems have evolved throughout human history. Primitive man relied on a subsistence economy, in which man provided for his own needs; this was known as direct, subsistence or traditional production. When specialisation developed, barter became the accepted practice of satisfying wants, known as 'indirect production'.

The failure of barter to satisfy wants stemmed from the problems of double coincidence of wants, rate of exchange disagreements, indivisibility and store of value. All of these problems were eventually overcome with the introduction of money.

While these above types of economic systems are still in existence in isolated parts in the world, the more recognised economic systems are:

› **Free market, capitalist, laissez-faire or unplanned economy**
› **Command, planned or collectivist economy**
› **Mixed economy.**

Free market system/market economy

Perhaps the simplest way to describe this system is 'free' from government ownership. A free market system has the following features:

- **A limited role for the government, which may provide law, order and ensure equity**
- **Households and firms make decisions based on self-interest, which means profit for the producers and satisfaction for the consumer**
- **Privately owned resources**
- **Allocation of resources and distribution of output achieved through the price mechanism, and determined by the forces of demand and supply**
- **Complete freedom of choice for producers and consumers with respect to production and consumption**
- **Consumer sovereignty, indicating that consumers rule since they possess the ability to use money to 'vote' for products that act as a signal to producers. No example of a pure market economy exists today, but the USA and Hong Kong have been cited as economies that closely resemble this model.**

While the market system is positive in many ways, it is not a perfect system and negative consequences may result. The negative consequences are regarded as market failures. See table 2.1.

Market economy evaluated

Table 2.1 Positive and negative aspects of a market economy

Positive	Negative
Freedom of choice for producers and distribution to consumers	Income and wealth in this system are not evenly distributed, creating few rich and many poor
Consumer sovereignty	Those who own the input factors earn more income than non-owners
Profit-driven enterprises encourage lower costs and keep prices low, which keeps the rate of inflation low.	High income earners dictate choice of goods and services produced through their buying power.
Competition promotes high quality and efficiency, and weak firms are eliminated from an industry.	Monopolies/sole producers can exist. They develop and may lead to objectives not in accord with general welfare, e.g., raising prices.
Resources are allocated to where there is high demand and where the rewards are accordingly high.	Public goods are not provided because no profit is possible when a good is collectively consumed and it is also impossible to exclude non-payers.
Profits are a source of finance for research and development, invention, innovation or product improvement.	Prices may be too high (shortages) or low (bumper crop) affecting consumers and producers.
Dynamic efficiency is a long-term concept associated with economic growth caused by inventions and innovation. Dynamic efficiency is efficiency in the long-term period, e.g., 50 years.	Fluctuation in economic activity leads to buoyant or contracting economies.
Unregulated market forces of demand and supply set prices when they are in equilibrium.	Rising prices result in inflation lowering purchasing power. Unemployment normally results from a contraction of an economy.
	Pollution (negative externality), environmental degradation and exhausting of non-renewable resources harm sustainable development.
	Over-consumption of demerit goods (e.g., alcohol) and under-consumption of merit goods (e.g., education and health) can happen in some economies.

Key points

A free market economy emphasises freedom from government ownership and promotes freedom for producers and consumers to choose. It also promotes self-interest, competition and private ownership, all of which allow the system to be self-regulating. It has other positive elements such as consumer sovereignty and efficiency in consumption and production.

Some weaknesses in this system are pollution control, a large gap between rich and poor, unemployment arising from a recession when markets fail (under or overproduction) and the creation of monopolies that operate contrary to the public interest. They may exert a powerful influence on prices and supplies and restrict competition.

Table 2.2 Evaluation of the free market economy

Economic problem	Free market solution	Method	Weaknesses
What to produce?	Freedom of choice and consumer sovereignty use money 'votes' to dictate the choice of good or service according to unregulated market forces of demand and supply.	High product demand influences prices and profit. Resources are thus directed to capitalise on high-profit opportunities and away from low-profit opportunities.	Undesirable goods such as alcohol and tobacco are a result of this process.
How to produce?	Producers buy input factors on the open market depending on the nature of the good.	High demand for products cause high related demand for labour or land to produce these goods, bringing up the price of labour (wages) and land (rent). In turn, more factors are supplied in a bid to capitalise on high wages and rent. Firms choose the least cost method.	Automation may cause labour unemployment. High factor prices can lead to inflation. Skilled labour is difficult to obtain in a short space of time.
For whom?	The price mechanism allows wants to be satisfied by the ability to pay the market price.	Goods and services go to those who can afford to pay with wages that they earn.	Wages, incomes and wealth are unevenly distributed; therefore, high income earners have a greater claim in the distribution of goods and services.

Key points

Table 2.2 provides a simplified explanation of how a market system attempts to solve the economic problem. It is referred to as the 'invisible hand', which is in the price system and dictates what, how or for whom goods are produced. How the price system works will also be explored in chapter 11 which looks at the price mechanism.

Planned, collectivist or command economy system

In a pure sense a planned economy is exactly what it implies, that is, it is planned and carried out by a central planning committee. There is no role for private enterprise. Further, what, how and for whom to produce are determined by a planning committee in a bid to ensure everyone shares equally in the output of national resources and that income and wealth are also evenly distributed.

Cuba is one of the few countries of the world that uses collectivist practices, although some free market elements have been recently introduced.

The features of a pure planned economy are:

› All economic decisions are undertaken by a central planning authority.
› There is no role for private enterprise.
› There is no private ownership of resources.
› What to produce is determined by the central planning authority and therefore there is no freedom of choice.
› Any profit earned by state controlled companies is shared with all citizens.
› There is, therefore, no competition.
› Prices are set for all goods and services by the central planning authority.
› The level of wages is determined by the central planning authority.
› Self-interest is replaced by the national interest.
› Apart from price setting, distribution is also determined by a quota system, queuing for items in short supply, a merit and voucher system for food and other basic necessities such as transport.

Planned economy evaluated

Table 2.3 Positive and negative aspects of a planned economy

Positive	Negative
The goal of this system is the welfare of all citizens.	Decision making is inhibited by bureaucratic procedures and bottlenecks.
Government possesses the information to direct resources to their best use.	There is no freedom of choice for consumers and producers.
Wasteful competition is avoided.	The system is rigid and not adaptable to changes. Shortages frequently occur.
The government can choose priorities, for example to emphasise equality for all citizens with respect to education, health and poverty elimination.	Specific production targets and lack of incentives lower worker morale and lead to poor productivity.
The government can choose, for example, greater protection for the environment under this system compared to others.	Goods and services are of poor quality due to lack of competition.
Greater growth rates may occur when a government central planning authority allocates more resources to capital than consumer goods.	Queuing is commonplace when shortages occur.

Table 2.4 An evaluation of the planned economy

Economic problem	Solution	Method	Weaknesses
What to produce?	The central planning authority surveys and information gathering determine needs rather than wants.	The information on what to produce is directed to production units, which allocate resources to meet production targets.	Shortages, poor quality goods and services.
How to produce?	The central planning authority has information on the nation's pool of resources and determines the factor combination based on the nature of the product or service.	Production units may mass produce using more labour than capital to boost employment.	Targets and lack of production incentives lower productivity.
For whom to produce?	The state oversees the distribution of output.	Distribution is based on need, merit and queuing.	Typically, a central state will be less efficient and flexible in its production choices.

Solving the economic problem with a planned economic system

Key points
A planned economy allocates resources through a central planning authority, which plans what, how and for whom to produce. The main objective of this system is to eliminate the weaknesses of the market system and to emphasise national welfare over individual welfare.

Weaknesses of this system are mainly bureaucracy, shortages, quantity rather than quality, and inefficient production.

Mixed economy

A mixed economy, as the name implies, is one in which decisions about what, how and for whom to produce are undertaken by private individuals, firms and the government. Both the planned economies and market economies have, in fact, given way to mixed economies to capture the strength of both systems while attempting to eliminate the weaknesses of each system. Except for Cuba, all Caribbean economies are 'mixed economies'.

Table 2.5 summarises the role of the market system and state system.

Table 2.5 Role of the market system and state system

Economic activity	State system	Market system
Transport	National transport company	Mini, maxi buses and rental taxis
Health	General state hospital	Private nursing homes
Education	Public schools	Private schooling
Housing	National housing authority	Private home construction
Employment	Government service	Sales, trades
Insurance	National Insurance	Barbados Mutual Company
Oil refinery	Nationalised oil co – Petrotrin	Private oil co – BP Amoco
Food	National fisheries	Private fishermen

The extent to which the state intervenes in the economy varies from country to country. Generally, the state attempts to influence or regulate the free market price system in order to achieve its objectives. This is done via subsidies (e.g., food, transport), taxes (indirect), and VAT (to discourage consumption of products such as alcohol and tobacco).

Regulation may take the form of zoning for traffic congestion, a prices commission to set minimum and maximum prices, and ombudsmen for insurance and banking.

Other more indirect means of intervention are achieved through the use of monetary, fiscal or exchange rate policy. In recent times there has been a deliberate strategy of giving a greater role to the private sector than the state to increase productivity and competitiveness, in order to improve economic performance.

Key point

Mixed economies incorporate both the private and public sectors in solving the economic problem, using taxation, legislation and regulation.

Chapter summary

Economic systems describe the model or method societies use to solve the economic problem. The roles of private and state enterprises vary in the three main models which are: the market economy; the planned economy; and the mixed economy.

Market economies make all economic decisions with very little state intervention. Planned economies are just the opposite.

Practice questions

1. In no less than four sentences explain what is meant by Adam Smith's 'invisible hand'.

2. Explain what is meant by the concept of 'the market'.

3 Tools of economic analysis

INTRODUCTORY ECONOMICS A TEXTBOOK FOR CAPE ECONOMICS STUDENTS

LEARNING OBJECTIVES

- Define model.
- Define assumptions.
- Distinguish between a variable and a constant.
- Distinguish between inductive and deductive reasoning.
- Distinguish between endogenous and exogenous variables.
- Define functions, relations and intercepts.
- Explain minimum and maximum values of a function.
- Explain tabular presentation of data.

REQUIRED KNOWLEDGE

An understanding of simple tabular presentations, diagrams, pie charts, bar graphs, time series and cross-sectional data, gradient and cross-section (usually done in geography at an early level).

TOPIC VALUE

A concept requiring an extensive written explanation can be summed up in a simple model, diagram or formula. It will assist in exercises in analysing life situations; for example, budgeting, playing a game, or thinking through a problem. It is an alternative language.

Model

A model is any mechanism that represents a theory, hypothesis or idea. It may take the form of a diagram, formula, table, equation or theory. In economics, models may explain a theory. For example, a demand curve may illustrate a theory that explains why consumers purchase more of a good at lower prices than at higher prices. It may be used to illustrate a law in economics under certain conditions. A map is really a diagram of a country. Models, therefore, help to explain, analyse and predict issues in economics or any other social science.

Assumptions

Assumptions are made in economics so that relationships can be examined, that is, certain factors have to be held constant in order to understand relationships between two variables. For example, if analysing consumer behaviour one must assume that everyone thinks or acts in a reasonable way, otherwise the analysis or theory is compromised by unreasonable behaviour. In economics these assumptions are called *ceteris paribus* assumptions, meaning 'all other things being equal'.

Variables

A variable is any measurable quantity that changes in time, for example, population changes, output levels, cost of production, or prices of goods and services (see table 3.1).

Table 3.1 **Measurable variables related to oranges**

Month	Quantity demanded (kg)	Price ($)
January	10	2.00
February	80	4.00
March	160	7.00
April	180	12.00

In the above example, note that both price and demand for oranges are variables that are changing in the first few months of the year. We may use the above table to theorise, analyse or predict the relationship between demand for oranges and changes in their price.

This type of reasoning may be called deductive because we make a general observation that leads to a specific conclusion: for example, there is a national shortage of oranges, so we may not be able to obtain any in our market. This is said to be 'top-down' reasoning, whereas inductive reasoning is the opposite: for example, prices of oranges are increasing in our market, so it looks like there is a national shortage.

Models may also lead to general conclusions that may arise from specific observations.

In economics, the study of how variables affect one another is common; for example, price and quantity, income and expenditure, cost and production. These are called functional relationships and may be expressed as a graph, table or an equation.

Linear function

A functional relationship shows how one variable is affected by one or more variables. As the word implies this function plotted on a graph is a straight line. For example, it is possible for the relationship between consumer expenditure and increases in income to have a linear function if we spend half of every extra dollar we earn. This linear function may be expressed as a formula, namely, $C = f(y)$; that is, consumer expenditure is a function of (depends on) the level of income earned. See table 3.2 below.

Table 3.2 **Linear function**

Income	Consumer expenditure
100	50
200	100
300	150
400	200
500	250

In this case, there is a functional relationship between changes in consumer expenditure and changes in level of income that is fixed which is 0.5 of income. This can also be expressed as $C = 0.5y$.

It can also be expressed as a graph as shown in figure 3.1.

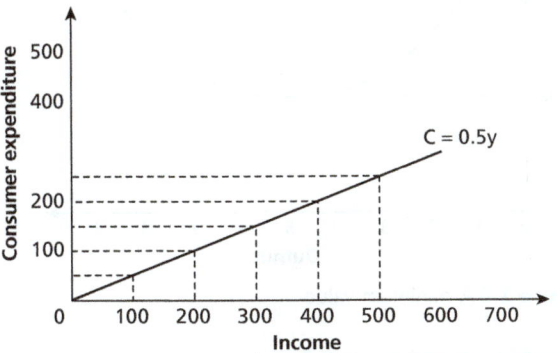

Figure 3.1 A linear function

Note that in figure 3.1, it is a straight line that is plotted and therefore a linear function.

A non-linear function

When the functional relationship between two variables takes place at a changing rate, as opposed to a fixed rate, the plotted graph will not be a straight line. For example, it has been observed that as our age increases so does our expenditure, until around 35–40 years of age when for each extra dollar we earn, we spend less but save more.

Furthermore, when we approach age 60 and beyond, our needs decrease and so does consumption expenditure. A consumption expenditure function may look like figure 3.2.

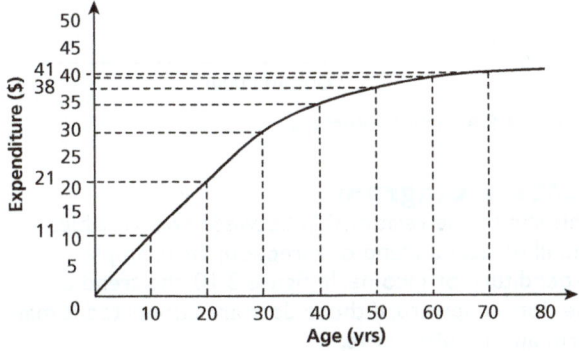

Figure 3.2 A non-linear function

A constant

A constant is different from a variable and is defined as a measurable quantity that never varies. Refer to figure 3.3 that illustrates fixed cost of production as a constant.

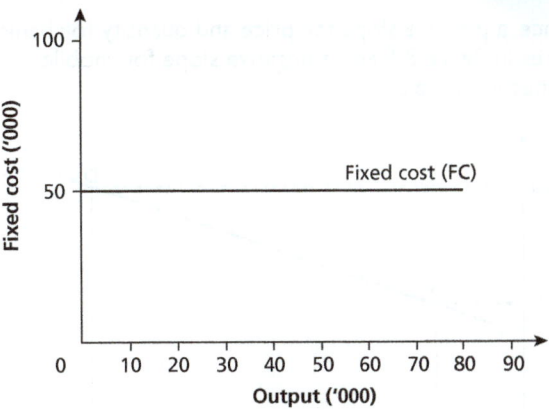

Figure 3.3 A constant function

Note that even at zero output the cost is $50,000 and any increase in output leaves the fixed cost unchanged.

Endogenous and exogenous variables

An endogenous variable is one determined by the model under analysis. For example, using demand theory, figure 3.4 shows how the quantity of ground provisions demanded depends on price factors. Quantity of ground provisions is the endogenous variable. The exogenous variable in this case is price, which is also called the independent variable; it is determined by factors outside the model such as the cost of growing provisions or the number of sellers. You may also see the word autonomous used in place of independent variable and induced used in place of dependent variable.

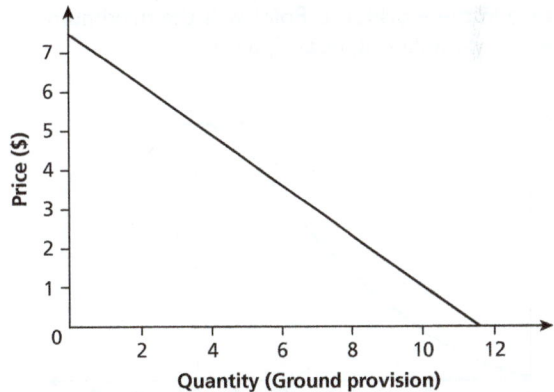

Figure 3.4 Endogenous and exogenous variables

Gradient

The gradient or slope of a function is simply the change in the vertical axis divided by the change in the horizontal axis. Note that when two variables move in the same direction the value is positive and if they move in opposite directions the value is negative.

Hence, a positive slope for price and quantity for bank shares in figure 3.5 and a negative slope for mobile phones in figure 3.6.

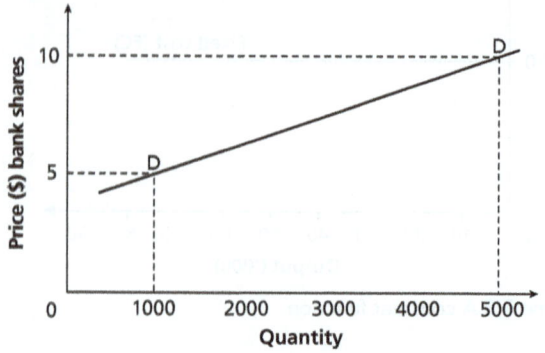

Figure 3.5 A positive gradient

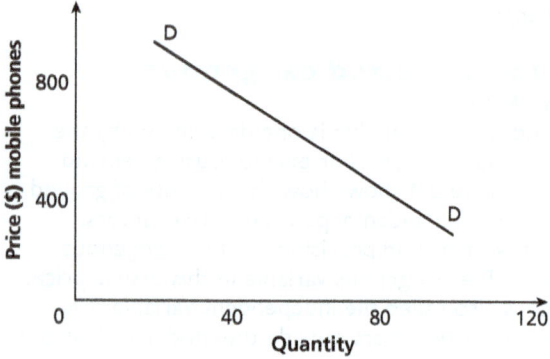

Figure 3.6 A negative gradient

Maximum and minimum values

Figure 3.7 shows how total output varies with an increase in the workforce. Point X is the maximum value of a variable output at Y_1 units.

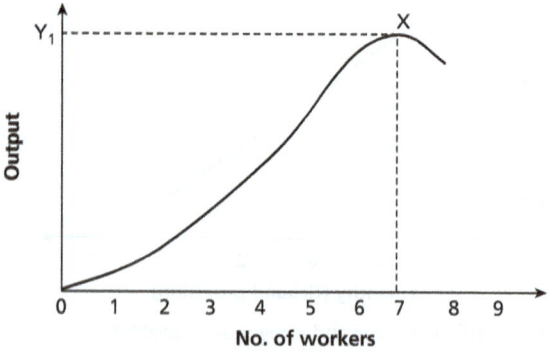

Figure 3.7 A maximum value

Figure 3.8 illustrates how average cost rises and falls as output increases from 0 to 9 units. Average cost of production is the lowest value of C_1 at output 5 units.

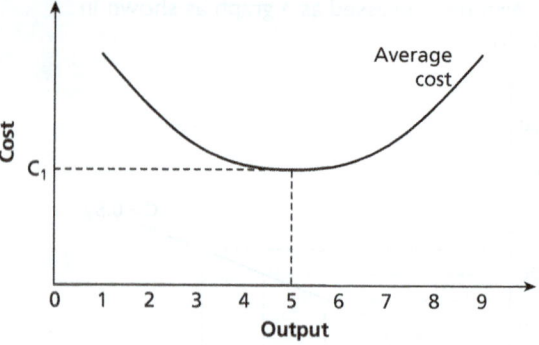

Figure 3.8 A minimum value

Vertical intercept

Where a variable being measured meets or intersects the vertical axis of a graph, it is called the vertical intercept. It reveals an important relationship between the dependent and independent variable in that it shows what the value of a dependent variable is when the independent variable is zero.

In figure 3.9, basic expenditure at zero income is $1,000, financed from past savings or borrowing.

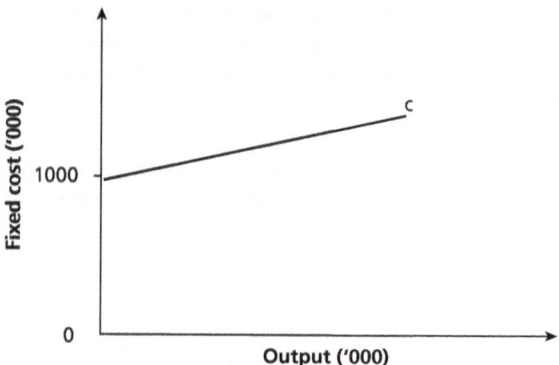

Figure 3.9 A vertical intercept

Scatter diagram

This shows the relationship between two variables and illustrates a trend or direction; for example, expenditure or income. In figure 3.10, the trend of the dots is upward; if those dots are connected it may form an irregular curve.

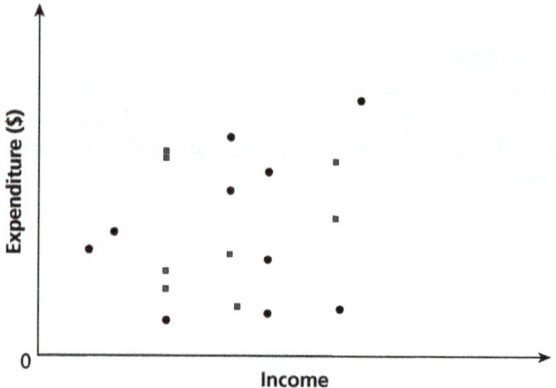

Figure 3.10 A scatter diagram

Chapter 3 Tools of economic analysis

Positive and normative statements

In the study of economics, statements may be normative or positive. One that can be proven by data or evidence is a positive statement. If a statement is an opinion and has a personal bias, it is normative.

Example 1: Consumer borrowings increase when interest rates fall.

Example 2: The government ought to redistribute income and wealth more evenly.

Chapter summary

- Models are the main tools of economic analysis.
- They are used mainly to represent an idea, hypothesis or theory in condensed form that is easily understood.
- Models enable social scientists to analyse, explain and predict economic issues.
- Expansive ideas or theories can be condensed for easy understanding with the use of tables, graphs, charts, curves, diagrams, formulae and equations.
- A model may change a qualitative analysis (written ideas) into a quantitative one (formula, table, equation or diagram).

Exam preparation questions

1. A variable is best described as:
   a. A fixed value
   b. A measurable quantity that is unchanged
   c. A magnitude
   d. A measurable quantity that varies.

2. Which of the following is a model:
   i) A graph
   ii) An equation
   iii) A theory
   iv) A table?
   a. iii
   b. i and iv
   c. ii and iv
   d. all of the above.

3. A functional relationship is defined as:
   a. The percentage change in a value
   b. The total value of a change in a variable
   c. A relationship between two variables
   d. A relationship between three variables.

4. I pay a rent of Bds$30.00 for my home phone even if I do not use it for the next 20 years; this is best described as a variable that is:
   a. A token charge
   b. A variable cost
   c. A constant
   d. A normal cost.

INTRODUCTORY ECONOMICS A TEXTBOOK FOR CAPE ECONOMICS STUDENTS

4 Theory of demand

Chapter 4 Theory of demand

> **LEARNING OBJECTIVES**
> - Explain the first law of demand.
> - Define effective demand.
> - Explain the conditions of demand.
> - Differentiate between total and marginal utility.
> - Explain the law of diminishing marginal utility.
> - Explain consumer equilibrium.
> - Explain the optimal purchase rule.
> - Identify applications of utility theory.
>
> **REQUIRED KNOWLEDGE**
> - Demand theory at the introductory level
> - Factors affecting demand.
>
> **TOPIC VALUE**

We demand on a daily basis because demand is related to the satisfaction of wants and needs.

Definition of demand

Demand is the willingness and ability to pay for a good or service at a given price over a given period. This is called effective demand.

A typical demand statement expresses demand for oranges as: 500 oranges at 50 cents per orange per week. The demand schedule in figure 4.1 is derived from table 4.1 and shows the quantity of oranges and the prices at which they are demanded.

Table 4.1 Demand schedule

Price ($)	Quantity
10	2
8	3
6	4
4	6
2	10

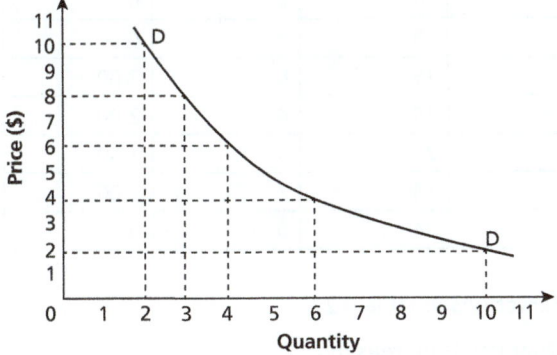

Figure 4.1 A demand curve

There are many different concepts of demand as well as effective demand. Other types of demand are:

› **Derived demand**, which is the demand for a factor of production related to the demand for what the factor can produce, e.g., a mechanic's services are demanded due to a demand for vehicle repairs.

› Joint demand is when one good is demanded together with another. It is also called a complementary good. Examples of goods for which there is a joint demand are printers and toners.

› Aggregate demand is the total demand for a country's national output.

Common error

Many confuse demand for a good with 'window shopping'. Demand must be supported by the ability to pay.

Factors which influence demand for a good or service

Consumers are influenced by certain factors to purchase a product. These factors may be separated into two categories, namely, price and non-price factors.

Price factors and non-price factors

Price factors refer to the actual price of a good. Many people are influenced by the price of a good when they make a purchase.

The non-price factors are:

› Level of income
› Prices of related goods, e.g., substitutes and complements
› Advertising
› Fashion and taste and habit
› Time
› Seasonal changes
› Expectations of the economy.

Non-price factors are also called the conditions of demand. When price changes are analysed, the non-price factors are held constant.

Key point

Effective demand is the willingness and ability to purchase a good or service at a given price over a given time period. If you refer again to the demand schedule a greater quantity of oranges is demanded at lower prices and less at higher prices. This is typical of most goods that are consumed and it is valid, provided the conditions of demand remain constant in that period.

The cardinalist theory of demand

A study of this topic gives a possible explanation of why you purchase more of a good when the price falls and vice versa. It also explains why you always look for a bargain.

The cardinalist approach to demand is so named because it assumes that cardinal numbers can measure satisfaction derived from consuming a good such as a chocolate bar. For example, if you consume a chocolate bar this theory assumes that satisfaction can be measured in the same way that a thermometer measures temperature. Other assumptions of this theory are:

› **Prices of other related goods are unchanged.**
› **Incomes are fixed.**
› **The consumer is rational, i.e., is able to make a decision based on self-interest.**
› **Consumers aim to maximise satisfaction.**
› **Tastes are unchanged.**

Utility

Cardinalists consider satisfaction to be represented and measured by utility. They identify two types of utility, total utility and marginal utility. Total utility is assumed to be the total satisfaction or usefulness gained from consuming a good or service.

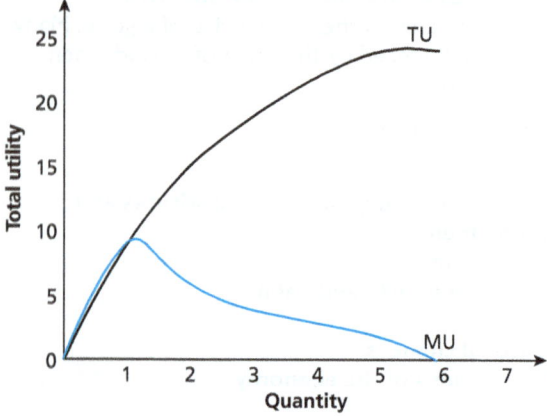

Figure 4.2 Total and marginal utility curves

Refer to figure 4.2, measuring total utility gained from consuming bars of chocolate. Although total utility (TU) is rising, whether we continue to consume depends on our desire to consume one more unit of the good or service to maximise total utility.

Marginal utility (MU) measures the satisfaction of consuming one more good and is measured by the change in TU when one more (or less) unit of a good is consumed. It is expressed in formula as change in TU/change in Q.

Utility is measurable in units of satisfaction or usefulness. For example, if three chocolate bars yield 19 utils of satisfaction and four bars yields 22 utils, the MU of the fourth bar is 3 utils. Refer to table 4.2.

Note:

› The TU for the first bar = 9 utils; TU for bars 1 and 2 = 15 utils; MU of bar 2 = 6 utils.
› MU is diminishing as more bars are consumed.
› The sixth bar yields zero MU.

The above observations explain the law of diminishing marginal utility, which states that 'as increasing units of a good are consumed, the marginal utility of each additional unit consumed diminishes until it reaches zero'.

Common error

Sometimes the law of diminishing marginal utility is mistaken for the law of diminishing returns. The law of diminishing marginal utility refers to consumption while the law of diminishing returns is related to production.

In figure 4.2, note that TU reaches a maximum of 24 utils when five bars are consumed and that MU is zero at six bars. The conclusion to be drawn is that when TU is at its highest MU will be zero.

How does the law of diminishing marginal utility explain the first law of demand?

In their personal judgement rational consumers equate satisfaction with price. In other words, satisfaction is equal to price (money given up). This is the basis of consumer equilibrium.

Equilibrium is simply defined as a balance between two forces, that is, satisfaction = money paid. Expressed another way, marginal utility equals price or P = MU.

For example, if you are willing to pay $1 for 2 utils of satisfaction then the price column in table 4.2 shows what you will be willing to pay for each additional chocolate bar. Note that as MU falls so does price. More of a good (1 to 6) is demanded at lower prices ($4.50 to $1.00).

Table 4.2 Total and marginal utility

Chocolate bars	TU	MU	Price willing to pay ($)
0	0	0	0
1	9	9	4.50
2	15	6	3.00
3	19	4	2.00
4	22	3	1.50
5	24	2	1.00
6	24	0	0

Observations in table 4.2:

› Quantity is increasing.
› TU is rising.
› MU is falling.
› Price is falling.
› When TU is at its highest, MU is equal to zero.

More of a good is demanded at lower prices, since MU is falling; prices also fall so that MU is equated to price.

Chapter 4 Theory of demand

Table 4.3 Total and marginal utility

Pizza				Soft drink			
Quantity	TU	MU	MU/price	Quantity	TU	MU	MU/price
1	20	20	10 (20/2)	1	11	11	11/1
2	35	15	7.5 (15/2)	2	20	9	9/1
3	45	10	5 (10/2)	3	27	7	7/1
4	50	5	2.5 (5/2)	4	32	5	5/1
5	52	2	1 (2/2)	5	35	1	1/1

The information in table 4.2 shows that more of a good will be demanded at lower prices and less at higher prices *ceteris paribus*. This is known as the first law of demand.

Summary

The more of something you consume, the less you are willing to pay for it because your satisfaction from each additional unit is diminishing. Since your satisfaction is measured in money terms (P = MU), you will therefore be willing to pay less. The first law of demand is explained by utility analysis. Although consumer equilibrium is explained for one good, it also explains the rationale for choosing several goods; for example, monthly grocery purchases.

The optimal purchase rule/law of equi-marginal returns

The optimal purchase rule explains the choice of the best combination of goods with a limited income. When shopping for grocery items, choices are made. The aim of the shopper is to buy the most items for the least expenditure.

The optimal purchase rule states that consumers allocate their expenditure on many items in such a way that the ratio of satisfaction per dollar spent (MU/p) is the same for all goods. In this way, total satisfaction (TU) reaches a maximum. Expressed in formula, it is:

$MU_x/p_x = MU_y/p_y = MU_z = p_z$

Where:

MU/x is the marginal utility of good x and px the price of good x.

MU/y is the marginal utility of good y and py the price of good y.

MU/z is the marginal utility of good z and pz the price of good z.

Try to follow this example, which refers to table 4.3. Let us again assume that satisfaction can be measured in utils. If the price of a slice of pizza costs $2.00 and gives you 20 utils of satisfaction then $1.00 = 10 utils or MU/p = 10. If a soft drink costs $1.00 and yields 7 utils then each dollar gives 7 utils or MU/p = 7. If you only have $10.00, what is the best combination of pizza and soft drink that you can purchase?

Consumers look for value (MU) for their money (price) and would rank the purchases that give the highest satisfaction or MU. The consumer will go down the ranking as far as income allows, ranking pizza and soft drink.

If a slice of pizza is $2.00 then the first pizza @ 10 utils per dollar = (20/2).

Choice 2 = second soft drink + first slice of pizza = $2.00 + $2.00 = $4.00 (utils per dollar) = (9/1+20/2)

Choice 3 = third soft drink + 2 pizzas = $3.00 + $4.00 = $7.00 (utils per dollar) = (7/1+15/2)

Choice 4 = fourth soft drink + 3 pizzas = $4.00 + $6.00 = $10.00 (utils per dollar) = (5/1+10/2)

Choice 5 = fifth soft drink + 2 pizzas = $5.00 + $4.00 = $9.00 (utils per dollar) = (1/1 +15/2)

Choice 4 is the best because the marginal utility per dollar in each case is 5/1 and the total income of $10.00 is spent. If you check the table you would readily observe that for this combination: Total utility = 4 soft drinks (32 utils) + 3 pizzas (45 utils) = 77 utils

Combination 3 is: 3 soft drinks 35 utils

    2 pizzas = 27 utils

    = 62 utils

Expenditure = $7.00

Combination 3 achieves less TU and $3 left over. The optimal purchase rule therefore underlines the highest value for money spent is 77 utils for $10.00.

Helpful hint: the ratio of prices must be matched by the ratio of marginal utilities of each good.

Whenever the MU/price ratio of good X is greater than the MU/price ratio of another good Y, the optimal purchase rule states that the rational consumer will restore equilibrium by consuming more of good X and less of good Y. In this way the MU of X will fall and the MU of Y will rise.

The reason for this is that consuming more of good X reduces satisfaction per price while consuming less of good Y raises MU/p. This falling and rising of the marginal utility to price ratio for both goods eventually brings them to equilibrium when their respective ratios of MU/p are the same. The same reasoning is applied to more than two goods consumed.

While the logic of utility theory is simple it may be criticised because it assumes that satisfaction can be measured when in, fact it, may not be the same for everyone. *Ceteris paribus* assumptions of price, income and other 'fixed' conditions of demand are also not fixed in a dynamic world.

Key points

A consumer will compare the marginal utility to price ratio, purchasing more of that good which has a high MU/price ratio and less of that good with a low MU to price ratio. Consumer equilibrium is achieved where:

$$\frac{MU_x}{P_x} = \frac{MU_y}{P_y} = \frac{MU_z}{P_z}$$

Purchasing more of one good lowers its MU while purchasing less of one good raises MU (people value things more highly when they have less of them). Eventually, when the marginal utilities are equal, equilibrium is achieved. This is called the optimal purchase rule. Although a theory, utility analysis may explain certain types of economic behaviour.

Applications of the theory

The very wealthy pay more income taxes than low income earners as a form of redistributing income. It is thought that a wealthy person places a low utility on the last dollar earned, while a poor individual values his last dollar highly. Redistribution of wealth by taxation, therefore, is reputed to be based on marginal utility analysis.

It is argued that product promotion and advertising promote value for a product that is more than the product really has. In other words, more 'satisfaction' is supposedly created by the advertising leading buyers to believe they are getting more 'utility' than they are paying for and therefore are more willing to buy more of the product. This creates brand loyalty.

The water/diamonds paradox exists because water is cheap and diamonds are expensive. One sustains life; the other is dispensable. Fewer diamonds exist so their value or utility is high, while water is plentiful so a low value is placed on the last unit. It is marginal utility not total utility that determines prices.

Consumer surplus

Consumer surplus is the difference between the prevailing market price of a product and the price consumers are willing to pay. If you were willing to pay $500.00 for a cellular phone but discovered that the actual price was $400.00, then your consumer surplus is equal to $100.00 in surplus satisfaction or utility.

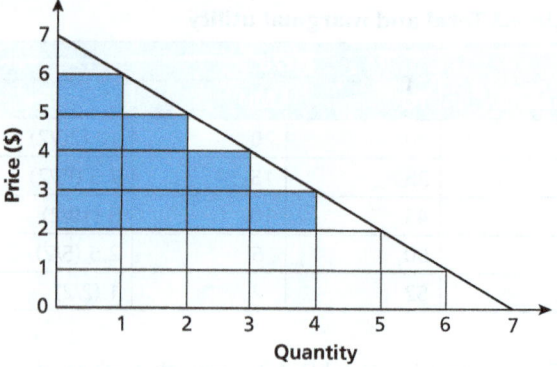

Figure 4.3 Consumer surplus

Diagrammatically, consumer surplus is identified as the area to the left of the demand curve and above the price line.

Figure 4.3 shows that when the price of a slice of cake is $2.00, five slices will be bought by a consumer. Total consumer surplus is the sum of each individual surplus gained for each slice.

For example, surplus on slice:

1 is $6.00 − $2.00 = $4.00
2 is $5.00 − $2.00 = $3.00
3 is $4.00 − $2.00 = $2.00
4 is $3.00 − $2.00 = $1.00
5 is $2.00 − $2.00 = $0

Total consumer surplus = $10.00

(a)

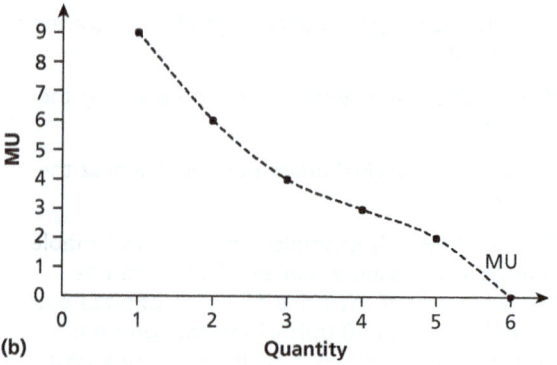

(b)

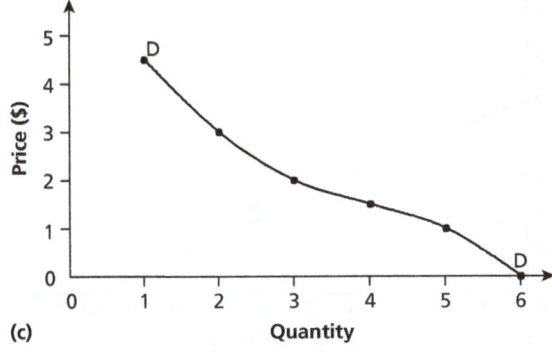

Figure 4.4 a, b and c The total and marginal utility and the related demand curve

The ordinalist theory of demand

Since it is difficult in practice to measure satisfaction, ordinalist or indifference curve, theory assumes satisfaction could be ranked first, second, third, and so on, and therefore provide an analysis closer to reality.

An indifference curve is a curve or line that shows different combinations of two items that yield the same level of satisfaction, *ceteris paribus*. The consumer is therefore 'indifferent' with respect to any combination because equal satisfaction is derived from any combination.

Table 4.4 Combinations of an indifference curve

	Cherries	Plums
A	40	1
B	30	2
C	22	3
D	16	4
E	12	5
F	11	6

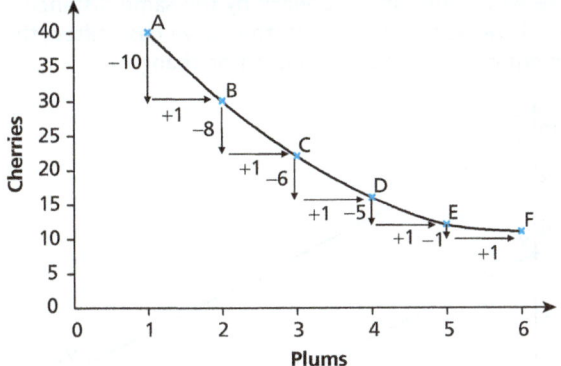

Figure 4.5 Indifference curve and marginal rate of substitution

The indifference curve illustrated in figure 4.5 is derived from table 4.4. Basic assumptions are:

› There are only two items of food to choose from: cherries and plums.
› The consumer is rational and a utility maximiser.
› Income and prices of the items are fixed.
› All other factors are assumed to be fixed (*ceteris paribus*).

Observe that combination A of 40 cherries and 1 plum yields the same satisfaction as combination D, that is, 16 cherries and 4 plums. Note also that changing from A to B involves the sacrifice of 10 cherries for 1 plum in order to sustain the same level of satisfaction.

Yet switching from combination B to C, 8 cherries are given up to achieve 1 extra plum. This rate of exchange is called the marginal rate of substitution (MRS) and is defined as the rate at which a consumer is willing to give up one good in order to consume the quantity of another good while maintaining the same level of satisfaction.

In the example shown in figure 4.5, observe how the rate of exchange starts at 10 cherries to 1 plum and subsequently diminishes to 1 cherry to 1 plum.

The reason for this is the familiar law of diminishing marginal utility. Sacrificing fewer cherries as the combinations changed, caused the MU of cherries to rise and the MU of plums to fall.

Key points

Indifference curves show combinations of two goods that yield equal satisfaction. It is similar in concept to a production possibility frontier in that it is a consumption possibilities boundary, given that income and prices are fixed. The rate of exchange of one good for the other is called the MRS and may be calculated as the slope or gradient of the indifference curve at any given point.

Other points about indifference curves to note:

› The curve normally slopes downward because to consume more of one good requires you to give up some of the other goods, since income is fixed.
› More of one good is required in compensation for the other good given up.
› The curve is convex because the MRS is diminishing, i.e., less of the good on the vertical axis is sacrificed for more on the horizontal axis.
› They cannot intersect since they would then represent two different levels of satisfaction and the point of intersection would also represent two different levels of satisfaction that are contradictory.
› They do not need to be parallel to each other.
› They cannot slope upward because, as in figure 4.6, you would consume more of both goods, therefore point B is superior to point A, contradicting the rationale of the indifference curve.

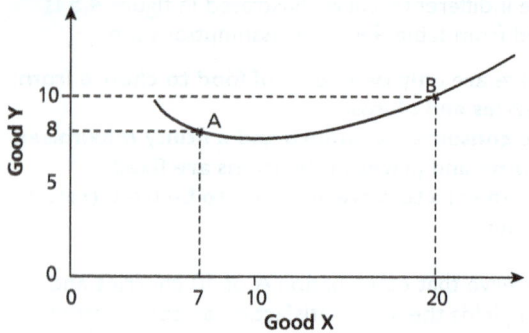

Figure 4.6 Upward sloping indifference curve

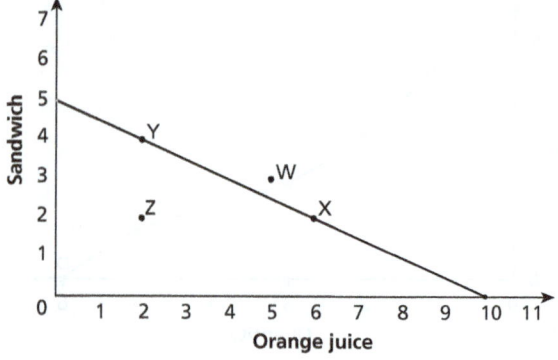

Figure 4.8 A budget line or constraint

Figure 4.8 shows a budget line of purchasing possibilities with an income of $20.00, when the price of a sandwich is $4.00 and the price of orange juice is $2.00.

Note:

> The ratio of prices is $4.00 to $2.00 and thus 2:1.
> The slope of the budget line is defined as 1:2, i.e., each sandwich given up gains two orange juices.
> Any point on the line is affordable and total income is spent. At point X, 2 sandwiches @ $4.00 = $8.00 and 6 orange juices @ $2.00 =$12.00, together equal $20.00. At point Y, 4 sandwiches @ $4 =$16.00 and 2 juices @ $2.00 = $4.00, together make $20.00 in all.
> At point W, 5 orange juices @ $2 = $10 while three sandwiches @ $4 = $12; total expenditure is equal to $22.00, which is not affordable. Hence, point W is unattainable as it is over the budget of $20. Point Z is attainable, i.e. 2 orange juices @ $2 = $4 and 2 sandwiches @ $4 = $8.00, together equal $12 but $8.00 remain.

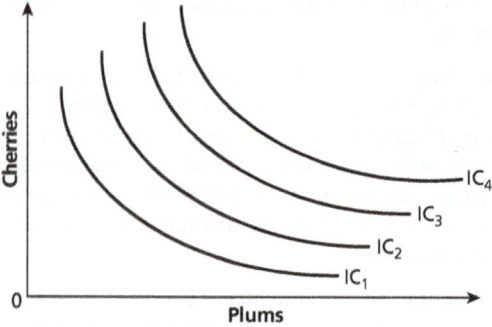

Figure 4.7 An indifference map

An indifference map, as illustrated in figure 4.7, consists of several indifferent curves extending outward from the origin indicating increasingly higher levels of total satisfaction. Rational consumers aspire to be on the curve furthest from the origin, that is, IC_4 because more of both cherries and plums are preferred to less of both.

Key point
The indifference map in figure 4.7 represents how consumers are likely to act in order to achieve the highest level of utility.

The budget line or constraint

While the indifference curve indicates consumer preferences, the quantity actually chosen will depend on the:

> level of income
> relative prices of the goods in question.

Refer to figure 4.8, where a budget line or curve shows the combinations of two goods that the consumer can actually buy, given their level of income and the relative prices of the two goods in question. If the consumer's income is $20.00 a day, a sandwich costs $4.00 and a drink of orange juice is priced at $2.00, then the choice of combination can be shown on a budget line to reflect this.

See figure 4.9. If the prices change, for example the price of a sandwich falls from $4.00 to $2.00 and the price of orange juice falls from $2.00 to $1.00, then the budget line will shift outward from XY to X_1Y_1. Similarly, if both prices remained at $4.00 and $2.00 respectively and income changes to $40.00 then the curve would also shift outward by the same distance. Note, however, that although the curve has shifted, the gradient or ratio of prices does not change.

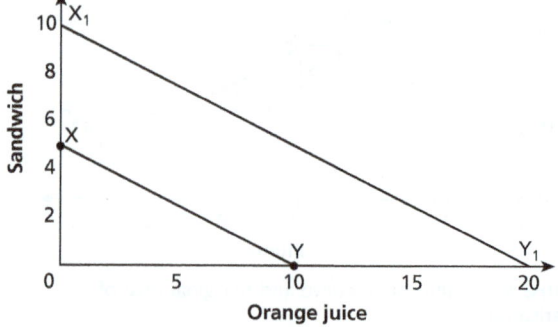

Figure 4.9 Shifts of the budget line

Chapter 4 Theory of demand

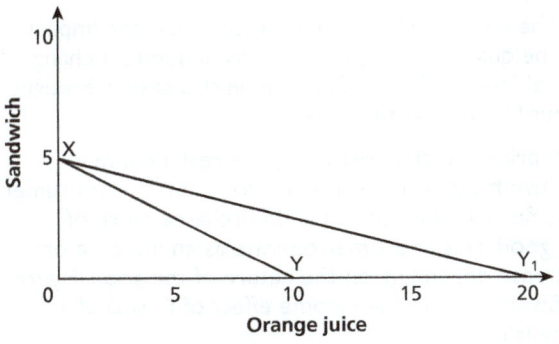

Figure 4.10 Budget line pivots (1)

If one price changes, however, for example the price of orange juice falls from $2.00 to $1.00, then the budget line would pivot as in figure 4.10 from XY to XY$_1$, changing the slope of the line from 1:2 to 1:4. The slope is also referred to as the relative prices of the two goods.

Similarly, if the price of a sandwich changed from $4.00 to $2.00 the budget line would pivot as shown in figure 4.11 from XY to X$_1$Y and the gradient or slope would reflect the change in relative prices from 1:2 to 1:1.

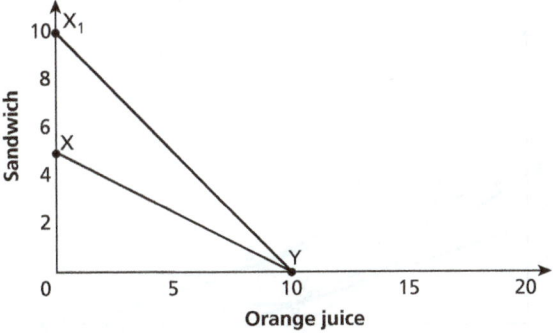

Figure 4.11 Budget line pivots (2)

Key points

The budget line represents a combination of two goods which is attainable with a given level of prices and income, *ceteris paribus*. Consumer equilibrium has yet to be explained but we now have the models to explain it. Since an indifference map represents possibilities that we wish for and a budget line represents what we can afford, bringing them together would reveal the best affordable combination. Consumer equilibrium in this way would maximise satisfaction from our income. Consider figure 4.12.

It is clear that indifference IC$_3$ is beyond our budget and IC$_1$ is affordable but we can go to a higher indifference curve IC$_2$ attaining higher satisfaction in so doing.

Note that IC$_2$ is tangential to budget line BL. At point O the gradients/slopes of the indifference curve and the budget line are the same and tangent to each other. Also the MRS (ratio of goods in exchange) is equal to the ratio of prices and can be expressed as:

$$\text{Ratio of goods} = \frac{\text{Mu of OJ}}{\text{Mu of SW}}$$

$$\text{Ratio of prices} = \frac{\text{Price of OJ}}{\text{Price of SW}}$$

Where:

OJ = Orange juice

SW = Sandwich

If the price of the orange juice changes from $2.00 to $1.00 then budget line BL would pivot to BL$_1$ as illustrated in figure 4.13.

When the budget line pivots to BL$_1$, it is now tangential to a higher indifference curve IC$_3$ and a new equilibrium at Y. Note a price fall in price from $2.00 to $1.00 for orange juice induces an increase in demand of six more orange juices. Hence, we can conclude that more of a good (orange juice) will be demanded at lower prices, *ceteris paribus*. We can proceed to derive a demand curve for orange juice using indifference curve analysis as shown in figure 4.13.

It has been derived from the equilibrium or tangential points of the indifference curves and budget line that pivoted as the price of the good fell.

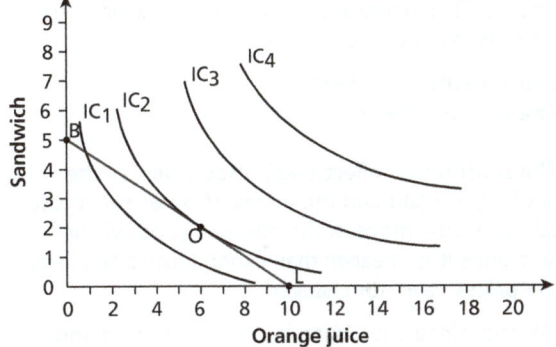

Figure 4.12 Consumer equilibrium

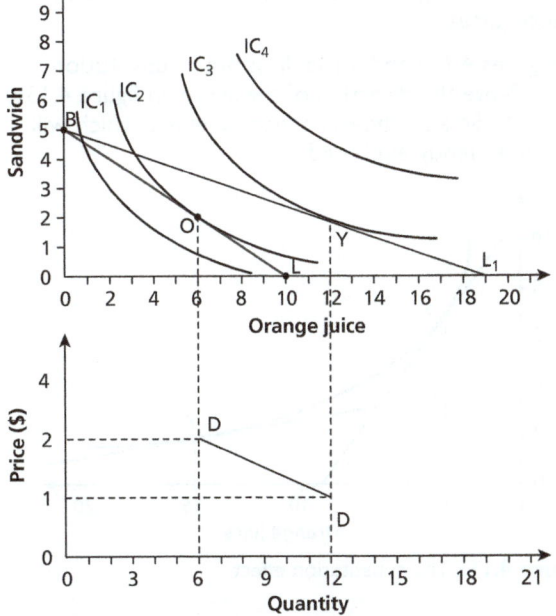

Figure 4.13 Deriving a demand curve for orange juice

As illustrated in figure 4.14, a line joining the equilibrium points A, B and C is called a price consumption curve.

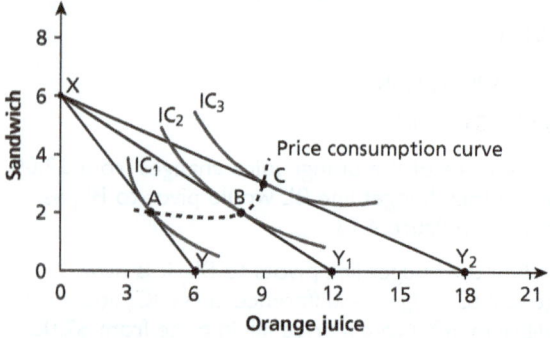

Figure 4.14 Price consumption line

The price consumption curve (shown in figure 4.14) connects all points of consumer equilibria.

Income and substitution effects

In figure 4.13 when the price of orange juice fell from $2.00 to $1.00, six more orange juices were purchased. This increase in quantity purchased is the result of two effects caused by a price change.

› The substitution effect
› The income effect.

The substitution effect takes place when, as the price of a good falls and the prices of other substitutes remain constant, more of the cheaper good will be bought since it is cheaper than other substitute goods whose prices have not changed.

We therefore substitute more of this good and less of others whose prices have remained constant but relatively higher. This is called the substitution effect of a price change; in figure 4.15a it is from X to Y = 11 orange juices.

Figures 4.15a and 4.15b illustrate a substitution effect. Note the direction of the arrow in figure 4.15b. Figure 4.15b also shows an income effect, which will be subsequently explained.

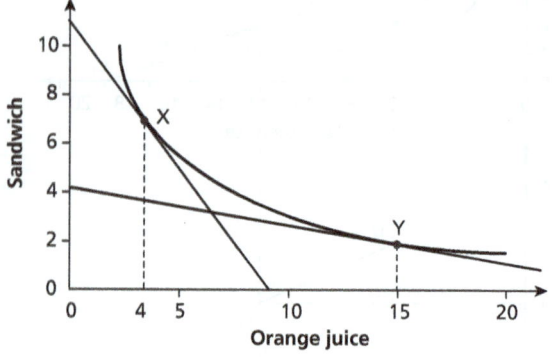

Figure 4.15a The substitution effect

The income effect of a price change is the impact on the quantity of a good purchased due to a change in real income. The real income in this case is brought about by the change in price.

If price falls then the change in real income is positive if other prices remain constant. The consumer feels financially better off and purchases more of the good. This effect may operate as an increase or decrease depending on the nature of the good. Figure 4.15b also shows the income effect of Y to Z of a price fall.

Referring to the figures illustrating both substitution and income effects, note the importance of the arrows that indicate the direction of the changes. In this case, both effects are in the same direction hence more orange juice is bought. Sometimes for different types of goods one effect may be stronger than the other, or one may counteract the other. A normal good is one that experiences an increase in consumption with positive changes in real income. This may come about due to a decrease in price or an increase in real income. For the fall in price of a normal good the substitution effect is always an increase in consumption.

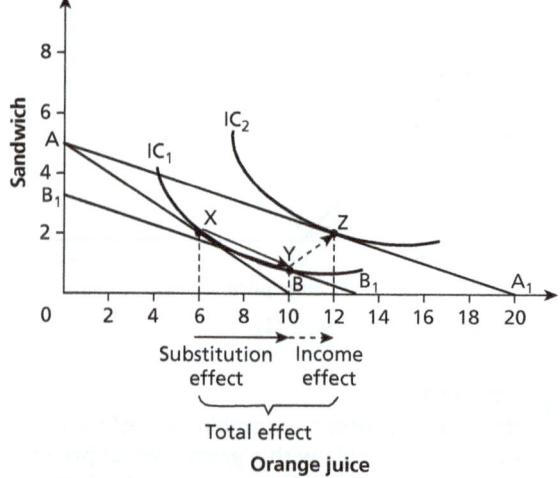

Figure 4.15b Income and substitution effects

Separating the substitution and income effects of a price change (fall) for a normal good

To determine which effect is more powerful it is possible to separate these two effects. Refer to figure 4.15b above.

› AB is the original budget line. The equilibrium point X denotes equilibrium quantity of six orange juices and two sandwiches. As a result of a fall in the price of orange juice from $2.00 to $1.00 the quantity demanded increases to 12. AA_1 represents the new budget line with a new price ratio of 1:4 which has pivoted to the right.
› Previous ratio of prices is 1:2.

- A new budget line B_1B_1 tangential to the original indifference curve IC_1 isolates the substitution effect by changing the gradient of AB (1:2) to reflect the new price ratio of 1:4 on the original indifference curve AA_1.
- X to Y is revealed as the substitution effect, which is equivalent to four orange juices (6–10). Note the direction of the arrow.
- The income effect is therefore from Y to Z and is equal to two orange juices and the distance between B_1B_1 and AA_1 represented by YZ. Note that where the substitution effect ends, the income effect begins.
- The substitution effect of four orange juices added to the income effect of two orange juices makes the overall total or price effect of six orange juices.
- In conclusion, the overall price or total effect is the summation of the substitution and income effects.

Income and substitution effect for inferior goods

Income and substitution effects of a price fall for a normal good operate in the same direction. This is not the case for an inferior good, which is defined as one that experiences a fall in demand when real income increases and therefore subject to a negative income effect. See figure 4.16.

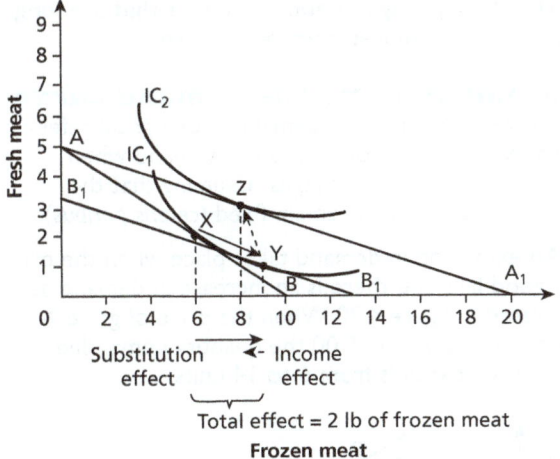

Figure 4.16 Income and substitution effect for an inferior good

Frozen goat meat may be cited as an example of an inferior good. With a price fall for frozen meat from $4 to $2, the increase in real income causes less frozen goat meat to be bought and a switch to buying fresh meat. Note the quantity of frozen goat meat bought is a reduction of one pound, compared to an increase of $3\frac{1}{4}$ lb of fresh goat meat purchased instead.

The substitution effect is X to Y, or 3 lb. Note the increase is always associated with the substitution effect.

The income effect is negative, that is −1, which erases part of the substitution effect. The sum of the effects are:

substitution effect = + 3
income effect = −1
Total or price effect = +2

The income and substitution effects of a price change (fall) for a Giffen good

A Giffen good is a special type of inferior good with an extreme negative income effect. Demand increases as its price increases and vice versa. The income effect moves in the opposite direction, completely erasing the increasing substitution effect. Demand for the product falls considerably with a price fall and vice versa. The demand curve for a Giffen good is upward sloping.

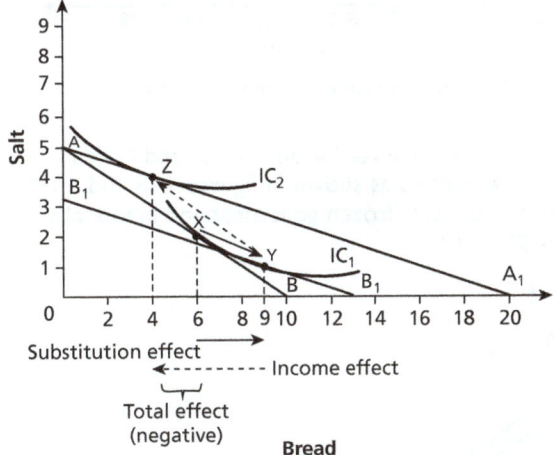

Figure 4.17 Income and substitution effects of a fall in price of a Giffen good

Sir Robert Giffen who authored the concept, cited bread as a Giffen good since more was consumed as its price increased. The reason is that since bread is a staple, when prices rose other goods could not be purchased so people filled themselves with bread. Note in figure 4.17, the substitution effect is equal to 3 (6 to 9 or X to Y) but negative income effect is equal to Y to Z or −5. Total effect is equal to −2.

Student hint

Separation of income and substitution effects and Giffen goods are topics that appear regularly in examinations.

Table 4.5 Income and substitution effects and quantity demanded for a fall in price

Type of good	Substitution effect	Income effect	Quantity demanded
Normal	Strong	Strong	More
Inferior	Weak	Fairly negative	Less than before
Giffen	Weak	Very negative	Very much less

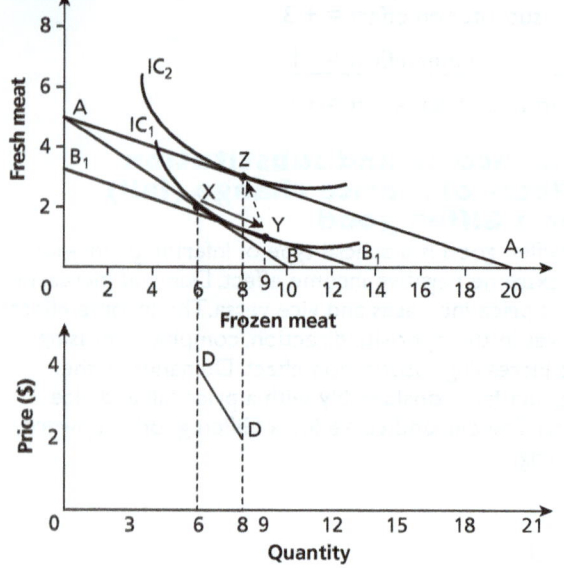

Figure 4.18 Demand curve for an inferior good

The demand curves for an inferior and Giffen goods are derived as shown in figures 4.18 and 4.19, when the price of frozen goat meat and bread falls from $4 to $2.

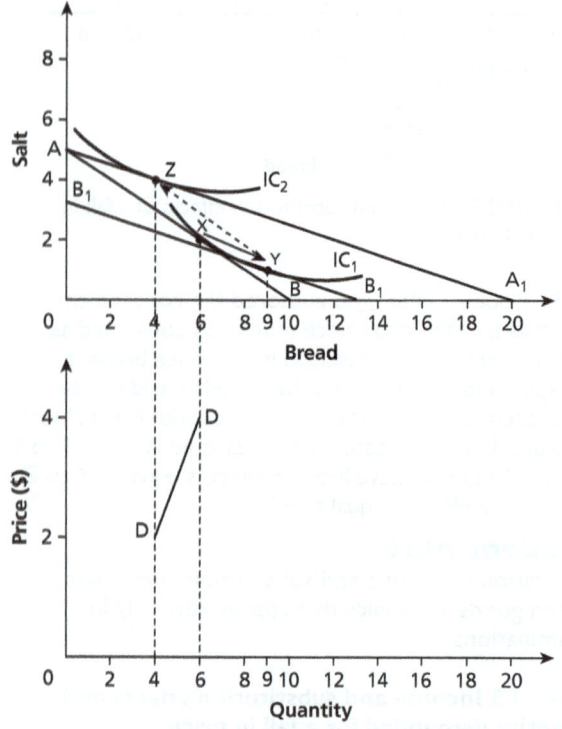

Figure 4.19 Demand curve for a Giffen good

Common error
There is much confusion when differentiating amongst normal, inferior and Giffen goods. Inferior and Giffen goods have negative income effects for price decreases. For a normal good, demand will rise because both income and substitution effects cause increases in quantity demanded.

Summary
Normal goods, inferior goods and Giffen goods have varying substitution and income effects. Inferior and Giffen goods experience negative income effects while for normal goods both effects are positive.

There are no examples of Giffen goods in the real world – beside bread and potatoes during the Irish Potato Famine – so they really only exist theoretically. Giffen goods are represented by an upward sloping demand curve. There are other demand curves which are also upward sloping, namely:

> Goods of ostentation convey status to the buyer and more of these goods are demanded at higher prices, e.g., a BMW motor car or brand name clothes and shoes
> High priced goods that indicate high quality
> Goods of speculation, e.g., company equities that are rising in price
> Rising house prices
> Goods of snob value, e.g., works of art

The limitations of indifference curve theory
While the indifference curve theory may be used to separate income and substitution effects and to derive demand curves, there are limitations to the theory.

> Satisfaction may be generated from advertising.
> Consumers do not always act rationally.
> The theory may not apply to goods that are long lasting, e.g., houses, cars, refrigerators.

Movement along the demand curve
A change in the quantity demanded of a good refers to an extension or contraction of demand when the price of the good changes, assuming that the conditions of demand remain fixed (*ceteris paribus*).

An extension in demand takes place when the price of a good falls and there is an increase in demand as illustrated in figure 4.20. When the price of good X falls from $10.00 to $5.00 the quantity demanded expands or extends from 6 to 14 units.

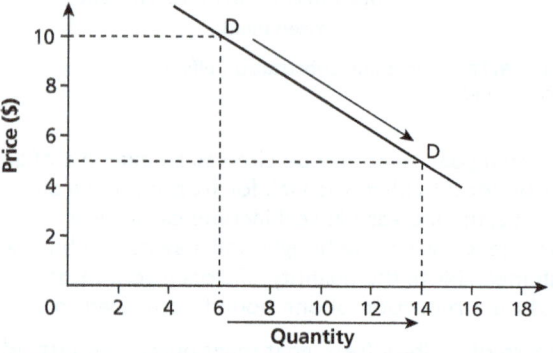

Figure 4.20 Movement along a demand curve

Note the direction of the arrows that reflect the extension in demand. Conversely, when the price

Chapter 4 Theory of demand

of a good rises from $5.00 to $10.00, the quantity decreases (contracts) from 14 to 6. This is called a contraction of quantity demanded.

Common error
There must be the assumption that the conditions of demand remain fixed when prices change, in order for extension and contraction to be observed. For example, if the prices of cell phones decrease and a condition of the demand also changes, for example level of income falls, then it is unlikely that more will be demanded. Similarly, if cell phone prices rise and there is also a change in another condition of demand, for example heavy promotional advertising of cell phones, more cell phones are likely to be purchased.

A change in demand
A change in demand is different from a change in quantity demanded. A change in quantity demanded is as a result of a price change only and leads to a movement along a demand curve, whereas a change in demand is a result of a change in quantity demanded at each and every price when non-price factors change. See figures 4.21 and 4.22.

If there is a change in the non-price factors, the demand curve will shift to the right or the left depending on the nature of the change.

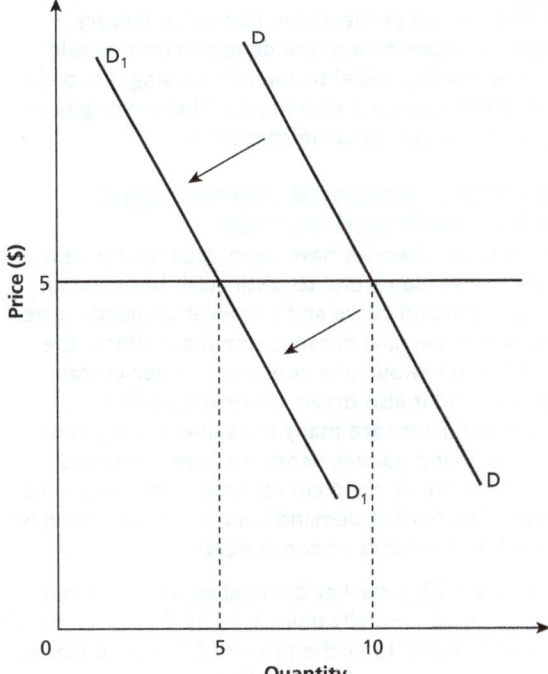

Figure 4.22 Shift in a demand curve to the left

The following factors will cause a change in demand, shifting the demand curve for a good such as cellular phones to the right. More of the good would be demanded at each and every price. The non-price factors of demand are:

1. An increase in income
2. A change in taste from landlines towards cell phones
3. A rise in the price of a substitute, e.g., email
4. A fall in the price of a complement good jointly used, e.g., phone cards
5. An increase in population size and structure. (If the population's structure is young, then there will be an increase in demand for cell phones among the young population.)
6. A longer time period will allow for better information to reach customers
7. Number of uses: if a product has multiple uses, demand would increase at all prices
8. Government law: if the state decrees that auto insurance is compulsory, there will be a significant change in demand
9. Change in seasons: demand for cricket bats will shift to the right in the cricket season
10. Change in distribution of income.

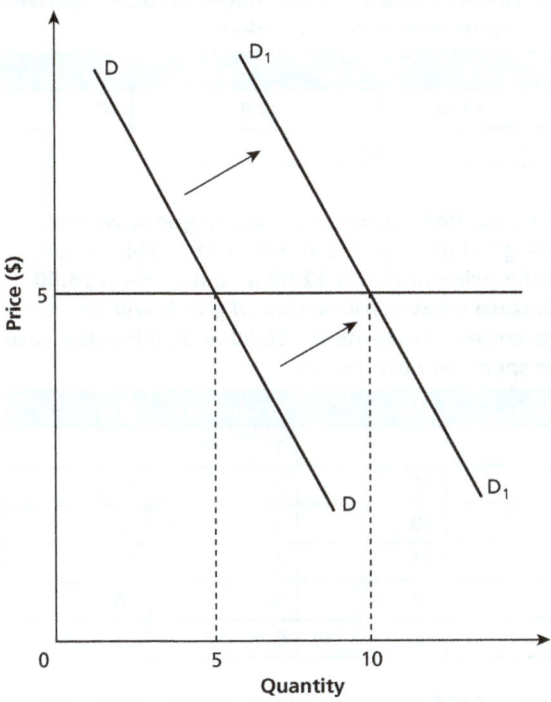

Figure 4.21 Shift in a demand curve to the right

If, however, all of the above non-price factors change the opposite way, the demand curve would accordingly shift parallel to the left, causing less to be demanded at each and every price. These changes are analysed in greater detail in chapter 8.

Individual demand curves and market demand curves

Now that two theories have been used to derive a demand curve, be careful to distinguish between an individual demand curve and a market demand curve. An individual demand curve is one that reflects the purchasing behaviour of a consumer under certain conditions and it also draws on *ceteris paribus* assumptions. There are many consumers in a given market so that a market demand curve is derived from adding the demand curves of all consumers in a given market. Market demand curves may, however, be derived for thousands of consumers.

In figure 4.23, a market demand curve is derived from adding horizontally units 3, 5 and 9 at price $5.00 and units 5, 9 and 15 at the price of $2.00. The market demand curve is therefore DD DD.

Key point
A market demand curve is derived by the horizontal addition of the individual demand curves in a particular market, for example tomatoes.

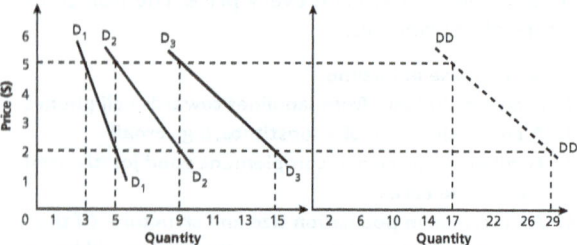

Figure 4.23 Deriving a market demand curve by horizontal addition

Chapter summary

> Demand is the willingness and ability to pay for a good or service at a given price and time period.
> Two main theories that explain demand theory are the cardinalist (using numbers) and ordinalist (using ranking).
> The cardinalist theory of the law of diminishing marginal utility explains that we pay less for more goods because marginal utility falls with each good consumed. Consumer equilibrium is given by the formula **MU = P**.
> The optimal purchase rule explains that in allocating expenditure among several goods, consumers aim to achieve the same level of satisfaction per dollar spent for each good. It is expressed by the formula.

$$\frac{MU_x}{P_x} = \frac{MU_y}{P_y} = \frac{MU_z}{P_z}$$

> Cardinalist theory overcomes the criticisms of utility theory's assumption that satisfaction cannot be measured by ranking bundles of goods.
> It asserts that more or less of a good is bought when there is a price fall due to a combination of substitution and income effects that complement or counteract each other.
> Normal goods have a positive income effect, unlike inferior and Giffen goods. The substitution effect operates consistently as an increase in quantity demanded.
> Extension and contraction of demand describe changes in quantity demanded due to price changes when non-price factors are unchanged.
> Changes in demand are changes in quantity demanded at each and every price. In both cases the demand curve changes its position when conditions of demand change.
> Market demand curves are the horizontal addition of many individual demand curves.

Practice questions

1. If a consumer purchases the snacks shown in the table below and is observing the optimal purchase rule, what is the marginal utility derived from purchasing two nutcakes?

Good	Price	Quantity	MU
Chocolate bar	$2	6	10
Nutcake	$3	2	X

2. A consumer wishes to purchase goods whose marginal utilities are shown in the table below. If the price of rice is $2.00 lb and chicken $4.00 lb, state what combination of goods will be purchased if income is $28.00 and all income is to be spent on both goods.

Q Rice	MU	Q Chicken	MU
1	38	1	24
2	29	2	23
3	19	3	22
4	11	4	12
5	7	5	10
6	6	6	8

3. Jill has $100 per month to spend on video games and novels. Video games cost $20 each and novels cost $20 each.
   a. (i) Define 'marginal utility'.
      (ii) Calculate Jill's marginal utility from:
         1) video games
         2) novels
   b. Draw a diagram showing Jill's budget constraint.

Quantity	Utility from video games	Utility from novels	Marginal utility		Marginal utility per dollar	
			Video games	Novels	Video games	Novels
0	0	0				
1	30	30				
2	40	38				
3	48	44				
4	54	46				
5	58	47				

c. (i) Calculate the marginal utility per dollar of Jill's consumption choices.
   (ii) State the optimal number of video games and the optimal number of novels that Jill will consume in a month.
d. State how each of the following will affect the quantity of video games and novels consumed by Jill:
   (i) An increase in the money she has to spend by $20, *ceteris paribus*.
   (ii) An increase in the price of ONE of the goods, *ceteris paribus*.

4. Brian has an income of $15.00 to spend on snacks and movies that are normal goods. Prices of snacks and movies are $1.00 and $1.50 respectively. The price of movies falls to $1.00.

   a. Draw a diagram to show income and substitution effects.
   b. Give the definition of a Giffen good.

INTRODUCTORY ECONOMICS A TEXTBOOK FOR CAPE ECONOMICS STUDENTS

5 Elasticity of demand

Chapter 5 Elasticity of demand

LEARNING OBJECTIVES

- Define elasticity of demand.
- Explain price, cross, and income elasticity.
- Calculate price, cross and income elasticity.
- Identify and explain the three types of elasticity.
- Explain the uses of the three types of elasticity.
- Apply the concepts of elasticity.

REQUIRED KNOWLEDGE

- Income and substitution effects
- Factors of demand
- Calculating percentages and calculating gradients.

TOPIC VALUE

This aspect of demand gives some insight into the reasons why people respond to changes in price in the way that they do. Some price changes result in significant changes in demand.

Introduction

Elasticity of demand is defined as the degree of responsiveness of quantity demanded of a good or service in response to changes in the three main influences on demand, namely price, income, and prices of substitutes and complements. Since elastic infers 'stretching', quantity demanded may 'stretch' or contract when price, income and prices of other related goods change.

Price elasticity

Refer to figure 5.1, which illustrates the changing equilibrium of a price change. In indifference curve theory you would observe that both income and substitution effects cause a significant change in quantity demanded. According to figure 5.1, the change is from Y_1 to Y_2 units of good Y.

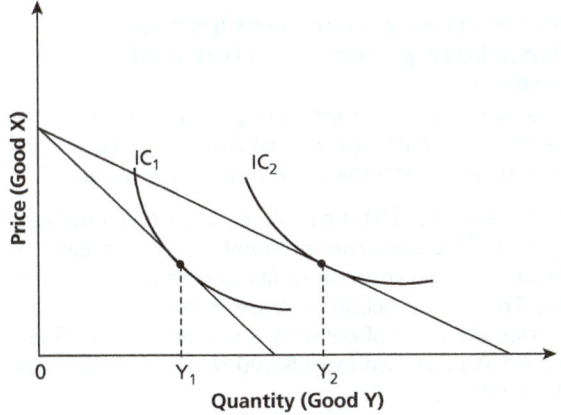

Figure 5.1 An elastic response

While the change seems significant, this response can in fact be measured quite accurately. There are two ways to calculate the elasticity or 'responsiveness' of quantity demanded due to price changes. They are:

1. **By formula**
2. **By change in total expenditure from a price change.**

Calculating elasticity by formula

The formula used to measure price elasticity of demand is:

$$\frac{\text{percentage change in quantity demanded of good A}}{\text{percentage change in price of good A}}$$

If the formula is applied, then a change from $4 to $5 (see figure 5.2) is now expressed as change in price, $4 to $5 = 1.

Percentage change = $5 - \frac{4}{4} \times 100 = 25\%$ or 0.25

Related change in quantity 3 to 2 = 1

Percentage change = $3 - \frac{2}{3} \times 100 = \frac{1}{3} \times 100 = -33\frac{1}{3}\%$ or -0.33

% Δ in Qd = $-33\frac{1}{3}\%$ or -0.33

% Δ in Price = $+25\%$ or $+0.25$

Price elasticity of demand therefore = $\frac{-0.33}{0.25} = -1.33$

Note a negative change in quantity equal to −0.33 is divided by a positive change in price of + 0.25, giving a negative answer of −1.33 (i.e., a $1 decrease in price leads to a 33 per cent increase in quantity demanded). All price elasticities of demand and downward sloping demand curves carry a negative sign but by convention the sign and the positive value is given. The negative sign is to indicate the inverse relationship between price and quantity demanded.

Two important aspects of the coefficient are the sign and the size. A coefficient therefore of −1.33 with a negative sign indicates that the slope is negative and the good in question is normal according to price.

The sign therefore indicates the category of the good, which may be normal or inferior. The size refers to the value 1.33 in the above example. If it is greater than 1 then the interpretation is an elastic response. An example of a good that is elastic in demand is branded lines of clothing or footwear.

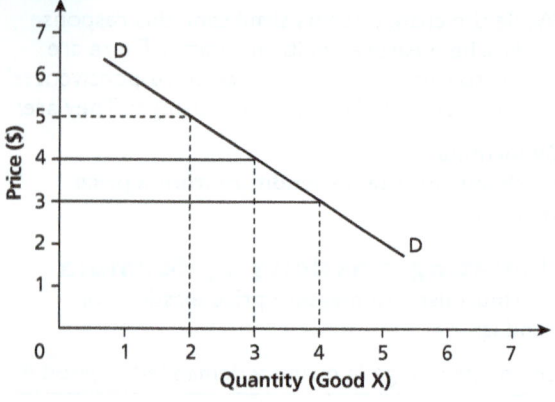

Figure 5.2 An elastic response measured

When the coefficient is less than one, the price elasticity of demand is said to be inelastic. In figure 5.3, a fall in price of good X from $10 to $5 induces a quantity change of 1 (4 − 5). Applying the formula will give the following:

$$\text{Price elasticity of demand (PED)} = \frac{\%\text{Change in } Q_d = \left(Q_2 - \frac{Q_1}{Q_1}\right) \times 100 = \left(5 - \frac{4}{4}\right) \times 100 = \left(+\frac{1}{4}\right) \times 100 = +0.25}{\%\text{ Change in Price} = \left(P_2 - \frac{P_1}{P_1}\right) \times 100 = \left(5 - \frac{10}{10}\right) \times 100 = \left(-\frac{1}{2}\right) \times 100 = -0.50}$$

$$\text{PED} = \frac{+0.25}{-0.50} = -\frac{1}{2} \text{ or } -0.5$$

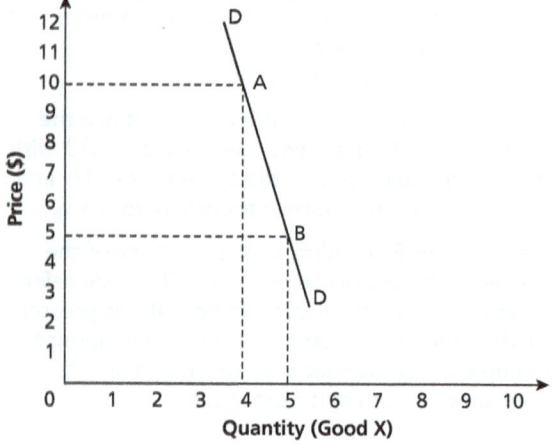

Figure 5.3 An inelastic response measured for good X

An example of a good that is inelastic in demand is electricity. Since the coefficient is less than 1 it is inelastic in demand. Note again that the sign categorises the type of good (normal) and size, plus the degree of responsiveness.

Common error
Guard against confusing the elasticity of demand of a point on the curve and elasticity of demand between two points. A demand curve that is a straight line has a constant slope mathematically, but the elasticity coefficients change along the points of the demand curve. Calculating price elasticity of demand is done for a segment or arc of the curve in percentage terms.

It is important to note that in figure 5.3 calculating price elasticity of demand from A to B is different for a price rise, compared to a price fall. When price falls from $10.00 to $5.00 the coefficient value is 0.5. However, a rise from $5.00 to $10.00 gives a different coefficient, that is, from $5.00 to $10.00 = $\frac{5}{5}$ = 1

The change in quantity is from 5 to 4 = 1

The % change is $\frac{1}{5}$ or 20%. The coefficient is 20% = $-\frac{1}{5}$ or − 0.2

Dividing $\frac{-20}{100}$% = − 0.2

For the same segment A B there are two coefficients, i.e., − 0.5 and − 0.2

To get around this problem the **average or midpoint** price elasticity of demand formula is applied by dividing formula 1 and formula 2 as follows:

1. $\frac{\text{change in quantities} \times 100}{\text{sum of quantities}}$

2. $\frac{\text{change in price} \times 100}{\text{sum of prices}}$

3. **Divide formula 1 by formula 2 to find point elasticity**

Summary
Elasticity of demand measures the responsiveness of quantity demanded to changes in price. Coefficients greater than 1 are elastic responses, while coefficients less than 1 are inelastic.

Since a rise and fall in price over a segment of the curve yield two different coefficients, this is solved using the midpoint or average formula. The sign preceding the coefficient is important because it reflects the type of good. A negative sign implies a normal good according to price while a positive sign implies a Giffen good. The size refers to the degree of responsiveness, that is, where the coefficient is elastic, inelastic, unitary, zero or infinite.

The total revenue method of estimating price elasticity of demand
The second method of estimating price elasticity of demand is the change in total revenue or total expenditure of consumers for a price rise or fall.

Total revenue (TR) is calculated as price multiplied by quantity. The basic rule of thumb is if an increase in price causes total revenue to fall, demand is said to be elastic. For a price fall, an increase in revenue indicates that price elasticity of demand is similarly elastic. See figure 5.4. A price rise from $5.00 to $8.00 yields a fall in TR as follows:

$$15 \times \$5 = \$75$$
$$4 \times \$8 = \$32$$

From a rise of $5 to $8 the fall in TR = $43

Chapter 5 Elasticity of demand

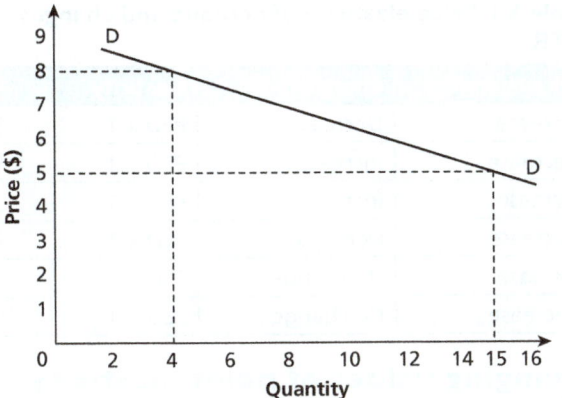

Figure 5.4 An elastic response: total revenue method

A fall in price will cause TR to rise by $43.00. In figure 5.5 a price rise or fall yields opposite results. A price rise in this instance causes TR to rise instead and a price fall causes TR to fall.

Example: 5 × $10 = $50.00
           4 × $20 = $80.00
Increase in TR = $30.00

Likewise, a price fall will cause TR to fall by $30. In this case, price elasticity of demand is said to be inelastic. There are instances when there is neither a rise nor fall but a constant coefficient = 1; in this case, it is called **unitary** elasticity.

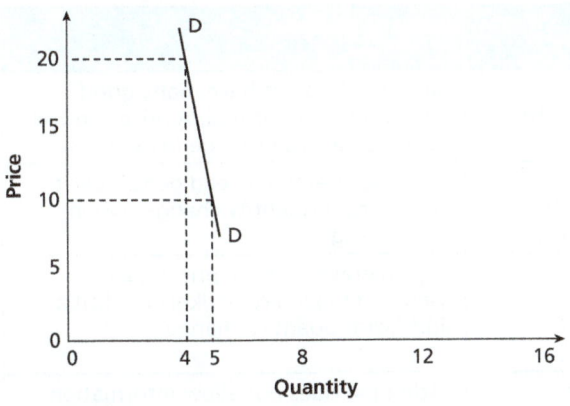

Figure 5.5 An inelastic response: TR method

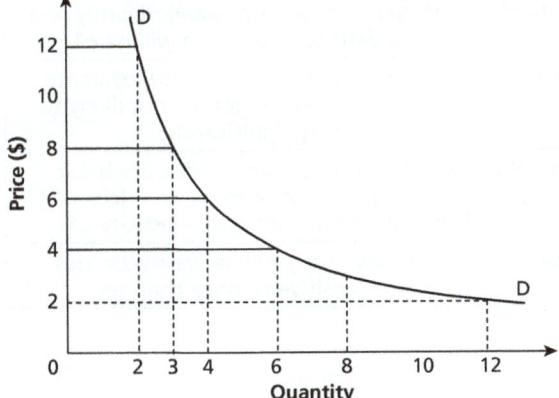

Figure 5.6 Unitary elasticity: TR method

In figure 5.6 any price multiplied by quantity would yield a TR of $24.00 whether prices are rising or falling. This is a unique feature of unitary elasticity. For example, at a price of $12.00 and quantity of two units, TR = $24.00. If the price falls to $6, the corresponding quantity would be 4. Therefore, TR = 6 × 4 = $24.00. Any price increase or fall will yield a TR = $24.00.

Extremes in elasticity

There are two extremes in price elasticity of demand. They are zero or perfectly inelastic demand and infinite or perfectly elastic demand.

Zero elasticity

As the coefficient implies the value is always equal to zero. Figure 5.7 shows that a rise in price will yield a coefficient as follows:

For a price rise of $2 to $3

Change in quantity = 0

% Δ in P = 0.5 or 50%

$$\frac{\% \Delta \text{ in Qd}}{\% \Delta \text{ in price}} = \frac{0}{0.5} = 0$$

For a price fall $3 to $2

% Δ in Qd = 0

% Δ in P = $\frac{1}{3}$ or 0.3

$$\frac{\% \Delta \text{ in Qd}}{\% \Delta \text{ in P}} = \frac{0}{0.3} = 0$$

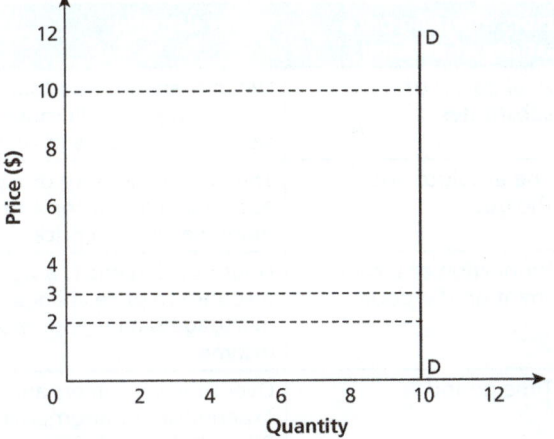

Figure 5.7 Perfect inelasticity

Any value divided by zero is equal to zero. An example of this type of elasticity may be observed for the price changes of insulin for persons suffering from diabetes. They would purchase the drug whatever the changes in price.

Perfect elasticity

In the case of perfect elasticity the price does not change but quantity does change. In fact, at a price of $10.00 an unlimited amount is demanded. Hence price elasticity of demand is infinite (∞). Figure 5.8 shows a horizontal demand curve at a price of $10.00. The curve is perfectly elastic.

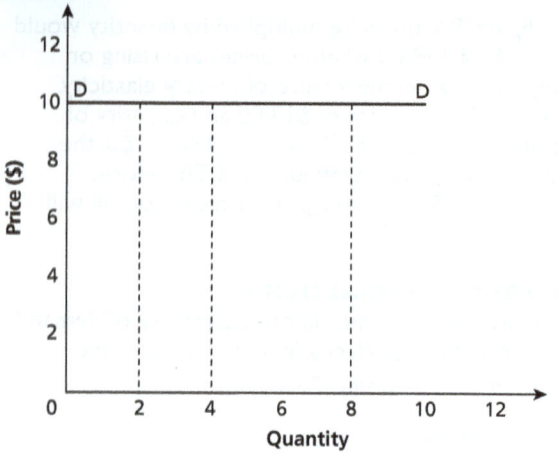

Figure 5.8 Perfect elasticity

Table 5.1 Price elasticity of demand and changes in TR

Price change	Change in TR	Elasticity
Increase	Decrease	PED > 1
Decrease	Increase	PED > 1
Increase	Increase	PED < 1
Decrease	Decrease	PED < 1
Increase	No change	PED = 1
Decrease	No change	PED = 1

Key point

There are two methods of estimating price elasticity of demand. They are the formula method and the change in TR method. They are invaluable to an entrepreneur who has to price his product according to the price elasticity of demand. An important point to note is that price elasticity of demand changes throughout the points of a linear demand curve.

Changing values of point elasticity of demand

The midpoint of the linear demand curve in figure 5.9 has a price elasticity of demand equal to 1. Note that price elasticity of demand starts at zero at point D on the horizontal axis and increases in value to point A on the vertical axis. Points to the right of B above have a value less than 1, while to the left of B values are greater than 1. At point B, the value is equal to 1.

Although price elasticity of demand at a point can be calculated by algebra, a quick way to measure it is at a single point, for example at point B. In order to estimate the elasticity at that point the distance BD is divided by distance BA, which is equal to 1. Price elasticity of demand at C will then be CD/CA = <1.

Table 5.2 Factors affecting elasticity of demand

Factors affecting price elasticity of demand	Elastic demand	Inelastic demand
1. Availability of substitutes	When there are good substitutes, a change in price will cause demand to fall significantly, e.g., soft drinks.	Gasoline does not have many good substitutes as a car fuel. A price rise will not cause a large change in demand.
2. The absolute price of the good	The higher the price of a good, e.g., automobile or laptop computer, the more elastic for a price rise or fall.	Low-price items like lead pencils elicit insignificant quantity changes when price changes.
3. Proportion of income spent on the good	House buying elicits a significant response to price changes, since a mortgage is a large proportion of income.	Buying erasers whose prices have risen and fallen are unlikely to elicit a significant quantity change.
4. Time period	Over time consumers adjust their expenditure to alternative products. Price elasticity of demand is >1.	Little time does not allow information on price changes to affect demand.
5. Durability of a good	If the good lasts for a short time people would need it quickly. Price elasticity of demand is >1.	Products like television sets and refrigerators are not changed easily and price elasticity of demand will be <1.
6. Advertising	Goods not promoted tend to have an elasticity >1.	Advertising may cause brand loyalty to increase. Price changes are not likely to affect quantity significantly.
7. Habit-forming goods and services	For goods that are not addictive or habit forming, e.g., clothing, price elasticity of demand is usually >1.	Alcohol, tobacco and coffee are habit forming and not sensitive to price changes, therefore price elasticity <1.
8. Necessities and luxuries	Luxuries, e.g., swimming pool, price elasticity of demand > 1.	Electricity and gasoline are necessities and not sensitive to price changes.

Chapter 5 Elasticity of demand

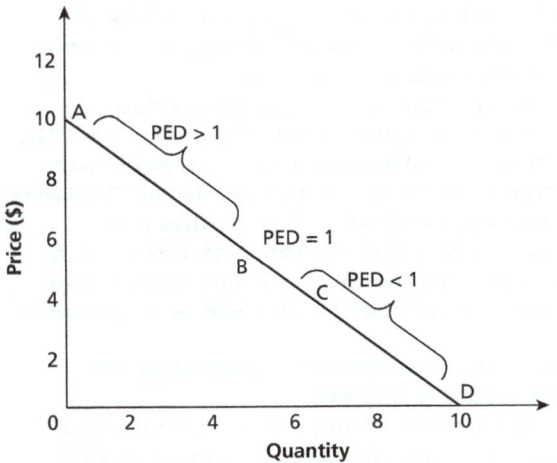

Figure 5.9 Point price elasticity of demand

Summary

Price elasticities of demand differ along different points on a curve. In a straight line linear curve the midpoint has a value of 1. To the left of the midpoint, values are greater than 1 in ascending value. Similarly, to the right of midpoint, values are less than 1 in descending value. A simple formula for determining point elasticity is the inverse of slope multiplied by price at any point of measurement.

The usefulness of price elasticity

- If price elasticity of demand is elastic, decreasing prices via discounts or bargain sales yield an increase in TR.
- If price elasticity of demand for a good or service is inelastic, a firm may raise prices to increase profit, e.g., alcohol, cigarettes, gasoline, electricity.
- Firms may separate markets with different elasticities to price discriminate, e.g., home and foreign markets or night rates for internet users versus daytime rates.
- Advertising creates brand loyalty, making demand inelastic as well as increasing market share for a firm. Successful advertising shifts the demand curve to the right.
- The government may raise taxes on habit-forming goods and services in order to raise tax revenues, e.g., gasoline, alcohol, tobacco and gambling.
- Unions may bargain for higher wages in industries whose products have an inelastic demand, e.g., water or electricity.
- A government may lower (devalue) the price of its currency to encourage an inflow of foreign revenue from the sale of exports with an elastic demand. Refer to chapter 33 for more information on exchange rates.

Cross elasticity of demand

If you were thinking of buying a watch but found out that the battery is just as expensive as the watch, you would rethink your purchase of the watch. The same goes for computers and printers, ink or compact discs.

Your concerns have to do with another significant influence on demand, that is, the change in the price of one good and how it affects the quantity demanded of a good related to it; for example, computers and printers are known as complements or goods used jointly. Relatedly, how does the price of frozen goat meat affect the quantity demanded of fresh goat meat, given that they are substitutes?

These concerns are all related to cross elasticity of demand (CED) or cross price elasticity of demand, which is defined as the degree of responsiveness of quantity demanded of one good in response to the price change in another related good. It is expressed in the formula:

$$CED = \frac{\% \Delta \text{ in Qd of good A}}{\% \Delta \text{ in price of good B}}$$

Once again the sign and size are very critical in categorising the good and measuring its price responsiveness. If the coefficient is a negative sign, the category of the good is said to be a complement.

See figure 5.10. When the price of a flashlight falls from $100 to $50, the quantity of batteries demanded increases from 50 to 125 units since more flashlights will be bought with a price fall, then CED of batteries is expressed as:

Δ in Qd of batteries = 125 − 50 = 75.

The % change is 75/50 × 100 = 150%

Δ in price of flashlight = $50 − $100 = $−50 or

$\% \Delta = \frac{-50 \times 100}{100} = -50\%$

CED therefore $\frac{+150\%}{-50\%} = -3$

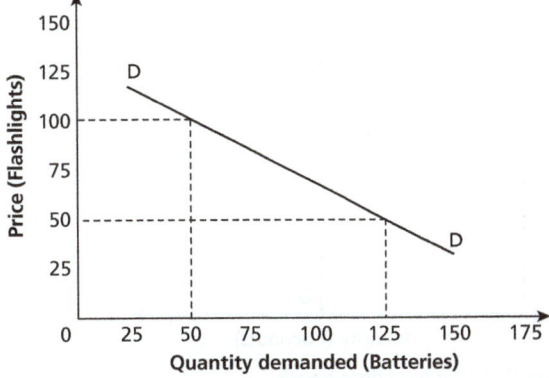

Figure 5.10 Complementary goods

Note the sign and the size denote a complement that is very responsive. Similarly, for substitutes, consider wheat flour and cornmeal flour. Refer to figure 5.11. If the price of a bag of wheat flour rises from $10 to $15 the demand for wheat flour will fall. The demand for a substitute, cornmeal flour, will rise.

The CED of cornmeal = % Δ in Qd of cornmeal

$= 20 - \frac{10}{10} \times 100 = +100\%$

% Δ in price of wheat flour = $15 - \frac{10}{10} \times 100 = +50\%$

$\frac{+100\%}{+50\%} = +2$

CED = +2

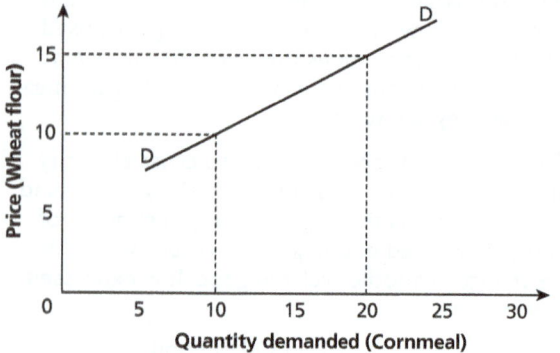

Figure 5.11 Substitute goods

Note again the positive sign associated with the category that is a substitute when whole wheat prices change and the quantity of cornmeal demanded increases. The size denotes how responsive cornmeal is as a good substitute for wheat flour.

Independent goods

Refer to figure 5.12. When goods are not related in any way they are said to be independent and carry a coefficient of zero.

Example: % Δ in Qd of coconuts = 0

% Δ in price of gold jewellery = −10%

Therefore CED = 0

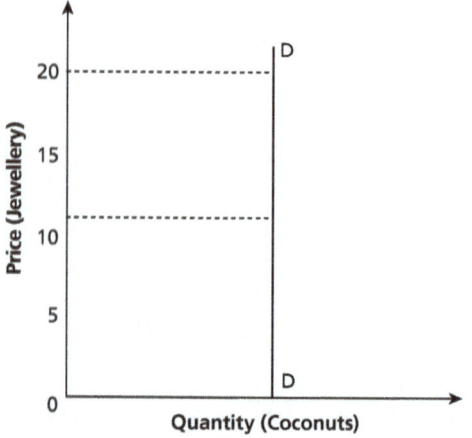

Figure 5.12 Independent goods

Summary

Cross elasticity of demand measures the percentage change in quantity demanded of one good when the price of another related good changes. For complements, the sign is negative; for substitutes, it is positive; and for independent goods, the coefficient is equal to zero.

> The main factor affecting cross elasticity of demand is the extent to which goods are close complements or substitutes.
> A high negative CED suggests very close complements; for example, CD players and CDs, although a fall in price of CDs may not impact strongly on the quantity demanded of CD players. Similarly, a CED with a high positive value suggests very close substitutes; for example, a peanut drink and chocolate milk drink, or two competing brands of toothpaste, or soap powder.

The value of cross elasticity of demand to a firm

It is important for a firm to know CED values for complements and substitutes. If there is high CED between hot dog sausages and hot dog bread, for example, and there is a price rise for hot dog sausages, firms may counteract the expected fall in demand for hot dog sausages by offering hot dog bread on sale, or selling them together at a bargain price. For example, you may observe that coffee is sometimes sold with cream in the same package for one price.

Similarly, if CD players increase in price a firm may counteract the expected fall in demand for CD players by offering free compact discs.

Cross elasticity of demand is largely influenced by the closeness in the relationship of substitutes and complements. A high value in both instances refers to a very close relationship between the products.

Income elasticity of demand

Since income is a main influence on demand, a change in real income, that is, a price fall or income rise without inflation, will very likely increase demand for goods and services.

Recall that an increase in income will cause a shift in the demand curve to the right for normal goods, whereas an increase in price induces changes along the curve. It was also noted that when incomes increased, there was a fall in demand for some type of goods called inferior goods.

Income elasticity of demand (YED) measures the percentage change in quantity demanded of goods and services in response to changes in income. Expressed in formula it is:

$$\frac{\% \Delta \text{ in Qd}}{\% \Delta \text{ in Income}}$$

A coefficient greater than 1 is said to be elastic, less than 1 inelastic and zero elastic if there is no change in quantity demanded when income changes. Once more the sign and size are important. A positive sign indicates a normal good according to income. See figure 5.13. A negative sign indicates an inferior good, as shown in figure 5.14.

Chapter 5 Elasticity of demand

Table 5.3 The relationship between type of good, price elasticity of demand, sign and demand curve

Type of good	PED (sign)	YED (sign)	CED (sign)	Demand curve
Normal	Negative	Positive	-----	Downward sloping: negative slope
Inferior	Negative	Negative	-----	Downward sloping: negative slope
Giffen	Positive	Negative	-----	Upward sloping: positive slope
Veblen, snob value or good of ostentation	Positive	Positive	-----	Upward sloping: positive gradient
Complement	-----	-----	Negative	Downward negative slope
Substitute	-----	-----	Positive	Upward positive slope

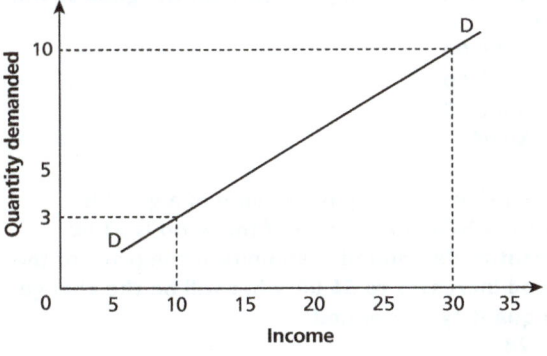

Figure 5.13 A normal good

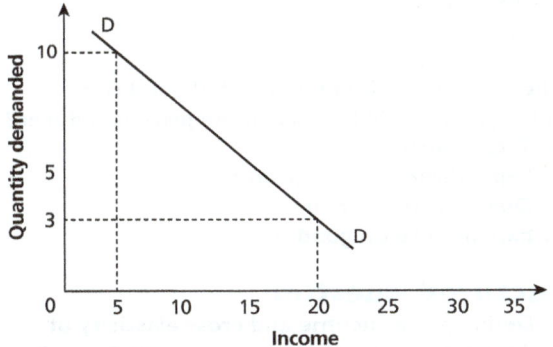

Figure 5.14 An inferior good

Note that there are occasions when real changes in income cause no change in quantity demanded. This is also called a zero income-elastic response. Moreover, a single good may, over time, experience all three types of income elasticities as illustrated in the Engel curve in figure 5.15.

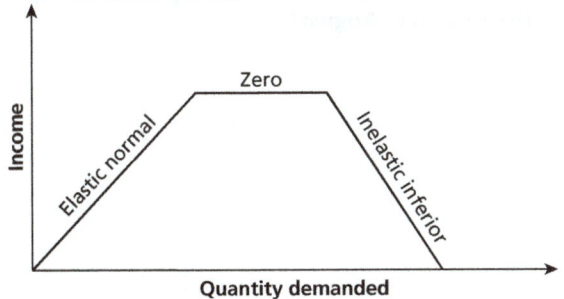

Figure 5.15 The Engel curve

If a newly employed person travels by bus to work, small income increases will cause his or her demand for bus travel to be stable. They may demand 20 hours a month of bus travel if their income is $5,000 monthly.

Yet, despite an improved income of $7,000, their bus travel stays at 20 hours, with perhaps carpooling as well. After 7 or 8 years and multiple income increases they may purchase a car and use less bus travel. Bus travel, therefore, could be a normal good with respect to income, zero elastic and an inferior good over a period of time.

Goods that respond positively to increases in real income are sometimes called superior or income-elastic goods. Some examples are houses, automobiles, swimming pools, expensive jewellery, plasma television sets, satellite dishes, upscale restaurant dining and foreign travel. There is an upsurge in activity in these markets when an economy is enjoying high-income changes in buoyant economic conditions.

Factors affecting income elasticity of demand

It is assumed that income responsive goods and services depend on levels of disposable income that are generally determined by rates of taxation. In addition, rates of inflation and expectation of inflation would temper consumers' demand for income-elastic goods. Expectations in an economy may also be a determining factor when crime rates are high and political stability not assured.

If a country has a high standard of living, as in developed countries, and consumers are accustomed to the purchase of income-elastic goods their income elasticity of demand may be high, for example foreign holidays.

Wealthy individuals react to increases in real income differently from average or low-income earners, since low-income earners may purchase only basic necessities.

In developing countries with steady economic growth, demand for inferior goods falls in favour of superior goods, such as tertiary level education.

Value of income elasticity of demand and decision making

> A firm may benefit from a knowledge of income elasticity of demand when economic conditions are positive and incomes are rising. Cars, house buying, foreign travel, upscale dining and real estate markets record high profit levels.
> In a recession when incomes are falling, firms may concentrate on selling inferior goods, e.g., basic goods and services. Firms trading in superior goods may target high-income earners or advertise extensively. Insurance and other financial products experience high demand during an economic boom.
> Caribbean hotels target markets in foreign countries whose economic growth rates are rising, because real incomes in those countries are likely to be rising as well.

Summary

Income elasticity of demand (YED) measures the relationship between changes in real income and quantity demanded as is expressed in the formula:

$$\frac{\% \Delta \text{ in Qd}}{\% \Delta \text{ in income}}$$

Negative and positive values of YED indicate inferior and normal/superior goods respectively. An Engel curve illustrates all three types of income elasticity.

Chapter summary

> Elasticity in economic language is the extent or degree of responsiveness of quantity demanded to a change in three significant determinants of demand: the absolute price of the good, level of income, and price of other related goods.
> It is calculated by formulae. For price elasticity of demand, changes in TR are also used.
> The average or midpoint formula is the most accurate measure of a segment of the curve because values are different for the same segment of a curve.
> Income elasticity measures the percentage changes in quantity demanded with respect to changes in income, while CED measures the extent to which goods are related.
> The sign and size are important in categorising and interpreting elasticities of demand.
> Elasticity is a useful tool of analysis for firms, governments and unions in predicting changes in the economic environment.
> Normal, inferior, Giffen, complements, substitutes and snob value goods all carry different PED, YED and CED.

Practice questions

Multiple choice questions

1. The price elasticity of demand of good X is 0.5. If the price of the good changes by 10 per cent what is the corresponding percentage change in quantity?
   a. 10 per cent
   b. 20 per cent
   c. 5 per cent
   d. 15 per cent

2. The demand for good X is perfectly elastic. 50 units are sold at Bds $3.00 per unit. If the price is raised to $4.00 expenditure on the good X will be:
   a. $150.00
   b. $200.00
   c. $600.00
   d. $0.00

3. The price elasticity of demand of a good is unitary. When the price of the good is $3.00, quantity demanded is 40 units. If the price of the good increases to $6.00, what will be the change in quantity demanded?
   a. 24
   b. 20
   c. No change
   d. 80

4. The price elasticity of demand of good B is unitary. What will increase if the price is reduced?
   a. Total revenue
   b. Expenditure on substitutes
   c. Quantity demanded
   d. Expenditure on good B.

Structured question

1. a. Define price, income and cross elasticity of demand. Support your answers with formulae, examples and appropriate diagrams.
   b. The Caribbean is a popular tourist destination. Identify three factors that may influence the price elasticity of demand for hotel accommodation in Barbados in the month of July. What factors may determine YED for holidays in Jamaica in the month of August?
   c. How may a hotelier in Antigua use a knowledge of CED to boost his profits during the month of August?

Chapter 6 How to produce: theory of supply I

INTRODUCTORY ECONOMICS A TEXTBOOK FOR CAPE ECONOMICS STUDENTS

LEARNING OBJECTIVES

- Identify the factors of production.
- Explain the periods of production.
- Explain the law of variable proportions.
- Explain and illustrate total, marginal and average product.
- Explain the relationships between TPP, MPP and APP.

REQUIRED KNOWLEDGE

Basic theory on:
- The short- and long-run periods of production
- The law of diminishing returns
- Economies and diseconomies of scale.

TOPIC VALUE

Producers create the supply to match the demand of consumers.

Production

Production is simply the act of converting inputs into output; for example baker + flour + yeast + oven = bread.

Units of production

A unit of production is a factory or plant, for example an oil refinery.

A unit of management is the firm's decision-making unit relating to the operations of the factory or plant.

Production function

The production function expresses a mathematical relationship which shows the maximum output that can be achieved by a number of combinations of inputs, as shown in table 6.1.

Table 6.1 **A production function**

Labour (units)	Capital (units)	Output (kg)
40	10	2,000
100	20	5,000

In table 6.1, note the ratio of labour to capital is 4 to 1 $\left(\frac{40}{10}\right)$ and 5 to 1 $\left(\frac{100}{20}\right)$, for outputs of 2,000 kg and 5,000 kg respectively.

The periods of production

The periods of production explain the ability of a firm to increase output when the variable and fixed inputs are varied. There are four periods of production.

1. The momentary or market period
2. The short-run period
3. The long-run period
4. The very long-run period.

In order to understand these periods of production, it is necessary to explain what are fixed and variable factors of production.

A fixed factor is one that is not easily changed, takes time to replace and exists whether or not there is any production. Also, it is unchanged during the process of production. For example, the ovens in a bakery remain unchanged after bread products are made. It could also be a furnace, building or land.

A variable factor changes as output changes; it is easily changed and may also be altered during production; for example, flour to bread, iron ore to steel, or sugar cane to sugar.

The momentary period of production is a period when output cannot be increased because it is impossible for the variable or fixed factors to be changed at a moment's notice. For example, if the bakery runs out of bread at the time you are there, you simply cannot get any in the momentary/market period. Perhaps in a three-hour time period you may return to purchase some bread. A filled car park, cinema and sold-out cricket match are other examples of situations when the capacity cannot be increased in the momentary period.

The short-run period of production is the period of production when output can be increased by changing the variable factors. During this production period, at least one fixed factor cannot be changed, for example in our previous bakery example more bread can be baked not by changing the ovens but by increasing the quantity of ingredients such as flour, and so on. For a filled car park, an adjoining empty lot may be rented within a week.

The long-run period is the time taken to change both variable and fixed factors in order to increase production. In our bakery example, running out of bread may mean the bakery is too small to accommodate the growth in customers. The profit-minded owners may therefore change their fixed factors – expand the premises, change to automatic ovens, or open a branch as well. In each case, all factors are changed to increase production. Note also that in the long-run since all factors can be changed they are then regarded as variable.

The very long-run is the period of time, which is usually very long, for example 30 to 50 years, during which output may be increased through new inventions, innovations or the emergence of new technology.

It is important to note that there is no fixed period in terms of time. The short-run is not three days or one week or the long-run two to three years. These production periods vary from industry to industry. For example, a coconut vendor's long-run is the time taken to replace a beast of burden or van, which is perhaps one month, whereas in the oil industry it may take five years to change an oil platform.

Chapter 6 How to produce: theory of supply I

Summary
Production functions show a mathematical relationship between inputs and output. This relationship may take place during four periods of production, namely, the momentary, short, long and very long-run periods. All periods show change in output and the ability to change the combination of inputs.

Table 6.2 Time allowed to change

Period of production	Fixed factor	Variable factor
1. Momentary	Cannot change	Cannot change
2. Short-run	Cannot change	Can change
3. Long-run	Can change	Can change
4. Very long-run	Can change easily	Can change easily

It is important in output theory to recognise the difference in the periods because the input/output relationships are different for each period.

The short-run
In this period of production, the input/output relationship is influenced by two laws.

1. The law of increasing returns to the variable factor
2. The law of diminishing returns to the variable factor.

Both laws may be represented by the law of variable proportions, which explains the relationship between the total physical product (TPP), marginal physical product (MPP) and average physical product (APP).

The law of variable proportions states that as increasing amounts of a variable factor, for example labour, are combined with a fixed amount of a fixed factor, for example land, returns to the variable factor will initially increase at an increasing rate (law of increasing returns) until they peak and then (law of diminishing returns) fall to zero.

Before these laws are discussed, different measurements of output need to be explained. Refer to table 6.3.

Table 6.3 Total, marginal and average product

No. of workers	Total physical product	Marginal physical product	Average physical product
1	12	12	12
2	27	15	13.5
3	44	17	14.7
4	58	14	14.5
5	69	11	13.8
6	77	8	12.8
7	82	5	11.7
8	82	0	10.25

Table 6.3 shows the input/output relationship of workers on a one-hectare farm of land in planting tomatoes. The total physical product refers to total output per time period. For example, worker number 1 in the above table plants 12 tomato plants per day.

The marginal physical product (MPP) measures the change in total physical product (TPP) when one additional unit of labour is added. It is expressed as ΔTPP/Δinput. The APP or average physical product is the total physical product divided by the quantity of inputs.

Observations
In table 6.3, note that the change from worker number 1 to 2 yields an MPP of 15, as TPP increases from 12 to 27 units. Workers (variable factors) are working on one hectare of land (fixed factor) banking the soil, fertilising and planting tomato seedlings.

Observe:

> - **The TPP is rising throughout from worker number 1 to 7, levelling off at 82 units.**
> - **The MPP is rising by increasing amounts, i.e., 12, 15, 17, etc. (increasing marginal returns) and then declining to 14, 11, 8, etc. (decreasing returns).**
> - **The APP is also rising and falling from 12 to 14.7 and 14.6 to 10.25 respectively.**

The last two measures of output are also related to productivity, which is different from production. Productivity expresses a rate of production, hence it is given by the formula, output/input, here tomato plants/worker. Production is simply total output per time period such as day/month or year.

Common error
Productivity is frequently confused with production. The way in which these concepts are related to each other can be seen in figure 6.1, which is drawn from table 6.3.

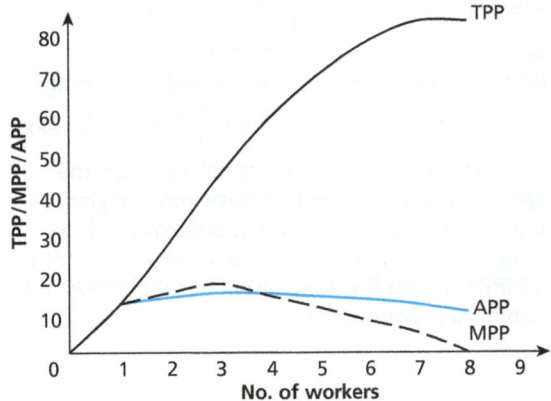

Figure 6.1 Total, marginal and average physical product

Observe in figure 6.1 that total physical product (TPP), marginal physical product (MPP) and average physical product (APP) all rise and fall.

- Even if MPP is declining but greater than APP, APP is rising.
- When MPP cuts the APP, the APP immediately declines but remains positive until it reaches worker number 8, when it becomes negative.

Reasons for increasing returns

- From worker 1 to 3, each has more of the fixed factor (land) with which to work.
- Specialisation, also called division of labour, may increase output, i.e., one worker banks the soil, a second fertilises and a third plants seedlings, etc.

Reasons for diminishing returns to the variable factor

- The fixed factor becomes overcrowded as the ratio of workers to land changes (variable proportions or ratios).
- The monotony of repetitive work, worker apathy, disruption in production on the assembly line if one worker is absent or injured.

Assumptions of the law of diminishing returns

- Technology is fixed.
- All variable inputs are equally efficient.
- The short-run period is the period of production in question.
- Factors of production are mobile.

Common error

The law of diminishing returns (LDMR) is often confused with the law of diminishing marginal utility (LDMU). The LDMR relates to production while LDMU relates to consumption.

When a marginal value is higher than an average value, the average value will be rising. This is a mathematical fact. For example, if there are ten students who are 17 years old in a classroom the average age is 17, that is, $\frac{170}{10} = 17$. If a teacher is 30 years old and enters the room (the marginal addition) the total age is 200 years and the average of the teacher and class would be $\frac{200}{11} = 18.18$ years.

Note the effect of a higher marginal value on the average value. The relationship between marginal and average product in figure 6.2 emphasises how the marginal value controls the average value, that is, when MPP>APP, APP will be rising but if MPP<APP it would pull APP downward.

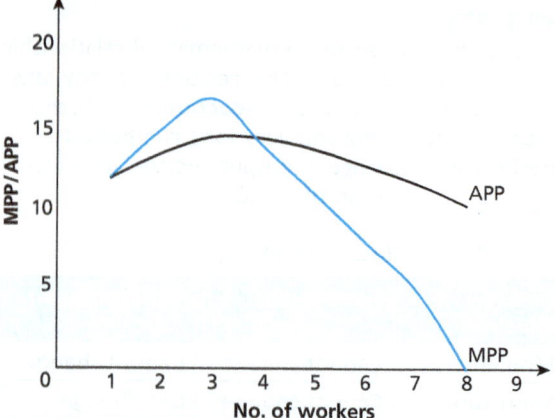

Figure 6.2 Average physical product and marginal physical product

The stages of production

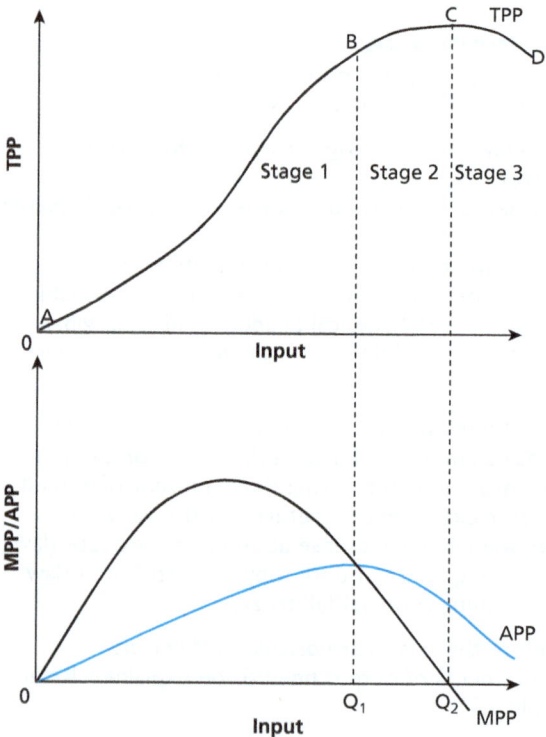

Figure 6.3 The stages of production

The TPP, APP and MPP illustrate three stages of production. Stage 1 is from A to B on the TPP curve. Stage 2 is between B and C on the TPP curve; AP is at a maximum when MPP is declining to 0. Stage 3 is from point C to D where TPP is declining because MPP is positive.

An entrepreneur would not produce at stage 3 because the TPP is declining and MPP is negative. Instead, a producer would produce at stage 1 (best returns) or stage 2 (where TPP is still increasing). Between stages 2 and 3, additional workers increase the total product until it declines.

Common error
The concept of increasing returns (to a variable factor) in short-run production is often confused with increasing returns to scale (due to the size of the firm). In the short-run the increasing returns are strictly to the variable factor, while in the long-run they are returns to all factors as the firm alters its scale of production.

Summary
The short-run period of production focuses on an important law relating to scarcity. It is called the law of diminishing returns or the law of variable proportions. It highlights three stages of production, stage 1 or 2 being the preferred stage for a profit-minded firm. It also diagramatically expresses the relationship between TPP, APP and MPP.

› A production function expresses a technical relationship between inputs and output; it is the maximum output from a range of combinations of inputs.
› There are four periods of production: the market period, short-run, long-run and very long-run periods of production.
› The law of variable proportions explains how and why variable inputs cannot continuously be increased to increase output.
› Returns to the variable factor increase because of division of labour and more of the fixed factor is available.
› Returns to the variable factors diminish because the fixed factor becomes overcrowded.
› Diminishing returns may cause a firm to engage in long-run production to satisfy excess demand, or if growth in customers outgrows the capacity of the firm.

A firm's attempt to satisfy expanding customer growth may be handicapped by diminishing returns to the variable factor in the short-run. It is for this reason that a firm will increase its capacity in the long-run by varying all of its factors, changing its scale of production as it does so. When both fixed and variable factors are changed such as, for example, in a bakery if the building is extended and oven and baking technology modernised, it is possible for output to increase by a greater proportion than the changes in inputs themselves.

Long-run production

Table 6.4 Increasing returns to scale

Capital (ovens)	Labour (bakers)	Output (loaves)
2	4	500
3	6	1,250

The long-run production function shown in table 6.4 illustrates that a percentage change in capital and labour of 50 per cent (2 to 3 ovens and 4 to 6 bakers) increases output by 150 per cent (500 to 1,250 loaves). When the percentage input change is exceeded by the percentage output change, this is called increasing returns to scale.

If a percentage change in output is less than the percentage change in input this is called decreasing returns to scale as shown in table 6.5.

Table 6.5 Decreasing returns to scale

Capital (ovens)	Labour (bakers)	Output (loaves)
2	3	500
4	6	600

Here, a 100 per cent change in capital and labour yields an output change of only 20 per cent. And if the percentage change in input yields the same percentage change in output this is called **constant returns to scale**. These three returns to scale are referred to as the **long run law of returns to scale**.

Both short and long-run production have profound effects on the costs of the firm and these effects will be explored in chapter 9.

Key point
In the long-run a firm is not hindered by rigidity of a fixed factor. In this time period all factors may be changed to increase output. Long-run production is influenced by the law of returns of three possibilities: increasing returns to scale; constant returns to scale; and decreasing returns to scale.

Chapter summary

› Production is the act of converting inputs into output.
› A unit of production is a factory or plant.
› A unit of management is the firm's decision making unit of a factory or plant.
› The production function expresses a mathematical relationship that shows the maximum output that can be achieved by a number of combinations of inputs.
› There are four periods of production: the momentary or market period; the short-run period; the long-run period; and the very long-run period.
› A fixed factor is one which is not easily changed.
› A variable factor changes as output changes.
› The marginal physical product (MPP) is expressed in formula as ΔTPP/Δinput. The Average Physical Product (APP) is represented as TPP/inputs.

› The law of variable proportions states that as increasing amounts of a variable factor are combined with a fixed amount of a fixed factor, returns to the variable factor increase and then decline to zero.
› Long-run production is influenced by the law of returns.

Practice questions

1. Diminishing returns are caused by:
   a. Some inputs being less efficient than others
   b. Too much of the fixed factor with which to operate
   c. Overcrowding of the fixed factor
   d. Total physical product falls below marginal physical product.

2. In the short-run:
   a. All factors are variable
   b. All fixed factors can be changed
   c. At least one factor cannot be changed
   d. The variable factors cannot be changed.

3. Which of the figures below illustrates short-run output?

   a.
   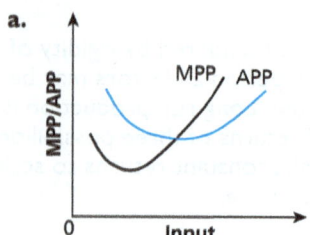

   b.
   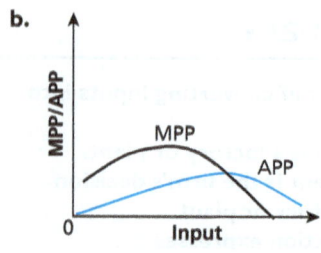

   c.
   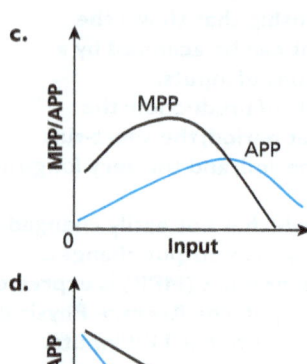

   d.

4. If increasing amounts of a variable factor are added to a fixed quantity of a factor, the marginal product will initially rise but thereafter decline. This is a statement of:
   a. The law of constant returns
   b. The law of diminishing marginal utility
   c. The law of diminishing marginal returns
   d. The law of decreasing returns to scale.

5. In which order do TPP, MPP and APP begin to decrease in short-run production?

	1st	2nd	3rd
a.	TPP	APP	MPP
b.	APP	TPP	MPP
c.	MPP	TPP	APP
d.	MPP	APP	TPP

Chapter 7 How to produce: theory of supply II

LEARNING OBJECTIVES

- Explain the shape of the supply curve for a firm and industry.
- Demonstrate and explain extension and contraction of supply.
- Demonstrate and explain shifts of the supply curve.
- Explain and calculate price elasticity of supply (PES).
- Calculate and interpret supply elasticities.
- Identify and explain periods of production.

REQUIRED KNOWLEDGE

Introductory knowledge of supply curves and the causes of their movements to the right or left.

TOPIC VALUE

When hurricanes and other natural disasters strike in Caribbean territories the prices of agricultural products rise. Stocking up on basic and survival items is a natural response. When items are in abundance prices are cheaper. This chapter provides an insight on supply.

Table 7.1 The supply schedule

Price ($)	Quantity (kg)
10	400
9	300
8	200
7	100
5	40

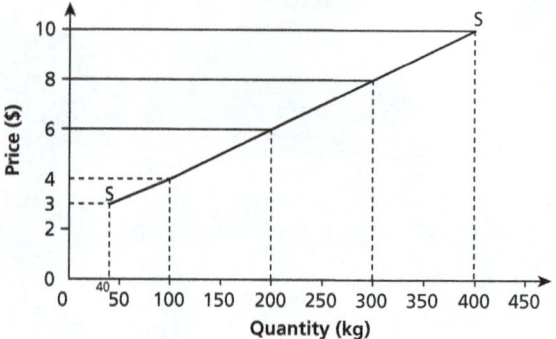

Figure 7.1 A supply curve

Introduction

Chapter 6 explored output theory in the short and long run. Important issues related to production were also examined. This chapter explores the issue of supply as it relates to providing goods and services for the markets.

Supply may be defined as the quantity of goods or services that firms are willing and able to offer to the public for sale at different prices per time period.

A farmer may reap just 200 peppers to offer for sale to his customers and leave the rest in his field. His supply is therefore 200 peppers; the remaining quantity is considered stock.

The supply curves of individual farmers are added together horizontally to reflect the market supply of goods for all farmers in that industry. Individual and market supply curves are typically left to right and sloping upward to the right to reflect the law of supply.

This law states that more of a good is supplied at higher prices and less at lower prices, all other things remaining equal (*ceteris paribus*). This positive relationship between quantity supplied and price may be explained by:

> Higher prices that offer better prospects for profit
> Firms that cannot survive at low prices enter with increased quantity when prices are higher
> Supplying more goods requires more factors of production, leading to higher costs which are reflected in higher prices.

A supply curve for watermelons (see figure 7.1) may be plotted from a supply schedule (see table 7.1).

Factors affecting supply

Factors that affect the supply of a good or service are: price factors; and non-price factors.

Price factor

This refers to the prevailing price of a good that, when high, is an incentive to produce in expectation of profit.

Non-price factor/determinants

These are also called the conditions of supply that affect supply in a positive or negative way. The conditions of supply are:

> The cost or prices of the inputs of production, e.g., land, labour, capital or raw materials
> Good or bad weather (for agricultural goods)
> Disease, pests or drought (for agricultural goods)
> Changes in technology
> Changes in the prices of other commodities
> The economic objectives of a firm
> Government indirect taxes, subsidies, regulations
> Time.

Movements along a supply curve

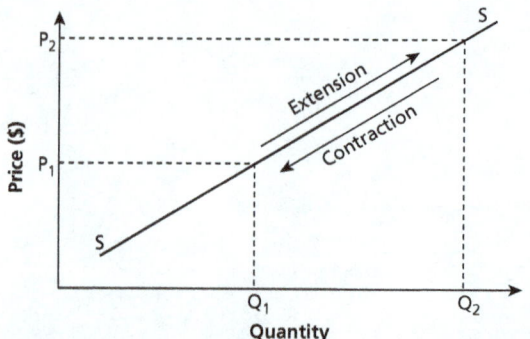

Figure 7.2 Movements along a supply curve

Chapter 7 How to produce: theory of supply II

In figure 7.2, an extension of supply is a movement from left to right along the supply curve in response to a price change. Non-price factors are assumed to remain fixed when prices change. Note the change from Q_1 to Q_2 when prices rise from P_1 to P_2. The assumption made in this analysis is the short-run period.

A contraction of supply is exactly the opposite of extension. When prices fall from P_2 to P_1 supply falls from Q_2 to Q_1 (non-price factors remain fixed).

A change in supply

A change in supply refers to a shift of the supply curve to the right or left, depending on whether the change is positive or negative. This shift may be caused by a change in any of the non-price factors, as shown in table 7.2 below.

Table 7.2 **Factors that cause a shift in the supply curve**

Non-price factors	Direction of shift
An increase in the cost of the factors of production. Output is reduced.	Shift to the left
New technology, innovation or invention and increased productivity, e.g., microchip revolution.	Shift to the right
Adverse weather conditions for agricultural produce. If drought affects crops, supply will decrease.	Shift to the left
Government indirect taxes, e.g., VAT will raise supply costs and negatively affect profit. Output is reduced.	Shift to the left
Government subsidies cause supply costs to fall. Firms raise output.	Shift to the right
If a substitute good becomes cheaper to produce, firms will switch away from the original product, e.g., from oranges to grapefruits if sold at the same price.	Supply curve for oranges shifts to the left
Goods in joint supply, e.g., beef and leather. The production of beef invariably coincides with the production of leather.	Supply curve for leather shifts to the right if beef production increases
Aim of producers: a firm plans to restrict supply to obtain a high price, e.g., the OPEC (Organization of the Petroleum Exporting Countries) cartel.	Shift to the left

Figure 7.3 shows rightward (increases in supply) and leftward shifts (decreases) in response to a change in non-price factors. Figures 7.4a and 7.4b show horizontal addition of individual supply curves to derive market supply curve.

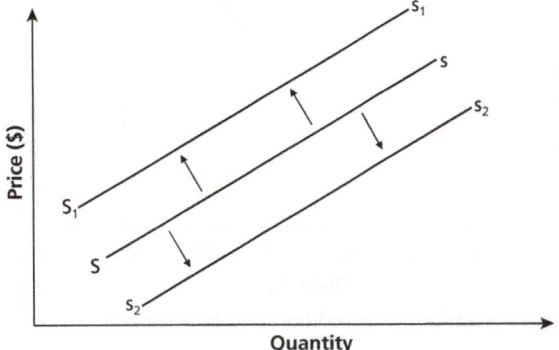

Figure 7.3 Shifting supply curves: left (S_1) and right (S_2)

If the supply curves of producer A, B and C are added horizontally, S_4 is the market supply curve as shown in figures 7.4a and 7.4b.

Key points

› Supply is defined as the quantity of goods or services offered for sale at given prices per time period.
› More is supplied at higher prices because: of expectation of higher profits; it costs more to supply more; firms enter the industry in the long run in response to rising profits.
› Extension and contraction of supply are caused by price factors.
› Changes in the conditions of supply shift the supply curve to the left or right.

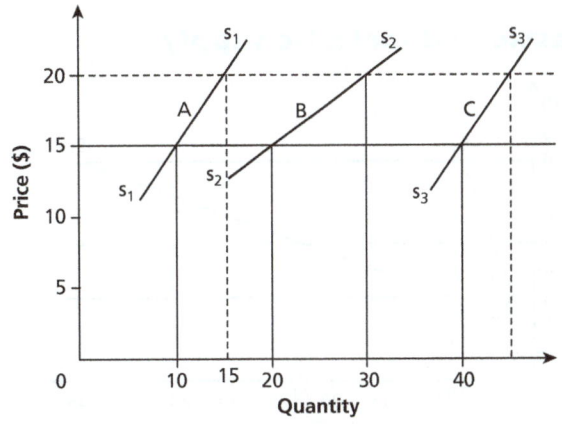

Figure 7.4a Supply curves of producers A, B, C

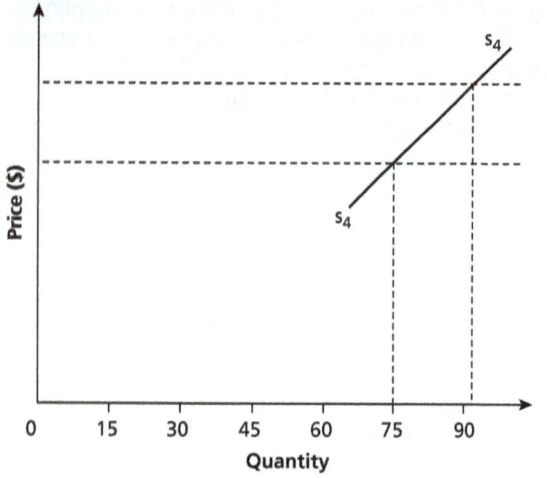

Figure 7.4b Horizontal addition of supply curves

Price elasticity of supply

An analysis of short-run and long-run output emphasises how time plays a vital role when firms change their level of output. This idea is essential to price elasticity of supply (PES).

PES is very similar to price elasticity of demand (PED) because it measures the degree to which the quantity supplied changes as prices change. It is expressed by formula as:

$$\frac{\text{percentage change in quantity}}{\text{percentage change in price}}$$

As in PED, the symbol and size are also important for PES. An upward sloping supply curve carries a positive symbol.

Elastic and inelastic supply

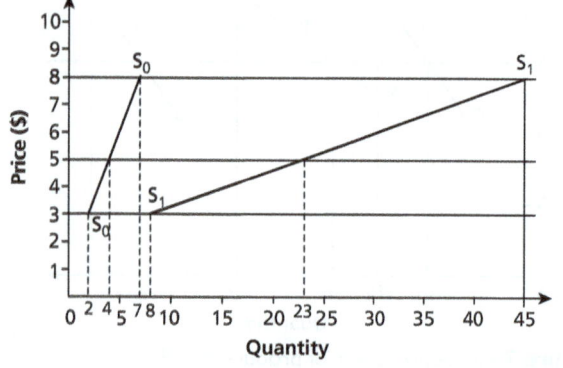

Figure 7.5 Changes in supply curve based on price changes

Figure 7.5 shows two different quantity changes when price changes from two different supply curves. For example:

The percentage price change from $5 to $8 on S_0 = $\frac{3}{5}$ = 0.6 or 60%

The percentage quantity change from 4 to 7 on S_0 = $\frac{3}{4}$ = 0.75 or 75%

Therefore, PES = $\frac{0.75}{0.6}$ = 1.25

Price change from $5 to $8 on S_1 = 0.6

Quantity change from 23 to 45 on S_1 = $\frac{22}{23}$ = 0.96

PES of price change $5 to $8 on S_1 = $\frac{0.96}{0.6}$ = 1.6

Determining price elasticity of supply other than by formula

The PES of a curve or any point or segment is determined by whether the curve is linear or non-linear. If a linear supply curve intersects the vertical axis the PES along the curve is greater than 1, as shown in figure 7.6.

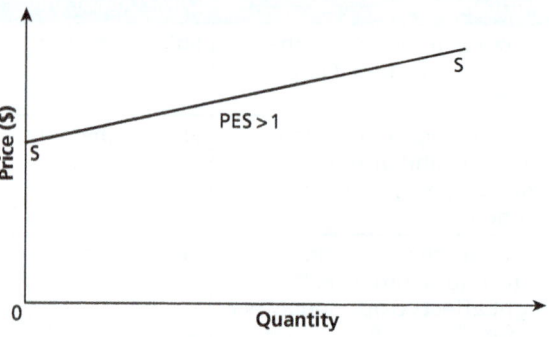

Figure 7.6 Price elasticity of supply > 1 (elastic)

If the supply curve intersects the horizontal axis the PES along the curve is less than 1. See figure 7.7.

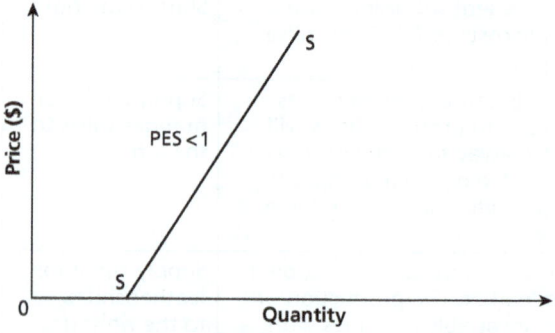

Figure 7.7 Price elasticity of supply < 1 (inelastic)

If the supply curve passes through the point of origin, PES along the curve = 1 in all cases. See figure 7.8.

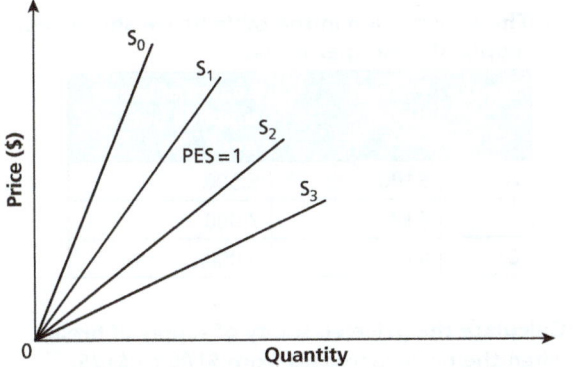

Figure 7.8 Price elasticity of supply = 1 (unitary elasticity)

If a supply curve is non-linear, price elasticity of supply is determined by a tangent to the point on the supply curve. See figure 7.9.

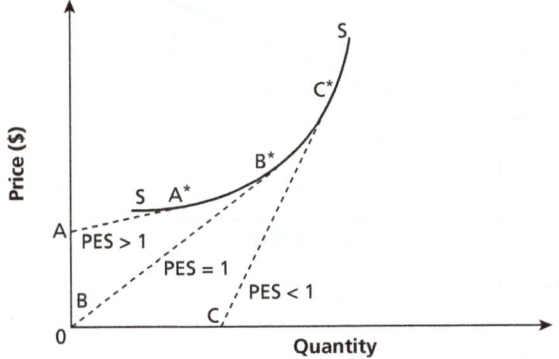

Figure 7.9 Point elasticity of supply

Note:

Tangent A* intersects the vertical axis, therefore PES > 1. Tangent B* reflects price

Elasticity of supply = 1 at point B. At point C, tangent C* reflects PES < 1.

Determinants of price elasticity of supply

How responsive firms are to price changes in the industry depends on the time period. In the momentary period it is not possible to change output. PES is therefore perfectly inelastic as shown in figure 7.10.

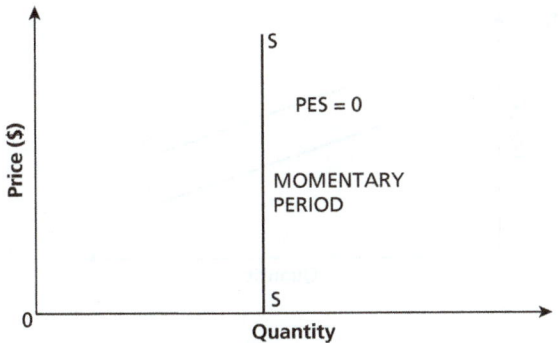

Figure 7.10 Price elasticity of supply in the momentary period of production

In the short run, price elasticity of supply may be greater than 1 because the short run allows for variable factors to increase output, while the fixed factor is unchanged as shown in figure 7.11.

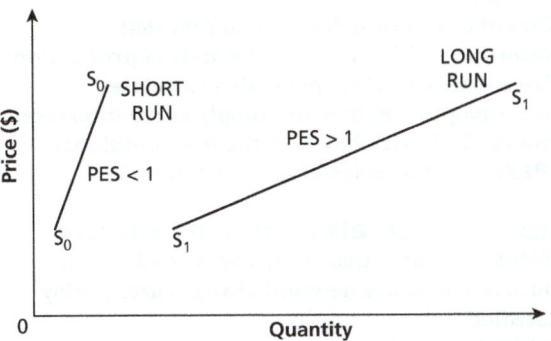

Figure 7.11 Price elasticity of supply in the short run and long run

In the long run when all factors can be altered, PES is very elastic. New firms may also enter the industry during this time period to capitalise on profit opportunities. See figure 7.11.

The supply curve pivots to the right as more time allows for the changing of variable and fixed factors. See figure 7.12.

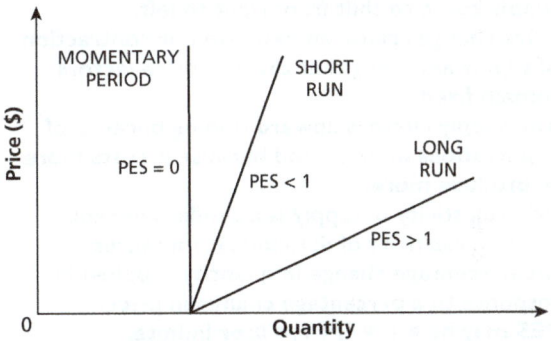

Figure 7.12 Price elasticity of supply in the three time periods of production

Other determinants of price elasticity of supply

The existence of stock when prices rise
If prices rise, firms can easily supply when they have stock; therefore, PES is greater than 1.

Spare capacity
Price elasticity of supply is greater than 1 if a firm has spare raw materials, labour and machines. It may respond quickly to capitalise on price increases. PES in agricultural or perishable goods is less than 1, since an entire growing season would be required to increase the output in flowers and fruits production. PES is less than 1 in the short-run period. The nutmeg crops in Grenada were destroyed by hurricane winds; it was estimated that to replace the trees would require 10–15 years. Price elasticity of supply of nutmeg therefore in the short run = 0 but in the long-run is greater than 1.

Key points

› PES measures the change in quantity supplied in response to changes in price.
› PES may be elastic, inelastic, unitary, zero, or infinite.
› One of the most influential factors that determine PES is the time periods of production.
› Price elasticity of supply is also calculated according to whether the supply curve intersects the vertical axis (PES > 1), the horizontal axis (PES, 1) or the point of origin (PES = 1).

Uses of price elasticity of supply

› If PES is greater than one, prices tend not to fluctuate because demand changes are quickly satisfied.
› If PES is < 1 prices may rise.
› If PES = 0, a price rise is wholly borne by the consumer.

Chapter summary

› Supply is defined as the quantity of goods and services that are offered for sale at a given price and in a given time period.
› Changes in the determinants of supply cause the supply curve to shift from right to left.
› Price changes cause an extension or contraction of supply assuming that the non-price factors remain fixed.
› The supply curve is upward sloping because of expectations of profit and because it costs more to produce more.
› Price elasticity of supply is a similar concept to price elasticity of demand. It measures the percentage change in quantity supplied in response to a percentage change in price.
› PES may be > 1; = 1; < 1; = 0; or infinite.
› PES is influenced by time, capacity, mobility of factors of production, nature of the good, storage capacity, and weather conditions for agricultural goods.

Practice questions

1. When the price of shirts increases from $5.00 to $6.00 each, the supply of shirts increases from 20 to 25.
   a. Draw the curve implied by this information.
   b. Write the formula for price elasticity of supply for shirts and calculate it.
   c. Based on your calculation of the price elasticity of supply for shirts, what will be the increase in the supply of shirts?

2. a. Define the term 'price elasticity of supply'.
   b. What is meant by the term 'the supply of bread is inelastic'?

   c. The information in the table below shows the supply of bread per week:

Week	Price of bread	Loaves of bread supplied per week
A	$100	6,500
B	$125	7,000
C	$150	8,000

   Calculate the price elasticity of supply of bread when the price increases from $100 to $125.

3. Identify the figure which shows the effect of a subsidy granted by the government, where S_1 moves to S_2.

   a.
   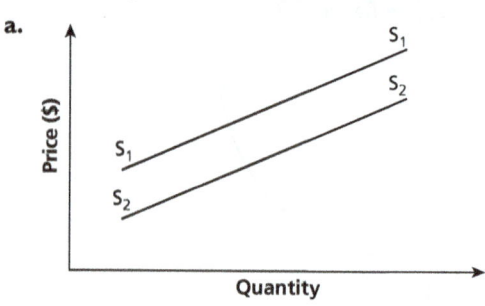

   b.
   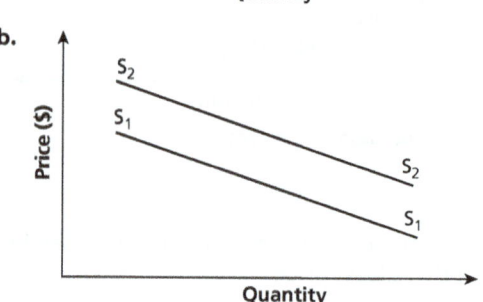

   c.
   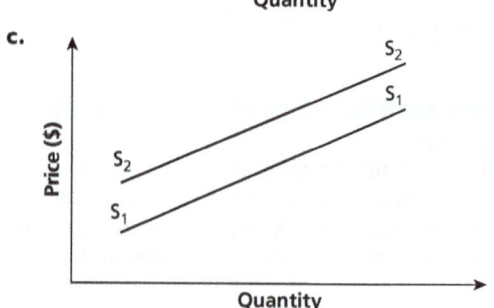

   d.
   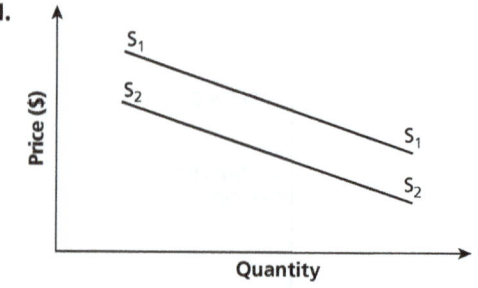

4. Identify the figure that illustrates a car park filled to capacity.

a.
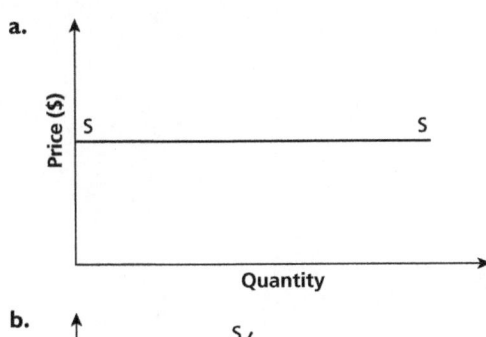

b.
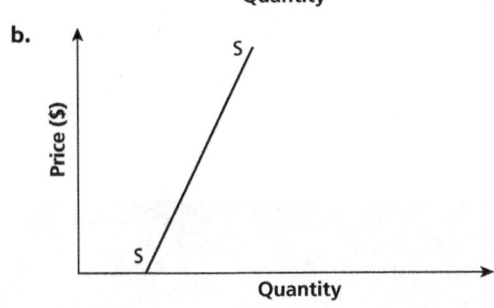

c.
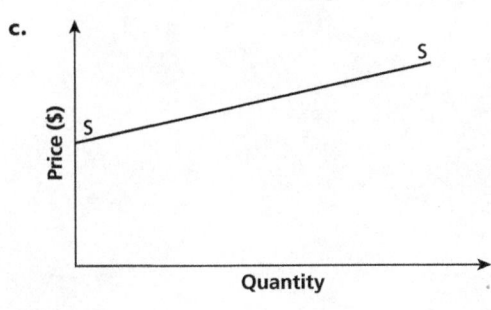

d.
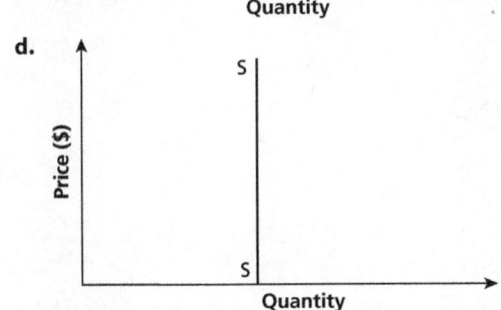

5. Identify the figure that illustrates a contraction of supply.

a.
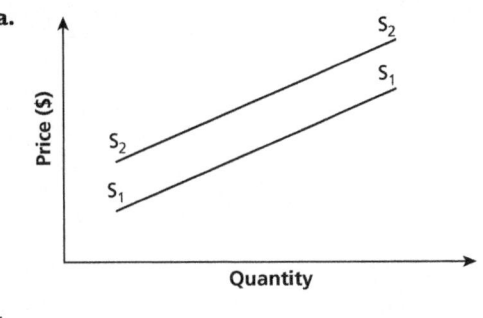

b.
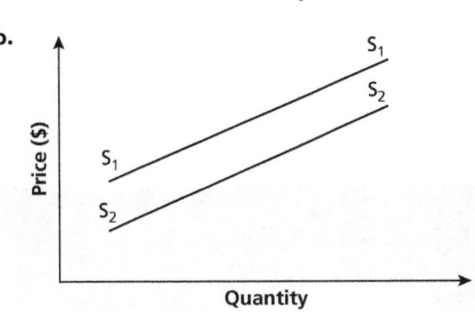

c.
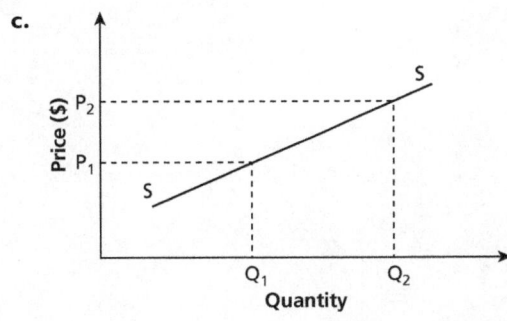

d.
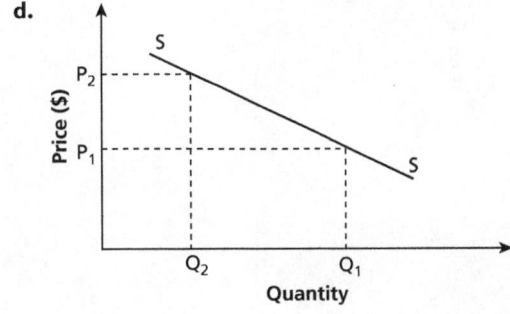

INTRODUCTORY ECONOMICS A TEXTBOOK FOR CAPE ECONOMICS STUDENTS

8 Market equilibrium

Chapter 8 Market equilibrium

LEARNING OBJECTIVES

- Explain equilibrium price.
- Explain changing equilibrium price.
- Explain and illustrate change in demand supply.
- Explain functions of the price mechanism.
- Define, illustrate and explain price ceiling, floors, and consumer and producer surplus.
- Illustrate the incidence of a tax.

REQUIRED KNOWLEDGE

- Demand and supply curves and the reasons for their shifting to right or left
- The role of government in the economy.

TOPIC VALUE

Consumers stock up on goods if they anticipate there will be a shortage in the future, to ensure they have a supply and to save money. This chapter aims to give you a better understanding of exchange rates, interest rates, the export sector, wages and rent.

Market equilibrium

A typical market may be represented diagrammatically by demand and supply curves. Chapter 4 distinguished between a change in demand and a change in quantity demanded at a given time. The former caused a movement of the demand curve.

Equilibrium in the free market is achieved when the plans of buyers are in perfect agreement with the plans of sellers, or where planned demand is equal to planned supply. There is no prearranged meeting between buyers and sellers to determine prices. It is simply brought about by unregulated market forces or the 'invisible hand' of the market.

The equilibrium price in figure 8.1 is where the demand curve and supply curve for pineapples intersect, because at this price the quantity demanded is equal to the quantity supplied.

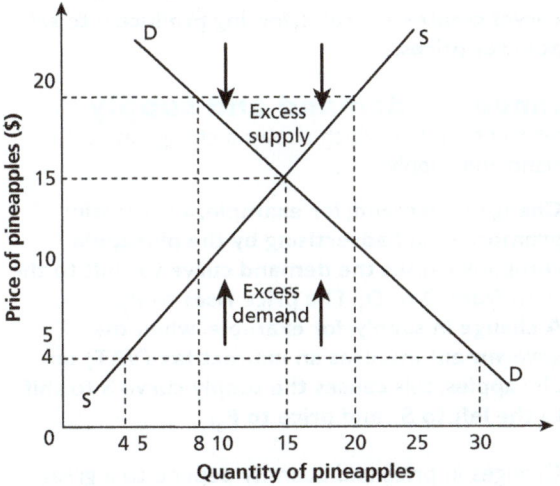

Figure 8.1 Market equilibrium

In figure 8.1, $15 is the equilibrium price. The equilibrium quantity is 15 pineapples. Equilibrium means a state of rest, or no tendency to change.

Before this equilibrium was reached, there was a disequilibrium at the price of $20 because at that price the quantity demanded was eight pineapples, while the quantity supplied was 20 pineapples. Twelve pineapples of excess supply will exert a downward pressure on the price, *ceteris paribus*, leading to a price fall. At the new lower equilibrium, quantity demanded is equal to the quantity supplied.

The same interaction takes place when the quantity demanded is greater than the quantity supplied. At price $4 the quantity demanded (Qd) = 30, while the quantity supplied (Qs) = 4. A market shortage of 26 pineapples would cause prices to rise, encouraging suppliers to supply a greater quantity at $15.

This interaction continues until the equilibrium price is reached at $15 where Qd = Qs. Sometimes this equilibrium process takes place quickly, but at other times it takes place slowly. As long as equilibrium is reached there will be no tendency to change unless the conditions of demand or supply change, or both change together.

An increase in price

A rise in equilibrium price may result from:

› **Change in conditions of demand, shifting the demand curve to the right**
› **Change in conditions of supply, shifting the supply curve to the left.**

The demand curve shifts to the right and upward if there is a change in one of the conditions of demand; for example, the demand curve for pineapples would shift to the right if tastes and preferences switch from citrus to pineapples (pineapple prices remaining constant) as shown in figure 8.2.

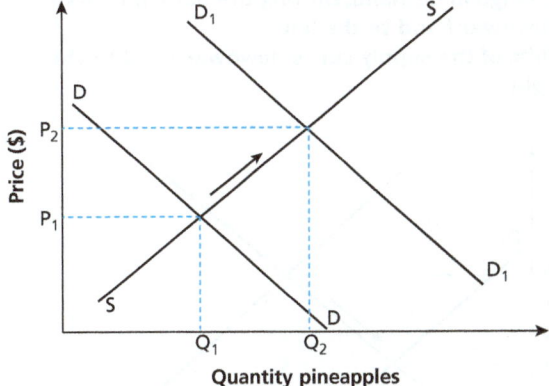

Figure 8.2 Increase in price shifts demand curve

Note:

› **DD shifts to D_1D_1**
› **Price changes from P_1 to P_2**
› **Quantity changes from Q_1 to Q_2**
› **D_1D_1 shifts along the supply curve SS.**

Summary
When DD shifts to D_1D_1 there is a shortage at P_1. Price rises to P_2 and suppliers increase their output of pineapples on the market. Note the movement along the supply curve and the direction of the arrow.

Change in condition of supply
In figure 8.3, there is a change in supply of pineapples due to bad weather and floods (assuming demand is constant).

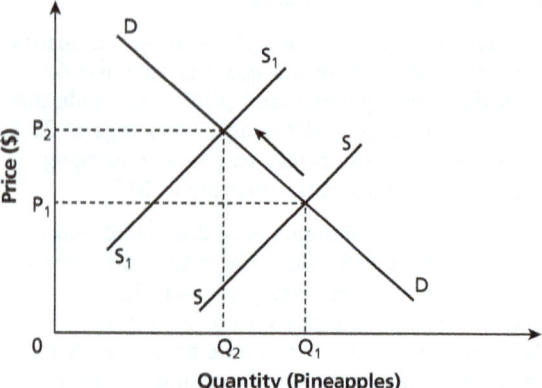

Figure 8.3 Change in conditions of supply shifts the supply curve

Note:
> SS shifts to S_1S_1 raising price from P_1 to P_2. Note SS shifts along the demand curve.
> Demand therefore contracts (contraction of demand) from Q_1 to Q_2. Note the direction of the arrow.

Both figure 8.2 and 8.3 illustrate a price rise from a change in demand and supply.

A price fall
A price fall may result from:

> Change in demand, shifting the demand curve downward and to the left
> Shift of the supply curve downward and to the right.

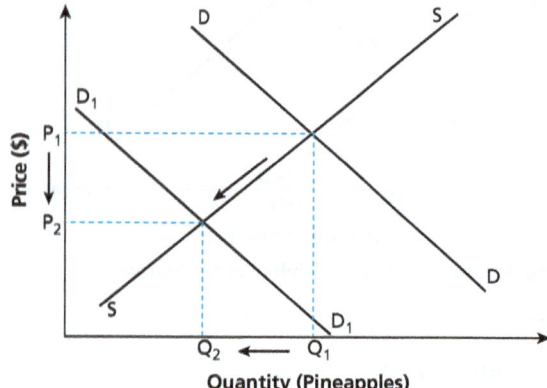

Figure 8.4 A decrease in price

In figure 8.4, a fall in the price of a substitute fruit, for example, watermelon causes the demand for pineapples to fall.

> DD shifts to the left to D_1D_1
> P_1 falls to P_2
> Q_1 falls to Q_2
> DD moves along the supply curve. Note the direction of the arrows
> Note the contraction of supply caused by low prices.

To achieve specific economic objectives, governments may provide a subsidy to producers or consumers, and this may impact on the price of a good or service offered in the market place, for example the price of gasoline. So, a subsidy could be defined as a government grant or transfer that serves to lower the price of a good and ease the burden of higher prices on consumers.

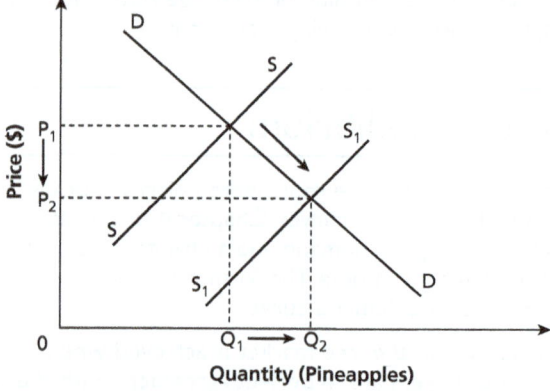

Figure 8.5 Increase in supply by a subsidy

In figure 8.5 a government subsidy increases the supply of pineapples:

> SS moves down to S_1S_1 along the demand curve.
> P_1 falls to P_2.
> Q_1 increases to Q_2. This is an extension of demand due to a decrease in price that is caused by a downward movement of the supply curve.
> Note that in each case, the movement of the curves creates a surplus, forcing producers to sell at lower prices.

Changes in demand and supply
Refer to figure 8.6, which shows a change in both demand and supply:

> Change in demand; for example, a successful promotion and advertising by the pineapple company causes the demand curve to shift to the right from D to D_1. The price rises to P_2.
> A change in supply; for example, when the government imposes an indirect tax (VAT) on pineapples, this causes the supply curve S to shift to the left to S_1, and price to P_3.

Changes in price and quantity depend to a great extent on which shifting curve moves to a greater degree than the other. In this case, note that the shift of the demand curve to the right in figure 8.6 is greater than the shift of the supply curve to the left.

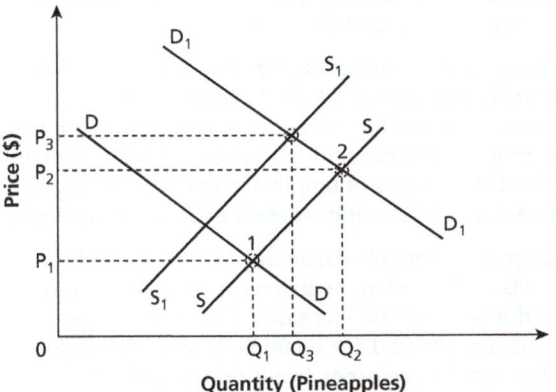

Figure 8.6 Change in both demand and supply

Summary

- Equilibrium market price is determined by the intersection of demand and supply curves. At this price Qd = Qs.
- When Qd > Qs, shortages develop that drive prices up, encouraging firms to supply more until Qd = Qs.
- When Qs > Qd the excess supply causes prices to fall; as a result quantity demanded increases until Qs = Qd.
- Changes in demand and supply alter the equilibrium price because these changes cause the curves to shift, achieving a new equilibrium.

The functions of the price mechanism

The price mechanism is the pivot around which the free enterprise system revolves. It is the principal mechanism for solving the economic problem in a free market economy. The price mechanism performs the following functions in a free enterprise economy:

- Signalling/informing
- Allocating/rationing
- Motivating
- Rewarding
- Coordinating.

What to produce

Consumers' wants and needs are communicated to sellers by high prices through a change in demand (shift to the right), for example a change in taste or fashion. Prices communicate changes in conditions of demand. This is crucial to sellers. Similarly, sellers indicate through high prices that raw materials are scarce or weather conditions are unfavourable.

Prices provide information or signals about the conditions of supply

High prices are caused by unfavourable conditions of supply in the same way that low prices are caused by favourable conditions of supply. This information is vital to customers with respect to choices they may wish to make.

Allocating/rationing function

Prices serve to allocate resources such as the factors of production to the production of goods and services that are in high demand. High prices are the result of high demand, among other factors.

Firms respond by increasing output to capitalise on profit. This would have a chain reaction on the markets for labour, land and capital. Factors of production are allocated to meet high prices caused by increases in demand or a decrease in supply.

The incentive function

High prices provide the incentives for profit-seeking firms to produce goods and services associated with high prices. High prices therefore act in a 'motivating' role.

A queue, rota system and lottery are other ways to ration goods and services. However, who will buy these goods will depend on how income is distributed.

Rewarding

Lastly, prices reward the factors of production for their use. For example, land receives rent, capital receives interest, labour receives wages and enterprise receives profit.

Coordinating

The way in which prices work takes on the role as coordinator. This is the invisible hand referred to by Adam Smith. A simple example of how the functions of the price mechanism solve the economic problem can be shown when the cricket season ends and the soccer season begins. Refer to figures 8.7 a, b, c and d.

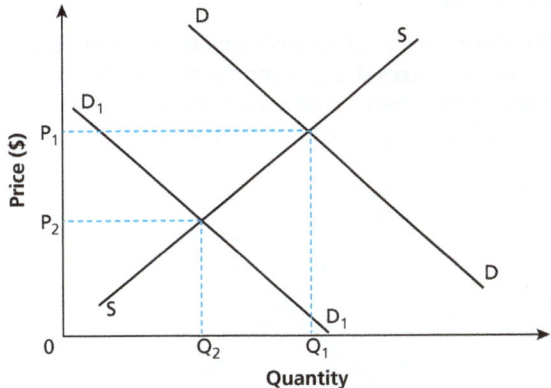

Figure 8.7a Cricket gear market

When the cricket season ends the demand curve for cricket gear shifts to the left from D to D_1. As a result quantity demanded falls from Q_1 to Q_2, and cricket gear prices fall from P_1 to P_2.

Increased demand for football goods and services, increases prices from P_1 to P_2 and quantity from Q_1 to Q_2.

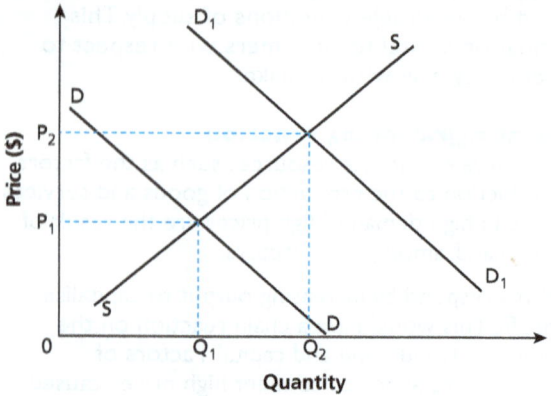

Figure 8.7b Football gear market

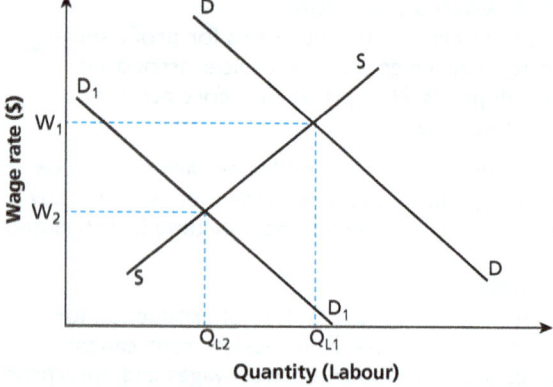

Figure 8.7c The labour market for cricket

When price, output and profit fall, the demand for labour, land and capital for cricket inputs (here, labour) fall from Q_{L1} to Q_{L2}.

The fall in demand for factors of production leads to a fall in wages from W_1 to W_2. Interest and rent act in a similar way. The owners of the factors of production seek higher rewards, shifting into the football market.

The rise in prices of football equipment, grounds, and so on, increases the demand for the factors of production. As a result, wages, interest and rent rise, attracting factor inputs into this market.

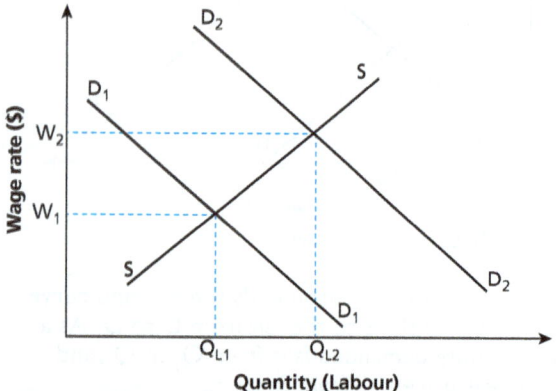

Figure 8.7d The labour market for football

Demand for labour related to football rises from W_1 to W_2. The rise in prices of football equipment grounds increases the demand for factors of production. As a result, wages, interest, and rent rise, attracting labour into this market.

Due to the cricket season ending, the demand for bats, balls and helmets fall, as do their prices, since the demand curve for these items will shift to the left. The labour market is similarly affected, that is, demand falls for the services of umpires, pitch preparers, gear repairers, and so on, and wages fall for these workers.

Once the football season begins the demand for footballs and all related equipment rises. Prices rise since the demand has increased. The other factor markets are affected, for example labour, and wages rise for coaches, referees, groundsmen and star players. The demand for capital goods also rises such as, for example, machines to cut the grass, mop up water, make nets and equipment, and their prices also rise.

Entrepreneurs are lured by the prospect of profit into the soccer industry because profits rise. Likewise, in the pursuit of their highest rewards, land, labour and capital respond to their self-interest and indirectly satisfy their wants and needs. Thus, it appears as if an 'invisible hand' is coordinating the factors of production.

Adam Smith advocated that the price mechanism is self-regulating and no intervention is required. The government, he argued, should only provide law, order, national security and ensure fairness.

Consumer/producer surplus

In chapter 4 the concept of consumer surplus was explored. As a reminder, it is the difference, or surplus utility that consumers receive when they pay a lower price for a good than, in fact, they were willing to pay.

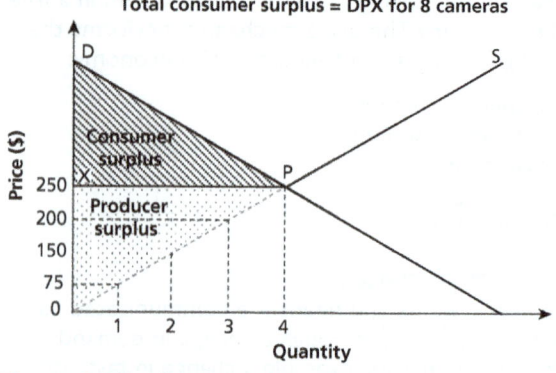

Figure 8.8 Producer and consumer surplus

Producer surplus is a similar concept. Surplus profit goes to a producer. In figure 8.8, the supply curve shows the price at which the producer is willing to supply his cameras. Camera number 1 is supplied at a cost of $75, but the market price is $250. The producer is making a profit of $175, which is his producer surplus for camera number 1. Similarly, the supply of camera number 2 results in a surplus for the producer, $250 − $150 = $100. Camera number 3 yields a surplus of $250 − $200 = $50, but number 4 = $250 − $250 = $0.

Total producer surplus is equal to the area under the price line and to the left of the supply curve or triangle OPX. Consumer surplus, on the other hand, is the triangle DPX. It is the area above the price line and to the left of the demand curve DP.

Finally, if both consumer and producer surpluses are added together, this gives the total surplus to society; it is also called total welfare and is given by triangle DPO.

Price control

Although equilibrium price and quantity are achieved when planned demand is equal to planned supply, such an equilibrium price may be a burden for low-income earners in the view of the government.

Government regulation, subsidy, or other forms of state intervention serve to reduce the impact of high prices on low-income earners, especially for basic food items such as milk, flour and bread.

The price mechanism is not perfect. The state is therefore obliged to correct this disadvantage of the price mechanism on the basis of equity.

Price ceiling

A ceiling is the highest part of a room in the normal sense of the word. A price ceiling is similar in that it is the highest price a consumer can be charged for a good or service by law. Ceiling prices are intended to be a form of a social safety net, income redistribution and poverty reduction.

In some shops or food stores, a schedule of prices is set by the government for basic food items such as flour, rice, bread and milk. It is also called a maximum price and is illustrated in figure 8.9.

A maximum price is set at $7.00, although the free market equilibrium price is $10.00. Sellers cannot sell at prices above $7.00 but can sell below that price.

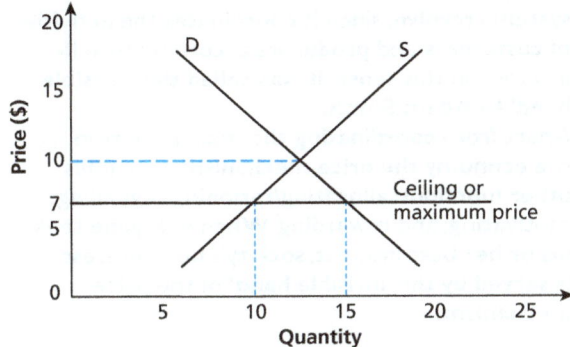

Figure 8.9 A price ceiling

Note: At price $7.00, the quantity supplied = 10 while quantity demanded = 15.

Shortages are associated with maximum prices that can lead to 'black market' prices that may go above the ceiling price. Rent control is an example of a ceiling price. Governments that set ceiling prices invariably resort to rationing the available low supply of a commodity.

Price floor (minimum price)

A price floor is one set by government that is the lowest or minimum price that can be charged for a good or service. It is meant to protect a producer from an equilibrium price that may be too low to sustain the business enterprise or provide an income for the seller. Farmers, in particular, suffer fluctuating prices when supply and demand are unstable. An example of a minimum price is the minimum wage. A worker is, in fact, a seller of his labour.

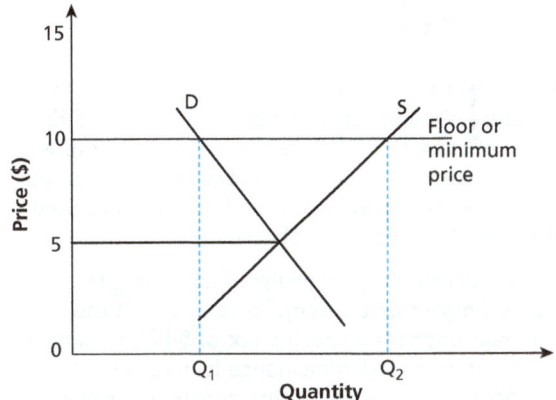

Figure 8.10 A price floor

In figure 8.10, note the equilibrium wage rate of labour is $5.00 per hour. This wage may be insufficient to sustain a person who earns a low income. The government accordingly sets a minimum wage of $10.00 per hour.

Note:

> Minimum prices create a surplus with respect to crops. The government may be obliged to intervene to purchase and finance the stock of such surpluses to maintain high prices.
> High guaranteed prices make firms inefficient as firms are assured of a high price. They are therefore not as profit-driven and may become complacent in their management.

Key points

> Ceiling and floor pricing are forms of government intervention to reduce the negative impact of high prices on customers and low prices on producers, e.g., flour and rice.
> A ceiling is the maximum price that can be legally charged for a good or service. It, however, creates shortages and black markets, defeating the purpose of interventions on consumers' behalf.

> A floor is a legally set minimum price at which a producer's output can be sold to protect against fluctuating prices and incomes, e.g., minimum wage.

The effects of taxes and subsidies on market equilibrium

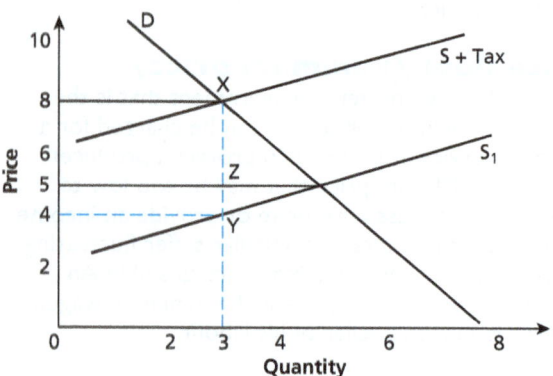

Figure 8.11 Effect of tax

An indirect tax is one that is levied on consumer expenditure; the impact of the tax can be passed on to consumers by the producer on whom it is imposed. An indirect tax may be a value added tax, for example, VAT, or it can be a specific tax such as a tax imposed on the sale of alcohol and tobacco.

An indirect tax may be analysed according to incidence (impact or burden). For example, if the government imposes a specific tax of $4.00 on a pack of cigarettes, the burden/incidence is determined by the proportion of the $4.00 that consumers pay and the proportion that the producer pays. Refer to figure 8.11 and note the following.

> The imposition of the tax causes the supply curve S_1 to shift upwards and to the left by the total amount of the tax YX, leading to a new equilibrium X.
> The price of the pack of cigarettes to the consumer increases from $5.00 (old equilibrium) to $8.00 (the new one).
> The buyer pays $3.00 out of the $4.00 tax (ZX).
> The producer only pays $1.00, i.e., $4.00 to $5.00 (YZ), which is the difference between the $4 tax and what the consumer pays, $5.
> ZX + YZ = XY

Observe that the consumers pay ZX of the total tax while the producers pay YZ. ZX and YZ are referred to as the incidence of the tax. The objective of the government may be to discourage the consumption of demerit goods for health reasons. The taxation of demerit goods is also an effective method of raising revenue for the government.

The effect of a subsidy on price equilibrium

The effects of a subsidy on price equilibrium were analysed in figure 8.5. In that explanation, the effect of the subsidy caused the price to decrease. Figure 8.12 and the explanatory note below show how the downward shift of the supply curve lowers price and identifies the parties who benefit from the subsidy.

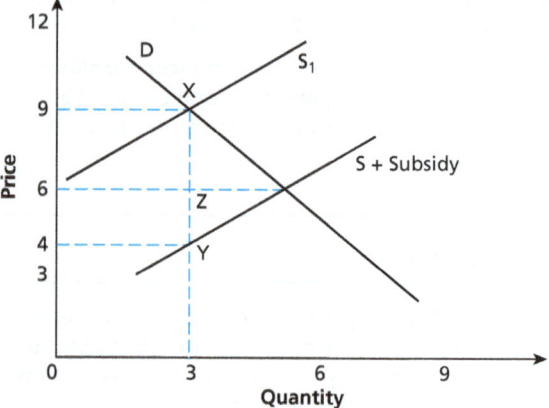

Figure 8.12 Effect of a subsidy

Note:

> The government grants a subsidy of $5.00 per gallon on gasoline to the travelling public.
> The supply curve S_1 shifts downward and to the right (S + subsidy).
> XY represents the extent of the subsidy.
> The equilibrium price falls from $9.00 to $6.00.
> The benefit to the consumer is therefore $3.00 (ZX).
> The benefit to the producer is $2.00 (ZY). The objective of a government subsidy is always to increase welfare and redistribute income to the needy.

Key points

> The price mechanism is an interplay of decisions made by consumers that affect the demand curve and producers that affect the supply curve. When the plans of both parties are the same, price equilibrium is achieved.
> The price mechanism of the free market is the main pivot around which the free market systems revolve, since it coordinates the activities of customers and producers according to self-interest. In this sense, it was called the 'invisible hand' by Adam Smith.
> Apart from coordinating the main players in the economy the price mechanism also fulfils other functions: allocating/rationing; signalling; motivating; and rewarding. When everyone seeks his or her best interest, society's best interest is served by the 'invisible hand' of the price mechanism.

- Consumer surplus is the difference between the price that a consumer is willing to pay and the equilibrium price. This surplus is surplus satisfaction or utility. It is generally identified as the region above the price line and to the left of the demand curve.
- Producer surplus is the difference between the price at which a producer is willing to supply goods on the market and the actual going market price. This surplus is also called his 'economic rent' or profit on each unit supplied.
- Producer surplus is also generally identified as the area to the left of the supply curve and under the price line.

Chapter summary

- Equilibrium in the free market is achieved when the plans of buyers are in perfect agreement with the plans of sellers.
- The equilibrium price is determined at the point where the demand and supply curves intersect.
- A change in demand is determined by price only.
- A change in demand is determined by non-price factors.
- Producer surplus is the difference between the market price of a good and the supply price.
- Ceilings and floor pricing are forms of government intervention to reduce the negative impact of high prices on consumers and low prices on producers.
- A ceiling is the maximum price that can be legally charged for a good or service.
- A floor is a legally set minimum price at which a producer's output can be sold.

Although price ceilings and floors are just two forms of intervention in a mixed economy, it is important to understand that such intervention is made to correct the imperfections of the unregulated price mechanism on the basis of equity. In these two instances, it is the negative effects on high and low free-market determined prices. There are other instances where the government feels it should intervene, regulate or assist.

In all such instances, actions are designed to cushion or resolve the imperfections of the price mechanism. Market failures (see chapter 14) will be examined in more detail after the analysis of markets has concluded in later chapters.

Practice questions

1. a. In no more than three sentences, explain what you understand by Adam Smith's invisible hand.
   b. List two functions that Adam Smith suggested government should perform.

2. The government has decided to put a ceiling on the price of milk. What effect will this have on the following?
   a. The demand for milk
   b. The supply of milk
   c. The quantity of milk sold.

3. Define the following concepts:
   a. Consumer surplus
   b. Producer surplus.

4. a. Draw a carefully labelled figure to show equilibrium in the market for compact discs.
   b. On the figure in (a) above, show how an improvement in technology is likely to affect the supply of compact discs, all other things being equal (*ceteris paribus*).
   c. State how an increase in population is likely to affect the market for compact discs.

Multiple choice questions

1. An indirect tax causes the:
   a. Supply curve to move to the right
   b. Demand curve to move to the left
   c. Supply curve to move to the left
   d. Demand curve to move to the right.

2. A rise in equilibrium price will cause:
   a. A reduction in consumer surplus
   b. A reduction in producer surplus
   c. An increase in consumer surplus
   d. No change in producer surplus.

9 The cost of production

Chapter 9   The cost of production

LEARNING OBJECTIVES

- Identify total costs.
- Identify short-run costs.
- Identify and explain total fixed and variable costs.
- Identify and explain average fixed and variable costs.
- Calculate marginal costs.
- Explain long-run costs.
- Explain and identify economies and diseconomies of scale (internal and external).

REQUIRED KNOWLEDGE

- Basic costs of a firm, for example fixed and variable costs
- Basic knowledge of economies and diseconomies of scale as the firm expands
- Short- and long-run output
- Marginal, average and total costs concepts.

TOPIC VALUE

Chapter 7 explored production in the short- and long-run periods. This chapter examines how output in these periods of production influences a firm's costs. A firm's cost of production is crucial to the level of profits it makes because lower costs enable higher profit.

The cost of production

A firm's costs are the payments it makes for the use of factors of production; for example, land, labour or capital. A firm may incur the following costs:

› **Opportunity costs**
› **Social or external costs**
› **Explicit costs.**

Opportunity costs, which were discussed in chapter 1, are also called implicit costs. Social costs are the costs imposed on society by firms, which they tend to ignore, for example pollution costs.

Explicit costs are the costs with which we are more familiar. These are fixed, variable, average, marginal, and total costs. In the short-run a firm will incur fixed costs, which are defined as those costs that are independent of production and hence do not change when production changes. Some examples of fixed costs are rent of premises, interest on bank loans, insurance payments and depreciation of assets. If you passed by a farm on a Sunday and it is closed, production will be zero, but fixed costs are running, nevertheless. They are also called overhead, indirect or sometimes sunk costs.

Table 9.1 **Total cost, total fixed and total variable cost**

Output	TFC (000)	TVC (000)	TC (000)
0	50	0	50
1	50	10	60
2	50	16	66
3	50	22	72
4	50	28	78
5	50	38	88
6	50	60	110
7	50	88	138
8	50	100	150
9	50	130	180

Figure 9.1 represents fixed costs (FC) of production. Note that at an output of zero FC is $50 and does not change as output changes. Hence FC is shown as a horizontal line.

The total variable cost curve (TVC) has a gradual, then a steeply sloping segment that reflects the law of diminishing returns. Increasing returns to the variable factor reduce costs, which causes TVC to rise slowly. However, when diminishing returns set in, TVC rises steeply. Both figures 9.1 and 9.2 are plotted from table 9.1.

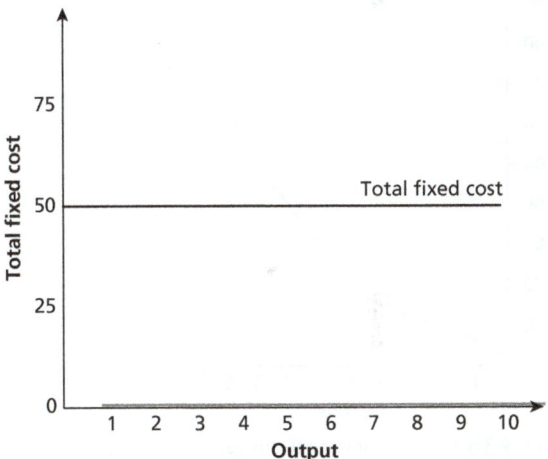

Figure 9.1 Total fixed cost curve

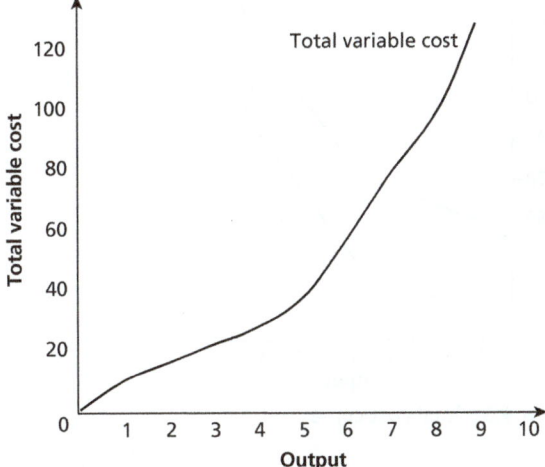

Figure 9.2 Total variable cost curve

Total cost

Total costs of production will therefore be: total fixed costs + total variable costs = total costs

Expressed in formula as: TFC + TVC = TC

Diagramatically it is shown below in figures 9.3a, b and c.

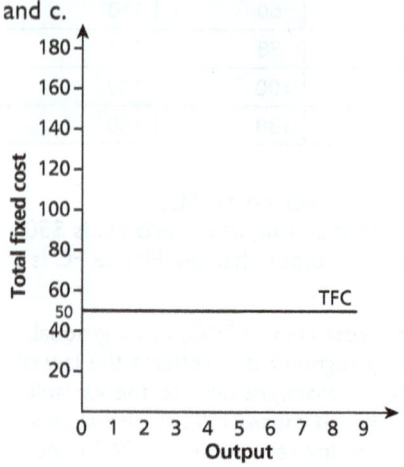

Figure 9.3a Total fixed cost curve

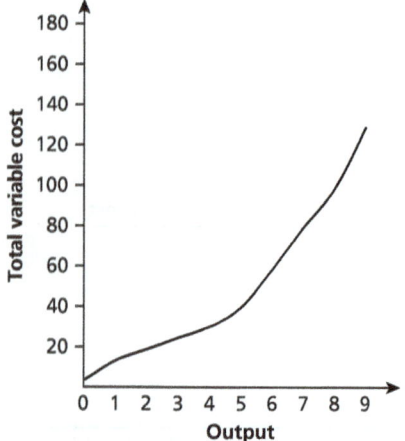

Figure 9.3b Total variable cost curve

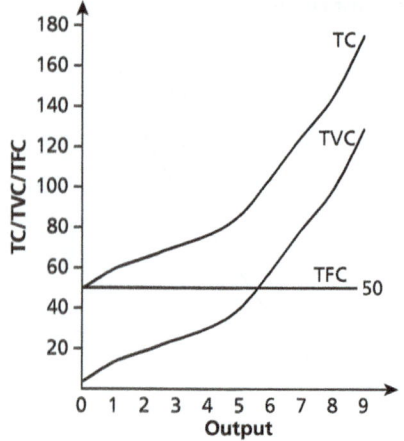

Figure 9.3c Total cost curve

Notes:

Observe the following:

FC = $50		at zero output
VC = $0		at zero output
Therefore	TC = $50	at zero output

TC starts at $50

Summary

Explicit costs are the firm's operating short-run total costs, not including implicit costs. Total fixed cost (TFC) is a horizontal line and TVC first rises slowly and then quickly to reflect the law of diminishing returns. Added together, TFC and TVC are equal to TC. Economists and accountants view costs differently. Economists include explicit and implicit costs, while accountants recognise only explicit costs.

Average total cost

If your contribution to a cake sale is a cake of 50 slices, how do you cost each slice? This is called the average total cost (ATC) of each slice, or simply the average unit cost (AC). If the cake costs $100 to make, then 50 slices would cost $2 per slice to make. If you sell each slice for $3 you would make a profit on each slice that is equal to $1. This simple experience is your best education in cost theory.

ATC = TC/q   or $100/50 = $2 (AC or unit cost)

There is another way to determine ATC by simply adding average fixed cost to average variable cost, that is, AFC + AVC = ATC.

If the fixed cost of the cake in the above example was $25, then AFC= FC/q or $25/50 = 0.50 cents.

VC would then be $75 and AVC = TVC/q or $75/50 = $1.50

Therefore, AFC + AVC = ATC or $0.50 + $1.50 = $2.00

These simple cost concepts are graphically presented in figures 9.4 a, b and c.

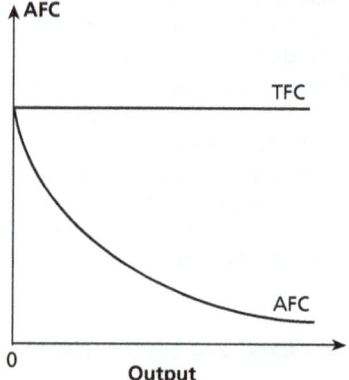

Figure 9.4a Average fixed curve

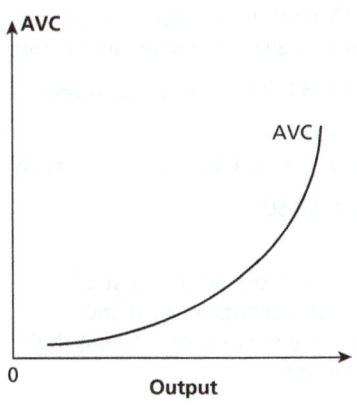

Figure 9.4b Average variable cost curve

Short-run costs

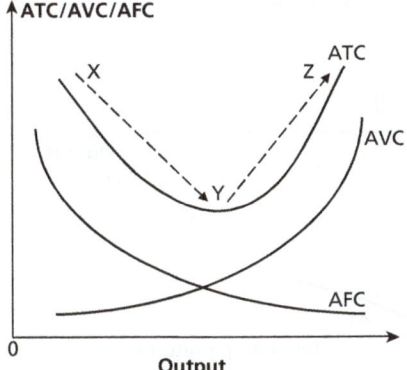

Figure 9.4c Average total cost curve

Notes:

The relationship between TFC and AFC is shown in figure 9.4a.
> AFC falls evenly because it is a fixed dollar value divided by increasing output in the short-run.
> AVC is derived by dividing TVC by Q.
> When AFC is vertically added to AVC in figure 9.4c, an ATC curve is derived.

The ATC curve is usually U-shaped because the downward segment, XY in figure 9.4c, is heavily influenced by the downward segment of AFC above AVC. Refer to figure 9.4c. The ATC curve is U-shaped because the upward segment YZ, is influenced by the AVC curve.

The average cost curve shows the lowest cost of production for any given level of output. Having explained TC, TCV, TFC and AFC, AVC and ATC, there is only one other very important short-run cost of production to consider, namely, marginal cost.

Marginal cost

Marginal cost is the change in the total cost of producing one more or one less unit and is expressed in formula as change in TC/change in Q (or $\frac{\Delta TC}{\Delta Q}$).

If the cost of ten pens is $100 and 11 pens cost $105 then the marginal cost of the eleventh pen is $5. By formula then it is:

$$\frac{\Delta TC = \$100 \text{ to } \$105}{\Delta Q = 10 \text{ to } 11} = \frac{\$5}{1} = 5$$

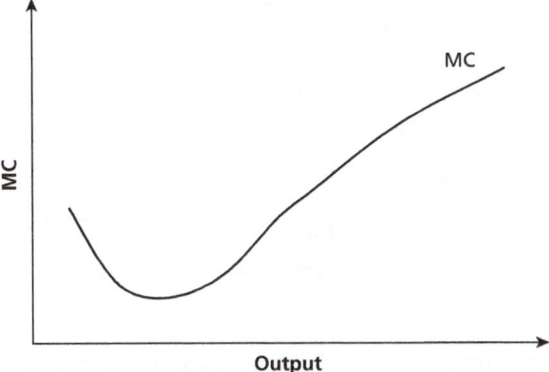

Figure 9.5 Marginal cost curve

One more or one less pen will therefore cost $5. Sometimes firms change quantities in batches rather than an extra one. MC can still be applied. For example, if the change in total cost is $100 to $120 when output changes from 10 to 20 units, then the change in TC is $20 and the change in output = 10.

$$MC = \frac{\$20}{10} = \$2.00$$

The marginal cost curve is easy to recognise in this instance. It looks like a hockey stick or the popular Nike logo, as shown in figure 9.5.

Note:

Marginal cost is really a change in variable cost as TVC changes after one more (or less) unit is produced, since fixed costs are unchanged, as the example shown in table 9.2 demonstrates.

Table 9.2 MC is related to VC

Output	TFC ($)	TVC ($)	TC ($)
10	20	30	50
11	20	40	60

MC = Δ TC ($60 − $50) = 10
       Δ Output (11 − 10) = 1

Note that the Δ in TVC = 10 and Δ in FC = 0

Marginal costs are very important to a firm if it plans to expand the production.

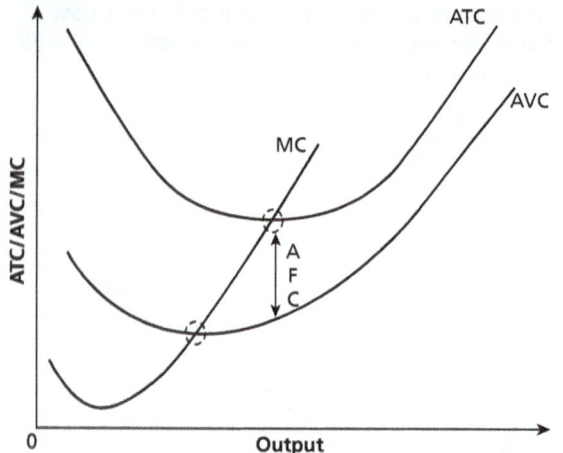

Figure 9.6 Marginal cost cuts average cost curves at minimum points

Note that in figure 9.6 the marginal cost curve cuts both AVC and ATC at their minimum points.

As soon as MC is greater than AVC, AVC immediately starts to increase. And as soon as MC > ATC, ATC immediately starts to increase. Although the ATC curve is derived by vertically adding AFC and AVC, another simple way to illustrate it is by a diagrammatic summary, showing how marginal physical product (MPP) and average physical product (APP) have an inverse effect on marginal cost and average variable cost.

See figures 9.7 a, b, c and d.

Student hint
This concept, which is frequently tested by examiners, is easy to prove:

If ten pies cost $100, then average cost of one pie = $10

If the marginal cost of the eleventh pie, is $12, then the total cost of 11 pies is 100 + 12 = 112; average cost of 11 pies = $\frac{112}{11}$ = 10.18

Short-run costs and short-run output
The diagrammatic summary in figures 9.7 a, b, c and d show how short-run production affects short-run cost.

> Note how diminishing marginal returns X_0, X_1, X_2 and X_3 cause MC to rise and hence cause AVC to be pulled up.
> Note the inverse relationship between MPP and MC and APP and AVC in figures 9.7c and 9.7d respectively.

It should be clear that increasing productivity will cause decreasing MC and AVC up to X_2 in figure 9.7c and X_3 in Figure 9.7d, and then decreased productivity will cause increasing MC and AVC.

The impact of productivity on cost of production is very clear cut and easy to prove; for example, if ten workers can cut 100 steel drums per day and the wage bill to the employer is $100, the unit labour cost per drum is $ $\frac{100}{100}$ pans = $1. If the same ten workers cut 200 steel pans the next day, on the owner's promise of a day off, then the unit labour cost of each pan is now $ $\frac{100}{200}$ pans = $0.50.

Summary
Increased productivity lowers the labour cost of production. Firms may make profits in local and foreign markets and become very competitive if their labour productivity increases.

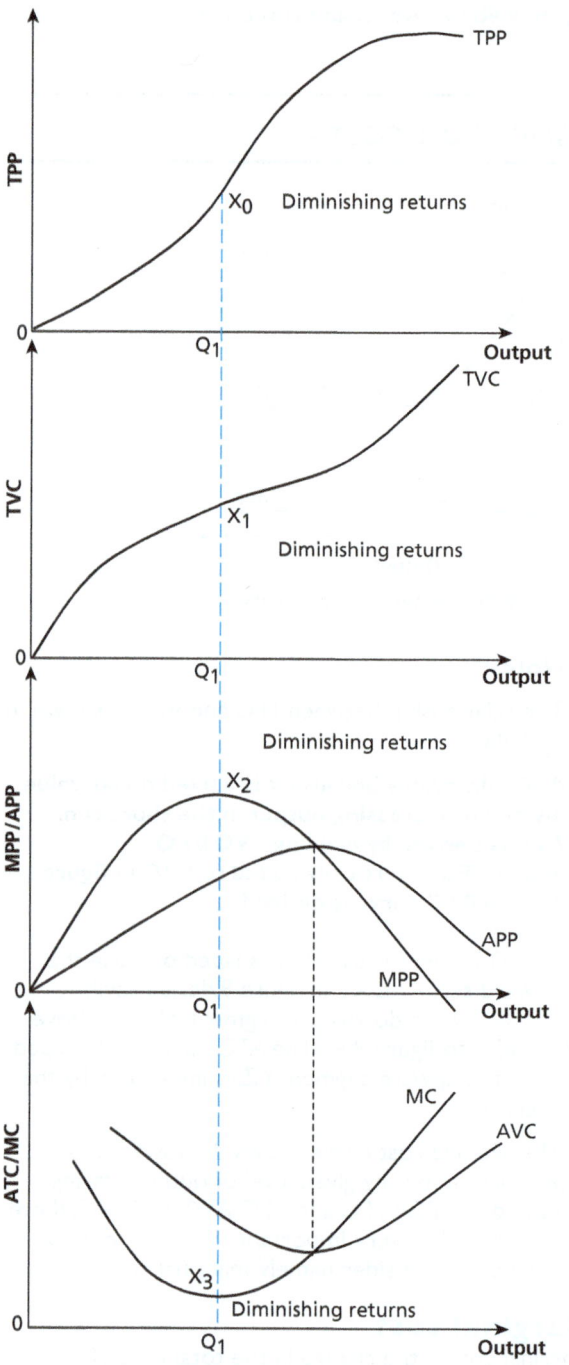

Figure 9.7 a, b, c and d The relationship between short-run output and costs

Chapter 9 The cost of production

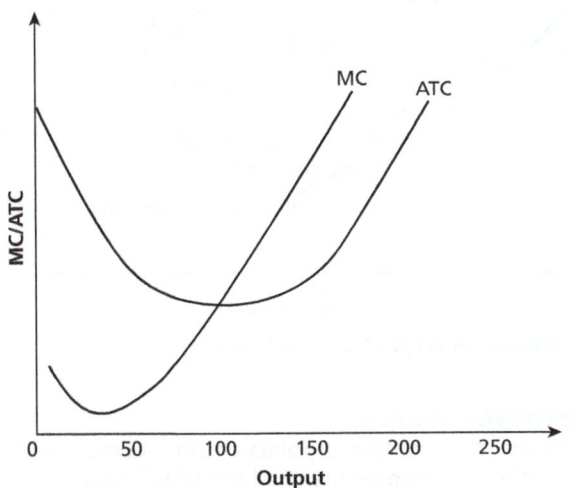

Figure 9.8 Short-run costs increases

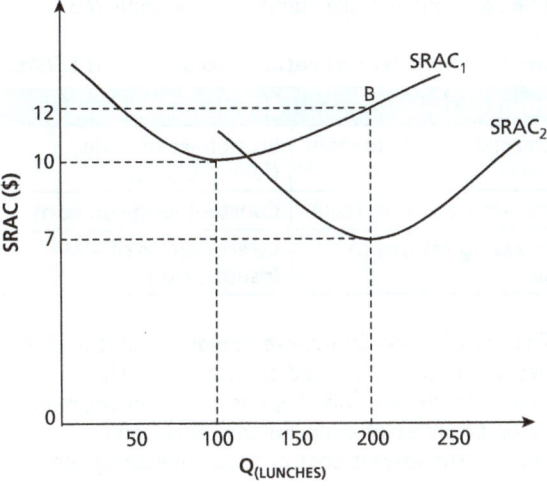

Figure 9.9 Increase in demand for school lunches

In the short-run when the fixed factor becomes overcrowded, diminishing returns cause AVC, MC and ATC to rise, increasing the cost of production. This is illustrated at output level 100 in figure 9.8. The firm could, however, enter long-run production by changing all factors of production, that is, making them all variable.

Refer to figure 9.9, which shows the cost curve of a caterer for school lunches. If there is an increase in demand due to growth of the business, a caterer for school lunches will wish to produce 200 lunches. Note that at 100 boxes the average cost per lunch is $10. Increasing production to 200 lunches, using existing fixed and variable factors, causes average cost to rise to B on short-run average cost 1 ($SRAC_1$) because diminishing returns increase AC. If the caterer changes all factor inputs and expands to 200 boxes, AC will fall to $7 on $SRAC_2$ when the plant is expanded.

If the caterer did not expand the plant, costs would rise to $12 using the first plant. The conclusion would be that expansion reduced AC. This reduction in long-run AC due to expansion is called internal economies of scale, or the cost savings of large-scale production. It also explains the phrase 'bigger is cheaper'.

In fact, the entrepreneur could keep on expanding output and be pleased that the long-run average cost is initially falling, remains constant, and then starts to rise, as shown in figures 9.10 and 9.11.

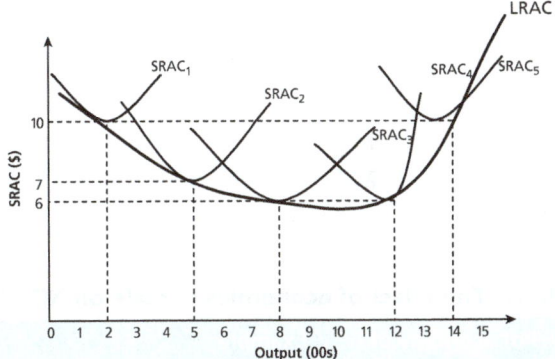

Figure 9.10 Reduction in average costs in the long-run

Now combine outputs and costs.

In chapter 6, which looked at long-run production, it was established that:

› **If percentage change in output > percentage change in input = increasing returns to scale**
› **If percentage change in output < percentage change in input = decreasing returns to scale**
› **If percentage change in output same as percentage change in input = constant returns to scale.**

These three relationships significantly influence long-run costs.

Notes for figure 9.10:

› **Increasing returns to scale from 200 to 800 reduces long-run average cost (LRAC) from $10 to $6. This cost reduction is called internal economies of scale.**
› **Further expansion from 800 to 1,200 units, LRAC is constant. This is referred to as constant economies of scale.**
› **From output 1,200 to 1,500, LRAC has risen, this is called internal diseconomies of scale.**
› **The least cost of output, 800 units, is called the minimum efficient size of production where all economies of scale have ended.**

The relationships are summed up in table 9.3.

Table 9.3 **The effect of returns to scale and LRAC**

Returns to scale	Effects on LRAC
Increased returns to scale	Economies of scale (falling LRAC)
Constant returns to scale	Constant long-run costs
Decreasing returns to scale	Diseconomies of scale (rising LRAC)

The LRAC curve is a curve tangent to all the SRAC curves and is also U-shaped, similar to the short-run average cost curves. This shape is due to economies and diseconomies of scale. Further, this curve represents the lowest cost of producing any given level of output.

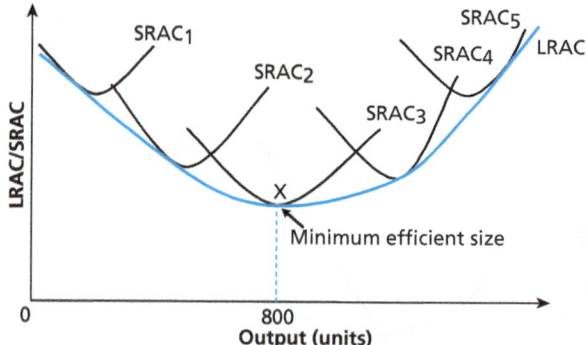

Figure 9.11 Average cost in the long-run

Common error

Note that these tangency points do not necessarily touch the minimum points of all the SRAC curves, except for $SRAC_3$.

Note:

› At output level 800, the minimum efficient size of operation is reached because economies of scale have come to an end. Output beyond this point achieves diseconomies of scale.
› The LRAC shown above is also called an envelope curve and is similar to a cost boundary.

Table 9.4 **The effect of economies of scale on AC of production**

Level of economy of scale	Example	Why AC falls
Indivisibilities	A large construction firm uses a tractor more often than a small company.	The cost of the tractor is the same if used three or eight times. If frequently used the AC of the job will fall.
Increased dimension	A 9-ton truck's capacity is three times that of a 3-ton truck. Also true of supertankers carrying crude oil.	A 9-ton truck does not cost three times the amount of a 3-ton truck, therefore saving money.
Linked process	Bringing together many stages of production in one plant reduces costs, e.g., oil refinery.	Same place and same time production reduces AC.
Principle of multiples	A soft drink factory uses a large integrated machinery operating at one speed.	Different machines operating at different speeds cause bottlenecks, but once integrated, bottlenecks and AC are reduced.
Division of labour	An auto plant uses mass production division of labour.	Increased productivity by specialisation reduces costs.
Purchasing	Large firms buy in bulk quantity.	Bulk buying of raw materials is done at discounted prices.
Financial	Raising capital by selling company stock or raising cheaper loans from banks due to the asset value of large firms.	Large assets enable financing and borrowing at reduced interest rates.
Managerial	Hiring specialists, e.g., advertising or legal specialists.	Specialists increase productivity and reduce costs of production. The cost of bringing in a specialist is spread over large increases in output.
Marketing	Transport and advertising.	These costs fall over large levels of output.
Research and development	Innovation and product improvement and packaging.	These costs are spread over large levels of output.

Internal economies of scale

Why do LRACs fall when a firm expands? The following examples are reasons why internal economies of scale are experienced by the firm itself when expanding.

Internal economies of scale may take place at different levels on a firm.

Internal diseconomies of scale

The output expansion of a firm beyond the maximum efficient plant size will cause LRAC to rise, causing internal diseconomies of scale (DOS).

Examples are:

- Coordination and control of a large workforce are difficult for managers. Efficiency falls and long-run costs rise.
- Internal communications are also not easily achieved, although information technology has since minimised this problem.
- Overspecialisation reduces productivity and increases long-run unit costs.
- Workers feel distanced from managers and interpersonal relations tend to lower worker morale and create poor industrial relations. Work stoppages increase costs.

External economies of scale

A firm may indirectly benefit from actions outside of its control. Growth in the industry may cause the LRAC of a large firm to fall. These are called external economies of scale.

Examples are:

- Improved infrastructure: e.g. road networks, power, water and telecommunications improvements by government and existing firms benefit new firms.
- Skilled labour pool, through siting of training schools in close proximity to industrial centres, or hiring skilled professionals from nearby firms.
- Agglomeration, which is the entry of new large firms to process waste, provide technical support, e.g., machine shops, catering, cleaning and security.

The above external economies of scale will cause LRAC to shift vertically downward.

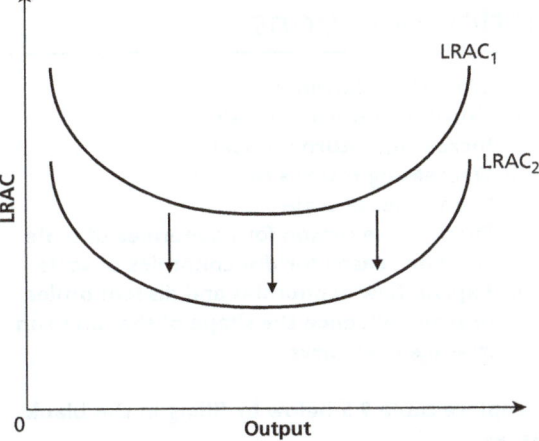

Figure 9.12 External economies of scale shift long-un average cost vertically downward

Large-scale expansion may also lead to external diseconomies of scale, that is, a vertical rise in the LRAC curve.

Examples are:

- Pollution
- Prices rise as firms compete with one another for services, labour, raw materials and land space
- Traffic congestion causes distribution delays.

Chapter summary

- A firm does not have a fixed factor restriction in the long-run, as it does in the short-run, because in the long-run it is possible to make the fixed factors variable.
- Output in the long-run is governed by the law of returns to scale. Scale means changing from a small level of output to a large level of output.
- Increasing, constant and decreasing returns to scale cause **LRACs** to decrease, remain constant and rise respectively.
- Falling **LRACs** are caused by economies of scale and represent the cost reductions as output expands, e.g., bulk buying, automation, increased dimension, and financial economies of scale. Economies of scale (EOS) may also be external.
- Diseconomies of scale cause long-run average cost to rise through difficulty in coordination and control of a large firm.
- When economies of scale come to an end, this point is called the minimum efficient size of production.
- Diseconomies of scale may also result from external effects such as traffic congestion and rising land, labour and raw material prices.

Practice questions

1. a. Explain the following:
   i. Constant returns to scale
   ii. Increasing returns to scale
   iii. Decreasing returns to scale
   iv. Economies of scale
   b. i. Discuss one reason for economies of scale and one reason for diseconomies of scale.
   ii. Explain how economies and diseconomies of scale influence the shape of the long-run average cost curve.

2. Complete table 9.5 below by filling in the blank spaces.

Table 9.5

Output	FC	TVC	Total cost	AFC	AVC	MC
0			10			
1			16			
2			24			
3			37			
4			46			
5			55			

3. A steel band craftsman produces five tenor pans at an average cost of TT$3,000 per pan. When he produces the sixth tenor pan the average cost falls to TT$2,900. What is the marginal cost of the sixth tenor pan?
   a. $1000
   b. $600
   c. $2400
   d. $483

4. a. State the law of diminishing returns and the law of returns to scale.
   b. Explain with the aid of figures how the two laws in (a) above, may cause both SRAC and LRAC to be U-shaped.

5. Explain, with the use of a figure, the relationship between the firm's short-run and its long-run average total cost curves.
   a. Define each of the following, or write the formula for calculating it.
      i. APP   ii. MPP   iii. AVC   iv. MC
   b. State what happens to APP and MPP as output increases.
   c. State what happens to AVC and MC as output increases.
   d. How will output be affected when a variable input is added to a fixed input?
   e. How do increasing levels of output affect costs?

Table 9.6

Units of output	TC (00)	TVC
0	150	
5	200	
10	230	
15	240	
20	270	
25	350	

6. The data given in table 9.6 above represents the costs of making coconut ice cream.
   a. Calculate the fixed cost of production and explain what is meant by fixed costs. Support your answer with examples of fixed cost for an ice cream producer.
   b. Calculate average fixed cost (AFC) at output 10 quarts and explain what will happen to AFC as output increases.
   c. What is meant by marginal cost?
   d. Calculate the marginal cost of the fifth quart of ice cream.
   e. Use data from the table to explain why marginal cost is equal, not only to a change in TC, but to a change in TVC as well.
   f. Briefly explain the likely shape of the AVC and ATC curves from the data given in table 9.6.

10 Market structures

LEARNING OBJECTIVES

- Identify the four market structures.
- Explain the differences between them.
- Identify barriers to entry.
- List and explain the characteristics of market structures.
- Explain perfect and imperfect competition.

REQUIRED KNOWLEDGE

- Demand
- Supply
- Price elasticity of demand and supply
- Price equilibrium
- Cost and output theory in the short- and long-run
- Business organisations.

TOPIC VALUE

Fundraising activities in schools (e.g. cake sales) are a good introduction to unit cost theory.

Introduction

Successful firms are profitable. Profit, however, is determined by the difference in the cost and sales of output in the short or long-run. Since short and long-run output and costs have been analysed in previous chapters, this chapter analyses how the revenue of a firm is determined.

The difference between cost and revenue will then determine profit or loss.

Sellers and buyers influence prices by their numbers and purchasing decisions. In essence, the number of buyers and sellers in a market may determine the degree of competition or market structure of the industry.

Market structure is determined by many factors that create competitiveness among the firms in an industry.

Factors that determine market structure are:

› **The ability to set or accept the going market price in the industry**
› **Barriers to entry**
› **The type of product sold**
› **The level of short- and long-run profit earned**
› **The number of sellers**
› **Knowledge of market conditions**
› **The number of buyers**
› **The demand curve that each market faces, depending on the market power of buyers**
› **The mobility of the firms, i.e., the ability to adapt or shift resources to other industries.**

These factors are further explained as follows.

The ability to influence price

This depends on whether the firm is a price taker or price maker. If prices are raised or lowered it may cause a loss or gain in sales. In other words, the ability to influence price is determined by how price elastic the good is and how dominant the firm is to set price.

Barriers to entry or exit

These are the difficulties or invisible barriers that new firms face trying to enter or leave an industry. Firms enter an industry easily or can make it difficult for new entrants. Some barriers are: legal patents, brand name or trade logos, control of raw materials, high advertising costs of existing firms, extremely high set-up costs (as found in the oil industry), extremely high cost of land, economies of scale of existing firms, and raising large sums of financial capital.

The number of buyers and sellers in the industry

If there are few sellers they may enjoy monopoly power, while many buyers provide them the opportunity to achieve market power.

Type of good offered for sale

If the good has very few good substitutes then demand will be inelastic and there will be little or no competition; for example, gasoline or electricity or telecommunications.

Level of profits

A few firms in an industry may record high profit levels. While few firms do earn high profit, the price elasticity of demand of the products that they trade in plays a major role in the profit earned. Profit may not be evenly shared among the firms in the industry.

Mobility of factors

The mobility of the factors of production enable firms to adapt to differing types of production such as, for example, when labour and capital on a farm shifts to being used at a factory instead.

These factors determine the level of competition in a market or industry and competition between firms is identified by four different market structures:

› **Perfect competition or a perfectly competitive market**
› **Monopoly**
› **Monopolistic competition**
› **Oligopoly.**

Although the four market structures represent different levels of competition, there are two extremes that should be examined first. These two extreme levels are perfect competition and monopoly.

Perfect competition

Perfect or pure competition describes an industry with absolute, total, or pure competition and has the following features:

› **There are so many sellers and buyers that the action of one buyer or seller is insignificant and therefore unable to influence the demand or** supply curve. Prices are therefore determined by pure competition and market forces.

> As a result of the large numbers of firms, each firm in the market brings an insignificantly limited supply to the industry and is therefore unable to affect prices. Firms are therefore price takers rather than price makers.
> Each firm's product is identical to the products of other firms in the industry. This is called product homogeneity. These products are therefore perfect substitutes for each other, taking competition to a very high level.
> There are no barriers to entry or exit to any firm in this industry, so there is absolutely no difficulty or obstruction to entering or leaving if the firm wishes. More firms create more competition.
> Perfect knowledge exists for all firms in this industry so no one firm has any information advantage with respect to raw material prices on other firms' costs of production. Buyers also have perfect knowledge of every price in every location or quality, size, colour, of every good anywhere.
> No firm will raise or lower prices since raising prices with a perfect substitute for competition will yield no sale. Price elasticity of demand being perfect, a firm will not lower prices because it is possible for the small quantity brought to the market to be sold at the ruling price. It would make no sense therefore to lower prices.

Perfect mobility is also another unique feature of a perfect market.

Factors of production are highly mobile and can therefore switch to another firm making an identical product with considerable ease. Factor mobility is therefore perfect. In the real world there are no perfect (pure) markets, but some aspects of perfect competition may be observed in some markets.

An example is the US currency market.

> All $5, $20 or $100 bills are pretty much identical.
> Knowledge is not perfect in the future but reliable on a daily basis, e.g., the exchange rate is quoted daily in newspapers.
> Barriers to entry and exit are very low. It is easy for someone to sell (exit) US dollars. Purchasing (entry) is easy at certain times but it may be difficult at times of currency shortages so this may be a barrier to entry.
> There are many buyers and sellers. It is not only banks that sell US currency. A currency buyer at a bank could also be a seller at the same bank.
> Each buyer is a price taker, but may have some ability to set price since US currency may at times be scarce. This market may be imperfect because buyers are sometimes unaware when US currency prices change overnight. Also, counterfeiting limits homogeneity. Barriers do exist for both buyer and potential seller because it is illegal to sell US currency in markets in some countries.

Monopoly

A monopolist is simply a sole supplier and is therefore the firm and industry at the same time. This is a pure monopoly. A legal monopoly is defined in some countries as any firm controlling 25 per cent of total market share. In a pure monopoly, there is no competition because of the following characteristics:

> There is one seller and there are many buyers.
> There are very strong barriers to entry, e.g., very high set-up costs; economies of scale enjoyed by monopolists bring about low prices, discouraging new entrants. There is also control of raw materials, legal barriers (in essential industries, e.g., water supply, electricity).
> The monopolist is a price setter.
> The monopolist's control over supply enables the firm to set price or quantity but not both because it controls supply not demand. So the firm can offer a certain quantity for sale and the demand curve would determine price or set a price and the demand curve would determine the quantity demanded. The firm would face a downward sloping demand curve as a result.
> Product branding (differentiation). A popular brand, e.g., Banks Beer of Barbados may pose a strong barrier to other competitors.

Apart from pure and legal monopolies, other forms of monopoly are:

> Monopoly by merger. In some instances, this is permitted by law and in some ways may act like a cartel.
> Natural monopoly. This is a monopoly with the ability to exploit economies of scale to such an extent that it is able to supply an entire industry's output at a lower cost than two or three firms together. Examples of this are the state-owned water supply and distribution or electricity.

Imperfect competition

Between the extremes of perfect competition and monopoly are market structures that compete imperfectly. These are monopolistic competition and oligopoly. Monopolistic competition takes place when:

> There are many buyers and sellers though not as many as in perfect competition, but numerous enough to ensure competition.
> The ability to influence price is not as strong as a monopolist, but a monopolistic competitor has a monopoly over its branded product and so has some influence on price.
> Products in this market are not identical but differentiated (branded) so there exists a small element of product monopoly power.

- Barriers to entry in this market structure are not as low as perfect competition but low enough to allow new entrants fairly easy entry into the market.
- The existence of firms with a similar product also means each competitor faces an elastic demand curve in the market. An example of this industry in the Caribbean are restaurants serving local cuisine.

Common error

A monopoly market structure is often confused with a monopolistic market structure. The phrase 'monopolistic competitor' may sound like a contradiction in terms but the term 'monopolistic' refers to the monopoly a firm has over its branded product.

A pure monopoly in theory refers to a single firm.

Oligopoly

An oligopoly is a market structure in which a few large firms dominate the industry; for example, insurance companies, commercial banks or paint companies. The features of this type of market structure are:

- Few firms and many buyers
- The ability to set price depends on whether there is a leader whose pricing strategy everyone will follow, or the oldest and most experienced firm.
- There is price rigidity in this type of market that suggests that competition is based on non-price factors, e.g., promotion, advertising or service.
- Interdependence. Each firm's strategy is determined by the way rival firms are likely to act.
- Firms cooperate informally, a strategy referred to as informal collusion.
- Oligopolists trade in similar goods or services that are branded (differentiated).
- Barriers to entry in this market structure are not easy to overcome so competition is strictly of a non-price nature.
- Some barriers are high level of technology, and economies of scale of over a large range of outputs.

Chapter summary

- Market structure describes the many different characteristics of firms that determine their ability to compete.
- The criteria that determine market structure include: the number of buyers and sellers, the nature of the product, barriers to entry and exit, the ability to influence output and price, the demand curve the firm faces, and the level of short- and long-run profit.
- The four main market structures are: perfect market, monopoly, monopolistic competition and oligopoly.

Monopolistic and oligopolistic firms engage in imperfect competition while firms in a perfect market engage in perfect competition.

- Imperfect competitors face a downward sloping demand curve, while competitive firms face a horizontal demand curve that is equal to marginal revenue and price.
- Price elasticity varies along a linear demand curve.

Practice questions

1. Define the term 'market structure'.
2. List four types of market structures that exist in the **CARICOM** region and give one example of each type.
3. Select two of the market structures listed in (2) above and compare them with respect to each of the following:
   a. Barriers to entry
   b. Number of firms and buyers
   c. Nature of the goods they produce
   d. Market power and control over price.

Chapter 11 Price, revenue and profit concepts

LEARNING OBJECTIVES

- Explain and illustrate total, average and marginal revenues in different market structures.
- Analyse the equilibrium of the firm and in an industry, in the short- and long-run and in different market structures.
- Explain profit maximisation, normal and above normal (economic) profit.

REQUIRED KNOWLEDGE

- Demand and supply
- Short-run output, cost
- Market structure
- Cost of production.

TOPIC VALUE

How are total, average and marginal revenue determined? Market structures differ in their ability to influence price because the demand curve each market structure faces is different. This fact largely determines the revenues of each firm in its respective market structure.

Market structure and revenue

In order to make pricing and output decisions a firm will need to calculate the revenue and cost of output and the price of this output. The main types of revenue that the firm would need to identify for these purposes are:

> Total revenue
> Average revenue
> Marginal revenue.

The relationship between total, average, and marginal values has already been identified in the chapters 4, 6 and 9 on utility, output and cost.

Total revenue (TR) is the total sales of the firm for a specific time period, calculated as price multiplied by quantity. For example, if a peanut vendor sells 200 packs of peanuts a day at $2.00 per pack, his TR will be $400.00.

Average revenue (AR) is the revenue earned for each unit sold and is calculated as: $\frac{TR}{q}$

AR for the peanut vendor will be $\frac{\$400}{200} = \$2.00$

Note that AR and price are the same concept. Marginal revenue (MR) is the revenue realised from the sale of an additional unit or one less unit of output; for example, if the peanut vendor sells 201 packs of peanuts the change in TR will be:

TR from 200 packs @ $2.00 = $400

TR from 201 packs @ $2.00 = $402

Change in TR = $2.00

Change in quantity sold = 1

Therefore MR = $\frac{\$200}{1}$ = $2.00

Similarly for 220 packs:

TR from 200 packs @ $2.00 = $400

TR from 220 packs @ $2.00 = $440

Change in TR = $40

Change in quantity = 20

MR = change in TR/change in quantity

= $\frac{\$40}{\$20}$ = $2

Revenue and output according to market structure

The three revenue concepts outlined above (TR, AR and MR) will depend on how output affects price. For a perfect market each firm's output is so small that supply is unaffected if firms enter or leave the market. It is the same with demand. There are so many consumers that no one can influence demand by themselves. The price is determined by market forces and firms in this market are price takers. See figure 11.1.

In figure 11.1, since a perfect competitor's output does not affect price, the price is taken from the market equilibrium. Hence the perfect competitor faces a demand curve that is a horizontal line or a perfectly elastic demand curve. For a perfectly competitive firm, TR in figure 11.1 will be as shown in table 11.1 and figure 11.2.

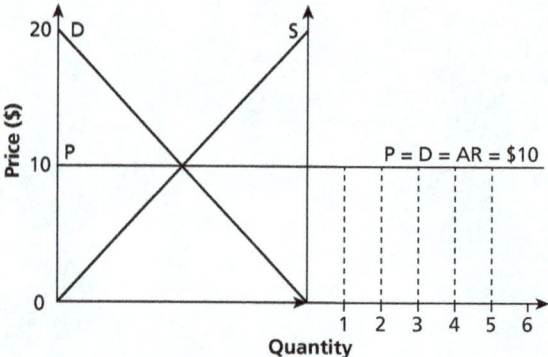

Figure 11.1 Price in a perfect market (price taker)

Table 11.1 Price and total revenue

Quantity	Price	TR
1	10	10
2	10	20
3	10	30
4	10	40
5	10	50

Chapter 11 Price, revenue and profit concepts

Note:

In Figure 11.1:

1. The firm is a price taker
2. An infinite number of products can be sold at the ruling market price.

Since the price is the same for every quantity sold, the TR is a linear curve, forming a 45 degree line through the point of origin. See figure 11.2.

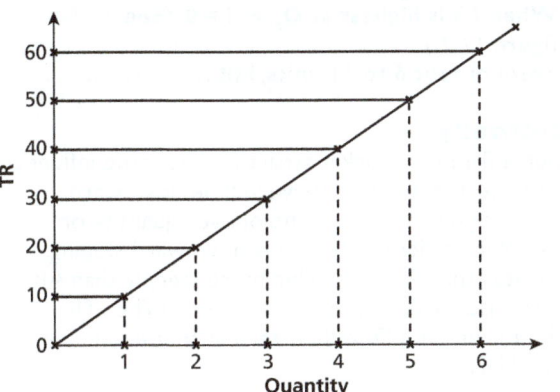

Figure 11.2 TR in a perfect market

Calculating AR when price is the same for each level of output or quantity sold, is found by the formula, TR/Q.

In figure 11.3 AR for the first unit is $10/1=$10. AR for unit 2 = $10 x 2 = 20/2 =$10. For units 3 through to 6, AR is the same. Hence price, AR and demand are the same. Thus in a perfect market P = AR = D.

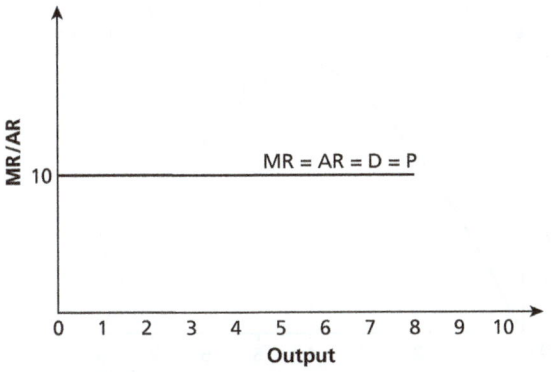

Figure 11.3 MR = AR = Price = D in a perfect market

Marginal revenue

See table 11.2. Since MR is the additional revenue gained from one more (or less) unit sold, the change in TR between units 1 and 2 is $10, that is, from $10 to $20. The extra revenue gained from the sale of the third, fourth, fifth or sixth unit is also $10, that is, the difference between $30, $40, $50 and $60. We can now conclude that if a demand curve is horizontal or perfectly elastic, the price (AR) and MR will be the same. The demand curve can now be written as P = D = AR = MR for any firm in a perfectly competitive market.

Table 11.2 The equality of P = D = AR = MR in a perfect market

Quantity	Price	TR	AR	MR
1	10	10	10	10
2	10	20	10	10
3	10	30	10	10
4	10	40	10	10
5	10	50	10	10
6	10	60	10	10

Summary

A perfectly competitive firm cannot influence price because there is a vast number of buyers and sellers in the market who individually have no influence over price. In all three other market structures, firms have some measure of influence over price. A monopoly, for example, has total control of quantity or price but not both. Both monopolistic competitors and oligopolists have varying ability to influence price in their markets.

Total revenue in a monopoly market structure

A monopolist controls supply but not demand and a greater output will be bought by consumers at lower prices than at higher prices. This single firm therefore faces a downward sloping demand curve in the marketplace. This is shown in the demand curve in figure 11.4, derived from table 11.3. The table also shows the MR, should the firm start to sell at $1 and move dollar by dollar to $10.

Table 11.3 TR and MR in a monopoly market structure

Price $	Quantity	TR $	MR $
1	10	10	–
2	9	18	8
3	8	24	6
4	7	28	4
5	6	30	2
6	5	30	0
7	4	28	–2
8	3	24	–4
9	2	18	–6
10	1	10	–8

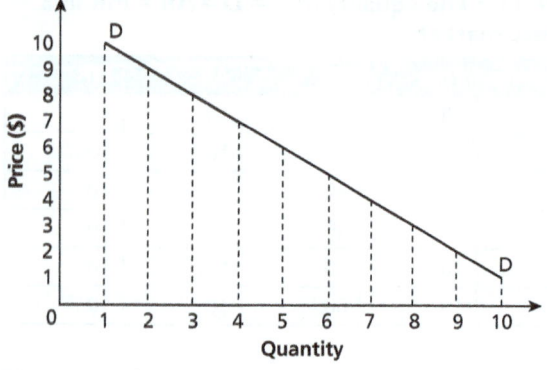

Figure 11.4 A monopolist demand curve

In such a case, TR is equal to price multiplied by quantity, as shown in table 11.3 and figure 11.5.

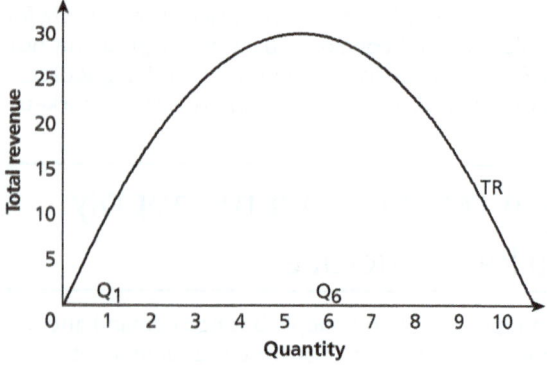

Figure 11.5 TR curve

Note that TR will rise, peak and then fall to zero as shown in figure 11.5.

Marginal revenue

The relationship between marginal and total utility was examined in chapter 4 and showed that when total utility is rising, marginal utility is falling. In the case of revenue it is similar. Note how TR is rising as long as MR is positive.

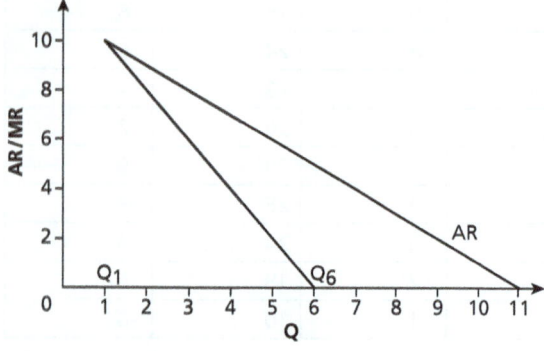

Figure 11.6 MR < AR for a monopoly

More importantly, even though both AR and MR are falling, MR is falling faster than AR. Figure 11.6 is plotted from table 11.3.

If AR or demand is a linear curve, computing the related MR curve will bisect the horizontal axis. A firm facing a downward sloping demand curve such as a monopoly, a monopolistic competitor or oligopolistic competitor, will have AR, MR and TR curves similar to those shown in figure 11.6.

Note

Refer to Figures 11.6 and 11.7. In summary:

› **AR = D = P is downward sloping.**
› **TR rises, peaks at Q_6, then declines to zero.**
› **MR falls more quickly than AR and is less than AR from Q_1 to Q_6.**
› **When TR is highest at Q_6, MR = 0.** (See figure 11.7.)
› **From output 6 to 11 units, MR is negative.**

Summary

When a firm in a market structure has some influence over price, the demand curve will be downward sloping because there is control over quantity or price. When a demand curve is downward sloping, MR is less than AR and falling more steeply than AR. TR will rise, peak and then fall to zero. When TR is at a maximum MR will be zero at that point. See figure 11.7.

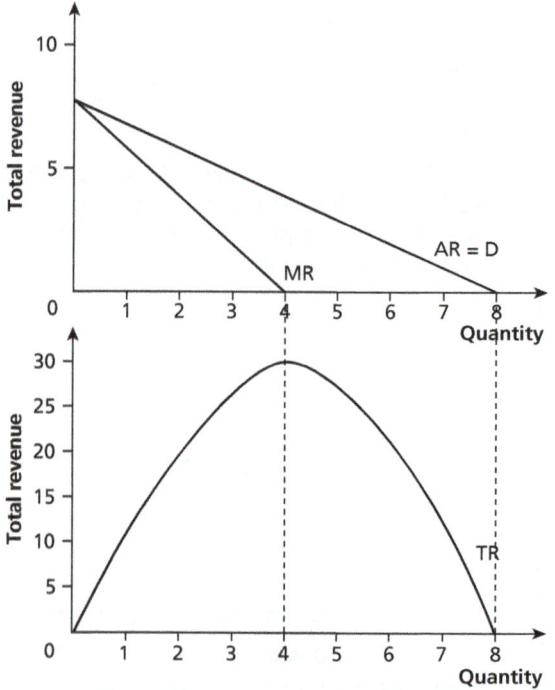

Figure 11.7 Where TR is maximum, MR = 0 for monopoly

Revenue and elasticity

› **If a demand curve is horizontal, price elasticity of demand (PED) is perfectly elastic for a firm in a perfectly competitive market.**
› **If the demand curve is downward sloping, recall that at the midpoint of a downward sloping demand curve PED = 1. PED to the left of midpoint is greater than one and PED to the right of midpoint is less than one.**

Chapter 11 Price, revenue and profit concepts

This is illustrated in figure 11.8.

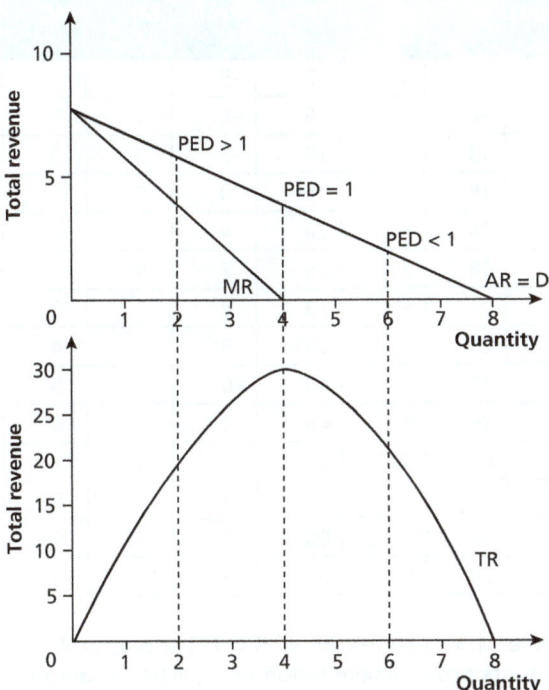

Figure 11.8 TR and price elasticity of demand

Note from figure 11.7 that at Q_2 PED >1 and AR and MR are positive. At Q_4 AR is positive but MR = 0. At Q_6 AR is positive but MR is negative. A firm therefore will not sell output where MR is negative. So it will set prices in the elastic portion of its demand curve.

Summary
Price elasticity of demand varies along a demand curve. Where PED = 1, MR = 0. A firm will not set price in the inelastic portion of a demand curve since MR will be negative.

Since elasticity varies along a downward sloping demand curve (AR), firms would set price in the segment of the curve that is elastic, or to the left of the midpoint where PED = 1 because in this segment MR is positive.

AR, TR and MR vary in the way each is determined by the different market structures.

- In a perfect market AR and MR are the same. AR in imperfect markets is downward sloping.
- Linear demand curves give rise to linear MR curves that bisect the horizontal axis in imperfect market structures.
- At the midpoint of a linear demand curve PED is equal to one.
- Imperfect markets have some influence over price setting. Their demand curves are therefore downward sloping.

Profit maximisation

Having analysed production and cost in the short- and long-run and revenue determination in each market structure, it is now easier to understand the concept of profit.

Traditional economic theory of the firm assumes that all firms aim for an output that achieves the highest level of profit possible. This is called the equilibrium output and the highest level of profit is called profit maximisation.

Profit maximisation takes place at an output level where there is the greatest positive difference between TR and total cost. At this level of output the marginal cost of production is also equal to marginal revenue, that is MC = MR.

Profit maximisation in a perfectly competitive firm
Figure 11.9 is plotted from table 11.4. Note that TR = Total revenue and TC = Total cost.

Table 11.4 Total revenue/total cost short-run analysis

Output	TC	AR = P	TR	Total profit
0	5	5	0	−5
1	10	5	5	−5
2	13	5	10	−3
3	15	5	15	0
4	16	5	20	4
5	18	5	25	7
6	21	5	30	9
7	26	5	35	9
8	30	5	40	10
9	36	5	45	9
10	43	5	50	7
11	51	5	55	4
12	60	5	60	0

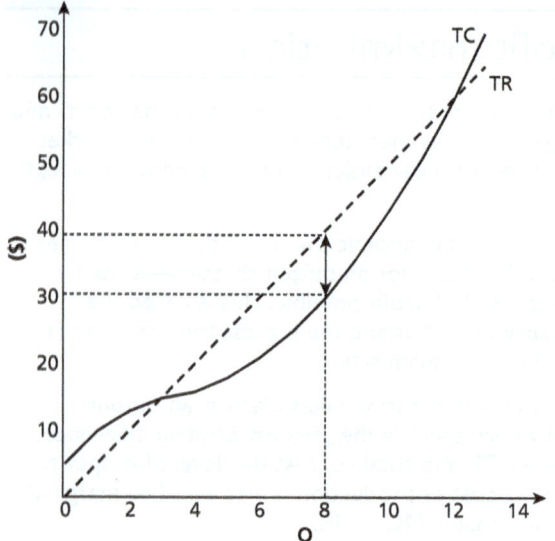

Figure 11.9 TR/TC short-run profit-maximisation analysis

Table 11.5 **Profit-maximisation MC/MR analysis**

Output	TC	AR = P	TR	Profit	MR	MC
0	5	5	0	−5	–	–
1	10	5	5	−5	5	5
2	13	5	10	−3	5	3
3	15	5	15	0	5	2
4	16	5	20	4	5	1
5	18	5	25	7	5	2
6	21	5	29	8	5	3
7	25	5	35	9	5	4
8	30	5	40	10	5	5
9	36	5	45	9	5	6
10	43	5	50	7	5	7
11	51	5	55	4	5	8
12	60	5	60	0	5	9
13	70	5	65	−5	5	10

The price of the product and therefore AR = D = P is $5.00. Since it is a perfect market there is only one price and hence a horizontal demand curve. Note well, the familiar total cost curve that was derived in chapter 9 on cost theory. Note also the 45 degree TR curve.

Profit maximisation is the assumed objective of all firms in microeconomic theory. In real life, profit maximisation may only be the objective of firms owned and managed by owners.

To summarise, profit maximisation is:

> **The equilibrium output for a firm in all market structures according to traditional economic theory.**
> **Achieved at an output where TR exceeds TC by the greatest positive margin and also where MC = MR.**

In figure 11.9, TR exceeds TC by the greatest amount at output 8 units, where TR = $40 and TC = $30. The highest level of profit is equal to $10.00.

Other observations:

> Between output level 1 to 3 there is a loss (TC>TR in figure 11.9).
> At output level 3, TC = TR; this is called break-even point. There is neither profit nor loss at this level of output.
> Between output levels 3 to 12 units, the perfectly competitive firm is making a profit (TR>TC).
> At output level 12 the firm is making zero profit, which is also called the break-even point (TR=TC).
> At output levels beyond 12 the firm is making a loss (TC>TR).

Table 11.5 illustrates how TR > TC at output 8 represents profit maximisation or equilibrium output. Figure 11.10 is plotted from table 11.5. It shows MC = MR at eight units.

When both total and marginal analysis are examined, note that at output level 8, TR exceeds TC by its greatest value and also that MC = MR = $5 as illustrated in figure 11.11.

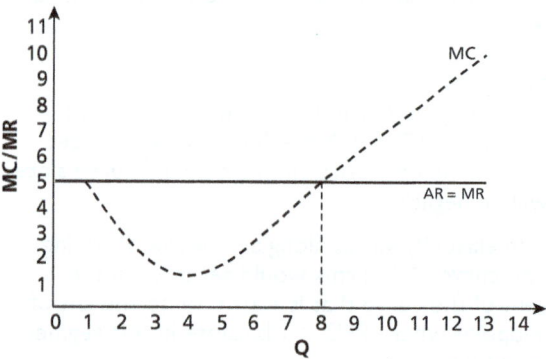

Figure 11.10 Profit maximisation by MC/MR analysis

Common error

Sometimes it is not easily grasped why MC = MR represents the highest level of profit. From figure 11.10 and table 11.5, you should be able to observe this relationship clearly.

Note:

Observe that MC = MR at output 1 and 8 units but profit is not maximised at output 1 unit because MC is falling at this level of output. At output 8 units MC is rising. Profit maximisation therefore occurs where MC cuts MR from below (at output 8).

In figure 11.11, from 3 to 8 units, profit is being made on each successive unit with an increasing gap between TR and TC. Should unit 9 be produced the firm would still make total profit overall but not on unit 9 itself, for which MC = 6 >, AR = 5.

As long as an extra unit of output adds more to revenue than to cost, a firm would increase output until the cost of one extra unit (MC) is equal to MR. At output 9 units MC > MR so the firm should reduce output to 8 in order to profit maximise.

11	25	27
11.5	24	24
13	28	22

Profit-maximisation for monopoly (TR/TC analysis)

See figure 11.12 and table 11.6.

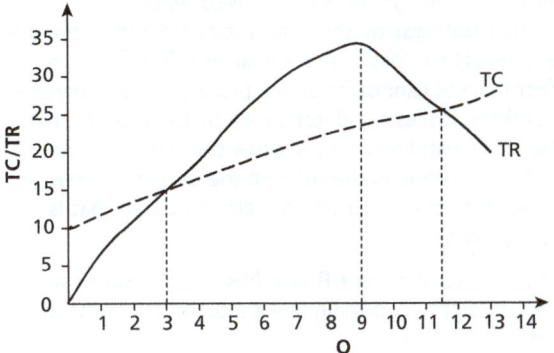

Figure 11.12 Profit-maximisation by TC = TR analysis for a monopoly

Since a monopoly can control output or price but not both, it will face a downward sloping demand curve in the market, selling more units if the price is reduced. Note the familiar shape of the total cost curve and the typically arched shaped TR curve and the greatest positive difference between TR and total cost is at output level 9 units.

> At output level 3 units, there is a break-even point, with TR the same as TC.
> Output level 11.5 units is also a break-even point, but profit is equal to zero.
> Between output levels 0 and 3 units the monopolist is making a loss.
> Between output levels 3 and 11.5 units the monopolist is making a profit, TR>TC.
> Beyond output levels 11.5 units the monopolist is making a loss once more, TC>TR.

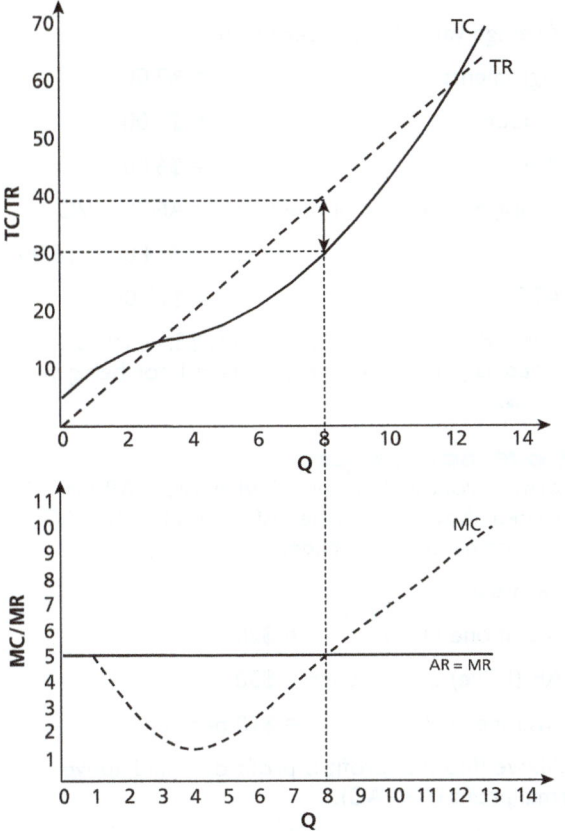

Figure 11.11 Profit-maximisation MC/MR analysis

Table 11.6 Profit-maximisation for monopoly (TR/TC analysis)

Quantity	TC	TR
0	10	0
1	12	7
2	13	11
3	15	15
4	17	19
5	18	24
6	20	28
7	22	31
8	23	30
9	24	34
10	25	31

MC/MR analysis of profit-maximisation for a firm trading as a monopolist

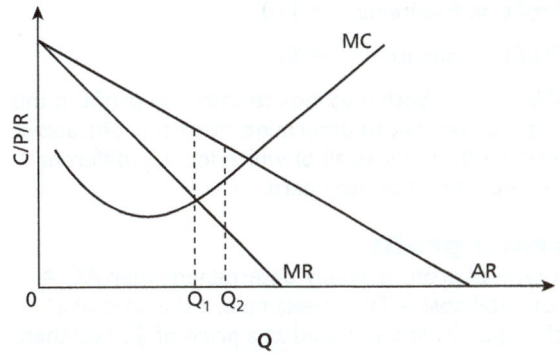

Figure 11.13 Profit-maximisation by MC = MR analysis for a monopolist

Observe the familiar AR and MR curves for a monopolist in figure 11.13. At Q_1, MC = MR. If the firm produces beyond Q_1 to Q_2 it would not make a loss overall but it would make a loss on that unit (Q_2), MC > MR, and it would not maximise profit since the additional unit adds more to costs than to revenue.

Summary

For both a perfectly competitive firm and a monopolist firm, profit is maximised where TR exceeds total cost by the greatest positive margin and where marginal cost is also equal to MR. Firms in a perfect market cannot influence price because they are price takers. Prices are determined by the free market forces of demand and supply. Since there is only one price for everyone in the market, the demand curve facing each firm is a horizontal demand curve that is perfectly elastic.

In a perfect market AR and MR are the same while TR is a straight 45 degree line through the point of origin.

Profit in the short-run

Normal profit, above normal profit, and loss

Although all firms maximise profit as a rule, the level of profit made is very much determined by the cost of producing a given level of output. This profit may be determined in two ways:

1. Total revenue minus total cost (TR – TC).
2. The unit price of one unit minus the unit cost (AR – average cost (AC)) of one unit multiplied by the equilibrium output. For example, if the total cost of five items @ a unit cost of $4 each is $20 and the TR of five items @ $6 is $30 then profit is equal to $30 – $20 = $10.

We could just as well find the profit on one unit and multiply it by the number of items sold in the following way:

Price of one item = $6
Unit cost of one item = $4
Profit on five items = $10
Profit on one item = $2

We will use both methods to calculate profit in this chapter as we seek to determine: normal profit, above normal profit, and loss, all of which identify different levels of profit a firm may earn.

Normal profit

This type of profit is simply determined when AC = AR or total cost = TR; for example, if the cost of a lunch is $20.00 and it is sold at a price of $20.00 then normal profit is being made. This may be confusing since both cost and price are the same. However, the cost of providing the lunch is a profit of $5.00, which is regarded as a fixed cost of production.

Example:
Average fixed cost per lunch:
Rent = $6.00
Interest on loan = $2.00
Profit = $5.00
Insurance = $1.00
Average fixed cost = $14.00

Average variable cost per lunch:
Ingredients = $2.00
Labour = $4.00
AVC = $6.00
Average total cost of one lunch = AFC + AVC
= $14.00 + $6.00
ATC = $20.00

Reminder: Profit on one lunch is $5, which is included as part of the firm's costs risk for being in business.

Above normal profit

If normal profit is determined when AC = AR (as explained above), then when AR is greater than AC above normal profit is made, that is

Example:
AC of one lunch = $20
AR (Price) of one lunch = $30
Average profit = $10 per box

Above l/normal profit is profit over and above normal profit (AR>AC).

TR/total cost approach of equilibrium output (30 lunches)
TC = 30 lunches @ $20 (AC) = $600
TR = 30 lunches @ $30 (AR) = $900
Above normal economic profit = $900 – $600 = $300
OR
30 lunches at profit of $10 per lunch = $300

Loss
A loss takes place when TC > TR or AC is greater than price (AR). If 30 lunches cost $20 to produce then TC = $600

30 lunches at price $10 TR = $300

loss = $300

Similarly if the price (AR) of one box =

$10 and the unit cost AC of one box =

$20 loss on one box lunch = $10

and loss on 30 lunches = 30 x $10

= $300

Chapter 11 Price, revenue and profit concepts

Normal, above normal profit and loss in a perfect market

It is quite possible for these three levels of profit to be made in a perfect market even if the vast number of firms accept the same price from the market. Clearly the level of profit in this type of market will be determined by cost rather than price.

Perfect competition

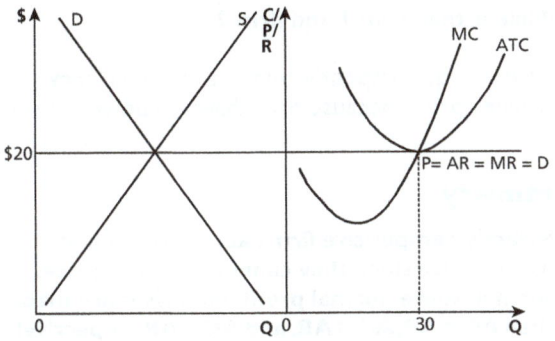

Figure 11.14 Normal profit for a perfect competitor

Figure 11.14 shows a firm in a perfect market accepting the price from the market since it is a price taker. The curves in the diagram representing the firm provide the following information:

MC = MR (equilibrium output of 30 lunches)

ATC = AR (the information needed to calculate the profit of 30 lunches)

On the vertical axis note the letters CPR for cost, price and revenue. To determine whether profit is normal, above normal or negative (that is a loss) follow these simple steps:

1. **Identify profit maximisation (equilibrium output), which is where MC = MR, i.e., at 30 lunches.**
2. **Identify the price of one lunch by drawing a line connecting 30 lunches on the horizontal axis up to the demand curve (AR) and it will reveal a price of $20 per lunch (the dotted line).**
3. **Find the cost of one lunch (AC) by connecting a line from equilibrium output (30 lunches) to the AC curve. Note the AC is also $20, therefore if AR = AC, then the firm is making normal profit.**

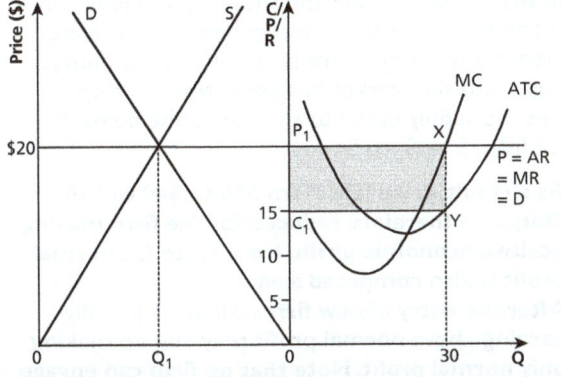

Figure 11.15 Above normal profit for a perfect competitor

In figure 11.15, above normal profit for a perfect competitor is calculated using the three steps outlined below.

> **Step 1: Identify profit maximisation equilibrium output, MC = MR (at X) = 30 lunches.**
> **Step 2: Identify the price of one lunch (AR) by connecting Q (30) to the AR or demand curve = $20.**
> **Step 3: Identify unit cost (AC) C1 of 1 lunch by connecting Q (30) to AC curve = $15 per lunch.**

Profit on one lunch = AR (price) − unit cost (AC) = $20 − $15 = $5 per box (average profit). Therefore, profit on 30 lunches = 30 × $5 = $150 or the shaded area $P_1 XYC_1$.

Loss

See figure 11.16.

Before going to the three steps for a firm making a loss, observe that at profit-maximisation output of 30 lunches, the AC of $25 is greater than the price of $20. At a glance the firm is making a loss. Proceed, nevertheless, using this three-step method:

> **Step 1: Identify profit maximisation output = 30 lunches**
> **Step 2: Identify price of one lunch (AR) by connecting Q (30) to the AR curve (D) price therefore = $20**
> **Step 3: Identify unit cost (AC) of one lunch by:**
> - **Connecting (Q) 30 lunches to the AC curve = $25**
> - **Loss on one lunch = $5 (loss)**
> - **Therefore loss on 30 lunches = $150 (loss) or shaded area.**

TR/TC method: TR/total cost approach of equilibrium output

$$TR = AR \times Q_1 = \$20 \times 30 = \$600$$
$$TC = AC \times Q_1 = \$25 \times 30 = \$750$$
$$Loss = \${-}150$$

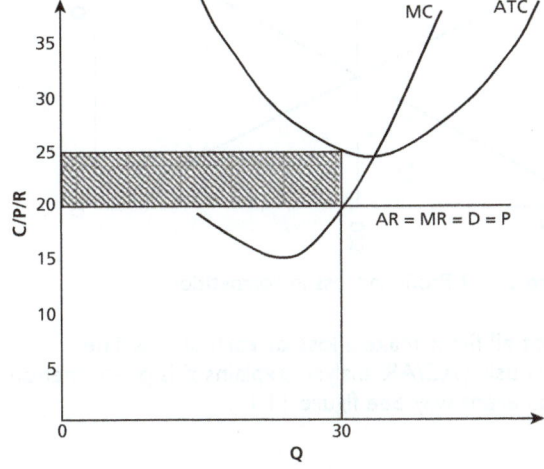

Figure 11.16 Loss for a perfect competitor

You may correctly question that at output 30 units a loss is incurred and that there is no profit. MC = MR is therefore not only where output is maximised but also where the firm's losses are the least. MC = MR is also loss minimisation output.

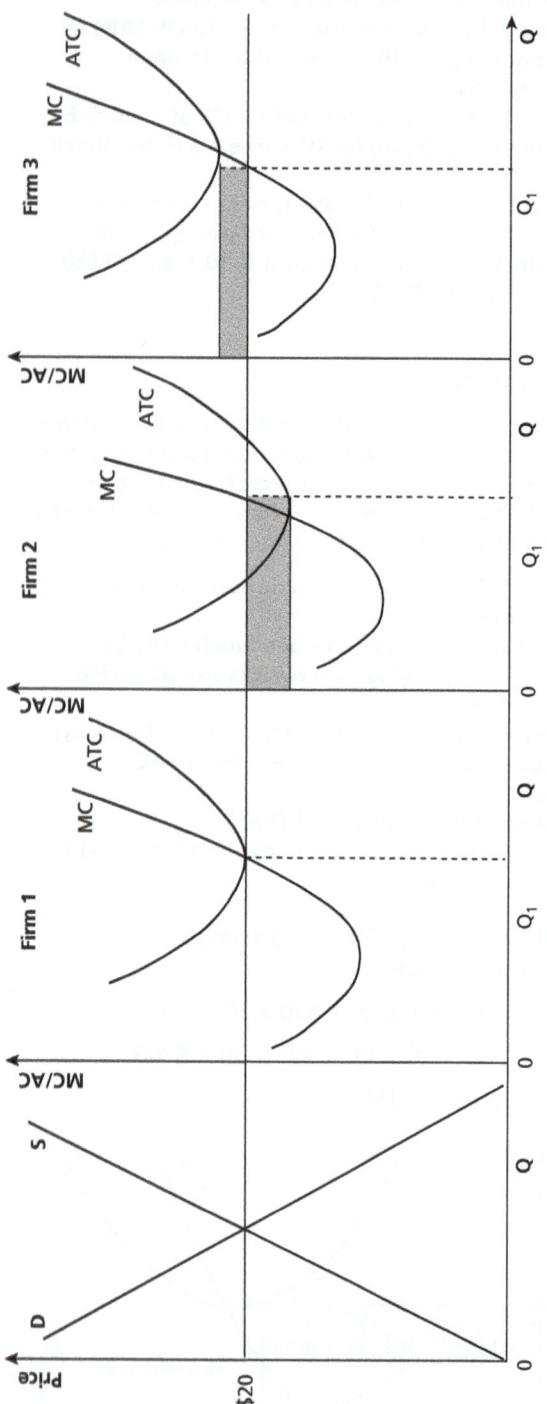

Figure 11.17 Profit and loss in competition

Not all firms make a loss or earn profits. The figures using AC/AR analysis explains this phenomenon in a different way. See figure 11.17.

Short-run profit
Note:
> All three firms in Figure 11.17 accept the ruling market price of $20
> Each competitor is a profit maximiser or loss minimiser, expanding production to where MC = MR
> All three earn different levels of profit: firm 1 normal; firm 2 above normal/positive economic profit; firm 3 loss. To conclude, firm 2 is more cost-efficient than firm 1, and firm 3 is less efficient than firm 1 and firm 2.

In a perfectly competitive market, cost efficiency determines profit because firms have no power to set prices.

Summary
> Perfectly competitive firms accept the ruling market price since they cannot influence price.
> Normal, above normal profit and losses are made when AC = AR, AC < AR, and AC > AR respectively.
> When a loss is made the firm produces where MC = MR to minimise loss. No profits are made at the equilibrium output.
> Profit may be estimated in three ways:
> (i) Average profit x Q
> (ii) TR – TC (iii) AR – AC
> Because a perfectly competitive firm cannot control price, which it accepts from the market, the level of profit is determined by the firm's cost performance.

The long-run equilibrium of perfect competition
With these three levels of profit in mind it is only above normal profit that attracts other firms into the industry, because it is assumed that firms outside the industry will already be earning normal profits. It is easy for new firms to enter another industry because:

> There are no barriers to entry.
> The resources of new entrants are mobile (easily moved and set up).
> Knowledge of the market is perfect.

What happens when new entrants enter the market is shown in figure 11.18.

In the transition from the short- to the long-run new entrants enter the industry because there are no barriers to entry. There is also increased output brought into the market by new entrants, which causes the supply curve to shift along the demand curve from S to S_1 to S_2.

> As a result, price falls from $50 to $40 to $30.
> Output is therefore reduced for the firm making positive economic profit, from Q_1 to Q_3; normal profit is also competed away.
> After the entry of new firms, all firms initially earning above normal profit may end up making only normal profit. Note that no firm can engage in long-run production earning a loss. It will have

to exit the industry in the long-run period if it is making a loss.

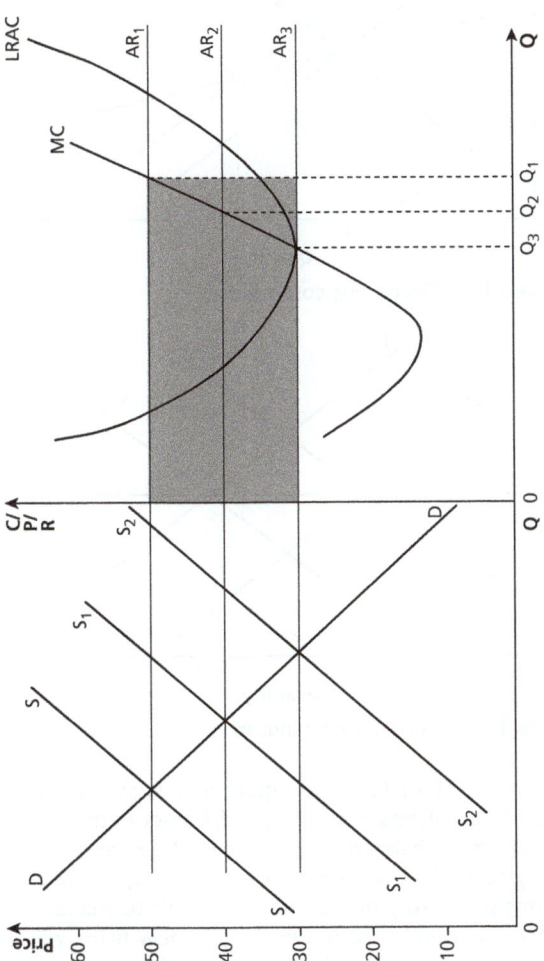

Figure 11.18 New entrants entering the industry (perfect competition)

Shut-down or exit conditions

If the price keeps falling and losses are made what should these firms do in the short-run period? Should they stay or exit? The answer is they can stay, even if making a loss, but the firms must cover their variable costs of production. The reason is simple. If a firm leaves or stays in the industry it still has to pay its fixed costs.

Variable costs will be zero since these are incurred by production. If the price is high enough to cover variable costs the firm may still survive, hoping that other loss-making firms who leave will cause the supply curve to start shifting to the left, causing prices to rise once more. Perhaps a simple case may enhance the grasp of shut-down conditions.

A very small catering firm has the following costs: FC = $1,000.00

VC = $5,500.00

Should the firm accept an offer of $6,000? At first glance, TC = FC + VC = $5,500 + $1,000 = $6,500.

It seems that the $6,000 offer cannot cover the firm's cost, but if the firm does not take the job it will not incur VC of $5,500 but must meet its FC of $1,000. Taking the offer, however, will cover VC of $5,500 and help to pay $500 towards the fixed cost. It will be making a smaller loss and help it to stay in business.

Summary

In the short-run a firm may remain in the industry provided it covers its variable cost. But if it can cover a little more than its variable costs this may help it to pay part of its fixed costs. If any firm fails to cover its average total costs, the firm may remain in the industry in the short-run but must leave in the long-run. See figure 11.19.

Note:

Figure 11.19 reveals the following:

> Price is falling as new firms enter the industry.
> The price has fallen to P_5.
> The firm is covering AVC at P_4.
> The firm is not covering AVC at P_5.

If the price falls to P_4 the firm may stay and not exit the market in the short-run.

If the price falls to P_5 the firm will have to exit in the short-run because it cannot cover AVC.

Leaving an industry is achieved by failing to replace worn-out machinery and allowing existing fixed factors to run down.

The short-run supply curve

Observe that in figure 11.19 the supply curve shifts downward along the demand curve as new firms enter the industry.

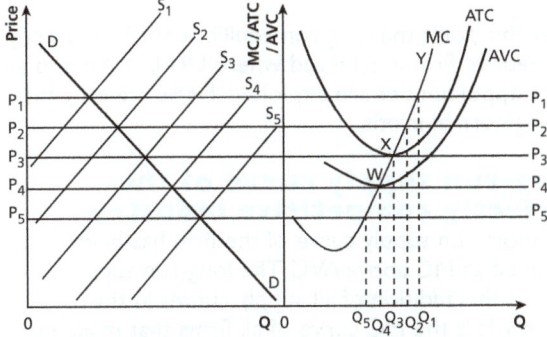

Figure 11.19 Short-run supply curve in a perfectly competitive firm

Price falls from P_1 to P_5 and quantity falls from Q_1 to Q_5. Note that as the price line moves along the marginal curve there are changes in quantity.

The marginal cost curve is effectively the supply curve of the firm since it links price with quantity supplied in a perfectly competitive market.

The supply curve of a perfectly competitive firm is therefore MC above AVC (W to Y) in the short-run.

The firm will not produce at a point where price (AR) is below AVC because here it is adding more to its costs than is gaining in revenue and so would exit the industry. Since all costs must be covered in the long-run, the long-run supply curve is MC above LRATC (X to Y).

Summary

A firm may remain in the industry even if it cannot cover its short-run ACs. The reasons are as follows:

> Whether it remains in production or shuts down it still has to meet its fixed costs of production.
> If AR or price can cover more than AVC it will have a little surplus to contribute to paying its fixed costs.

By this reasoning, the firm's supply curve in a perfect market is its MC curve above AVC in the short-run but MC above LRATC in the long-run, as shown in figure 11.19.

Long-run equilibrium for a perfectly competitive firm

The shifting of the supply curve in the short-run as new firms enter a perfectly competitive industry moves the firm into a long-run equilibrium. To re-emphasise, although in the short-run period some firms may make a loss and still remain in the industry, losses cannot be made indefinitely. In the long-run, all firms must cover all their costs that is LRAC must be equal to AR.

In the long-run, if all firms are making normal profit then:

> No new firms will enter to earn normal profit, as they are already earning this elsewhere.
> All loss-making firms will exit.
> All scope for economies of scale will have ended.

At this point the long-run equilibrium of a perfectly competitive firm is achieved where LRAC = AR and all profit opportunities are exploited. Firms are only then making normal profit.

Long-run supply curve of the perfectly competitive industry

The short-run supply curve of the firm has been identified as MC above AVC. The long-run supply curve is the addition of all supply curves in the industry. It is the MC curve of all firms that make up the industry.

The long-run supply curve is shown in figures 11.20, 11.21 and 11.22.

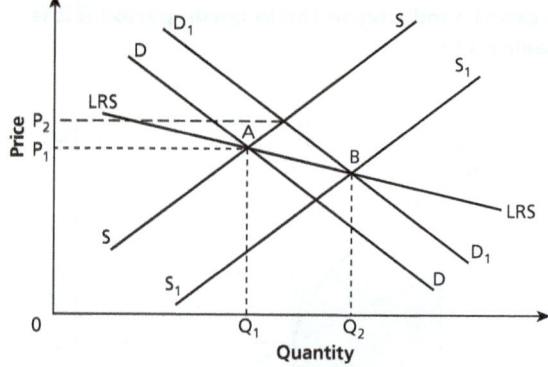

Figure 11.20 Decreasing cost industry

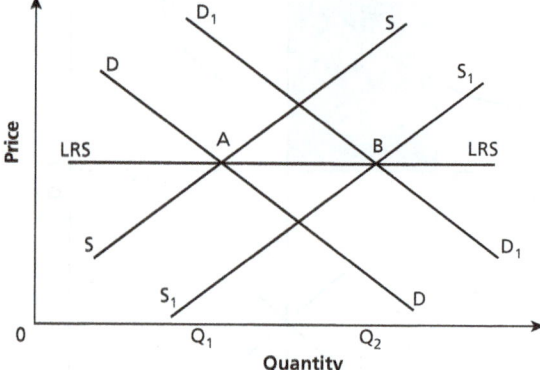

Figure 11.21 Constant-cost industry

In figure 11.20, long-run equilibrium is at industry price (P_1) and firms output (Q_1). If, however, this equilibrium is changed by the forces of demand shifting to $D_1 D_1$ then a new price of P_2 will allow all firms previously making normal profit to make positive economic profit. Once again, new firms will be attracted into the industry, causing the industry supply curve to shift to the right (SS to $S_1 S_1$). Note the increase in output is Q_1 to Q_2. The long-run supply curve (LRS) is simply derived by joining equilibrium A and B. Although it is approximately horizontal it may be upward or downward sloping. If the LRS curve were horizontal this would imply a constant-cost industry.

If the LRS curve is upward sloping then it will be an industry of increasing costs (Figure 11.22). If the LRS curve is downward sloping it will be a decreasing cost industry (Figure 11.22).

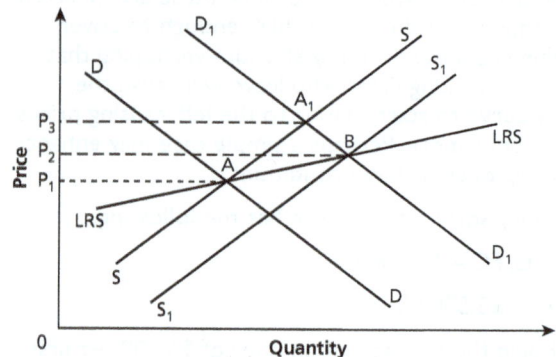

Figure 11.22 Increasing cost industry

Chapter 11 Price, revenue and profit concepts

The same applies to figure 11.22.

> Short-run equilibrium **A**
> Demand increases, so **DD** shifts to D_1D_1 and new equilibrium A_1 and higher prices P_3.
> New firms enter as P_2 offers positive economic profits, so **SS** shifts down to S_1S_1, as new entrants enter the industry. The long-run supply curve is **LRS/AB**.

See figure 11.21. This long-run curve equilibrium results in a constant-cost industry.

Key points

> In the long-run all firms must cover their costs of production. Therefore, long-run equilibrium is where **AC = AR** and firms are only making normal profits.
> All entry and exit of firms have ended. There is no entry of firms when all firms are only making normal profit.
> All economies of scale have ended at the minimum efficient plant size of production.
> If this equilibrium is changed in the short-run period through a change in demand or supply, high prices will enable positive economic profit and, once again, new entrants shift the supply curve downwards.
> Constant, increasing and decreasing costs are reflected in the **LRS** curve when equilibrium points are connected.

Chapter summary

> Firms may earn normal profits, above normal profits or a loss depending on how cost-efficient their operations are.
> Normal profit is determined as **AC = AR**. A fixed profit level is considered a component of fixed cost of production, so that if revenue is equal to cost, profit is assured. Above normal profit/positive economic profit is calculated as **AR > AC**.
> Loss is sustained when **AR < AC**.
> In a perfectly competitive industry firms earning positive economic profit attract new entrants into the industry, increasing output in the short-run and causing industry prices to fall.
> Economic profit is competed away in the long-run for a perfectly competitive firm.
> Loss-making firms may stay in the industry in the short-run provided variable costs of production are covered by revenue.
> Loss-making firms also produce where **MC = MR**. **MC = MR** also determines the loss-minimising output level of a firm.
> The short-run supply curve of the firm is **MC** above **AVC** since any firm producing below **AVC** must exit the industry in the short-run.
> The equilibrium level of output for the industry is where all firms would be making only long-run normal profits.

> If in the long-run demand changes positively, then economic profit is achieved through a high price and would again encourage new entrants into the industry until a new equilibrium is achieved.
> The **LRS** curve to a firm is **MC** above **LRAC**.
> The **LRS** curve to a perfectly competitive industry is determined by a connection of two equilibrium points.

Practice questions

1. a. Define the term market structure.
   b. List any two market structures and state one way in which they are different.
   c. In which market would you place gasoline stations in your country?
   d. The diagram below shows the marginal cost curve (MC), the average total cost curve (ATC), and the average variable cost curve (AVC) for a perfectly competitive firm.
   e. Reproduce this diagram in your booklet.
   f. Label each of the cost curves in the diagram you have drawn.
   g. In your diagram, clearly indicate the firm's supply curve.

Increasing cost industry

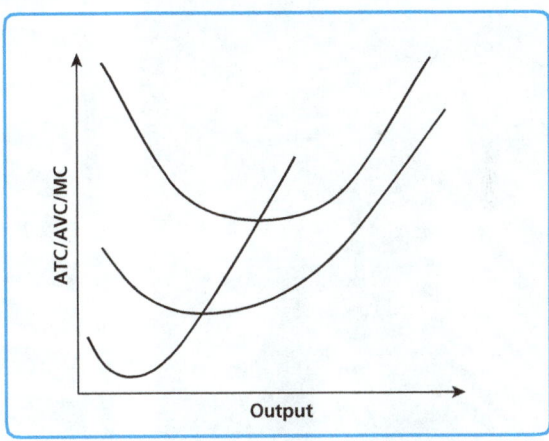

2. a. Define the term 'market structure'.
   b. State four assumptions on which perfect competition is based.
   c. State three types of market structures other than perfect competition and give an example of each.
   d. Explain how each of the types you mentioned in (c) above differs from perfect competition.
   e. In a perfectly competitive industry, firms are making positive economic profit (above the normal profit).
      (i) Draw a diagram showing this situation. Label the axis, the cost and revenue curves and indicate the profit made by the firms.
      (ii) Explain what will happen to profit, the number of firms and output in the long-run.

12 Monopoly and monopolistic competition

Chapter 12 Monopoly and monopolistic competition

LEARNING OBJECTIVES

- Explain short-run equilibrium.
- Explain long-run equilibrium.
- Explain price discrimination.
- Describe natural monopoly.
- Explain the effect of taxes and subsidies on monopoly market structure.

REQUIRED KNOWLEDGE

- Features of monopoly
- Revenue theory
- Cost theory
- Profit maximisation concepts
- Normal, positive economic profit and loss.

TOPIC VALUE

Monopoly power has been the focus of many large companies, and governments try to regulate their behaviour.

Introduction

A monopolist is a sole supplier. It differs from perfect competition because monopolies have:

› **The ability to set price**
› **Very strong barriers to entry faced by other firms**
› **A differentiated product**
› **A downward sloping demand curve**
› **No competition as only one firm in the market.**

Short-run equilibrium

In the short-run a monopolist's profit is determined by the cost efficiency of the firm. Low-cost firms make above normal profit and high-cost firms may, at best, earn normal profit and, at worst, make a loss.

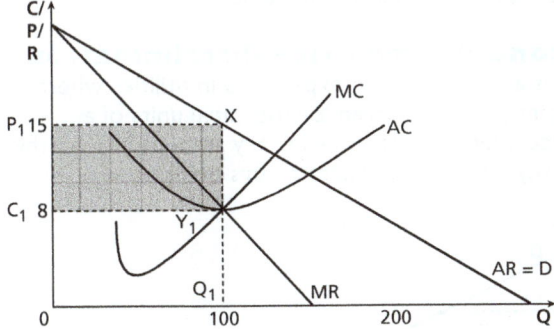

Figure 12.1 Monopolist making above normal profit

Note: C/P/R denotes costs, price and revenue.

Positive economic profit is earned when total revenue is greater than total cost or when AR is greater than AC.

In figure 12.1 the monopolist is making positive economic profit according to the following steps.

› **Step 1: Identify profit maximisation output (MC = MR) at equilibrium output, 100 units.**
› **Step 2: Identify the price at that level of output (connect 100 to AR curve), $15.**
› **Step 3: Identify the cost of 1 unit (AC) (connect 100 to AC curve), $8.**
› **Step 4: Calculate profit on one unit, $15 – $8 = $7.**

Therefore, profit on 100 = 100 × 7 = $700

Above normal profit = $P_1 X Q_1 O - C_1 Y_1 Q_1 O = P_1 X Y_1 C_1$ (the shaded area)

In Figure 12.2 the monopolist is making normal profit. Note AR = $15 and AC = $15 (follow steps 1 through to 4, as for figure 12.1). Average profit = 0

Or TR = 1,500 (15 × 100)
   TC = 1,500 (15 × 100)

Therefore profit = normal

Remember that businesses include a certain level of profit as part of their fixed costs, so that when total revenue is equal to total cost they have still secured 'normal' profit. Refer to chapter 11 for revision of this point.

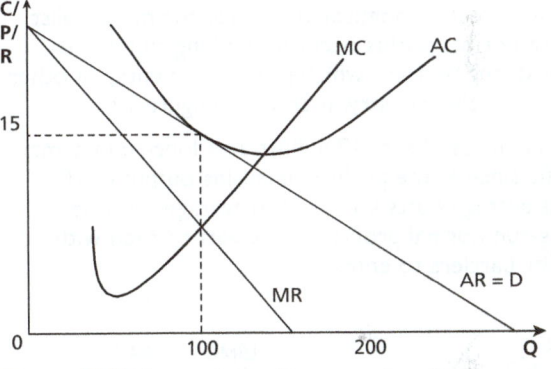

Figure 12.2 Monopolist making normal profit

A monopoly may incur a loss if it is inefficient. Some state enterprise monopolies that are not profit-driven make losses, as shown below in figure 12.3 (again, follow the steps outlined above).

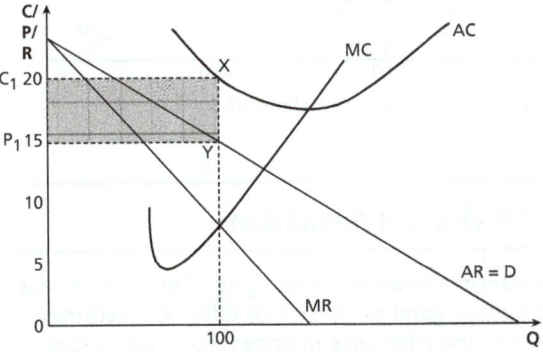

Figure 12.3 Monopolist making losses

Profit maximisation/loss minimisation
MC = MR = 100

Price (AR) of one unit = $15

Cost (AC) of one unit = $20

Loss on one unit = $5

1) Loss on 100 units = $500
   Since   TR = $15 × 100 = $1,500
                  TC = $20 × 100 = $2,000
2) Loss = –$500
3) The loss is represented by the shaded area C_1XYP_1

Student hint
Remember, in an examination choose which of the three measures of loss you prefer. Do not attempt to explain all three and waste precious time.

Long-run equilibrium
For monopolists, in the long-run, strong barriers to entry exclude possible entrants. Since the monopolist is a sole producer, above normal profit may persist in the long-run. When the firm expands its operations it will benefit from economies of scale. It is also possible for higher-cost producers to earn normal profits but, as for all firms in all markets, long-run costs must be covered and loss makers must exit the industry in the transition to long-run production.

This is a basic difference between a monopolist and a perfect competitor, that is, for the monopolist above normal profits occur in the long-run due to very strong barriers, which prevent the entry of other firms into the industry, as shown in figure 12.1.

In contrast, figure 12.4 illustrates long-run normal profit, since at the profit-maximising output of 100 units average costs are equal to average revenue. Long-run normal profits may be earned even with strong barriers to entry.

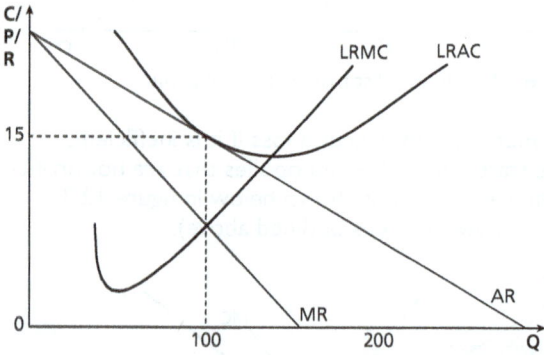

Figure 12.4 Long-run normal profits for a monopolist

Price discrimination

Price discrimination is the charging of different prices for the same good or service to different customers. Note that the difference in prices must not be due to differences in costs of production. The cost of producing the good for all customers must be the same. If you attended a football game, paying a lower student price than adults, but everyone sat in the same area that would be an example of price discrimination. The same applies if you attended a cinema show where children were charged lower prices than adults, yet all were seated together in the same area.

For a monopolist to price discriminate certain conditions must apply. The seller must be a monopolist because if there are other sellers he or she may not be able to raise his price for fear of losing customers and profit. Other conditions are:

› **Two distinct markets must be identified**, e.g., children or adults for a cinema show.
› **The good or service must be the same**, e.g., a football match and accommodation are the same for everyone.
› **There must be barriers between the two markets** because enterprising individuals may purchase the good cheaply and resell for a profit, taking away the monopolist's profit. Barriers may be age (children and adults), gender (offers for women that exclude men, e.g., cheap ladies night in a club), distance (foreign versus local cars), time (a night rate different to day rate for an internet service); and
› **There must be differing elasticities of demand between the two markets**, i.e., one market more or less elastic in demand than the other.

There are three different types of price discrimination, i.e., first, second and third degree price discrimination.

First degree price discrimination
This takes place if the seller can charge every customer a different price. For example, a doctor in a small community may know everyone intimately and may be able to charge everyone a fee he or she knows they can afford to pay.

Accordingly, the doctor may charge a wealthy person a high fee and a low-income earner a low fee for the same service. In this way the doctor secures all the consumer surplus of his clients.

Second degree price discrimination
This is a fairly common experience in utilities where a higher price is charged for the initial units of a service, then a lower price for any amount beyond this quantity. Figure 12.5 illustrates this point.

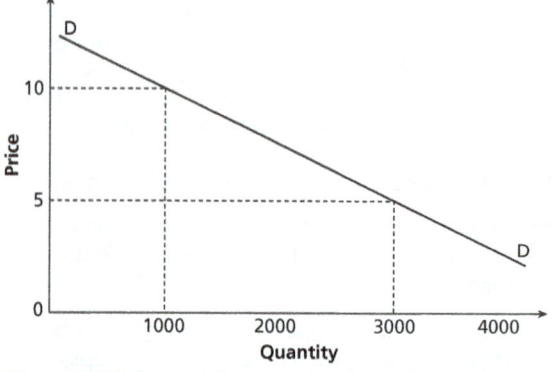

Figure 12.5 Second degree price discrimination

In figure 12.5, the first 1,000 units of a service such as, for example, electricity, are sold at $10 and beyond 1,000 at $5 per unit. Again, the aim of price discrimination is to increase profit by a transfer of consumer surplus to the producer.

Third degree price discrimination

This is the most common form of price discrimination. The monopolist aims to sell the firm's profit-maximising output in two well-separated markets with different elasticities, rather than as a single firm and single market. The monopolist can then charge a high price in the more inelastic market and a low price in the more elastic market. Adding the profits in two markets earns a higher level of profit, compared to selling in one market only. See figure 12.6.

In market A the firm can make a total revenue of $5,000 (500 × $10). However, if 500 units of profit-maximising output are split into markets B and C the following will result.

Market B : TR = 400 × $9 = $3,600 (figure 12.7)

Market C : TR = 100 × $20 = $2,000 (figure 12.8)

Market B + C = $5,600 (figure 12.6)

(Market A = $5,000)

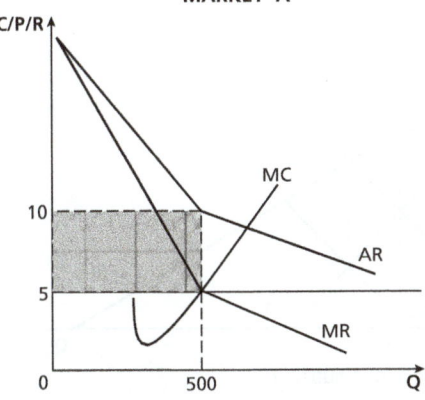

MC=MR is 500 units at price $5
TR = 500 × $10.00 = $5000

Figure 12.6 Third degree price discrimination market A

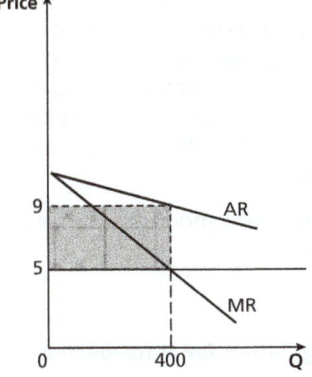

MC=MR is 400 units at price $5
TR = 400 × $9.00 = $3600

Figure 12.7 Third degree price discrimination market b

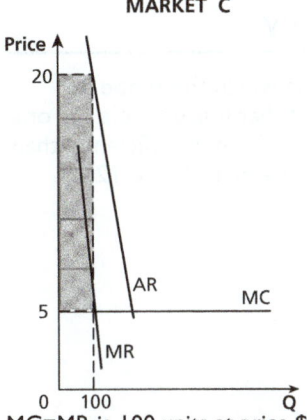

MC=MR is 100 units at price $5
TR = 100 × $20.00 = $2000

Figure 12.8 Third degree price discrimination market c

Increase in TR = $600

Observe that summation of market B and C results in odd-shaped AR and MR curves in market A.

Advantages and disadvantages of price discrimination

The advantages and disadvantages of price discrimination are given in table 12.1.

Table 12.1 Advantages and disadvantages of price discrimination

Advantages	Disadvantages
Consumers would be able to afford a high-priced good at a lower price.	Welfare (consumer surplus) is transferred from consumer to producer.
	A price-discriminating monopolist may use price discrimination to drive out competitors by lowering prices and raising them once the competition has exited the market.
Profits may enable price-discriminating monopolists to enter a new market, promoting competition.	Some price-discriminating monopolists use surplus output to sell cheaply in a foreign market. This is called dumping and is considered unfair competition.
Price discrimination may assist a failing monopoly to earn profit.	From the analysis of price discrimination, it would seem price discrimination is more in the interest of consumers than producers.

Natural monopoly

A natural monopoly is one in which the scope for economies of scale is so vast that it is possible for one firm to service the entire market more efficiently than two or more firms together. Refer to figure 12.9.

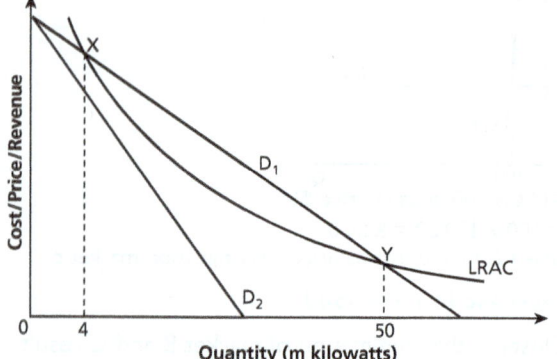

Figure 12.9 A natural monopoly

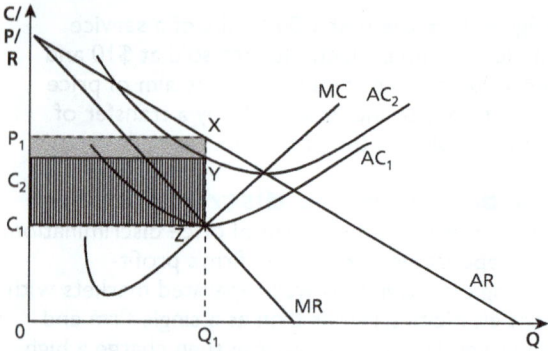

Figure 12.10 A lump-sum tax

Demand curve D_1 represents the demand curve of the electricity industry. A monopoly experiences extensive economies of scale between 4–50 million kilowatts of power, where long-run average cost is less than average revenue.

If another company were to enter to provide half of the industry's needs, long-run average cost would be greater than D_2, which is the demand curve facing two firms. Both firms would experience a loss at all levels of output.

A natural monopolist's long-run average cost curve is so shaped to reflect gradually falling long-run average costs because firms of this type incur very high set-up costs or fixed costs. However, because of high levels of output, these costs can be afforded and spread out. The falling curve reflects economies of scale.

Typically, such a firm may want to charge a high price, since in most instances they may provide an essential service with fairly inelastic demand, for example electricity. It is for this reason that natural monopolies are regulated by the government in the national interest, and in the most cases they are majority shareholders in these strategic industries.

Regulation of monopolies

Effect of taxes and subsidies on monopoly profits as a form of regulation

A lump-sum tax is a tax equal to a fixed sum that is imposed to regulate monopoly power. A lump-sum tax will affect the average cost curve of a monopolist since it will become a fixed cost of production. The average cost curve will therefore shift vertically upward, reducing the firm's level of profit. Refer to figure 12.10.

In figure 12.10 profit maximisation is at Q_1 and above normal profits are represented by the rectangle P_1XZC_1. However, a lump-sum tax shifts AC_1 vertically upward to AC_2. Profits are now represented by the rectangle P_1XZC_2. Therefore, a lump-sum tax reduces profit by P_2YZC_1.

An indirect tax, for example VAT, shifts the MC curve upward and, in the manner of a supply curve and a subsidy, shifts the MC curve downward to the right. See figure 12.11. If the firm is a profit maximiser, price would change from P_1 to P_2 if an indirect tax is imposed.

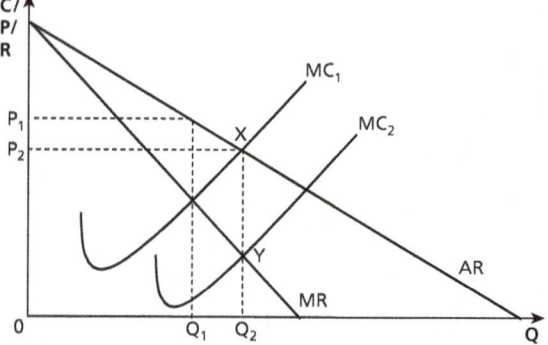

Figure 12.11 Effect of a subsidy

Effect of a subsidy

Governments can attempt to regulate price by providing a subsidy, which causes the MC curve to shift downward and to the right to MC_2.

Note in figure 12.11, profit maximisation output is Q_1 and at price of P_1. If the government wishes to regulate prices to a low of P_2 it must grant a subsidy equal to XY. Now, after the subsidy, profit maximisation moves to output Q_2. At a price of P_2 the subsidy may be financed by a lump-sum tax.

Apart from taxes and subsidies, monopolies may be regulated in the following ways:

› **Price controls**
› **Nationalisation**
› **Privatisation and deregulation for state-owned monopolies**
› **Disintegration, i.e., breaking up a large monopoly into smaller units**

- Reducing entry barriers by inviting competition from abroad
- Outsourcing, i.e., when monopolies raise prices local importers are granted licenses to import cheaper goods and services.

Monopolies evaluated

The benefits and costs of a monopoly are outlined in table 12.12.

Table 12.2 The benefits and costs of a monopoly

Benefits	Costs
Economies of scale may mean low costs and low prices.	Monopolists restrict output. Price rises and there is loss of consumer surplus.
	The monopolist is not an efficient producer because output is less than the productive optimum.
Monopoly profits may be used to assist a company that is part of a monopoly.	Monopolists may engage in predatory or low pricing strategy to discourage or drive out competitors.
Price discrimination may make the good available at a cheaper price to low-income earners.	

Comparing perfect competition with a monopoly

Efficiency in resource allocation may be measured in the following ways:

1. Technical efficiency
2. Cost efficiency
3. Allocative efficiency.

Technical efficiency is achieved when a given level of output is produced with the least-cost input combination. This type of efficiency leads to cost efficiency that is producing not only at an output level at the lowest point on the average cost curve, but also on the lowest average cost curve possible.

Allocative efficiency is simply the use of scarce resources to produce the right combination and quantity of goods that society wishes to consume. A level of output where P = MC is identified as allocative efficiency.

Efficiency is discussed in greater detail in the chapter 14 on market failures.

The best way to compare these two market structures is to note what happens when thousands of small firms either merge or are taken over by a monopoly. They differ in the following ways:

- Price
- Output
- Consumer surplus
- Efficiency.

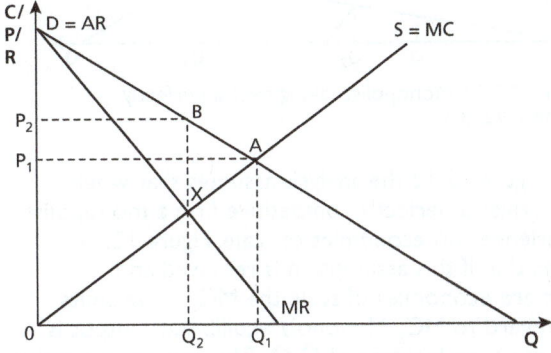

Figure 12.12 Comparing perfect competition with monopoly

Refer to figure 12.12. To convert perfect competition to a monopoly the following curves need to be identified for a monopoly: MC, MR, AR. Since S = MC and D = AR, MR is drawn intersecting the midpoint of the horizontal axis. Note that the demand curves AR and supply curves S = MC reflect perfect competition.

The changes are:

1. Equilibrium output of perfectly competitive industry = Q_1

   Equilibrium of monopoly = Q_2

   Therefore a loss of Q_1Q_2 in output

2. Price under perfect competition = P_1

   Price under monopoly = P_2

   Conclusion: a monopoly charges higher prices

3. Consumer surplus in perfectly competitive industry = Triangle DAP_1

   Consumer surplus under monopoly = DBP_2

   Reduction in consumer surplus (welfare) = P_2BAP_1

4. Output Q_2 is not technically cost efficient. Perfectly competitive industry produces where P = MC. A profit-maximising monopolist produces where P is greater than MC (Q1), hence allocatively inefficient. The assumptions for this model are no economies of scale.

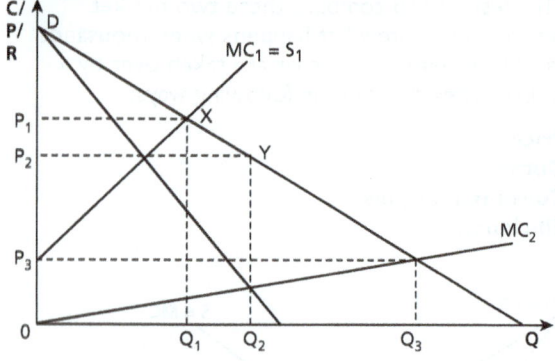

Figure 12.13 Monopolist taking over a perfectly competitive firm

In figure 12.12 the analysis assumes that when taking over a perfectly competitive firm a monopolist experiences no economies of scale. Figure 12.13 shows that if this assumption is removed and there are economies of scale the MC_1 curve shifts downward to MC_2. Monopoly equilibrium output is now at Q_2, an increase of Q_2Q_1. The consumer surplus in a perfectly competitive industry is DXP_1, but consumer surplus under monopoly = DYP_2. Increase in welfare (consumer surplus) P_1XYP_2.

However, there remains the allocative and technical inefficiency of the monopolist as a result of the change.

Other differences

> A perfect market is more unstable than a monopoly because of numerous changes in the perfectly competitive industry.
> Firms in perfectly competitive industries do not achieve the level of economies of scale that monopolists do.
> When all firms in an economy are simultaneously in long-run equilibrium in all possible markets, this is called a general equilibrium. When this is achieved there is allocative, technological and dynamic efficiency – and with full employment there will also be Pareto optimality. The economy will be on the production possibility frontier. A monopoly will not achieve this result. A perfectly competitive industry will, however, achieve this.
> The success of a perfectly competitive industry or economy is very much dependent on an equitable distribution of income.

Summary

> A monopoly is a sole seller with an imperfect market structure because it has the ability to set price, while firms in a perfectly competitive industry cannot do so.
> Monopolists earn normal, positive economic profit, or loss in the short-run, but only normal and positive economic profit in the long-run because of the barriers to entry to other firms.
> A monopolist may practise price discrimination to increase profits. This practice entails selling the same good or service to different customers at different prices. There are first, second and third degree price discrimination.
> A natural monopoly is one with such extensive scope for economies of scale that one firm is able to supply an entire market at a cheaper cost than two or more firms.
> Governments may regulate monopolies by taxing their profits or granting subsidies to increase output.
> A monopoly is a less efficient market than a perfectly competitive industry. It is allocatively and technologically inefficient. It is, however, more dynamically efficient than a perfectly competitive industry.

Monopolistic competition

Although different from monopoly, monopolistic competition bears some similarities to both perfect competition and monopoly. It is similar to perfect competition because there are very low barriers to entry in this type of market. Also, there are a large number of firms – though not as many as a perfectly competitive industry.

There are similarities to monopoly in that these firms have a monopoly over the product they sell because of its branded nature. The clothing industry is an example of this market structure.

The main feature of this market therefore is product differentiation (branding) and promotional advertising geared towards establishing brand loyalty. Brand loyalty is not only restricted to a 'product' but a service that is unique in some way.

Brand loyalty is something that is very well known. Many believe that 'good things are not cheap' and 'cheap things are not good'. Brands have exclusive value. For example, students enjoy going to downtown locations or 'the mall'. The demand curve facing these firms are downward sloping and fairly elastic, since each firm's product is a reasonable substitute for another competitor's product. Note, as with all market structures, three forms of profit are possible, that is, short-run normal, above normal profit, and loss.

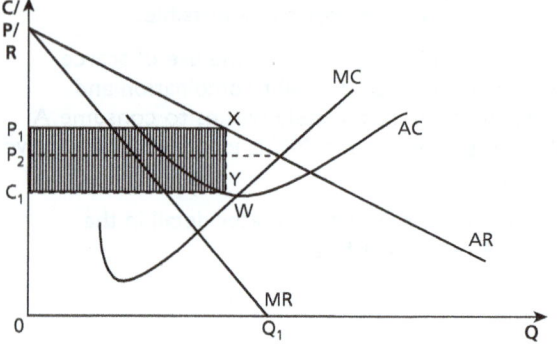

Figure 12.14 Monopolistic competitor earning above normal profit in the short-run

Figure 12.14 represents a monopolistic competitor earning above normal profit (P_1XYC_1) in the short-run. As in other market structures, other firms in the industry may also make normal profits and loss.

Note:

- **Equilibrium or profit maximisation output is Q_1 where MC = MR.**
- **Above normal profit is P_1XYC_1.**
- **Output Q_1 is not cost efficient as production is taking place to the left of minimum average costs. There is therefore excess capacity of Y to W. This is an inefficient use of resources.**
- **The firm is not allocatively efficient since output is sold at P_1 and not where P = MC at P_2.**

In the transition to the long-run, new firms easily overcome entry barriers and as a result they take profits away from profit-making firms – in a similar manner to what happens in perfect competition. When this happens the demand curve shifts to the left and is also more elastic. This leftward shift in the demand curve brings the demand curve of the monopolistic competitor tangential to long-run average costs. Therefore, only normal profits are earned in the long-run. Refer to figure 12.15.

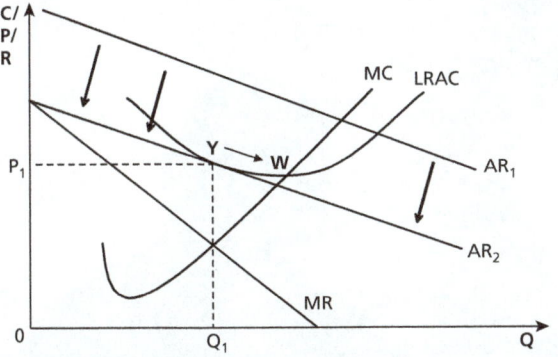

Figure 12.15 Monopolistic competitor in the long-run as new firms enter

In figure 12.15, note:

- **Profit-maximising output Q_1.**
- **Normal profit (AR_2 = LRAC).**
- **Excess capacity of Y–W (see arrow).**
- **The firm is both technically and allocatively inefficient.**
- **The demand curve AR has shifted to the left due to the entry of new firms competing with existing ones.**
- **Long-run equilibrium is at Q_1 where LRAC is tangential to AR_2.**
- **Normal profit is earned at price P_1.**

Chapter summary

› A monopolistic competitor shares some features with perfectly competitive markets and a monopoly.
› Because of product differentiation it has some degree of control over price, in a similar way to a monopoly.
› AR = demand is downward sloping, similar to a monopolist.
› In the short run, normal profit, positive economic profit and loss can be made, as in perfect competition.
› In the long-run, only normal profit is made as positive economic profit is competed away by new entrants entering the market, similar to perfect competition.
› The shifting of the AR (demand) curve is caused by new firms 'stealing' customers from other profit-making firms.
› Monopolistic competition is inefficient, technically and allocatively in the short- and long-run, similar to a monopoly.
› Firms operate with unused or excess capacity, similar to a monopolist.

Practice questions

1. Explain why economists prefer perfect competition to monopoly. Illustrate your answer with the use of a diagram.

2. With the aid of a diagram, state the effect of monopolies on producer and consumer surplus.

3. a. Define the term price discrimination.
   b. Define the term normal profit.
   c. Can a firm in perfect competition make above normal profit in both the short- and long-run?
   d. Define the term monopoly and give an example of a monopoly in your country.
   e. How does the output and price of a firm under a monopoly differ from the output and price of a firm under perfect competition?

INTRODUCTORY ECONOMICS A TEXTBOOK FOR CAPE ECONOMICS STUDENTS

13 Oligopoly and contestable markets

Chapter 13 Oligopoly and contestable markets

LEARNING OBJECTIVES

- Define oligopoly.
- Distinguish between different types of oligopolies.
- Explain price rigidity and non-price competition.
- Define and explain collusion.

REQUIRED KNOWLEDGE

- Output, cost and revenue theory
- Profit maximisation.

TOPIC VALUE

After exploring the issues in this chapter, you should understand how and why the Organisation of Petroleum Exporting Countries (OPEC) cartel controls the price of oil in the world.

Introduction

An oligopoly is a market structure dominated by a small number of large firms. It is the most common form of market structure to be found in the real world, because as firms grow, fewer firms remain in the industry (mostly as a result of mergers) and it is more difficult for new firms to enter the market.

Features of an oligopoly

Features of an oligopoly include:

› Few sellers but many buyers
› Each firm may sell differentiated products
› Strong barriers to entry
› Short- and long-run positive economic profit
› Interdependence, collusion and price rigidity: firms tend to engage in non-price competition.

Examples of oligopolistic firms are banks, insurance companies, newspapers and automobile companies. There is one model of oligopoly behaviour, but economists have identified a few different types.

Most models, however, exhibit the following behaviour.

Interdependence

Since a few firms dominate the industry, any action by one firm will affect the others. Firms' decisions are therefore based on how their rivals are likely to react.

Price stability/rigidity

This follows from the previous point. Firms will not risk a price war that may adversely affect the few in the market, so when one firm raises prices others tend to follow; for example, commercial banks' interest rates and insurance companies' rates. High and low prices could both trigger an unnecessary price war.

Non-price competition

Firms compete with each other through advertising or promotions. Product promotion is the advertising strategy of choice. Giveaways, after-sales service, branding and credit arrangements are other non-price strategies that are commonly employed.

There are sometimes very effective non-price barriers to entry, such as branding of products. Also, large-scale production enables the achievement of economies of scale, which makes the long-run average cost curve 'L' shaped rather than 'U' shaped.

Collusion

A few firms in an industry will cooperate directly (formally) or indirectly (informally). This behaviour is referred to as formal and informal collusion.

Formal collusion takes the form of cartel arrangements that are openly agreed upon and formalised; for example, OPEC oil cartel.

Informal collusion involves no formal arrangements but certainly 'an understanding' between firms on output and pricing decisions.

Models of oligopolistic behaviour

The Sweezy model

The Sweezy model of oligopolistic behaviour explains two common features of oligopoly:

1. Interdependence
2. Price rigidity.

Figure 13.1 represents a firm in an oligopoly. Note the peculiar, irregular, kinked shape of the demand curve that the firm faces. It is shaped this way to reflect how rigidly firms would react if prices were raised above or below point X of the demand curve.

If the firm raises its price above P_1 to P_2 other firms would not follow. There would be a loss of market share from Q_1 to Q_2 (large fall in quantity demanded) making that position of the curve price elastic for the price-raising firm.

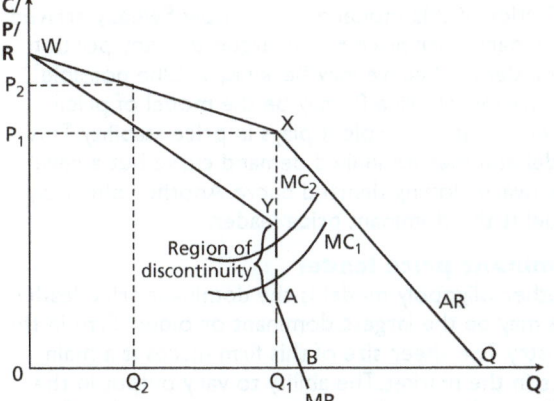

Figure 13.1 The Sweezy model of oligopolistic behaviour

If the price is lowered, other rivals will follow to prevent the firm from benefitting from the fall in price. No customer would respond to this firm's particular price reduction since their actions are matched by their rivals. The demand curve under P_1 is therefore price inelastic. In this case, price P_1 remains 'rigid' or stable.

Another aspect of the model that explains price rigidity is the peculiar marginal revenue curve, which is derived from the average revenue curve WX. The marginal revenue curve AB is derived from average revenue curve XQ. The broken line YA is called the region of discontinuity caused by the 'kink' at point X, a result of computing MR from AR values. Since the oligopolist is a profit maximiser and would set output at MC = MR, then MC = MR is at Q_1 and price P_1 at point X on the demand curve. Note that MR is represented by WYAB.

Even when costs increase, that is, from MC_1 to MC_2, prices do not rise because MC is moving along the vertical line YA. Price and quantity are therefore unchanged as a result of the increases in costs.

Even if demand for the product increases, price would still be rigid in the Sweezy model. Refer to figure 13.2.

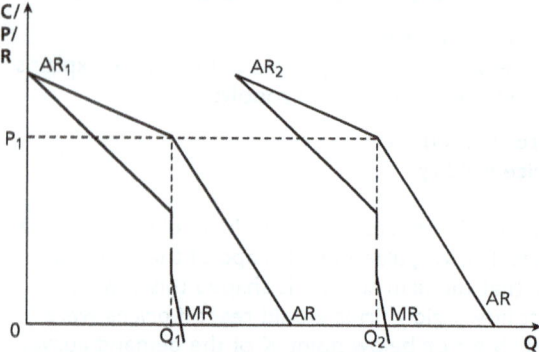

Figure 13.2 Price rigidity of Sweezy's model

Increased demand causes AR_1 to shift to the right to AR_2.

Price remains at P_1 although output has changed from Q_1 to Q_2.

Critics of this model question how Sweezy arrived at the particular price P_1 and argue that any portion of the demand curve may be 'kinked'. One possible explanation of price P_1 may be the model of price leadership and the role it plays in price stability. This model assumes no kinked demand curve but a regular downward sloping demand curve. Another oligopoly model is the dominant price leader.

Dominant price leader
Another oligopoly model is the dominant price leader. This may be the largest, dominant or oldest firm in the industry. The sheer size of this firm makes it a main force in the market. The ability to vary output in the market makes this firm a dominant price setter. Other rivals not producing this quantity of supply may simply comply with this firm's price setting.

Barometric price leader
A barometric price leader is one who has the best knowledge of market conditions, especially demand. Out of a respect for this knowledge, other firms will follow its lead.

Cartel
When a few firms agree formally to limit competition between themselves this is called a collusive oligopoly. Price fixing and quotas are formally agreed upon. OPEC is an example of a cartel in oil production and distribution. The agreement removes the threat of under- or over-pricing or retaliation. This type of oligopoly functions like a monopoly, since in banding together they are in practice one firm.

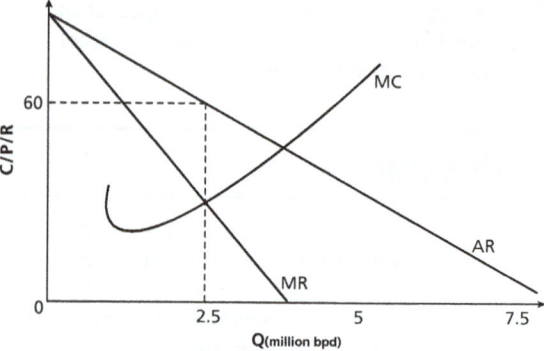

Figure 13.3 Market structure for a cartel

In figure 13.3, note that:

> AR = D is the market demand curve facing the cartel.
> MC is the horizontal addition of all firms, MC curves.
> A price of $60 is agreed upon with 2.5 million barrels of oil per day the corresponding output, which supports a price of $60. The 2.5 million bpd is then divided up among members in quotas according to:
- Market share
- Costs of production
- Capacity, e.g., firm A provides 1 million bpd, firm B provides 1 million bpd, and firm C provides 0.5 million bpd.

If any member over-produces, for example, producing an output of 3 million, price will fall accordingly.

Oligopoly evaluated
The advantages and disadvantages of an oligopoly are given in table 13.1.

Table 13.1 The advantages and disadvantages of an oligopoly

Advantages	Disadvantages
Above normal profit helps to finance research and development and new products with a branded 'edge', e.g., cell phone technology (cameras etc.).	Oligopolists act like monopolists who manipulate price and output for profit.

Chapter 13 Oligopoly and contestable markets

Advantages	Disadvantages
Non-price competition favours the consumer.	Oligopolists who may not be as large as other rivals may not achieve economies of scale.
	They profit maximise but are neither cost nor allocatively efficient.

Summary

> An oligopoly is a market dominated by a few large firms.
> The unique features of an oligopoly are: interdependence; price stability; collusion and non-price competition; large-scale production and selling of a differential product.
> There are many models of oligopolistic behaviour but the main models are: Sweezy's 'kinked' demand curve; dominant price leader; barometric price leader; cartel.
> Oligopolists behave similarly to monopolists with the similar benefits and costs to society.

Contestable markets

W. Baumol, an American economist, developed a theory of contestable markets in the 1980s. In a contestable market the role of barriers to entry and exit play a crucial role, even if it is a monopoly.

The threat of competition may act as actual competition, forcing a firm to keep its profit normal; this discourages new entrants from entering and capitalising on profit opportunities.

For example, if a school's cafeteria is the only supplier, the school's principal may experiment with external vendors once per month. Immediately, the cafeteria owner realises that it is possible for other firms to contest the school market. As a result, the cafeteria changes its complacent behaviour and lowers prices, improves quality and renders efficient service.

Note that it will cost very little for an ice cream, peanut, pie vendor or a mobile barbeque vendor to 'roll in' and 'roll out' of a school. The cost of entry and exit is therefore small compared to the profit they can all make. In this case, threat of competition forces the cafeteria to behave as if competition existed.

A contestable market is therefore one in which the cost of entry and exit is very low. This causes prices and profits to remain low. Perfect and monopolistic competition have elements of contestable markets, as do monopolies and oligopolies, because barriers are easily overcome.

Contestable markets have the following characteristics:

> **Costless entry and exit**
> **Normal profit and low prices in the short- and long-run**
> **One or many firms in the market**
> **No collusion**
> **Profit maximisation.**

Table 13.2 Market structures compared

Market type	No. of firms	Barriers to entry & exit	Type of good & service	Control over price	Demand curve	Profit in short-run/long-run	Efficiency allocative/technical	Example
Perfect	Many	None	Identical	None	Perfectly elastic	Normal profit, above normal profit, and loss in the short- and long-run. SR: NP ANP and loss. LR: NP	Technical: yes Allocative: yes	Foreign currency markets
Monopolistic	Many	Very weak	Differentiated	Some	Fairly elastic sloping downward		Technical: no Allocative: no	Shoestore
Oligopoly	Few	Strong	Similar or different	Mostly price taker	Downward sloping	SR: NP, ANP and loss LR: ANP NP	Technical: no Allocative: no	Banks
Monopoly	1	Very strong	Very differentiated	Price setter	Inelastic downward sloping	SR: NP, ANP and loss LR: NP NP	Technical: no Allocative: no	Water distribution
Contestable	1–20	Very weak	Differentiated	None	Downward sloping	SR: NP, ANP and loss	Technical: yes Allocative: yes	Airlines

Note: SR: Short-run   LR: Long-run   NP: Normal profit   ANP: Above normal profit

The role of costless entry and exit in this theory is crucial. If a firm knows it cannot recover its costs, for example selling equipment or not recovering certain costs (sunk costs), it may think twice about entering an industry. If, however, it can move in and out freely it will always be optimistic about its choices in a market where profit is made.

For example, if a natural monopoly is making profits, more firms will not be able to compete with it for a long time. If, however, a firm can enter and exit freely it may be able to enter and exit for $3 million but make $10 million in one year, before the natural monopolist lowers its price in a price war to drive out this competitor.

Thereafter, the natural monopolist is likely to keep prices and profits low because of the 'threat' of competition. 'Hit and run' entry and exit therefore may force an existing monopolist to keep its prices low. Even if it lowers prices to get rid of a competitor who leaves, and it raises its price once more, another entrant will make a costless entry and exit to temporarily 'steal' some market share.

An evaluation of contestable markets

Free entry and exit of firms – called contestable markets – into a monopoly situation may lead to low prices. This is so, because as new firms enter, existing firms may lose market share, causing a fall in demand for their product and a fall in price.

Since monopolists may be reduced to perfect competitors, cost and allocative efficiency may serve to resolve the issue of excess capacity or inefficient management associated with a profit maximising monopoly.

This is so, because if long-run profits are normal, average cost will be equal to average revenue (productive/technical and cost efficiency) and MC will also be equal to average revenue or price (allocative efficiency). In the real world sunk costs are usually high, especially for large firms undertaking foreign direct investment. Sunk costs may, in practice, be difficult to recover.

Contestable markets theory ignores aggressive monopolies who make it known that new entrants would be engaged in a serious battle for market share.

Some barriers, in effect, make entry into some industries very difficult. Specialist enterprises such as telecommunications require knowledge of advanced technologies that are not easy to obtain since a firm's research and development are not usually in the public domain.

Summary

› Contestable markets are markets in which entry and exit are virtually costless or free. This creates a 'threat' of competition for monopolists or oligopolists who will be obliged to discourage new entrants by keeping prices low and profits normal.

› Contestable markets enable the best of both perfect and imperfect competition and hence promote efficiency. In fact, since perfect competition seems not to be of the real world, contestable markets may be a better alternative, since they do not require government intervention in markets.

The strengths and weaknesses of the marginalist approach

The marginalist principle refers to economic decision-making at the margin. It is assumed that all decisions are made with respect to maximisation of resources to achieve this goal. For a consumer, satisfaction is maximised according to whether one more or one less should be consumed. This will take place where marginal utility = price, that is, the satisfaction gained from consuming one more will only be achieved if marginal utility is equal to price.

Similarly, the producer will observe this principle as well. The firm will produce where MC = MR or hire labour where the MC of labour (wage or marginal input cost) = the MRP of labour.

The marginalist approach to pricing and output discussions therefore refers to the concept of short-run profit maximisation. This is the assumption of traditional economics.

In practice, however, it is difficult to determine marginal product or marginal cost if factors of production are employed jointly such as, for example, for taxi and a taxi driver.

Making the highest level of profit in the short-run will be the objective of a firm if ownership and control lie in the hands of the owner. It is more likely to depend on the business type. If the business is a sole trader, partnership or private limited company, short-run profit maximisation may be the preferred objective of the firm, assuming that the firm is knowledgeable about other objectives and chooses to profit maximise.

A family type business may choose profit maximisation in order to achieve growth in the long-term. Growth is usually achieved by sacrificing short-run profit.

Profit maximisation may be the objective if profits are reinvested for future growth and profitability. Shareholders, customers, public interest groups may all be at odds with each other. Pricing and output decisions then may simply be based on factors that determine:

> Market structure
> Government intervention (taxes and subsidies)
> The long-term growth of the firm
> The state of the economy (short-run) or the long-term prospects of the economy
> Factors which influence demand and supply
> Objectives according to those who control the firm, for example, shareholders and directors
> Costs of production especially labour and raw materials or the ability to achieve economies of scale.

The following arguments may be advanced to support objectives other than profit maximisation.

> **Firms may indeed seek to maximise profits in the long-run by sacrificing short-run profits.**
> **Determination of demand is arbitrary even if market research is undertaken. In addition, changes in demand may be unpredictable.**
> **If there is a recession, a firm may simply try to survive.**
> **It may be difficult to compute fixed costs when a firm has a diversified product range because there will need to be a fixed cost for each product.**
> **The average total cost may not actually be 'U' shaped. For example, an oil refinery producing several products, e.g., gasoline, paraffin, aviation fuel, benzene kerosene, diesel fuel. The ATC in these examples is likely to be saucer-shaped with an elongated LRAC.**

Objectives other than profit maximisation

Managerial utility

Profit maximisation, according to economists, may not be achievable because of lack of information on marginal costs but also firms may have other objectives.

Generally, a firm's objectives tend to be determined by ownership. If one person owns the company it is likely that profit maximisation may be the primary objective – but it may depend on their personality, lifestyle and commitments. If, however, the firm is owned by shareholders then they would normally wish to earn the highest possible level of profits and hence dividends.

Managers, however, tend to reward themselves, that is, 'perks' or non-salaried benefits because their control is largely unquestionable.

In the final analysis, a level of profit to satisfy the owners (the stakeholders) and to justify their non-salaried benefits of the directors leads to an objective called managerial utility.

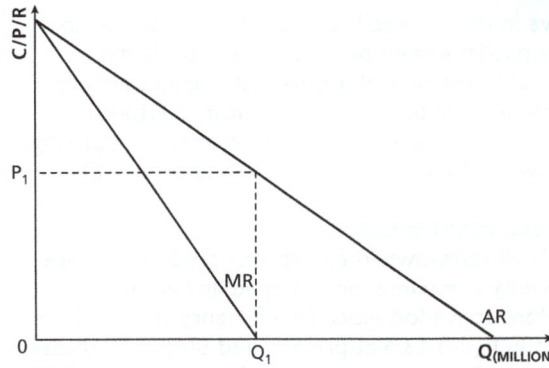

Figure 13.4 Sales revenue maximisation

Sales maximisation

Another type of objective is sales maximisation, as advanced by W. Baumol (a contestable market theorist). He theorised that the volume of sales and managers' salaries are positively related so corporate managers, particularly in insurance companies, are paid according to the volume of sales of their workforce. An increased volume of sales elevates a firm in terms of market position and provides an incentive for the sales force to maximise effort. Sales or sales revenue maximisation is achieved where TR is the highest, MR = 0 and price P_1 as shown in figure 13.4.

Management by objectives

H.A. Simon theorised that there are many competing groups in and out of the firm that all influence the firm's objectives. Managers, workers, shareholders, unions, environmental groups and consumers all have different objectives.

The dominant group will, in the end, determine the objective of the firm. In many cases, however, a target is set for each group in order to harmonise competing interest. Such a policy may be management by objectives.

Growth maximisation

This objective closely resembles sales maximisation in that growth is assured through sales, which in turn may mean lowering prices and therefore profits to achieve the goal of prestige, status or managerial utility.

Other growth objectives may be achieved through mergers and takeovers.

In nearly all objectives the customers' growth is achieved through investment that requires retained profit.

Conservative policy

Some firms are 'risk averse', that is, cautious in decision-making and therefore stick to tried and tested methods of conducting business. This is readily observed in family firms that inherit practices that have been handed down.

Survival

All of the above objectives are unrealistic if the firm faces any additional competition and cannot survive in the market. Therefore, firms tend not to overly publicise their profit or, alternatively, may make sufficient normal profits that may not attract the attention of potential competitors. Output is therefore set where AC = AR or average cost pricing, as shown in figure 13.5 at price P_2 and output Q_2.

Welfare maximisation

Nearly all state-owned enterprises tend to operate with welfare maximisation in mind and would therefore strive for allocative efficiency (P = MC), as shown in figure 13.5 at price P_1 and output Q_1. Note that price (P) measures the benefit to society and MC the cost to society in alternative production so that when P is equal to MC, society is getting the quantity of goods it desires and at the price it wishes to pay.

At price P_1 (refer to figure 13.5) welfare is maximised since P = MC, which means that P, the benefit to society, is equal to MC, the cost to society.

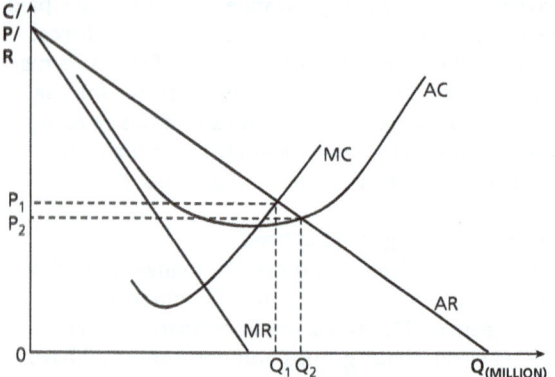

Figure 13.5 Average and marginal cost pricing

Profit/consumer maximisation

This is the objective of a producer or consumer cooperative whose primary objective is the interest of its members. Average cost pricing may be the preferred form of the firm's output.

Table 13.3 The different operating objectives of firms

Firm's objectives	Pricing/output
Profit maximisation	To satisfy shareholders or owners of small enterprises MC = MR
Managerial utility	To satisfy shareholders or owners of small enterprises MC = MR
Growth max. Prestige status etc.	Setting a minimum target for competing groups in a firm may also come close to MC = MR. (H. A Simon)
Conservation survival	Normal profits so as not to attract new competitors, therefore AC = AR
Consumer/ producer utility	The objective of consumers' and producers' cooperatives

The objectives of firms other than short-run profit maximisation and outlined above are not an exhaustive list but rather a few of those in actual observable practice. Perhaps the most popular objective would be long-run instead of short-run profit maximisation, that is, the building of a business over the long period.

Pricing and output strategies of multinational corporations

As the term suggests, multinational corporations (MNCs) operate in many countries at the same time, and they are responsible for the majority of world trade in some industries, for example manufacturing products and some service industries. Common features of MNCs are:

> They have significant market power by their sheer size.
> The operations and decision-making of such firms are managed from a home country and are therefore centralised.
> Financial strategies are geared towards tax avoidance and low cost.
> In recent times, especially through globalisation, the world is regarded as a single market in which MNCs can sell the same product, e.g., KFC, Nestlé products, Macfoods Hamburgers, or oil companies like BP/Amoco.
> Pricing and output strategies are geared naturally towards profit using a strategy called transfer pricing. This is achieved, for example, by setting prices above or below market prices to avoid paying taxes. If a host country has a high corporation tax on profits, MNCs will set a low market price to achieve lower profits, and less taxes.

MNCs may also overstate their costs in a high-tax country to artificially raise their expenses and avoid paying taxes. Equally, they may understate the price of a good in a 'high-tax' country from where they import, to avoid paying tariffs on those imports. This is one way an MNC is able to earn very high profits while paying low taxes.

Advantages of producing in a foreign country for MNCs

The advantages of producing in a foreign country are:

> A reduction in transport costs of inputs and of output distribution.
> Can deal with the threat of competition to their products better when in close contact with the market in a foreign country.
> Exploit low wages and low costs of inputs (raw materials).
> Avoidance of import restrictions, e.g., building a plant in a foreign country.
> Qualify for recognised assistance if they set up in grant-assisted locations.
> Exploit where employment legislation is less onerous/costly.

- Environmental health and safety standards are lower for MNC.
- Government policy of industrialisation by invitation offers benefits such as: cheap sources of energy; tax holidays; and infrastructure.

These issues will also be raised in chapter 35, which focuses on foreign direct investment.

Table 13.4 Effects of MNCs on host countries

Benefits for host country	Cost to host country
Employment	Elimination of domestic producers
New technology	Replacement of labour
New management techniques	Natural non-renewable resources are depleted
Export growth	Their sheer size makes them insulated from many government policies
Tax revenue	They may not strictly adhere to health or safety standards
Corporate sponsorship	They send their profits to their home countries
Good quality, low prices of products	They can shift production around the world and in this way exert influence on negotiations with unions or host governments

Market concentration and market structure

Concentration ratio

To understand market concentration, pause to consider the word 'concentration'. A very concentrated market is dominated by industries or markets where a monopolist or a few firms dominate the industry and produce, for example, 90 per cent of output/sales, while 20 or more firms share 10 per cent. This industry is very concentrated indeed.

By this reasoning, a pure monopoly is considered totally concentrated because one firm accounts for total market share. Monopolistic competition, on the other hand, is less concentrated than an oligopoly since the market share is divided up among many firms, each with a small share of the market. The least concentrated market will therefore be a perfectly competitive industry.

Market share is determined by the number of customers or clients that a firm serves as a percentage of the total market of customers.

Table 13.5 Concentration ratios

Firm	% of Industry output
1	28
2	20
3	16
4	15
5	14
All other	7

In table 13.5 the concentration ratio of the three largest firms is 64 per cent (28 + 20 + 16). For four firms or a C4 the concentration ratio is 79 per cent (64 + 15). A five firm concentration ratio is 93 per cent (79 + 14). This is a concentrated oligopoly market.

Herfindahl-Hirschman Index

The Herfindahl-Hirschman Index (HHI) is another measure of market concentration that gives a more accurate measure of market concentration than the concentration ratio. To calculate the index, the percentage of each firm is squared and added up.

Taking a monopoly as an example, since it would control 100 per cent of the market the HHI would be = $(100)^2 = 10,000$.

This is the highest value of the HHI and gives an indication of degree of equality or inequality in market share in a monopoly. A market is said to be unconcentrated if its HHI is less than 1000, but concentrated if the HHI is greater than 1,800.

In this case, market share of this market is totally dominated. As the value of the HHI falls, the market share is more equally distributed and less dominated by a few firms.

In the above example, an HHI for the five firms would be: $(28)^2 + (20)^2 + (16)^2 + (15)^2 + (14)^2 = 784 + 400 + 256 + 225 + 196 = 1,861$

Compared to the maximum HHI of 10,000 and given the number of firms in this market the value of 1,861 suggest that the market is fairly concentrated.

Concentration ratios have been criticised on the grounds that the measure presents an incomplete picture of concentration in markets. The measure does not include the market shares of the entire industry, nor provide information about the distribution of firm size. If there is a change in market share in the industry, concentration ratio should reflect this.

Chapter summary

Oligopoly and monopolistic competition are market structures that lie between the two market extremes of perfect competition and monopoly.

Monopolistic competition is very similar to perfect competition except for the differentiated product and therefore some ability to set price. The demand curve is elastic but downward sloping. Further, long-run output is achieved with excess capacity and therefore productively inefficient. It is also allocatively inefficient since P is not equal to MC in the long-run.

Oligopoly is a market structure dominated by a few firms. The main features of this market are: price rigidity; interdependence; collusion; non-price competition; a differentiated product; and strong barriers to entry.

Competitors are sometimes price takers or price makers. These different types of oligopolies are: Sweezy's 'kinked' curve; dominant price leader; barometric price leader; and cartel.

The degree to which a few firms dominate a market may be calculated by the percentage of total output or sales represented by the five or six largest firms expressed as a concentration ratio. An alternative measure of a market concentration is the HHI, which is calculated by squaring the respective market shares of the major producers in one industry.

Multinational corporations (MNCs) produce in different countries. Their pricing and output decisions are designed to maximise profits by avoiding taxes using a transfer pricing. Away from MNCs, many firms do not maximise profits but may opt to maximise growth: welfare, output, sales or managerial utility. They may also focus on survival or act conservatively. Meanwhile cooperatives seek the interest of their members.

Practice questions

1. The condition necessary for normal profit is that:
   a. Marginal cost must be equal to marginal revenue
   b. Average cost must be equal to marginal cost
   c. Average cost must be equal to marginal revenue
   d. Average cost must be equal to average revenue.

2. Which of the following is responsible for the 'kink' in the demand curve of the oligopolistic firm?
   a. Rival films in an oligopoly match price cuts but not price increases
   b. Rival firms in an oligopoly match price increases but not price cuts
   c. The products sold by oligopolistic firms are substantially different from each other
   d. The products sold by oligopolistic firms are slightly different from each other.

3. Which of the following best describes the 'marginalist principle'?
   a. Average cost equals average revenue
   b. Marginal cost equals average revenue
   c. Average cost equals marginal revenue
   d. Marginal cost equals marginal revenue.

4. The point at which the firm in perfect competition covers its variable costs is called the:
   a. Closing down point
   b. Variation point
   c. Economies of scale point
   d. Long-run equilibrium point.

5. Compare the short-run and long-run situations of a monopolistically competitive firm with respect to the following:
   a. Price
   b. Output
   c. Profit.

6. Define the following terms:
   a. Cartel
   b. Natural monopoly.

7. Explain how a cartel can be less stable than a natural monopoly.

8. Explain why each of the following features is present in a monopolistically competitive industry.
   a. High advertising costs
   b. Inefficiency in the long-run-equilibrium.

9. Explain why the price in an oligopilistic industry might be sticky upward and downward.

Multiple choice question

1. Monopolistic competition takes place when:
   a. There are barriers to entry.
   b. All firms are making long-run super normal profits.
   c. Sellers face a perfectly elastic demand curve.
   d. There are differences between the products of the firm.

2. Firms are more likely to collude if:
   a. Products are very different.
   b. Products are standardised.
   c. There are many firms in the industry.
   d. There is a sudden change in demand.

3. Prices are sticky in the 'kinked' demand curve because:
   a. The AR curve is elastic above the kink and inelastic below it.
   b. The AR curve is inelastic above the kink and elastic below it.
   c. Marginal revenue is discontinuous at the kink portion of the curve.
   d. Elasticity is infinite at the 'kink'.

14 Market failure

INTRODUCTORY ECONOMICS A TEXTBOOK FOR CAPE ECONOMICS STUDENTS

LEARNING OBJECTIVES

- Define market failure and the concept of economic efficiency with special emphasis on Pareto optimality.
- Explain allocative and cost efficiency.
- Identify cases of market failure: monopoly, public and merit goods and why they fail.
- Define social and private costs/benefits.
- Distinguish between negative and positive externalities.
- Identify and explain imperfect information, adverse selection and moral hazard.

REQUIRED KNOWLEDGE

- Scarcity
- Efficiency and productivity
- Least cost combination
- Allocative efficiency
- Consumer and produce surplus
- Markets
- Private costs of production.

TOPIC VALUE

Noisy neighbours, dogs that disturb the peace, steelbands practising near your school or home are all stressful situations, and their economics are examined in this chapter.

Introduction

In chapter 1, which considered scarcity and the economic problem, choices concerning the three basic problems of what, how and for whom to produce were posed, since resources have to be put to their best use. Further, the 'best' use of these scarce resources is achieved if the three basic questions are answered by achieving Pareto efficiency.

The word 'best' describes the concept of efficiency, that is, on what to produce, how to produce it and for whom, but it is also a normative judgment.

The best combination of goods and services, the best factor combination and the best way to distribute output are the three main ideas connected to economic efficiency, which was briefly outlined in chapter 10, which looked at market structures. See figure 14.1.

Economic efficiency consists of:

› Allocative efficiency
› Productive or technical efficiency.

Allocative efficiency concerns solving the 'what to produce' problem or providing the goods and service and the quantities that people wish to buy.

Productive efficiency concerns the most efficient method of production for these goods. In simple terms, the goods that people wish to buy must be produced with the least amount of resources.

Productive efficiency

If a firm can achieve the maximum output from a given combination of input factors then it would also be producing at its lowest cost. For example, if five bakers and two ovens produce 1,000 loaves when it is within their capability to produce 1,500 loaves then production and cost are inefficient. Having analysed output in four market structures, any market that produces at the minimum efficient size (the lowest point on the LRAC) is therefore productively and cost efficient.

Allocative efficiency

As long as society's producers are able to produce goods that consumers wish to buy and in the quantities they desire, then allocative efficiency is achieved as far as the 'best' combination of goods or services is concerned. If insufficient goods or services or none at all are produced, this may be due to allocative inefficiency in production. For example, the inability to purchase tickets to a 'one day' international cricket match.

Allocative efficiency is achieved when output is produced where P = MC. Price is the value that society places on a good or service and MC is the cost to society of providing this good in alternative production. If the value placed on a good is greater than the cost to society of providing it then society is indicating it wishes to have more.

Similarly, if the cost to society of providing another unit of a good exceeds the value buyers place on it, then society is indicating that it wants less of the good. Only when the value placed by buyers on a good is the same as the cost to society, will allocative efficiency be achieved.

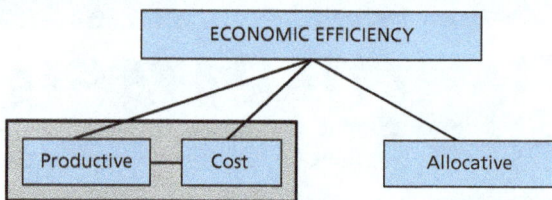

Figure 14.1 Economic efficiency

Figure 14.2 shows that at an output of 100 boxes society values the 100th box at $20, but the MC of the 100th box is only $8. Society wishes more. It is only when 150 boxes are produced that the value placed on the 150th unit is equal to the cost of that unit. At an output of 200 the cost to society (MC) of the 200th unit is $20 while society places a value of $10 on the 200th unit, indicating that society desires less of the good. Both the values and cost to society are the same at output 150 units and a price of $15.

Chapter 14 Market failure

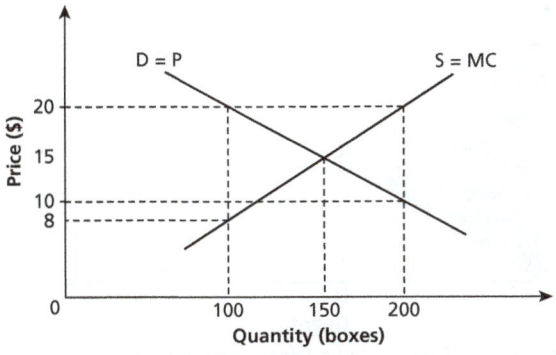

Figure 14.2 A market for boxes

Key points

> Efficiency is a concept that expresses the best or most efficient use of resources when it satisfies the 'what', 'how' and 'for whom' to produce question.
> The 'what' question is solved by allocative efficiency.
> The 'how' question is solved by productive efficiency.
> The 'for whom' question depends on methods of distribution, e.g., the price mechanism, queues, lotteries, quotas, stamps, etc.

Efficiency and consumer and producer surplus

Allocative efficiency is also achieved when consumer and product surplus is maximised.

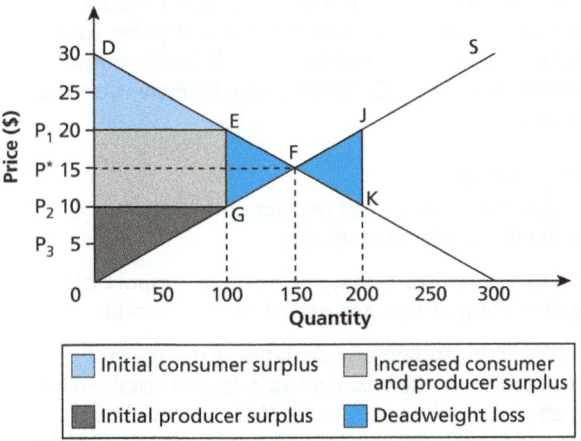

Figure 14.3 Efficiency and consumer and producer surplus

In figure 14.3, when price P_1 is $20 consumer surplus is only DEP_1. Consumer surplus is increased to DFP^* at a price of $15.

> Producer surplus at P_2 $10 is OGP_2
> It is maximised at price P^* $15 and represented by triangle OFP^*.

When consumer surplus (DFP^*) is added to maximum producer surplus OFP^* the welfare of society's resources is maximised, that is, triangle DFO. At Q 150 there is allocative efficiency. The cost and benefit to society are equal.

Deadweight loss

When output is 100, triangle EFG represents the loss of welfare or efficiency to society. This is also called a deadweight loss. Deadweight loss therefore is the loss of welfare when output is not allocatively efficient. Output 200 is beyond allocative efficiency and triangle JFK is again lost welfare.

Key points

Allocative efficiency is achieved when P = MC where buyers place a value on a good that is equal to the cost of using the resources to produce it, that is, marginal cost. If output is greater or less than this optimal output there is a deadweight loss.

Efficiency and Pareto optimality

Recall that the concept of Pareto optimality was first raised in chapter 1 when discussing the 'best' use of resources.

The concept of Pareto optimality was advanced by V. Pareto, an Italian economist. He theorised that when resources are allocated in a way that no one loses, a Pareto improvement is achieved. When such improvements come to an end, it would only be possible to make someone better off by making someone else worse off.

A production possibility frontier may help to clarify the concept in figure 14.4. Point X yields 30 units of consumer goods and 20 units of capital but at point X_1 more of both is achieved. This is a Pareto improvement.

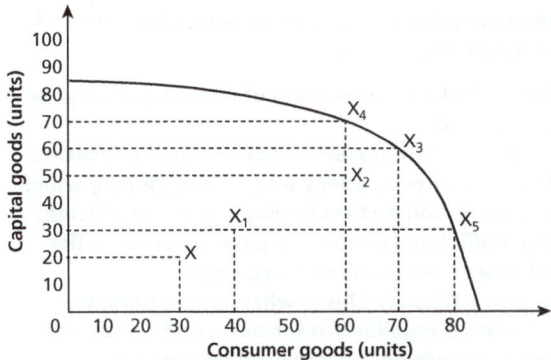

Figure 14.4 Efficiency and Pareto optimality

Even moving from point X_2 of 60 units of consumer goods and 50 units of capital goods to X_4 does not reduce the quantity of consumer goods but instead increases capital to 70 units. This is an improvement. But trying to produce more consumer goods from X_4 to X_3 involves a loss of ten units of capital goods to gain ten units of consumer goods.

From point X_4 to X_5 the same result is achieved, which is a loss of 40 units of capital goods to gain 20 units of consumer goods. All points on the PPF are Pareto optimal points because it is not possible to gain without losing.

The link between Pareto optimality and efficiency, therefore, is that efficiency leads to a Pareto optimal resource allocation. Accordingly, when productive and allocative efficiency are achieved in every possible market in the system, Pareto optimality is achieved as well.

For example, if the food industry is not producing at its lowest cost (using more resources than it should) and every other industry is productively efficient, then merely becoming productively efficient would yield more output without affecting other industries. All industries would then be productively efficient.

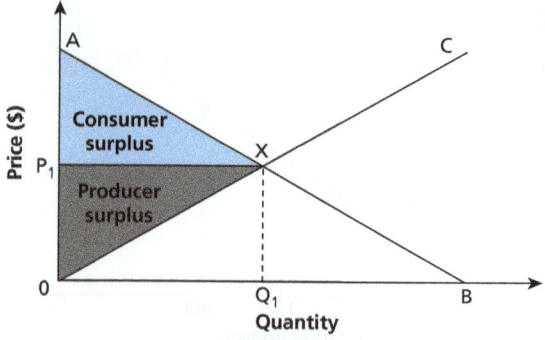

Figure 14.6 Efficiency and perfect competition

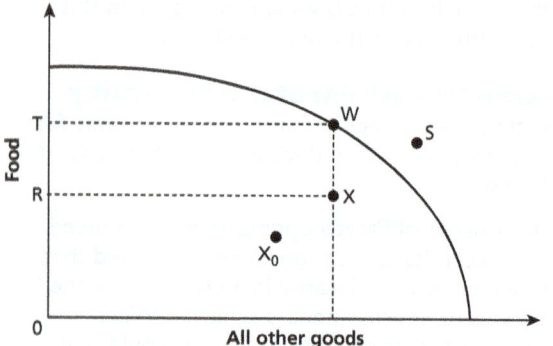

Figure 14.5 Pareto optimality and efficiency

In figure 14.5, the food industry could produce TR of more food without giving up other goods and services on the horizontal axis by moving from point X to point W. The food industry is then productively efficient at point W.

Allocative efficiency is also achieved on any point of the production possibility frontier. Other types of efficiencies include:

› **Static efficiency:** allocation of resources in a given time period
› **Dynamic efficiency:** efficiency through allocation of resources over a very long period during which time invention and technology improve efficiency
› **Social efficiency:** when marginal social benefits and marginal social costs are equal
› **Private efficiency:** this is when consumers are in personal equilibrium for one good or several goods and where marginal private cost = marginal private benefit.

Key point
Pareto optimality is achieved through efficiency.

Efficiency and perfect competition
If all markets operate in a perfectly competitive market structure, this will ensure efficiency or Pareto optimal resource allocation. For example, allocative efficiency is achieved under perfect competition because in the long-run P = MC. The reasons are clear:

› **All consumers face the same choice.**
› **All consumers have perfect knowledge of prices.**
› **Any firm operating where P > MC will have no customers because perfect knowledge allows all other firms to achieve P = MC.**

Refer to figure 14.6, which represents a perfectly competitive industry. Allocative efficiency emphasises that consumers purchase goods they wish to consume and in the quantities they desire, that is, Q_1.

The demand curve or price measures the value that society places on a good and marginal cost measures the cost that society places on the good. The buyers involved in this particular good are represented by AX on the demand curve because they all value the good above the market price.

XB represents buyers who value the good less than the market price, hence showing no interest in the good. Sellers whose costs are less than the price will profit, hence OX represents the sellers who participate in this market. XC of the supply curve represents sellers whose cost price is above the market price and are therefore not participating in this market.

In this situation, at P_1 consumer and produce surplus are equal, but they will not always be. Total welfare to society is the triangle AXO. Any output to the left or right of Q_1 is therefore inefficient or loss of welfare to society.

Key points
Long-run equilibrium of perfect competition is a model for market 'success'.

The assumptions that are made in support of perfect competition are not of the real world.

Notwithstanding, any deviation from perfect competition is likely to lead to a loss of total welfare or efficiency when output levels in the market are not in accord with P = MC or minimum LRAC. When the allocation of resources causes a loss of efficiency or welfare, market failure is said to have taken place. When this occurs, the good in question may be overproduced, underproduced or not produced at all, resulting in loss of welfare maximisation.

In nearly all instances, this 'incorrect production' or market failure is not Pareto optimal because conditions of Pareto optimality have not been met. To conclude, market failure takes place when there is a failure to achieve economic efficiency and welfare maximisation in the allocation of resources.

The causes of market failure

In many cases of market failure note how it may be caused by conditions not conforming to perfect competition, for example, monopoly.

Imperfect market structure

Refer to figure 14.7. Since monopoly is almost the opposite of perfect competition, market failure in monopoly is due to:

- Incorrect output Q_2
- The practice of profit maximisation at MC = MR, instead of P = MC
- Price P_1 is higher than the efficient output price P_2
- Consumer surplus is not maximised. It is YXP_1 instead of YKP_2
- P_1XKP_2 is lost in consumer surplus
- The firm/industry is also productively inefficient since output Q_2 cuts LRAC at Z, which is to the left of minimum LRAC (W); this therefore reveals excess capacity.

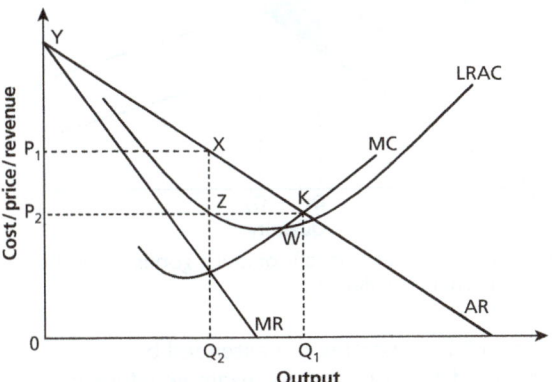

Figure 14.7 Market failure caused by imperfect market structure

Monopolistic markets and oligopoly are market failures for the same reasons as for a monopoly. In these markets, there is a failure to meet conditions of perfect competition in price, output, knowledge, mobility and type of good. Price discrimination is also an example of a monopolist operating in conditions of market failure.

Public goods

A public good is one which has two distinct characteristics. First, it is non-rivalrous and non-excludable, for example, street lights and street signs. Non-rivalrous means that consumption of one unit does not leave one less for others since the supply is unlimited.

The non-excludable feature of public goods

This means that a public good, e.g., streetlights can be enjoyed by all at the same time and place. It is an example of a market failure simply because if left to private enterprise, the good would not be provided because there is no profit in providing it. For example, if you erect a streetlight with a coin slot in a dark street near to a bus stop, and you insert a coin to put on the light everyone would use the illumination free of charge. This is called the 'free rider' problem.

Even if consumers wanted to pay there would be difficulty in measuring the quantity of light consumed. Since the quantity of the service cannot be measured and cannot exclude others from their purchase, no one will buy illumination and there will be no profit to be earned.

Since it is valued by society, however, the government may use tax revenues to install these lights for the safety and peace of mind of the public. Market failure in this case is due to the free rider problem and a failure of the incentive function of the price mechanism in this market, resulting in a total failure of the market since no output is produced.

Private goods

A private good is one that is excludable and rivalrous. In other words, consuming one unit leaves less for others to consume. For example, if you purchase a lunch box, there will be one less for others. In addition, no one else can free ride on your lunch. You can exclude them. Compare this box lunch with a public good, which is quite the opposite.

Common error

A public good is sometimes described as one that is used by the public and provided by the state, but this is insufficient. The non-rival and non-excludable nature of the good should be highlighted. To understand the nature of a public good it should be compared to a private good that is rivalrous and excludable.

Merit goods

A merit good is one that gives rise to indirect extended benefits, or positive externality to society, beyond the benefit to the buyer and which is under-provided and under-consumed out of ignorance. If left to the free market, output produced would be less than the efficient quantity because the demand for merit goods is weak due to ignorance of the benefits. This is a market failure of information. Hence, an incorrect quantity of a merit good is produced.

Health and education are commonly cited examples of merit goods. Since an ill or illiterate person is considered a burden to society and a healthy, educated one an asset, the state assumes a paternalistic role by providing both public and merit goods on the basis of need or merit (e.g. by making the ill healthy) and financed by taxation revenue.

Since demand is weak and price low, there is little scope for profit. Prices do not react to what is good or bad for society; they only signal profit opportunities. Weak demand is due to information failure of the price mechanism.

Demerit goods

These types of goods are over-provided by the free market and over-consumed out of ignorance. In addition to providing a 'benefit' to the user, a demerit good has an overall negative effect or externality on society. Common examples are alcohol, tobacco, addictive drugs and gambling.

Apart from being over-consumed, output is beyond the efficient level where P = MC. Once again, the price mechanism strictly reflects a want. Prices are therefore high, presenting opportunities for profits. The reason for demerit goods being a market failure is that over-consumption takes place through lack of information about the associated negative effects.

Governments regulate or tax the consumption of such goods, as well as provide state-sponsored education programmes to provide information on the dangers of consuming the products.

Externalities

Private, external and social costs

Merit goods provide extended positive benefits/externalities to society, while demerit goods extend negative cost/externalities to society. Since buyers are not concerned about these benefits and costs when choosing goods, they are called spillover, indirect third-party effects or externalities. Figure 14.8 shows the demand for education.

If EMB is added to PMB this will shift the PMB curve to the right by the amount of the EMB (as in figure 14.9) to achieve social marginal benefit (SMB). This reflects the full benefit of the purchase.

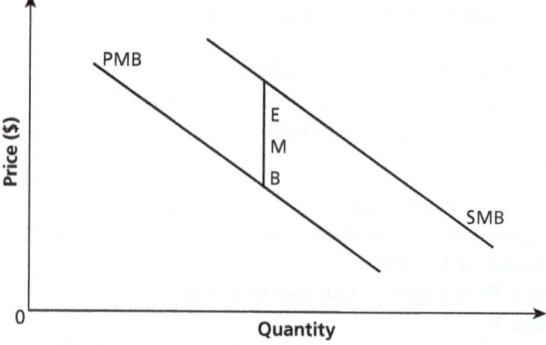

Figure 14.9 PMB + EMB = SMB

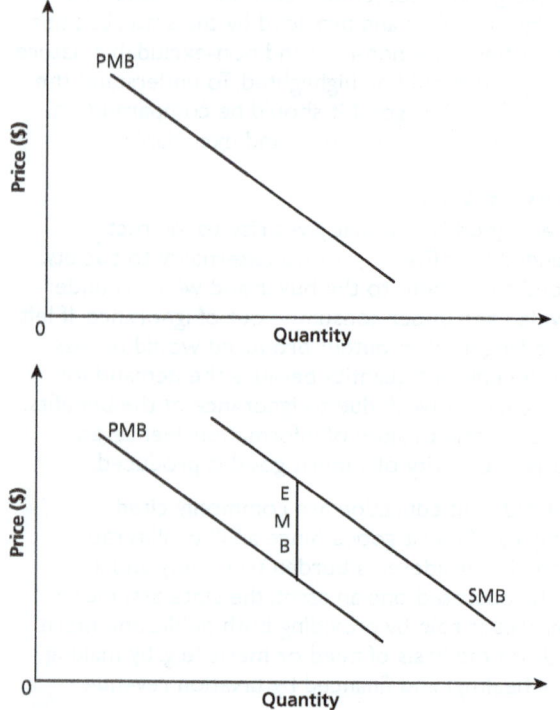

Figure 14.8 Private marginal benefit for education

A demand curve reflects private marginal benefit (PMB) (Utility theory) as in figure 14.8. However, if the spillover benefit of education to society can be measured it is called external marginal benefit (EMB) and should be added to the PMB of the buyer.

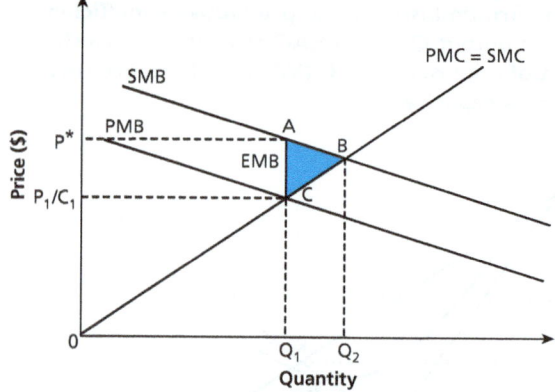

Figure 14.10 Extended benefit of merit goods (education). The good is under-produced

Figure 14.10 illustrates the extended benefit/externality of a merit good, for example education, which is under-produced. The socially optimal level of output is Q_2 rather than Q_1.

Note that at Q_1, the benefit (P*) is greater than the cost to society (C_1). The extended benefit is denoted by EMB, which measures the extended benefit and causes the PMB to shift to the right to SMB. Note the correct quantity or socially optimal quantity of education is Q_2 while the incorrect quantity is Q_1.

Similarly, the supply curve reflects private marginal cost (PMC). Any spillover cost/externality from a transaction is called external marginal cost (EMC). If the EMC is added to the PMC it would cause the PMC to shift to the left by the vertical distance of the EMC.

When a negative spillover, third-party or indirect negative effect is imposed on society the good is over-produced and over-consumed. See figure 14.11; when EMC is added to PMC, social marginal cost is achieved.

An example of a positive externality is to imagine a contractor building your neighbour's fence on the property next to your own; your neighbour receives a benefit, but it spills over to you since you do not have to build a fence and you do not pay for it. The price your neighbour pays fails to reflect the indirect benefit you receive as shown (figure 14.12).

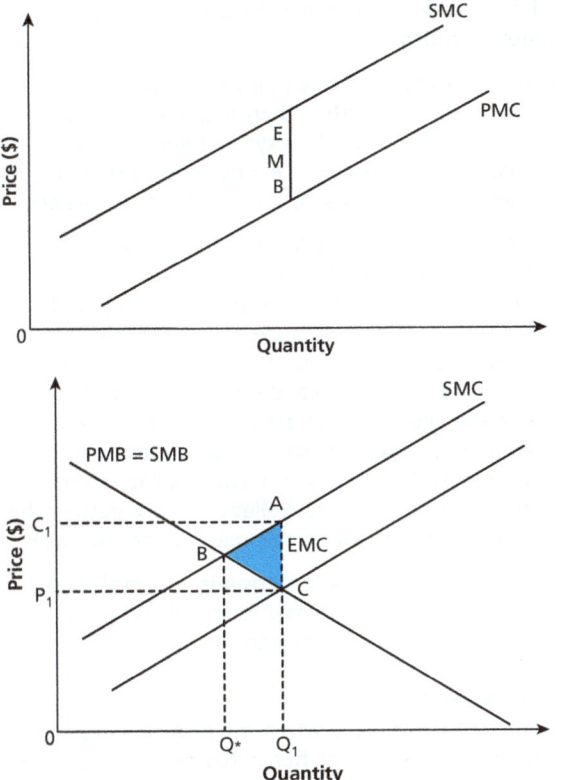

Figure 14.11 PMC + EMC = SMC (demerit goods: alcohol)

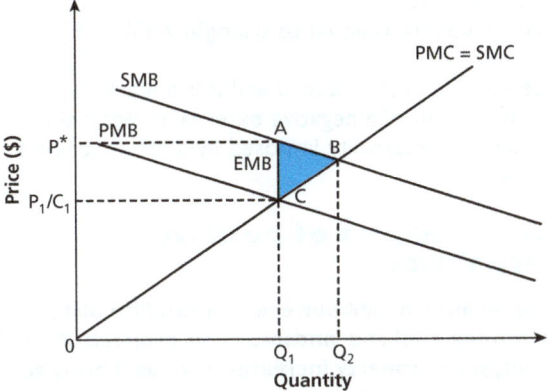

Figure 14.12 The extended benefit of the neighbour's fence

Note:
- Q_1 is the quantity of fence bought at price P_1
- EMB reflects the spillover benefit
- Q_2 is the optimal quantity of fencing, therefore the good is underproduced by the quantity Q_1Q_2.

Further at Q_1, note that the value placed on the good P^* is greater than the cost to society = C_1. Loss of welfare is triangle ABC.

In this example, the positive externality is caused by the contractor (producer), with you (the consumer) receiving it.

Negative externality (pollution)

Producers can also impose a negative externality on consumers; for example, if a sugar producer burns a sugar cane field in preparation for harvest, the wind may blow the ash into a residential neighbourhood. The supply curve of the sugar produced does not reflect this external cost (figure 14.13).

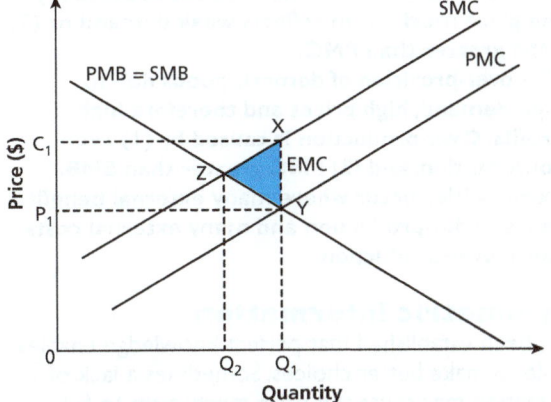

Figure 14.13 The external marginal cost of pollution

Figure 14.11 illustrates the incorrect quantity of alcohol produced at Q_1.

When negative spillover effects from alcohol (EMC) are added to private costs of (PMC) production, the social marginal cost of producing output Q is obtained.

Note:
- Q_1 – suboptimal quantity (the market is in equilibrium but there are social costs)
- Q_* – the 'correct' quantity.

At Q_1 the cost to society (C_1) is higher than the value (P_1) buyers place on Q_1 units, since the 'correct' equilibrium is Q_*. ABC of welfare is lost by producing Q_1; the good is therefore overproduced by Q_*Q_1.

The spillover, third-party or indirect effects previously explained are also referred to in economics as externalities. Negative externalities are external marginal costs or negative extended costs that are not reflected in the supply curve of a firm. Positive externalities are external marginal benefits that are not reflected by a demand curve when a good is bought.

Although merit and demerit goods are examples of a good with positive and negative externalities respectively, there are many other real-life examples that perhaps you may have observed. These can be classified according to those who cause the effect and those who receive the effect.

Note:
- Q_1 and P_1 are the original quantity and price.
- When EMC of pollution is added to the supply curve PMC, the new equilibrium is at Z and optimal quantity Q_2.
- Further at Q_1 the cost to society at X on SMC is greater than the value buyers place on the last unit Y on PMB.
- Loss of welfare is equal to triangle XYZ.

The good is overproduced and it is a market failure as a result of a negative externality. Again this illustrates the externality imposed by a producer on a consumer.

Other examples of positive externalities

- Your wealthy neighbour erects a satellite dish, swimming pool and landscapes his property. As a result, your property increases in value. This is an example of a positive externality from consumer to consumer.
- If warm water from a power plant provides ideal breeding conditions for fish, the fishermen in that area will have received a positive externality for which they do not pay. This is an example of a positive externality from producer (power plant) to producer (fishermen).

Key points

An externality is a positive or negative spillover or third-party effect not reflected in demand or supply curves, hence not included in the price mechanism. If these effects are not included in the price mechanism, market failure will result from under- or over-production of output. The cause of this is market failure, that is, failure of the price mechanism to include EMC or EMB.

So far we have identified market failure caused by:

- Imperfect markets that practise profit maximisation instead of producing where P = MC or allocative efficiency.
- Non-provision of public goods, which is a failure of the incentive function of the price mechanism.
- The under-provision of merit goods because (1) the price mechanism reflects weak demand or (2) SMB greater than PMC.
- The over-provision of demerit goods due to high demand, high prices and therefore high profits. Over-production is caused by (1) over-consumption, and (2) MSC greater than SMB.
- Externalities occur where many external benefits cause under-production and many external costs cause over-production.

Asymmetric information

It has been established that perfect knowledge enables people to make better choices. Sometimes a lack of information may cause the price mechanism to fail, causing market failure as in merit and demerit goods. Such informational failure may be observed with asymmetric information.

In any transaction, if one person has more information than the other, then this is known as asymmetric information. This type of informational failure has been the focus of economists in recent times because it causes a failure of different markets.

For example, if you pay for a private economics tutor, it is assumed that he or she has more information and mastery of the subject than you do. Also if you go to a doctor, lawyer, or mechanic you assume he or she possesses more knowledge than you do. In these cases you are the principal and your mechanic the agent. Asymmetric information takes place when your agents such as your doctor, lawyer, or mechanic perform a task for you. Your ignorance of these skills may lead you to believe you are getting the best value for money when this may not be the case.

This principal–agent interaction is observable in two common examples of asymmetric information, moral hazard and adverse selection.

Moral hazard

Moral hazard takes place when the principal in a transaction changes his or her behaviour in a careless or irresponsible way, resulting in an external marginal cost and hence a market failure. A classic example may be observed when a person purchases fire or burglary insurance and becomes careless in securing his property (not remembering to turn off the gas or the iron). Careless and complacent attitudes have caused many fires and thefts to take place, imposing a social cost on society and a waste of resources. In this case, the principal has more information than the agent since the agent is unaware of the principal's poor attitude towards securing the insured item.

Adverse selection

People who apply for insurance (the principals) have more information about their health than the insurance company (the agent). As persons with hidden health problems are most likely to purchase insurance than those in good health, the price of insurance is therefore likely to reflect the cost of people who are of below average health.

This price will therefore not reflect the cost of insurance for a healthy person. A healthy person will not be deservedly charged a low rate of insurance because he or she is included in the group with hidden health problems.

Similarly, a person who wants to sell an old car may not get the correct price for it, even if it is in good condition, because it is assumed that an old car will be defective, hence it is likely to be sold as if it were a 'lemon'. In this case, the buyer is the principal and the agent is the used-car salesman with knowledge of the product's defects and who will only pay a low price for the car because of the possibility that it is defective.

Adverse selection in banking

A bank will hesitate to lend to a new borrower because it may not have the information to ascertain their ability to repay the loan. The bank's attitude will be different with a customer of 20 years' good standing, since the bank knows his or her financial capability if their salary is deposited there. A new borrower carries a higher risk of defaulting on a loan than the average borrower. In this case, the borrower is the principal and the loans officer the agent.

Chapter summary

Market failures are caused by a failure to achieve economic efficiency and therefore failure to achieve Pareto optimality. When this happens there is over-, under- and non-provision.

Some examples of market failure are imperfect market structure, externalities, no provision of public goods, few/shortage of merit goods, over-production of demerit goods, pollution and asymmetric information.

Practice questions

1. Define each of the following. Give an example of each.
    a. Asymmetric information
    b. Moral hazard
    c. Adverse selection.

2. a. Explain and give an example of each of the following terms:
        i. Public goods
        ii. Externalities
        iii. Asymmetric information.
    b. Explain how each of the concepts listed in (a) above causes a market to fail.

3. Define the following terms and explain how asymmetric information may lead to each of them.
    a. Adverse selection
    b. Moral hazard.

INTRODUCTORY ECONOMICS A TEXTBOOK FOR CAPE ECONOMICS STUDENTS

15 Role of government and market failures

Chapter 15 Role of government and market failures

> **LEARNING OBJECTIVES**
>
> - Identify and explain state action to correct market failure.
> - Taxation and subsidies.
> - Regulation and anti-trust legislation.
> - State ownership: privatisation and deregulation.
> - Limitations of government action.
> - Identify the pros and cons of government measures used in an attempt to correct market failure.
>
> **REQUIRED KNOWLEDGE**
>
> - Efficiency
> - Pareto optimality
> - Price mechanism
> - Private costs
> - Utility
> - Deadweight loss.
>
> **TOPIC VALUE**
>
> This topic explains why the free market system fails the poor and needy when the distribution of income is uneven, and why the state has to impose penalties on firms and individuals to correct and regulate the failures of the market system.

Introduction

It was Adam Smith who advocated non-intervention in the free market, which he insisted was self-correcting. Government intervention became necessary as a result of the great depression of the 1930s. Market failures started to plague many of the world's economies.

Government intervention

Government intervention in a free market may assume different forms such as:

- Taxation
- Subsidies
- Regulations and deregulation
- Direct provision
- Legislation
- Privatisation/nationalisation
- Anti-trust policy
- Market creation, e.g., tradeable permits.

Market failures and government measures

Monopoly

The government regulation of monopolies is re-emphasised in this chapter. Since monopolies are profit maximisers, their profits may be subjected to a lump sum tax and then redirected to the poor and needy. (Refer to Figure 12.10 in chapter 12 for an illustration of the effect of lump-sum taxes.)

A government can purchase a majority shareholding in a private monopoly, set price where P = MC and achieve allocative efficiency in this way. This form of action is called nationalisation, and may be done, in particular, if the industry is a strategic one such as, for example, oil or airline.

Government may also partially privatise nationalised companies on the basis that profit-driven enterprises are more likely to be productively efficient, as is the case of Powergen Limited and T+TEC in Trinidad and Tobago. In this instance, the method of correction is taxation, regulation and privatisation.

Public goods

Governments intervene to solve the total failure of important markets such as public goods by direct supply, and financed through taxation. Public goods give rise to positive externalities. The objective of state action is efficiency.

A government will have the effect of reducing the price to the consumer. The objective of the correction may be efficiency (providing education and training), promoting positive externalities, promoting equity (fairer income distribution) or paternalism (promoting civic mindedness, libraries and museums).

Imperfect information (informational failure)

In seeking to provide consumers with information that enables better choices, governments may enact strict laws on and instructions for use, and so on. They may also enable the following:

> - **Strict advertising standards, particularly for persuasive advertising rather than informative advertising**
> - **Government grants to research institutions, e.g., CARIRI, the Caribbean Research Institute provides information to entrepreneurs. In addition, Central Bank and Government's Statistic Department provide up-to-date information on the economy for better business planning.**

In some Caribbean territories there is legislation to ensure transparency in government undertakings, such as via the Freedom of Information Act.

Management information systems have provided a boost for restricting information failure. In this regard, information technology is provided to all public institutions to serve the public more efficiently and easily. Likewise, tax relief is granted for information technology as an incentive for organisations to become technologically efficient in their use of information.

Adverse selection and moral hazard

These types of informational failures are corrected by the state-funded Bureau of Standards and Ombudsman offices and relate to goods and services traded in the insurance and financial sectors. Government-approved information programmes are managed by an information ministry. The objectives of correction in this case are efficiency. The method of correction is legislation, regulation and direct provision.

Labour immobility

Labour immobility is a cause of a failure of the labour market. Surplus labour may accumulate when a person is either occupationally or geographically unable to fill a vacancy. Surplus labour creates unemployment and leads to a misallocation of human resources.

Governments in critical situations may adopt the following corrective measures:

> Manpower information on job vacancies
> Retraining of idle labour through government training programmes
> Free education of all types: primary, secondary and tertiary
> Regional policy, i.e., industrial zones set up near to high areas of unemployment
> Legislation enabling the transfer of pension rights to encourage the free movement of labour
> Promote free movement of labour within the region via CSME, a Caribbean Government agreement
> Government housing policy, i.e., siting housing settlements near to industrial activity
> Reduction of direct taxes to encourage participation in the labour force.

The objectives of corrective government action are:

> Labour worker efficiency (efficiency)
> Redistribution of income (equity)
> Positive externalities (efficiency).

The methods of correction are:

> Legislation
> Direct provision
> Regulation.

Inequitable distribution of income

One of the primary reasons for market failure is the uneven distribution of income. Since high-income individuals can use their buying power to influence the 'market', lower income earners are at most times unable to participate in the market on even terms. This is clearly a failure of the free market and government correction is undertaken to level the playing field or ensure equity (fairness). One common measure is the redistribution of wealth from rich to poor people via progressive taxation.

Price control

To protect against the negative effect on markets of high prices a government may institute a price ceiling to protect consumers, especially for necessities such as food (the schedule of food prices) and housing (rent control).

For sellers, farmers may be given a guaranteed price for their produce in order to stabilise their income. In times of a bumper crop, the government buys the excess amount on the market and releases it in times of crop failure or flood.

In addition, workers' incomes are protected against the effects of low wages (below poverty line) by minimum wage legislation. Indirect taxes such as, for example, specific taxes on alcohol, tobacco and gambling serve to raise prices intended to discourage consumption. Since demand for these goods and services is inelastic the government raises revenue. Consumption of these types of demerit goods can only be controlled if demand is elastic. See figure 15.1.

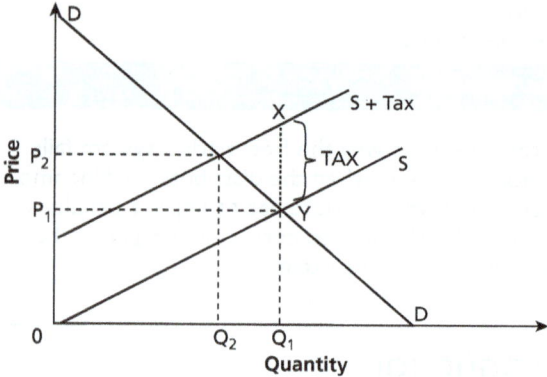

Figure 15.1 A demerit good

Note:

Output Q_1 of cigarettes at price P_1 changes to output Q_2 at a high price P_2 when an indirect tax of XY is imposed on the seller (S more than S + Tax). Q_2 is therefore the optimal quantity of cigarettes sold.

Equity and efficiency

Equity and efficiency are highly desirable outcomes for any society but attempting to achieve either of them may cause one to conflict with the other.

For example, one of the biggest equity issues is the redistribution of income. The chief means of doing so is redistributing income from the rich to poor. The incentive for both parties to increase productivity is removed when progressive taxes take more from the rich to give to the poor, via transfers such as unemployment benefits. Both wealthy and unemployed have no incentive to work harder.

Similarly, trying to be 'fair' using subsidies distorts the market mechanism. Allocative efficiency (P = MC) may not be achieved because the price may be below marginal cost. In addition, setting a minimum wage may increase production costs.

In addition, price ceilings aimed at achieving equity cause shortages to develop and black markets to push prices higher, worsening equity and increasing allocative inefficiency.

In the Caribbean, government provision of merit goods such as education aims to promote equity. This

Chapter 15 Role of government and market failures

may, however, unintentionally create opportunities for 'brain drain' syndrome. As a result of the exodus to other countries, there may be a shortage of skilled labour in Caribbean countries.

The provision of government housing programmes, merit and public goods, and infrastructural projects may divert scarce resources away from private enterprise, creating shortages and high prices. Surpluses arising out of a bumper harvest may ruin a farmer when prices plunge below marginal costs.

Other forms of state intervention to correct market failure

Privatisation

Economists tend to regard privatisation and deregulation as supply-side measures, since they are designed to foster production efficiency. Privatisation is the sale or transfer of ownership and control of state companies to the private sector, mainly by the sale of shares. Privatisation is also considered to be:

> **Sale of housing to tenants.**
> **Outsourcing of contracting services at state-run organisations**, e.g., laundry, cleaning, security and catering services are delivered by private companies in hospitals.
> **Creating competition for state-owned companies to make them more profit driven**, e.g., DIGICEL competing with Telecommunications Services of Trinidad and Tobago.
> **Compulsory competitive tendering by state-run enterprises.**

Table 15.1 Privatisation evaluated

Advantages	Disadvantages
Privatisation removes bureaucratic management and promotes cost and production efficiency.	Private monopolies may be formed under privatisation.
Choice and quality are promoted through privatisation and lead to allocative efficiency.	Profits of private companies are no longer remitted to the state.
Private firms have more incentive to innovate and create new products, promoting dynamic efficiency.	State shares are sold below market value to encourage participation, thereby not optimising revenue.
Political interference is avoided when the private sector takes control of national companies.	After privatisation, shares are usually sold to private shareholders who then own large blocks of shares.
The sale of state companies is a source of revenue to government. Government borrowing is reduced.	Privatised companies are inclined to focus more on profits than social objectives (e.g. preserve the environment).
A wider cross-section of the country may become shareholders in a public limited company.	Some strategic industries are not appropriate for private sector management, e.g., rural bus routes that are not profitable but a necessary public service.
	Buyers for loss-making state enterprises are difficult to identify, especially when heavy liabilities are left behind.

Deregulation

Deregulation is the removal of rules and regulations which constitute barriers to competition between firms. For example, insurance companies and banks once had clearly drawn lines of operation, but most Caribbean governments have deregulated the finance industry to allow insurance and other financial institutions to compete for deposits and loans. Similarly, it is not uncommon to find a pharmacy selling food and other grocery items.

Deregulation promotes competition, with the objective of lowering costs and increasing productive efficiency. The dismantling of tariff barriers also falls into this category. The removal of protective trade barriers enables trading companies to increase productivity and hence lower their costs. Deregulation also means fewer rules and less bureaucracy, which is a known impediment to productivity. Another form of deregulation is the removal of subsidies on goods and services provided by state-managed corporations, which imposes on the firm the need for efficient cost-cutting strategies.

The main drawbacks to deregulation seem to be that deregulated firms tend to operate where risk is very much less and market share assured; for example, transport on highly travelled routes, or in goods where demand is inelastic such as private nursing and health services.

Government correction of market failure: the limitations

The limitations of the government actions are given in table 15.2.

Table 15.2 The limitations of state correction of market failure

Market failure	Government actions and their limitations
Monopoly	Imposing lump sum taxes may reduce dynamic efficiency, although output and price are interchanged. A subsidy should be used together with a lump sum tax. Cost and revenue curves differ among firms and separate taxes and subsidies would be needed. Corrective action is impacted. Privatisation (see disadvantages in table 15.1 above).
Public goods	Decisions to provide public goods involve cost–benefit analyses when both private and social costs and benefits are assessed. The calculation of external benefits and costs is subjective and inexact. In addition, governments may borrow to provide public goods, competing with private enterprise for scarce resources. Construction may cause negative externalities.
Merit goods	Support for merit goods via a subsidy, but which may need to be financed by government borrowing. The limitations are similar to those for public goods. Merit goods are provided by the state in the 'best interest' of people and are therefore paternalistic. Free will is not exercised; therefore, it is a normative judgment. Once expenditure on merit goods is started it is difficult to reverse or stop. Recipients of state-funded education may migrate.
Demerit goods	Imposing indirect taxes will only reduce consumption if demand for demerit goods is elastic. In real life, demand for these goods is inelastic. Indirect taxes are also a distortion of the price mechanism.
Negative externalities and divergence between private and social cost and benefits	Pollution in many cases continues, although at a reduced rate. • It is very difficult to measure pollution and assess costs to the environment. • Banning the product leads to a welfare loss. • Monitoring may be cost prohibitive, e.g., hiring trained inspectors. • Property rights may only affect a small group. • Pollution is still present despite tradeable permits. • Legal action may only be afforded by the wealthy. • Pollution laws are largely unenforceable, e.g., Litter Act, noise.
Positive externalities	Although they are highly desirable and in the 'interest' of society they are financed by tax revenue or state borrowing, both of which have negative consequences; e.g., borrowing creates a debt to society and raises interest rates. In addition, indirect taxes may adversely affect low-income earners more than others, e.g., VAT.
Informational failure	The method of collecting and analysing government information is not always reliable. As such, it is also not always helpful to business planning. Adverse selection and moral hazard are difficult to monitor. Since the economy is always changing, information may become outdated.
Low wages/high prices	**Ceilings and floors** cannot always prevent shortages and surpluses. They require further action to achieve their objective with respect to equity and intervention buying of surpluses. They also distort the allocating function of the price mechanism. Employers may resist the minimum wage, which it is argued causes costs of production to rise.
Labour mobility	Government strategies to increase labour mobility may not be effective if participation in the labour force is frustrated due to the disincentive effects of taxation or high prices. Housing projects may depress property values. Funding for training programmes may not be sustainable.
Inequitable income distribution	Transferring income from high- to low-income groups remains an elusive goal of most governments. Subsidies create dependency, complacency and a burden to the taxpayer.

The reasons for market failure, methods of correction used and examples are given in table 15.3.

Table 15.3 The reasons for market failure and method of correction

Market failure	Reason for failure	Method of correction	Example of market failure and method of relief
Imperfect market	Failure due to allocative/ productive inefficiency	Taxation, regulation, deregulation and legislation	Monopoly, lump sum taxes on profit, regulation, legislation. Anti-trust laws.
Public goods	Total failure, allocative inefficiency	Direct provision	Streetlights, street signs, drainage, law and order. State provision.
Merit goods	Partial failure, allocative inefficiency, under-consumption and production	Subsidy and/or direct provision, legislation (paternalism)	High cost of private education and health. Government borrowing and tax revenue to provide tertiary level subsidies.
Demerit goods	Allocative inefficiency, over-production and consumption	Indirect taxes, legislation, information (paternalism)	Alcohol, tobacco, over-consumption. Specific taxes, prohibition for minors, public education.
Negative externality (divergence between private and social costs and benefits)	Allocative inefficiency, over-production	Taxation, regulation, legislation	Industrial, air, water pollution. Legislation (anti-pollution law), regulation (quotas banning, permits), indirect taxation.
Positive externality	Allocative inefficiency, under-production	Subsidy	Professional training grants (subsidy) to companies to provide training, museums, libraries.
Information	Allocative inefficiency	Legislation, direct provision, regulation	Adverse selection: used car market. Bureau of standards (regulation), advertising (legislation against false advertising), job vacancies (provision of information, manpower control), Ombudsman.
High prices	Inequity	Legislation	Low wages. Ceilings (minimum wage laws and rent control laws).
Low prices	Inequity	Legislation	Farm produce. Maximum prices for farmers. Redistribution of incomes.
Inequitable distribution of income	Inequity	Subsidies, transfers	Squatting settlements. Unemployment benefits, merit goods, free school books and education, subsidised housing, scheduled prices of basic food items.
Labour immobility	Allocative inefficiency	Direct provision, subsidy	Business failure and unemployment. Retraining schemes, regional policy (industrial zones), legislation for transfer of pensions.

Private sector intervention in the correction of market failures

Private sector measures to regulate and reduce market failures may be summarised as:

> Corporate code conduct which governs issues such as waste disposal and adherence to health and safety standards.
> Social responsibility such as ensuring that marketed products are safe, providing multilingual information on safety and storage and expiry date information. Recycling of waste products falls into this category.
> Company voluntary agreements (CVA) are agreements that allow failing companies to renegotiate their debts to prevent insolvency and protect the interests of their clients.
> Corporate ethics is related to issues such as insider trading, false advertising, industrial espionage, bribery and money laundering.

Chapter summary

> The government is obliged to correct market failure to ensure market efficiency.
> Market failure is corrected by intervention, regulation, legislation, public education, taxation, direct provision and market creation.

Practice questions

1. Explain and give an example of each of the following terms:
   i. Public goods
   ii. Externalities.

   Explain how each of the concepts listed above may cause a market to fail.

Multiple choice questions

1. Economic efficiency in production occurs when:
   a. All firms are maximising profits and producing where MC = MR.
   b. There is spare capacity.
   c. The output of one good cannot be increased without reducing the output of another good.
   d. The economy does not have to depend on imported goods.

2. Which combination best describe examples of privatisation?
   a. Deregulation and franchising
   b. Contracting out and regulation
   c. Deregulation and nationalisation
   d. Ceiling prices and regulation.

3. The concept of 'adverse selection' implies that
   a. Persons who have insurance may tend to be less careful and thus increase risks.
   b. Persons who take out insurance are those with the highest risk.
   c. Those who sell insurance policies are less well informed than those who buy them.
   d. Those who choose insurance policies are often the same ones who do not really need them.

16 Theory of income distribution

LEARNING OBJECTIVES

- Identify the rewards to the factor inputs.
- Explain the demand for labour.
- Explain derived demand and marginal revenue productivity theory.
- Evaluate criticisms of marginal revenue productivity.
- Explain the supply of labour.
- Explain and illustrate the backward bending supply curve.
- Explain equilibrium price and labour.
- Explain wage differentials.

REQUIRED KNOWLEDGE

- The price mechanism
- Short-run production and marginal physical product
- Profit maximisation
- Perfect and imperfect markets
- Income and substitution effects
- Derived demand.

TOPIC VALUE

People earn different wages, so there are rich and poor people all around us. These everyday observations and their causes may be explained by wage theory.

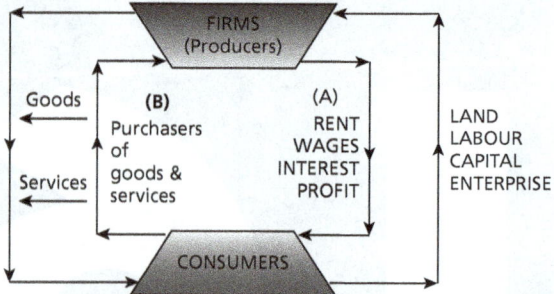

Figure 16.1 A two-sector counter circular flow of income and the rewards to the factors

Introduction

Distribution of incomes refers to the incomes that are earned by the relevant factor of production, such as, for example, wages paid for labour. This is referred to as the functional distribution of income, because it shows how incomes are distributed for the relevant factor input. This chapter seeks to explain how the factors of production earn their rewards. These factor rewards are as follows:

> **Wages are the rewards for labour.**
> **Rent is the reward for land.**
> **Interest is the reward for capital.**
> **Profit is the reward for enterprise.**

Wages, rent, interest and profit are also called factor incomes. Each of these factors of production is demanded and supplied in their respective markets in a way that is similar to the goods market, although in factor markets the roles are reversed. For example, in the goods market, consumers demand goods and services and producers supply them. In the factor markets, producers demand land, labour, capital and enterprise, which are supplied by consumers who are also called households. This exchange is illustrated in figure 16.1.

Figure 16.1 shows how the goods and factor markets are linked in a simplified exchange. Firms demand factors of production to produce goods and services for sale and households provide these factor inputs for reward, for example, rent for land, wages for labour, interest for capital and profit for enterprise.

This is the factor market at work, labelled 'A', on the right-hand side of the figure. On the left-hand side, firms employ the factor inputs to create goods and services for sale. Households use their factor incomes to purchase this output at 'B'. In chapter 22, which discusses national income, the government and the international sector is added to these two sectors and the entire four-sector model is explained in more detail.

The section labelled 'A' explains how wages, for example, are determined with respect to labour. In the labour market, labour is determined by the demand and supply for labour

Derived demand

The demand for labour (as with the demand for any factor of production) is called a derived demand; this is defined as the demand for any factor of production that is related to the demand for what the factor can produce. For example, the demand for teachers is linked to the demand for education. Similarly, the demand for capital such as gardening tools, for example, is related to the demand for food. The derived demand for carpenters, masons, engineers, welders and bricklayers is each linked to the demand for houses or buildings.

The demand for labour is typically downward sloping, as in the goods market. This means that when wages are high, the demand for labour is low. The opposite is also true. In the same way that consumers demand more goods at lower prices, producers demand more labour when wages are low, as shown in figure 16.2.

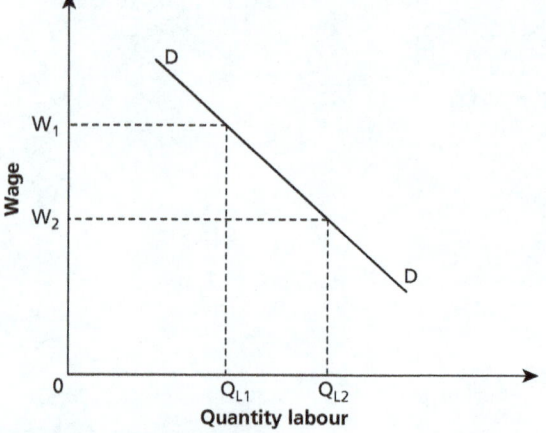

Figure 16.2 The demand for labour

Chapter 16 Theory of income distribution

Traditional economic theory of wages: the new classical theory

Traditional economic theory seeks to explain that factor rewards are determined by the marginal revenue productivity theory (MRP); this simply states that wages are based on the productivity of each additional unit of labour. The assumptions of this theory are that:

- Labour's output is sold in a perfect product market, meaning that there is one ruling price (see chapter 11 for revision).
- Labour is hired in a perfect labour market (see below for explanation).
- The firm is a profit maximiser.
- Production takes place in the short-run period.
- Technology is fixed in this period.

A perfect labour market is explained as one in which:

- Each worker has the same skill as any other worker (homogeneous).
- Each firm is a wage taker, because there are many sellers of labour and many buyers of labour who cannot by themselves influence the wage rate.
- There is perfect mobility of workers, i.e., workers can transfer into any other job with ease.
- Perfect knowledge exists, i.e., a worker knows immediately where every job exists and its going wage rate.
- There are no barriers to entry into any profession.

Marginal revenue productivity theory states that a profit-maximising firm would hire an additional worker as long as the marginal worker contributes as much to the revenue of the firm as the wage paid to him or her. The wage rate is called the marginal input factor cost. In other words, if your wage is $100 and the value of your output sold is $100 or more, then you would be hired. The theory is based on two simple factors:

1. The marginal physical product (MPP)
2. The marginal revenue product (MRP).

The marginal physical product

Figure 16.3 (below) shows the short-run product curve, the marginal physical product of labour (MPPL). The curve is downward sloping due to diminishing returns. Converting each worker's marginal output, the value of the marginal product (VMP) is calculated by multiplying the marginal physical product of the worker by the price of the output, that is:

MPP × P = VMP

Marginal revenue product (MRP), however, is determined by multiplying MPP by MR. Just as in a perfect market, P and MR are the same, the VMP and MRP are the same in a perfect labour market.

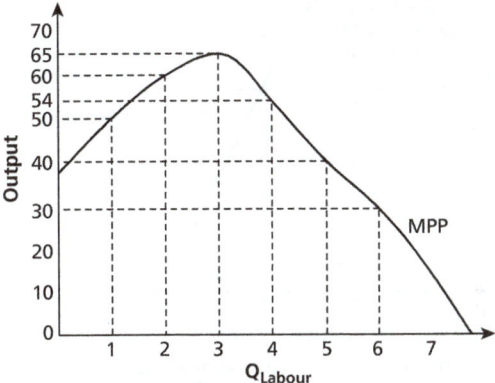

Figure 16.3 The marginal physical product of labour

Common error

Do not confuse the VMP with the MRP. Remember that VMP = MPP × P and MRP = MPP × MR. However, in a perfect market P = MR, so here VMP and MRP are the same.

Table 16.1 shows that it is possible to calculate VMP and MRP from information supplied in the table. See columns 5 and 6.

Refer to Table 16.1. The marginal physical product and MRP curves may be derived from the values in columns 3 and 4. To calculate VMP, simply multiply MPP by price, which in this example is the price of labour's output, equal to $2.

Table 16.1 Calculating VMP and MRP

No. of workers (1)	TPP (2)	MPP (3)	Price per unit (4)	VMP (MPP × AR) (5) = (3) × (4)	MRP (MPP × MR) (6) = (3) × (4) (P = MR)	Wage rate (7)
0	0	0				
1	16	16	$2.00	32	32	$30.00
2	35	19	$2.00	38	38	$30.00
3	60	25	$2.00	50	50	$30.00
4	84	24	$2.00	48	48	$30.00
5	105	21	$2.00	42	42	$30.00
6	120	15	$2.00	30	30	$30.00
7	128	8	$2.00	16	16	$30.00
8	130	2	$2.00	4	4	$30.00

Examples:

Worker 1 = output 16 × $2 = $32. To calculate MPP × MR in this example is the same as MPP × P.

Worker 2 = output 19 × $2 = $38. Remember, in a perfectly competitive market, MR and P are the same.

Since the firm is a profit-maximising firm it will hire where MC = MR, that is, the marginal input cost of labour (wage rate) is equal to MRP. Therefore, six workers will be hired at wage rate of $30.

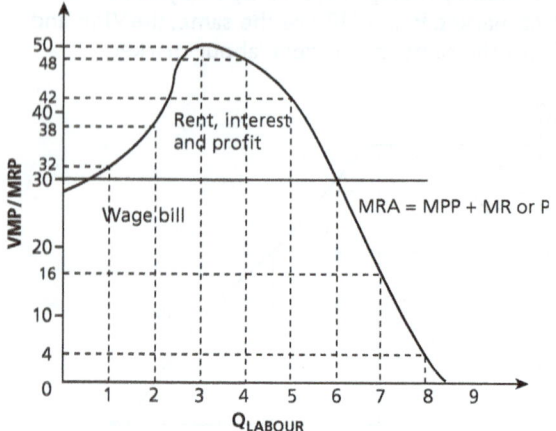

Figure 16.4 The value of the marginal product (VMP) and marginal revenue product (MRP)

Note in figure 16.4:

> The price of the product is $2.00.
> The wage rate is $30 for all workers.
> MPP is rising and falling due to increasing and diminishing returns to the variable factor. Note the rise and fall of MPP and that MRP is also following the same shape.
> VMP (MPP × P) and MRP (MPP × MR) are the same in a perfect market since P = MR.
> From worker 1 to 5 the MRP = VMP is higher than the wage of $30 (marginal input factor cost).
> Worker 6 is adding as much to cost as he or she does to revenue.

In figure 16.5, as the supply of labour increases, the wage rate falls and more workers are hired as a result. In other words, the MRP curve shows how much labour is demanded when the wage rate changes. It therefore functions as the short-run demand curve for labour, according to traditional economic theory.

The long-run demand curve for labour in an industry

The long-run demand curve of the industry is not the addition of the MRP curves of firms in the competitive industry. It is computed differently. Refer to figure 16.6.

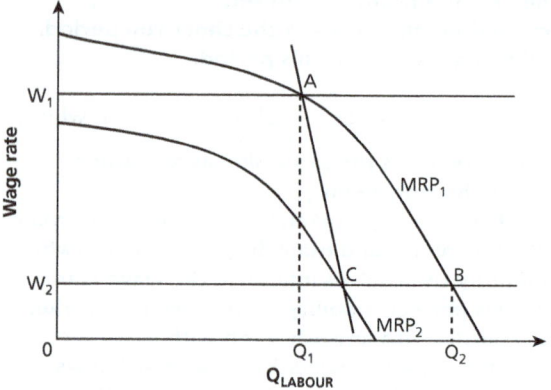

Figure 16.6 Long-run demand curve for labour in an industry

Note in figure 16.6:

> As the wage rate of W_1 falls to W_2, the quantity of labour hired increases from equilibrium A of Q_1 workers to equilibrium Q_2. Since this low rate applies to all employers, they will all hire more workers.
> The resulting increase in output would cause the price of the good in a competitive market to fall. This fall in price would cause the MRP_1 to shift to the left to MRP_2 and a new equilibrium of C.
> A line connecting equilibrium points A and C becomes the new industry curve.

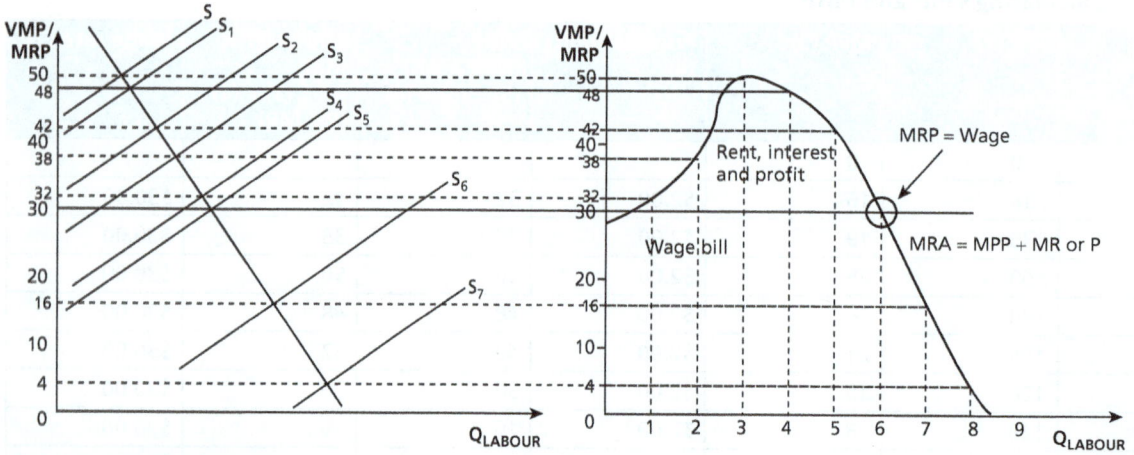

Figure 16.5 Hiring where MRP = Wage (profit maximisation)

> A shift in the MRP or demand curve for labour to the right will take place if productivity of labour or the price of the good changes positively.

MRP and the imperfect labour market

The demand curve or MRP curve for labour faced by a firm in an imperfect product market is different from that of a perfect market. If we change the assumption of MRP theory to an imperfect product market, the MRP curve would be to the left of the VMP. See Figures 16.7a, b and c.

Figure 16.7a shows marginal revenue in an imperfect product market. Figure 16.7b shows the VMP_1 (MPP × P) and MRP_1 (MPP × MR). Since MR is less than P in an imperfect market, the VMP and MRP are likewise not the same. The MRP curve will be to the left of the VMP_1 curve. Compared to a perfect market, less labour will be hired by a profit-maximising firm when the output is sold in an imperfect market. See figure 16.7d. At a wage rate of W_1, the quantity of labour demanded in an imperfect labour market (QL^*) is less than that demanded in a perfectly competitive labour market (QL_1).

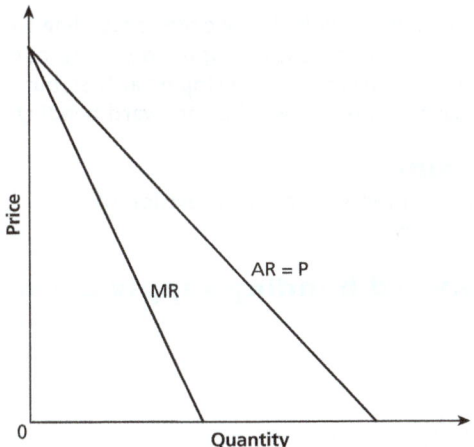

Figure 16.7a Imperfect product market

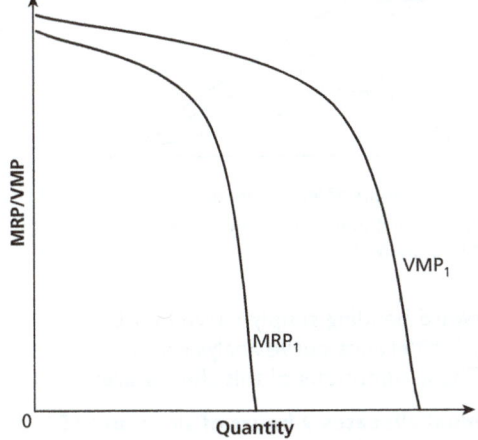

Figure 16.7b Imperfect labour market

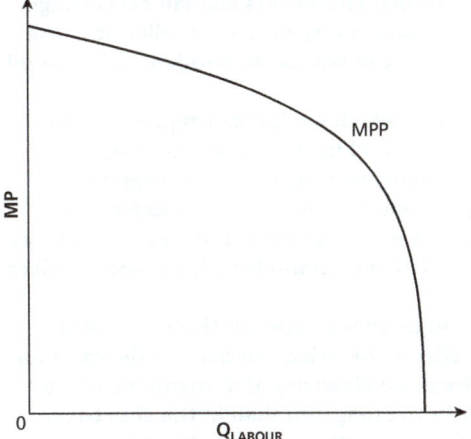

Figure 16.7c Marginal physical product

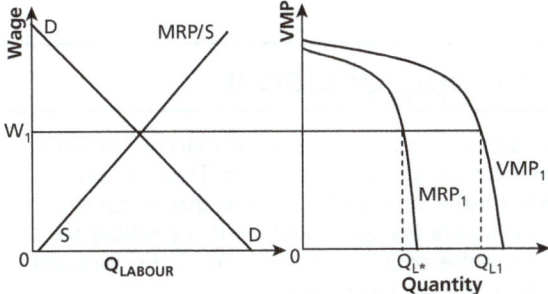

Figure 16.7d Less labour hired in an imperfect product market

Key points

The demand curve for labour in a perfectly competitive firm, according to traditional new classical theory, is the MRP curve. Since this curve determines the quantity of labour hired by a profit-maximising firm, labour will be hired where MRP = wage (MR = MC). Changes in productivity and prices will cause MRP_2 to shift to the right or left.

In an imperfect market the VMP and MRP are different because P and MR are not the same in an imperfect product market. Accordingly, the MRP curve will be to the left of the VMP_1, causing less labour to be hired, compared to a competitive labour market.

The price elasticity of demand for labour

Elasticity of demand for labour may be expressed as percentage change in quantity of labour divided by the percentage change in wage. There are four main factors that affect the elasticity of demand for labour. These are:

1. **The wage elasticity of demand for labour is linked to price elasticity of demand for the good or service that labour produces.** If, for example, demand for gasoline is inelastic then demand for petroleum engineers will be similarly so.
2. **The percentage of total cost of production that labour represents affects the elasticity of demand for labour.** In the oil industry, for example, if labour costs are small compared to capital, then elasticity of demand of labour is less than one. If

labour, therefore, represents a small percentage of total cost then a wage increase will not cause a fall in quantity of labour demanded, as in the oil industry.

3. The ease with which capital can replace labour makes the demand for labour elastic; for example, mechanical sugar cane harvesters replacing human labour. To further explain, if labour can be easily replaced then a rise in wages will cause a fall in demand for labour and a switch to capital.
4. The time adjustment between the short- and long-run affects the price elasticity of demand for labour. The price elasticity of demand for labour is greater in the long-run than in the short-run because the longer time period allows for a greater flow of information and decision making.

The supply of labour

So far only one side of the labour market has been explained, that is, the demand side. This section focuses on the supply of labour so that when the two curves are brought together, it is possible to determine the equilibrium wage rate in perfect and imperfect market structures.

The supply of labour may be analysed in four ways:

1. Individual supply curve
2. Supply curve facing the firms
3. Supply curve facing the industry
4. Supply curve of the country.

The individual supply curve

In figure 16.8, the individual supply curve simply shows the number of hours that an individual is willing to supply to a firm at a given wage per time period, for example $10 per hour per 12-hour day. Expectedly, the curve would slope upward from left to right.

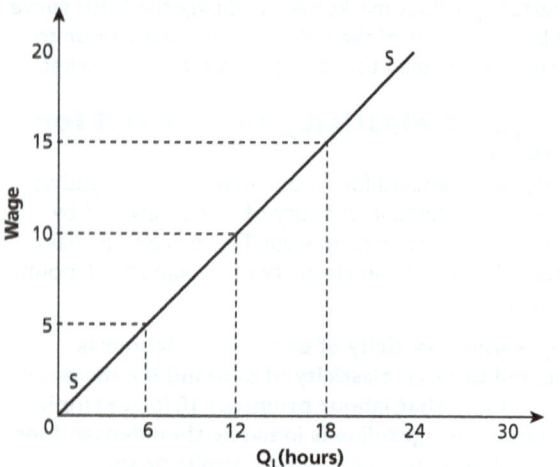

Figure 16.8 Individual supply curve

This implies that more hours will be supplied at a higher wage. A rational person will want higher wages for more work simply because work is a disutility, that is, not entirely enjoyable and involves a sacrifice of leisure.

Working more hours requires the equivalent compensation of wages. This reasoning is explained by income and substitution effects. When wages rise, a rational worker will choose to work more since not working means giving up income and consumption. The worker is therefore substituting work for leisure hours.

This is called the substitution effect of wages. The worker also experiences an income effect of wages. More hours of work earn a higher income, which could be used to purchase leisure. For this reason, when incomes or wages become increasingly higher, the income effect leads to increased hours of work. These combined effects explain the upward sloping curve.

In practice, this may not be so. Many people prefer to work fewer hours when wages increase. A negative income effect may cancel out the substitution effect. It is the same reason workers choose not to work on Christmas Day or any special holiday because they value leisure over more work.

Key points
The supply curve of an individual worker, according to classical theory, is left to right and upward sloping, but in real life it is likely to be upward sloping at first, but after an increase in wages it will be backward bending.

Student hint
Refer back to chapter 4 for a quick revision of indifference curves.

The backward bending supply curve of labour

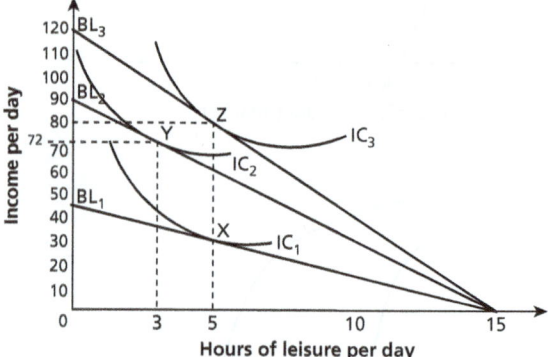

Figure 16.9 Backward bending supply curve: indifference curve analysis

The backward bending supply curve may be explained by indifference curve analysis as in figure 16.9. The assumptions of this theory are:

› An individual allocates 9 hours of sleep and 15 hours of work and leisure in a 24-hour day.
› If, for example, he or she chooses 5 hours of leisure, then they will choose to work 10 hours.

Chapter 16 Theory of income distribution

The individual's choices can be illustrated on an indifference curve, which shows different combinations of work (income) and leisure that yield the same level of utility. These curves are convex to the origin, similar to those in demand analysis, indicating that as leisure is given up it must be compensated for by higher income. These three curves move outward from the point of origin to indicate increasing levels of utility. The budget lines show combinations of income (work) and leisure that are affordable.

At a wage of $3 per hour, a sugar cane worker chooses between $45 (15 × $3) and 15 hours of leisure and selects point X, a combination of 5 hours of leisure time and 10 hours of work ($30), shown on BL_1 and the indifference curve IC_1.

On budget line BL_2 and indifference curve IC_2, when wages are raised to $6 an hour the choice is between $90 (15 × $6) or 15 hours of leisure. Point Y is chosen on the budget line BL_2 increasing working hours from 10 to 12 hours, the worker therefore opting for 3 hours of leisure and earning $72 per day.

When, however, the wage rate is increased to $8 per hour the individual now has to choose between $120 (15 × 8) and 15 hours of leisure. On this occasion, combination Z or 10 hours of work is equal to $80. Since an increase in income causes the individual to work fewer hours, the income effect of this increase is negative. Working more (12 hours) at $6 an hour is called the substitution effect.

Figure 16.10 shows how the supply curve of labour in this example is actually a backward bending supply curve, because the downward negative income effect is stronger than the upward substitution effect of the curve from wage rate $6 to $8 per hour.

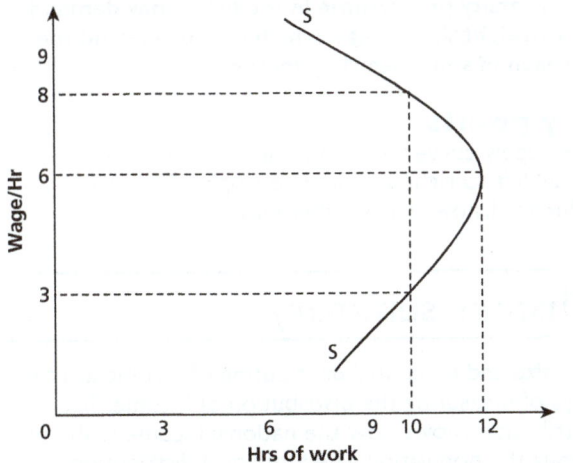

Figure 16.10 The backward bending supply curve of labour

Key points
When a worker supplies more hours of labour when the wage rate is increased, this is called the substitution effect of a wage increase. If the wage is increased further, workers may feel they can work fewer hours because they value their leisure. This is called the negative income effect of a wage increase. The supply curve is therefore backward bending.

The supply curve of labour to firms
Since the firm in a perfectly competitive industry is one of very many, it cannot influence the wage rate by itself and therefore becomes a wage taker. The supply curve of labour to the firm indicates the price of labour to the firm, which is the wage rate set by the perfect labour market as shown in figure 16.11.

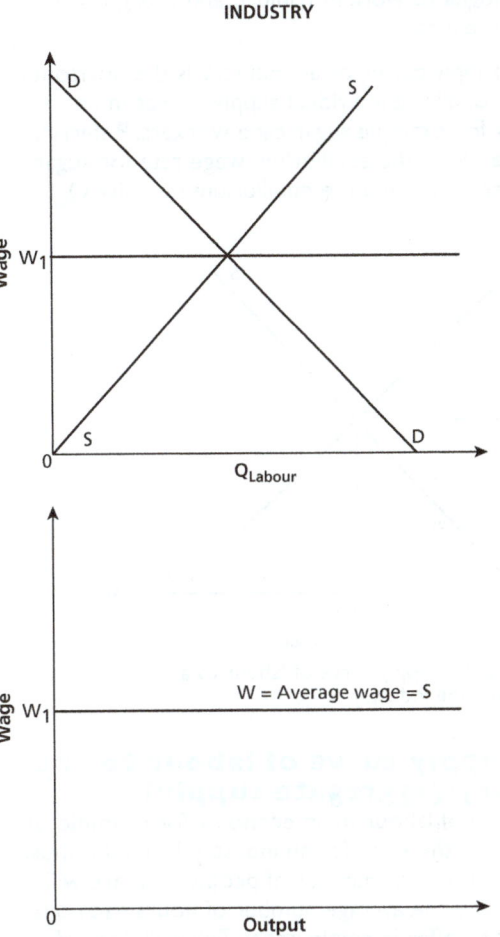

Figure 16.11 The supply curve of labour to a perfect market

The supply curve of labour to an industry
This supply curve will be upward sloping because high wages will attract more hours of labour. Whether the curve shifts to the right or left would depend on the conditions of supply. For example:

› The skill and experience of the worker
› Job satisfaction/dissatisfaction
› The conditions of the working environment
› Non-salaried benefits, e.g., 'perks', such as medical insurance/pension schemes
› The elasticity of supply to a particular occupation.

The two main factors in this case that affect the price elasticity of supply are occupational and geographical mobility.

Occupational mobility is the ease with which a person can move from one job to another. In a perfect market, a worker is considered completely mobile because he or she is as multi-skilled as all other workers.

Geographical mobility is the ease with which someone can shift to another job in another location or region. If a worker is not unduly concerned about social ties or the inconvenience of moving, he or she is geographically mobile; for example, moving from Antigua to work in Trinidad and Tobago with considerable ease.

The supply curve for an industry is the horizontal addition of all the individual supply curves in an industry, for example sugar cane workers. Referring to figure 16.12, the equilibrium wage rate for sugar harvesters is W_1 and the equilibrium quantity Q_{L1}.

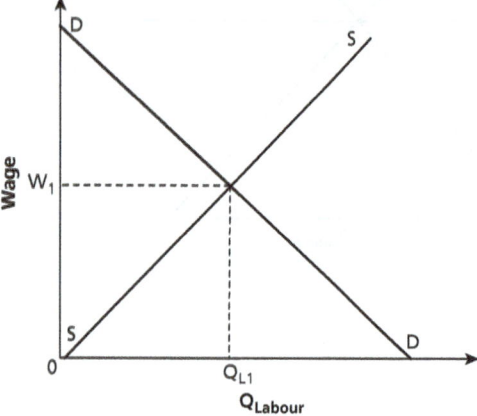

Figure 16.12 Supply curve of labour to a country's sugar cane industry

The supply curve of labour to the country (aggregate supply)

The supply of labour to an economy, for example, St Lucia, is not the same for an industry. Instead it must recognise the total number of people who are willing to work and the average number of hours each one is willing to offer in employment. This will depend therefore on the following factors:

- Size of the population: this will determine the supply of labour to all industries.
- The age composition of the population: there are different age groups in the population. Some populations have a high proportion of old to young. This is an important factor that determines the supply of labour.
- The labour force: this consists of people who are of the legal working age, for example, from 18 to 60 years and who offer themselves for work. They are also called the economically active population. This issue will be considered in a little more detail in the chapter 18.
- The length of the working week and number of holidays available to the labour force are also factors that determine the number of hours supplied for employment.
- The activity rate, or the labour force participation rate, is the percentage of the population in the labour force.

- The rate of income taxes has a discouraging effect on low-income workers who feel 'overtaxed' and alienated. Taxes are a disincentive to work and may be a factor that determines the number of hours offered in employment (see the Laffer curve in chapter 26).
- The availability of unemployment benefits may also act as a disincentive to work, since a person who collects $200 a week in unemployment benefits may not be encouraged to take up employment paying $230 per week. The reasoning is that working 8 hours for an extra $30 is not worth the sacrifice.

Elasticity of supply for labour

As in the goods market, the elasticity of supply of labour is the percentage change in quantity of labour supplied divided by the percentage change in wages. The supply of labour can be elastic, inelastic, infinite, unitary or zero elastic depending on the following factors.

- The level of unemployment: an unemployed pool of labour makes the supply of labour elastic if there is small change in the wage rate, since available labour can be sourced very quickly.
- The level of training: doctors and lawyers tend to take long periods in training before joining their industries, hence the price elasticity of supply of labour is inelastic if the wage rate is increased.
- The occupational and geographical mobility of labour: this determines how quickly a vacancy can be filled if the wage rate increases.
- Qualifications and skills required for employment: if qualification and skills for a job are high, the price elasticity of the supply of labour will be inelastic. For example, pre-qualification to a university programme in medicine may demand a straight 'A' average, which may be beyond the reach of some aspiring doctors.

Key points

The supply curve to a firm, industry and country are all left to right and upward sloping. They are influenced, however, by different factors.

Chapter summary

The size and functional distribution of income are two ways of measuring the distribution of income. Size distribution shows how the national income is shared among the population. The functional distribution shows how the national income is distributed among the factors of production.

Derived demand is defined as the demand for any factor of production related to the demand for what the factor can produce. The demand curve for labour in a perfectly competitive firm is the MRP curve. For a profit-maximising firm, labour will be hired where MRP = wage (MR = MC). Changes in productivity and prices will cause MRP to shift to the right or left.

The supply curve of an individual worker is left to right and upward sloping. In real life it is likely to be upward sloping at first, but after an increase in wages it will be backward bending.

Practice questions

1. Outline the marginal productivity theory.
2. Use the marginal productivity theory to explain the demand curve for an input under a competitive market structure.

Number of workers	Output (units)	Marginal revenue product ($)	Total revenue ($)
1	10	100	100
2	28	80	180
3	24	60	240
4	28	40	280
5	30	20	300

3. Examine the table above and answer the following questions.
   a. What is the marginal product of the third worker?
   b. Calculate the price of the product.
   c. If the wage rate is $20 per worker, how many workers will be hired?

Multiple choice questions

1. Which of the following will cause the demand for labour curve to shift to the right?
   a. A decrease in the price of the product
   b. An increase in the price of a substitute factor of production
   c. A rise in the wage rate
   d. A decrease in the production of labour.

2. Which of the following terms explains the relationship between factor rewards and costs of production?
   a. Inverse
   b. Direct
   c. Indirect
   d. Negative.

3. The MRP curve slopes downward because:
   a. A firm will pay more to attract factors from other uses.
   b. Less of a factor is demanded at lower prices.
   c. More of a factor is supplied at lower prices.
   d. The marginal physical product is constantly falling.

4. Which of the following is explained by the theory of income distribution?
   a. How wages and salaries are earned among income earners
   b. How factor rewards are allocated to the factors of production
   c. Government's attempt to address the problem of income inequalities
   d. Government's efforts to redistribute incomes to the poor.

5. Which one of the following could cause a perfectly competitive firm's marginal revenue product curve for labour (MRPL) to shift to the right?
   a. An increase in wages
   b. A fall in productivity
   c. An increase in the labour supply
   d. A rise in the price of the final product.

INTRODUCTORY ECONOMICS A TEXTBOOK FOR CAPE ECONOMICS STUDENTS

17 The interaction of labour markets and unions

Chapter 17 The interaction of labour markets and unions

LEARNING OBJECTIVES

- Explain wage determination in perfect and imperfect markets.
- Analyse the effect of unions on labour markets.
- Differentiate between transfer earnings and economic rent.

REQUIRED KNOWLEDGE

- Demand and supply of labour
- Marginal revenue productivity (MRP) theory
- Consumer and product surplus.

TOPIC VALUE

Those people who wish to be paid a high salary set about pursuing lucrative occupations. But what determines wages is not so straightforward. Some of these issues are explored in this chapter.

Unions are important to the working class since they seek the interest of the worker.

Wage determination

Introduction
Since prices are determined by the forces of demand and supply, the same forces apply to the labour market. In some industries, however, wages are determined partly by the actions of labour unions representing given categories of workers.

Wages in a perfectly competitive industry
As figure 17.1 illustrates, Q_{L1} of labour is demanded at a wage of W_1. In this perfectly competitive market all firms are wage takers. The equilibrium wage rate is W_1 and the number of workers employed is Q_{L1} of workers.

The demand curve (the MRP) will shift to the right if there is a:

- Productivity increase
- Rise in the product price
- Rise in the price of capital, requiring substitution of labour.

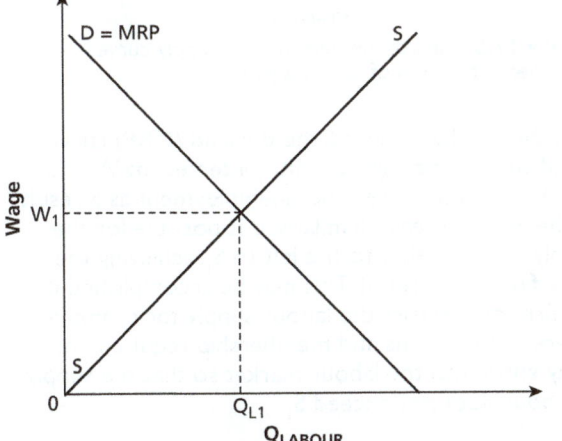

Figure 17.1 The equilibrium wage rate in a perfectly competitive labour market

The supply curve for labour will shift to the right indicating an increase if:

- There is an increase in the size of the population.
- Conditions in other industries worsen, causing occupational movement of labour.
- Perks or job satisfaction exist in one industry compared to others.

Figure 17.1 shows the manner in which wages are determined in a competitive market, and figure 17.2 shows how they are determined in an imperfect labour market.

Wages in an imperfect labour market

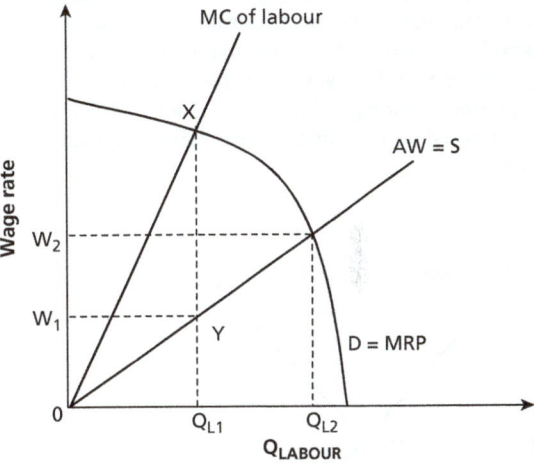

Figure 17.2 Wage determination in an imperfect labour market

An imperfect labour market means the firm is a sole buyer of labour. In this case the firm is not a monopolist but is instead called a monopsonist. For example, Caribbean Airlines Ltd is the main purchaser of pilot services in the Caribbean and therefore may be called a monopsonist. See figure 17.2.

In figure 17.2, the demand curve for labour is the familiar MRP curve. Note, however, the supply curve of labour is not a straight line, as in perfect competition, but an upward sloping supply curve.

Note again that the MC of labour is higher than the average cost (AC) of labour because, in order to attract a new worker, a higher wage must be paid as an incentive to join the firm. If the new worker is paid this higher wage, then the workforce must also be similarly paid. The change in the wage bill is not only for the extra worker but the other workers as well. For example, if ten workers are working for $9 an hour the wage bill is $90. If an eleventh worker is given a wage of $10 then it is assumed that the entire workforce will also be entitled to receive $10 an hour.

The total wage bill will therefore be 11 × $10 = $110, a change of $20. The MC of labour is $20, while the average wage is $10. The MC curve in figure 17.2 is therefore higher than the average wage curve.

The profit-maximising firm will hire labour according to MRP = MC at point X, resulting in QL_1 of labour being hired. They are then paid the lowest or average wage W_1 (connect QL_1 to the AC curve to get W_1). Note if this firm operates in a perfectly competitive labour market, the equilibrium wage would be W_2 and the quantity of labour QL_2.

The introduction of a union in a perfect labour market

Labour unions seek the best interests of workers whom they represent. They focus on issues such as fair wages, promotion, working conditions, protection against unfair dismissal and discrimination against workers. These are among their many and other varied functions. Primary among these functions are wage negotiations. In Figures 17.3 and 17.4 the introduction of a union in a perfect labour market is analysed.

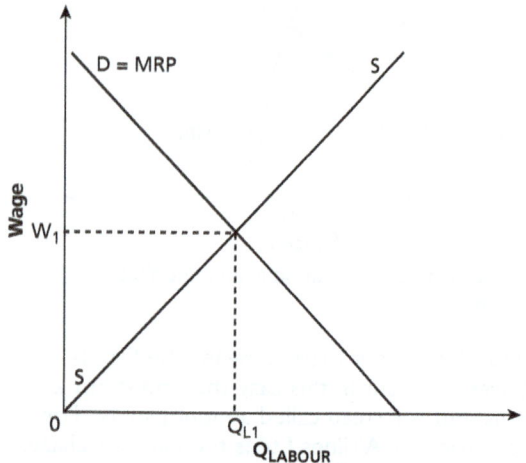

Figure 17.3 Before union-negotiated wage rate

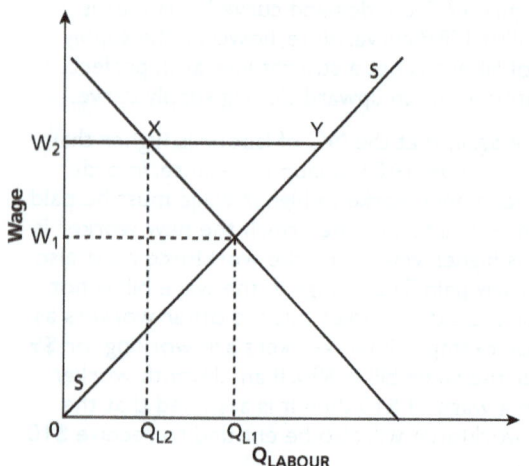

Figure 17.4 After union-negotiated wage rate

Before the introduction of a union, the equilibrium quantity of labour and wage rate was QL_1 and W_1 respectively. Figure 17.4 shows that the union seeks to raise the wage rate above W_1, causing demand for labour to fall at the newly negotiated wage rate of W_2. Since no labour will be supplied under the wage rate W_2 then W_2 XYS is, in effect, the new supply curve of labour. Note also there is an excess of labour at wage rate W_2, equal to XY. If the union has total control over the surplus labour XY, then the wage rate will be W_2. If not, then some or all of this surplus labour may cooperate with the firm to work for less than W_2, and therefore weaken the union's bargaining position.

It is not necessarily true that there will be a reduction in the quantity of labour hired by a firm if a union-negotiated wage of W_2 is accepted. It would be possible to leave employment unaffected if the demand curve shifts to the right or the supply curve to the left, thereby preserving the equilibrium quantity of W_1. Refer to figure 17.5.

Recall that the demand curve is the MRP curve and would shift to the right under certain conditions, which are:

> **An increase in productivity**
> **An increase in the price of the product or service**
> **A rise in the price of capital requiring a substitution of capital for labour.**

It is possible for the union and the monopsonist to agree to a productivity deal or a price increase, particularly if price elasticity of demand for the good is inelastic.

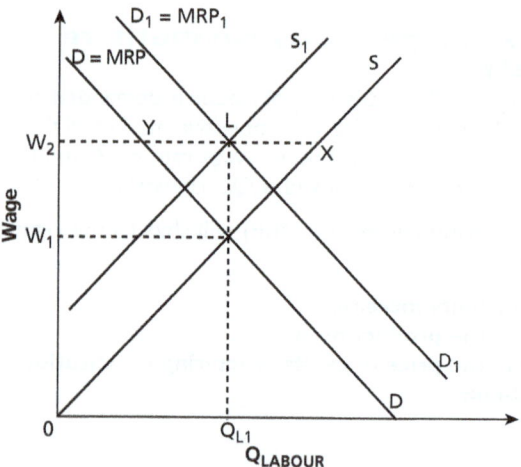

Figure 17.5 Shifts of the demand and supply curves to preserve the level of unemployment

If this can be achieved, the demand (MRP) curve could shift to the right to MRP_1 intersecting W_2 XS at L. In this way, there is no unemployment as a result of the wage increase. Similarly, it is possible for the supply curve to shift to the left to S_1, achieving the same favourable result. This may be accomplished if the firm can restrict the labour supply, for example, where qualifications and membership requirements delay entry into the labour market so that the supply of labour does not exceed S_1.

Unions and an imperfect labour market

A union could also negotiate a higher wage rate with a monopsonistic buyer of labour and, in fact, increase both wage and employment in the firm. Refer to figures 17.6 and 17.7.

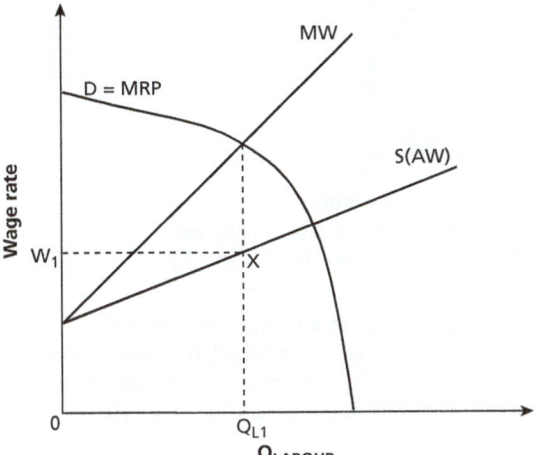

Figure 17.6 Before union intervention

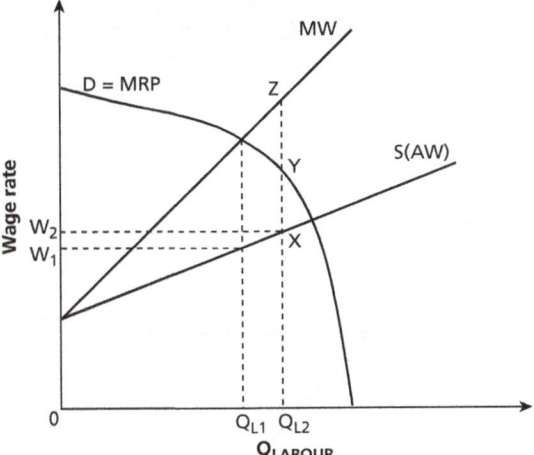

Figure 17.7 Post union intervention

Figure 17.6 represents the familiar monopsonist wage of W_1, when MW is equated with MRP. QL_1 of labour is paid the average wage of W_1. With the entry of a union, a wage of W_2 is negotiated above the non-union wage of W_1, in effect, making W_2XS the new supply (AW) curve, as shown in figure 17.7.

Note that the upward MW curve is drawn to reflect the AW curve (it is higher). A new AW curve (W_2XS) requires a new MW curve as well. The horizontal position of W_2XS also functions as the MC of labour or marginal wage.

To construct a MW curve related to the upward sloping portion of the AW curve XS would result in the MW curve ZMW.

The MW curve related to W_2XS consists of two portions, W_2X and ZMW. The dotted line connecting these two gives an odd-shaped MW curve, W_2XZ (MW). The odd reconstruction of the MW curve results in a profit-maximising QL_2 of labour because this is where MW = MRP; QL_2 of labour are then paid W_2 (connect QL_2 to the AW curve).

The conclusion is that an increase in wages from W_1 to W_2 has also raised employment from QL_1 to QL_2. It should be noted, however, that the ability of unions to influence wages may also be determined by:

› Public support
› The extent of a strike fund
› The elasticity of demand for the product and labour producing it
› Solidarity with other unions
› The state of the economy
› The strength or power of the union itself
› Government industrial relations law
› The role that employer organisations play collectively by banding together to counteract union demand for high wages.

Key points

A union-negotiated wage increase may affect labour markets differently. In a perfect labour market employment may fall, but if the demand and supply curves can shift to the right or left there will be no loss of employment. In a monopsonistic labour market it is possible for both wage rate and employment to increase.

Transfer earnings and economic rent

The transfer earnings of a factor of production are the minimum payments necessary to keep that factor in its current employment. It is also the supply price of a factor of production.

For example, a taxi driver in St Vincent will operate a taxi on a particular route provided that he makes the minimum amount of EC$100 a day. This is a transfer earning to labour to prevent him from 'transferring' his taxi to another use. However, if he makes EC$250 when a tourist hires him for a day to go to the beach, then he not only makes a transfer payment but an extra EC$150, which is called economic rent.

Economic rent is therefore any surplus over a factor's transfer earnings.

Common error

Do not confuse transfer earnings with transfer payments, which are money transfers paid without an equivalent exchange of goods or services, for example old age assistance.

If a firm cannot make normal profit it must leave the industry. In this case, for the factor of production enterprise, normal profit is the transfer earnings of the firm and above normal profit is the economic rent of the firm because it represents the surplus of profit over normal profit. With land and capital it is the same. If a landlord gets more than the asking rent for his land then he or she realises not only his transfer earnings, but also economic rent.

Diagrammatically, transfer earnings are identified as the area to the right and under the supply curve. The area above and to the left of the supply curve and under the price line is known as economic rent. It is also called producer surplus. See figure 17.8.

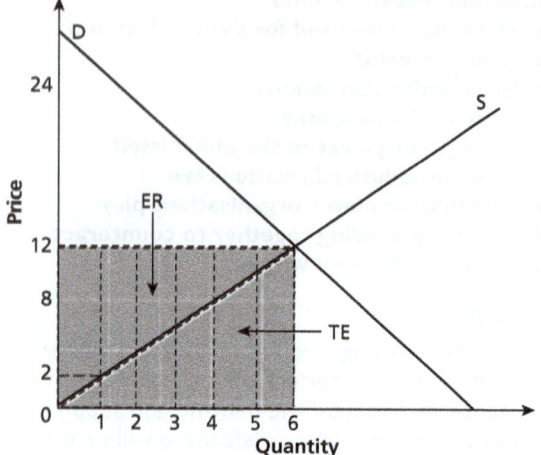

Figure 17.8 Transfer earnings and economic rent for fried chicken

In the market for fried chicken, 1 snack box may be supplied for $2 by the firm, but the market price is $12. The transfer earnings are $2 and economic rent is $10. Similarly, for the fourth unit transfer earnings are $8 and economic rent $4 ($12−$8). There is no economic rent for the sixth unit, but the firm is making its transfer earnings. Totalled together, the vertically shaded triangle above the supply curve is the sum of economic rent.

Transfer earnings, economic rent and elasticity of supply

Transfer earnings and economic rent vary with elasticity of supply in any market. See figures 17.9 and 17.10.

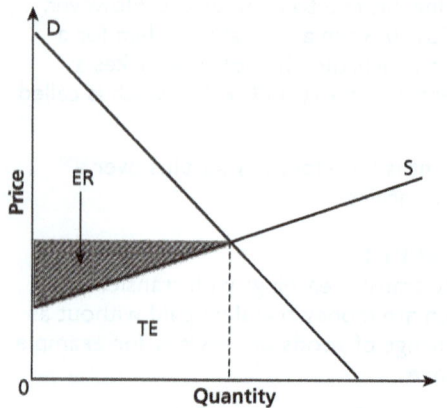

Figure 17.9 When PES > 1 economic rent is low

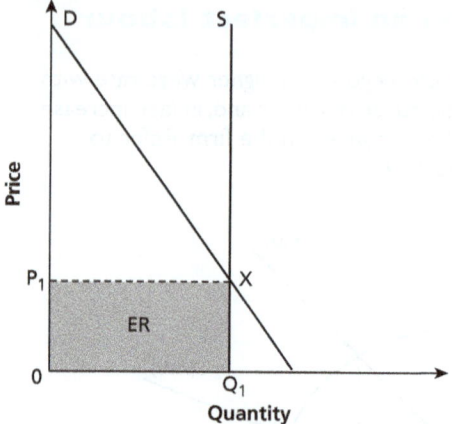

Figure 17.10 When PES = 0 economic rent is low economic rent is maximised (TE = 0)

The figures show that an elastic supply will cause economic rent to be reduced, but when price elasticity of supply = 0 economic rent is maximised and transfer earnings equal zero (figure 17.10).

Price elasticity of supply

In figure 17.11 when price elasticity of supply is infinite (perfectly elastic) transfer earnings are maximised by the area $P_1 X_1 Q_1 O$. When economic rent is temporary it is referred to as quasi-rent.

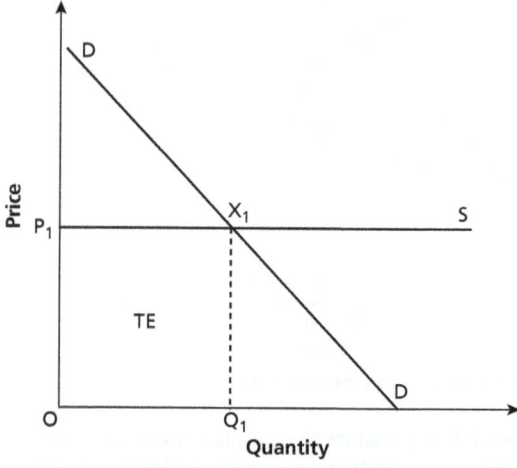

Figure 17.11 Maximum transfer earning

Key points

Transfer earnings are the rewards to factors of production in their next best employment. Alternatively, they are the payment to a factor that is necessary to prevent it 'transferring' to another use. Any surplus over transfer earnings is called economic rent. Supply elasticity is a main determinant of economic rent. Therefore, for superstars like Usain Bolt, Chris Gayle, Brian Lara and Rihanna, who have unique talents, their earnings are mostly economic rent.

Wage differentials

There would be no difference in wages if all labour markets were perfectly competitive. However, in real life everyone makes a different wage. Traditional economic theory states that when wages are higher in one industry than another, there will be a movement from the low-wage to the high-wage industry over time. In the long-run equilibrium everyone will earn the same wage.

However, this analysis assumes perfect competition. In reality, perfect labour markets do not exist and the majority of wage differentials stem from the imperfection of many labour markets existing alongside each other. It is for this and other reasons that differences in wages exist. The main reasons are:

- Imperfect labour markets
- Separation of labour markets by barriers
- Different demand and supply conditions, and elasticity of demand and supply, in different markets
- Net maximum advantage of a job where the non-wage benefits may outweigh low wages, e.g., high job satisfaction or ease and convenience of commuting.

Imperfect labour markets and wage differentials

A monopsonist as sole buyer of labour has the power to influence the wage rate. See figure 17.12.

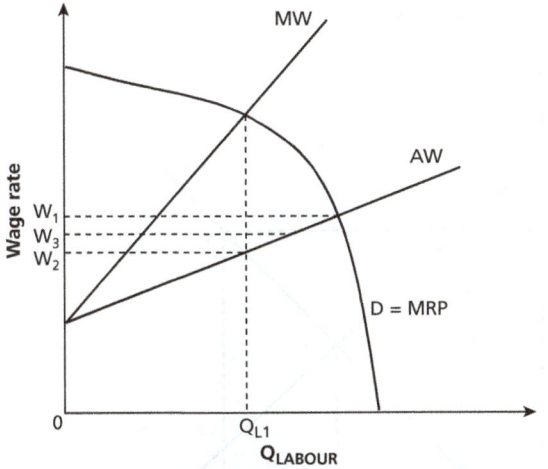

Figure 17.12 Wages determined by a monopsonist labour market

Note that under a monopsonist the wage is W_2, whereas in a perfect labour market it is W_1; therefore, the difference in wages is due to monopoly (monopsony) power.

Also, a strong union (which is in fact a monopoly supplier) may also bargain for higher wages. In figure 17.12, the union-negotiated wage may be W_3.

Thirdly, a monopolist in the goods and services industry may pay a high wage simply because the price of the product is high. This would influence the marginal revenue product of the worker.

The high wage may also act as an incentive, increasing the productivity of the worker. Both productivity and the price of the output influence the MRP of a worker and therefore the demand curve. If a powerful union is bargaining with this particular monopolist, higher wages could be negotiated from higher profits in a productivity deal.

The separation of markets and wage differentials

Owing to occupational and geographical barriers, workers may be unable to cross over into another industry to take advantage of higher wages that exist there. As a result, that market may be insulated from free entry of labour and competition for jobs. Here are some examples.

Long internships and apprenticeships for young doctors, lawyers and in some craft industries are common in most societies, and these restrict the free flow of labour into these markets.

Likewise, very high qualifications for a job, or membership association requirements, can cause high wages to persist in those sectors, even in the long-run. For example, the medical and legal professions require membership enlistment in order to practise.

And finally, there may be ethnic or gender discrimination in a market, which results in lower than average wages for these groups; and this too may be a barrier to entry.

Different demand and supply conditions and elasticities of various labour markets and their link to different wages

Most of the factors outlined in respect of separation of markets also apply to supply conditions that may be different in each market. Gender and ethnic discrimination, qualifications, long internships, duration of training and occupational and geographical mobility, are all factors that impact on the supply of labour and indeed the elasticity of supply.

There are other factors that may affect supply conditions. For example, different workers have various skills, talents and abilities that cause their supply to be very restricted; for example, famous sportsmen such as Argentinian Lionel Messi and Brazilian Neymar have unique talents that not only cause their supply curve to be positioned to the left but to be very inelastic indeed. See figure 17.13.

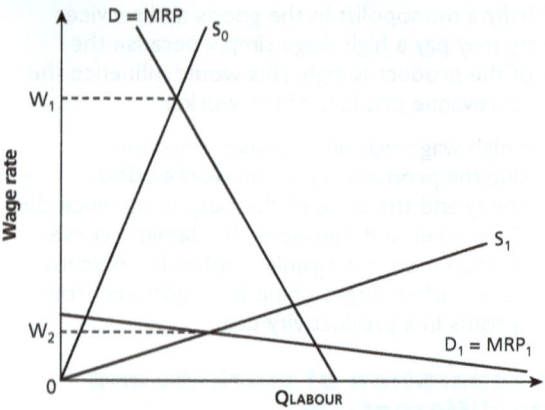

Figure 17.13 Difference in wages due to elasticity of demand and supply for labour

For a superstar, the supply curve is very much to the left and very inelastic in supply. Whereas the supply curve S_1 for a janitor is very much flatter and to the right, since there are many people with a similar skill level and experience who can do that job.

Note the position of the demand curve for the superstars or someone like a brain surgeon. It is to the right, since they are very skilled, talented and productive and, as a result, their fees are very high. Their MRP curve is therefore to the right. It is also inelastic in demand because they are not easily replaced by either man or machine.

The demand curve for a janitor is also influenced by productivity. Since the skill level for a janitor is low, his productivity and MRP are also low, resulting in the MRP curve D_1 positioned to the left and very elastic because demand for his services is elastic. Note their different wages: W_1 for superstars and brain surgeons, and W_2 for janitors.

Net maximum advantage and wage differences

Job seekers always consider other aspects of a job rather than just its wages. If a job's wage is low but gives considerable job satisfaction, provides security, is near to home, and the conditions of work or worker morale are pleasing, all of these benefits compensate for low wages and maximise the worker's 'advantage'. Similarly, if the above conditions are absent an employer may pay a higher wage to compensate for the disadvantages of the job.

Hence the reason for higher wages in dangerous jobs, for example miners, oil-well drillers, drivers of vehicles carrying radioactive waste or crop dusters. Higher wages are also paid as compensation to persons working in isolation, or extended hours. These differences in wages are referred to as 'compensating or equalising differentials' according to Adam Smith. Wages may also differ in the same profession due to:

› Security
› Gender
› Qualification and experience
› Flat rate versus piece rate of pay.

Differences in wages are also noticeable in private versus public sectors, in rural versus urban industries and in a boom economy versus a recessionary economy.

Key points

Wages differ because labour markets are imperfect. The power of unions, different demand and supply conditions and elasticities, the barriers between markets, and the maximum net advantage, are some of the factors that may explain why wages do not tend towards equality.

Minimum wage

A national minimum wage is one enacted by law to help raise the living standards of workers who would be vulnerable to low incomes. The national minimum wage is therefore a floor or minimum price for the sellers of labour and represents the government's attempt to redistribute incomes and solve the free market's failure to distribute incomes more equitably.

To work effectively, the floor wage will have to be set above the wages of the lowest paid workers in the economy.

According to traditional economics, the effect of a minimum wage on the labour market is similar to a union-negotiated wage in a competitive labour market.

The three basic consequences of the minimum wage rate could be identified as the effect on the:

› **Number employed**
› **Number unemployed**
› **Level of earnings.**

See figure 17.14.

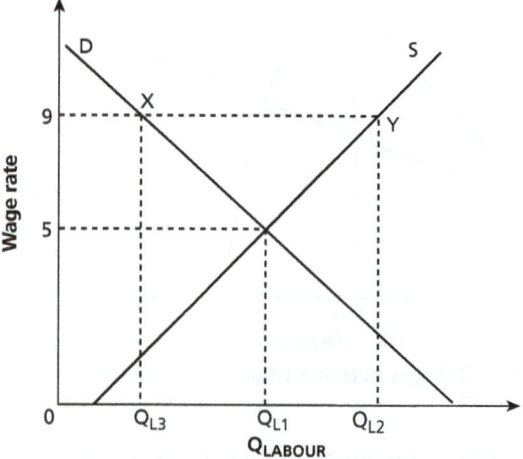

Figure 17.14 Introduction of minimum wage in a perfectly competitive labour market

The current rate of employment is QL_1 before the floor wage is introduced. When a minimum wage of $9.00 per hour is introduced QL_2 is supplied; therefore, $QL_2 QL_3$ represents unemployment or surplus labour. Earnings for QL_2 of labour, however, will rise from $5.00 to $9.00 per hour. In spite of this theoretical argument, there have been arguments for and against a national minimum wage. These are presented in table 17.1.

Table 17.1 **Arguments for and against a national minimum wage**

For	Against
Employment may be increased by a firm with monopsonist power. Firms do not release workers because of high recruitment costs and would train their workers to earn their new wage.	A minimum wage causes unemployment.
Minimum wage would not necessarily cause inflation, e.g., if workers regard minimum wage as a boost to their job security and therefore work harder, increasing productivity.	It causes inflation since wages are a high percentage of firms' costs.
There is unlikely to be a ripple effect, as minimum wage affects only those at the very bottom of the pay scales.	Persons who work for less than the minimum wage will become unemployed because they are not worth the new minimum wage.
Minimum wage does not necessarily cause export uncompetitiveness because other countries also have minimum wage laws.	Minimum wage would cause a ripple or demonstration effect, pushing other higher wages further up to maintain gaps in wages.
Foreign direct investment is unaffected as this generally uses high-skilled workers, rather than low-skilled ones.	Minimum wage discourages foreign direct investment. Higher wages may cause a firm to be uncompetitive in export markets.
	Minimum wage does not raise living standards because the unemployed are unaffected by it.

Chapter summary

Minimum wages represent government action to solve the problem of labour market failure caused by an inequitable distribution of income. It is an example of a price floor that is intended to: raise the living standard; redistribute income; and correct equity market failure.

Traditional economics theorises that a minimum wage causes surplus labour and unemployment but raises earnings for those who remain employed.

Practice questions

1. **Using demand and supply curves, illustrate and explain how a minimum wage law will affect the labour market.**
2. **Define the term 'value of the marginal product of labour'.**
3. **Explain the difference between labour force and potential labour force.**
4. **Distinguish between size and functional income distribution and classify the distributions.**
5. **John operates a small business that accumulated revenues totalling $980,000 in 2005. He paid $49,000 to his landlord, $147,000 to the bank and he had $196,000 remaining after paying his staff. Using the four major economic factors of production, answer the following questions.**
   a. **State how much was earned by each factor of production.**
   b. **Name the reward accruing to each factor.**
   c. **Indicate the percentage of the revenue received by each factor of production.**

INTRODUCTORY ECONOMICS A TEXTBOOK FOR CAPE ECONOMICS STUDENTS

18 Interest, profit and rent

Chapter 18 Interest, profit and rent

LEARNING OBJECTIVES

- Define, explain and illustrate interest, profit and rent.

REQUIRED KNOWLEDGE

- Concepts of demand and supply
- Marginal revenue productivity theory
- Profit maximisation
- Derived demand.

TOPIC VALUE

Interest, profit and rent play a vital role in our ability to create wealth for ourselves and, by extension, for the economy.

Introduction

According to conventional marginal revenue productivity theory, the rate of interest is the price of capital, in much the same way that wages are the price of hiring labour. In fact, interest is much more than the price of capital, it is also the price of borrowing money or financial capital that may finance any kind of expenditure.

The interest rate is explained by the demand for and supply of loanable funds in the same way that prices are determined in a perfectly competitive market.

The supply of loanable funds

Loanable funds consist of money not spent but saved; for example, consumers who decide to give up consumption and put their money into the bank as a form of savings. Similarly, firms and the government may contribute to this 'pool' of loanable funds by depositing funds into a bank. The reward for this sacrifice is the rate of interest paid by the bank.

The supply curve of loanable funds is therefore upward sloping, left to right, and reflects that increasing amounts of deposits, and hence sacrifices, require equally higher compensations for loss of consumption.

According to marginal revenue productivity theory, the demand for these loanable funds depends on a firm's demand for capital goods such as machines or equipment. As in marginal revenue productivity theory of wages, the marginal revenue productivity of capital is downward sloping because the marginal physical product (MPP) is also downward sloping due to diminishing returns to capital.

These diminishing returns, or output when sold in a perfect market, will give the marginal revenue product of each machine expressed not in money, but as a rate of return expressed in percentage terms. The demand curve for capital is called the marginal efficiency of capital or MEC and is derived when the firm estimates the net profit of each machine expressed as an annual percentage rate of return. Note again that the percentage rate of returns fall due to diminishing returns to capital – in the same way that they do for labour. This percentage yield is called the marginal efficiency (productivity) of capital. See figure 18.1.

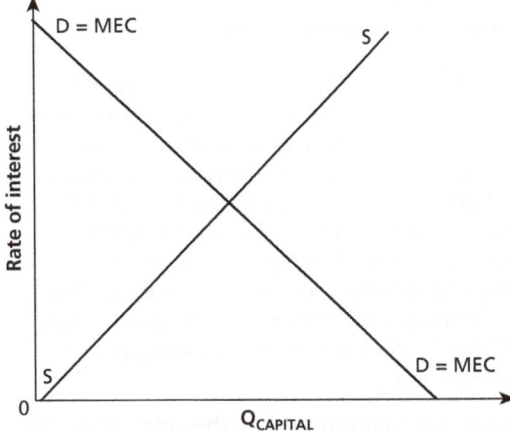

Figure 18.1 Determination of interest

As long as the MEC of a machine is higher than the rate of interest (marginal input factor cost) a profit-maximising firm will hire or purchase the capital good. Note therefore that the MEC curve is the demand curve for capital, because as the rate of interest falls the firm hires more capital, and vice versa.

As you might expect, criticisms of the theory are the same as those advanced for the marginal revenue productivity theory of wages. A movement of the MEC curve is achieved if:

› **The productivity of capital is increased.**
› **There is an increase in the price of the output created that it helps.**
› **Business expectations are very positive and firms' spending on capital goods increases.**

Summary

Interest is the price of capital, according to traditional distribution theory. This classical theory explains the rate of interest as determined by the demand and supply of loanable funds. The demand for loanable funds is assumed to be used for the purchase of capital goods, and is referred to as the MEC.

Profit

Profit concepts such as above normal, normal and loss, and profit maximisation were analysed in some detail in chapter 11. As a reward to the factor of production enterprise, profit is the reward for taking uncertain risks.

In most cases, the greater the degree of risk, the greater the level of profits; for example, oil exploration. Unlike the other factor rewards, which are determined before production starts, profit is determined after output is sold. Many factors other than risk may affect the level of profits. These may be:

› **Ability to set price**
› **Barriers to entry**

- Demand elasticity of the product or service
- Monopoly power and the level of competition at home and abroad
- State of the economy
- Level of taxation
- Cost of production
- Existence of economies of scale.

According to conventional marginal revenue productivity theory, profit levels are determined by the supply and demand for entrepreneurs, which is taken to mean the number of firms in an industry. Profit is therefore determined according to the degree of competition in the different market structures, starting with many firms in perfect competition to one firm in a pure monopoly. The supply of firms or entrepreneurs is mainly related to risk. Other factors which affect the supply of entrepreneurs are:

- Access to start-up capital, i.e., the rate of interest
- State of the economy: more entrepreneurs are attracted into business when the economy is growing
- Rate of taxation on profits
- Government support for business enterprises, e.g., small business development
- Number of individuals trained in business education
- High prices and profits which attract entrepreneurs into certain types of industries
- Ease of entry and exit from an industry
- For foreign direct investment, the supply of entrepreneurs is determined by government regulation, infrastructure, government policy, profitability of output, price elasticity of demand of the output, the level of competition.

Demand for entrepreneurs is a derived demand and is linked to the demand for a good or service. The number of firms in an industry depends to a large extent on the productivity and skill of the firm's owners, since entrepreneurship is a determinant of the supply and success of firms in an industry.

Too many firms in an industry will also lead to diminishing returns since resources are finite. The number of firms in an industry is determined in the long-run by the number that can cover their costs, in much the same way that labour and capital equate marginal input cost with their revenue product.

The functions of profit are:

- Reward for risk-taking
- Source of financing and therefore an alternative to borrowing
- Incentive to innovation
- Measure of efficiency
- Price, in that it allocates resources from loss-making industries to profitable ones
- Signal to new entrants in an industry.

Key point

Profit is the reward to the entrepreneur for taking risk. According to marginal revenue productivity theory, it is determined by the supply (number of firms in an industry) and the level of demand (derived) for goods and services. The demand for entrepreneurs is linked to the productivity of the firm or the entrepreneur and is also influenced by the law of diminishing returns.

Land

The concept of rent was analysed, along with transfer earnings and economic rent, as a factor payment to the landlord for the use of the factor of production, land in chapter 17.

As with the other factors of production, marginal revenue productivity theory holds that rent is determined by its supply and demand, that is, of land. As expected, the demand for land is derived from the demand for food, housing, recreation and/or other commercial or industrial needs.

The demand curve for land is derived from the MPP of land multiplied by its marginal revenue. It is downward sloping, since the productivity of land is subject to the law of diminishing returns.

The supply of land is assumed to be fixed, although some types of land may have more variable supply than others in response to demand/high prices. The amount of land given to agriculture, for example, will depend on the marginal revenue productivity of the land's agricultural output. Rents will differ according to demand and price. For example, if the demand for land is very high for residential housing, the marginal revenue productivity of the land will also be high.

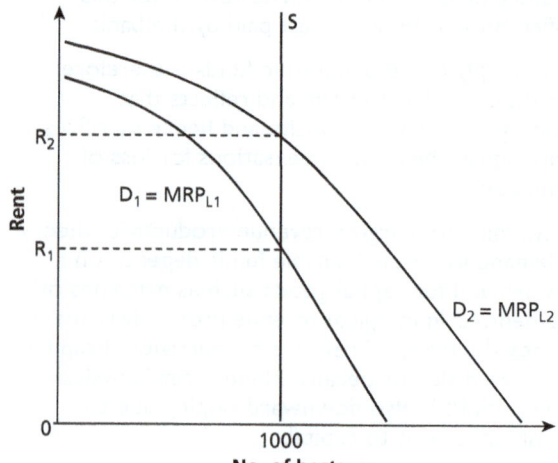

Figure 18.2 Determination of rent for land

Note that in figure 18.2, the rent for 1,000 hectares of land is R_1, yet when $MRPL_1$ shifts to the right as a result of an increase in demand for land, rent is now equal to R_2.

Summary

The marginal revenue productivity of land depends on its productivity and price. If demand for use of land is greater for residential housing than for food, the rent for land will be higher for housing.

Table 18.1 Factors of production compared

Similarities	Differences
They all earn a reward when hired or purchased.	Wages, interest and rent are calculated before production while profit is calculated after wages and rent have been paid.
Land and capital are similar since developing land requires capital. Raw material may be land but once mined it is capital.	Land is fixed in supply to a greater extent than labour and capital.
It is difficult in practice to determine the marginal revenue productivity of the four factors of production since they are frequently employed jointly, e.g., machine and operator.	The marginal revenue productivity of labour is expressed in a monetary value while the marginal revenue productivity of capital is expressed as a percentage return on investment.
It is possible to increase the productivity of all the factors of production, e.g., labour with education and training; capital with automation; land with drainage and fertilisation (agriculture), infrastructure and development (residential); entrepreneurship with managerial and organisational training and experience.	Land is geographically immobile. However, it may be occupationally mobile, i.e., shift from being used for agriculture to industrial or residential use with ease. Labour and entrepreneurship may be both occupationally and geographically mobile.
All factor inputs are subject to diminishing returns.	Net maximum advantage plays a significant role in the determination or difference in wages, rent or interest.
Transfer earnings and economic rent for all factors are determined by the price elasticity of supply.	Capital, labour and the entrepreneur are the only factors with a fixed life span.

Similarities	Differences
The demand for a factor input is a derived demand.	Land is regarded as the most crucial factor input since nothing can be created without land.
Labour, capital and entrepreneurship play a significant role in adding value to land.	

The labour force

The labour force consists of those between the legal working age and the retirement age, who offer themselves for employment. The potential labour force consists of those between the ages of 18 and 60 who have the capability and potential to work. In CARICOM countries the legal working age is 18 and the most common retirement age is 60 years. The labour force is also called the working population.

Economically active population

Not everyone between the legal working age and retirement age is economically active: many are working while others are looking for jobs. The economically active includes those who are employed plus those who are actively searching for employment.

The economically inactive population may therefore be those who have retired or those at, or over, the legal working age but perhaps in tertiary education or not looking for a job. Also, some women may temporarily leave the workforce to raise children, and they too are economically inactive.

The activity or participation rate

The activity or participation rate of labour is simply the labour force of the country expressed as a percentage of the population.

For example; if population = 1,000,000, number employed = 500,000, unemployed = 100,000: then the labour force activity or participation rate is:

$$\frac{600,000 \times 100}{1,000,000 \text{ (population)}} = 60\%$$

Chapter summary

Interest, profit and rent play a vital role in our ability to create wealth. Interest is the reward paid to capital according to traditional distribution theory. A reward to enterprise is profit and it is the reward for taking uncertain risks.

The supply of firms or entrepreneurs is mainly related to risk and on the productivity and skill of the owners. The demand for entrepreneurs is a derived demand and is linked to the demand for a good or service.

The marginal revenue productivity of land depends on its productivity and price.

The labour force consists of those between the legal working age and the retirement age, who offer themselves for employment.

Practice questions

1. Outline the marginal productivity theory.
2. Use marginal productivity theory to do each of the following:
   a. Derive the demand curve for an input under a competitive market structure.
   b. Explain the demand for capital.
3. What do you understand by the term 'minimum wage rate'?
4. Discuss two reasons why it is necessary for governments to set minimum wage rates for gas station attendants and cinema workers.
5. Explain the minimum wage rate and discuss the effect of a minimum wage rate on:
   a. Employment
   b. Unemployment
   c. Earnings.

19 The distribution of income

LEARNING OBJECTIVES

- Identify the factor rewards.
- Differentiate between size and functional distribution of income.
- Illustrate the Lorenz curve.
- Identify/describe factors that cause income inequality.
- Explain the concept of poverty.

REQUIRED KNOWLEDGE

- Wages
- Interest
- Profit
- Rent.

TOPIC VALUE

There are rich and poor among us, a feature described as inequality in the distribution of income. This chapter explains this problem and how it is resolved.

Introduction

The concept of functional distribution of income was introduced when the factors of production and their rewards were analysed. In other words, factor inputs earn incomes according to their productivity. When wages, interest, rent and profit are added together, with a few adjustments, this total income is known as the national income.

The other measure of distribution of national income is how incomes are distributed among the population. This is known as the size distribution of income, and the most common ways of measuring the size distribution are the Lorenz curve and the Gini coefficient.

The Lorenz curve

In figure 19.1 the Lorenz curves measure the equality in the size distribution of income. The horizontal axis measures the cumulative percentage of the population and the vertical axis gives their percentage share of total income.

Under a 45-degree line, the poorest 20 per cent of the population receives 20 per cent of the total income in the country and 60 per cent of the population receives 60 per cent of the income, and so on.

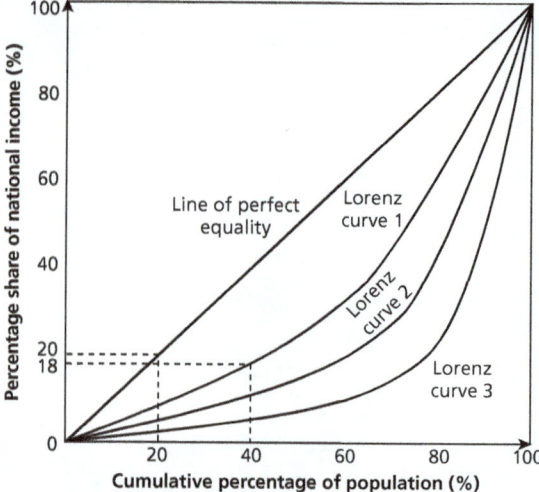

Figure 19.1 The Lorenz curve

The 45-degree line is therefore called a line of perfect equality (LOPE), that is, it has a perfectly even distribution of income. (It is assumed that the income is pre-tax.) In reality, however, this is never the case.

What is more likely is that the income distribution will form what is called a Lorenz curve, beneath the 45-degree line. In figure 19.1, under Lorenz curve 1, 40 per cent of the population is only earning 18 per cent of the total income of the country. Note that Lorenz curves 2 and 3 show increasing inequalities in the distribution of income. Indeed, the further to the right that the Lorenz curve moves, the greater will be the inequality of distribution. But the nearer the curve is to the LOPE, the distribution of incomes will be more even.

Although one may be able to determine inequality from a Lorenz curve at a glance, it is a less precise measure than the Gini coefficient.

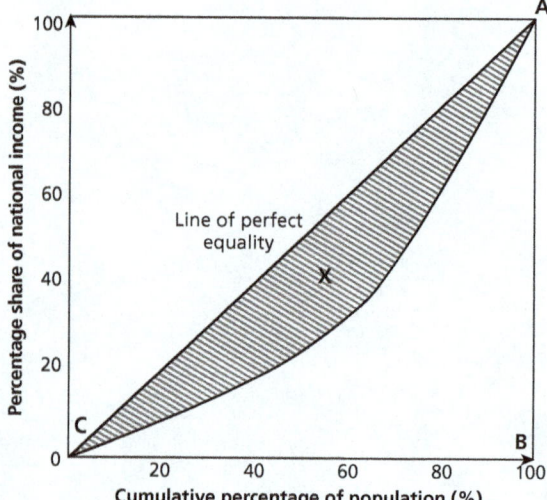

Figure 19.2 The Gini coefficient

The Gini coefficient

The Gini coefficient is calculated by expressing area X as a ratio of area ABC, and if the Lorenz curve is nearer to the LOPE the fraction will be smaller. The value of the coefficient lies in a range between zero and 1. For example, if the Lorenz curve is equal to the LOPE, then the Gini coefficient will be zero. If the Gini coefficient is 1, then the distribution of income is perfectly uneven. A Gini coefficient of 0.25 is a more even distribution of income than 0.45. The Gini coefficient may be measured before or after taxation.

If income is measured after taxes, the Gini coefficient is a post-tax measurement and therefore a more accurate and realistic measure of income equality. As a post-tax Lorenz curve moves closer to the LOPE, it may be inferred that income redistribution adjusted for taxes has improved the distribution of income.

Gini coefficients, however, are not without their limitations because they only measure one aspect of inequality. They fail to take into account wealth, undisclosed income and non-income benefits. Some samples of Gini coefficients in the Caribbean in the year 2003 were: Jamaica 0.38; Barbados 0.49; Trinidad and Tobago 0.40 (according to the UN Food and Agriculture Organization).

Summary

The Gini coefficient and Lorenz curve are the two most common measures of inequality of income.

Factors that cause income inequality

The functional distribution of income is not likely to be even. Some countries' wages may account for a greater share of national income than profits, rents or interest. In the analysis of wage differentials, reasons why different levels of wages are paid to labour are identified. In the majority of cases it is because of imperfect market structures. The factors that cause income inequality in the size distribution of income are as follows.

Human capital and education

Higher incomes are often earned by workers with more education, qualifications, skills and training (human capital).

Household size

Where there are large families, the income per person will be low if total 'take home' pay is not significant. Likewise, if some adults stay at home to assist in the management of the household, the potential for earning is reduced.

Marital status

A single parent earns less than a gainfully employed married couple. Unmarried persons who live alone have little margin for savings.

Age and seniority

The older one becomes, the greater will be the potential earnings through promotion and seniority. Older persons tend to be in more positions of management than younger persons.

Geographical location

Workers in urban areas tend to have higher incomes than those in rural areas because the demand for skilled labour in commercial districts attracts higher wages; examples include doctors, plumbers and welders working in the country, versus those working in towns. Likewise, some regions may be dominated by lower-earning agricultural industries compared to, for example, petrochemicals, bauxite or natural gas.

Ability

Highly skilled individuals often experience a high demand for their skills and earn high incomes; for example, oil fire fighters, gifted athletes, underwater welders, and financial management experts.

Inheritance

Persons inheriting or having accumulated wealth can often use their wealth to enlarge their income (and wealth) further.

Work intensity

Men tend to earn higher wages than women based on a combination of gender discrimination, more stable employment (because they don't bear children and do less child rearing) and the fact that because they stay longer in employment, they are given more training. They work in higher-value industries such as banks and energy industries. The majority of women tend to work in service industries as, for example, secretaries, sales assistants in flower shops and waitresses, although this trend is changing as women are beginning to enter professions previously dominated by men.

Discrimination

Minorities tend to earn less in multicultural societies due to ethnic and religious discrimination.

Rate of pay

Individuals who are paid a flat rate earn less than those whose wages are based on their productivity. A distinction should be made between wealth and income. Income is a flow of earnings per time period; for example, monthly, weekly wages. Wealth is a stock of capital at any point in time and may consist of assets that are both financial and physical in nature; for example, savings, equities, property, works of art and precious metals.

Measures designed to reduce income inequality: benefits in cash and kind

In the analysis of correcting market failures in chapter 15, many examples of government activities to remove inequalities were identified. Note that equality and equity are not the same. Equality refers to receiving the same treatment, whereas equity has to do with fairness. Since free markets do not recognise social values, market forces reward those who command higher wages and use their money to enjoy greater quantities of goods and services.

In its role of promoting a just society, the government can take the following measures to correct the unequal distribution of income.

Progressive taxation
This is based on 'vertical equity', that is, persons who earn more pay a greater share of their income in taxes. (Under horizontal equity those who earn the same amount should have the same liability/pay the same taxes.)

Price ceilings
Price ceilings are maximum prices for basic necessities to life; for example, food and basic items for proper nutrition such as flour, rent control for housing.

Price floors
These are are minimum prices in favour of sellers with fluctuating incomes; for example, farmers, and minimum incomes.

Subsidies
These help to reduce prices of chosen goods, to make them more affordable to persons earning low incomes, for example, gasoline and food.

There are also subsidies for basic medicines purchased at pharmaceutical outlets, as well as government scholarships for education and professional training; for example, teachers and the Dip. Education, and subsidised school books.

Direct provision
Direct provision of goods and services by the government includes:

> Merit goods; for example; education, libraries, museum, sporting facilities, health facilities
> Assistance to vulnerable groups, for example, single parents, the disabled
> Old age assistance
> Care for unwed mothers
> 'Smart card' voucher for the purchase of basic amenities
> Bus transport for pensioners and school children
> School meals
> Public goods
> Vocational training, for example, self-help and other state-funded training.

Poverty
Correcting inequalities in income by the government is made not only to address the issue of equity or fairness itself, but also to allow low-income families and individuals to satisfy their most basic needs. Food, water, shelter, clothing and transport are some examples of basic necessities to human life.

Poverty may be viewed as absolute or relative.

Absolute poverty and relative poverty
Absolute poverty defines poverty in absolute terms; for example, no access to food, water, clothing and transport. In some countries these basic necessities are called the 'poverty line' and anyone living below the poverty line is considered poor. A common measure of poverty is a daily energy intake of less than 2,400 calories.

Relative poverty is experienced if someone is living below an average standard of living for that country. For example, in developed countries a basic standard of living may be ownership of a house, car, refrigerator, television, washing machine, home computer and other labour-saving devices such as a microwave oven and a vacuum cleaner. In contrast, in the CARICOM region, food, shelter, clothing, water, and access to public and merit goods may constitute a basic standard of living.

If individuals do not own these goods and services, they are relatively poor. Relative poverty may mean the inability to access an average level of consumption. Persons who are the poorest are: the elderly; single-parent families; the physically challenged; persons who have no marketable skills; and the very young who may be orphaned.

The costs of poverty
The costs of poverty include:

> Lower output caused by unemployed human resources
> Government expenditure on poverty alleviation measures, which might otherwise be used for development
> Poorer health, due to the overcrowding of some urban districts
> Potentially more criminal activity, and social dislocations such as marriage breakdown and depression.

Measures to reduce poverty fall into two basic categories:

1. Benefits in cash
2. Benefits in kind.

Benefits in cash
Cash benefits are available to persons falling below a specified income level; for example, those where annual income is $24,000 or $2,000 a month. Persons

applying for such benefits are therefore required to show proof of income. Some examples of cash benefits are unemployment benefits, child support grants and single-parent grants. However, cash benefits do not guarantee relief from poverty since individuals' income shortfall may be very large, and how they spend any benefits is their choice and they may spend these grants on demerit goods.

Benefits in kind

Benefits in kind, by direct state provision, are a more effective way of reducing poverty. Examples of benefits in kind are:

> **Health services provided free of charge in public hospitals or health centres**
> **Education**
> **School meals, books, bus passes.**

In addition to these free or subsidised provisions, the government may provide housing to remedy housing shortages, or to alleviate squatting on state lands. Employment strategies are another main area of provision by governments in the CARICOM region.

While state-funded education and training provide employment indirectly, the state is also a major employer in the public sector and may run programmes that create short-term work opportunities.

Means-tested benefits: some limitations

Not all those who are entitled to benefits receive them because of lack of information; for example, failure to disclose personal information, ignorance, illiteracy and pride. And vulnerable groups such as the physically and mentally challenged are not necessarily included in the social safety net.

However, some people who receive benefits may not see the need to work for a living and may therefore become dependent on the state and become economically inactive.

Much of the discussion concerning the inequality of the distribution of income and wealth and measures to reduce poverty invariably focuses on the important issue of social welfare. However, social welfare must be seen as not only the best allocation of resources, but also the best distribution. Equity and efficiency are insufficient. The state must therefore engage in social welfare programmes to reduce poverty and increase welfare.

The benefits of any social welfare programme funded by the state may be for reasons of:

> **Welfare equity**
> **Beneficial externality**
> **Voter maximisation.**

Welfare equity was advocated by Adam Smith in order to promote a fair society. The beneficial externality is the provision of education and health. As they are merit goods, their benefits to society go beyond the direct benefit to the recipient; for example, education and health promote productivity to the benefit of society in total. Welfare programmes have been criticised by economists and other commentators for creating a dependent society and negatively impacting on a person's pride and self-respect.

Voter maximisation is the use of state resources to earn political support for a government in office.

Key points

The inequality of the distribution of income and wealth and measures to reduce poverty are important issues of social welfare.

Absolute poverty defines poverty in absolute terms; for example, no access to food, water, clothing and transport. Measures to reduce poverty fall into two basic categories: benefits in cash and benefits in kind. Benefits in kind are a more effective way of reducing poverty.

Measuring poverty

The poverty line is one way of measuring poverty. It may vary among countries, but it is generally held that on average a family needs to spend approximately one-third of its income on food. This cost is multiplied by three to arrive at the official poverty line, which is adjusted for family size.

Aside from measuring poverty, other methods for measuring the standard of living are the Measure of Economic Welfare (MEW) (Nordhaus and Tobin), which emphasises the net welfare from positives (goods) and negatives (bads) when national income figures are computed. A more detailed analysis of this measure is provided in chapter 21, which discusses national income.

There is also the basic needs measure, that is, the inability to access food, shelter and clothing.

The UN's Human Development Index (UNDP HDI) takes into consideration the life expectancy, per capita income, adult literacy rates and school enrolment rates.

Chapter summary

All factors of production earn rewards: land, labour, capital and enterprise earn rent, wages, interest and profit respectively. According to traditional theory, the reward to a factor is determined by the forces of supply and demand. The demand curve of a factor of productivity is the marginal revenue product (MRP) curve of the factor.

The distribution of income may be viewed in two ways: functional distribution of income and size distribution of income. Two measures of the size distribution of income are the Lorenz curve and the Gini coefficient.

The main government actions to reduce inequality of incomes are: benefits in cash (e.g., old age assistance) and benefits in kind (e.g., public and merit goods). Social welfare involves the most efficient allocation of resources and the best distribution of those resources. Social welfare programmes are designed by the government to alleviate poverty and reduce inequalities.

Poverty may be absolute if a person's income cannot purchase the basic necessities of life. The poverty line is calculated under the assumption that an individual spends a third of their income on food. That number is multiplied by three and adjusted for family size. Apart from the poverty line, the HDI, and MEW are other measures of welfare or standard of living.

The objectives of government welfare programmes may be based on equity, poverty reduction, beneficial externality, paternalism and vote-getting.

Equity and equality are not the same. Equality means same quantity while equity means fairness. While equality is based on fact, fairness is based on judgment, which varies according to society's expectations and standard of living.

Practice questions

1. a. Give two cases of the high levels of poverty in the Caribbean.
   b. The Gini coefficient in Dominica changed from 0.34 to 0.46 between 1998 and 2000. Explain what this change implies about the dynamics of poverty in Dominica in that period.
   c. Suggest one policy measure that may be useful in reducing poverty in the Caribbean.

2. Critically assess the role that government should play with respect to each of the following:
   a. The housing market
   b. National security
   c. Environmental degradation.

3. Explain the meaning of each of the following terms:
   a. Functional distribution of income
   b. Inequality
   c. Gini coefficient
   d. Lorenz curve.

Chapter 20 Macroeconomics

20
Macroeconomics

LEARNING OBJECTIVES

- Define macroeconomics.
- Illustrate and explain the circular flow of income.
- Identify and explain the fundamentals of the economy.

REQUIRED KNOWLEDGE

- Basic understanding of inflation, unemployment and exchange rates
- Definition of imports and exports
- Interest rate
- Economic growth.

TOPIC VALUE

It is in our interests to interpret changes in our economy to plan for the future.

Introduction

Microeconomics is the study of the components of the economy, and analyses how they relate to each other.

The word aggregate, meaning total, is used when studying all firms, industries, markets and their output.

Macroeconomics

Macroeconomics is not only the study of the workings of an economy as a whole, but also how that economy relates to other economies around the world through external trade.

Typical macroeconomic issues are employment, economic growth, exchange rates, inflation, interest-rate policy, balance of payments and balance of trade.

Macroeconomic cycle or circular flow diagram

In the microeconomic chain a rise in demand will, *ceteris paribus*, cause prices to rise and hence profits. These are microeconomic issues and are illustrated in figure 20.1.

In figure 20.2 the circular flow diagram shows 'The Big Picture', that is, how the four main participants in the economy – firms, consumers, government and external trade – relate to one another.

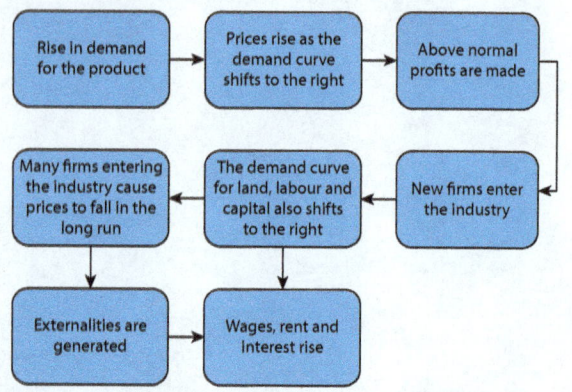

Figure 20.1 A simple microeconomic chain assuming supply is constant

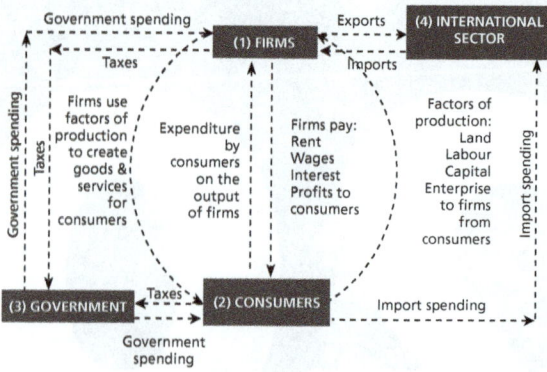

Figure 20.2 A simple four-sector circular flow of income (open economy)

Key point

Microeconomics is the study of the individual parts of the economy; for example, the demand, output, cost and revenue of individual firms and an industry in the short- and long-run. Macroeconomics is the study of the whole economy and focuses on issues such as employment, national output, overall price level, economic growth, exchange rates and economic development.

The major macroeconomic variables

A country's 'health' is determined by its 'fundamentals' or major economic variables. These are the achievement of:

› Nearly full employment, or 2 per cent unemployment
› Positive and sustained rate of economic growth of the national output of the country of about 5–8 per cent per annum
› Low rate of inflation of about 2 per cent per annum
› Satisfactory balance of payments position, meaning earnings from exports and other inflows should be sufficient to sustain imports for 6 months
› Stable exchange rate.

Macroeconomic objectives defined

Although all five macroeconomic objectives are discussed in much detail in later chapters, a brief overview is necessary to provide a basic understanding of each variable.

A sustained rate of economic growth means a 5–8 per cent increase in the monetary value of goods and services provided in a country in a given year, compared to the previous year. For example, if Barbados produced Bds$40 billion of output in the year 2006 and 42 billion in 2007, then the growth rate is calculated as 42 bn – 40 bn = 2 bn.

Percentage growth rate is: $\dfrac{2 \text{ bn} \times 100}{40 \text{ bn} \times 1} = 5\%$

The growth should be due to an increase in total production and not an increase in price.

In most cases economists are interested in real growth, which is growth adjusted for inflation.

Economic growth is possible if a country can increase its output by employing its idle resources to increase capacity in the long-term. In addition, if existing resources yield more output through productivity of labour or technology, or improved quality of land, growth would also be achieved.

A low rate of unemployment is also considered a high priority for all countries in the Caribbean, in particular, since unemployment is linked to a low standard of living and poverty. High rates of unemployment are also the cause of some social problems. The rate of unemployment is calculated by dividing the number of persons unemployed by the labour force:

$$\frac{\text{number unemployed} \times 100}{\text{labour force} \times 1} = \text{rate of unemployment}$$

If the labour force in a Caribbean island is 80,000 and the unemployed number is 10,000, then the rate of unemployment is 12.5 per cent.

The achievement of price stability is another important macroeconomic objective because inflation negatively affects consumer confidence. Price stability is taken to mean a rate of inflation of 2 per cent per annum. Formally, inflation is defined as the persistent rise in the average price level. It reduces the purchasing power of money over time, for example people's savings. The increase in the general price level is measured by a retail price index.

Another important objective is a healthy balance of payments. The balance of payments is a record of monetary inflows and outflows of a country that result from trade, investment or other transfers with the rest of the world. Inflows may, for example, be due to the export of goods and services or financial investments coming into a country. Outflows may be due to the importing of goods, services and investing in financial products overseas.

Over a period of time the government will try to ensure that expenditure on imports does not exceed revenues gained from exports. Why? Because if expenditure on imports exceeds revenue gained from exports this would result in a balance of payments deficit, and if those debts cannot be paid they would create indebtedness to other countries that require 'servicing' (interest payments to pay for) such debts.

The exchange rate of a country is the price it pays to purchase a unit of currency of another country. For example, the rate of exchange between the US and Trinidad and Tobago is TT$6.40 for US$1. Exchange rates may be either fixed by the government (similar to a price ceiling) or 'flexible', when they are determined by free market forces. Exchange rates are discussed in more detail in chapter 33.

The relationship between macroeconomic variables

The government may identify different strategies to achieve the five macroeconomic objectives. For example, they may use policy tools such as taxation, government spending, monetary policy or a combination of these. However, it is necessary to examine these policies in a little more detail before embarking on an analysis of how these variables work.

Generally though, it is not an easy task to achieve all these objectives together. For example, economic growth and full employment tend to complement each other, since growth requires the employment of labour resources. When growth takes place, incomes thus created may stimulate spending at home and abroad, causing demand inflation and balance of payments deficits. Macroeconomic variables are more fully explored in later chapters in this book: inflation (chapter 29); unemployment (chapter 30); exchange rates (chapter 33); balance of payments (chapter 34); and growth (chapter 36).

Chapter summary

Economic growth is a yearly percentage measure in the value of output of a country. A low rate of unemployment is considered to be between 2 and 3 per cent of the labour force and is measured as:

$$\frac{\text{number unemployed} \times 100}{\text{labour force}}$$

A low rate of inflation is taken to mean 2 per cent. The retail price index is used to measure the rate of inflation.

The balance of payments is a record of the financial transactions of one country with the rest of the world. The rate of exchange between one country and another is the price paid for each other's currency to facilitate external trade. There are five main objectives that governments seek to achieve in managing the economy. They are:

› **Low rate of unemployment of 2 per cent**
› **Low rate of inflation, e.g., 2 per cent**
› **Sustained economic growth of approximately 5–8 per cent per annum**
› **Reasonable balance of payments position that is sufficient to purchase imports for 6 months**
› **Stable exchange rate.**

Practice question

1. Which of the following is not considered a macroeconomic objective?
   a. Full employment
   b. Sustained economic growth
   c. High levels of productivity
   d. Low rates of inflation.

21 National income: the circular flow of income

Chapter 21 National income: the circular flow of income

LEARNING OBJECTIVES

- Define the different variations of national income: gross domestic product (GDP), gross national product (GNP) and net national product (NNP).
- Differentiate between national and personal income.
- Explain the measures of the national income.
- Describe and explain the income, expenditure and output method of calculating national income.
- Identify the important uses of national income statistics.
- Identify the limitations of national income statistics.

REQUIRED KNOWLEDGE

- Basic knowledge of the circular flow model.

TOPIC VALUE

There is much interest in the 'Budget' that is presented to Parliament annually, since it affects the lives of people directly.

Introduction

National income is the monetary value of the total flow of output resulting from the economic activity of a country, measured on an annual basis. Adjustments for depreciation and inflation are also made to this figure.

It should be noted that income is a different concept to money. Money is the amount of income we have at a particular point in time and, like wealth, it is a stock concept. Income may be added to or subtracted from this stock and therefore may be described as a flow concept.

In order to determine whether the economy is growing, stagnating or contracting it is necessary to measure the yearly output. Perhaps the best-known measure of a country's final output is gross domestic product (GDP). As the name implies, gross means total, product means output, and domestic refers to home.

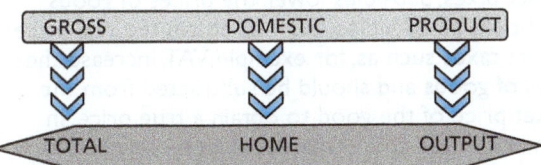

Figure 21.1 Gross domestic product

Formally, GDP is the monetary value of the flow of output produced within the land and maritime boundaries of a country over a 12-month period. It matters not who produces this output. It may be local or foreign factors of production operating together; GDP measures economic activity in a calendar year.

Gross national product (GNP) is another method of expressing the national output of a country. GNP, however, measures only the value of the output of factors of production of the home country, wherever these factors are in operation throughout the world. The reasoning is simple. Many foreign companies who operate in a country send their profits and other income back to their home country. This is an example of property income going abroad.

Similarly, a local firm may have a subsidiary in a foreign country; for example, if Banks Beer of Barbados operates a company in Jamaica then its profits earned in Jamaica will be repatriated to Barbados. Property income coming into the country is simply called property income from abroad.

GNP will then be calculated as GDP plus net property income from abroad.

Another measure of the national income/output of a country is net national product (NNP), which is calculated as GNP less depreciation.

Depreciation, or capital consumption, takes place when capital assets depreciate over the 12-month period, or become outdated and therefore replaced. An allowance is made for replacing outmoded equipment.

Replacement of capital goods is a part of current production. The assumption is that capital goods are produced to maintain a capital stock by replacing it.

There are, therefore, three measures of the national output of a country and which one is chosen depends on the reason why these calculations are needed.

For example, if the government is concerned about the productivity of the factor inputs of the country, GDP will be used. However, GNP is the most realistic measure for the Caribbean region, based on the fact that there is much foreign direct investment in the Caribbean, much of which is repatriated to the home countries.

Key point

The value of the flow of national output of a country is expressed in three ways: GDP, GNP and NNP. GDP is the value of all output within the land and maritime boundaries of a country measured over a 12-month period. GNP is calculated as GDP plus net property income. NNP is calculated as GNP less depreciation.

Calculating the value of output

A very simple and useful method of understanding the value of national output is a circular flow of income diagram, which was briefly introduced in chapter 16 to explain factor rewards and the functional distribution of income. Figure 21.2 shows how the income earned by the factor inputs is used to purchase the output of firms, all other things being equal. Hence, the three ways in which the output of a country is measured are the income, expenditure and output methods. The assumption of this model is that the money spent on the output of a country is equal to the expenditure on this output, which is equal to the value of the output.

These three measures may be explained by using an example of grocery shopping with $1,000. Spending an income of $1,000 = income = one's grocery bill (expenditure) = value of items in the shopping cart (output). All three are therefore the same value as illustrated in figure 21.2.

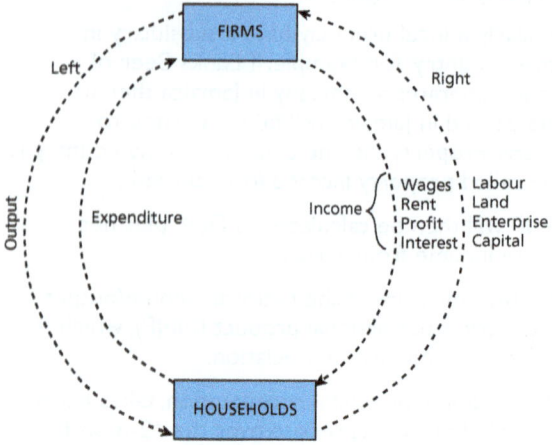

Figure 21.2 The circular flow in a two-sector circular flow diagram

Figure 21.2. shows an exchange of money for non-monetary items in what is known as a two-sector economy, consisting of producers and consumers. The flow between these two sectors is called the main flow of a closed economy.

On the right-hand side of the figure note that consumers supply factor inputs to producers who pay wages, interest, rent and profit in return for labour, capital, land and enterprise.

Producers then create output, which is purchased by consumers using factor incomes paid to them by firms. Wages, interest, rent and profit are equal to national income, and the purchase of firms' outputs are equal to expenditure and output respectively.

Two more sectors can be added to this simplified circular flow of income in the form of the government and international sectors to create a four-sector model.

The income method

In order to understand the income method of calculating national income, recall that it consists of the incomes that factor inputs earn when they are sold to producers.

The income method of calculating national income is as follows:

Income from employment

plus

Income from self-employment

plus

Gross trading profits of companies

plus

Gross trading surpluses of public corporations and government enterprise

plus

Rent

plus

Interest

plus

Imported charge for consumption of non-traded capital

equals

Total domestic income

less

Stock appreciation

equals

GDP

plus

Net property income from abroad

equals

GNP at factor cost

Less

Capital consumption (depreciation)

equals

NNP at factor cost

Notes on the income method

Income from employment represents wages, then profits from private and public companies. Rent is added as what is called 'imputed rent', which is really an estimated rental value of private homes. Total domestic income is further adjusted for stock appreciation, which represents price increases of stock over the year in question.

Factor cost is an adjustment for subsidies and indirect taxes. Subsidies lower the prices of goods and should be added to GDP to obtain the real price. Indirect taxes such as, for example, VAT, increase the prices of goods and should be subtracted from the market price of the good to obtain a true price. In summary, factor cost = market prices – sales taxes + subsidies. Net property income, represents the difference between outflows and inflows of interest, profits or dividends to obtain a net figure. Capital consumption is also deducted.

Common error

When income is paid and no output is created or exchanged, it is called a transfer payment (not transfer earnings). A transfer payment is not counted in the income method of calculating GDP because no corresponding economic output is created; for example, old age security or pension payments.

Chapter 21 National income: the circular flow of income

The expenditure method

The expenditure method of calculating the value of national output is calculated by adding up the final expenditure by the four main purchasers, that is, consumers, firms, the government and the foreign sector. It is possible to derive a simple formula for this method.

The following formula represents a concise way of measuring the value of a country's output using the expenditure method:

$C + I + G + (X - M) = Y$ (national income)

Where:

C is consumer spending

I is investment spending

G is government expenditure

X is exports (i.e., foreigners buying the national output)

M is imports (i.e., expenditure on output outside the country)

In the official records of the government the expenditure method would appear as follows:

Consumer expenditure

plus

General government final consumption

plus

Gross domestic fixed capital formation

plus

Value of the physical increase in stocks

plus

Exports of goods and services

equals

Total final expenditure

less

Imports

equals

GDP at market prices

less

Indirect taxes

plus

Subsidies

equals

GDP at factor cost

plus

Net property income from abroad

equals

GNP at factor cost

less

Depreciation

equals

Net national product at factor cost (or NI)

Notes on expenditure method

The value of physical increases in stock and work in progress is part of the flow of output produced and must therefore be counted, even if it is not sold.

GDP at market prices means GDP at the value sold in the market and not adjusted for the effects of subsidies and indirect taxes.

The output method

The output method totals the output of the different sectors of an economy. Output in agriculture, forestry, fishing, manufacturing, construction, distribution, transportation in the public and private sectors are all included in this measure.

Importantly, calculations of output may be inaccurate due to double counting. For example, logs are an input in furniture and manufacturing; therefore, the value of both logs and furniture cannot be counted. Either the final price is taken or the value added between each stage. For example, if cut logs are sold to a lumber yard for $200 and processed and sold for $600, the value added is $400. If a furniture shop uses the lumber to create a finished product, which is sold for $1,000, then the value added at this stage is $400. Note the added value is $1,000 ($200 + $400 + $400), which is equal to the final price.

Notes on measuring national income

When measuring national income:

› **Consumer durables are counted at final value at the end of the year in which the purchase was made.**
› **Capital consumption is purely an estimate.**
› **Government services are valued at cost.**
› **Imputed income for dwellings is estimated but the estimates for the value of vehicle rental and other consumer durables are not included in this category.**
› **Double counting is avoided.**
› **The black economy is not recorded.**

In both income and expenditure methods care must be taken to avoid transfer payments, which have already been explained. Some examples of transfers are:

› **Shares sold on the stock exchange**
› **Pocket money (personal allowances).**

The value of second-hand goods, e.g., a second-hand car is not counted although the salesman's commission is counted since it is payment for a service rendered in the year of output.

Uses of national income statistics

National income statistics are used as follows:

> They may be used to calculate the standard of living in a country by dividing the real national income by the population to obtain average real income per person. This is also called per capita income.
> Increases in national income from year to year are used to measure short-term economic growth. This may be misleading since an increase in national income may simply be brought about by an increase in prices but no change in output.
> National income statistics are used to calculate the standard of living and to compare standards of living between countries.
> They are used by government to guide economic planning since they will reveal which sectors are growing and which are in decline.

Private sector business development and planning also rely heavily on national income statistics because they provide an indication of the business climate and prevailing economic conditions, which influence business decisions.

Limitations of national income statistics

Although per capita income is used to measure the standard of living in a country, it fails to accurately and realistically reflect factors that do determine the standard of living. Some salient factors that affect standard of living in a country that per capita income fails to reflect are:

> Distribution of income as measured by the Lorenz curve or Gini coefficient
> Extent of the hidden economy, i.e., the illegal or underground economy
> Output created by 'do it yourself' activities and hobbies such as a vegetable garden or home improvement projects undertaken by the homeowner
> Level of pollution, e.g., air, noise, water
> Life expectancy, infant mortality and literacy rates
> Access to doctors per thousand population, or access to health care
> Length of the working week and conditions of employment
> Level of criminal activity in a country
> Many countries spend large sums on defence. This may serve to increase GDP but the welfare effect on the citizens of a country is questionable.

International comparisons

GDP and per capita income statistics are used to measure standard of living between countries. This may be misleading on the following grounds:

> Two countries may have similar GDP or national income statistics but differ significantly in terms of distribution of income.
> Countries differ in their methods of compiling national income statistics; therefore, there is a need for a standard method of measurement if the standard of living between two countries is to be compared.
> The composition of a country's output may be a significant factor in measuring standard of living. For example, defence or military output may not significantly affect a country's standard of living, but will feature in its national accounts.
> The quality of goods and services, the level of externalities and working conditions of individuals in different countries may differ widely.
> More money is spent on coping with climate changes in countries that lie in the temperate zone than in countries in the tropical zone.

Alternative measures of standard of living

Since real GDP or per capita income may be unrealistic measures of standard of living, a number of other measures have been developed to reflect the quality of life. The Human Development Index (HDI) was developed as a Measure of Economic Welfare by the United Nations, and is based on an index measuring three key indicators. These are literacy levels, life expectancy and real GDP (at PPP exchange rates).

Another commonly used measure is the measure of economic welfare (MEW, developed by Nordhaus and Tobin) which adjusts GDP for 'goods' and 'bads' as follows.

GDP	+ Goods	– Bads	= MEW
100 billion	+ 30 billion	– 10 billion	= 120 billion

Examples of 'goods' are positive externalities and other variables such as hobbies, value of labour-saving devices and recreation.

Examples of 'bads' are negative externalities and crime.

Nominal and real GDP

Nominal or money national income measures GDP without any adjustment for price increases. This type of GDP is called GDP at current prices. Consider the simple example given in table 21.1a below of a country producing only two goods, oranges and bananas.

Chapter 21 National income: the circular flow of income

Table 21.1a Nominal GDP Country X in year 2013

Goods	Quantity	Unit price	Total value	Nominal GDP
Oranges	5m	$4.00	$20m	$20m
Bananas	6m	$5.00	$30m	$30m
GDP			$50m	$50m

The GDP at current prices is calculated as price multiplied by quantity and is called nominal or money GDP.

For example, note that in table 21.1a the value of oranges and bananas in the year 2013 is $50m.

Real GDP is equal to production of goods in a selected year multiplied by the price of these goods in a selected base year.

GDP deflator

The GDP deflator is a measure of the changes in the prices of goods in a given time period. It is expressed in formula as: Nominal GDP/Real GDP × 100.

Refer to table 21.1a to calculate nominal GDP. To compute real GDP in year 2 to the price level of year 1, proceed as in the example in given in table 21.1b as follows.

For example, in year 1 nominal GDP is calculated as price multiplied by quantity, which is equal to $50 million.

Table 21.1b Nominal GDP in year 1 at year 1 (2013) prices

Year	Goods	Quantity	Unit price	Nominal GDP
1	Oranges	5m	$4	$20m
1	Bananas	6m	$5	$30m
				$50m

In year 2 (table 21.2), with an increase in the quantity of oranges to 8m and a decrease in the quantity of bananas to 5m and a change in prices from $4 to $5 (oranges) and $5 to $6 (bananas), the nominal GDP for year 2 is now $70m.

Table 21.2 Nominal GDP in year 2 (2014) at year 2 prices

Year	Goods	Quantity	Unit price	Nominal GDP
2	Oranges	8m	$5	$40m
2	Bananas	5m	$6	$30m
				$70m

Real GDP in year 2 (2014) at year 1 (2013) prices is calculated by valuing output in year 2 ($70m), at year 2 prices, and dividing the answer by year 2 quantity multiplied by year 1 prices. (In this sense year 1 is the base year from which price levels will be measured.) In table 21.3 year 2 output at year 1 prices is $57m, while year 2 output at year 2 prices in table 21.2 is $70m.

Table 21.3 Real GDP in year 2 (2014) at year 1 prices

Year	Goods	Quantity	Unit price	Nominal GDP
1	Oranges	8m	$4	$32m
1	Bananas	5m	$5	$25m
				$57m

GDP deflator for year 2 with base year 2013 at year 1 prices is :

$$\frac{\text{Nominal GDP (2014)}}{\text{Real GDP (2014)} \times 100} = \frac{70m}{57m} \times 100 = 122.8.$$

Chapter summary

National income is the monetary value of the total flow of output of a country measured in a year. The value of the flow of national output of a country is expressed in three ways: GDP, GNP and NNP.

GDP is the monetary value of output produced within the land and maritime boundaries of a country over a 12-month period. GNP, however, measures only the value of the output of factors of production of the home country.

GNP is calculated as GDP plus net property income. NNP is calculated as GNP less depreciation.

A very simple and useful method of demonstrating and calculating the value of national output is a circular flow of income diagram. This method of calculating the value of national output is carried out by adding up all final expenditure of the national output by the four main purchasers. They are consumers, firms, the government and foreign direct investment.

The output method totals the output of the different sectors of an economy and includes agriculture, forestry, fishing, manufacturing, construction, distribution and transportation, all in the public and private sectors.

Practice questions

1. Explain the difference between gross domestic product (GDP) and gross national product (GNP).

2. Explain why each of the following is not counted in GDP calculations:
   a. Transfer payments
   b. Second-hand sales.

3. Outline the main difference between the expenditure approach and the income approach of determining GDP.

4. Briefly describe how each of the following is calculated:
   a. Net domestic product
   b. National income.

5. Define the following:
   a. GDP deflator
   b. Factor cost.

Note: Questions 6 and 7 refer to the following table.

Item	$ (m)
Exports and net property income from abroad	80
Imports and property income paid abroad	65
Taxes	25
Subsidies	18
Total domestic expenditure at market prices	260

6. Refer to the above table and calculate the gross national product at the following factor costs.
   a. $253m
   b. $267m
   c. $268m
   d. $275m

7. Refer to the above table and calculate the gross national product at the following market prices:
   a. $245m
   b. $268m
   c. $275m
   d. $448m

8. State the components of GDP (expenditure-based) that would be affected by each of the following transactions:
   a. A family buys a new refrigerator
   b. Aunt Jane buys a new home
   c. Your parents buy a bottle of French wine
   d. The city council repairs a main highway.

9. State one limitation of GDP as a measure of economic well-being.

10. Briefly describe how each of the following terms is calculated:
    a. Gross domestic product
    b. National income
    c. Disposable income.

Chapter 22 National income: determination

LEARNING OBJECTIVES

- Define national income equilibrium.
- Explain and demonstrate equilibrium in a two-sector economy.
- Explain a three-sector equilibrium.
- Explain a four-sector equilibrium.
- Identify and explain injections and linkages and planned and unplanned investment, and disinvestment.

REQUIRED KNOWLEDGE

- The circular flow of income.

TOPIC VALUE

The economy may be likened to an inflow/outflow model of a water tank. There are inflows (injections) and outflows (withdrawals) from the tank (main flow).

Introduction

This chapter begins with an explanation of the Keynesian model of the economy. From the outset the Keynesian model assumes an economy with:

1. Less than full employment
2. A given level of stocks
3. Spare capacity
4. Output at constant prices, i.e., no inflation
5. Wages assumed to be constant.

Basically, Keynes asserted that aggregate planned demand (C + I + G + X – M) determines the level of economic activity and that fluctuations in the economy were due to a difference in the amount that firms and households invested or saved respectively.

In figure 22.1 the familiar circular flow diagram represents a two-sector economy and shows how the national income is determined. The two sectors illustrated are households (consumers) and firms (producers).

It is assumed that $100 m will be paid as wages, interest, rent and profit to households in exchange for labour, capital, land and enterprise. These factors of production are then assumed to be employed to create an equivalent of $100 m in output.

Households then spend the same factor incomes of $100 m to purchase $100 m in output, with savings equal to zero and investment by firms also zero.

If the planned expenditures of households and firms (C + I) are equal to planned income or output (Y), then equilibrium is said to exist, and expressed as C + I = Y. Equilibrium is a balance between two forces, that is, aggregate demand (C + I) and Y (output), or aggregate supply.

The flow between these two sectors is the main flow in the model. Into this main flow are planned injections (J) and out of this main flow are planned withdrawals or leakages (W).

An injection is any income in addition to the circular flow of income in a given year that is not provided by households. It may also be viewed as expenditure on the national output of a country, except for domestic consumer spending.

For example, in a two-sector model of the economy, an injection would be investment spending, that is, firms' spending on the output of other firms such as raw materials.

In a four-sector model, injections would be investment, government spending, and exports (summarised as I + G + X), all of which are assumed to be independently or autonomously determined and hence not influenced by changes in national income.

A withdrawal or leakage is any income earned in the circular flow (wages, interest, rent, and profit) that is not returned to firms in the year of production; in the two-sector model this would consist of savings, because it is assumed that income not consumed is saved. In a four-sector model withdrawals would comprise savings, imports and taxes (summarised as S + M + T).

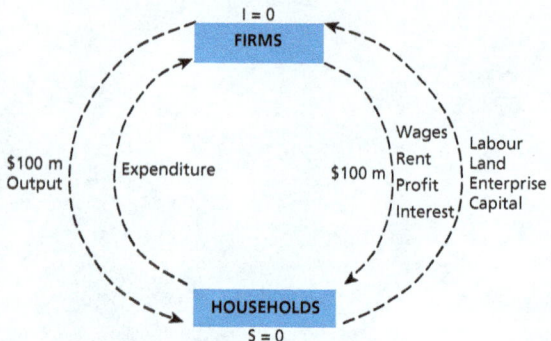

Figure 22.1 Two-sector circular flow diagram: determining national income

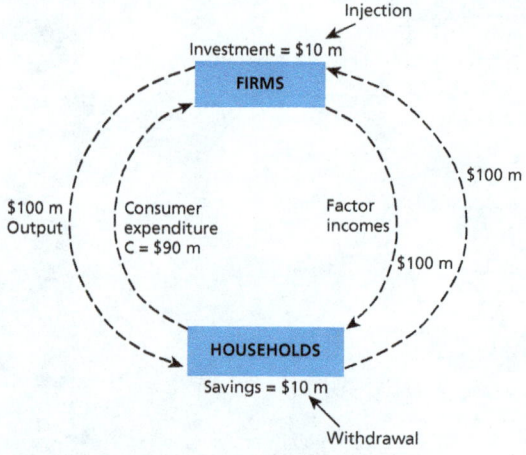

N.B. – 'm' denotes millions

Figure 22.2 Two-sector circular flow diagram: national income equilibrium

Chapter 22 National income: determination

Key points
For national income to be in equilibrium two conditions must be satisfied:

1. **Planned expenditure = planned income**
2. **Planned injection (J) = planned withdrawals (W).**

Notes:
In figure 22.2, consumption is equal to $90 m because $100 m is paid to households and $10 m is saved. Note also investment = $10 m.

For the first condition, equilibrium national income is planned expenditure = planned income C + I = Y $90 m + $10 m = 100 m.

The first condition of equilibrium is satisfied.

Condition number 2 requires planned injection (J) = planned withdrawals W

I = $10 m

S = $10 m

$10 m = $10 m

To conclude, the economy is in equilibrium.

Common error
Be careful not to confuse planned expenditure (C + I + G + X − M) with actual expenditure, which is what is actually spent in the country after a year has passed. Firms try to predict (take risk) what the level of planned expenditure is, based on the previous year, in the same way that all firms make their purchasing plans from month to month.

Basically this Keynesian model assumes that changes in national income are caused by changes in the expenditure that make up the aggregate demand in the economy.

Although equilibrium of the economy may exist as long as planned expenditure and injections are equal to planned output and leakages, there may be changes in the behaviour of households that may cause the equilibrium to change, leading to a change in the level of national income.

Disequilibrium

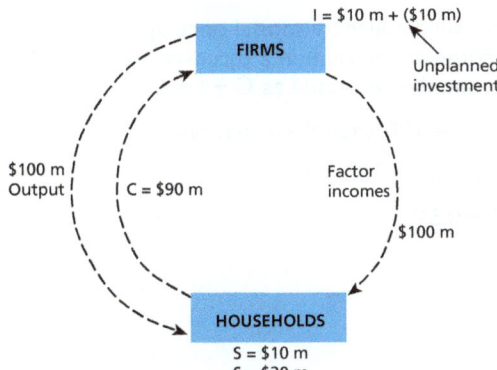

Figure 22.3 National income disequilibrium 1: by increasing savings (two-sector economy)

Refer to figure 22.3.

Recall that in the previous equilibrium:

C + I = Y

Or 90 m + 10 m = 100 m

And J = W

10 m = 10 m

Imagine now that the plans of households and firms are different; for example, households save some of their income and spend less than firms anticipate.

There will be a disequilibrium, as follows. Firms buy $100 m of factors of production from households and pay $100 m in factor incomes. They then produce $100 m in output to match the previous year's aggregate expenditure.

If households increase their savings from $10 m to $20 m then C + I < Y because consumption will now be $80 m, since $20 m is saved from the $100 m paid.

That is, C + I is then 80 m + 10 m = 90 m, which is $10 m less than 100 m output produced by firms.

This $10 m of excess output is added to firms' stocks (an assumption of this theory). This is called unplanned investment. Note that actual investment totals $20 m, while planned savings is also $20 m. Is this then an equilibrium? The answer is no, because $10m of investment is unplanned.

Yet, you should appreciate that $20 m of investment is equal to $20 m of savings, although this will not give an equilibrium according to the criteria previously set out: that is, planned C + I = planned Y; or planned J = planned W.

It is also possible for a disequilibrium to be caused when firms increase their planned expenditure on capital goods (investment), resulting in planned I > planned S. Refer to figure 22.4 below.

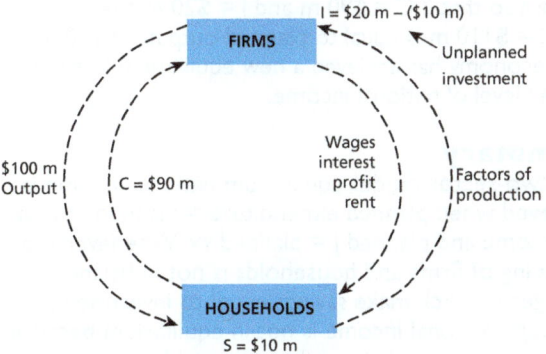

Figure 22.4 National income disequilibrium 2: by increasing investment (two-sector economy)

The figure shows the following

C + I = 90 + 20 = 110

Y = 100

Therefore C + I > Y.

Increasing investment (two-sector economy)

In this case, firms must meet the extra $10 m in excess aggregate demand from their stocks. This is called unplanned disinvestment.

Note that when firms do so, total actual investment is equal to $10 m, since actual investment will be equal to planned + unplanned investment, that is, $20 m − $10 m = $10 m.

Once again, an injection of $10 m (I) is equal to leakages of $10 m, but national income is not in equilibrium because $10 m of investment is unplanned.

Return to equilibrium

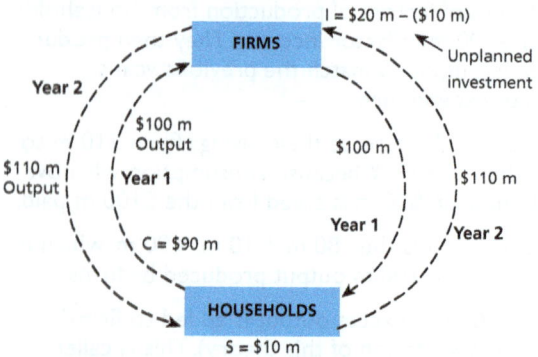

Figure 22.5 Return to equilibrium

Refer to figure 22.5. Since a planned injection is greater than a planned leakage and C + I > Y ($90 m + $20 m = $110 m > $100 m) the level of national income would rise in the next year. This is because firms would base their output on the previous year's aggregate demand of C + I = $110 m. They will, therefore, hire more factor inputs, increasing employment in the economy by paying out $110 m in factor incomes and producing $110 m in output.

The following will result. If $110 m is paid to households who continue to consume $90 m, as they did in the previous year, then S = 110 m − 90 m = 20 m. Note also that if C = $90 m and I = $20 m, then C + I = $110 m is equal to planned output = $110 m. The economy has achieved a new equilibrium but at a higher level of national income.

Summary

In a two-sector model, equilibrium national income is achieved when planned expenditure = planned output, or income and planned J = planned W. Whenever the spending of firms and households is not in balance, changes in stock make savings equal to investment, although national income is not in equilibrium because planned savings is not equal to planned investment.

At this point in the analysis, the equilibrium of a two-sector model may also be expressed in simple algebra. There is no government sector, so there are no taxes to deduct and, therefore, no disposable income.

Suppose that export expenditure = 60, and imports = 40, the equation then becomes:

C + I = Y; and C = 40 + 0.5y; and I = 60

Then algebraically, equilibrium is expressed as:

40 + 0.5y + 60 = Y

Solving 100 + 0.5y = Y

100 = Y − 0.5y

$100 = \frac{1}{2}Y$

Y = 200

For the injections and leakages approach the algebra is also simple; for example:

J = W

or I = S

Therefore, if 60 = −40 + 0.5y (savings function)

then 60 + 40 = 0.5y

100 = 0.5y

y = 200

Note that S = −a + 0.5y because

C = 40 + 0.5y

A three-sector equilibrium

A three-sector economy is also known as a closed economy because it is closed to international transactions. In a three-sector economy the government sector is added to the economy; for example, C + I + G

Where:

C is consumption

I is investment

G is government expenditure.

Not all government expenditure is related to national output; for example, transfers are not payment for services, but simply a transfer of income.

A major part of government expenditure is made to factor inputs and, therefore, legitimately counted in the national output/income.

Using the simple algebra model once again, national income equilibrium in a three-sector (closed) economy is simply expressed as C + I + G = Y.

Suppose G = 100, then the equation is:

40 + 0.5y + 60 + 100 = Y

200 = Y − 0.5Y

200 = ½ Y

Y = 400

In an equilibrium of a four-sector or open economy, the activities of foreigners are factored into the aggregate demand functions. Foreigners purchase local goods and services, particularly those which are part of the Caribbean tourism industry and from related sectors such as, for example, food and entertainment. This is referred to as export expenditure. Remember, however, that goods from abroad are called imports. This should not be counted in the national income because it is injected into another economy.

Suppose export expenditure is equal to 60 and imports equal to 40, the equation would then be:

$C + I + G + (X - M)$

$40 + 0.5y + 60 + 100 + 60 - 40 = Y$

Chapter summary

The Keynesian model assumes an economy with: less than full employment; a given level of stocks; spare capacity; output at constant prices, that is, no inflation; and wages assumed to be constant.

If the planned expenditures of households and firms (C + I) are equal to income or output (Y), then national income equilibrium is said to exist.

The flow between these two sectors is called the main flow and into this main flow are planned injections (J) and from this main flow are planned withdrawals or leakages (W).

An injection is any income received by firms not provided by households in the domestic economy. It may also be viewed as expenditure on the national output of a country, except for domestic consumer spending autonomously determined and hence not influenced by changes in national income.

A withdrawal or leakage is any income earned in the circular flow (wages, interest, rent and profit) not returned to firms in the year of production. Any unplanned addition to stock is called unplanned investment. Unplanned reductions from stock are called unplanned disinvestment.

Practice question

1. a. State the formula for national income equilibrium in a four-sector economy.
   b. **Identify and illustrate three injections and three leakages in a four-sector economy.**
   c. **Distinguish between unplanned investment and unplanned disinvestment.**

INTRODUCTORY ECONOMICS A TEXTBOOK FOR CAPE ECONOMICS STUDENTS

23 Consumption and savings

LEARNING OBJECTIVES

- Define, illustrate and explain the consumption function.
- Define and explain autonomous and induced spending.
- Calculate and illustrate the marginal propensity to consume (MPC) and the average propensity to consume (APC).
- Explain shifts of the consumption function.
- Explain other theories of consumption, e.g., life-cycle hypothesis.
- Distinguish between permanent and transitory income.
- Explain the relationship between consumption and savings, the marginal propensity to save (MPS) and average propensity to save (APS).
- Explain the role of consumption and savings on economic activity.

KNOWLEDGE REQUIRED

- Price and non-price factors that determine aggregate demand
- Endogenous and exogenous variables
- Movements along, and shifts of the aggregate demand curve
- Marginal and average values, and their relatedness.

TOPIC VALUE

Even with zero income we will need to sustain life and therefore continue to consume food. We may finance this consumption from past savings, obtain a loan or sell our possessions. We tend to increase our consumption spending as our incomes increase. We spend in our early years of work, and tend to save more in our middle years.

The role of consumption and savings on economic activity

Introduction
The expenditure method of measuring national income identified the buyers of the national output in a simple equation C + I + G + X − M = T. This is known as aggregate expenditure, or aggregate monetary demand. Each variable will be examined in turn, starting with consumption.

Consumption
Consumption is expenditure on goods and services that yields utility; for example, food, clothing, transport and entertainment. It is regarded as the largest component of aggregate expenditure or aggregate monetary demand (AMD).

This explanation of consumption is one advanced by the noted economist John Maynard Keynes. He asserted that the consumption we undertake is based on our current income, that is, the income we are earning at the present time. He refers to this income as absolute or disposable income, hence, his theory of consumption is called the absolute income hypothesis. If government taxation is excluded from the analysis

then all income earned becomes disposable income. Keynes's idea was that consumption consists of two parts: (1) fixed or autonomous consumption and (2) induced consumption. This he expressed in a simple equation:

$$C = a + bY_d$$

Where

C is consumption

a is fixed or autonomous consumption

b is the fraction of every additional dollar earned that is consumed, also called the MPC (explained below)

Y_d is disposable income

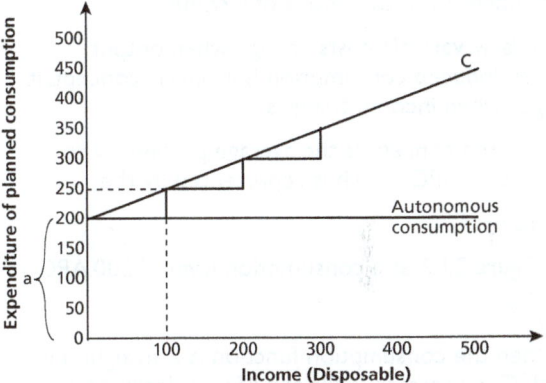

Figure 23.1 A consumption function

In figure 23.1, note that at zero income, consumption is $200. At this level of income, consumption is financed from past savings or borrowing. At zero income, or at any other level of income, the level of autonomous consumption is fixed. The letter 'b' in the equation above represents the fraction of every additional dollar earned that is given to consumption; it is called the marginal propensity to consume, or the MPC.

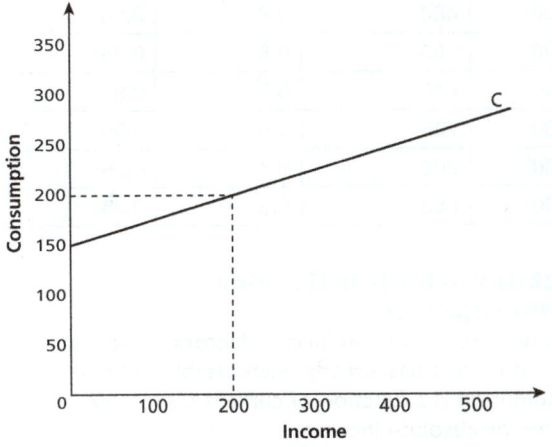

Figure 23.2 Average propensity to consume (APC)

Consumption is induced by increased income (we spend more when we earn more) but we do not spend it all. If our income increased from

$300 to $400 and our change in consumption is $50, this means that we are consuming $50 out of this additional $100 or 0.5. The letter 'b' therefore represents this fraction of every dollar earned that is consumed or the MPC. Note that the MPC also represents the gradient of the consumption function.

In figure 23.1 it is 50/100 or 0.5, and may be calculated as the change in C divided by the change in Y ($\Delta C/\Delta Y$). The consumption function could now be rewritten as:

$C = a + bY$ or $C = 200 + 0.5Y$

This concept is similar to the topic of fixed and variable costs, discussed in microeconomics. Remember that fixed costs are independent of production. In this case, fixed consumption is independent or autonomous of income.

Similarly, variable costs change when output changes. Induced consumption is a similar concept; it changes when income changes.

A related concept is the average propensity to consume or APC, which is represented by the formula $\frac{C}{Y}$.

In figure 23.2, at a consumption level of 200 APC is $\frac{200}{200} = 1$

When the consumption function is a straight line the MPC is constant, while the APC is declining in value throughout. See table 23.1.

Table 23.1 The MPC and APC

Income	Consumption	MPC ($\frac{\Delta C}{\Delta Y}$)	APC ($\frac{C}{Y}$)
0	80	0.8	0
100	160	0.8	1.6
200	240	0.8	1.2
300	320	0.8	1.06
400	400	0.8	1.00
500	480	0.8	0.96
600	560	0.8	0.93
700	640	0.8	0.91
800	720	0.8	0.90
900	800	0.8	0.89
1000	880	0.8	0.88

Factors which influence consumption

Income factors and non-income factors influence consumption. It has already been established that consumption is a function of current disposable income or absolute income.

Non-income factors which influence consumption are as follows.

Wealth
The more wealth people have in the form of homes, cars or stocks and shares, the more likely their spending out of current income will increase. This is also true of property, which people use as collateral security in order to finance consumption.

Interest rates
Falling interest rates cause not only stock values to rise but borrowing to increase as well, thereby financing increased consumption.

Access to easy borrowing
Automatic teller devices and other access to easy credit stimulate consumer spending out of current income, hence some people get into debt easily.

Rates of taxation
High levels of taxation reduce disposable income and dampen spending out of current disposable income. If taxes are increased, consumption will accordingly fall. It is the opposite for low rates of taxation.

Expectations of inflation
If consumers feel there will be inflation in the future, they may purchase in the present when money has more purchasing power. In a related way, if there is an expectation of a future increase in incomes, people will be more likely to spend more on that expectation.

The composition of households
Young income earners are heavy spenders compared to middle- and upper-income earners.

Tastes
If people have expensive tastes they will spend more out of disposable income.

Key points
Determinants of consumption are income and non-income factors. Non-income factors include wealth, distribution of income, rate of taxation, expectations of inflation in the future and the cost and availability of credit.

Refer to figure 23.3, which shows that a change in someone's disposable income is likely to cause a movement along the consumption function, while in figure 23.4 a change in some of the non-income factors may cause an upward or downward shift of the entire consumption function.

Chapter 23 Consumption and savings

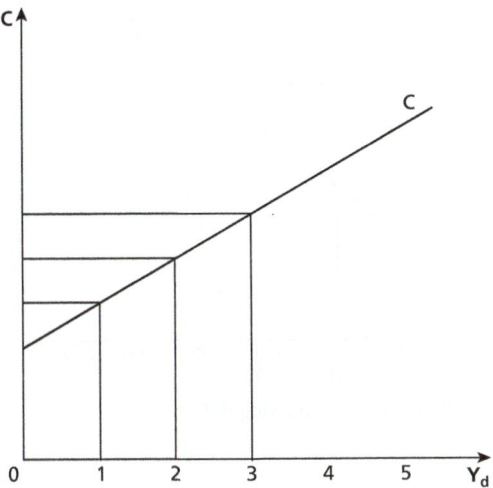

Figure 23.3 Change in disposable income

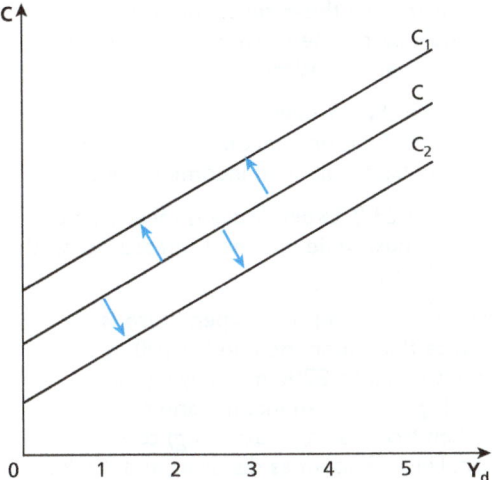

Figure 23.4 Change in non-income factors

Other theories of consumption

John Maynard Keynes's absolute income hypothesis theorised that the level of consumption in a society was based on the prevailing level of current income. Other theories of consumption are not in agreement with this explanation.

Life-cycle hypothesis
The life-cycle hypothesis by Modigliani and Ando theorised that people's patterns of consumption are based on their future earnings over their working years. Individuals make decisions about the level of expenditure at each period of their lives. For example, young professionals borrow extensively in their early years, save in their middle years and sell assets in their retirement years to augment their pensions. At the age of 35, a person knows his or her future stream of income, so will pay for a mortgage based on 20–25 years of future income. Also, the fact that insurance and other pension products are bought early in our working years suggests a consumption pattern with a long-term view.

Permanent income hypothesis
This hypothesis by Milton Friedman is similar to the life-cycle theory because it asserts that current consumption is based not on current income but permanent income, which is average income over a lifetime. A related idea is transitory income, which is a windfall, or temporary unplanned income, and is assumed by long-term theorists to be saved rather than spent.

Relative income hypothesis
J.S. Duesenberry believed that consumption patterns are influenced by the spending patterns of the social group to which one belongs. If friends are spending on foreign vacations, swimming pools or expensive cars, others will spend to 'keep up' with their friends. In effect, consumption is also based on past peak incomes, since people find it difficult to reduce their standard of living.

Key points
Although Keynes suggested that current income was a significant determinant of consumption, others such as Friedman and Ando and Modigliani suggested that consumption is based on future earnings. Duesenberry suggested that consumption is based on 'keeping up with a social group or the pattern of past earnings'.

Savings

Saving is defined as income not spent on consumption. Hence saving is expressed as:

$Y - C = S$

Where:

C is consumption

Y is income

S is savings

In the analysis of consumption the relationship between consumption and income was expressed in equation form, that is:

$C = a + bYd$

Savings are therefore equal to

$S = -a + sYd$

Where:

S = savings

s = 1 − b

− a = negative savings (money needed to finance autonomous consumption)

s = the fraction of every extra dollar earned that is saved. This is called the marginal propensity to save (MPS); also expressed as (1−b) where b is the MPC. If the MPC is 0.5 then the MPS is 0.5 because MPC + MPS = 1

Yd = disposable income

Figure 23.5 illustrates a savings function that shows the relationship between savings and changes in national income.

From the figure it is observed that savings S is induced by increasing income, since increasing income enables saving. The MPS is the fraction of every additional disposable dollar earned that is given to savings and is expressed in formula as $\Delta S/\Delta Y$. For example, if $S = -a + 0.5y$, the MPS is 50 cents out of every additional dollar earned. The APS is the average level of savings and it is expressed as S/Y. In figure 23.6 at income level $30m the APS is equal to 5/30 = $0.16.

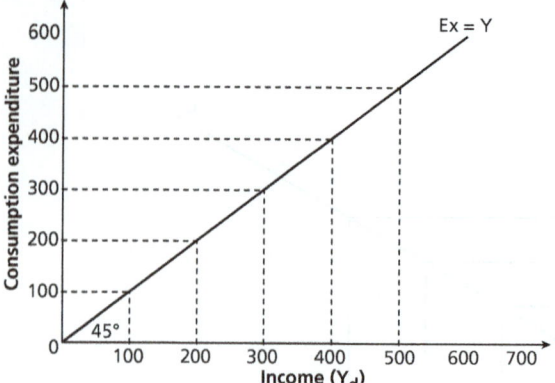

Figure 23.7 45-degree line showing different equilibrium points

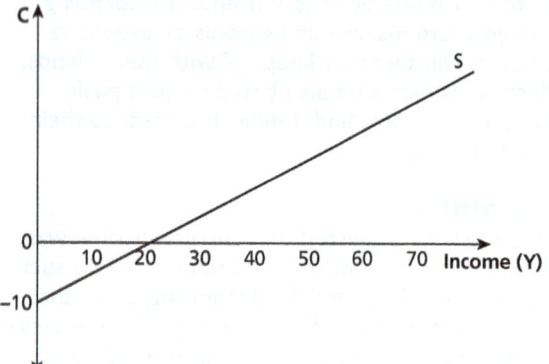

Figure 23.5 The savings function

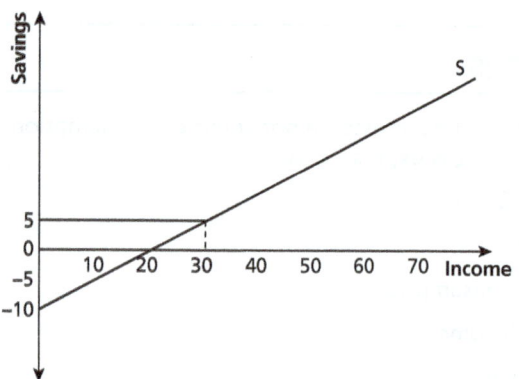

Figure 23.6 Average propensity to save (APS)

The relationship between consumption and savings expressed as an equation is:

$S = Y - C$.

Therefore, $C = Y - S$.

Diagrammatically the relationship between C and S is better understood if a 45-degree line is used.

In equilibrium, national income planned expenditure is equal to planned income or output (when national income is measured by these three methods). In figure 23.7 a 45-degree line is used to show how equality can be diagrammatically expressed.

Every point on the 45-degree line represents an equilibrium point of national income where planned expenditure is equal to planned income or output.

Refer to figure 23.8. Expenditure is measured on the vertical or Y axis, while income is measured on the X or horizontal axis.

However, only consumption expenditure is measured. Note that when income is $100 m, consumption is equal to $200 m, implying that consumption is greater than income and that $100 m is taken from savings (dissaving) to finance consumption. This is known as dissaving and it takes place during a level of income between $0 and $300 m. Within this range consumption is greater than the 45-degree line, which represents income.

At national income $300 m, however, C = Y, meaning that S = 0. From $300 m onwards, savings are positive because consumption is less than income. This is represented by the shaded area to the right of equilibrium point X.

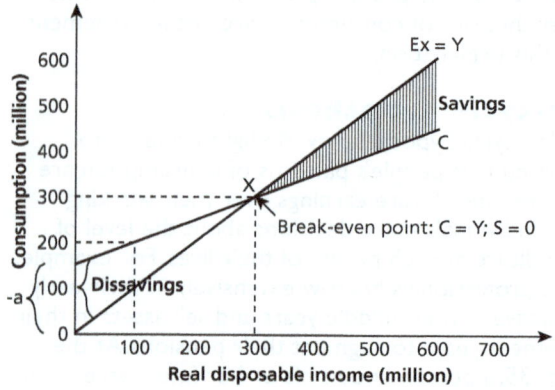

Figure 23.8 Income equilibrium (planned income equals planned expenditure)

In figure 23.9, the relationship between consumption and savings is clear. Area A shown in the consumption function corresponds to area B of the savings function; both indicate negative savings.

Beyond income level 300 m, savings are positive. Factors that influence savings are income and non-income factors.

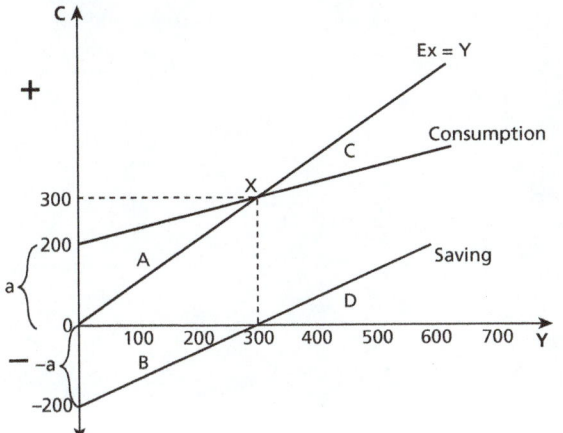

Figure 23.9 Relationship between consumption and savings

The most influential factor on savings is the level of disposable income. Increased income enables savings, especially at high levels of income. Also note that:

> The rate of interest is also an influential factor.
> At higher rates of interest savers increase their savings, with a view towards earning higher interest income for their deposits.
> The rate of inflation is more likely to discourage savings, because money deposited in the bank may lose value when inflation is taking place (if the rate of inflation is higher than the rate of interest).
> If inflation is anticipated, people are more likely to spend their money before inflation erodes the purchasing power of their money.
> Attitudes towards thrift is another determinant of the level of savings, because a high consumption society may prefer leisure over savings. This may cause the level of savings to be low.
> The range and reputation of finance institutions may also encourage or deter savings. If there is confidence in the banking sector people will be motivated to save.
> Relatedly, if there is a variety of savings institutions such as insurance, trust companies, credit unions or mutual fund companies offering competitive rates for deposits, the competition for funds may be higher, savings rates may increase and the level of savings may rise.
> Government policies such as tax concessions on insurance products also serve to stimulate the level of savings.

Key points
Government policies such as tax concessions on insurance products also serve to stimulate the level of savings.

Chapter summary

Determinants of consumption are income and non-income factors. Non-income factors include wealth, distribution of income, rate of taxation, expectations of inflation in the future and availability of credit.

A change in disposable income is likely to cause a movement along the consumption function, while a change in any of the non-income factors may cause an upward or downward shift of the consumption function.

Savings and consumption are opposite sides of the same coin. If the MPC = 0.8 then MPS = 0.2.

MPC + MPS = 1 because total income can only be consumed or saved.

Saving is defined as income not spent on consumption. Hence savings is expressed as $C - Y = S$.

Practice questions

1. Distinguish between consumption, savings and investment.
2. Briefly explain the concept of the relative income hypothesis.
3. Distinguish between the average and marginal propensities to consume and save.
4. Express the Keynesian consumption function as an equation.
5. What is the mathematical significance of the 45-degree line with respect to the consumption function?
6. What is meant by autonomous consumption?
7. What does the slope of the consumption function represent?
8. Derive a savings function from $C = a + bY$.
9. Distinguish between permanent income and transitory income.
10. Briefly describe the life-cycle theory of consumption.
11. List other influences upon consumption.

INTRODUCTORY ECONOMICS A TEXTBOOK FOR CAPE ECONOMICS STUDENTS

24 Investment

Chapter 24 Investment

LEARNING OBJECTIVES

- Explain the nature of investment.
- Identify the types of investment.
- Explain the reasons for investment.
- Explain and evaluate the two main theories of investment.
- Explain the accelerator theory.
- Explain the marginal efficiency of capital.
- Define, and explain public investment and cost benefit analysis.

REQUIRED KNOWLEDGE

- National income accounting (expenditure method)
- MRP theory (as a basis for understanding marginal efficiency of capital, MEC)
- Aggregate demand
- Investment and savings
- Concepts of gross and net values.

TOPIC VALUE

A higher standard of living carries a sacrifice, which is that of saving part of your income and giving up some consumer spending in the present. Savings are loaned to firms to enable the replacement of worn out capital and investment in new technology. Saving now enables future consumption.

Introduction

Investment is the second component of aggregate demand. Furthermore, investment represents producers' demand for capital goods and is considered to be part of the national output.

By definition, investment is defined as a flow of expenditure on capital goods, which adds to a nation's stock of capital in a given year for the creation of wealth in the future. It is a flow, rather than a stock concept, since there are additions and subtractions to the nation's stock of capital.

Gross fixed capital formation, physical increases in stock and work in progress appear in the expenditure method of calculating the national income. These are both examples of investment in capital.

Common error

We tend to use the word investment to describe spending on stocks, equities and financial products. However, these are all savings instruments and are not investments in the economic sense.

It is only when savings are used to purchase capital goods in the production process that investment expenditure takes place.

While investment represents a demand for current output, similar to consumption, government spending and exports, it is different in a very important aspect.

The main difference lies in the ability of investment to increase a nation's capacity to produce in the future and hence promote economic growth. In addition, while the other components are fairly stable over time, investment is the most unstable component of aggregate demand for the reasons outlined in this chapter.

Important terms
Gross investment

Gross investment is also called total investment, or gross fixed capital formation. It refers to the total output of capital goods produced in a given year. It includes not only the addition of new capital to existing stock, but also the replacement of worn out or outdated capital.

Depreciation

Depreciation is the term used to measure the value of worn out capital. The term obsolescence refers to the value of replacing outdated capital; for example, replacing a typewriter with a computer and printer, or a power saw replacing an axe.

Net investment

Net investment is a flow of expenditure on new additions to the capital stock. Replacement capital is not included in net investment. Note that net investment and replacement are important to the country's productive capacity, since replacement investment maintains the size of existing stock and therefore maintains the country's productive capacity. Net investment, however, increases a country's productive capacity and is regarded as a significant factor in economic growth.

Physical and human capital

Physical capital should be distinguished from human capital. Physical capital is expenditure on new plant and machinery, whereas human capital is expenditure on training and upgrading the skills of the workforce.

Autonomous investment

This type of investment is independent of national income.

Induced investment

Induced Investment is investment expenditure undertaken due to changes in income, that is, a change in the growth of sales or national income as a whole.

Planned investment

This represents the expenditure on capital that firms plan to make in a given year.

Unplanned investment

This explains additions to stock when aggregate supply of output is greater than aggregate demand.

Unplanned disinvestment

This explains subtractions from stock by firms when aggregate demand is greater than aggregate supply.

Categories of investment

Since investment is undertaken for many different reasons it may be necessary to classify them. Plant and factory buildings, machinery and vehicles represent capital that may both be new additions to existing stock, or replacement of worn-out capital.

Categories of investment include the following:

- **Additions to stock** such as finished goods and raw materials are regarded as investment, since they form part of current output, although not consumed during the period under review.
- **Construction** is also considered an addition to the stock of capital.
- **Construction of residential and commercial buildings** is considered a part of investment, since they add to the productive capacity of a country.
- **Work in progress and semi-finished goods** also have productive capacity and are regarded as investment as well.
- **Public investment** refers to state expenditure on infrastructure, which adds to productive capacity. Pubic and merit goods such as roads, ports, schools, police stations, public buildings and drainage are all considered as public investment.
- **Residential investment** is also considered capacity creation.

Factors which determine the level of investment

Level of profits
If firms' expectations of profit in the economy are positive, private investment is likely to increase.

Business optimism
This is related to the above point. Business optimism is based on future demand patterns. If a firm foresees a growing market share and future demand for their product, it will invest in more capital to meet this demand.

Many factors influence business optimism, chief among which are expectations created by economic growth, government economic policy, political stability and trends in regional and global trade.

Technical progress
Since firms will want to maintain a competitive edge, they will invest in modern technology. If new inventions and innovations are introduced, this will provide an incentive to invest. Similarly, new techniques of production, together with new technology, may lower a firm's cost of production.

If capital is cheaper than labour, a firm may choose to invest in capital instead of labour, assuming that the supply of capital is elastic.

Economies of scale
Economies of scale, both at the plant and firm level, may be a stimulus to investment for a firm because of the potential for cost savings and profit.

The rate of interest
Since the rate of interest is the cost of borrowing funds to finance commerce, low rates of interest will allow a firm to undertake an investment project with a percentage rate of return on the project that is higher than the rate of interest. Many firms operate with large overdraft facilities.

In this instance, the rate of interest represents the rate of servicing this debt. This concept is discussed in more detail in the analysis of marginal efficiency of capital.

Government incentives
If the government provides incentives to firms such as depreciation taxes, subsidies or grants, these will reduce costs and increase the rate of return on investment. Investment will accordingly rise.

Corporation taxes
This is an extension of the point made in favour of government incentives. If corporation taxes are reduced, a firm's return after taxes may provide an incentive for increased investment.

Marginal efficiency of capital and the marginal efficiency of investment

While analysing marginal revenue productivity theory, it was established that a profit-maximising firm would hire additional units of labour until the last unit adds as much revenue to the firm as the cost of hiring this factor.

The same reasoning applies to the demand for capital. In this case, the price of capital is the rate of interest of borrowed funds for the purchase of capital, and the marginal revenue productivity of capital is the sale of the capital's output.

However, capital is different from labour, since labour is usually hired for its output in the present and will work long into the future, up to 40 years.

Capital has a limited life and an investment project may take several years to complete before output and profit begin to accrue. Firms face a range of potential projects that yield different returns on their investment and face a downward sloping demand curve for capital. As investment increases, returns on investment will decline due to the law of diminishing returns to capital. The return on investment may be expressed in monetary terms; for example, a one million return on a ten-million investment is equal to a 10 per cent return. Similarly, a loan instalment may be expressed in percentage rather than monetary terms. If the expected future returns on investment (the internal rate of return) is greater than the cost of the investment (rate of interest) the investment is deemed profitable. These expected returns are the marginal efficiency of capital (MEC) and are sensitive to business confidence.

The marginal efficiency of investment is a schedule, when taking all firms together. Firms invest to earn a profit, which varies according to the viability of the investment. The rate of return may be high or low. This rate of return, or marginal efficiency of capital (MEC) in the economy at large, varies from one investment project to another. For the economy, the investment schedule can be calculated and expressed according to the prevailing rate of interest. Planned investment may be expressed as a function of the interest rate. Refer to table 24.1, which shows a marginal efficiency schedule for the economy as a whole.

Table 24.1 The marginal efficiency of capital for the economy as a whole

MEC % (per year)	Planned investment ($ bn per year)
30	5
20	10
10	15
5	20

A planned investment function or curve may be derived from the figures given in table 24.1.

Note that there is an inverse relationship between the rate of interest and the marginal efficiency of investment. At a rate of return of 30 per cent, only $5 bn of investment is profitable. In contrast, when the marginal efficiency of capital is 5 per cent, $20 bn of investment is possible because the cost of borrowing (5 per cent) is low, allowing a previous unattainable investment to take place; while at 30 per cent this cost of borrowing may be difficult to cover in terms of returns.

Note also, just as in marginal revenue productivity of labour, the downward shape of the marginal efficiency of investment schedule is due to diminishing returns to capital and the fact that increased output lowers the price and affects the future expected returns on the project.

Key point
According to the marginal efficiency of capital theory of investment, firms will demand capital for investment as long as the rate of return on the life of the investment is greater than rate of interest over the life of the project.

Criticisms of MEC and interest-determined investment

› The rate of interest is a determining factor for investment, but it ignores the fact that firms may finance a project from retained profit. However, if the rate of interest is high, a firm may obtain a higher rate of return if retained profit is saved, rather than invested.
› Firms' planned investment takes into account small changes in interest rates in their yearly business planning.
› Much of a firm's financing is undertaken through trade credit and is not wholly dependent on the rate of interest.
› Interest rates may be written off as an expense to firms when calculating net profit and therefore are not a significant factor of investment.
› Even when interest rates are low, assuming that the demand for capital is high, the supply of capital may be inelastic.
› Firms may not be able to capitalise on low interest rates if the government's monetary policy is focused on consumer spending and not on firms.

Factors which influence planned investment
The planned investment schedule may shift to the left or right in the manner of most demand curves, under certain conditions that are similar to factors that increase investment. These are as follows.

Expectations of the economy
If investment planners have a pessimistic view of the economy, they will anticipate a fall in the future rates of return and reduce investment spending as a result. Keynes referred to the expectations of a firm as 'animal spirits', which he determined to be a key factor in investment. If expectations are negative, the planned investment schedule will shift to the left.

Cost of capital
The cost of capital goods influences the rate of return. If the cost of capital goods rises, the rate of return would fall and so would the level of planned investment.

Technological change
This increases the productivity of capital and hence the rate of return. Planned investment will rise at all levels of interest rates, *ceteris paribus*.

Government incentives
If the government provides incentives to firms such as a depreciation tax, subsidies or grants, this will reduce costs and increase the rate of return on investment. Planned investment will accordingly rise.

Corporation taxes
This is an extension of the point made in favour of government incentives. If corporation taxes are reduced, a firm's return after taxes may provide an incentive for increased investment.

Level of profit

A firm's rising level of profits may stimulate the demand for capital. This will shift the planned investment schedule to the right, as illustrated in figure 24.1.

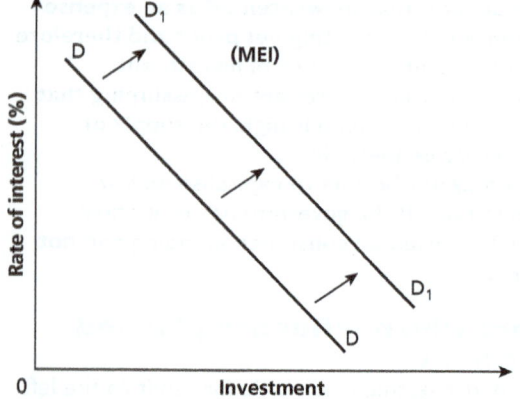

Figure 24.1 Increased demand for capital shifts investment schedule (D to D_1)

The accelerator principle of investment

The accelerator principle is different from the marginal efficiency of capital as a theory of investment, because it theorises that investment spending is induced by the rate and magnitude of a change in national income or output over time. The principle states that if the rate of increase in consumption is maintained, the level of investment will not change. This theory therefore seeks to explain induced investment.

The level of a firm's planned investment will be 'accelerated' by the rate of change of output and income from the previous year. This may be interpreted as a change in demand. This happens because firms are assumed to keep a fixed capital to output ratio. For example, if a firm requires $4 of capital to produce $1 of output, the capital output ratio is 4:1 or simply 4. This is known as the accelerator coefficient.

Assuming there is no replacement capital for a firm producing cement, an output of $1m of cement therefore requires $4 m of capital. If the demand for cement increases from $90 m to $100 m the firm is required to invest $40 m in capital. If there is a change in demand for cement from $100 m to $110 m, this will also require a change in investment of $40 m of capital.

Further, if this demand for output increases to $130 m of cement, 80 new units of capital are now required because the change in cement/output is now $20 m more, which requires 80 units of capital (4:1).

Note that a change in output or demand of 18 per cent (from $110 m to $130 m) accelerates investment to 100 per cent (from 40 to 80 units). If output changes from 130 to 180 units, the change is 50 units of cement requiring 200 units of capital (50 × 4).

The change in investment is now 80 to 200 or 150 per cent, which is induced by a change in output of 50 units (130 to 180) or 38.4 per cent. When, however, the demand for cement increases from 180 to 200 bags or 11 per cent, investment plunges from 200 units of capital to 80, a fall of 60 per cent.

The conclusion to be drawn from this exercise is that when the rate of demand/output increases at an increasing rate, the rate of change in investment will be accelerated by a greater percentage.

If the same figure is used for an economy, the change in output or sales can be taken to represent the change in national income. If the dollar ratio is used then $4 of capital are required to create $1 of output. A simplified formula for the accelerator principle is:

$$In = a\ (\Delta NI)$$

Where:

In = net investment,

a = capital output ratio

ΔNI is the change in national income.

Table 24.2 The accelerator

Year (t)	NI (m)	Net investment (m) (I_t)
2010	100	–
2011	110	40 (10 × 4)
2012	130	80 (20 × 4) = 100% increase
2013	180	200 (50 × 4) = 150% increase
2014	200	80 (20 × 4) = 60% decrease

Note:

Table 24.2 may be summarised as follows:

› An increase in investment from $110 m to $130 m (18%) induces investment from $40 m to $80 m (100%).
› An increase in investment from $130 m to $180 m (38%) induces investment from $80 m to $200 m (150%).
› An increase in investment from $180 m to $200 m (11%) induces a significant fall in investment by 60%.

The conclusion to be drawn from this table is that it is not the increase in national income that induces an accelerated rate of investment but the rate and magnitude in the change in national income. Note that although the change in national income is positive between the years 2003–2004, the rate of change is less than in the previous years. In short, the national income is not increasing at an increasing rate.

Key points

The accelerator principle suggests that if the change in national income is increasing at an increasing rate from one year prior to the year in question ($Y_t - 1$)

Chapter 24 Investment

to the year in question (Y_t), the rate of change in net investment (I_t) will accelerate at a greater percentage than the change in national income.

If the rate of change in national income falls, the change in investment falls significantly by a greater percentage than the change in national income.

Limitations of the accelerator theory

> - The theory assumes that firms have no spare capacity to accommodate an increase in demand in the short-run.
> - It also assumes that firms will respond to increases in demand by investing in new machinery.
> - Firms may determine that increase in demand is temporary and may use the factors of production more intensively, e.g., working 24-hour shifts.
> - Even if demand is permanent, the supply of capital in the short-term may be inelastic in supply.
> - Capital output ratios are not constant and may vary to a greater degree in the short-term when excess capacity exists in a recession, rather than a boom when the firm's capital is fully employed.
> - There are time lags that are associated with changes in investment as a result of changes in national income that are intended to induce changes in net investment.

The volatility of investment

The unstable nature of investment may be attributed to a variety of causes.

J.M. Keynes pointed out that the role of the expectations of the business sector is a key explanation of the volatile nature of investment. In computing the marginal efficiency of capital, there is much guessing and forecasting. Business expectations are strongly influenced by confidence and optimism, which may rise and fall as the business sector interprets economic signals and trends.

If business confidence increases, the business sector will expect a future increase in profit and revenue streams of investment they may be planning. This will shift the marginal efficiency of capital upward and to the right as illustrated in figure 24.1.

A collapse of business confidence will cause a downward estimation of future profits and revenues from planned investment, and cause a shift in the marginal efficiency of capital downward and to the left.

Business expectations also tend to be variable, which in turn cause investment to be variable. Many factors influence business confidence. Mainly, there is a lack of information on investment decisions that is related to demand for goods and services in the future.

Changes in taste and fashion, changes in government policy, the pressures of globalisation, the rate of inventions and innovations, and shocks to the economic global environment and natural disasters are some factors that affect future demand.

Spending on durable goods, such as motor vehicles and other capital goods, is heavily influenced by the state of the economy.

The accelerator principle also provides reasons for volatility of investment. Since a change in the rate of income or sales can induce such large increases and decreases in investment, then significant changes in national income have the potential to initiate further changes in the economy.

Key points

The volatility of investment is explained by the rise and fall of business expectations of future profit, which causes planned investment to shift to the right or left. The uncertain nature of future demand will cause a downward revision of estimated future profit. The sudden changes in investment caused by the accelerator principle are other reasons advanced for the volatility of investment.

Public investment

Public investment is undertaken by the government and focuses on infrastructure such as road building, ports, drainage, dams, public buildings, schools and police stations.

The feasibility of a government investment is undertaken by a technique called cost benefit analysis. A simplified explanation of cost benefit analysis involves:

> - **Identifying the costs and benefits of the project, e.g., a roadway exchange**
> - **Identifying positive and negative social benefits**
> - **Assigning a monetary value to the costs and benefits identified**
> - **Calculating a value for future costs and benefits and discounting them to the present**
> - **If benefits exceed costs, the investment project should be undertaken.**

Possible benefits of a roadway exchange

> - **Time saving**
> - **Decrease in vehicular accidents**
> - **Less traffic congestion**
> - **Less mental stress**
> - **Increase in private property value**
> - **Increase in profits for transport-oriented companies through efficient distribution**
> - **Increase in worker productivity**
> - **Increase in punctuality.**

Possible costs of the roadway exchange

> - **Construction noise and dust**
> - **Inconvenience to nearby residents.**

Problems related to assigning monetary values to benefits

In order to attribute a monetary value to time saved, the value of an hourly wage may be used; this is a technique called shadow pricing. However, this may be inexact if the road is used to attend leisure activities, such as going to the beach, since saving time is not associated with leisure activities.

The value of the reduction in accidents may be quantified using workman's compensation values. Saved lives may be valued by life insurance rates using shadow-pricing.

Problems associated with cost benefit analysis

Prices may not always be a reliable or available method for putting a cost on something.

First, double counting may occur. For example, the profits of companies cannot be counted together with time savings, since time savings are included in the contribution to profit.

Additionally, the responses to questionnaire surveys may not be accurate or truthful, since responses may vary due to subjective evaluation. It is hard to assign a value to the negative effects of, for example, pollution, so its calculation becomes subjective. And finally, inflation may distort prices – as would monopoly power in an industry.

Key point

Public investment is undertaken when a cost benefit analysis shows that the private and social benefits of the project are greater than the private and social cost.

Chapter summary

Investment is the most unstable element of aggregate demand, caused by expectations of future profit and the accelerator principle. It is defined as a flow of expenditure on capital over a period of time. The categories of investment are machines, building, inventories, additions to stock, construction and work in progress.

Investment may be determined according to the MEC, or induced by an increasing rate of change in national income according to the accelerator principle. Public investment is undertaken when a cost benefit analysis estimates that the aggregate private and social benefits of a project are greater than the aggregate private and social costs.

The volatility of investment is explained by the rise and fall of business expectations of future profit, which cause the planned investment curve to shift to the right or left.

The uncertain nature of future demand will cause a downward revision of estimated future profit. The sudden changes in investment caused by the accelerator principle is another reason for the volatility of investment.

The accelerator principle suggests that if the change in national income from one year prior to the year in question (Y_t-1) to the year in question (Y_t) is increasing at an increasing rate, the rate of change in net investment (I_t) will accelerate at a greater percentage than national income.

Practice questions

1. a. Explain what is meant by the accelerator principle.
   b. Is it capable of explaining all investments in a Caribbean economy of your choice?

2. a. What are the influences on the level of savings in your country?
   b. Suggest ways in which the level of savings may be increased.
   c. Analyse the economic consequences of an increase in the level of savings in your country.

3. a. What do economists mean by 'investment'?
   b. What are the main determinants of investment in your country?
   c. Why is investment considered important?

4. a. Distinguish between autonomous and induced investment.
   b. State four reasons why investment is considered volatile.
   c. Explain and comment on the measures that the government of a selected Caribbean economy has taken to increase investment.

Multiple choice questions

1. The basic assumption underlying the acceleration principle is that:
   a. Investment is sensitive to the rate of interest.
   b. Investment depends on the willingness of banks to make advances.
   c. Firms maintain a fixed ratio between capital employed and borrowed funds.
   d. There is a target relationship between the level of output and the capital stock.
   e. The rate of growth of output exceeds the rate of growth of the capital stock.

2. What would cause the value of the accelerator to increase?
   a. A reduction in tax rates
   b. An increase in the capital-output ratio
   c. An increase in the saving ratio
   d. An increase in the marginal propensity to consume.

25 National income equilibrium: Keynesian cross model

INTRODUCTORY ECONOMICS A TEXTBOOK FOR CAPE ECONOMICS STUDENTS

LEARNING OBJECTIVES

- Define, explain and calculate the multiplier.
- Explain the balanced budget multiplier.
- Identify output gaps.
- Define and explain inflationary and recessionary gaps.

REQUIRED KNOWLEDGE

- Consumption
- Savings
- Basic understanding of inflation
- Unemployment
- Injections and leakages.

TOPIC VALUE

The concepts of inflation and unemployment are directly related to our standard of living.

Introduction

Figure 25.1 represents a Keynesian cross model of a two-sector economy without government, which illustrates the $C + I = Y$ approach to national income (while figure 25.2 represents the injection and leakages approach). Note that an autonomous increase in investment of $20 m results in an increase in output from Y_0 to Y_1. If a further $20 m of investment is added ($C + I_2$), the new equilibrium will be X_1, at output Y_2.

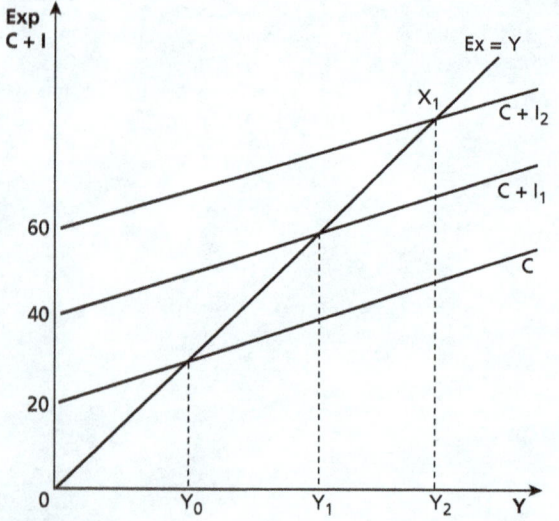

Figure 25.1 Keynesian analysis of national income

In figure 25.2 note the autonomous upward shift of the investment function from I_1 to I_2 in the injection and leakages model. Observe that both models graphically illustrate the economy in two different ways but yield the same result of a change in national income from Y_1 to Y_2. Very importantly, the analysis assumes that injections I, G and X are autonomous and not determined by income, whereas leakages (savings, taxation and imports) are, in fact, determined by changes in income.

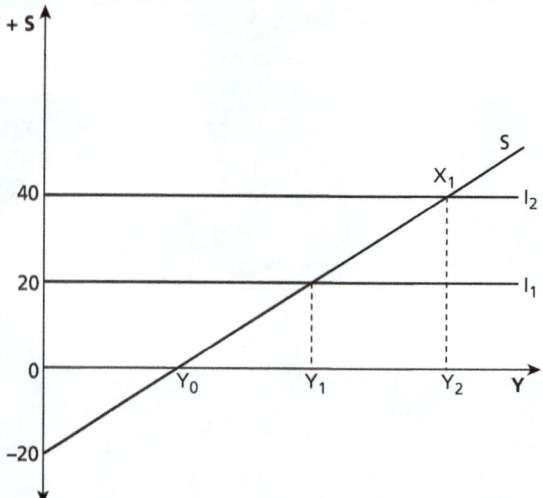

Figure 25.2 Injections and leakages approach to national income

A three-sector Keynesian cross model of equilibrium

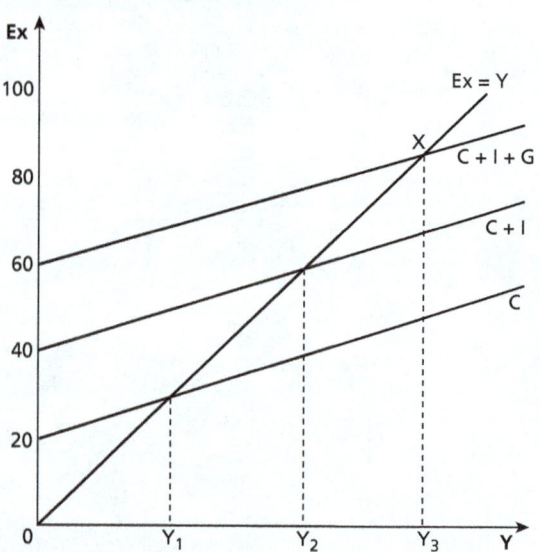

Figure 25.3 Keynesian cross: government spending increases national income

Figure 25.3 of the Keynesian model shows that autonomous government expenditure of $20 m moves the $C + I$ function upward and parallel to $C + I$ and causes an increase in national income from Y_2 to Y_3 at point X. Note this function is now $C + I + G$.

Correspondingly, figure 25.4 shows that the autonomous government function added to the investment function also causes the national income equilibrium to increase from Y_2 to Y_3 at point X*. Note also that the change in the model $C + I + G = Y$ is the same result as $I + G = S + T$; that is, a change in national income from Y_2 to Y_3 because it represents different models that explain the same concept.

Chapter 25 National income equilibrium: Keynesian cross model

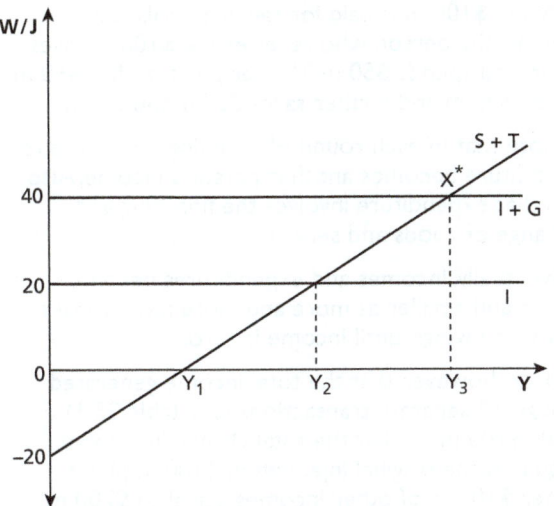

Figure 25.4 Injections and leakages approach: government spending increases national income

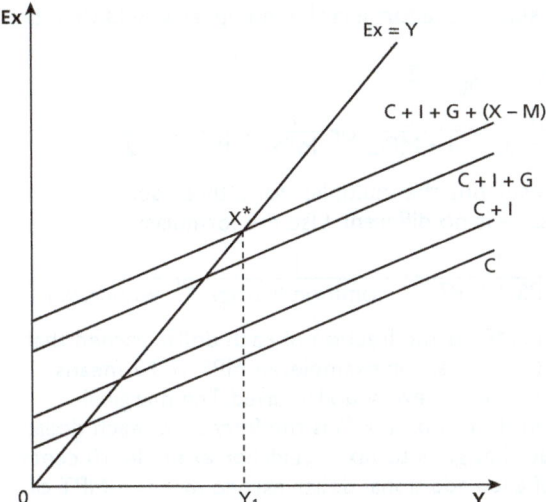

Figure 25.5 Keynesian cross four-sector national income equilibrium

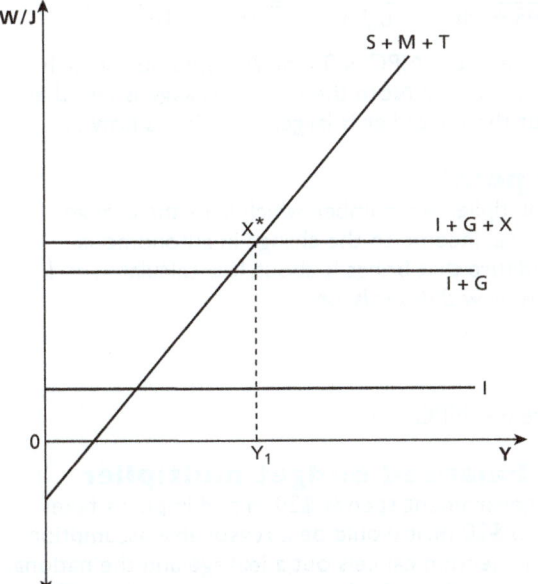

Figure 25.6 Injections and leakages approach four-sector national income equilibrium

A graphical model of a four-sector economy is illustrated in figures 25.5 and 25.6. These two figures illustrate national income equilibrium: first, without injections and leakages; and second with the injections and leakages. That is, $C + I + G + (X - M) = Y$, corresponding to $I + G + X = S + M + T$ at equilibrium Y_1 in both cases. Note that the foreign sector brings exports and imports into the model. If exports are greater than imports, the AD function shifts upward to a new equilibrium X^*.

The multiplier

Note that in figures 25.7 and 25.8, a change in autonomous expenditure of $20 m of investment causes income to increase from $20 m to $70 m. This is caused by the multiplier process. It would appear as if the $20 m of investment has expanded to $70 m in some way.

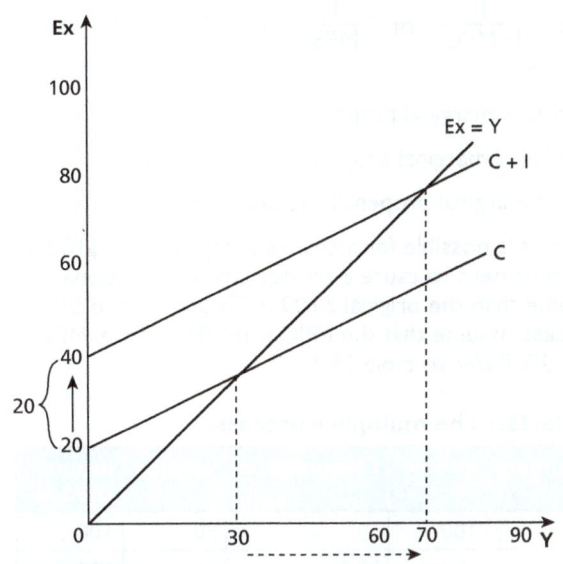

Figure 25.7 Keynesian cross – calculating the multiplier (K)

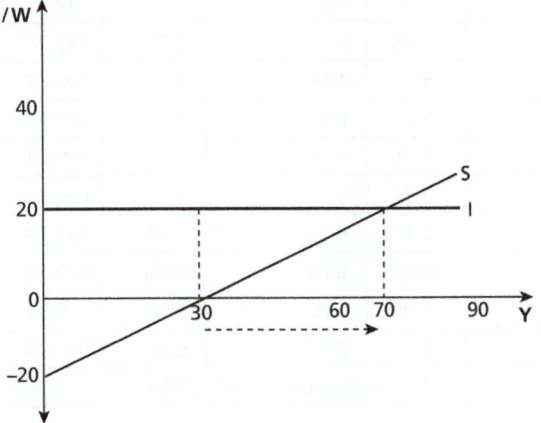

Figure 25.8 Injections and leakages approach – calculating the multiplier (K)

The multiplier (k) is a number that links the change in national income to the change in autonomous spending, such as government spending or investment, which causes it. From this definition we may view the multiplier as:

$$k = \frac{\Delta Y}{\Delta I}, \frac{\Delta Y}{\Delta G}, \frac{\Delta Y}{\Delta C}$$

Where:

ΔY is the change in income

ΔI is the change in investment

ΔG is the change in government expenditure

ΔC is the change in consumption.

Referring to figures 25.7 and 25.8, the multiplier would be:

$$k = \frac{\Delta Y = 40}{\Delta I = 20}$$

Therefore, $k = 2$

The more formal way to calculate the multiplier for a two-sector economy, however, is achieved using the formula:

$$k = \frac{1}{1-MPC} \text{ or } \frac{1}{MPS} \text{ or } \frac{1}{1-b}$$

Where:

MPS is marginal propensity to save

MPC is marginal propensity to consume

b is marginal propensity to consume.

So, it is possible for a change in injection of $100 m of investment to cause a greater change in national income than the original $100 m. To understand this process, assume that the MPC is 0.5. Therefore, MPS is also 0.5. Refer to table 25.1.

Table 25.1 The multiplier process

Spending	Income	Consumption	Savings	Income created
1	100	50	50	100
2	50	25	25	150
3	25	12.50	12.50	175
4	12.5	6.25	6.25	187.5
5	6.25	3.12	3.12	193.75
6	3.12	1.56	1.56	196.87
7	1.56	0.78	0.78	198.43
8	0.78	0.39	0.39	199.21
9	0.39	0.19	0.19	199.60
10	0.19	0.09	0.09	199.79
11	0.09	0.04	0.04	199.88
12	0.04	0.02	0.02	199.92
13	0.02	0.01	0.01	199.94
All other rounds 0.06 = 200				

Table 25.1 shows how $100 m of investment could create an additional $100 m in national income, assuming the MPC and MPS of all income recipients are 0.5. In the above table 'All other rounds = 0.06' means the spending rounds of 0.06 cents that completes the creation of the additional 100 million of income.

When $100 m is paid for raw materials, for example, the person who receives the $100 m saves $50 m and spends $50 m. The recipient of that $50 m spends $25 m and further saves $25m, and so on.

Note that in each round of spending one person's expenditure becomes another person's income. Also note that expenditure involves the financing and exchange of goods and services.

Eventually, incomes and expenditures become smaller and smaller as more and more money leaks away into savings, until income is zero.

Note, however, that the total income generated through 12 separate transactions (see table 25.1) equals $100 m so that the total change in income is equal to the original injection of $100 m plus a further $100 m of other incomes, equal to $200 m. The conclusion to be drawn is that $100 m creates an additional $100 m, or a grand total of $200 m.

Based on the formula the multiplier would then be:

$$\frac{\Delta Y}{\Delta I} = \frac{200}{100} = 2, \text{ or}$$

$$\frac{1}{1-b} \text{ or } \frac{1}{1-MPC} \text{ or } \frac{1}{MPS} = \frac{1}{0.5} = \frac{1}{1/2} = 2$$

Calculating the multiplier for a three-sector economy is no different. Use the formulas:

$$\frac{1}{MPS + MPT} \text{ or } \frac{1}{\text{common leakage}} \text{ or } \frac{1}{\text{withdrawals}}$$

The MPS is the fraction of each dollar earned that goes to savings. For example, an MPS of 0.2 means 20 cents out of every dollar saved. The marginal propensity to tax (MPT) is the fraction of each dollar earned that goes to taxes paid. For example, 10 cents out of each additional dollar earned means a MPT of 0.1. Note that there is now another leakage in the form of taxes, so the multiplier becomes:

$$\frac{1}{MPS + MPT} = \frac{1}{0.2 + 0.1} = \frac{1}{0.3} = \frac{1}{1/3} = 3$$

In this case, the MPC is 0.7 or 70 cents out of each additional dollar. Note the rate of leakage is less than 0.5, but the multiplier is larger than 2; it is now 3.

Key point

The multiplier is a number which links the change in national income to the change in autonomous expenditure that brings it about. It is calculated as 1 divided by withdrawals, or

$$\frac{1}{1-b}$$

Where $b = MPC$

The balanced budget multiplier

If the government spends $20 m and imposes taxes equal to $20 m, it would be a reasonable assumption that an injection cancels out a leakage and the national income would not, in the circumstances, change. There is, however, an increase in the national income.

This increase occurs because government spending is subject to the effect of the multiplier, but taxation does not cause a full decline of $20 m. Assuming a MPC of 0.75, the effect of taxes is to reduce consumption spending, which will limit the multiplier effect.

For example, if the MPC is 0.75 then a $20 m increase in income would result in a spending increase of $20 m × MPC, that is, $20 × 0.75 = $15 m. In this case, however, the reverse occurs: a $20 m increase in taxation (a leakage) reduces consumption by the same amount, that is, 0.75 × $20 m = −$15 m. Note that the value of the multiplier is 4. ($1 / (1 − MPC)$)

And since $K = \Delta Y / \Delta I$, i.e. $\Delta Y = K \times \Delta I$

This means that the fall in income via taxation of $20 m = 15 × 4 = −$60 m.

Meanwhile, if the government spending of $20 m is subject to the multiplier, then its increase in income is 20 × 4 = 80. To summarise, an increase in government spending equal to $20 m, together with an increase of taxation equal to $20m, actually increases the national income by $80 m − $60 m = $20 m.

Therefore, a combined J + W of $20 m increases the national income by $20 m making the overall multiplier = 1.

The multiplier also works in reverse. A fall in an injection or increase in a leakage could have a reverse effect on national income, in the same way as an increase in injection and a fall in leakages. A simple formula for calculating the balanced budget multiplier (the tax multiplier is how much GDP increases after a fall in taxation, or vice versa) is:

Balanced budget multiplier = − MPC/MPS + 1/MPS (government spending multiplier) = 1

Key point
When government expenditure and tax increases are the same, and the MPCs of all income recipients and taxpayers are the same, there will be a change in national income by the amount of the expenditure, because the multiplier does not work to reduce consumption by less than the increase in government spending. The balanced budget multiplier is therefore = 1.

Inflationary and deflationary gaps
It is necessary to first understand what is meant by the full employment level of national income in order to fully comprehend the concepts of inflationary and deflationary gaps. The full employment level of national income is simply the level at which all the productive resources of the economy are fully utilised. In other words, there are neither spare capacity nor idle factors of production at this level of national income.

This full employment level of national income is also referred to as the potential level of national income and represents a ceiling on the attainable level of output in the economy. Keynesian theory assumes that this level of national income is the goal of all economies because the labour force will be fully employed and aggregate expenditure is just sufficient to absorb the maximum output of the economy. In figure 25.9b this level of income is represented as Y_{FE}.

However, suppose the aggregate expenditure function ($C + I + G + X − M$) as shown in figure 25.10a produces an equilibrium level of national income Y_1 that is less than the full employment (Y_{FE}) level, then this leads to a phenomenon referred to as a deflationary or recessionary gap.

Figure 25.10a shows that the deflationary gap is denoted by the vertical distance XY. Expressed another way, XY represents the amount by which aggregate expenditure must increase in order to achieve the full employment level Y_{FE}.

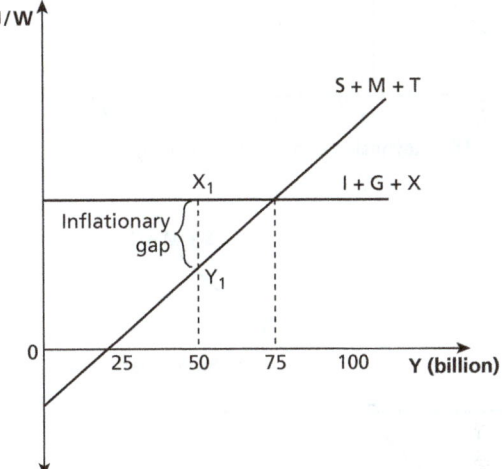

Figure 25.9a Injection and leakages inflationary gap

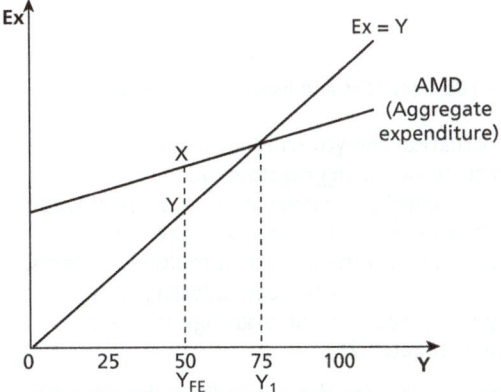

Figure 25.9b Economy operating beyond full employment level of national income

Also note that when the deflationary gap is represented by the injections and leakages model in figure 25.10b, this shows that leakages (S + M + T) exceed injections (I + G + X) at the full employment level Y_{FE}. This level of national income is also associated with recessionary conditions such as a high rate of unemployment, aggregate demand less than aggregate output, and consumer and business confidence very low, which leads to business closures and greatly reduced external trade.

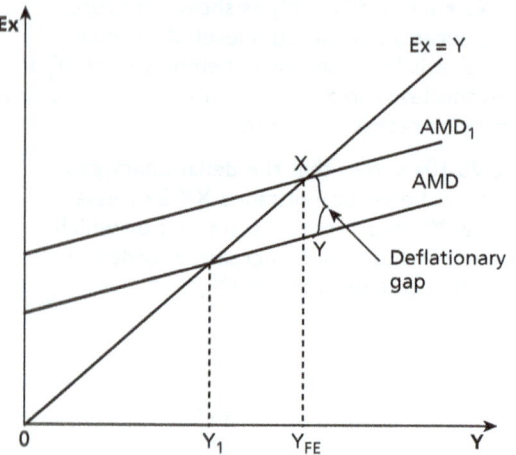

Figure 25.10a Keynesian cross deflationary gap

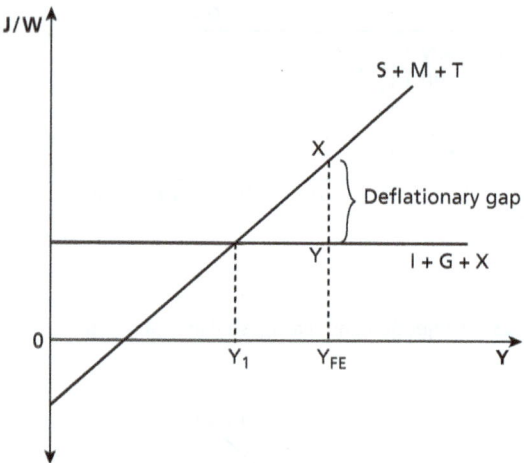

Figure 25.10b Injections and leakages deflationary gap

In this situation the government may initiate measures to stimulate aggregate expenditure to increase consumption or investment – or increased government spending – in order to close the deflationary gap with the attendant multiplier effects. Alternatively, it may seek to reduce leakages by employing measures to reduce savings and taxes (discussed in chapter 26).

It is also possible for the expenditure function to produce an equilibrium national income at a level that exceeds the full employment level (Y_{FE}). This occurs simply because there is excess demand for goods and services that cannot be produced because all resources are already fully employed. As a result, this leads to a rise in the general price level, as excess demand is actually being satisfied not in real terms, but in monetary terms. This explanation also represents the Keynesian view of how inflation is caused.

Figure 25.11 clearly illustrates this point. Note that the vertical distance XY is called the **inflationary gap** and also represents the amount by which aggregate expenditure must be reduced in order to achieve the full employment level Y_{FE}.

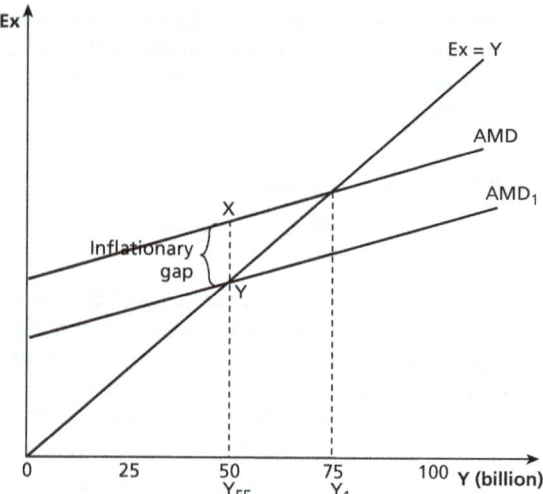

Figure 25.11 A Keynesian cross inflationary gap

This may be achieved if the government reduces its spending, by reducing an injection to reduce consumption, for example, or by increasing direct taxes, or increasing interest rates, which will also dampen investment spending.

Note in figure 25.9a that at YFE the inflationary gap is where injections (I + G + X) are greater than leakages (S + M + T) by the vertical distance X_1Y_1. In both figures 25.10 and 25.11 the vertical distance XY and X_1Y_1 are ways to illustrate the inflationary gap.

Key points
An inflationary gap refers to the increase in aggregate expenditure that cannot be accommodated since the economy is operating beyond its full employment capacity. Demand inflation is created in this way when the average price level is pulled up. It also measures the amount by which expenditure must fall to achieve full employment.

A deflationary or recessionary gap refers to the aggregate expenditure required to carry the economy to full employment. The shortfall in aggregate demand leads to unemployment.

Output gaps
An output or GDP gap is the difference between actual and potential GDP. For instance, if actual GDP is less than potential GDP, the resulting output gap is referred to as a recessionary or deflationary gap. If, on the other hand, actual GDP is greater than potential GDP the output gap is referred to as inflationary.

The inflationary gap may come about as a result of using fully employed factors of production more intensively, in order to satisfy an increase in aggregate demand. Since all factors of production are already fully employed the actual GDP exceeds potential GDP.

The short- and long-term in macroeconomics

The short-run in microeconomics is defined as the time during which at least one fixed factor cannot be changed, while variable factors can be mobilised to increase production. The long-run is defined as the period during which firms can increase output by changing all factors, and all factors become variable.

The short-run in macroeconomics is the period during which wages and prices are inflexible to changes in economic conditions such as aggregate demand and aggregate supply. In macroeconomics, there are two types of equilibria: short-run and the long-run. As economic conditions change, prices (including wages) may not adjust quickly enough to maintain equilibrium in markets in the economy. Inflexible prices are slow to achieve equilibrium level, creating prolonged periods of shortage or surplus. Wage and price stickiness inhibit the economy from achieving its natural level of employment and its potential output. In the short-run, price or wage inflexibility is an obstacle to full adjustment.

On the other hand, the long-run in macroeconomic analysis is a period in which wage and price flexibility do allow employment to move to its natural level, represented by the vertical long-run AS curve, and, after full market adjustment has been achieved, real GDP returns to its potential. The long-run also allows disequilibrium between different sectors within the economy to be in equilibrium, as well as the external economy, where different rates of interest, wages and exchange rates eventually leads to equilibrium.

Chapter summary

National income equilibrium is achieved when planned expenditure is equal to planned income; an alternative expression is that national income equilibrium may be achieved when planned injections are equal to planned leakages.

The multiplier (k) is a number that links the change in national income to the change in expenditure that causes it. The formula for a two-sector economy is 1/1–b or 1/MPS and for a four-sector economy it is 1/total leakages. The balanced budget multiplier is equal to 1.

The MPS is the fraction of each dollar earned that goes to savings. The marginal propensity to tax is the fraction of each dollar earned that goes to taxes paid.

An inflationary gap represents the amount by which aggregate expenditure must be reduced in order to achieve the full employment level of national income. A deflationary or recessionary gap refers to the aggregate expenditure required to enable the economy to achieve full employment.

The short-run in macroeconomics is the period during which wages and prices are inflexible to changes in economic conditions such as aggregate demand and aggregate supply. The long-run in macroeconomic analysis is the period during which wage and price flexibility do allow employment to move to its natural level, represented by the vertical long-run AS curve.

Practice questions

1. State four major determinants of aggregate demand.

2. State four major determinants of aggregate supply.

3. Discuss three factors that account for the volatility of investment.

4. Explain the relationship between 'savings' and 'investment'.

5. Using the standard Keynesian 45-degree diagram, explain the difference between inflationary and recessionary gaps.

INTRODUCTORY ECONOMICS A TEXTBOOK FOR CAPE ECONOMICS STUDENTS

26 Fiscal policy

Chapter 26 Fiscal policy

LEARNING OBJECTIVES

- Define, describe and differentiate between automatic and discretionary fiscal policy.
- Explain the Budget presentation.
- Differentiate between Keynesian and monetarist fiscal policy.
- Explain fiscal policy and the macroeconomic objectives.
- Explain budget deficits and surpluses.
- Identify fiscal policy time lags.
- Explain and evaluate the potency of fiscal policy.

REQUIRED KNOWLEDGE

- Basic theory of taxation
- Government expenditure and the role it plays in the economy
- Multiplier theory
- The components of aggregate demand
- Accelerator theory
- Inflationary and deflationary gaps
- The downward-sloping aggregate demand curve
- The upward-sloping aggregate supply curve
- Macroeconomic fundamentals.

TOPIC VALUE

Everyone wants a high standard of living, and part of this is determined by the government's fiscal policies, that is, their policies on taxation and expenditure, which are analysed in this chapter.

Introduction

Fiscal policy is the deliberate use of government expenditure and taxation, supported by the national debt and transfers, to achieve the government's short- and long-term objectives. Fiscal policy, therefore, is a tool of economic management that is used to regulate economic activity.

Fiscal policy is strongly linked to Keynesian economic prescriptions. Keynes believed that the economy, left on its own, would lead to micro and macroeconomic market failures, as happened in the USA in 2008 when financial institutions collapsed through a lack of state regulation.

Keynes also believed that a lack of government intervention allowed the Great Depression of the post 1930s to take place. He, therefore, strongly advocated government regulation of economic activity. Keynes's main argument was that the government's use of fiscal policy greatly influences the components of aggregate demand (C, I, G, X and M) to achieve the main macroeconomic objectives of the government.

In particular, he advocated budget deficits and surpluses to cure deflationary and inflationary gaps respectively, and was more concerned about short-run rather than long-run objectives.

Monetarist fiscal policy differs from the Keynesian approach, in that it focuses on the microeconomic objectives of the economy and advocates monetarist supply-side fiscal measures, which are designed to impact on the long-run aggregate supply curve.

Some of these long-term objectives are regulation of monopolies, privatisation, productivity in all factor markets, competition, and promotion of efficiency via incentives to work, save and invest. Figures 26.1 and 26.2 show how Keynesian and monetarist fiscal policies were intended to achieve their respective short- and long-run objectives.

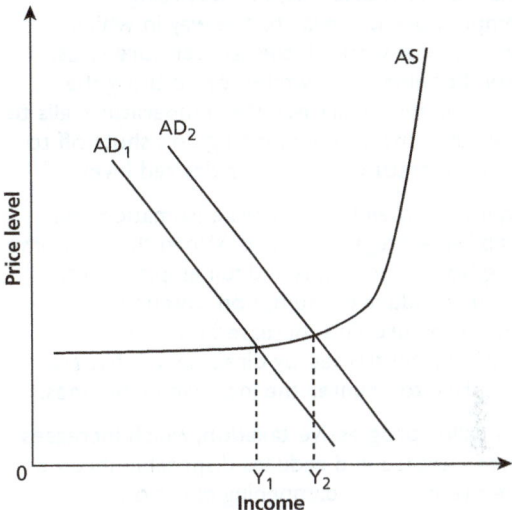

Figure 26.1 Keynesian fiscal policies

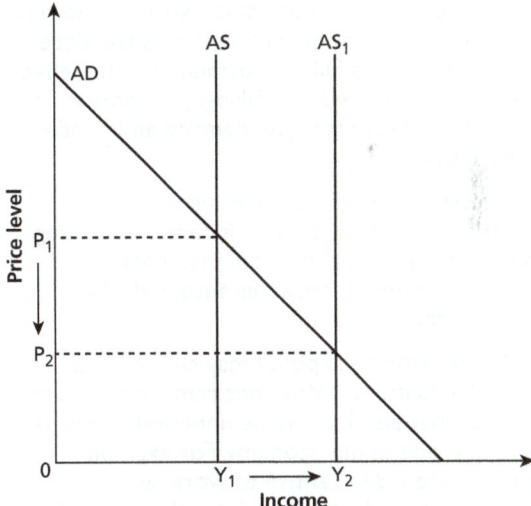

Figure 26.2 Monetarist fiscal policies

Note that in the figure 26.1, Keynesian remedies focus on short-term aggregate demand, while monetarist prescriptions (figure 26.2) target the shifting of the aggregate supply curve in the long-run.

Keynesian fiscal policy

Keynesian fiscal policy targeted aggregate demand in order to achieve full employment, economic growth, price stability and a sustainable balance of payments position.

In order to understand how fiscal policy affects aggregate demand and expenditure it is necessary to explain two aspects of fiscal policy: automatic and discretionary fiscal policies.

Automatic fiscal policy

This policy is also referred to as stabilisation policy, since specific measures are put in place to act automatically to prevent large fluctuations in economic activity and hence to stabilise the economy.

The role a thermostat plays in stabilising room temperature is similar to the way in which stabilisation policy works. If the temperature rises, the air conditioning unit switches on to bring the temperature down. Similarly, if the temperature falls to a very low level, the air conditioning unit shuts off to allow the temperature to rise to a desired level.

The question then is how does automatic fiscal policy stabilise aggregate demand? When the economy is enjoying boom conditions and full employment, rising incomes induce consumption, creating inflationary pressure. This increased consumption is automatically neutralised by direct taxes that are already in place to counter the increase in incomes.

This is called progressive taxation, which increases as incomes increase, and reduces disposable income and therefore creates a dampening effect on consumer spending. Demand inflation is accordingly controlled. In addition, government expenditure on transfer payments during a boom is also automatically reduced. Unemployment benefit payments fall, since the country is close to full employment. The net effect of rising progressive taxes and falling government expenditure stabilises aggregate demand and hence economic activity.

In a recession, the reverse takes place. As incomes fall, reduced taxation on incomes and rising government expenditure (transfer payments and unemployment benefits) together automatically stabilise aggregate demand.

While automatic fiscal policy may cushion the severity of fluctuations, it does not remove them and such a policy may also have some undesirable effects on the supply-side of the economy. For example, high taxes create a disincentive to work, while unemployment benefits tend to deter the search for employment. In addition, an economy may be stabilised in a recession at an undesirable level of income such that if there is a start of a recovery, the reduced size of the multiplier, caused by automatic fiscal policy, may delay the recovery process.

During a recession, however, as government expenditure automatically increases and falling incomes are cushioned by reduced taxes through progressive taxation, the net effect is a reduced leakage and increased injection.

The traditional roles of automatic fiscal policy have therefore been to:

› Cushion the fluctuations of the trade cycle
› Reduce the time delays between fiscal action and desired effect on the economy.

Discretionary fiscal policy

Since automatic fiscal policy only reduces the extent of fluctuations in aggregate demand, it is left to discretionary fiscal policy to actively manipulate, or alter aggregate demand, using changes in taxation and government expenditure.

Discretionary fiscal policy is therefore the deliberate use of taxation, government spending, transfers and the national debt to directly regulate economic activity. In this respect, this type of fiscal policy becomes a major policy tool of economic management in much the same way that the gears in a vehicle speed up, or slow down, the rate of movement of a vehicle.

Changing government expenditure

If the government increases expenditure on public works, this will cause the aggregate demand curve to shift upward, via a full multiplier effect.

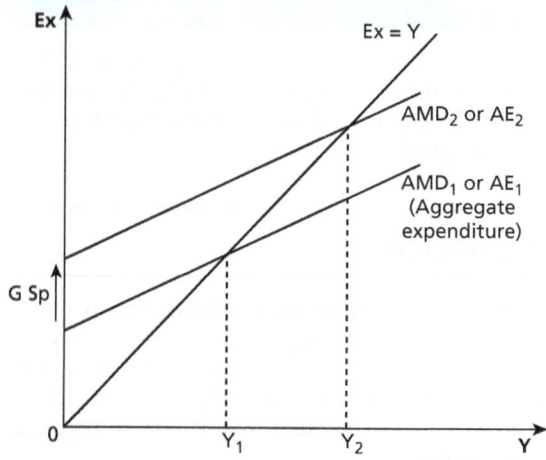

Figure 26.3 Discretionary fiscal policy: changing government expenditure

Note, in figure 26.3 discretionary fiscal policy of increased government expenditure has shifted the aggregate demand function upward, causing an increase in national income.

Changing taxation

If income taxes are reduced, for example, disposable incomes will rise and so will consumption spending (provided prices are constant). Aggregate demand will therefore also rise. When expenditure increases and/or tax reductions are employed, this is called an expansionary fiscal policy. A contractionary fiscal policy includes expenditure reductions and/or tax increases.

The aims of fiscal policy

Earlier in this chapter, reference was made to Keynesian and monetarist fiscal policy. The demand side of Keynesian fiscal policy and the supply-side nature of monetarist fiscal policy were also highlighted. The two-sided nature of fiscal policy is worth repeating before examining the effect of fiscal policy on the macroeconomic fundamentals.

The aims of monetarist fiscal policy are supply-side in nature, which include regulation of monopolies, productivity and efficiency increases, promoting competition and marketisation, privatisation, and resolving externalities. These are all discussed in chapter 31 on supply-side economic management.

Discretionary fiscal policy and aggregate demand

A reduction in taxes is likely to increase consumption, since disposable incomes will rise. If corporation taxes are reduced, investment is also likely to increase. Increased government expenditure will also affect consumption through the multiplier effect.

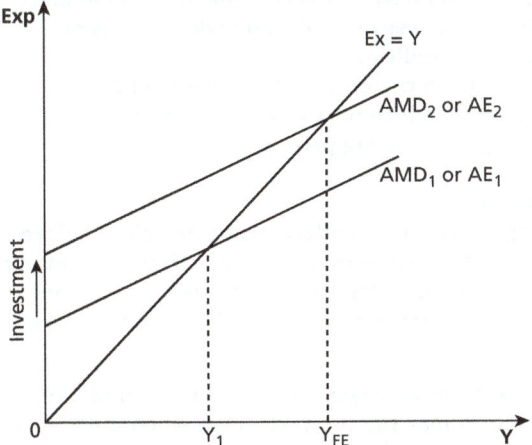

Figure 26.4 Discretionary fiscal policy and aggregate demand/expenditure

Since this will lead to growth, business optimism will cause investments to rise. This is all the result of expansionary fiscal policy, which was discussed earlier in the chapter. Note in figure 26.4, the shift of the aggregate demand function upward and to the left as a result of the increase in investment expenditure and that full employment is achieved at Y_{FE}.

Discretionary fiscal policy and unemployment

An expansionary fiscal policy may be achieved by a budget deficit. This is achieved when government expenditure exceeds government tax revenues. The deficit may be financed by borrowing from the central bank, the capital markets or from the public. When a budget deficit is employed, it may remove a deflationary gap. When aggregate demand is less than aggregate supply at full employment, the deflationary gap may be closed when increased government expenditure increases national income through the multiplier effect.

Note that in figure 26.4 the economy has reached full employment, causing the demand for labour and other factors to increase employment. A tax cut also has an incentive effect, in that it provides an incentive to work and in this case helps to counteract the poverty trap. Much has been written on the tax cut as a supply-side effect by Professor Laffer, who used the Laffer curve to illustrate his point.

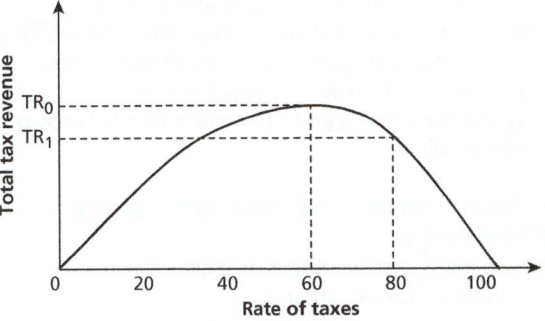

Figure 26.5 The Laffer curve

In figure 26.5 the vertical axis measures the total revenue collected from taxes, while the horizontal axis measures the rate of taxes from 0 to 100 per cent. When the tax rate is 0 per cent, total tax revenue is also zero and at a 100 per cent rate of tax, there is no incentive to work, so here total tax revenue is also zero. Between these two extremes, tax revenues rise steadily as tax rates increase, reaching (TR_0) maximum at a 60 per cent rate of tax. Any increase in the rate of tax after 60 per cent yields less tax revenue (TR_1) since workers have a disincentive to work and drop out of the workforce, reducing the revenue collected. If taxes are reduced there will be an incentive to work and, instead of losing tax revenue, the government will gain as more workers will return to the workforce.

Discretionary fiscal policy and economic growth

The very same analysis also applies to economic growth, since the multiplier and accelerator effects of an expansionary fiscal policy or a budget deficit will lead to a high increase in national income and hence economic growth.

Discretionary fiscal policy and inflation

An inflationary gap is removed by a deflationary fiscal policy and may cure demand inflation. An inflationary gap exists when aggregate demand is greater than aggregate supply at the full employment level of national income.

The removal of the gap may be achieved by a budget surplus when government expenditure is less than government revenues. In such a case, expenditure falls, leading to a reverse multiplier effect, bringing the level of national income to full employment. An increase in direct taxes may also cause a similar contractionary effect.

Discretionary fiscal policy and the balance of payments

The balance of payments is in deficit when external financial outflows exceed inflows. If government expenditure is reduced and the national income falls via the reverse multiplier effect, the marginal propensity to import will accordingly fall, *ceteris paribus*. A reduction in imports can reduce the deficit.

Increased tariffs also help to curb import spending. Both measures are fiscal in nature and may be employed to resolve a balance of payments deficit. The government may also grant subsidies to exporters, or may enter the market as a buyer. A reverse strategy may be employed in the event of a balance of payments surplus.

The limitations of discretionary fiscal policy

There are many disadvantages associated with this type of fiscal policy, which are:

- **Government spending is 'sticky' downward,** meaning that expenditure committed to maintaining new assets (recurrent expenditure) is difficult to cut. Once built, a school or hospital or road needs future upkeep. A school or hospital cannot simply stop functioning.
- **Government spending financed by borrowing is likely to raise interest rates,** since the government competes with private finance institutions for funds and will need to increase its rate to encourage borrowers to this end. In this case, borrowings 'crowd out' private investment.
- If the government spends heavily on large public works it will compete with private firms for material resources, causing their prices to rise; for example, cement, steel and skilled labour. This is referred to as resource crowding-out.
- Government spending on resources may cause shortages. Prices may rise in the construction sector, adding to cost-push inflation.
- Government spending may also have inflationary effects if the economy is at full employment.
- An expansionary fiscal policy may achieve full employment and economic growth but may also cause inflation, trade and balance of payments deficits and a weakened exchange rate. This is known as policy conflict. The use of different policies for different objectives is an alternative policy known as Tinbergen's Rule. In short, each policy must be aimed at a specific target without negative side-effects on other objectives.
- Direct taxes may reduce disposable income and lower the standard of living. They are also a disincentive to work, save and invest. Indirect taxes, for example value added tax (VAT), are regressive in effect. They also raise prices and create inflationary pressure.
- Multiplier and accelerator effects may be difficult to predict because they fluctuate when the expectations of the economy vary.
- Fiscal policy may be affected by time lags, in that by the time measures to counteract recession take effect, the economy may already be in the upswing phase, in which case the recovery may be adversely affected. These lags are discussed further in this chapter.

The potency of fiscal policy

The degree to which fiscal policy is effective depends on the following:

- **Accurate forecasting** in terms of predicting what changes are likely to take place with the components of aggregate demand (C + I + G + X)
- The extent to which a budget deficit or surplus will impact on injections and leakages, bearing in mind that an increase in some injections may be nullified or dampened by leakages
- The accurate determination of the size of the multiplier and accelerator effects, since these may change when expectations in the economy change
- Successful linking of fiscal changes to changes in aggregate demand, in order to achieve changes in the desired objectives; for example, reducing demand inflation by a successful increase in direct taxation and removal of value added taxes on basic commodities
- Determining the disincentive effects of fiscal policy on the incentive to work, save and invest
- Solving the time-lag problem.

Time lags

Time lags, which are the delay that takes place before a fiscal measure achieves its planned effect, are a major problem of fiscal policy. The effect may take too long to achieve, or even worsen the problem it is seeking to solve.

For example, a budget deficit intended to reflate the economy may start to take effect when the economy has already recovered and is expanding. In this case, expansionary fiscal policy makes the situation worse by creating inflation and balance of payments problems. Similarly, deflating the economy to head off inflation may only start to take effect when the economy has moved into recession. A budget surplus would, in this circumstance, worsen the recession.

There are five time lags associated with fiscal policy. These are as follows.

Information to recognition lag

This lag refers to gathering research or information confirming the economic problem, for example a deflationary gap. The government will only act if it is certain there is a recession. This may take some time for the economic researchers to determine.

Recognition to decision lag

Having confirmed the problem, for example inflation, the government must be certain about its strategy, which may involve economic decision-making with technocrats.

Decision to mobilisation lag

The government may need time to mobilise its resources to implement its economic strategy.

Mobilisation to implementation lag
A strategy of expansionary fiscal policy may require time to implement. These changes will require mobilising the Inland Revenue department for example. Having accomplished this, tax changes may take a further 3 to 6 months to carry out.

Implementation to achievement lag
A tax cut or an increase in government spending may take a while to bring about a desired result. For example, consumption may respond slowly if expectations of the economy are not optimistic, or a tourism promotion in a CARICOM state may take a few years to bring in more tourists. If time lags can be kept to a minimum, fiscal policy will reduce fluctuations in the long-term.

Key points
Fiscal policy's discretionary element has many disadvantages. Some of these are policy conflicts, downward stickiness of government spending, disincentives, crowding-out effects and time lags.

The national debt

The national debt consists of both internal and external borrowings of the government or its agents, that is, municipal bodies such as borough councils. When the government or its agents spend more money than they receive in revenue in a fiscal year, they are obliged to make up the deficit by borrowing.

This deficit is called the Public Sector Net Cash Requirement (PSNCR). When these deficits persist and accumulate over a period of time they become the national debt.

Common error
Be careful to distinguish between the PSNCR and the national debt. While they are related concepts, they are not the same. The national debt is an accumulation of the PSNCR of several previous years.

The PSNCR may be financed by:

- **Government printing money.**
- **Borrowing from the banking sector by selling bonds, treasury bills or securities.**
- **Borrowing from the non-bank public, e.g., selling bonds.**
- **Borrowing from foreign sources.**

The public sector debt repayment (PSDR) occurs when the government achieves a surplus, that is, government revenue exceeding expenditure. The excess revenue is used to repay an accumulated debt. The PSDR should not be confused with financing the national debt, which concerns the way the debt is financed, that is, bonds, and so on.

The debt ratio
The debt ratio expresses the national debt as a percentage of gross domestic product (GDP). In this way, it reflects a high- or low-debt ratio. A low-debt ratio of $10 billion to $100 billion GDP, or 10 per cent, suggests that the debt does not contribute a significant burden to taxpayers. Sometimes the external debt (the 'principal' in the formulas below) is expressed as a percentage of export revenue, once again reflecting the ability to repay the debt. The formula for calculating the debt ratio is as follows:

$$\frac{principal + interest \times 100}{GDP}$$

or

$$\frac{principal + interest \times 100}{valued\ exports}$$

The debt trap
A debt trap refers to an unusually high-debt ratio that persists for many years and which requires the government to commit revenue, usually reserved for management of the economy, to servicing the debt. When infrastructural development is postponed through committing funds to repay debt, growth in the economy is reduced.

The burden of national debt
The question of whether the national debt is a burden to present or future generations depends on how the debt is perceived. Usually, a debt payment is a sacrifice of income. A government debt, however, cannot be viewed in this way because it is actually borrowing from lenders in a country; for example, government bonds. The repayment of this debt many years later is financed by citizens from the same country. In effect, it is only a transfer of wealth from one to the other.

The real burden may have been on those who lived 20 years ago, when the loan was taken out, for whom resources could have been put to other uses.

Borrowing from overseas residents, however, does incur a loss since interest payments are made in foreign currency, which is earned through the sale of exports and therefore means a sacrifice of home resources.

If, however, the external debt was incurred to purchase technology or capital resources, the debt may yield future revenue from the investment and therefore not be viewed as a burden. In spite of these arguments, it can be said that the national debt does carry some costs.

These costs are summarised as follows:

- **Financing a debt via the PSNCR may cause financial and resource crowding-out. This may raise interest rates and have an inflationary impact on the construction sector.**
- **Raised interest rates act as a drag on capital formation.**

- Raising taxes to finance debts may have disincentive effects to work, savings and investment. This is called the excess burden of taxes.
- Borrowing from the banking sector adds to liquidity. Inflation may result if there is excess aggregate demand in the economy when it is close to full capacity.
- When interest payments increase as the national debt increases, the deficit created becomes difficult to control.
- Payment of interest for debt servicing is a diversion of finance away from the infrastructural development of a country.

Key point
Although it is argued that the national debt is a transfer of wealth within the country, the national debt does incur costs to the country in payments to overseas residents and can act as a drag on private investment at home.

Managing the debt
It is important to manage the national debt of a country to prevent it from becoming a burden. There are a variety of ways to manage the debt, which are explained as follows.

Debt refinancing
Debt refinancing is a process that converts an existing debt, including arrears and future payments, into a new loan. In effect, the creditor pays off the debtor's debt and starts a new loan arrangement.

Debt rescheduling
In this case, there is a lengthening of the time to repay the debt so that new and long-dated securities are applied to the outstanding balance. In effect, the debtor nation is granted debt relief. In some cases, the lending agency may reduce the debt service requirements of the debtor.

Debt restructuring
Debt restructuring is a strategic plan to prevent the debtor from incurring further debts. This may involve closing down state-owned firms that are a drain on the public purse, heavily indebted or are making huge losses.

Debt for equity swap
A debt for equity swap takes place when a creditor agrees to cancel all or a portion of debt owed in exchange for a share in a profitable state-owned firm.

Debt write-off
A debt write-off takes place when a creditor nation cancels the debt obligations of a debtor nation. In the majority of cases the debtor nation is usually a poor nation in terms of earning foreign exchange.

Debt retirement
Debt retirement is the repayment of a debt in full.

Government expenditure
The government is the single largest spender in the economy because it plays a dominant role in the economy. There are four main categories of government expenditure. These are:

1. Capital expenditure
2. Current expenditure
3. Transfer payments
4. Debt interest.

Common error
Do not confuse transfer payments with transfer earnings. Transfer earnings are the supply price of a factor of production, while transfer payments are payments made without the exchange of goods and services.

Capital expenditure
Capital expenditure refers to government spending on infrastructure and social capital; for example, schools, hospitals, police stations, ports, reservoirs, roads, and so on. Most Caribbean territories have a public sector investment programme (PSIP), to which the majority of the capital expenditure is allocated. It is therefore the creation of new assets.

Current expenditure
Current expenditure is government spending that maintains assets already created; for example, wages paid to public employees such as doctors, nurses, teachers and policemen. Highway maintenance and other public goods, for example parks, absorb most current expenditure.

Transfer payments
Transfer payments are incomes received without the exchange of goods or services, such as unemployment benefits and subsidies for sugar and gasoline, for example, in some Caribbean territories.

Debt interest
Debt interest is the payment of interest to holders of government debt.

The reasons for government spending
The objective of government expenditure may be placed in four categories:

1. Social
2. Economic
3. Demographic
4. Technological.

Social reasons
The government allocates expenditure to maintain law and order, especially when criminal activity increases. Government spending in this category also focuses on poverty alleviation, reducing vagrancy, tackling homelessness, improving health care and providing a

social safety net to ensure a basic standard of living for vulnerable groups in society – single parents, the elderly or physically challenged.

The government also allocates expenditure on public education and social issues such as contagious diseases, tobacco and alcoholism consumption, and teenage pregnancy. State spending also seeks to promote a fair society; for example, promoting wealth and income distribution, school meal plans, and free medicine, transport and school books.

Economic reasons

The government allocates expenditure for economic reasons to:

- **Manage the economy**, e.g., to promote economic growth and development. The government in this case may provide infrastructure to accommodate the private sector, e.g., roads, ports, power, water and communication. The provision of infrastructure is necessary to increase overall productivity in the economy.
- **Retrain idle labour** with the objective of increasing occupational mobility.
- **Accommodate regional policy**, i.e., the development of underdeveloped regions by establishing industrial zones.
- **Promote export development**, especially in the tourism sector.
- **Boost export sales** by financing trade missions.
- **Finance the provision of public and merit goods** as the economy grows.
- **Government spending on debt repayment** increases if the rate of interest increases.

Difficulty in cutting government expenditure

Government expenditure may be difficult to cut because:

- Debt repayments are contractual.
- Expectations in society are difficult to change, e.g., people get used to free health and education, and the social safety net.
- The structure of the population is constantly changing.
- State assets are in continuous need of maintenance.
- A fall in government spending may cause a downturn in the economy.
- Wages in the public sector are difficult to cut because unions are powerful and can be militant.

Taxation

A tax is a charge or levy on individuals and firms by the government, in order to raise revenue to carry out government spending. It also achieves economic and social objectives. A tax is also called a surcharge, tariff, duty or levy.

Types of taxes

A tax may be direct or indirect. A direct tax is one that is levied on income and wealth. The impact of the tax is fully borne by the person upon whom it is levied. An indirect tax is a tax on expenditure. The impact of the tax may be shifted from the person on whom it is levied to someone else; for example, VAT may be passed on to buyers by firms.

Summary

A tax may be differentiated by the incidence, burden or impact on the person on whom it was intended. If it cannot be avoided, it is a direct tax. When the burden of a tax can be shifted to someone else, it is said to be indirect.

Aims of taxation

Taxes are imposed for reasons that may be economic or social.

Economic reasons

Taxes are imposed for economic reasons to:

- **Raise revenue** for the purpose of financing government spending, e.g., public and merit goods.
- **Curb demand inflation.** Raising taxes tends to dampen consumer spending.
- **Regulate monopolies** by imposing taxes on profits.
- **Protect infant industries** from unfair competition, particularly in open economies. In addition, a country may wish to promote the consumption of local output, e.g., to reduce the food import bill.

Social reasons

Taxes are imposed for social reasons to:

- **Discourage the consumption of demerit goods** such as alcohol, tobacco and gambling
- **Redistribute income** from rich to poor by way of progressive taxation
- **Discourage negative externalities** such as noise, air or water pollution. In some countries they are called green taxes. In most Caribbean territories taxes are imposed on firms that pollute the environment.

Summary

Taxes are levied to achieve efficiency, equity and to realise micro- and macroeconomic objectives.

Qualities of a good tax

In his book, *The Wealth of the Nations*, Adam Smith outlined the necessary qualities of a tax. According to Adam Smith taxes should be:

- **Fair**, i.e., based on the ability to pay the tax. According to the law of diminishing marginal utility, a rich man values his last dollar lower than a poor man. Therefore, government should take it away from him and redistribute it to a poor person. This is called vertical equity. Horizontal equity refers to the people in the same economic status paying the same quantity of taxes.

- **Certain.** Taxpayers should know exactly how much they should pay, how to pay it and when and where it should be paid.
- **Convenient.** It must be easy to pay a tax. Complicated procedures should be avoided at all cost, including the time and method of payment.
- **Economical.** The cost of collecting the tax should not exceed the amount of the taxes collected for the taxpayer or administrator (Inland Revenue).

Apart from the four 'canons' of taxation above, there are other qualities of a good tax. It should be:

- **Difficult to avoid**
- **Flexible** to adapt to changing economic circumstances
- **Efficient**, i.e., achieve what it sets out to achieve, e.g., to redistribute income.

Key point
Taxes should be fair, economic, certain, convenient, flexible, difficult to evade and efficient.

The effects of taxes
Refer to figures 26.6, 26.7 and 26.8. A tax may be progressive, regressive or proportional.

Under a progressive tax, a greater percentage of taxes is taken as the income of a person increases. An example of a progressive tax is PAYE (pay as you earn) or income tax. See figure 26.6.

A regressive tax is one that has greater impact on lower incomes than higher incomes, for example VAT. For example, if a high income and low income person purchase an item for $100.00 and pay 15 per cent VAT on the item, they will both pay a total of $115.00. But if the poor man is earning $5,000 a month, for him the tax represents 0.3 per cent of his income, while for the wealthy buyer earning $50,000 per month the $15 is just 0.03 per cent of his income. Figure 26.7 illustrates a regressive tax.

A proportional tax is a fixed percentage of one's income, as shown in figure 26.8.

Direct taxes and the negative effects of taxation have already been discussed but are summarised here.

Summary of direct taxes and the negative effects of taxation

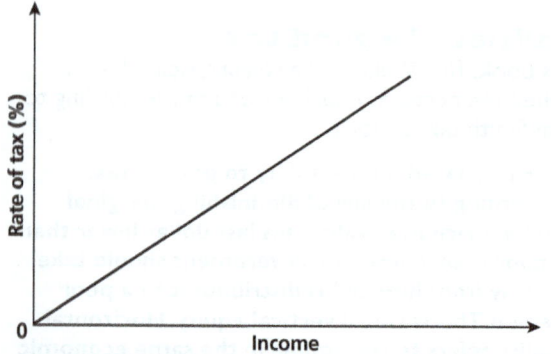

Figure 26.6 A progressive tax

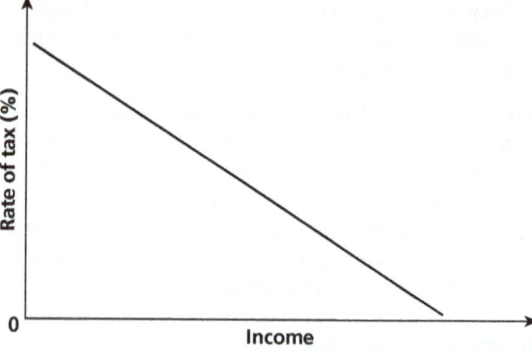

Figure 26.7 A regressive tax

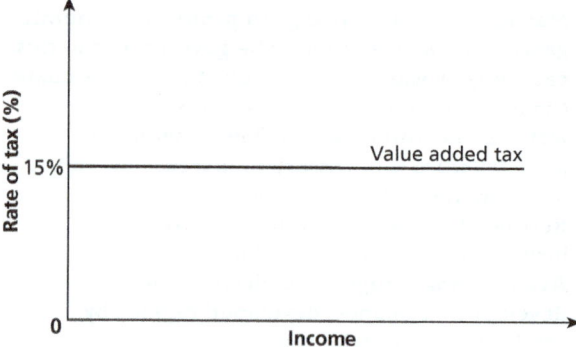

Figure 26.8 A proportional tax

- A direct tax is a disincentive to work, save and invest. E.g., high corporation taxes are a drag on investment.
- Direct taxes lower disposable income, negatively affecting consumption and adversely affecting the ability to save. Living standards are also affected.
- High taxation (direct) may act as a drag on the recovery phase of an upswing in the economy.
- Direct taxes lead to unemployment traps. The unemployed will prefer to collect unemployment benefit than work at low wages to pay high taxes.
- Taxes discourage upward mobility of labour. A middle manager may refuse to accept a promotion because the job puts him in a higher tax category.
- High corporation taxes are a disincentive to foreign direct investment on which most CARICOM territories depend for economic development. This issue is explored in more detail in chapter 35 on foreign direct investment.
- High indirect taxes (e.g. VAT and duty) raise the prices of local goods and services, which further become uncompetitive in external markets.
- Indirect taxes can be inflationary. In the short-term, citizens would purchase cheaper foreign substitutes (import substitution) leading to a possible balance of payments deficit. In the long-run business closures may also result, leading to high levels of unemployment.
- Indirect taxes such as VAT or tariffs distort the price mechanism to the extent that the price may no longer reflect the real preferences of consumers or producers.

- Tariff barriers inhibit free trade, leading to a lack of competitiveness in external markets and also to inefficiency on the part of home producers.
- Indirect taxes are also regressive. Low-income earners carry a greater relative burden than high income earners.

Key point

There are many disadvantages of direct and indirect taxation. These effects are felt in the micro- and macroeconomy and are summarised above.

Sources of government revenue other than taxation

Other sources of government revenue apart from taxation and the PSNCR are:

- Gross banking profits of state-controlled companies
- Sales of nationalised industries (privatisation)
- Rent from government-owned enterprises
- Sale of government goods and services, e.g., passports, licensing of vehicles
- Interest and dividends earned from government investment.

Chapter summary

Fiscal policy, which is linked to Keynesian economic prescriptions, is the deliberate use of taxation, government expenditure, transfers and the national debt to achieve the government's short- and long-term objectives.

Automatic fiscal policy is also referred to as stabilisation policy, since measures are put in place to act automatically. Discretionary fiscal policy is therefore the deliberate use of taxation, government spending, transfers and the national debt to achieve the objectives of the government. Fiscal policy's discretionary element has many disadvantages, some of which are policy conflicts, downward stickiness of government spending, disincentives, crowding-out effects and time lags.

The national debt consists of both internal and external borrowings of the government or its agents, that is, municipal bodies such as borough councils. Although it is argued that the national debt is a transfer of wealth within the country, the national debt incurs costs to the country in payments to overseas residents and can act as a drag on private investment at home.

There are four main categories of government expenditure. These are capital expenditure, current expenditure, transfer payments and debt interest. Government expenditure is undertaken for social, economic, demographic and technological reasons. It is very difficult to cut due to entrenched expectations and other irreversible conditions.

Practice questions

1. Discuss the fiscal policy tools available to Caribbean countries that can be used to increase and decrease output and employment.

2. Which of the following best defines 'fiscal policy'?
    a. An instrument to change the national debt
    b. A means of changing government spending
    c. Government making decisions on interest rates
    d. Changes in taxation and government spending to regulate economic activity.

3. The government places a tax on gasoline in country X. This is an example of:
    a. Expansionary trade policy
    b. Expansionary regional policy
    c. Expansionary monetary policy
    d. Contractionary fiscal policy.

4. When a government spends more than it collects from tax revenues, this results in a:
    a. Trade surplus
    b. Budget surplus
    c. Balance of payments deficit
    d. Budget deficit.

5. Which of the following is an automatic fiscal stabiliser?
    a. State required pension
    b. Tax rebates paid to Inland Revenue
    c. Contribution to National Insurance
    d. Unemployment benefits.

INTRODUCTORY ECONOMICS A TEXTBOOK FOR CAPE ECONOMICS STUDENTS

27 Money and banking

Chapter 27 Money and banking

LEARNING OBJECTIVES

- Define money.
- Identify the characteristics of money.
- Identify different types of money.
- Explain the demand for and supply of money.
- Explain liquidity preference theory.
- Identify the money stock and factors affecting the supply of money.
- Explain the determination of interest rates.
- Demonstrate credit creation.
- Identify the function of the central and commercial banks.

REQUIRED KNOWLEDGE

- Basic money and banking theory
- Functions of commercial and central banking.

TOPIC VALUE

Most individuals seem to be preoccupied with possessing money, because it is linked to the satisfaction of wants, standard of living and quality of life.

Introduction

So far, most aspects of the economic problem have been analysed without mentioning the monetary aspects of the economy. Money is merely a claim to wealth.

Money without output would be as useless as finding a million dollars on a deserted island. It would not make you any better off.

Money is anything acceptable that can perform the following functions:

› Medium of exchange
› Measure of value
› Store of value
› Standard for future payment.

The nature and types of money

A medium of exchange
Money enables trade to take place. Before money was used, the exchange of goods and services was carried out by the system of barter in primitive economies. But to carry out an exchange successfully, the wants of the barterers had to coincide; frequently, this did not occur and the satisfaction of wants became frustrated as a result. With money, goods could be acquired even if wants did not coincide.

Measure of value
Money fixes a value or price on a good so that the value of goods can be 'rated' against other goods. For example, if a pen costs $5.00 and a fish costs $20.00, we could say that a fish is worth four pens. It is precisely this problem that caused much disagreement between barterers but was subsequently solved with the money system. Money as a measure of value is also known as a unit of account.

A store of value
Long ago individuals wished to save some of their output for future use, but its quality deteriorated as time passed. Since a dollar today will be the same dollar one year from today, it performs the function of a store value for future spending, provided that the general price level does not rise and cause the value of the dollar to fall.

A standard for future payment
If you wish to make a purchase today but have to make payments over a period of time, it would be difficult to calculate the exact amount to be paid in the future. However, money allows an exact calculation of credit instalment and therefore enables the satisfaction of 'wants' now, but payment over a period of time in the future; for example, 5, 10 or 20 years.

The characteristics of money
Anything commonly valued and acceptable as money can function as money, but it must also have certain characteristics or qualities. Money must be:

› **Acceptable:** everyone must agree to accept a certain form of money.
› **Durable:** it must not change its form or deteriorate, causing people to lose confidence in it.
› **Divisible:** in barter it was difficult to make small payments because it was difficult to trade the part of a whole, for example the leg of a goat; smaller units of money allow small purchases.
› **Uniform:** all types of money must be the same.
› **Scarce:** money must be scarce in order to have value. If leaves of a common tree were used as money, it would require too many leaves to enable a transaction because everyone would have much of it.
› **Portable:** money should be easy to carry around to facilitate trade.
› **Difficult to copy or duplicate:** if money is easy to reproduce it would cease to become scarce and there would be a loss of confidence in that form of money.

Money and liquidity
The ready acceptance of money in cash form allows valuables or assets that are easily turned into money to take the place of money. When an asset can be easily converted into cash without delay, or at a very low cost, such an asset is said to be a liquid asset.

Travellers' cheques, bankers' drafts, certain types of jewellery, a fixed-time deposit in the bank are some examples of liquid assets. Cash or units of currency, plus notes and coins, are 100 per cent liquid.

Types of money circulating in an economy
Many assets can act as money. The following is a summary of different types of money.

Commodity money

In the prison system where notes and coins are of no value, cigarettes or illegal cellular phones or illicit drugs are commonly held by the inmates as a form of money. In this case, the assets function as commodity money because they have other basic values; for example, cellular phones can be used as a medium of exchange as well as to communicate.

Convertible bank notes

These are bank notes that in the recent past were backed by gold to the extent that it was possible to 'convert' these notes into gold.

Fiat money

Fiat money is the currency that the government authorises; it is also known as token money.

Fiat money is the money currently in use and consists of notes and coins that are not backed by gold but function as units of money according to government law. It is also called legal tender and, like commodity money, the notes and coins have no real value but are commonly acceptable as legal.

How commercial banks create money

Fiat money is money printed by the government and used as legal tender. Commercial banks similarly create money known as bank deposits, which function as claims to currency.

Customers transfer bank deposits from the commercial bankers, using cheques as instructions to their bankers to make payments on their behalf. However, because a banking customer may require part of his or her bank deposit in cash, banks keep a stock of currency to satisfy this need.

This quantity of cash when expressed as a percentage of the total bank deposits is called the cash ratio, and each bank determines over time how much the ratio ought to be. Even if more cash is needed, the bank can convert some of its liquid reserves to fulfil this need. The central bank of a country retains the right to set a cash ratio according the monetary policy it wishes to carry out. (See chapter 28 on monetary policy for more details on the cash reserve ratio.)

How bank deposits are created

Bank deposits are created in a variety of ways. When a customer makes a deposit in the bank, his or her account is credited by the amount of the deposit. No money is actually created at this stage, since the sum deposited has assumed a different form. The deposit, for example $1,000, is both an asset and a liability to the bank, since if loaned to the bank it is an asset but it is also owed to a depositor and therefore a liability.

This form of money fulfils two main functions of money, a unit of account and store of value, and is therefore referred to as near money. Time deposits pay a higher rate of interest than current or savings accounts and function mainly as a store of value. In most cases, a week's notice of withdrawal or 'breaking' the deposit is necessary before it may be withdrawn.

Money and credit cards

The use of credit cards or 'plastic money' has been widespread as a means of payment, or as a medium of exchange, over the last three decades. It should be noted that credit cards are not money, but instruments that allow a cardholder to access money immediately, such as in a transaction in a grocery or department store.

Credit cards are therefore substitutes for money. It is only when a bank issues a loan to a client on a credit card that money is created. Since the loan increases the liability of the bank, the debt is also an asset of the bank. As the principal means of making money is in the form of interest paid on loans, banks tend to lend as much of their deposits as they possibly can.

The banking multiplier

The government acts as a regulator of money circulating in the economy, by employing a monetary policy. However, it is necessary to understand how a commercial bank can cause an expansion of money circulating in the economy.

This is known as a credit creation or a banking multiplier, and is similar in many respects to the multiplier discussed in chapter 22 on national income determination. To simplify matters, assume there is only one bank in a small economy. Assume also that the government (via the central bank) directs that 10 per cent of bank deposits must be retained with the bank and not loaned out. This is called the cash reserve ratio (CRR) or the reserve requirement ratio.

If, for example, someone deposits $100 in the bank, this deposit will expand according to the formula:

$$\text{Deposit} \times \frac{1}{\text{Cash ratio}} \quad \text{or} \quad \text{Deposit} \times \frac{1}{10\%}$$

In this case it is equal to $100 \times \frac{1}{10\%}$

$$= \$100 \times 10 = \$1,000$$

Just as the investment or government spending multiplier, the $1,000 consists of the initial $100 + $900 in successive rounds, as given in table 27.1.

Table 27.1 The banking multiplier

Deposit	CRR (10%)	Loaned
First, 100	10	90
Second, 90	9	81
Third, 81	8.10	72.90
Fourth, 72.90	7.29	65.61
Etc.		

Assume initially that there is one bank in a system and CRR = 10 per cent. Further, assume that when $100 is deposited the bank retains $10 and makes a loan of $90, which then returns to the bank resulting in $9 retained and $81 in loans. Eventually, the $100 will be reduced to zero through successive spending rounds, but will have expanded the money in circulation by a further $900.

Since a total of $100 of the $1,000 retained by the bank amounts to the 10 per cent CRR, this type of banking is called fractional reserve banking.

The liquidity assets ratio

The liquidity assets ratio is the obligation of commercial banks to maintain a percentage of liquid assets. For example, if these include short-term securities, treasury bills, of say $10 million the bank will still be able to lend $100 million in loans, by maintaining a liquid assets ratio of 10 per cent. If it becomes necessary the bank could convert the $10 million of liquid assets into cash.

A simple balance sheet of a commercial bank

Let us assume a rich relative has died and left you $100,000 in his will, which you deposit into a commercial bank. The $100,000 is an asset and liability to the bank. It is an asset because it is part of the reserves of the bank and it is a liability because the bank owes you this sum of money. The balance sheet will show the following information:

ASSETS	LIABILITIES
Reserves of currency $100,000	Current account deposits $100,000

Assume that the bank has a reserve requirement of 10 per cent, then the bank is bound to set aside the sum of $10,000.

The remaining $90,000 is called excess reserves of currency, or current account deposits that are surplus to the reserve requirement. Now suppose that a firm wishes to expand and needs $90,000 to do so, it may apply to the bank for this sum, which by chance is exactly what is required. The balance sheet will now appear as follows if the loan is granted.

ASSETS($)		LIABILITIES($)	
Currency Reserves	100,000	Current accounts deposits	100,000
Loan	90,000	(on behalf of firm)	90,000
Total	190,000		190,000

Note that it is only when $90,000 out of the $100,000 are lent that money is created and increases the money supply of a country. The money supply is the total quantity of money circulating in the economy and consists of financial assets that fulfil the functions of money. Since the money supply of a country is directly related to total expenditure on output, it is a key target of control for most governments, especially to prevent inflation.

Although notes, coins and current account deposits are primarily used as a medium of exchange, there are financial assets that are not used as a medium of exchange but which can be converted into liquidity quite easily. Examples are saving accounts, time deposits or treasury bills. The money supply may therefore consist of narrow measures, which are liquid and used as a medium of exchange, and broad measures, which are illiquid and function more as a store of value. Common measures of a country's money supply are:

Narrow money (very liquid), M_0 = notes, coins in public circulation plus banks' till money

$M_1 = M_0$ + current account deposits

$M_2 = M_0 + M_1$ + savings accounts deposits + time deposits + foreign-earned deposits

It is possible to keep on measuring the broad money stock that functions as a store of value and which mainly earns interest. In some Caribbean territories the money supply measures are much simpler than those of advanced industrialised nations.

In Trinidad and Tobago for example:

MI_a consists of M_0 + current account deposits

MI_b and MI_c consist of MI_a + saving account deposits

MI_c includes time deposits

Factors affecting the money supply

The government's budget surplus or deficit

A government budget deficit will facilitate capital, current and transfer expenditure, which will enter the banking system in the form of deposits on which banks will lend. The money supply will therefore increase.

The expenditures of the non-banking public

With respect to imports and exports, import spending reduces the money supply, whereas export earnings increase the money supply.

Commercial bank policy

The commercial banks' reserve requirement determines their ability to lend and therefore influences the growth of the money supply. A low reserve requirement will facilitate greater lending than a requirement that is high.

The demand for money

The demand for money is based on the quantity of money that firms and individuals wish to hold to carry out the functions of money.

One such function is the purchasing of assets, as a store of wealth. Assets may be physical or financial. Physical assets represent wealth in the form of houses, cars, plasma televisions, vacation cottages or jewellery.

Financial assets, by comparison, may take the most liquid form of cash. Current account deposits, time deposits or stocks and bonds have a lesser degree of liquidity, or are 'less liquid'.

The demand for money to hold as an asset, however, also means foregoing earned interest or dividends or profit if the money can otherwise be invested. There is, therefore, an opportunity cost of holding money.

The Keynesian view of money demand: the liquidity preference theory

J.M. Keynes described the demand for money as liquidity preference and theorised that money was demanded for three main purposes: the transaction demand, the precautionary demand, and the speculative motive.

The transaction demand
See figure 27.1.

The transaction demand for money is related to our use of money as a medium of exchange. This comes about because individuals are paid money at one time and spend it at different times. For example, payment may be made at the end of the month, or weekly or fortnightly. If an individual is paid on the 31 December he or she is likely to spend this income every day until 31 January comes around.

Factors that determine our transactions demand are: the level of income, the frequency of pay and spending patterns.

The level of income
As incomes rise so will expenditure (the upward sloping consumption function). The more individuals and firms spend, the more money is needed to complete transactions.

The frequency of pay
Changing the frequency of pay days will change the demand for money even if the income itself does not change. For example, if you earn $70 a week and spend it evenly at $10 per day then the average weekly transactions demand will be $35 and for the year $70 × 52 weeks = $3,640. However, if payday is at the month's end, $280 will be paid every 4 weeks and if $10 is spent evenly per day, the average holding would now be $140, yet your yearly income is unchanged at $3,640.

Spending patterns
If expenditure was carried out at the same time that money was received, there would be no demand for money to make daily transactions by firms and individuals. Purchases are, however, made in the period between pay days and money is therefore demanded to make these purchases. If our spending patterns vary, so will our transactions demand.

The precautionary demand for money
The precautionary demand for money is caused by the unplanned events of firms, by slow business days, and by unexpected opportunities or expenses, for example an illness, among individuals.

If someone is optimistic, this motive will not be very strong. A strong determinant of this motive is the level of income, because high-income earners will demand higher balances to provide for unplanned emergencies.

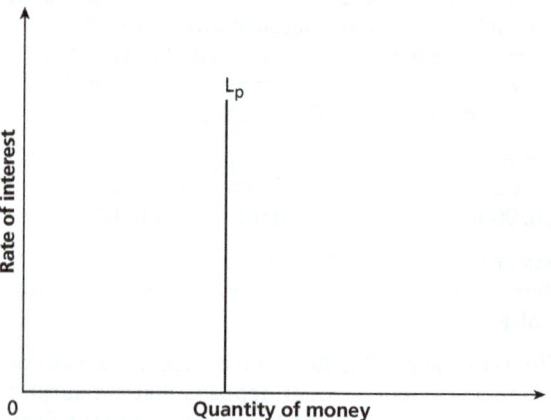

Figure 27.2 Precautionary demand for money

Overdrafts, credit card facilities and automatic teller machines have reduced the demand for these balances in recent times. Both the precautionary and transaction demand for money are not likely to change in the short-run. They are also unresponsive to interest-rate charges. Since they are held to carry out spending they are also called *active balances*. Note that in figure 27.2 the precautionary demand is also inelastic with respect to the rate of interest.

The speculative motive: the liquidity preference theory
J.M. Keynes also identified a speculative motive for demanding money, not as a medium of exchange but as a store of wealth. He identified only two forms of wealth, money or bonds. The speculative motive was focused on whether to hold money or bonds, or the reverse. Holding bonds involves risk because when bond prices fall the holder of the bond incurs a loss. Holding money means giving up the chance to earn interest with bonds. If bond prices are expected to fall, money is a better store of wealth and if bond prices are expected to rise they will be preferred to money.

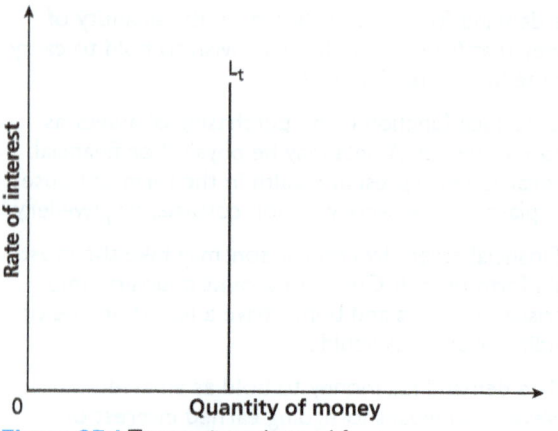

Figure 27.1 Transactions demand for money

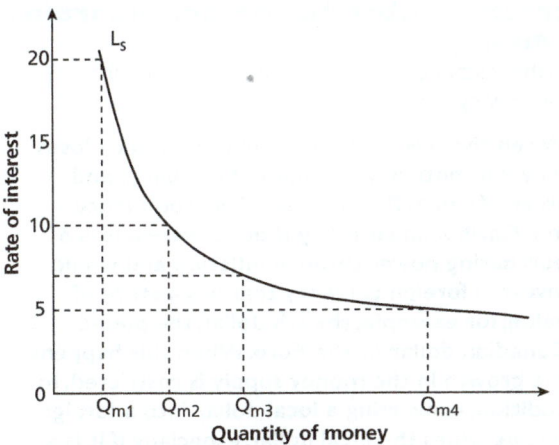

Figure 27.3 Speculative demand for money

This is a significant dilemma because bond prices and interest rates tend to move in opposite directions to each other, that is, a rise in interest rates will cause bond prices to fall. For example, consider a fixed rate bond, with a face value of $100 and at a rate of return of 10 per cent.

This implies a $10 return. To obtain the market rate or yield we express: $\frac{\$10}{\$100} \times \$100 = \$10$

The yield or the market rate is a very important concept. It is the yearly income expressed as a percentage of the bond. If the bond has a market price of $50 then the current market rate of interest will be:
$\frac{\$10 \times 100}{\$50} = 20\%$

Again, if the market price is $200 then the market rate of interest is: $\frac{\$10 \times 100}{\$200} = 5\%$

These rates are summarised in table 27.2.

Table 27.2 **Bond prices and the interest rate**

Bond price	Market rate of interest (%)	Fixed yield
$50	20%	$10
$100	10%	$10
$200	5%	$10

Note: In table 27.2 bond prices move in opposite directions to the market rate of interest.

According to Keynes, investors base their decisions to hold money or bonds on what they perceive to be the normal rate of interest, that is, the expected rate at any given time based on their 'instincts', and the prevailing rate. If the normal rate is above the prevailing rate, for example 10 per cent is greater than 6 per cent, they will anticipate a rise in the prevailing rate. If they expect a rise in the prevailing rate they will prefer to hold their wealth in money, since an upward moving rate of interest implies a loss in bond value. In table 27.2, a rise from 5 to 10 per cent causes a loss of $100 (from $200 to $100).

If, however, the normal rate is 6 per cent and the prevailing rate is 10 per cent the expectation would be a fall in the rate. The reverse happens and bonds will be preferred to money. Again, note what happens when a decrease in the rate of interest from 10 to 5 per cent causes bond prices to rise, making a profit for the holder. It is for this reason the speculative motive is drawn left to right and downward sloping, as shown in figure 27.3.

At a rate of 20 per cent, bonds are preferred to money as the rate of interest is expected to fall, so only Q_{m1} of money is demanded. At a rate of interest of 5 per cent, money is preferred to bonds to avoid a loss, so a significant Q_{m3} of money is demanded.

The liquidity preference schedule

Since both the transaction motive (L_t) and the precautionary motive (L_p) are assumed to be unchanged in the short-term and are also assumed unresponsive to the rate of interest, they are drawn as identical curves, or regarded as interest-rate inelastic.

If the three demand schedules for money are added together, a liquidity preference schedule is derived as in figure 27.4.

The liquidity preference schedule may be used to show how the Keynesian rate of interest is determined.

How demand responds to changes in the rate of interest

See figure 27.4.

In liquidity preference theory, the money supply is assumed to be fixed by the central bank and therefore unaffected by short-run interest-rate changes. If the rate of interest is ROI_1 the demand for money will exceed supply by XY. In order to meet this extra demand for money, the rate of interest will rise to ration the shortage. It should be noted that the central bank can either manipulate the interest rate, or the money supply, but not both.

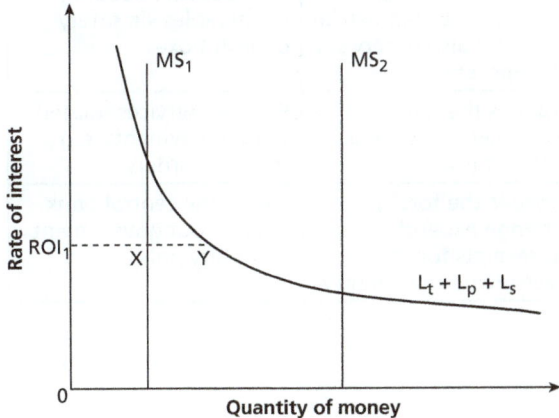

Figure 27.4 The liquidity preference schedule

Further, if the money supply is expanded to MS_2 there will be no significant change in the rate of interest, although everyone expects the rate to rise.

They will accordingly prefer to hold money instead of bonds. This is called the liquidity trap because the interest rate is unresponsive in the flat region of the demand curve.

Note that the liquidity preference theory assumes that factors other than rate of interest remain unchanged. These factors are:

› Changes in output and income
› Changes in price level
› Expectations will cause a shift in the liquidity preference schedule.

The portfolio balance

So far, the ways in which interest rates affect our decisions on whether to hold money or our wealth have been analysed. Our wealth may be arranged in a manner that shows the most liquid asset to be the least in terms of liquidity. Most people would attempt to find a proper balance in holding their assets according to liquidity, risk management factors, convenience and yield over time.

The functions of the central and commercial banks

The functions of the central and commercial banks are given in table 27.3.

Table 27.3 Functions of central and commercial banks

Central bank	Commercial bank
The sole authority with respect to printing money	Lends money to individuals and firms
Implements the government's monetary policy	Accepts deposits from citizens and firms
Manages the government's accounts (receipts and payments) and the government debt	Gives financial advice to clients
Performs the role as banker to the commercial banks and also supervises their operations	Provides safe-keeping of valuables via safety deposit boxes
Arranges the sale of government stock, e.g., treasury bills	Provides services related to debt payments, e.g., standing orders
Manages the foreign exchange expenditures and receipts for the government and country	Assists the central bank to carry out government monetary policy

Currency substitution and hoarding of money

In many instances people invest in foreign currency for the following reasons:

› When there is a threat of inflation money loses its value, both as a medium of exchange and store of value. People would lose confidence in a Caribbean currency if there were a loss of purchasing power through inflation and would invest in foreign currency that has a store of value; for example, the US dollar, the pound, Canadian dollar or the Euro. When this happens, the growth in the money supply is restricted. In addition, converting a local dollar into a foreign one devalues the local dollar, especially if it is a free or partially floating currency.
› Currency substitution also occurs when individuals and firms expect their currency to devalue against another foreign currency to which it is tied, e.g., $TT to the $US. If there was a threat of the US dollar devaluing to $8.00 TT, citizens and firms would move swiftly to purchase US dollars, effectively further weakening the local dollar.
› Hoarding of a currency would also take place if the government instituted exchange controls and attempted to ration scarce foreign exchange. In such an instance, a black market for foreign currency would develop.
› Confidence in currency would fall if there were political instability. Not only would local currency be converted to foreign ones, it may also be taken out of the country, leading to capital flight. In many instances, this is the plight of small Caribbean nations.
› The demand for foreign exchange in cash is also high when there is illegal activity. Persons engaged in illicit activities resort to cash finance in order to avoid leaving a 'paper trail'.
› During a recession when expectations in the economy are pessimistic, citizens may retreat into a foreign currency to avoid financial insecurity.
› Very high rates of taxation may also force individuals and firms to substitute the local currency for foreign ones.
› If the interest rate in a foreign country is higher than domestic rates, there will more than likely be a flight into foreign currencies to exploit high interest returns.

Chapter summary

> - Money is anything acceptable that can perform the functions of money.
> - The functions of money are a medium of exchange, a measure of value, a store of value, and a standard for future payment.
> - Money must be acceptable, durable, divisible, uniform, scarce and portable.
> - The credit creation multiplier is expressed as 1/cash reserve ratio.
> - The money measures are designated as M_0, M_1 and M_2 and apply to small economies.
> - The three types of demand for money are for transactions, precautionary and speculative motives.

Practice questions

1. Explain how banks 'create' money.
2. What is the money multiplier and how is it calculated?
3. List the three main functions of money.
4. List three desirable characteristics of money.

INTRODUCTORY ECONOMICS A TEXTBOOK FOR CAPE ECONOMICS STUDENTS

28 Monetary policy

Chapter 28 Monetary policy

LEARNING OBJECTIVES

- Define monetary policy.
- Analyse the effects of monetary policy on aggregate demand (Keynesian and monetarist views).
- Analyse monetary policy and the macroeconomic fundamentals.
- Identify and explain the weapons of monetary policy.
- Explain the lags of monetary policy.
- Evaluate the potency of monetary policy.

KNOWLEDGE REQUIRED

Elementary understanding of the role and functions of the central and commercial banks.

TOPIC VALUE

Monetary policy influences our ability to borrow for purchasing houses and cars because it is linked to the interest rate.

Introduction

Monetary policy consists of a set of measures that are designed to regulate the money supply and the level of interest rates and exchange rates to achieve the five macroeconomic objectives.

The processes by which changes in the interest rate or money supply cause changes in aggregate demand are called transmission mechanisms, which may be either Keynesian or monetarist in the manner in which they operate. A transmission process is similar to a chain reaction.

How monetary policy works

Observe in figure 28.1 that there is a change in the interest rate from ROI_1 to ROI_2 as a result of an expansion in the money supply. This will induce a change in interest-sensitive investment from I_1 to I_2 and a positive multiplier effect on aggregate demand.

The investment function is shifted upward as a consequence. An increase in output from Y_1 to Y_2 of GDP is achieved.

This is an example of the monetarist transmission mechanism at work. Note that monetarists firmly believe that the money supply plays a pivotal role in the economy because it stimulates aggregate demand, and the link between the two is strong, stable and predictable.

See figure 28.1. Investment is very responsive to a fall in the interest rate according to monetarist thinking (see the marginal efficiency of capital theory in chapter 24). This fall in interest rates induces a pronounced change in investment, which has an expansionary effect on the economy.

Investment

Since monetarists believe that investment is interest-elastic, firms will react to low interest rates by borrowing to finance expansion or diversification. Lower rates of interest lower the cost of financing a business enterprise.

Housing construction is also considered to be investment. Lower interest rates will therefore cause mortgage rates to fall, enabling first-time house buyers to have the opportunity to build or buy a house. Housing investment is also linked to other markets; hence suppliers of construction materials, house furnishings, home appliances and expenditure related to home furnishing will receive a similar boost in market activity.

Government expenditure

Although government expenditure is not associated with changes in the interest rate and is autonomously determined, a fall in the interest rate reduces the government's real debt in terms of repayment and financing deficits.

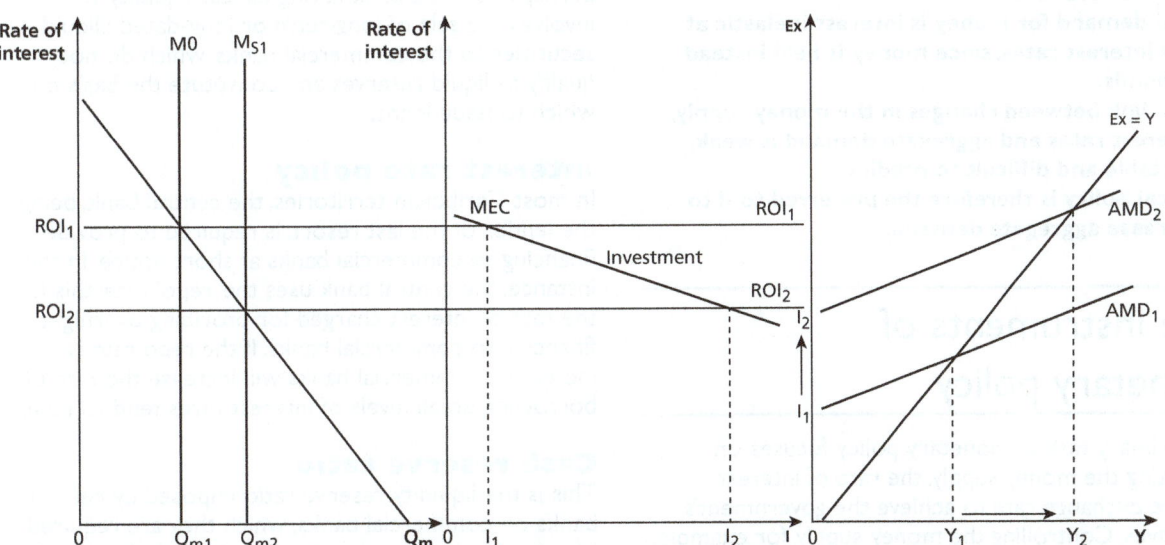

Figure 28.1 Monetarist transmission mechanism

Exports

The rate of interest has a significant effect on a country's exchange rate. If interest rates fall, this may reduce borrowing costs to finance import spending, raising demand for foreign currency.

A change in the rate of exchange such as, for example, from TT\$6.30 to US\$1 to TT\$8.00 to US\$1.00 works in favour of foreign buyers, who may increase their demand for domestic exports, thereby creating export multiplier effects. An extended benefit is also linked to local output and employment; with most Caribbean economies seeking to diversify their tourism-based economies, the rate of interest is an important issue. A unified flexible monetary policy may also be worthy of consideration by Caribbean monetary strategists.

Monetarist transmission mechanism

Monetarists firmly believe that the money supply plays a pivotal role in the economy because it stimulates aggregate demand, hence the link between the two is strong, stable and predictable.

Despite the differences in the Keynesian and monetarist schools of thought, present-day governments use a combination of Keynesian fiscal and monetarist supply-side polices to achieve their economic objectives

The Keynesian transmission mechanisms

Keynesian theorists do not share the monetarist view that investment is sensitive to changes in the interest rate. They hold the opposite view, that is, a fall in the interest rate has a minimal impact on investment and hence national income. Their main arguments are:

1. **The impacts of the money supply on aggregate demand are not direct but pass through the capital market and then to investment and national income.**
2. **Investment is responsive to confidence in the economy and has little to do with reductions in the interest rate.**
3. **The demand for money is interest-inelastic at low interest rates, since money is held instead of bonds.**
4. **The link between changes in the money supply, interest rates and aggregate demand is weak, unstable and difficult to predict.**
5. **Fiscal policy is therefore the preferred tool to increase aggregate demand.**

The instruments of monetary policy

The primary task of monetary policy focuses on regulating the money supply, the rate of interest and the exchange rate to achieve the government's objectives. Controlling the money supply, for example, will necessarily involve targeting the bank deposits of commercial banks, since these are created through the lending activities of the banks.

The central bank may target a bank's liquid assets because the extent of bank lending is determined by its liquidity. Apart from regulating the supply of money, the central bank may seek to influence the demand for money directly by regulating the rate of interest, which it has the authority to do.

The main instruments of monetary policy are as follows.

Open-market operations

This is the sale of government securities to the public, including the banking sector. When these financial products are bought and paid for, there will be an outflow from the commercial banks to the central banks. The effect of this is to reduce the bank's liquid asset ratio and further to restrict the amount banks can lend. However, some banks may have excess liquidity and this measure may not be effective in reducing their lending.

Conversely, if the central bank buys securities from the public and banking sector, there is a payment injection into the commercial banks that they are able to lend, since there is a greater proportion of liquid to illiquid assets.

Special deposits

The central bank has the authority to instruct all commercial banks to lodge a portion of their liquid assets with the central bank. This reduces the banks' liquidity and also their ability to lend. If increased lending is the objective of the central bank, it will release special deposits placed at the central bank to the commercial banks, increasing the liquidity of the commercial banks as they do so.

Funding

This monetary instrument is used when open-market operations and special deposits may be ineffective, perhaps due to a bank having excess liquidity. It involves the sale of long-term or long-dated illiquid securities to the commercial banks, which do not qualify as liquid reserves and constitute the basis on which to issue loans.

Interest rate policy

In most Caribbean territories, the central bank, being the lender of the last resort, is required to provide financing to commercial banks at short notice. In this instance, the central bank uses the 'repo' rate; this is the rate of interest charged for providing overnight financing to commercial banks. If the repo rate is increased, commercial banks will increase the rate of borrowing, so all levels of interest rates tend to go up.

Cash reserve ratio

This is the liquidity reserve ratio imposed by central banks on commercial banks, which they are required to set aside as a percentage of their bank deposits. It therefore restricts their ability to lend. For example, if a bank has deposits of $10 bn and the reserve ratio is increased from 10 to 20 per cent, the bank is then required to set aside $2 bn, which in effect restricts its lending.

Quantitative controls
These are currency quantity ceilings imposed on commercial banks by the central banks, with respect to the amounts that banks are able to lend.

Qualitative guidelines
The central bank may issue directives to commercial banks about the type of borrower they engage; for example, consumers or firms. To stimulate investment, the government may favour lending to firms and issue directives accordingly.

Moral suasion is an open declaration of the central bank's plans and objectives, which acts as a signal to commercial banks to encourage compliance with government's monetary policy.

The targets of monetary policy
The tools of monetary policy, previously outlined, do not directly achieve the government's five objectives. They need to connect to more than one target as a transmission mechanism before the five objectives are realised.

There are five main targets of monetary policy involved in the transmission mechanism:

1. Banks' liquid assets
2. Structure of interest rates
3. Money supply
4. Volume of bank credit
5. Exchange rate.

For example, if the government wishes to slow the rate of inflation, they may use the following instruments and targets (see figure 28.2).

Raising the repo rate (instrument) raises the structure of interest rises (1st target), domestic consumer spending is dampened (2nd target) and the rate of inflation slows (final target). There is also a time lag associated with these transmission mechanisms.

INSTRUMENT	1st TARGET	2nd TARGET	OBJECTIVE
Repo rate (rise)	→ Interest rates (rise)	→ Consumer spending (fall)	→ Demand inflation slows

Figure 28.2 The targets of monetary policy

Monetary strategy
Monetary strategy may be contractionary (tight money policy) or expansionary, depending on the objective the government wishes to achieve. Reducing inflation or resolving a persistent balance of payments deficit may require a tight money policy of high interest rates. High interest rates are also likely to deter import spending through the use of bank credit, but also have the capacity to attract overseas capital into a country, strengthening its external position.

Lags associated with monetary policy
The lags that are associated with fiscal policy also apply to monetary policy, since economic policies by themselves cannot yield results overnight. Monetary policy lags, however, are shorter in duration since changes in the rate of interest will have a quicker impact or consumption, investment and exports. The lags are as follows.

The recognition lag
It will take time to realise that a problem exists, for example inflation.

The information lag
To determine the extent of the problem will require information.

The decision lag
The monetary authority will need time to consult with the Minister of Finance about the strategy for controlling inflation; for example, to determine if it is cost-push inflation or demand-pull inflation. (For a detailed explanation see chapter 29 on inflation.)

The mobilisation lag
It will take some time to muster resources to deal with the problem, that is, statisticians, economists and computers.

The execution or implementation lag
It will take time to reduce liquidity in the financial system through open-market operations.

The achievement lag
This is the most significant of all lags, because if a repo rate is used that increases interest rates, this will not matter in a boom cycle when people are not sensitive to interest rates.

The potency of monetary policy
Monetary policy may be limited in effect in many ways:

> - **Interest rate control.** Interest rates are used to dampen consumer demand, e.g., during periods of demand inflation. If, however, consumers hold an optimistic view of economic conditions, high interest rates will not dampen consumer borrowing.
> - **The real rate of interest.** If inflation is running at 12 per cent and the prevailing rate of interest is 18 per cent then the real rate of interest is 6 per cent. High nominal interest rates will therefore not necessarily be effective as a control of consumer demand.

- High interest rates increase the cost of debt burden and may be inflationary. They may also raise mortgage and consumer credit rates.
- High interest rates may encourage high capital inflows. The resulting high exchange rates may make exports uncompetitive.
- To avoid control of liquidity, banks may borrow from other sources, or may sell some of their investments.
- Financing the public sector net cash requirement (PSNCR) by the government may be self-defeating, since it may reduce the liquidity of banks and cause interest rates to rise.
- The objective of controlling the money supply is related to the need to control total expenditure, which in turn depends on the velocity of money. For this to happen, the velocity of money must be constant or predictable. There is no certainty that velocity would be constant even in the short-run. Monetary or liquidity control will be successful if the demand for money is predictable.

Many factors related to speculation about the economy may make money demand unstable. Some examples are:

- Anticipation of a devaluation may cause an increase in demand for domestic currency to purchase foreign currency.
- During inflationary periods the demand for money will rise, e.g., for forward buying.
- Measures to control liquidity will not be effective if banks have surplus liquidity.
- Commercial banks may avoid control of their lending by using branches in other countries.
- Regulating the interest rate cannot ignore prevailing interest rates in a region where there is free capital movement. Monetary independence is not therefore guaranteed.
- Monetary policy may require some fiscal collaboration in order to achieve an economic objective. For example, to re-flate an economy that is coming out of a recession will not only require low interest rates, but also will need to accommodate government spending and lower taxation.

Chapter summary

Monetary policy involves implementing a set of measures designed to regulate the money supply or the level of interest rates, in order to achieve the five macroeconomic objectives.

- Apart from regulating the supply of money, the central bank or monetary authority may seek to influence the demand for money by regulating the rate of interest.
- The means by which changes in the interest rate or money supply cause changes in aggregate expenditure and aggregate demand are called transmission mechanisms.
- A transmission process is similar to a relay race. Monetary policy needs to connect to more than one target as a transmission mechanism before the five objectives are realised.
- The lags that are associated with fiscal policy also apply to monetary policy.
- Monetary policy may require some fiscal collaboration in order to achieve an economic objective.

Practice questions

1. Identify four instruments of monetary control used by central banks and explain why each of these may not always be effective in the context of the Caribbean.
2. Discuss why residents in many Caribbean countries choose to save in US currency rather than that of their own country.
3. Using a graph showing the theory of liquidity preference, explain how monetary policy can be used to increase the level of output and employment in an economy.
4. Discuss the fiscal policy tools available to Caribbean countries that can be used to increase and decrease output and employment.

Multiple choice questions

1. What is the most likely outcome of the central bank directing financial institutions to increase the rate of interest?
   a. Savings will rise
   b. Spending will rise
   c. Investment levels will rise
   d. The demand for a firm's product will rise.

2. What is the most likely effect of a rise in interest rates?
   a. An increase in bank lending
   b. A fall in the savings rate
   c. An increase in the external value of a currency
   d. An increase in investment.

3. Which of the following activities undertaken by the central bank best defines 'open market operations'?
   a. Issues long-term securities and fewer short-term securities, thereby reducing the bank's liquid assets.
   b. Issues compulsory loans that are demanded from the banks, thereby reducing their liquid assets.

c. Sets an upper limit on the volume of bank lending, reducing banks' liquid assets and raising interest rates.
d. Sells government securities, reducing the banks' liquid assets and raising interest rates.

4. A worker uses money to pay cash for a meal that costs $200. Which functions of money are being addressed in the above statement?
   a. A medium of exchange and a store of value
   b. A unit of account and a standard for deferred payments
   c. A standard for deferred payments and a store of value
   d. A medium of exchange and a unit of account.

5. Which of the following is a monetary policy measure?
   a. Fall in taxation
   b. Rise in government spending
   c. Fall in government spending
   d. An increase in the reserve ratio.

6. Using open market operations, the central bank sells government securities. What effect will this have on the interest rate and the money supply?

	Interest rate	Money supply
a.	fall	rise
b.	fall	fall
c.	rise	fall
d.	rise	rise

INTRODUCTORY ECONOMICS A TEXTBOOK FOR CAPE ECONOMICS STUDENTS

29 Inflation

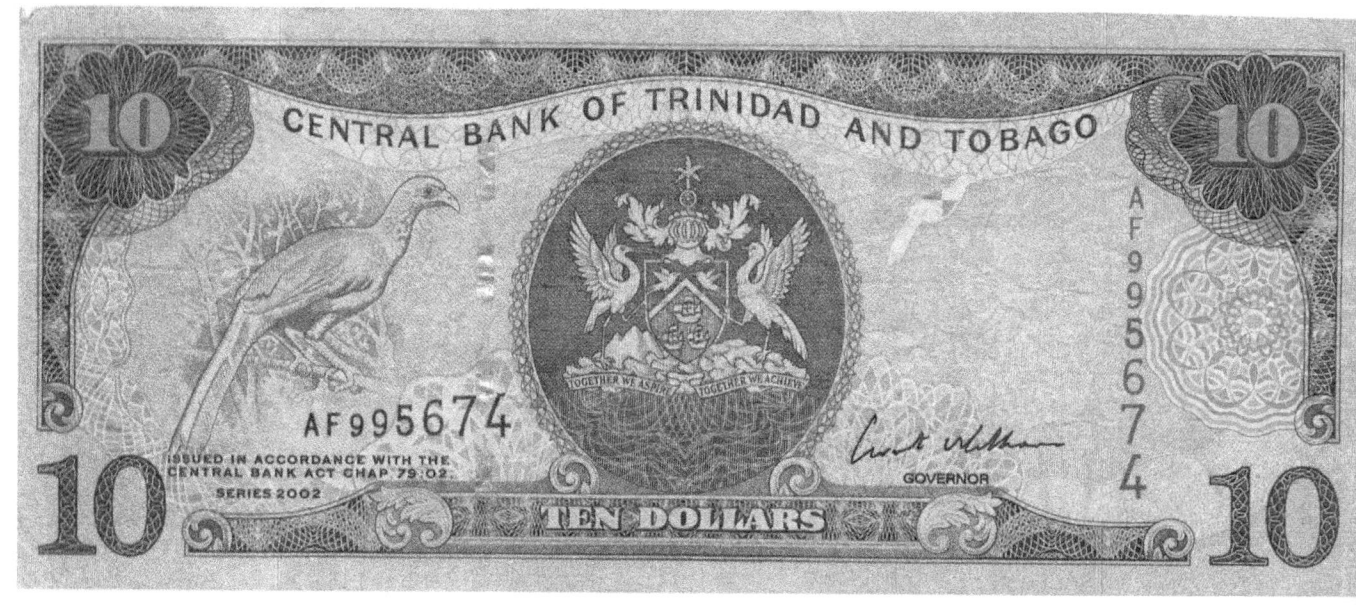

Chapter 29 Inflation

LEARNING OBJECTIVES

- Define inflation.
- Identify the causes of inflation.
- Explain the consequences of inflation.
- Explain the remedies for inflation.
- Explain Keynesian and monetary theories of inflation.
- Explain quantity theory.

REQUIRED KNOWLEDGE

- Inflationary gap, aggregate supply (AS) and aggregate demand (AD) curves
- Injection and leakages
- Potential or full employment output
- Cost theory
- Productivity
- Deflationary monetary and fiscal policy and supply-side management policies.

TOPIC VALUE

We are always seeking ways to preserve the purchasing power of our dollar, for example by purchasing gold. Inflation is the main cause of loss of purchasing power.

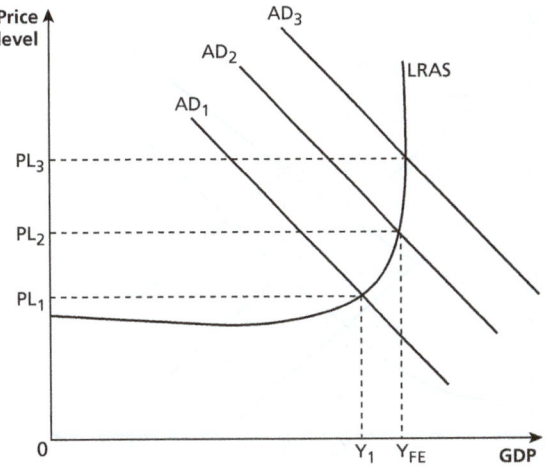

Figure 29.1 Demand-pull inflation

Introduction

Of the five main macroeconomic objectives, arguably most attention is given to inflation.

Inflation is defined as a persistent increase in the average level of prices over time, which reduces the purchasing power of a domestic currency. A singular increase in food prices at Christmas time does not in itself constitute inflation, since it implies a single increase in a short-time period. It may, however, start an inflationary trend.

A simple way to determine whether inflation has taken place is to compare the prices paid for food, clothes, cars, and so on, 30 years ago with the prices paid for these goods today.

A low rate of inflation is considered to be 1–2 per cent annually and does not have any harmful effects to the economy. If it is growing out of control at 30–50 per cent, it is called runaway inflation. The rate of inflation is measured by the retail price index, which is analysed in detail in this chapter.

Inflation is also classified according to core and headline rates. Core inflation measures the price increases of all items except food and energy (it removes items that exhibit price variations from month to month), whereas headline inflation measures changes in food prices only.

Figure 29.1 illustrates demand-pull inflation. Equilibrium national income is achieved at Y_1. When aggregate demand increases and shifts to the right along the long-run aggregate supply curve (LRAS) from AD_1 to AD_2, the increase in GDP is achieved with a PL_1 to PL_2 rise in the price level and full employment equilibrium (LRAS is at its maximum).

Note, however, that when the AD curve shifts from AD_2 to AD_3 the full employment level (FE) is exceeded. Note that there is no change in real GDP but a rise in the price level from PL_1 to PL_2. The reasons why the excess of aggregate demand over aggregate supply may cause a rise in the price level are:

> **Expanding fiscal policy by increasing government spending, and expanding monetary policy by decreasing interest rates may both be employed to achieve economic growth. This action may, however, stimulate excess demand and lead to demand inflation at the full employment level.**
> **If the rate of investment is greater than the rate of savings, or indeed any injection is greater than a leakage, e.g., X > M or G > T, or a combination of all three injections is greater than a combination of withdrawals, this is likely to cause a multiplier effect that may cause aggregate demand to exceed aggregate supply at full employment. It should be noted that demand inflation over time involves an interaction between aggregate demand and aggregate supply, contributing to a gradual but persistent increase in the price level.**

Demand-pull inflation: the inflationary spiral

Although the inflationary gap is an acceptable explanation of demand-pull inflation, it falls short of explaining the price spiral over time.

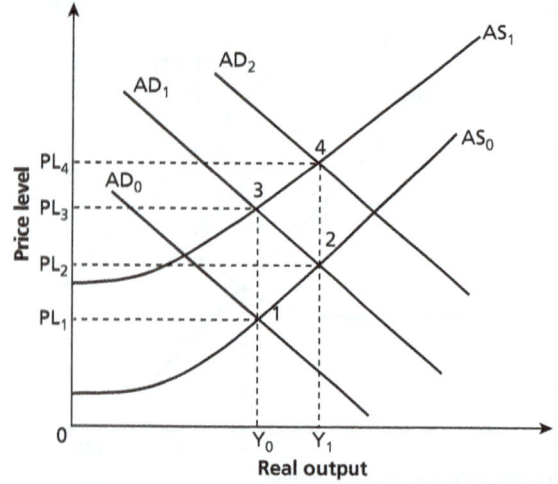

Figure 29.2 Demand-pull inflationary spiral

Figure 29.2 shows the dynamics of the spiral. Any increase in aggregate demand may be started when an injection is greater than a leakage at full employment; for example, when government spending is greater than taxation. If such spending is financed by borrowings from the banking sector this may:

› Increase the money supply
› Lower the rate of interest
› Increase the level of consumption.

In figure 29.2, AD is equal to AS at Y_0 output, at PL_1 price level at equilibrium 1. An increase in aggregate demand, due to a rise in government spending, will cause aggregate demand to shift to the right to AD_1, causing an equilibrium output of Y_1 at equilibrium 2 and a rise in the price level to PL_2.

This rise in the price level is likely to cause workers to demand wage increases. If unions are aggressive and the country is near to full employment the wage increases may be granted. This wage increase will, however, cause the aggregate supply curves to now shift to the left from AS_0 to AS_1, resulting in equilibrium 3 as producers seek to protect their profits.

Output is once again at Y_0 but the price level is now at PL_3, which is higher than before. Furthermore, when the wage increase is spent this causes the aggregate demand curve to once again move to the right to equilibrium 4, moving the price level to PL_4 and continuing the spiral already created.

Note that although there is a dynamic interaction of aggregate demand and aggregate supply it is aggregate demand that initiates this wage price spiral, and hence the inflation is called demand-pull inflation.

Cost-push inflation

Cost-push inflation is caused in a similar way to demand-pull inflation as the AS and AD curves shift. Independent increases in costs of production that are unrelated to demand push up prices, leading to cost-push inflation.

The following factors may also by themselves, or collectively, cause the aggregate supply curves to shift initially to the left, initiating a price spiral and causing real output to fall.

› Monopoly union power
› Indirect taxes, for example VAT
› Wage increases unrelated to productivity
› A devalued currency
› An increase in imported raw material prices.

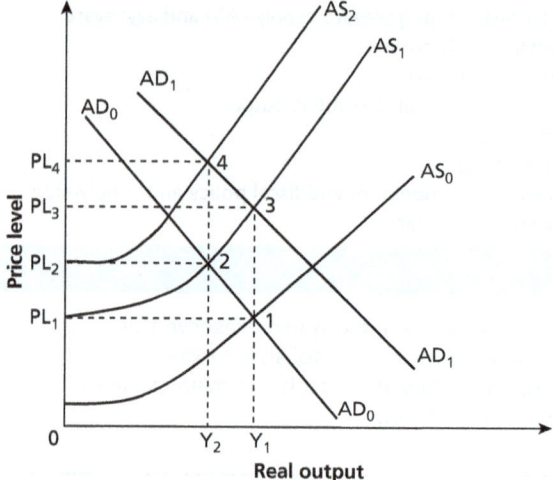

Figure 29.3 Cost-push inflation

Figure 29.3 illustrates the cost-push phenomenon. Initially, the economy is at equilibrium at output Y_1 and price level of PL_1. Wages paid as a result of new wage agreements cause an increase in the cost of production and create a ripple effect. Firms are likely to be affected.

AS_0 will therefore shift to AS_1 and a new price level of PL_2 and output Y_2. Spending the higher wages paid will cause AD_0 to shift to AD_1 and prices to increase to PL_3 but output remains at Y_1. The spiral continues when PL_3 leads to fresh demand for increased wages, shifting the AS_1 curves to AS_2, and so on. This phenomenon is also referred to as the wage price spiral.

Cost-push inflation may also be attributed to a wage/wage spiral when wages in one industry cause workers in other industries to demand increases in wages that are unrelated to rates of productivity. When wages are raised in one sector, unions are eager to preserve the differential between different sectors without corresponding increases in productivity. Firms also try to protect their profit levels after wage increases by increasing prices. Inflation may also be imported from other countries when imports of raw materials that have risen in prices are purchased, or when a devaluation causes import prices to rise.

Monetarist theories of inflation

Monetarist economic theorists disagree with Keynesian theories of inflation. In particular, they argue that any rise in cost does not necessarily mean a rise in the price level, unless there is an increase in the money supply to facilitate it, a phenomenon called monetary validation.

To comprehend the monetarist line of reasoning, it is necessary to first understand the quantity theory made famous by American economist Irving Fisher, which is still the oldest explanation of inflation.

The theory claims a direct and proportional relationship between changes in the rate of growth in the money supply and corresponding changes in the price level. The quantity theory is represented in a simple equation $MV = PY$ or PT where:

- M is the money supply
- V is the income velocity of money, i.e., the number of times money changes hands to purchase the final output of a country
- P is the average price level, i.e., total value of output divided by the total number of final transactions
- Y is the total volume of final output produced.

Originally, the equation was simply $MV = PT$. The difference between the two equations is that Y represents final output, whereas T represented intermediate inputs as well as final output. The double counting associated with the $MV = PT$ equation makes this version of the theory less accurate than the $MV = PY$ version.

$MV = PT$ is also called the transaction version of the equation, whereas $MV = PY$ is called the income version. Whichever version one may choose, it is clear that both sides of the equation express the same concept, that is, the money spent is equal to the value of the goods or services received in exchange, hence the theory has been called the Fisher theory of exchange. The equation then is a truism.

The velocity variable perhaps needs further clarification. The $20 you spend when buying lunch from a vendor enables the vendor to finance a $20 purchase himself, and the receiver of this income also spends it, and so on. When the same $20 bill is used repeatedly this is called velocity of money.

To further simplify, think of an economy whose only output is ice cream, which makes 500 ice cream cones per year at $2.00 per cone. The value of total output of an ice cream economy would be $1,000.

If the money supply in this economy was $100 then the number of times 100 dollars can be used to purchase $1,000 worth of ice cream is 10, that is, $1,000/$100 = 10 or GDP/Money supply = velocity.

Quantity theorists argue that V changes very slowly over time and also that the level of output in the long-run is also constant, since the LRAS curve is assumed to be perfectly inelastic.

When, therefore, the money supply is increased without an accommodating level of output, prices will rise. Monetarists further claim that factors that increase output in the long-run such as, for example, capital formation, technology, innovation, and so on, change very slowly over the long-run period. Since a long-run increase in output is not possible, a rising level of prices will require more money to finance the same level of expenditure. Monetarists argue, therefore, that only if the money supply is increased to meet this excess demand would equilibrium be restored.

Keynes's criticism of the quantity theory

J.M. Keynes argued that V and P are able to adapt and are therefore not constant. Keynes was not preoccupied with the long-run. In fact, he asserted that changes in M could bring idle factors into production through income-induced demand. In this case, T is variable.

Even if M does not change, a greater output is possible by more intensive use of the factors of production and productivity increases. V is also variable, he asserts, because increases in the money supply lead to a liquidity trap when interest rates are unresponsive to such increases. In a recession also, expectations are not one of consumption.

The consequences of inflation

The consequences of inflation depend on whether it is anticipated or not. If inflation is anticipated proactive action may be taken; for example, unions will use the rate of inflation to argue their claims, and firms may adjust their pricing to include the rising price level. The banking industry has, in the past, adjusted interest rates with an 'inflation cover' to recoup lost purchasing power when loans are advanced to clients. Government economic management tools of monetary, fiscal or exchange rate policy will also reflect an adjustment to rising rates of inflation.

The effects of unanticipated inflation

When inflation in an economy is not anticipated there are internal and external effects, which are summarised as follows:

Internal effects

The main internal effects of inflation are redistributive in nature, meaning that some income is redistributed from one source to another. For example, borrowers in the financial markets gain at the expense of lenders because the rate of inflation rises faster than the rate of interest.

- **Workers in less aggressive labour unions benefit from the aggressive negotiations of strong unions who seek to recover purchasing power for their members when real incomes fall during periods of inflation.**
- **The government will receive more tax revenue during periods of inflation as prices, profits and incomes rise. This form of redistribution is**

from firms and individuals to government. The government will also benefit during periods of inflation with respect to the national debt, as the real debt burden will fall. The redistributive effect in this instance is from the holders of government debt to the government.
- Individuals on fixed incomes are negatively affected through reduced purchasing power. Individuals who are not on fixed incomes but receive commissions and have index-linked salaries are beneficiaries in this redistributive process.

Apart from redistributive effects, other internal effects of inflation are:

- High domestic prices cause a shift in demand to lower-priced foreign import substitutes, causing domestic firms to struggle to survive. Some may go into receivership from business losses.
- The investment climate will be less optimistic for weak firms. Investment levels will therefore fall during inflationary periods.
- Menu costs may rise for all firms. This means that all businesses will need to make new pricing adjustments during periods of inflation. This price information will have to be sent to advertisers, suppliers, VAT collection agencies, etc.
- Well-established firms may enjoy soaring profits during inflationary times, since most of their costs are contract-based and fixed. In such cases, revenues will exceed costs. Firms may capitalise on excess demand during periods of demand-pull inflation to engage in what is called 'price gouging', i.e., raising prices to a higher than reasonable level, but which some consumers are still able to pay.
- A phenomenon called fiscal drag takes place, when the inflationary effect on wages puts more workers in higher income tax brackets, which are slow to adjust upwards for inflation.
- Inflation will affect the view of money as a measure of value, causing consumers to suffer from money illusion, i.e., confusing nominal income with real income.
- Economists identify one of the effects of inflation as shoe leather costs because of wearing out one's shoes by making many trips to the bank.
- During periods of inflation, the expectation of rising prices causes consumers and firms to purchase in advance to avoid higher future prices. In essence, this worsens the rate of inflation.
- House owners benefit during periods of inflation when property prices rise by more than the rate of inflation.

External effects
High rates of domestic prices will increase the demand for cheaper imported substitutes. Import spending is likely to exceed export earnings. The three external effects are:

1. Balance of trade deficit
2. Balance of payments deficit
3. Falling exchange rate that is floating freely. These effects are discussed in chapters 33 and 34.

Governments tend to raise interest rates to curb demand inflation. This is likely to encourage inflows of foreign capital to boost the external accounts.

During periods of inflation lesser-developed countries experience capital flight when individuals and firms convert domestic currency into relatively stable reserve currencies such as, for example, the US dollar, the euro or the pound. The main reason for this type of capital flight is loss of confidence in a domestic currency.

Counter-inflation policy
Having first analysed the destabilising effects of inflation on an economy, particularly in a lesser-developed country, it becomes a priority to slow down the rate of increase in the price level. Any policy designed to control the rate of inflation may first seek to counteract the symptoms before the cause is determined. Generally though, the immediate measures that may be employed to combat inflation before determining the causes are:

- Indexation: this simply involves an index that determines the increase in inflation and makes the necessary adjustments to prevent loss of purchasing power. For example, a cost of living allowance of 10 per cent of a salary may be paid to workers when the rate of inflation is 10 per cent. Indexation simply keeps par value, by preserving purchasing power.
- Floating exchange rates may reflect external effects of inflation. For example, if an exchange rate is freely floating, assuming an elastic demand for goods and services, the demand for exports will fall, causing the exchange rate to fall and making exports competitive once more. (Refer to chapter 33 on exchange rates.)

A time lag is attached to this measure, however. In such a case, both the balance of trade and balance of payments are positively influenced.

- Since rising wages may cause cost-inflation, an immediate limit may be placed on wage increases. An incomes policy is likely to accomplish this objective in the short-term.

When the root cause of inflation is determined, the government will then employ measures that are specific to the targeted cause. For example, if inflation is caused by excess demand, the government may reduce aggregate demand by using deflationary monetary and fiscal policies.

Since the time lags associated with monetary policy are shorter than those of fiscal policy, monetary policy is likely to be the first policy of choice to control demand inflation. The control of the money supply using interest rate management is likely to reduce consumer spending. An increased interest rate will also strengthen the exchange rate through the increased inflow of financial capital and reduced import spending.

With respect to reduced consumer spending, this would be achieved since savings are likely to increase with increased interest rates.

Figure 29.4 represents a contractionary monetary policy designed to reduce aggregate demand and the price level from PL_1 to PL_2. If interest rates are increased in a contractionary strategy, this may cause aggregate demand to shift from AD_1 to AD_2, with a fall in the price level from PL_1 to PL_2.

There are drawbacks to the use of interest rates in this manner, since a rise in interest rates may negatively affect interest-sensitive investment and consumption. With a fall in consumption, investment and exports all taken together, it is likely that aggregate demand will fall, with a negative impact on economic growth. Unemployment is likely to follow. With unemployment, however, increases in the price level are likely to decrease.

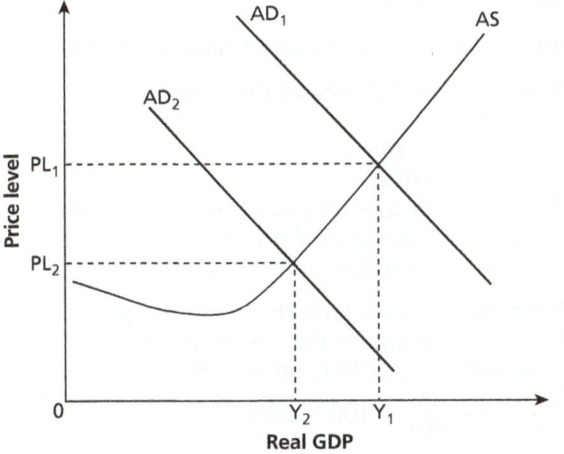

Figure 29.4 Contractionary monetary policy

Deflationary fiscal policy

A deflationary fiscal policy is also likely to control rising price levels. A cut in government spending, together with an increase in direct taxes such as income and corporation taxes, are likely to have a contractionary effect on aggregate demand through the reverse multiplier and accelerator effects.

A budget surplus will achieve the desired deflationary effect necessary to control demand inflation. There are, however, drawbacks to the use of fiscal policy in this way. These are:

> Cutting government expenditure, particularly recurrent expenditure, is difficult to achieve.
> Decreasing transfers will especially affect the vulnerable in society.
> Increasing income taxes create disincentives to work, save and invest.

Measures to combat cost-push inflation

Measures to curb cost-push inflation may be summarised as:

> A freeze on prices and incomes to prevent wage/price inflationary spirals. The drawbacks associated with this measure are that such measures are only temporary and are, in effect, a tinkering with the price mechanism. When restrictions are relaxed the cost pressures immediately build up again.
> Reducing indirect taxes such as VAT and import duty is another direct way to reduce cost inflation initiated by indirect taxes. However, they are both revenue earners and to compensate for loss of revenue the government may be obliged to resort to the public sector net cash requirement (PSNCR) and budget deficits. The removal of import duty may also leave infant industries vulnerable to aggressive competitors.
> Subsidising the production of goods during inflationary periods may work in the short-term but may also lead to complacency and inefficiency and the subsidy may require debt financing. In addition, exporting subsidised products may breach 'dumping' trade regulations set down by the World Trade Organization (WTO, a trade regulation body).
> If cost inflation is caused by an increase in imported raw materials or other inputs to domestic production, an upward revaluation of the exchange rate may, in effect, lower the cost of imported raw materials to domestic producers. An obvious drawback to this measure is that the level of export revenue may fall in the short-term, leading to external deficits. On the other hand, there is likely to be a payback in the low costs of exported goods.

The measures outlined above may be short-term measures. Long-term measures designed to reduce the rate of price level increases over time are linked to measures that increase productivity through monetarist supply-side measures.

Figure 29.5 shows how supply-side measures in the long-run shift the $LRAS_1$ curve to the right to $LRAS_2$, lowering the price level from PL_1 to PL_2 and increasing GDP from Y_1 to Y_2. Supply-side measures are, however, under review with the collapse of the capital markets throughout the world during 2008.

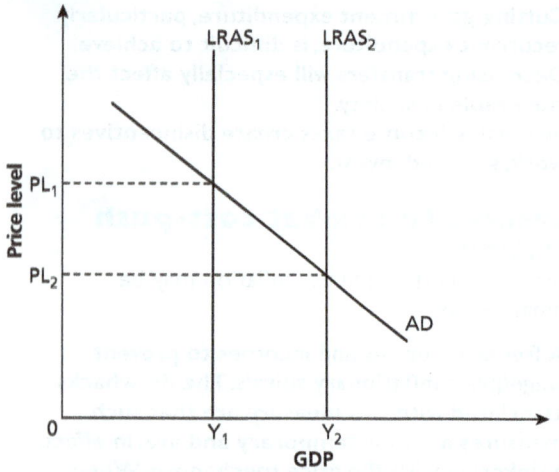

Figure 29.5 The long-run AS curve

Measuring inflation

The retail price index

Index numbers are used to measure price changes from one year to another. If the price levels of a single good, for example a fruit such as an orange, change from $2.00 in 2013 to $3.00 in the year 2014 the percentage change in price can be calculated quite easily:

$$\frac{\text{price in 2014 (\$3.00)} - \text{price in 2013 (\$2.00)}}{\text{price in 2013 (\$2.00)}} \times 100 = 50\%$$

However, inflation is not measured with one price change but the general price level over time. There is a statistical procedure that economists use to calculate the change in the general price level, as follows:

› A random sample of households is chosen.
› An expenditure survey is undertaken of a typical basket of about 1,000 items commonly purchased by households.
› A weight is assigned to each good. This represents a percentage of the budget. For example, if $600 out of $1,000 are spent on transport, the weight out of 100 would then be 60.
› A weight, therefore, indicates how important the good is in terms of the total expenditure. Weights may add up to 10, 100, 1,000 or 10,000. A simple example is given in table 29.1 below.

Table 29.1 The retail price index

Good	$ Price	Quantity	Total expenditure	Weighting
X	20	5	100	10
Y	30	10	300	30
Z	40	15	600	60
			1000	100

› The next step is to select a base year, which is the year that we compare price level changes to. The base year should ideally not be too far from the year of measurement, i.e., if the price level is being measured in 2008 the base year could be the year 2005, for example.
› Every good or service measured is given a value of 100 in the base year. For example, if transport prices rose by 10 per cent in 2014, then the prices in the base year index should be represented by 100 in the year 2011, and the index for 2014 = 110, which shows that transport prices rose by 10 per cent since the base year. The change is, therefore, reflected in the index in the year being measured. Refer to table 29.2.

Table 29.2 The RPI: retail price index

Good (A)	Base year 2011 index (B)	2014 index (C)	Weight (D)	Weighted index (C × D)
W	100	110	10	1,100
X	100	120	20	2,400
Y	100	100	30	3,000
Z	100	90	40	3,600
			100	10,100

Step 1. Multiply the 2014 index by the weights for goods W, X, Y and Z

Step 2. Add up total weighted index = 10,100

Step 3. Divide this total by the total of weights (100)

Therefore, $\frac{10,100}{100} = 101$

The rise in the average price level is 1 per cent because the average level of prices in 2014 is 1 per cent higher than the base year 2011.

If the average price level rises by 105 in year 2012 then the change in the average price level between 2011 and 2012 is calculated as $\frac{105 - 101}{101} = \frac{4}{101} \times 100 = 3.9\%$

Limitations of the weighted retail price index

The limitations of the weighted retail price index include:

› The index may fail to include new goods and services entering the market place, e.g., video games and personal computers.
› Weights may differ between families with different incomes, because low-income groups tend to spend a higher proportion of their monthly earnings than high-income groups.
› It is difficult to choose an average basket of items, because pensioners' expenditure may be different from a young married couple or single parent.
› Changes in the economy may affect consumer expenditure patterns, because such expenditure

tends to decrease more in a recession than in a boom. The weighted index may then be inaccurate.
- Sometimes information provided to researchers may not be true or accurate.
- The types of outlets used by consumers must be carefully monitored. Large retail supermarkets are the norm in developed countries but are beginning to emerge in Caribbean economies as well.
- Consumption patterns change over time, e.g., people are living healthy lifestyles, so that expenditure on tobacco or meat products is giving way to expenditure on exercise equipment and healthy eating.
- The retail price index ignores changes in the quality of goods and services over time. Plasma televisions are superior in quality to black and white models.

Other measures of the price level

Other measures of the price level include:

- The tax and price index measures the average household purchasing power and how changes in direct taxes affect purchasing power.
- The producer price index measures changes in material and product prices.
- The pensioners' retail price index measures price changes of goods and services purchased by pensioners.
- The GDP deflator is a measure of inflation for both consumer and producer goods.

Stagflation

Stagflation refers to a phenomenon in which economic recession and inflation occur together.

This occurred during the early period of the 1970s, caused by soaring oil prices that had the effect of raising the cost of production and creating unprofitable enterprises. The slowing of economic growth that followed the price increases was counteracted by expansionary monetary policy, which created a wage price spiral and inflation, as illustrated and explained in figure 29.3. Stagflation, therefore, was the result of trying to counteract a recession with expansionary monetary policy.

Chapter summary

- Inflation is defined as a persistent increase in the general price level over time, which reduces the purchasing power of a domestic currency.
- Independent increases in costs of production, unrelated to demand, push up prices, leading to cost-push inflation.
- Inflation is also classified according to core and headline rates. Core inflation measures the price increases of all items, whereas headline inflation measures price increases in food, utilities and fuel.
- Demand-pull inflation takes place when aggregate demand exceeds aggregate supply at the full employment level of national income.
- Cost-push inflation is caused in a similar way. Independent increases in costs of production, unrelated to demand, push up prices, leading to cost-push inflation.
- The quantity theory explains the direct and proportional relationship between changes in the rate of growth in the money supply and the proportionate changes in the price level in the equation $MV = PY$.
- J.M. Keynes argued that V and P are able to adapt and therefore not constant.
- The consequences of inflation depend on whether they are anticipated or unanticipated.
- When inflation in an economy is not anticipated there are internal and external effects.
- A deflationary monetary policy together with a deflationary fiscal policy is more likely to bring about control of the rate of growth in the price level.
- Stagflation occurs when inflation and unemployment occur together as a result of an external shock followed by a wage price spiral. An expansionary monetary policy that is used to reverse a recession creates more inflationary pressure.

Practice questions

1. Define the term inflation.
2. Explain the difference between cost-push and demand-pull inflation.
3. How is inflation measured?
4. How accurate is the measure of inflation?
5. What are the effects of inflation?
6. What measures should the government take to control inflation in your country?

INTRODUCTORY ECONOMICS A TEXTBOOK FOR CAPE ECONOMICS STUDENTS

30 Unemployment

Chapter 30 Unemployment

LEARNING OBJECTIVES

- Define and explain unemployment.
- Explain underemployment.
- Define and calculate the natural rate of unemployment.
- Identify causes and categories of unemployment.
- Identify the consequences of unemployment.
- Explain the remedies for unemployment.
- Explain the Phillips curve relationship between unemployment and inflation.

REQUIRED KNOWLEDGE

- Activity or participation rate
- Deflationary gap
- Fiscal, monetary and supply side economic management.

TOPIC VALUE

Unemployment lowers our collective standard of living, our pool of savings and the country's GDP growth. Unemployment is, therefore, of critical concern to the government.

Introduction

Unemployment refers to the total number of people who are of working age (over 18 years) who are willing, able and available to work at current wage rates but cannot find a job. Working-age persons may not work but may be enrolled in tertiary education. They are referred to as economically inactive.

The working population is merely the number of people who are employed plus those who are unemployed.

The labour force consists of a individuals of working age and below retirement age who are participating workers, employed or looking for work.

The rate of unemployment is expressed simply as:

$$\frac{\text{number unemployed} \times 100}{\text{labour force (employed + unemployed)}}$$

Unemployment

Note that the composition of the labour force can also be derived as the labour force = number employed + number unemployed.

A simple example will help to clarify the formula. A labour force of a CARICOM country may be 800,000 persons consisting of 100,000 unemployed and 700,000 employed.

The rate of unemployment therefore is:

$$\frac{100 \times 100}{(100 + 700) \times 1}$$

$$\frac{10,000}{800} = 12.5\%$$

It is also useful to point out that there are constant additions to and subtractions from the labour force. Accordingly, unemployment is a stock concept just like investment.

Claimant count

An alternative method of defining unemployment is the claimant count, which is the number of people who claim unemployment benefits. In most developed countries, this count may be used to calculate the rate of unemployment.

The different types of unemployment

The different types of unemployment may also be viewed as the causes of unemployment. As the ensuing explanations of the different causes of unemployment make clear, disequilibrium in the labour markets is almost always the reason for unemployment. Figure 30.1 shows the macroeconomic equilibrium of the labour market, with Q_{L1} of labour and a wage rate of W_1. If the wage rate becomes W_2, there is an excess supply of labour equal to $Q_{L2} - Q_{L3}$.

In this disequilibrium of the labour market, although the supply of labour exceeds the demand for labour there is no downward pressure on wages, as unions and others resist such downward pressures even in a recession. Wages are therefore said to be rigid or 'sticky' downward.

There are many reasons why such a disequilibrium condition may exist. When the rate at which workers join the labour force exceeds job vacancies, there will be an excess supply of labour on the market.

Trade union power or minimum wages may also lead to this disequilibrium condition. Both Keynesian and classical explanations point to a disequilibrium in the labour market.

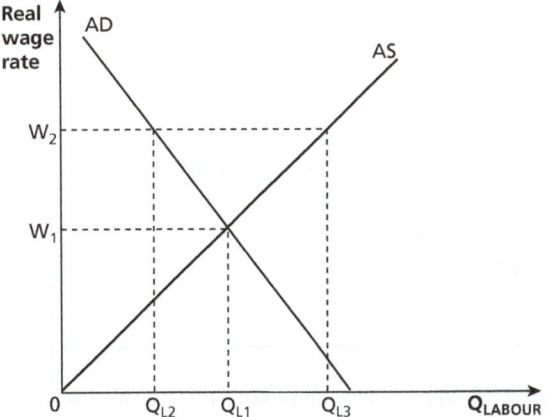

Figure 30.1 Classical disequilibrium unemployment

Keynesian, demand-deficit or cyclical unemployment

A deflationary or recessionary gap may exist when aggregate supply exceeds aggregate demand at the full employment level of national income. Refer to figure 30.2.

The deflationary gap XY gives rise to unemployed labour resources, since aggregate demand is insufficient to absorb aggregate supply. If the economy is in equilibrium below the full employment level, there will be unemployed labour resources. Insufficient demand, therefore, leads to a fall in aggregate supply and hence reduced demand for labour.

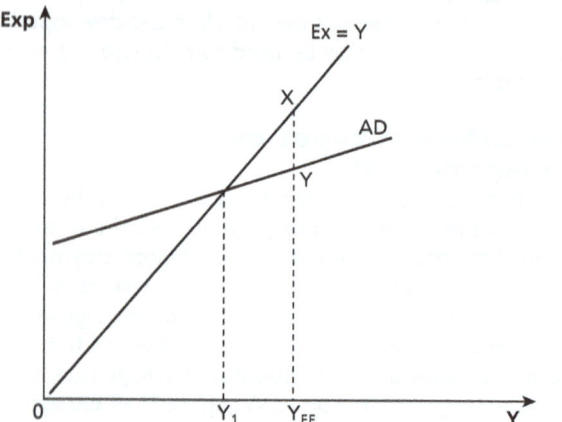

Figure 30.2 Demand deficient unemployment

The economy is at equilibrium national income at Y_1 but below the full employment level of national income Y_{Fe}. According to Keynesian thinking, this deficiency of aggregate demand can be overcome if an expansionary fiscal policy is employed.

The trade cycle in figure 30.3 highlights the same problem.

In figure 30.3, which represents the trade cycle, the linear curve labelled *PG represents potential economic growth, which is the optimal capacity of the economy, while *ST represents short-term economic growth. Whenever short-term (actual) growth is less than capacity growth (the shaded areas) this coincides with unemployment.

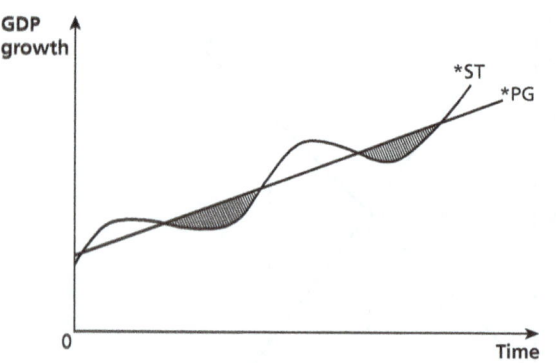

Figure 30.3 Cyclical unemployment illustrated by the trade cycle

Note:

*PG = potential growth (capacity growth)

*ST = short-term or actual growth.

Classical unemployment

Classical unemployment may be explained by figure 30.1. The downward 'stickiness' of high wages causes unemployment to persist, preventing market forces from forcing down wages.

Classical economists attribute this resistance in the market to unemployment benefits being too near existing wage rates and the lack of incentives to enter the labour market. Supply-side incentives that may achieve this entry into the labour market are the reduction, or elimination, of unemployment benefits and a cut in direct taxation to provide people with an incentive to enter the job market. Legislation to reduce labour market monopoly by unions may also be introduced.

Structural unemployment

Structural unemployment arises when there is a fall in the demand for labour due to a decline in an industry or a particular labour market. For example, if the all-important Windward Islands banana industry were to collapse, structural unemployment in these territories would rise. Similarly, if oil prices fall significantly, as they did in the early 1980s, small economies such as Trinidad and Tobago would experience structural unemployment. One remedy for such a development may be long-term diversification of the economy.

Regional unemployment

Structural unemployment may also take place if industries such as oil and gas, bananas and tourism are located in a particular region. Regional unemployment is therefore a form of structural unemployment, due to a fall in demand for labour. The hurricane devastation of the nutmeg crop in Grenada is a case in point, where the industry is likely to take 15 to 20 years to recover.

Technological unemployment

This is another type of structural unemployment because technological advances cause a fall in demand for labour. If combine harvesters are introduced to harvest sugar cane in sugar-producing economies of the Caribbean, the demand for unskilled 'cane cutters' will lead to unemployment in this labour market. In such a case, retraining may be a possible remedy to redirect this type of surplus labour into some other aspect of agricultural production or related industries.

International unemployment

This is another form of structural unemployment and is related to a fall in demand for goods and services due to international competition. For example, where economies of scale in developed countries reduce costs, for example beet sugar, it is difficult for Caribbean economies to compete in the sugar market with high-cost cane sugar.

High rates of inflation combined with a fall in productivity in Caribbean economies may cause exports to become uncompetitive, leading to business closures in these economies and eventually to international unemployment.

Seasonal unemployment

This type of unemployment is typical of industries with a seasonal demand, for example tourism. Much of the tourism in the Caribbean occurs during the winter months of North America or Europe.

Likewise, the entertainment industry in the Caribbean, particularly calypsonians and steel pan players, are unemployed after Trinidad Carnival, Barbados Crop Over celebration or Vincy Mas festivities. This type of labour sometimes finds employment in the 'off season' in other parts of the world, such as, for example, the Notting Hill Carnival, UK or Caribana celebration in Toronto, Canada.

Frictional unemployment

Frictional unemployment is not directly related to disequilibrium in labour markets but to the occupational and geographic immobility of labour. Job vacancies in one region may be available but remain unfilled because of immobility of labour in other areas, or their lack of experience and skill levels.

Search unemployment

Search unemployment is an aspect of frictional unemployment. In this instance, the unemployed do not take the first available job but 'search' until the best job is found. This is usually found in economies enjoying boom conditions. A reduction in this type of unemployment may be achieved through job-information services. Policies to reduce specific types of unemployment are given in table 30.1 below, but generally most focus on:

Table 30.1 **A summary of policies designed to reduce unemployment and related disadvantages**

Type of unemployment	Policy	Disadvantages
Classical disequilibrium	Supply-side policies, e.g., eliminating unemployment benefits and decreasing income taxes that are ineffective in the short-term.	1. Cutting government expenditure is 'sticky' downward and difficult to achieve. 2. Lower income taxes reduce the revenue base of the state, which may resort to the public sector net cash requirement, a high interest rate and the creation of debt.
Keynesian cyclical or demand-deficient unemployment	1. Expansionary fiscal and monetary policy that raise government expenditure and decrease taxes, or lower rates of interest, all of which expand the economy via multiplier effects. 2. Supply side policies, e.g., retraining of idle labour.	Increased government spending may be inflationary and also have a negative impact on the external accounts. Reducing the rate of interest has a similar effect.
Structural/ regional	A regional policy, i.e., providing employment opportunities where there is unemployment, e.g., industrial parks, or taking workers to the workplace, e.g., using housing initiatives: › Retraining of immobile labour › Long-term diversification of the economy (especially Caribbean territories) › Foreign investment.	Both regional policy and retraining of idle labour may take time to be effective. In addition, financing such initiatives may involve state borrowing. Diversification is a long-term initiative, sometimes in conflict with short-term political objectives. Foreign direct investment has benefits but also disadvantages.
Frictional or search	Supply-side, e.g., improving job-information services such as labour bureaus or job-information centres. Withdrawal of unemployment benefits.	The time lag involved in this exercise is likely to delay the impact of this measure. Supply-side measures are generally long-term. Withdrawing benefits may be politically undesirable.
Technological	Supply-side, retraining of idle labour together with diversification initiatives. Indigenous economic activity, e.g., micro enterprises linked to agriculture.	Much formalised planning and mobilisation of resources are needed. The time lag may be a consideration as well.
International unemployment (Lack of international competitiveness)	Monetary, fiscal and exchange rate policies are necessary in the short-run. › In the long-run, supply-side and diversification initiatives may increase competitiveness. › Import protection for declining industries.	Lack of competitiveness may be due to inflation. Deflationary fiscal and monetary policies may lead to negative growth. Raising taxes and interest rates may impact negatively on housing markets and investment generally. Import protection may encourage complacency.
Seasonal	Diversification of the economy and retraining of labour to be multi-skilled in the 'off season'. Entertainers and musicians may be used to export culture, and 'off-season' sugar and other workers may be absorbed into the tourism sector with training.	Difficulties associated with immobility of labour may weigh against policy measures, e.g., unemployed unskilled workers may be functionally illiterate.

- Fiscal policy
- Monetary policy
- Wage subsidies
- Retraining programmes
- Investment tax credit
- Employment tax credits
- Government employment programmes and reducing market imperfections.

Consequences of unemployment

The consequences or costs of unemployment depend on the duration of the period of unemployment in question. Nevertheless, whether short- or long-term the costs may be summarised as:

- **Loss of tax revenue to the government**, e.g., **PAYE** and **VAT**, and therefore there may be a need for the government to either raise taxation or use the public sector net cash requirement (**PSNCR**) to manage the economy. If the **PSNCR** is financed by the banking sector this may cause a rise in interest rates, causing investment and consumption to fall and negative economic growth and unemployment in the medium-term.
- **High levels of unemployment** render labour an idle resource and therefore an opportunity cost of foregone production. The output gap is therefore negative. Such lost production is irretrievable.
- **High rates of unemployment** increase the level of government spending when, for example, providing unemployment relief. The government may need to become an employer in 'make work' schemes, which are usually short-term in nature. A dependency syndrome may develop. Expectations of government financial support become entrenched and spending on such programmes is not sustainable.
- **High rates of unemployment** also relate indirectly to social fallout such as crime, alcoholism and domestic violence, all of which require increased government expenditure on crime reduction and social services.

The natural rate of unemployment

The natural rate of unemployment (NRU) is a concept associated with the monetarist school of thought. The NRU is considered to be that rate of unemployment where the labour market is in equilibrium at prevailing wage rates. Any unemployment during this period relates purely to those who voluntarily withdraw their labour because of the disincentive effects of high taxes, or labour-market imperfections such as informational failure or frictional unemployment.

Unemployment and inflation

Professor A.W. Phillips in 1958 proposed an inverse relationship between the rate of unemployment and the rate of inflation. His research of inflation and unemployment rates for roughly a 100-year period led him to conclude that when the rate of inflation was high, the level of unemployment was low and vice versa. He originally identified a relationship in the rate of change in wages and unemployment.

His reasoning was that any time the wage rate increased it led to inflation, based on the fact that 70 per cent of costs of production are accounted for by wages. Higher wages and higher costs usually lead to higher prices, initiating a chain reaction in the economy, and eventually to higher inflation.

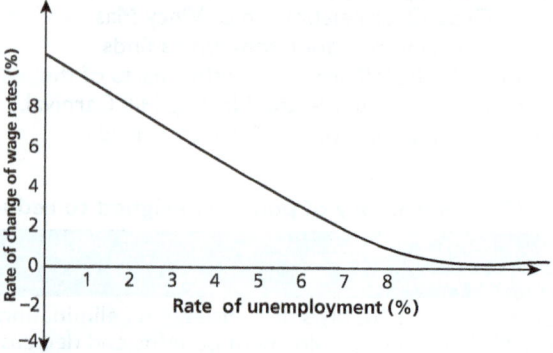

Figure 30.4 The Phillips curve

Figure 30.4 illustrates the concept of the Phillips curve.

The Phillips curve identified trade-off options to manage the economy. If a government opts for a low rate of unemployment it will invariably have to accept high rates of inflation as well.

This model proved popular and held true for a while, but later research showed that there was a breakdown in the relationship. Many economists have theorised that the Phillips curve was a peculiar event of the period 1958–66.

In Figure 30.5 in the Keynesian model shown, note that expanding AD_1 to AD_2 increases growth in the economy of Y_1Y_2. The creation of increased output provides jobs for the unemployed. Note the rise in the price level from PL_1 to PL_2. Inflation and unemployment can in fact coexist.

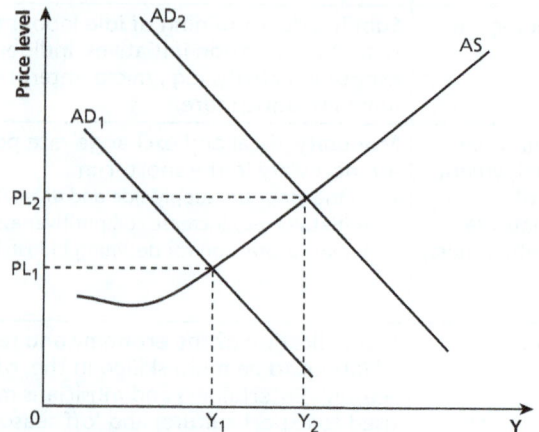

Figure 30.5 Inflation with employment

Underemployment

Underemployment is typical during a recession, or when business activity slows down. It refers to workers who wish to work full-time but can only find part-time work. It also relates to workers who are working full-time and kept on the job during a slump in sales, but not given enough work to do.

This situation may arise because of a firm's reluctance to lay off workers in a slowdown, based on the fact that to lay them off is more costly than keeping them in the firm doing little, since if business activity resumes it would be very costly to hire and train a new worker.

Chapter summary

> Unemployment refers to the total number of people who are of working age (over 18 years) who are willing, able and available for work at current wage rates but cannot find a job.
> The working population is merely the number of people who are eligible to work, having reached the working age and not above retirement age.
> The labour force, on the other hand, is the total number of the working population who are able and available for work at existing wage rates.
> The rate of unemployment is expressed simply as:

$$\frac{\text{number unemployed} \times 100}{\text{labour force (employed + unemployed)}}$$

> Disequilibrium in the labour markets is almost always the reason for unemployment.
> Classical unemployment may be explained by the stickiness of high wages, which causes unemployment to persist, preventing market forces from operating.
> Structural, real wage, seasonal, regional, cyclical and technological employment are some common types of unemployment.
> Cures for unemployment are usually based on fiscal, monetary, and supply-side policies.
> The **NRU** is considered to be that rate of unemployment where the labour market is in equilibrium at prevailing wage rates.
> The **Phillips curve** identified a trade-off of between low rates of unemployment and high rates of inflation.

Practice questions

1. Explain why unemployment exists in the Caribbean with reference to the Keynesian and classical views of unemployment.

2. Explain how foreign direct investment companies (FDIs) can be beneficial in reducing unemployment in the Caribbean.

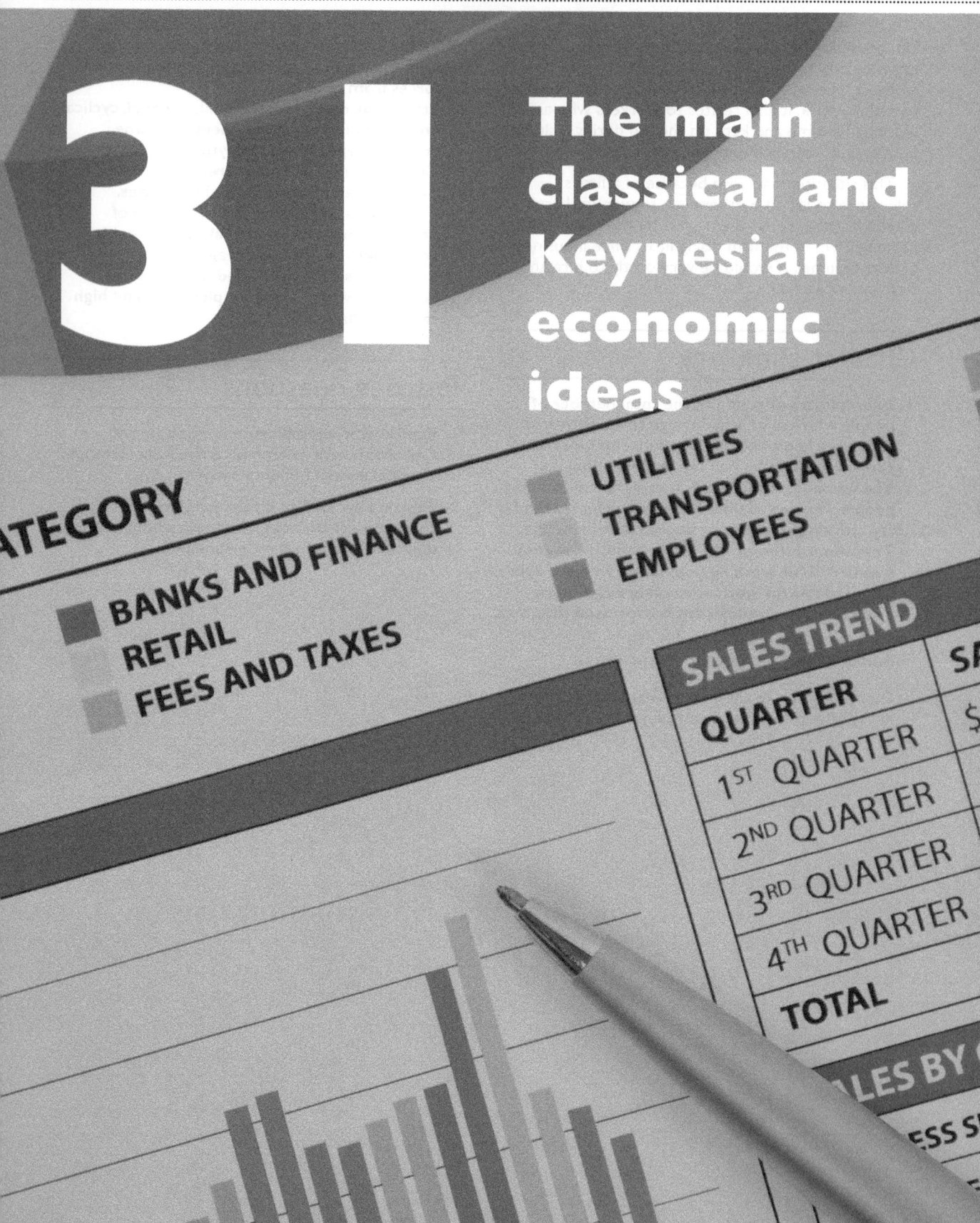

31 The main classical and Keynesian economic ideas

Chapter 31 The main classical and Keynesian economic ideas

> **LEARNING OBJECTIVES**
>
> - Define Keynesian and classical concepts.
> - Identify similarities and differences between Keynesian and classical concepts.
> - Explain classical and Keynesian remedies.
> - Explain trade liberalisation.
>
> **REQUIRED KNOWLEDGE**
>
> - Keynesian and fiscal monetary supply-side theories.
>
> **TOPIC VALUE**
>
> The reasons behind the collapse of the US financial markets in 2008 may be attributed to failed supply-side measures.

The main classical and Keynesian economic ideas

The fifteenth century was noted for mercantilism, which was an economic policy of sourcing wealth externally. Merchants were in a sense economic advisors to the king or prince of the time. It was Adam Smith, however, in his ground-breaking book, *The Wealth of Nations*, who recognised a natural order.

Smith, regarded as the father of modern economics, promoted the idea of an economy free from government interference. He believed the 'invisible hand' of the market would automatically solve the economic problem, based solely on self-interest and with no intention of promoting society's interests. All economic philosophers who embraced the predominant role that markets played were called classical or *laissez-faire* economic thinkers.

Classical economic thought was the reasoning behind the predominant method of economic management until the Great Depression of the early 1930s. During this time, massive unemployment, economic stagnation and poverty were rampant in all economies of the world; a similar condition existed for economies after the year 2008.

Classical economics failed to find solutions to these problems. The period that preceded the Great Depression was one characterised by rapid industrialisation. The Industrial Revolution and balanced budgets of the Victorian era were seen as the forces driving industrialisation.

It was another eminent economic thinker John Maynard Keynes, who revolutionised economic policy by advocating the intervention of the state to inject aggregate demand into the system by borrowing money and spending it on public works to 'jump start' stagnating economies.

Keynes's economic ideas were very much in opposition to the classical idea of a free market. Classical economic thought placed firm emphasis on the microeconomic working of all individual markets without state control.

Keynes's ideas became the standard for macroeconomics management. In a nutshell, Keynes identified the many weaknesses of the price mechanism, which caused unemployment and economic stagnation, and he is renowned for proposing the correction of these imperfections by state intervention. He advocated government spending and taxation or fiscal policy as tools of economic management.

The school of thought called monetarism attributed the cause of inflation to the increases in the money supply. This monetarist approach was based on the use of money policies as a tool of economic management.

A new classical ideology emerged in the early 1970s, highlighting policy tools that promoted efficiency in all markets. The new classicists were referred to as supply-siders, in contrast to Keynes who advocated aggregate demand management.

Since the 1980s supply-side management has become the economic management strategy of almost all countries. Reaganomics and Thatcherism were named after the supply-side policies of American President, Ronald Reagan, and the British Prime Minister Margaret Thatcher. They both achieved some measure of economic success with their monetarist policies.

The aggregate demand/aggregate supply model of the economy

Before an analysis of classical economic issues is undertaken it is necessary to explain the aggregate demand/aggregate supply (AS/AD) model of the economy, which was advocated by Keynesian and Classical economists. Note that the circular flow and the algebraic models are other ways to explain macroeconomic analysis.

Figure 31.1 is an AS/AD model of the economy, which looks like the demand and supply curves encountered in analysing the price equilibrium. In this macro model, however, note that the vertical axis represents the general or average price level of all goods and services in the economy. The horizontal axis represents real GDP output. The figure, therefore, shows how the entire economy can reach equilibrium, where AD = AS (as opposed to a microeconomic demand and supply curve of an industry).

Figure 31.1 shows an aggregate demand curve that is downward sloping, meaning that an increased quantity in real GDP is demanded at lower price levels in the economy.

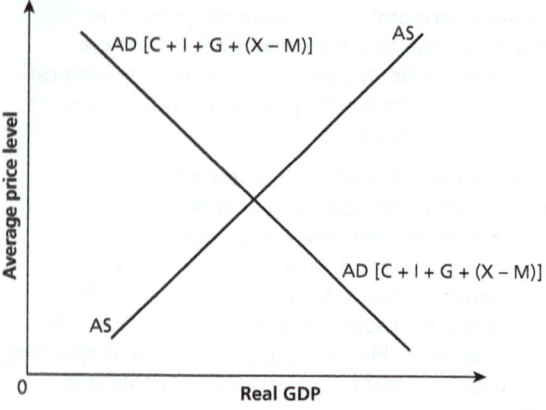

Figure 31.1 The AS/AD model

Since aggregate demand is represented by C + I + G + (X − M) it should be simple to see how more GDP is demanded at lower price levels.

Consumption

As price levels fall, consumers are able to purchase more goods and services with their income, which now has greater purchasing power.

If the price level increases, then their purchasing power is reduced as fewer goods and services will be demanded. On the other hand, rising prices require increased demand for money to meet normal everyday transactions, resulting in a rising interest rate. Rising interest rates increase mortgage and other loan instalments, so consumers are unable to demand other goods and services. In addition to pushing up interest rates, the increased demand for money also has an impact on the level of investment.

Investment

In the same way that higher levels of prices raise the interest rate, lower price levels lower the interest rate, enabling firms to undertake investment that previously would not have yielded a profit for them. Lower interest rates also lower the cost of borrowing for raw materials. For those reasons, firms' demand for real output (capital) increases at lower price levels.

Lower price levels will make domestic goods cheaper on the export market provided that these goods have an elastic demand. Foreign demand for local goods is likely to fall if the price level at home is higher than the price levels of trading partners. If exports are cheaper than imports, spending on imports with an elastic demand will fall, but demand for exports will rise if exchange rates are at a fixed level.

The conclusion is that there is a greater aggregate demand (C + I + GX + M) for real output at lower price levels than at higher price levels. Note that government spending is independent of price levels so that the government's demands for output do not depend on whether the price level is high or low.

So far, movements along the aggregate demand curve have been discussed. Non-price level factors will cause the aggregate demand curve to shift to the right or to the left, depending on the nature of the non-price level factors listed below. For example, if the price level is unchanged, the following factors will shift the aggregate demand curve to the right.

› **Consumers expect boom conditions in the economy**, e.g., when oil prices are high.
› **If consumers expect the future to be bright**, they will increase their consumption expenditure, e.g., buying a house or other big ticket items.
› **An increase in government spending with multiplied income-spending effects** will inject money into the economy. More government spending increases the demand for output at the existing price levels.
› **If the business climate is optimistic**, i.e., the economy is on a growth path, then firms will invest at the prevailing price levels.
› **If the growth in the economy or government spending impacts favourably on employment**, the available income will increase aggregate demand.
› **If the government engages in an expansionary fiscal policy**, i.e., increased government spending together with lower direct and indirect taxation, then aggregate demand is likely to increase.
› **If the distribution of wealth in the country is even**, this will impact positively on aggregate demand.
› **The age structure of the population will also have an impact on AD.** An ageing population may have less of an impact on AD than a young population.

The level of technology may also have an influence. Online buying opportunities can increase commerce, and other technologies that maximise credit purchases also have a favourable impact on aggregate demand.

If the factors outlined above are reversed, the aggregate demand curve will expectedly shift to the left.

The average price level and the AS curve

The similarity between microeconomic demand and macro aggregate demand also applies to microeconomic supply and aggregate supply. Note that at the macro level, we are considering AS and the price level. Also, for the short- and long-run periods of production, the supply curve has a different shape. In macroeconomics it is similarly so. The AS curve is upward sloping to reflect the fact that more will be supplied by the economy if price levels are rising. As firms' labour costs are fixed in the short-run, rising prices enable them to earn high profits. Firms may introduce 24-hour shifts and incentives to the labour force to increase productivity. The short-run at the micro level is the period during which factor inputs are fixed. In seeking to increase productivity, firms may offer higher inducements that may raise their costs of production. In addition, they may supply at higher prices if demand for certain types of output is inelastic. Another factor is that since in the short-term some factors cannot be altered, diminishing returns may cause costs to rise.

Chapter 31 The main classical and Keynesian economic ideas

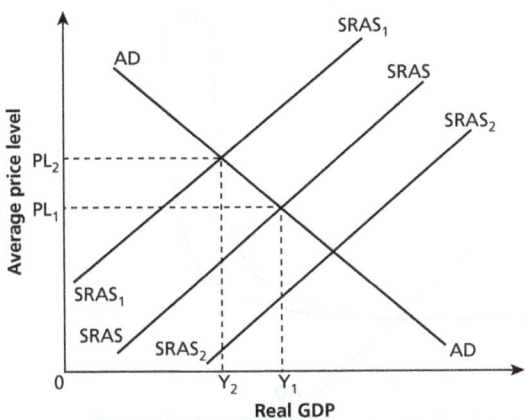

Figure 31.2 Shifts in the short-run aggregate supply curve: classical model

In figure 31.2, a shift of the AS curve to the right is caused by factors other than the price level, such as a government subsidy for certain types of goods and services.

A shift to the left may be caused by an indirect tax such as VAT. An increase in raw material prices will similarly shift the AS curve to the left, as will an increase in wage rates. If a country's exchange rate were to devalue or the costs of imported goods were to rise, these two would be likely to shift the AS curve to the left.

Figure 31.3 shows how an increase in AD (for example, an increase in government spending or a reduction in interest rates) may shift the curve to the right, causing an increase in output from Y_1 to Y_2 and the price level from P_1 to P_2.

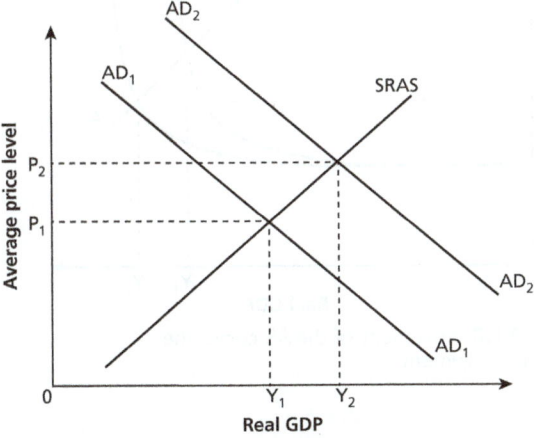

Figure 31.3 Shifts in the aggregate demand curve: classical model

Figure 31.2 shows an AS curve that has shifted to the left, perhaps due to government's imposition of indirect taxes, high raw material prices or failing labour productivity. In this case, output has fallen and the economy has contracted from Y_1 to Y_2.

Long-run aggregate supply curve

Classical long-run aggregate supply curve

Classical economists believed the LRAS curve to be vertical at the level of full employment. In the short-run, unemployed workers may feel the economy will improve and they will become employed eventually. Eventually, wages do fall and workers become employed, although at lower wages. Not only labour, but also the other factors of production would experience the same disequilibria and become fully employed in the long-run through a lowering of interest rates for capital and rent for land.

See figure 31.4.

Since the economy will be operating at full capacity in the long-run (Y_{FE}), increases in aggregate demand caused by lower taxes, low interest rates or increased government spending would cause the AD curve to move up the vertical AS curve, resulting in a rising price level from PL_1 to PL_2.

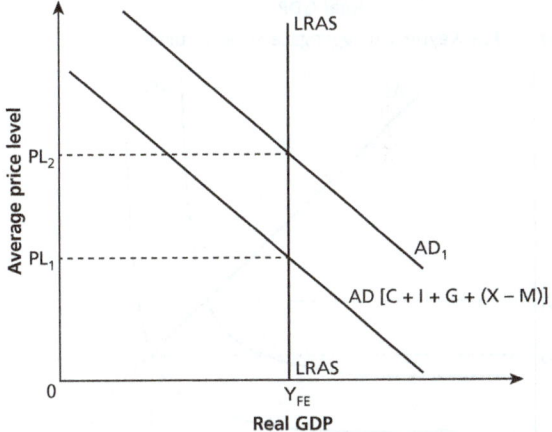

Figure 31.4 Rising price level in the long-run at full employment

The Keynesian long-run aggregate supply curve

Keynesian economists identify two stages of LRAS. See figure 31.5. Stage 1 is where, at lower levels of GDP, there are unemployed resources and the supply of resources is therefore perfectly elastic. Stage 2 is where the economy has grown and all factors of production are fully employed at the full employment level. Keynesians therefore reasoned that at stage 1, real wages will not fall because existing workers will get increases in wages as the economy grows slowly. Keynesians, however, also assert that in the long-run the economy may be in an equilibrium at less than full employment, as indicated at Y_1 in figure 31.5.

At Y_1 the economy is in equilibrium, although below full capacity employment at Y_{FE}. Note that Keynesians point out that when the economy is in stage 1, with high levels of unemployment, it is aggregate demand that moves the economy along a growth path from Y_1 to Y_3, with small changes in the price level but positive changes in real output. Any further increase in AD beyond Y_3 leads to faster rising price levels or inflation. Classical economists, on the other hand, recommend that measures to increase the AS curve would increase the productive capacity of the economy, with a falling price level and increased output/growth (figure 31.6). These supply-side measures are outlined in this chapter.

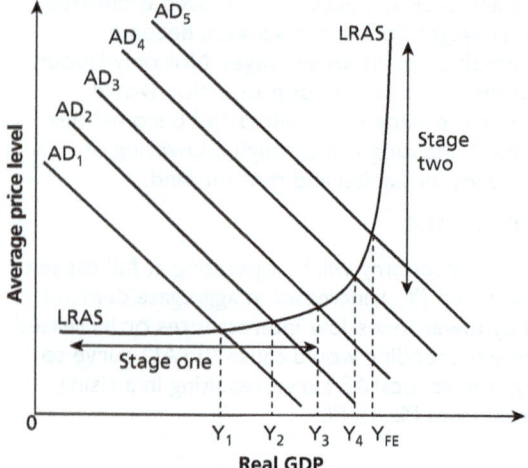

Figure 31.5 Keynesian aggregate supply curve

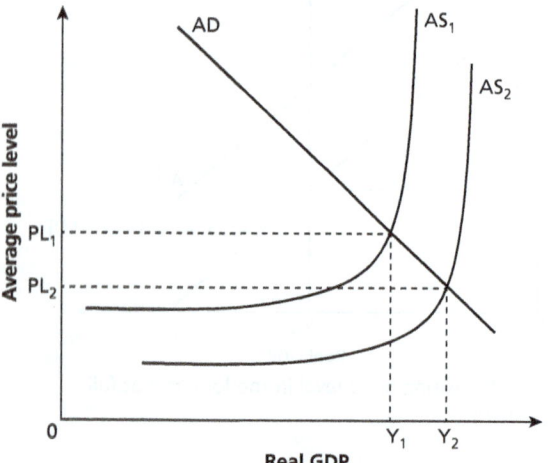

Figure 31.6 Increase in output, decrease in price level through classical supply-side measures

However, Keynesians argued that since the economy could be at an equilibrium below full employment, a shift of the AS curve would not affect output or the price level, as shown in figure 31.7.

If the economy is in equilibrium at Y_1 any movement of the AS curve (AS_1 to AS_2) leaves output unaffected.

Further, Keynesians argued that at the AD curve 1 in figure 31.8 there would be an increase in output from Y_1 to Y_2 and a lower price level from PL_1 to PL_2 if the AS curve shifts to the right.

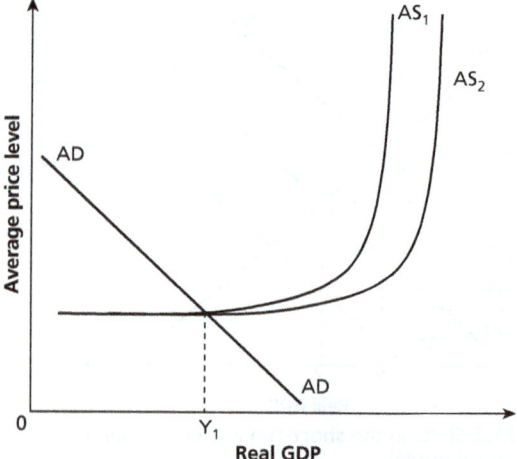

Figure 31.7 Price level unaffected by the expanded AS curve

The conclusion to this debate is simple. In a recession, Keynesians claim measures designed to shift AS to the right will not affect output. Measures to increase AD, however, will increase output and employment. The impact of the AS curve on the economy depends on its position on the AD curve, as shown in figure 31.8. They further assert that demand management will increase output to full employment, but once reached, the shift of the AS curve is then necessary as shown in figure 31.8.

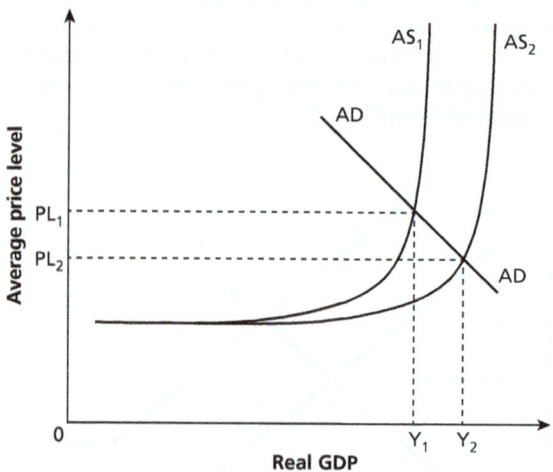

Figure 31.8 Movement of the AS curve: the Keynesian argument

Supply-side measures

The supply-side measures promoted by classical and supply-side economists are measures to increase efficiency in all the factor markets and promote market forces in an economy. The main measures are: privatisation, deregulation, liberalisation of trade and making the economy more competitive and market driven (with the state playing the role of facilitator by providing incentives to working, saving and investing).

These measures are summarised below.

Measures to increase efficiency in labour markets

- Increased occupational and geographic mobility: retraining of idle labour; and regional policy.
- Incentives to work: cutting direct taxes; and reducing and eliminating welfare and unemployment benefits, as an incentive to return to the labour force.
- Job information: manpower planning at job information centres.
- Movement within CARICOM (CSME): removal of barriers to entry in labour markets; reducing the power of unions; minimum wage legislation; making pensions transferable.

Measures to increase efficiency in capital markets

- Increasing competition among finance institutions (e.g., insurance companies, banks and credit unions) by removing barriers to competition (e.g. mortgage rates)
- Removal of taxes on interest, to expand the pool of capital for investment
- Tax holidays for foreign investors
- Introduction of deposit insurance to boost confidence in the capital markets
- Tax incentives for savers (insurance relief)
- The provision of state training for the occupationally immobile
- Exchange rate controls to encourage the movement of capital intra-regionally
- Decreased government spending on unemployment benefits to encourage a return to work and active participation in the workforce
- Full access to investment funds
- Reorganisation of the Stock Exchange
- Providing banking and insurance ombudsmen to seek depositors' interest
- Depreciation allowances.

Other supply-side policies

Privatisation

Privatisation of state-owned or controlled enterprises is also a supply-side measure much in evidence in CARICOM countries. Privatisation is traditionally considered to be the transfer of state assets to private ownership.

Privatisation refers to de-monopolisation, in that in a bid to control monopolies in the economy, the government introduces competition to curb monopolistic power.

Outsourcing

This concept involves the introduction of private firms to carry out operations normally undertaken by state firms, which have become inefficient for one reason or another. For example, laundry and provision of meals in some hospitals are undertaken by private firms, as is dispensing of drugs for patients. And in Trinidad and Tobago, annual motor vehicle inspection is undertaken by private garages.

Trade liberalisation

Trade liberalisation is another supply-side policy that promotes the reduction of tariff barriers to allow free competition. It is believed that competition encourages productivity and optimal use of resources. Some CARICOM countries, however, have argued that removal of tariff barriers may expose infant industries to unfair competition. Opposing voices have, however, pointed out that infant industries never become mature when they are protected by competition.

Classical economic theory summarised

Classical economic theory is founded on the freedom of all markets to reach equilibrium of aggregate demand and aggregate supply without government intervention.

Classical economics is based on the following main ideas:

- All markets are self-regulating, based on Say's law of markets (explained further in this chapter) which explains how the price mechanism would function to eliminate any temporary disequilibrium in any market.
- The economy would tend towards full employment in the long-run, due to flexibility in wage rates.
- Equilibrium in the capital markets would be achieved through flexibility in the interest rate.
- Equilibrium in international trade would be achieved by exchange rate flexibility.
- The aggregate demand curve is left to right and downward sloping.
- The aggregate supply curve is vertical at long-run full employment.
- The economy is driven by the supply-side of the economy.
- The role of the government is to keep a stable stock of money to finance aggregate demand, so that output can be absorbed. Classical theorists therefore believe that the appropriate tool for economic management is monetary policy.

The classical theory of output and employment

Classical economists maintained that the unregulated price mechanism would ensure that there would be no unemployment in the long run. Insignificant involuntary unemployment would be the only consequence. They based this reasoning on two concepts:

1. The unregulated price mechanism bringing all markets into long-run equilibrium, including the labour market.
2. Say's law of markets.

The short-run equilibrium: how free market forces bring the labour market into equilibrium

In its simplest form, classical theorists claim that if unemployment existed, then according to the free market forces the supply of labour would be greater than the demand for labour.

To fully explain this, note that in figure 31.9 the aggregate demand for labour is downward sloping from left to right as in microeconomic theory, but the vertical axis shows real wages, which represents purchasing power.

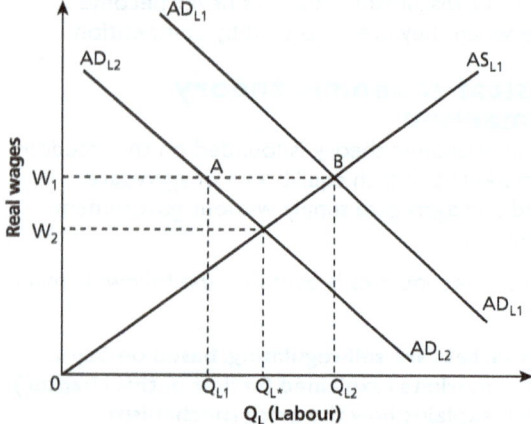

Figure 31.9 The flexibility of wage rates to eliminate unemployment

If aggregate demand for labour falls and the aggregate demand curve shifts to the left, then at the real wage of W_1 there would be surplus labour equal to Q_{L1} to Q_{L2}.

This classical or real wage unemployment would be eliminated because workers would be anxious to keep their jobs and would reduce their wage demands. Firms would realise that their labour costs are now reduced and in expectation of profit would hire low-cost labour, thus eliminating surplus labour. The sequence is as follows:

1. The supply of labour is greater than demand.
2. Wage levels are pushed down as a result.
3. Seeing that labour costs are low, firms will demand more cheap labour to make a profit.
4. Surplus labour is therefore employed.

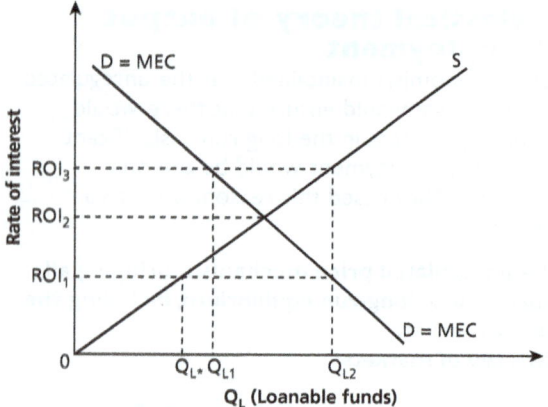

Figure 31.10 Flexibility of interest rates making savings = investment

Apart from the flexibility of the wage rate responding to changes in demand and supply of labour, the classicists also advanced the idea that the market for loanable funds, that is, money and capital, would also tend to equilibrium, making savings equal to investment.

Figure 31.10 explains how savings become equal to investment. First, all loanable funds are depositors' funds that banks lend to firms. The demand for loanable funds is assumed to come from firms that wish to invest. In the real world, consumers and governments demand loanable funds, but classical theory assumes this demand to be the demand for capital, as explained by the MEC curve.

To simplify matters, the demand for loanable funds is greater at lower, rather than higher rates, of interest. The supply curve represents depositors who would deposit more into banks as the rate of interest increases. The rate of interest is the market price for loanable funds.

Once again, if the rate of interest is ROI_3 there would then be a surplus of funds to the $Q_{L1}Q_{L2}$ supplied. Banks would therefore be forced to lower the rate of interest (price) to attract borrowers. A situation called excess liquidity is said to exist.

Eventually, the clearing prices or equilibrium would make demand equal to supply. Similarly, if the rate of interest is ROI_1 the demand would in this case exceed supply, forcing the rate of interest upward, attracting more savings and equilibrium with investment.

External market equilibrium

When import spending was greater than export earnings, according to past practice the resulting deficit was usually paid in gold from a country's reserves. In response to the outflow of gold, the country reduced its money supply, and hence its total expenditure, creating output and labour surpluses.

According to the classicists both prices and wages would fall as a result, making domestic production cheaper. This would provide a stimulus to exports and a disincentive to imports.

A simpler classical explanation is also based on the fact that when import spending is greater than export earnings, the resulting deficit would cause a fall in a country's exchange rate (provided it is flexible) and make exports competitive once again.

Key point

The flexibility of prices in the labour market (i.e. wages), the loanable fund market, and external trade (exchange rates) ensures there would be equilibrium in the final analysis, according to classical economic thinking. There is, therefore, a built-in tendency towards full employment equilibrium in the long-run.

Say's law of markets

J.B. Say was a French economic thinker who was greatly influenced by Adam Smith. He famously advanced the idea that unemployment should never exist, since supply created its own demand.

The simple reasoning was that according to the circular flow of income, payments to households of wages, interest, profit and rent became the financial means to purchase the output created by firms in a two-sector economy.

In other words, the act of supplying goods and services would always cause factors of production to be hired. The rewards from this employment enabled the purchase of outputs from firms, in which case aggregate demand should always be equal to aggregate supply.

As a result, employment should always be guaranteed. Even if savings, imports and taxes withdrew from the circular flow, this would be compensated by injections into the economy of investment, government spending and exports.

Key point

Say's law of markets advanced the idea that it is not possible for the economy to be in disequilibrium and to have unemployed resources because supply will always create its own demand. Creating output involves paying out earnings to purchase the very same output.

The Keynesian view

Keynesian economic ideas were, in the main, not in accord with the classical ideas outlined above. The main focus of Keynesian theory was the correction of market failures such as unemployment, inflation, negative growth and balance of payments deficits. In short, Keynes proposed state regulation of the economy since the state was a very influential force. The ideas will now be explored.

It is possible to advance the views of J.M. Keynes, now that some of his concepts have been analysed. Keynesian economic thinking held contrasting views to the classical economists. These are:

- In the short-run the labour market will not achieve equilibrium as classicists claim.
- An increase in savings will not cause an increase in investment in the loanable funds market. Therefore a disequilibrium will exist.
- The quantity theory of money advanced by the classical economists postulated that there is a direct relationship between the money supply of a country and the rate of inflation. However, an increase in the money supply will not necessarily lead to an increase in inflation, according to Keynes.
- Say's Law of markets is not valid.
- Fiscal rather than monetary policy should be the choice of economic policy. It is aggregate demand that drives the economy not aggregate supply.
- Unregulated markets do not create sufficient aggregate demand.

Keynes's explanation of the labour market and unemployment

Why surplus labour will not lower wages (the classical claim)

Basically, Keynes theorised that when the supply of labour was greater than the demand for labour the wage rate would not fall quickly enough to clear the labour market. Unemployment would accordingly persist. Keynes believed that it was possible for the economy to reach an equilibrium with unemployment in the economy. He theorised that the downward 'stickiness' of wages was due to workers resisting wage decreases, causing the surplus of labour (AB in figure 31.9) to last longer than was originally expected.

In figure 31.9 note that the fall in aggregate demand for labour as a result of a recession moves the wage rate downward from W_1 to W_2, the demand curve from AD_{L1} to AD_{L2}, and the quantity of labour falls from Q_{L2} to Q_{L*}. Further, note the disequilibrium employment indicated by the distance AB.

Classical economists advocated wage cuts when such a situation arises. Keynes, however, argued that wage cuts were ineffective since lower wages meant less consumer spending, causing firms to reduce their demand for labour. Unemployment would then become worse.

The market for loanable funds

Why low interest rates do not always cause investment to increase

See figure 31.10.

Keynes also disagreed with the classicists with respect to the loanable funds theory.

He asserted that savings will not necessarily become equal to investment. He explained that when savings increase, investment demand will decrease because more savings leads to less consumption. In these circumstances, firms will undertake less investment. Even though the rate of interest falls, this fall does not cause investment to rise.

Keynes believed that business optimism or expectations are a major determinant of investment and when interest rates fall, business confidence is similarly low. Keynes's solution to this situation of deepening recession was for the government to intervene in the economy by increasing aggregate demand through borrowing money to finance government spending. Lower taxes should also be used to stimulate aggregate demand. Accordingly, aggregate demand will shift to the right, leading to growth and employment with multiplier effects.

Keynes and the quantity theory

Why is the quantity theory not a stable relationship between money and output?

Classical economists believed that regulating the money supply regulated the economy and any excessive increase in the money supply would result in inflation. Keynes countered this argument by proposing that increases in the money supply would lead to an increase in savings, hence the velocity of money would slow down and prices would not necessarily rise.

He further reasoned that as long as there were idle resources in the economy, any increase in the money supply would instead increase output rather than prices.

Keynes and Say's law of markets

Since Keynes based his ideas on creating increases in aggregate demand, he disagreed with Say's law. Instead of supply creating its own demand, Keynes reasoned that it was the other way around. Demand, he insisted, would create supply, since firms respond to increased demand by creating more output. More labour, he asserted, will then be demanded.

Main Keynesian criticisms of classical economics

The main Keynesian criticisms of classical economics are as follows:

- If there is a disequilibrium in the labour market it will not automatically return to equilibrium, because wages are not downward adjustable as the classicists claim. Unions are militant; unemployment will persist.
- Savings will not automatically be equal to investment through the interest rate mechanism in the capital market as classicists claim. Investment responds to expectations in the economy, not the interest rate, according to Keynes.
- The foreign exchange market also does not change automatically; disequilibrium will persist.
- Classicists claim that Say's law of markets is valid. It is supply that creates demand. Keynesians think it is aggregate demand not aggregate supply that drives the economy.
- Fiscal policy is the main tool of economic management not monetary policy, as classicists claim.
- The government using fiscal policy should be the manager of the economy, not the private sector and monetary policy as classicists claim.
- The economy should be managed by macroeconomics, not microeconomics or the supply-side as the classicists claim.
- The quantity theory MV = PT is invalid because velocity (V) and transactions (T) are not constant in the short-run. Classicists claim that V and T are constant.
- Inflation is caused when aggregate demand exceeds aggregate output at the full employment level, not by increases in the money supply, as classicists claim.

Chapter summary

This chapter has discussed classical economic theory and Keynes' criticisms of the theory.

Classical economic theory is founded on the freedom of all markets to reach equilibrium of aggregate demand and aggregate of supply without government intervention. Classicists consider that all markets are self-regulating, based on Say's law of markets that supply creates its own demand.

Classical theorists also believe:

- **The price mechanism functions to eliminate any temporary disequilibrium in any market.**
- **The economy would tend towards full employment in the long-run due to flexibility in wage rates.**
- **Equilibrium in the capital markets is achieved through flexibility in the interest rate.**
- **Equilibrium in international trade is achieved by exchange rate flexibility.**
- **The aggregate demand curve is left to right and downward sloping. The aggregate supply curve is vertical at long-run full employment.**
- **The economy is driven by the supply-side of the economy.**
- **The role of the government is to finance aggregate demand so that output can be absorbed.**
- **The appropriate tool for economic management is monetary policy.**

Keynes asserted that:

- **If there is a disequilibrium in the labour market it will not automatically return to equilibrium.**
- **Savings will not automatically be equal to investment through the interest rate mechanism in the capital market.**
- **The foreign exchange market does not change automatically; disequilibrium will persist.**
- **It is aggregate demand not aggregate supply that drives the economy.**
- **Fiscal policy is the main tool of economic management not monetary policy.**

Chapter 31 The main classical and Keynesian economic ideas

- The government using fiscal policy should be the manager of the economy, not the private sector and monetary policy.
- The economy should be managed by macroeconomics, not microeconomics or the supply-side.
- The quantity theory MV = PT is invalid.
- Inflation is caused when aggregate demand exceeds aggregate output at the full employment level.

Practice questions

1. Outline the classical model of:
   a. Employment
   b. Price determination.

2. Explain why unemployment exists in the Caribbean with reference to the Keynesian and classical views of unemployment.

3. Explain how foreign direct investment companies (FDIs) can be beneficial in reducing unemployment in the Caribbean.

4. Explain the reasons why J.M. Keynes disagreed with Say's law of markets and the quantity theory.

32 International trade

INTRODUCTORY ECONOMICS A TEXTBOOK FOR CAPE ECONOMICS STUDENTS

Chapter 32 International trade

LEARNING OBJECTIVES

- Explain specialisation and trade.
- Explain the basis of trade.
- Explain the importance of exports and imports in a small open economy.
- Identify factors affecting exports and imports.
- Explain the gains from trade: absolute and comparative advantage.
- Identify the benefits and costs of trade.
- Explain protectionism.
- Explain trade liberalisation.
- Explain the terms of trade.

REQUIRED KNOWLEDGE

- Barter
- Specialisation
- Opportunity cost
- Productivity
- Production possibility frontier
- Economies of scale
- The role of exports and imports.

TOPIC VALUE

Our standard of living is directly affected by our ability to import foreign goods and services and to earn foreign currency from the sale of exports and other inflows.

Introduction

International trade is the buying and selling of goods and services between countries, with payment for the goods made in the currency of the seller. The islands of the Caribbean have a long history of regional trade.

The basis of trade

Perhaps the single most compelling reason for trade is the fact that world resources are unevenly distributed. Other reasons include:

> **Resources, especially land, are immobile, while labour and capital are not easily mobilised across international borders.**
> **Certain types of goods and services require specialised types of resources, e.g., wheat is grown in temperate countries. Some countries have resources while others do not. In the Caribbean, Trinidad and Tobago have oil, gas and asphalt, while the Windward Islands rely on banana production and tourism.**
> **If nations do not have resources to manufacture goods, then the goods themselves, wherever they are produced, are mobile and can move across borders.**
> **Some countries produce at a lower cost than others, e.g., beet sugar versus CARICOM sugar.**

In much the same way that Usain Bolt has a natural talent for sprinting, some countries are naturally endowed with resources that enable them to produce certain types of goods and services.

The role of exports and imports

From a theoretical viewpoint, exports are injections into, and imports withdrawals from, the main circular flow. As injections, exports have the potential to generate growth in the economy via the multiplier effect. Many countries have used export-led growth as their model of economic development. Japan and many Southeast Asian 'tigers' have adopted this form of growth model.

Furthermore, the sale of goods and services to trading partners means that the national output of a country is not wholly consumed in the home market. Similarly, the expenditure of households and firms may also favour foreign goods and services.

It should be noted that while exports reduce the available output to domestic households and firms, imports increase the output available domestically. Importantly, exports earn income for a country while imports earn income for trading partners. Exports and imports are not only goods, but also services. Other financial flows such as interest, profit and dividends are known as capital flows, which are earned in an open economy.

If export revenue from physical goods and services and financial inflows exceeds the outflows of a similar nature, the resulting net inflow of money places a country in a position with sufficient import cover to purchase goods and services that are not produced domestically. In addition, raw materials and specialised technology serve to increase a country's export capacity and long-term growth. On both counts, a country's standard of living will be increased.

When an open economy can earn enough from export revenue and other invisible inflows to finance import spending, self-reliance is achieved and external debt greatly reduced. If not, a country may suffer a foreign exchange shortage and may need to borrow from lending agencies such as the International Monetary Fund (IMF).

International trade and small open economies

Small open economies are usually classified as lesser-developed countries that depend heavily on imports.

The Group of Eight are the world's leading industrialised countries and comprise the USA, Canada, the UK, France, Italy, Germany, Japan and Russia. The relationship between the 'North' and the 'South' is linked to historical trading links.

The impact of external trade on developing countries is influenced by the following factors.

The technology and capital gap

Northern open economies have not only advanced technologies, but also more capital resources than small open economies.

In the Caribbean, labour-intensive products that are linked to the primary sector are manufactured. In an earlier period, coffee, cocoa, sugar cane and bananas were the main exports – apart from tourism. In addition, small open economies sold primary products to the North, where value was added to be resold to the providers of the primary products. Since northern economies had superior technology, they benefited from economies of scale and mass produced cheap goods. As a result, smaller economies have been unable to compete with these goods in the international market. Sri Lanka's rubber industry collapsed when synthetic rubber was manufactured in northern economies. In the same way, beet sugar was more cheaply produced as a result of research and development in the technologically advanced North.

This relationship, where small open economies depend on the North for their goods and services, has been characterised by some economists as a dependency syndrome. Since imports generally exceed exports for small economies, they are frequently in debt. In addition, in order for small economies to develop their infrastructure, they borrow to finance their development. As a result, there is a net outflow of interest from loan payments and profits sent back to home countries from foreign investment.

Foreign direct investment in the Caribbean is a case in point. Most of the investors are companies of the North, harvesting primary resources; for example, oil, gas, alumina. Even when an economy such as oil-rich Trinidad and Tobago is able to reap windfall rents from high oil prices, such prices are a cost of production to first world countries, which they pass on through the products in which they trade. The real purchasing power of the oil rents is therefore diminished.

The gains from free trade: the case for trade liberalisation

It was Adam Smith who focused attention on specialisation and the gains a country could achieve through free trade. Specialisation and trade internationally increase world output and makes a greater diversity of goods and services available to the world.

There are four main gains from trade, which are:

1. Greater availability and diversity of products now available to trading partners
2. Increased competition between countries
3. Scope for economies of scale where demand comes from very large markets, e.g., North American Free Trade Area (NAFTA) has 360 million people
4. Comparative advantage, which is trade made possible when one country produces a good at a lower opportunity cost than its trading partner.

There are other gains from trade that may be added to the four already identified. These are:

1. The spread of technology.
2. External trade may enable a country to develop export industries, providing jobs and contributing to economic growth and development.
3. There are welfare gains to be derived from trade when prices are lowered.

Absolute and comparative advantage

These two concepts, especially comparative advantage, are the foundation of international trade that was first identified by David Ricardo in the early nineteenth century. The assumptions of the theory are:

> Two countries A and B, each produces only two goods: sugar and bananas.
> Each country may have a different quantity of resources.
> Resources can move very easily from sugar to banana production on a 1:1 ratio.
> The level of technology is fixed.
> There are no transport costs.

Absolute advantage

As the term suggests, absolute advantage exists when a country can produce more of a good than another country using the same quantity and quality of resources. Note that absolute advantage is based on superior productivity. If two countries each have an absolute advantage, it is possible for each to specialise according to its superior productivity and gain from trade. Table 32.1 summarises the concept.

Table 32.1 **Absolute advantage**

	Sugar (tonnes)	Bananas (kg)
A	6	4
B	8	2
	Total 14	Total 6

If a worker in country A can produce 6 tonnes (sugar) and 4 kg (bananas) and a worker in country B can produce 8 tonnes (sugar) and 2 kg (bananas), then A has an absolute advantage in banana production and B has an absolute advantage in sugar production.

Note their combined output is 14 tonnes of sugar and 6 kg bananas. If they specialise, however, according to their absolute advantage and allocate all their resources to only one good, their production is likely to double, since they are using twice the quantity of resources, all things being equal. Table 32.2 below shows what will happen.

Table 32.2 **Production after specialisation**

	Sugar (tonnes)	Bananas (kg)
A	0	8
B	16	0
	Total 16	Total 8

It is now possible for country B to trade 7 tonnes of sugar with country A in exchange for 5 kg of bananas. The new arrangement will therefore be as shown in table 32.3.

Table 32.3 Gains in trade (absolute advantage)

	Sugar (tonnes)	Bananas (kg)
A	7	5
B	9	3
	Total 16	Total 8

Note that they are both better off after trade than they were before.

When, however, a country has an absolute advantage in both goods, trade according to absolute advantage is not feasible. However, trade can take place according to which country produces their output at a lower opportunity cost, or the country making the least sacrifice in terms of resources.

Comparative advantage, therefore, is achieved when a country can produce a good at a lower opportunity cost per unit resource than another country.

Perhaps an analogy may simplify the concept of comparative advantage. Let us assume that cricketer Chris Gayle can service the carburettor of his sports car in 2 hours, but he can also earn US$50,000 endorsing a product in the same time. Further, his 15-year-old nephew who is mechanically minded, can service the same carburettor in 5 hours, but he can also sell oranges to earn 100 dollars in 5 hours. Chris Gayle would sacrifice $50,000 to service his carburettor, while his nephew would sacrifice $100.

The best arrangement that makes both of them better off is for Chris Gayle to do the endorsement for $50,000 and pay his nephew $300 to service the carburettor. This is how comparative advantage works in favour of two parties.

Comparative advantage

Comparative advantage may be explained using a table or production possibility frontier (PPF). Let us assume that two CARICOM countries, Guyana and Barbados, are engaged in trade and Barbados has 10 units of land, while Guyana has 20 units. Further, Barbados can use one unit of land to produce 10 kg of sugar or 9 kg of rice, while Guyana can use one unit of land to produce either 5 kg of sugar or 2 kg of rice. Table 32.4 below summarises the production possibilities of each country.

Table 32.4 Production possibilities before trade (per unit of land)

	Sugar (tonnes)	Rice (kg)
Barbados	10	9
Guyana	5	2

It is clear that Barbados has an absolute advantage in both products. In the absence of trade, the two countries must produce both goods in order to become self-sufficient.

Using all 10 units of land Barbados could produce 100 tonnes of sugar (10 units × 10 tonnes) and zero rice, or 90 kg of rice (10 units × 9 kg) and zero sugar. Similarly, Guyana is capable of utilising its 20 units of land to produce 100 kg of sugar (20 units × 5 kg) and zero rice, or 40 kg of rice (20 units × 2 kg) and zero sugar. Table 32.5 below summarises these trade possibilities.

Table 32.5 Production possibilities before specialisation

	Sugar (tonnes)	Rice (kg)
Barbados	100	90
Guyana	100	40

The table can also be expressed as a trade possibilities frontier, as shown in figures 32.1 and 32.2.

Although Barbados produces 90 kg of rice or 100 kg of sugar, it must provide both goods with its resources without trade.

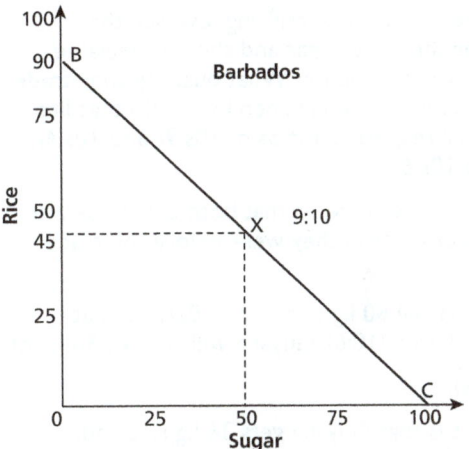

Figure 32.1 Production possibilities (Barbados)

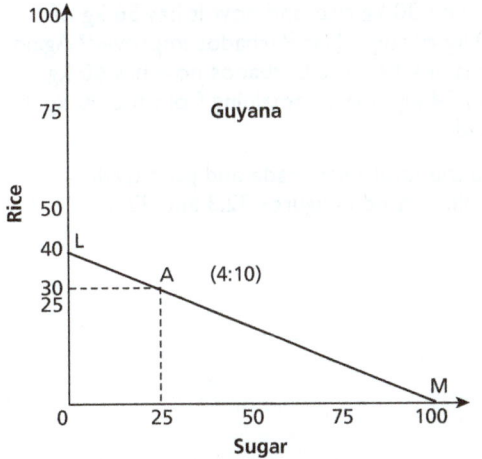

Figure 32.2 Production possibilities (Guyana)

Point X in figure 32.1 is such a combination, that is, 50 kg of sugar and 45 kg of rice are within its capability.

Similarly, Guyana must provide both goods without trade. Such a point being A along the PPF curve LM, yielding 30 kg rice and 25 kg sugar.

Neither Barbados nor Guyana can trade according to absolute advantage but can, however, trade according to comparative advantage. Trade takes place according to which country has a lower opportunity cost in sugar and rice production.

The opportunity cost ratios are as follows.

1. **Barbados: 9 rice: 10 sugar**
   Or cost of 1 rice = 10/9sugar (1.9 sugar)
2. **Guyana: 4 rice: 10 sugar**
   Or cost of 1 rice =10/4 sugar (2.5 sugar)

Barbados therefore has the lower opportunity cost in rice (10/9) and should specialise entirely in rice production. Guyana meanwhile has a lower opportunity cost than Barbados in producing sugar. Let us see how this is so.

1. Barbados: 10 sugar cost 9 rice
2. Guyana: 10 sugar cost 4 rice

Therefore, Guyana is sacrificing less rice than Barbados for the same sugar and should specialise entirely in sugar production. What quantity they trade, and at what terms, is determined by a ratio that lies between their respective ratios of 10s:9r and 10s:4r, for example 10s:6r.

Let us begin the trade so that both countries will become better off than they were before the trade took place.

Let Guyana sell 60 kg of sugar to Barbados at 10 sugar for 6 rice (10:6). Guyana will receive 36 kg of rice ($\frac{60}{10} \times 6$).

The result is that Guyana gets 36 kg rice and, having sold 60 kg of sugar, now has 40 kg of sugar remaining from the original 100 kg. Has Guyana improved? The answer is yes, because originally it had 25 kg sugar and 30 kg rice, and now it has 36 kg of rice and 40 kg of sugar. Has Barbados improved? Again the answer is yes, because Barbados now has 60 kg of sugar and 54 kg of rice remaining from the 90 kg it originally had.

Observe the entire pre-trade and post-trade scenario as illustrated in figures 32.3 and 32.4.

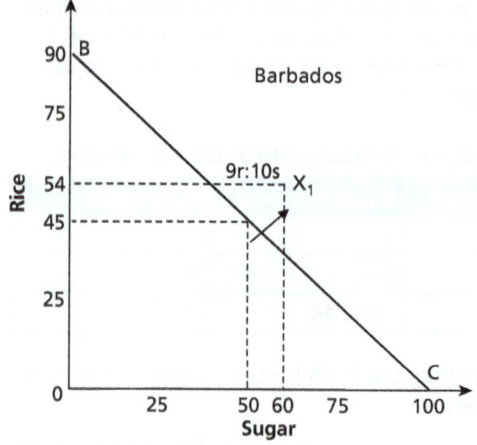

Figure 32.3 Gains from trade (Barbados)

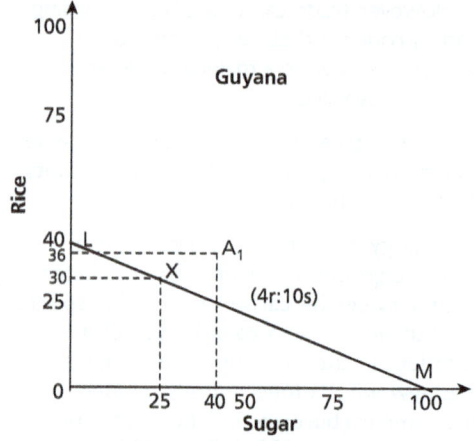

Figure 32.4 Gains from trade (Guyana)

In conclusion, for Barbados, point X_1 of 60 kg of sugar and 54 kg of rice was previously unattainable, whereas after specialisation and trade, according to comparative advantage, it achieved this combination. Similarly, Guyana's preferred point A_1 was beyond its capability, that is, 40 kg sugar and 36 kg rice. After trade through comparative advantage, both countries have also secured superior and preferred combinations.

Table 32.6 A summary of gains from trade

Barbados before trade	After
Point X 45 kg rice + 50 kg sugar	54 kg rice + 60 kg sugar
Guyana before trade	**After**
Point A 30 kg rice and 25 kg sugar	36 kg rice and 40 kg sugar

Chapter 32 International trade

Criticisms of the theory of comparative advantage

Criticisms of the theory of comparative advantage include:

> In practice countries produce more than two goods.
> Opportunity costs are in reality not constant because resources tend to be immobile, or some resources are more suited to certain types of goods.
> Exchange ratios, called terms of trade, usually do not lie between domestic opportunity costs.

What tends to influence exchange ratios are demand and supply factors of the trading countries.

> The theory also assumes that domestic ratios (e.g. 10:6) reflect domestic prices. This is not so if imperfect markets exist, since monopoly or monopolistic power will determine prices.
> Technology, in fact, differs significantly between lesser-developed countries (LDCs) and more developed countries (MDCs) to the extent that economies of scale may influence cost and price.
> Transport costs are a significant factor in trade and it is unrealistic to hold this variable constant in real life.

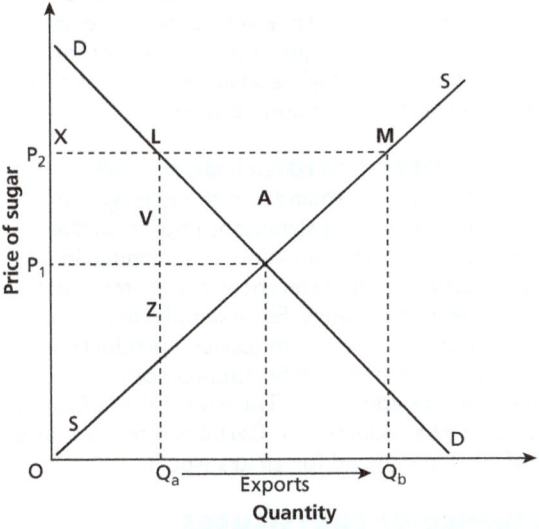

Figure 32.5 Gains and losses from export trade

Gains and loss from international trade

Figure 32.5 illustrates the welfare gains and losses when a country engages in exports trade. Before trade the domestic price of sugar was P_1.

The world price of sugar is P_2 and when the country engages in trade, price P_1 rises to meet world price P_2. At the world price of P_2 demand is reduced to OQ_a and supply increases to OQ_b with the surplus Q_aQ_b exported at the price P_2.

The welfare gain and losses are as follows:

> Before trade: consumer surplus = X + V
> Before trade: producer surplus = Z
> After trade: consumer surplus = X; therefore a loss of V
> After trade: producer surplus = Z + V + A; therefore a gain of V + A

Summary

The total welfare to society (consumer + producer surplus in figure 32.5) is equal to X + V + Z + A. The gain by producers exceeds the loss of consumers by the area A. Overall, society has gained in welfare (A) through exports.

Gains and losses through imports

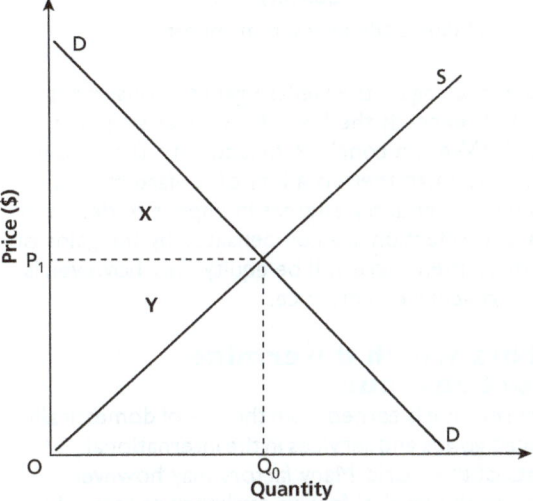

Figure 32.6 Gains and losses through import trade

Figure 32.6 shows the pre-trade scenario of a sugar economy. P_1 is the equilibrium price equating domestic demand and supply.

Total pre-trade welfare = Consumer surplus area X + producer surplus area Y.

Engaging in trade reveals the following:

(See figure 32.7.) The world price P_2 is lower than the domestic prices P_1; therefore, the price of sugar to the world falls to P_2. At price P_2, domestic demand increases from Q_0 to Q_b, while supply falls from Q_0 to Q_a. The demand shortage Q_aQ_b is imported. The welfare gains and losses are:

> Before trade, consumer surplus = X
> After trade, consumer surplus = X + Y + W
> Gain in consumer surplus = Y + W
> Before trade, producer surplus = Y + Z
> After trade, producer surplus = Z
> Loss = Y
> Total welfare to society = X + Y + Z + W

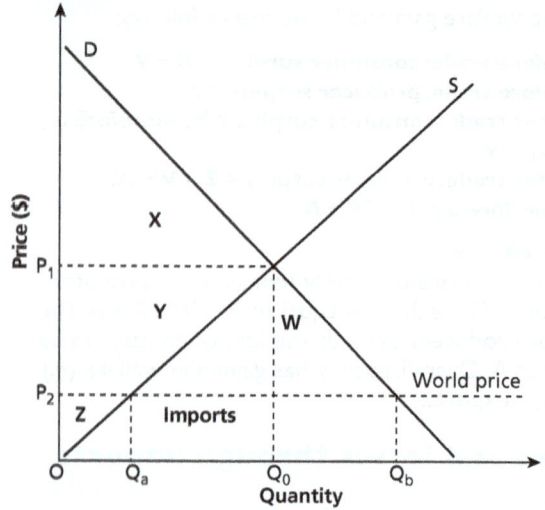

Figure 32.7 Post-trade-losses from imports

Note once again the welfare gain to consumers X + Y + W exceeds the loss of producer surplus Y by area W. We can conclude that society as a whole benefits, although there is a loss of welfare by one group when a country engages in import trade. If the losses of production are compensated by the gains of consumers then there will be equity. This, however, is difficult to achieve in practice.

Factors which determine export revenue

Export revenue is earned from the sale of domestically produced goods and services in the international markets of the world. Many factors may, however, determine the level of foreign exchange generated.

International prices

The price of the good or service in the international market is determined by demand and supply factors and factors related to market structure.

Demand factors are closely related to the elasticity of demand for the product. For example, tourism in the Caribbean is very price elastic because there are many other tourism destinations in the world. Hoteliers in the Caribbean must therefore consider this factor when pricing their holiday packages. Competition is a key element in international pricing. The size of a firm, comparative advantage and production levels, inflation and exchange all play their part in international pricing.

Most countries with a comparative advantage would also be able to have some degree of price-setting power in the international market. For example, the demand for (OPEC) oil is inelastic, allowing the cartel price-setting powers. Jamaican Blue mountain coffee is a specialty on the international market, since only a small quantity is produced in any given period. Supply is also inelastic, hence the reason for the high price of the coffee.

Domestic production

Another limiting factor is domestic production; this is linked to the capacity for economies of scale, but this factor is closely related to the size of the firm and the mass demand for the product.

The sale of a product to a mass market, therefore, is crucial to reap the advantage that scale economies offer. In this respect, access to and penetration of foreign trading blocs like NAFTA, with 360 million people, will benefit CARICOM countries. For example, domestic production is determined to a high degree by the availability of factors of production that may not be obtainable in sufficient quantity in a developing country.

Domestic prices and exchange rates

Domestic prices and exchange rates are also significant factors that determine export prices. Domestic prices are partly determined by cost factors such as specialisation and economies of scale; costs of production are to a large extent influenced by productivity levels and rates of inflation.

High domestic rates of inflation may be caused by demand-pull or cost-push factors. Exchange rates are determined by whether such rates are fixed or freely floating. Exchange rates are, however, in the main determined by the international demand for and supply of a country's currency, with exports being a main item. Inflation and interest rates are other determinants of a country's exchange rate, as they are related to demand for a country's currency.

Shifts in international demand

Shifts in international demand and the emergence of substitutes can make a significant impact on the international demand for an exported product. In some cases, changes in preferences and tastes cause demand patterns to change. For example, there has been a market shift away from tobacco products and a surge in products that are health promoting, for example exercise equipment. The World Trade Center disaster caused a reduction in Caribbean tourism as a result of a fall in demand for air transport.

Emergence of substitutes

The emergence of substitutes, another determining factor affecting export revenue, was very evident in the fall in demand for Caribbean sugar, when cheaper beet sugar was produced by European countries.

International activity

A wide range of international activity is also cited as something that affects exports. For example, sports, cultural and other related activity are determining factors for Caribbean tourism. The Cricket World Cup in the Caribbean in 2007 is one such example. Cultural events such as the Trinidad Carnival, Barbados Crop Over and Vincy Mas are export-generating opportunities. Business travel may be added to these factors that have linkages to food and hence agriculture, hotels, transport, entertainment and ecotourism.

Level of international incomes

Lastly, the level of international incomes may affect the demand for exports, particularly for income-elastic goods and services. Tourism is again a good example of this type of demand.

Positive economic growth in a country and the rising incomes associated with increasing real GDP provide a stimulus for export demand. Negative growth does the opposite. Because all countries are interdependent in trade, negative growth tends to have adverse feedback effects on trading partners, as the recession in USA demonstrated in 2008/09.

Summary

The single most compelling reason for trade is the fact that world resources are unevenly distributed.

In the past, small open economies sold primary products to the North where value was added.

> Exports reduce the available output to domestic households and firms; imports increase the output available domestically.
> When export revenues from physical goods and services and financial inflows exceed the outflows of imports of a similar nature, the resulting net inflow places a country in a position with sufficient import cover to purchase goods and services that are not produced domestically.

Terms of trade

Terms of trade is essentially a price concept and refers to the rates of exchange between one country's output and another country's output. If Barbados can exchange 2 kg of sugar for 1 kg of rice from Guyana then, all things being equal, 1 kg of sugar will be half the price of 1 kg of rice. The terms of trade would therefore be 1:2.

In the real world, however, when more than one good is traded, the terms of trade are expressed in the formula as: average price of exports × 100 divided by average price of imports.

The average prices of exports are calculated in a similar way that we measured inflation price levels. For example, 200 exported items may be selected and the price changes measured from a base year. Weights are also assigned. The same is done for import prices. The terms of trade is determined by the average of the export prices divided by average import prices.

Common error 1

The terms of trade is often mistaken for a volume or quantity concept. It should be emphasised that the terms of trade is a price concept, that is, the average price of exports compared to the average price of imports.

If the base year selected is 2012 and the average price index for exports in 2014 is 110, it means that the average price of exports rose by 10 per cent. If the index of import prices was 100 then the terms of trade are 110 × 100 = 110.

When the value of the terms of trade is greater than 100, it is said to be favourable. It could mean that export prices have risen compared to import prices. It is said to be favourable because if export prices rise compared to import prices then fewer exports will be sold in order to purchase any given quantity of imports. It is equivalent to a rise in real income for a country.

A favourable terms of trade may be possible for the following reasons:

> **Export prices are rising, while import prices are falling.**
> **Export prices are rising, while import prices are constant.**
> **Export prices are rising faster than import prices.**
> **Import prices are falling faster than export prices.**
> **Export prices are constant, while import prices are falling.**

The same reasoning is applied to an unfavourable terms of trade, which is indicated by a value of under 100. In this case, as long as import prices are relatively higher than export prices the terms of trade will be less than 100.

Common error 2

Once again, note the relative average price changes of exports and imports, and the quantity changes. If, for example, there is a rise in the average price index for exports, quantity changes will depend on the elasticity of demand for the product.

Revenue gained is also dependent on the price elasticity of demand. For example, if exports are elastic, a rise in the average price of exports is likely to cause a reduction in the quantity of exports traded and a fall in total revenue.

If the terms of trade are favourable and elasticity of demand for exports elastic, there is likely to be a balance of trade deficit, since rising export prices render exports uncompetitive relative to cheaper imports prices.

Protectionism

Arguments for restricting trade

Although there are gains or benefits achieved through international trade, countries employ methods to restrict imports into their domestic economies. The reasons for doing so are as follows.

The infant industry argument

This is the oldest argument for protectionism. Industries in their 'infancy' are unable to compete in the international markets with more established industries in MDCs, because infant industries need time to grow. This process of growth is necessary to achieve a high-volume output that generates economies of scale and low costs in order to successfully compete in the trading area.

Costs of production are usually high for infant industries; they need time to master production techniques and consolidate markets, and there is a time lag associated with this process of development.

Opponents of the infant industry argument point to the fact that infant industries do not 'grow up' because they are not driven by the effects of competition to increase their productivity.

There may perhaps be no need for protection since initial losses in the short-term are necessary for long-term growth. This argument is applicable to Caribbean countries because foreign investors are reluctant to establish manufacturing industries in the Caribbean. Instead, they establish commercial ventures that extract raw materials such as oil, gas methanol, urea, ammonia, bauxite and asphalt.

Governments can establish new industries by selectively using grants, subsidies and state resources to overcome risk.

The need to protect sunset industries

In many cases both developed and developing countries have industries that are in long-run decline but possess enough potential for profit, provided they are given the opportunity to 'get back on their feet'. Even the US automobile market has seen its industry superseded by Japan and the US government has employed tariff barriers to protect its industry.

Job protection

This is yet again a contradictory argument for restricting trade. If a local industry loses out to foreign competition, unemployment will result for a region or economy. But protecting these industries will limit consumer choice. Governments abroad may retaliate by also erecting barriers of their own. Everyone is disadvantaged.

It is further argued that unemployment is a cost of long-term development, since purchasing imported goods transfers incomes to another country, enabling those countries with the means to purchase other products from established domestic industries.

Unfair competition

The most common problem associated with this argument is the issue of 'dumping'. This is a form of predatory pricing, or underpricing, by some firms with surplus goods and high disposal costs, or no market.

Firms may sell below average total costs, ensuring that the variable costs are covered. Sometimes excess capacity may create this problem or a sudden change in demand. These goods are dumped on other economies to recoup losses.

Dumping may also take place if a good is produced cheaply as a result of a state subsidy and competes with substitutes that are not subsidised. It is argued that this is an unfair advantage. Although this is true, the consumer will benefit from the low price. There are regulations in place to prevent dumping in international trade.

Cheap labour

Since, on average, labour accounts for approximately 70 per cent of total costs, cheap labour enables a competitor to increase its market share in an industry. In recent times, China has made giant strides in world markets for this reason. An argument against this is that cheap labour is a vital resource of a country and it should not be penalised for having a low-cost resource that enjoys a comparative advantage.

Protectionism used to bargain in trade

Many countries use trade barriers, but some signal an intention to erect a trade barrier as a threat to another, which then causes another country to remove its barrier (a variation of monopolistic behaviour).

The key industry

Many developing countries, similar to those in the Caribbean Single Market and Economy (CSME), depend on a single revenue earner. When the price of this commodity fluctuates, the levels of foreign revenue fall. The threat of unemployment caused by international competition is an added cause for concern. Guyana's and Jamaica's bauxite, Barbados's sugar and the Windward Islands' bananas are all examples of this one-crop dilemma.

Diversifying an economy to overcome this threat carries a time lag in the medium- to long-term. In the short-term, however, LDCs see the need to protect their earnings and levels of unemployment to guard against this phenomenon. These arguments, however, do not hold sway with the World Trade Organization (WTO), who advocate reform in the external trade sector.

The external deficit

This is where the the level of imports is greater than exports in LDCs with weak exchange rates and where an external deficit is persistent. In response, a country's short-term policy would be to restrict imported goods in order to reduce the external deficit. Long-term supply-side measures may eventually cure the persistent deficit. Opponents of this argument, again view subsidies as a better method to remedy this problem than tariff barriers.

Externalities

Many countries import and export products that give rise to negative externalities. Examples of such products are cars without processes to remove harmful carbon monoxide, or chemicals that eventually enter the food chain, such as auto batteries that contain lead. In these cases, pressure groups have raised arguments in defence of the environment.

The restrictions to trade identified in this section are the focus of the WTO, that is empowered to reduce trade restrictions via negotiations and trade rounds.

Methods of protection

Methods of protection include tariffs, quotas, voluntary export restraint, government purchasing policies, subsidies, import deposits, and exchange controls, which are described as follows.

Tariffs

A tariff is a form of indirect taxation on imported goods or services. It is also called a customs duty. It may be a specified sum, for example $100, or an *ad valorem* percentage, similar to VAT. The main effect of a tariff is to cause the price of the import to rise.

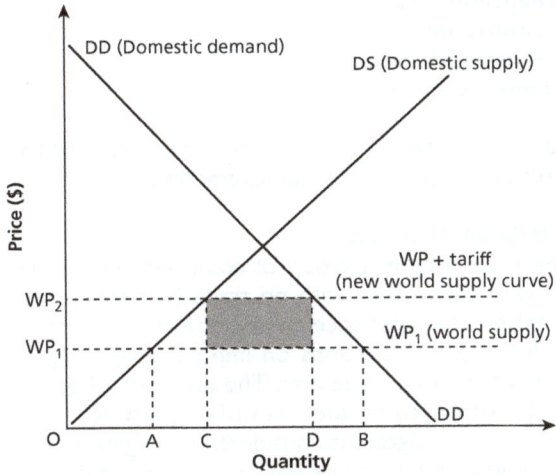

Figure 32.8 The effect of a tariff on producers and consumers

Figure 32.8 illustrates how a tariff raises the price of imports. WP_1 is the price of the good on the world market. WP_2 is the price when the tariff is added to the price. At price WP_1, OA is supplied and OB is demanded. At price WP_2 demand falls to OD.

Note that prices are determined where world supply WP_2 equals domestic demand (DD). Note also that domestic production increases from OA to OC, an increase of AC, while demand falls from OB to OD, by the quantity DB. Note that imports have fallen to the quantity CD, whereas without the tariff the quantity imported was AB. Tariffs not only restrict imports, but also raise revenue for the government.

Quotas

Figure 32.9 explains how a quota raises the price of an imported good and restricts the quantity imported. A quota is a specified quantity of a good that the government decrees should be imported. Before the quota the world price is Pw where domestic demand is O_{Q4} and domestic supply O_{Q1}. O_{Q1} to O_{Q4} is the excess demand that is imported.

To reduce this quantity imported, a quota of O_{Q2} to O_{Q3} is imposed on importers but which raises prices locally to Pd. Note that domestic demand is reduced to O_{Q3} while domestic supply increases to O_{Q2}.

Note that domestic supply plus the quota equals demand at Q_3.

The government will only raise revenue by this method if import licences are granted. In terms of welfare gains and losses, consumer surplus, originally DD DdPw, is now reduced to DD CPdd, a loss of PdCDdPw. Producer surplus, originally PwAO, has increased to PdBO, a gain of PdBAPw. The deadweight loss to society, which is lost to both consumers and producers, are triangles ABE and CDdF. Observe also that licensed importers gain revenue BCFE.

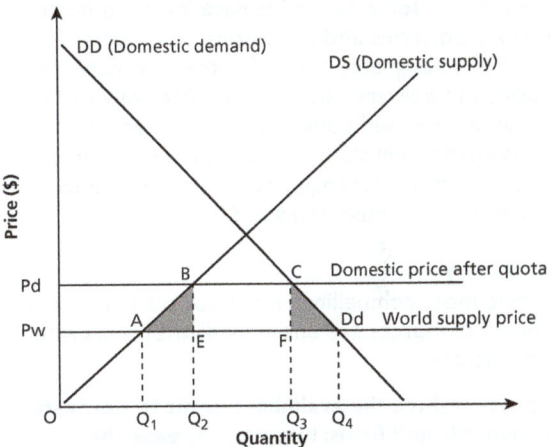

Figure 32.9 Non-tariff barriers

Voluntary export restraint

Voluntary export restraints (VERs) are another form of quota that are agreed upon (voluntarily) by exporters and importers. VERs operate in the same way as quotas, with the same consequences in terms of raised prices for consumers and profits for licensed importers. Producers also profit from higher prices than the pre-quota price. VERs are a preferable quota system to a government set of quotas, because buyers and sellers agree that it is in their mutual interest.

Government purchasing policies

Since the government is a major spender it may use this purchasing power to buy goods from local producers, even if the price is above the ruling world price. This is a form of non-tariff barrier since, in effect, foreign sellers are excluded from this non-competitive buying.

Subsidies

State subsidies for domestic exporters accomplish two benefits for domestic producers. First, it makes it easier for these producers to establish a foothold in foreign markets, as well as reducing the cost of production and hence prices, domestically. Effectively, on both counts foreign producers are at a disadvantage. In recent years, subsidies have been a contentious issue with respect to dumping in foreign trade.

Import deposits
Import deposits require an importer to remit to the government a proportion of the value of the quantity imported. This reduces the profit of the importer and acts as a disincentive to importers. The level of imports is accordingly reduced.

Exchange controls
This method of trade restriction targets the method of financing imports as a means of reducing the volume imported. If foreign currency has to be applied for, the government could effectively allow only the sale of foreign currency for selective imports and restrict others.

Other forms of protection
In recent years, some countries have imposed harsh regulations on terms and conditions of imports. Sometimes a designated port of entry may increase transport and delivery costs, which effectively raise the price of imported goods. In other instances, rigorous environmental, health and safety standards, language and other packaging regulations serve to raise the prices of imported goods.

Summary
The single most compelling reason for trade is the fact that world resources are unevenly distributed. Other reasons include:

- **Exports reduce the available output to domestic households and firms; imports increase the output available domestically.**
- **When export revenue from physical goods and services and financial inflows exceed the outflows or imports of a similar nature, the resulting net inflow places a country in a position with sufficient import cover to purchase goods and services not produced domestically.**
- **Small open economies export primary products to the North, where value is added and resold to the providers of the primary products.**
- **There are four main gains from trade, these are: greater availability and diversity of products now available to trading partners; increased competition between countries; scope for economies of scale; and comparative advantage.**
- **Although there are gains and benefits through international trade, countries employ methods to restrict imports into their domestic economies. The reasons for doing so are mainly to protect home industries and prevent job losses.**

Economic integration

The movement towards free trade between countries was given a boost with the introduction of General Agreement on Tariffs and Trade (GATT). GATT ensured that no country attempted to unilaterally erect tariff barriers that ultimately led to trade disputes. After numerous rounds of global negotiations involving many trading partners, GATT finally gave way to the WTO in 1995, as the new authority on promoting free trade negotiations.

The driving principle of the WTO is the liberalisation of international trade through the establishment of rules and regulations governing trade and the arbitration of trade disputes.

Regional integration
Trade agreements in the very recent past have focused on a few countries in close proximity to one another; for example, NAFTA, the European Union (EU), the Andean Pact Countries in Latin America, and the Asian Pacific Group.

Four basic groupings of regional trade agreements exist today. These are:

1. **Free trade area**
2. **Customs union**
3. **Common market**
4. **Economic union.**

All of these agreements are sometimes referred to as preferential trading or multilateral trade.

Free trade area
A free trade area is a group of countries engaged in trade with each other with no trade barriers among themselves. However, each retains the right to set individual trade restrictions on imports originating outside of the free trade area. The attention of each member is focused on the rules of origin, which govern whether a good is considered to originate from a member country or not, in order to assess the need for tariff charges. This underlines the need for rules of origin. The free trade area best known to the Caribbean economies is NAFTA, comprising 360 million people living in the USA, Canada and Mexico.

Customs union
The customs union is similar to the free trade area in that there is free trading among members of the union. However, there is a common tariff agreed to by all members, which is imposed on imports originating from outside the union. In these circumstances, members do not have the liberty to set individual import tariffs on non-member countries.

Common market
A common market has all the features of a customs union but goes further to include common agreements on:

- **Taxation on goods within the union. Ideally taxes should be the same for all members whether direct or indirect in nature.**
- **The same laws governing employment, trade and marketable products and safety standards.**

Economic union

An economic union is an extension of the common market. Integration extends to a common currency and hence a common monetary authority or central bank. Further, exchange rates are harmonised and monetary policy is commonly agreed upon. Indeed, macroeconomic policies are decided jointly between members to ensure uniformity of policy.

Economic effect of trade integration: customs union and common market

The economic effects of trade integration include the creation and diversion of trade as discussed below.

Trade creation

Trade is 'created' when all tariff and non-tariff barriers are removed as member countries of a region join a customs union or common market. The obvious reason is that members selling at the lowest cost will gain market share in the union. Specialisation and comparative advantage will obviously be at work in this instance.

For example, let us assume that before joining a customs union, Jamaica and St Lucia were exporting bananas in the Caribbean region. Further assume that St Lucia imposes a 60 per cent tariff on all bananas coming into the island. This makes Jamaican bananas expensive. When both countries from the union remove all tariffs, St Lucians will find that Jamaican bananas are cheaper. Jamaican producers experience an increase in trade because it is more efficient in banana production and will put its land resources to best use.

Trade has been increased by the removal of tariffs. Jamaicans may also find that St Lucian vegetables are now cheaper to import. Both producers will have benefited from specialisation, comparative advantage and efficient resource allocation.

Trade diversion

Trade diversion takes place when a country shifts from trading with a low-cost producer to a high-cost producer on joining a customs union. In the same way that removal of barriers enable trade creation for domestic producers in a union, imposing a common external tariff on products entering the union raises prices, effectively discouraging trade. This denies consumers of the union the chance to purchase low-priced products.

This would happen if consumers in Jamaica, Barbados, St Lucia and St Kitts purchase low-priced imports from a country outside the customs union in the Caribbean such as, for example, China. When the common external tariff increases the price of Chinese products that were formerly cheaply priced, the tariff causes a diversion of trade away from cheap Chinese products. Although producers of a customs union may benefit from trade creation from a world perspective, tariffs distort the allocating function of the price mechanism. The allocation of resources globally is therefore inefficient.

The net gain to the countries within the union may offset this global loss if the volume of trade creation is very high compared to trade diversion.

The gains from trade creation

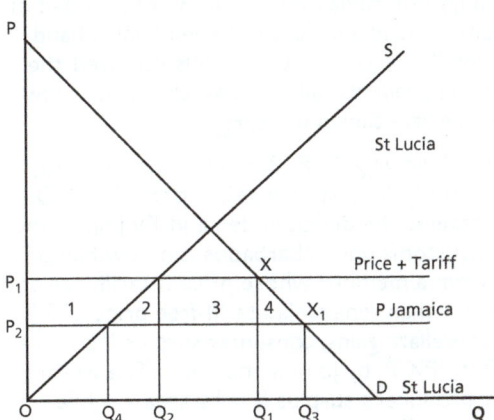

Figure 32.10 The gains from trade creation

These are the gains from trade creation via a customs union: Jamaica has the lowest price as a producer of bananas in the world at a price of P_2. If a tariff is imposed, St Lucia as a price taker and importer of bananas must pay P_2 plus the tariff, which is equal to P_1. At P_1 St Lucia produces OQ_2, demands OQ_1 and imports OQ_2 OQ_1. When the tariff is removed, price P_1 falls to P_2. The quantity demanded increases from OQ_1 to OQ_3 and St Lucian production falls from OQ_2 to OQ_4. Imports increase customer surplus from PXP_1 to PX_1P_2, that is, the areas 1 + 2 + 3 + 4. There is also a loss of producer surplus of area 1, and government revenue of area 3, so a net overall gain to all areas of 2 and 4.

Costs and benefits of trade diversion

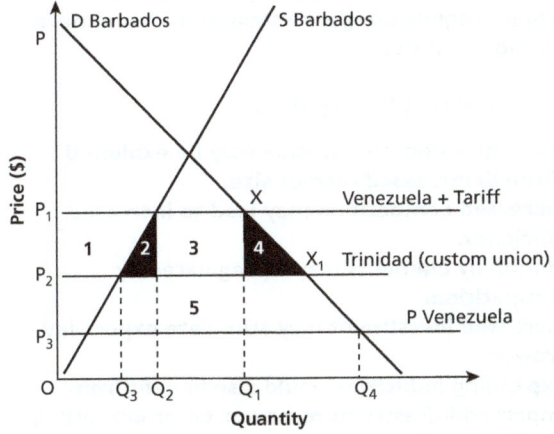

Figure 32.11 The costs and benefits of trade diversion

Figure 32.11 shows the gains and losses of trade diversion for oil products. Assume that Venezuela is the world's cheapest exporter of oil products but remains outside the customs union in the Caribbean with a price of P_3. Assume also that a tariff imposed on oil products raises the price to P_1 and, further, that Trinidad and Tobago, before joining the customs union, has a similar tariff imposed on its oil products, resulting in the very same price of P_1. Barbados, however, buys Venezuela's oil products at P_1 instead of buying from Trinidad and Tobago. When Trinidad and Tobago joins the union and the tariff is removed, the price of its oil products fall to P_2, which is not as low as a tariff-free Venezuelan price, P_3.

Note the following. At P_1 Barbados consumes Q_1 and produces Q_2 domestically and imports Q_1 to Q_2 which represents the deficit in demand. By joining the Caribbean customs union, Barbados can now buy oil products from a member whose price is tariff-free at P_2 (still higher than Venezuela's tariff-free price of P_3). In terms of welfare gains, consumer surplus increases from PXP_1 to PX_1P_2 by joining the union. The welfare losses are: producer's surplus falls by area 1, while government tariff revenue, which previously was area 3, is now reduced to zero since there are no tariffs in the customs union.

Summary of the costs and benefits of a customs union, common market or economic union

The costs (disadvantages) are:

- Firms within the union may try to take advantage of low wages in member countries, leaving short-term unemployment in their own countries.
- Integration may encourage mergers and oligopolistic behaviour in order to retain price control and profits.
- Beyond a certain size, expanding firms may, in the longer term, experience diseconomies of scale.
- There may be environmental costs from the free movement of large scale capital projects.
- There may be a net transfer of resources from large to small economies, e.g., the administrative budget requires larger contributions from more developed states.

The benefits (advantages) are:

- Internal economies of scale may be exploited through increased market size.
- Increased competition may lead to increased efficiency.
- Monopoly elements may be regulated by competition.
- Increased investment may stimulate export-led growth.
- Expanding industries would also benefit from improved infrastructure, power, communication, banking and insurance.
- Over the longer term, there is likely to be technological transfer between member countries.
- The single market concept enables members as a collective body to engage in trade bargaining and better terms of trade.

Regional integration in the Caribbean

Regional trade has existed in the Caribbean since the period of colonisation of Caribbean states by European countries. Initiatives towards formalising trade in the region had their earliest beginnings during the West Indian Federation of 1958.

The end of the West Indian Federation in 1962 signalled the first serious attempt at regional cooperation and trade. It was in 1962 that a common services conference was convened by Caribbean leaders to discuss the establishment of: the University of the West Indies, which was founded in 1948: and shipping services involving two ships donated by the Canadian Government, the *Federal Maple* and *Federal Palm*. In that year, Trinidad and Tobago proposed the idea of a Caribbean community not only of ten members who were in the West Indian Federation, but also other states in close proximity.

In 1965, Barbados, British Guyana and Antigua entered into discussions concerning the establishment of a Caribbean free trade area, called CARIFTA. Shortly afterwards, Trinidad and Tobago, Jamaica and both the Windward and Leeward islands joined CARIFTA. The next significant step towards multilateral regional trade was made in 1972 at the seventh Heads of Government Conference at Chaguaramas, Trinidad, where a proposal was made for the establishment of a common market (which in fact was a customs union). Initially, three areas of activity were earmarked for implementation, namely:

1. **Trade integration through a common market**
2. **Common services and functional cooperation**
3. **Harmonisation of the region's foreign policy.** Basically the customs union that was envisaged proposed the elimination of import restrictions among the member states and a common external tariff and protective policy exports of members in the customs union.

Consideration was also given to:

1. The development of regional integrated industries in less developed states in the union.
2. Rules of origin governing regional trade, i.e., percentage of input that originated in the union as opposed to being brought in from non-members.

Other worthy dates in the evolution of regional trade into what is now the CSME are:

- 1966: CARIFTA widened to include Grenada, Dominica, St Kitts/Nevis, Anguilla, St Lucia, St Vincent and Montserrat.
- 1968: The establishment of the Caribbean Regional Secretariat in May 1968 and the Caribbean Development Bank in 1968, in Guyana and Barbados respectively.
- 1973: At the eighth Heads of Government Conference, CARIFTA was disbanded to make way for CARICOM, formalised by the Georgetown accord.
- 1983: The Bahamas joined CARICOM.
- 1989: At the 10th Annual Conference of the Regional Heads of Government in Gran Anse Grenada, all parties agreed to deepen the integration movement into a single market economy on a phased basis as a means of fitting into an increasingly globalised world.
- 1991: British Virgin Islands, Turks and Caicos joined CARICOM.
- 1992: The instruments and technical arrangements and administrative procedure were introduced to the Heads of Government at their 13th Annual Conference in 1992.
- 1995: Suriname joined CARICOM.
- 1996: The establishment of the Assembly of Caribbean Community Parliaments (ACCP) in Barbados in May 1996. The AECP included Antigua, Barbuda, Barbados, Bahamas, Belize, Domonica, Grenada, Guyana, Jamaica, St Kitts/Nevis, St Lucia, Trinidad and Tobago and Turks and Caicos.

The CSME has evolved from the 1958 federation initiative and the main objective of this common market agreement is to present a united front to the other trading blocs of other regions of the world. This collective approach is seen as the most prudent way forward in terms of successfully treating with the competitive pressures of globalisation. Over time, it is felt that LDCs may benefit from an association with more developed economies in the common market.

Specifically, there is to be a free movement of labour, capital in all its forms, and goods and services within the common market, creating a borderless Caribbean economic village of 7 million people. Over time, fiscal, monetary exchange rate and other macroeconomic policies will become harmonised and, hopefully, will evolve into an economic and, finally, a political union. The achievement of political union, however, is more easily said than achieved, as it may compromise the sovereign independence of each state.

A summary of the benefits of the CSME for the region are:

- Free circulation of factors for production among member countries, including joint ventures, mergers and new business development in services such as banking and financial services
- Increased economic strength as a region when trading with states outside the single market economy
- Presenting a common position for the Caribbean region in trade matters with other trading blocs
- Accelerated, coordinated and sustained economic development
- Improved living standards for all in the region
- Enhanced competitiveness for regionally manufactured goods and services
- Net positive impact on the profitability of regional companies
- Access for producers to the entire CARICOM market and hence scope for scale economies.

Arrangements for Caribbean economies

The recent banana dispute between the Windward Islands and banana companies in the United States and the reduction of the sugar quota for Caribbean sugar, are just two factors that highlight the need for negotiation as a region. The CSME is seen as such a negotiating vehicle.

Currently, the negotiations of Free Trade Area of the Americas (FTAA) involving the entire Latin America region, the Caribbean, the USA, Canada and Mexico emphasise the need for the region to speak with one voice. Such a trade zone, stretching from Northern Canada to Southern Chile, would be the largest trading bloc of the world with 800 million people. It would need skilful negotiation on behalf of the Caribbean region.

Chapter summary

- International trade is the buying and selling of goods and services between countries with payment for the goods made in the currency of the seller.
- The most compelling reason for trade is the fact that world resources are unevenly distributed.
- Absolute advantage exists when a country can produce more of a good than another country using the same quantity and quality of resources.
- Comparative advantage is achieved when a country can produce a good at a lower opportunity cost per resource unit than another country.

- Exports reduce the available output to domestic households and firms.
- Terms of trade is expressed as index of export prices/index of import prices.
- Protectionism occurs when countries employ methods to restrict imports into their domestic economies.
- Tariffs, quotas and voluntary restraints are some of the measures used as forms of protectionism.
- A free trade area is a group of countries engaged in trade with each other with no trade barriers among themselves.
- A customs union is one in which there is free trading among members of the union but has tariff barriers to non-members.
- A common market has all the features of a customs union and also includes common agreements on taxation and safety standards.
- An economic union is an extension of the common market. Integration extends to a common monetary authority. Further, exchange rates are harmonised and monetary policy is commonly agreed upon.
- Trade is 'created' when all tariff and non-tariff barriers are removed as member countries of a region join a customs union or common market.
- Trade diversion takes place when a country shifts from trading with a low-cost producer to a high-cost producer on joining a customs union.

Practice questions

1. Developing economies may resort to protectionist measures to:
   i. Prevent the collapse of export earnings
   ii. Explain the importance of exports and imports
   iii. Accurately calculate the balance of payments
   iv. Respond to controls imposed by other countries
   a. I and II only
   b. I and III only
   c. I and IV only
   d. II and III only.

2. Distinguish between:
   a. Customs union and economic union
   b. Quota and tariff
   c. Absolute and comparative advantage
   d. Trade creation and trade diversion
   e. Terms of trade and balance of trade.

33 Exchange rates

LEARNING OBJECTIVES

- Define the exchange rate.
- Explain exchange rate determination.
- Define fixed, flexible and managed exchange rates.
- Explain the advantages and disadvantages of the three types of exchange rates.
- Define nominal, real and trade-weighted exchange rates.
- Explain purchasing power parity.
- Explain the relationship between the exchange rates and balance of payments.
- Explain the relationship between the exchange rate and inflation.

REQUIRED KNOWLEDGE

- Demand and supply analysis
- Elasticity of demand
- International trade
- Terms of trade
- Balance of payments
- Ceilings, intervention, purchasing and selling.

TOPIC VALUE

We all value foreign goods and services such as, for example, brand name products, cell phones or viewing cable television of international events. This chapter explains the different types of exchange rates and their effects on prices.

Introduction

Issues in international trade, terms of trade and balance of payments have already been examined in this book. This chapter analyses the pricing of trade through exchange rates.

The exchange rate is the rate at which one country's currency exchanges for another; for example, US$1 = TT$6.30. The exchange rate could be calculated in another way. If US$1 = TT$6.30 then a TT$1 is worth US$0.16 (1/6.30 = $0.16).

Pounds, francs, marks, rupees, East Caribbean dollars (EC), Jamaican dollars, bolivars or euros are different currencies that all represent foreign exchange. The market for foreign exchange is therefore worldwide, where many millions of currencies are traded on a daily basis. Exchange rates are necessary because, while internal trade requires domestic currency, external trade requires foreign currency. Perhaps a simple model may assist your understanding. Figure 33.1 illustrates there are many countries buying from and selling to each other. Each buyer must pay for goods and services in the currency of the seller.

Figure 33.1 Financing trade between countries

For example, a Trinidad and Tobago student who wishes to pay for university tuition fees in the USA will go to a bank and purchase US dollars at TT$6.30 for US$1. If college fees are US$1,000, they will cost TT$6,300. Similarly, a Jamaican coffee producer may wish to sell the popular Blue Mountain coffee to a firm in the USA. The American buyer will need Jamaican dollars to conduct the transaction. A British tourist who wishes to attend test match cricket in Antigua has to change pounds into EC dollars, in order to pay for the tickets and accommodation. It is possible therefore for a country's currency to be bought at any bank. These transactions are represented in figure 33.1.

One of the reasons why a Jamaican coffee producer may wish to be paid in Jamaican dollars for coffee bought by an American buyer is that Jamaican dollars are needed to pay the workers and to make purchases within Jamaica to manage the business. Sometimes banks may have a shortage of a particular currency. For example, rupees may not be available in a bank in St Kitts. In such a case, a vehicle currency may be used. The US dollar is accepted anywhere in the world and is such a currency.

Exchange rate determination

Exchange rates are simply the price of a currency and, like other prices, are determined by the free market forces of demand and supply. The exchange rate may also be fixed by the central bank, or a combination of free market forces and government decree, called a managed float.

The demand for a foreign currency

The demand for a foreign currency is linked to the demand for: imported goods, investment in foreign securities, and holdings of it as financial assets. It is therefore a derived demand.

The demand curve for foreign currency is left to right and downward sloping. It is negatively sloped, since more foreign currency is demanded at a lower rate of exchange. For example, if a Trinidadian wished to go on vacation in Gran Anse Grenada at a cost of EC$100 at an exchange rate of TT$3.00 for EC$1.00, this would cost TT$300.00. If, however, the rate of exchange is TT$2.00 per EC$1.00 it would now cost TT$200.00, illustrating that the lower the price of a currency the lower would be the expenditure on an imported good or service.

If the demand for Grenadian exports is elastic, a lower exchange rate for the EC dollar could give rise to an increase in demand for Grenadian exports and hence increased demand for EC dollars. Similarly, if the price of an EC dollar is high, fewer Grenadian exports would be demanded and therefore fewer EC dollars.

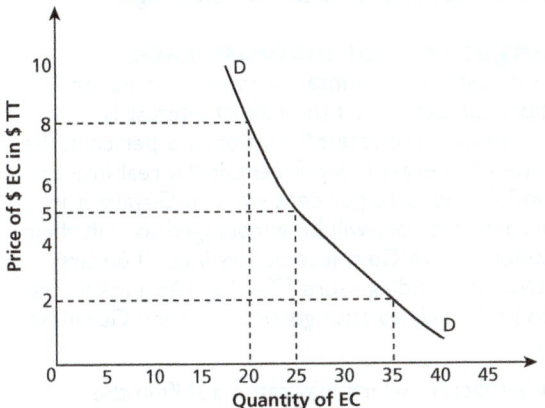

Figure 33.2 Foreign currency demand curve

Table 33.1 **A demand schedule for EC dollars**

Price of EC$	Quantity demanded
8.00	20,000
5.00	25,000
2.00	35,000

Refer to figure 33.2 and table 33.1. Note that a fall in the price of EC dollars from $5 to $2 results in an increase in the demand for EC dollars from $25,000 to $35,000.

In figure 33.2 illustrates Trinidadian dollars demanding EC dollars for the purchase of imports.

The supply of foreign exchange

The supply of EC dollars to the foreign exchange market is left to right but upward sloping to reflect that more EC dollars will be supplied at a high exchange rate than a low rate. For example, more EC dollars may be supplied because of a demand for Trinidadian goods and services by an Antiguan resident or firm. An Antiguan hotelier who wishes to expand hotel capacity may order cement from Trinidad. More EC dollars will be supplied at higher exchange rates, since if the rate of EC dollars to TT dollars is EC$1.00 = TT$1.00 then TT$1 million worth of imports would cost EC$1 million. At EC $1.00 = TT$2.00, the same TT$1 million worth of imports would now cost the Grenadian importer TT$500,000; and at EC$1 = TT$4, TT$1 million worth of imports would cost the Grenadian importer only EC$250,000.

Chapter 33 Exchange rates

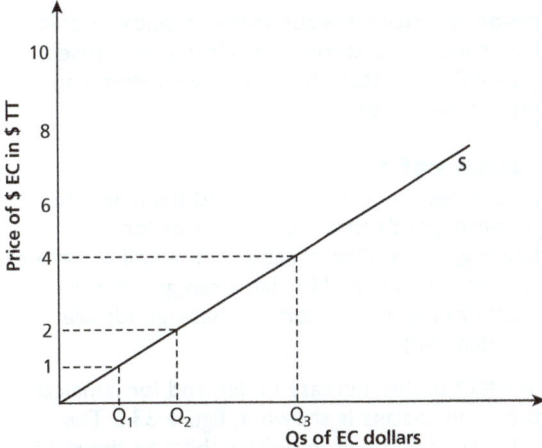

Figure 33.3 Foreign currency supply curve

See figure 33.3. At a higher rate of EC dollars to TT dollars more EC dollars will be supplied because Trinidadian imports would be cheaper as the exchange rate increases from EC$1.00 = TT$1.00 to EC$1.00 = TT$4.00. Note in figure 33.3 that as the price of the EC dollar rises from TT$2.00 to TT$4.00, the quantity supplied increases from Q_2 to Q_3.

The equilibrium rate of exchange

In figure 33.4, note that DD is the demand curve for EC dollars and SS the supply of EC dollars. At any point in time there is only one rate of exchange between the EC dollar and the TT dollar, which is the equilibrium rate, where the demand for EC dollars is equal to the supply of EC dollars. The equilibrium rate is TT$3.00 and the equilibrium quantity is $25,000.

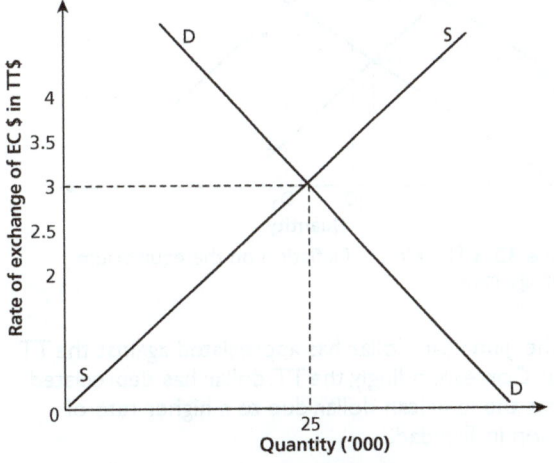

Figure 33.4 Foreign exchange equilibrium

Factors which affect the demand for foreign currencies

As with the price of goods and services, the conditions of demand may also cause a shift of the demand curves for foreign currencies to the left or right. The conditions of demand, which are also called the non-price factors, are summarised below. A shift of the demand curve to right or left may be caused mainly by inflation rates, changes in real income and changes in interest rates.

Inflation rates

If inflation rates are higher in Trinidad than Jamaica, then Jamaican goods that are substitutes for Trinidadian goods will be cheaper. There will therefore be an increase in demand for Jamaican goods and hence Jamaican dollars (assuming these goods are elastic in demand).

The effect of this increase in demand for Jamaican dollars by Trinidadians is shown in figure 33.5. The demand curve for Jamaican dollars shifts to the right, causing an appreciation of the Jamaican dollar, or a depreciation of the Trinidad dollar from 1:2 to 1:3.

However, this equilibrium price of TT$3 dollars for JM$1.00 is not the total picture. Since Jamaican goods are now cheaper than Trinidadian ones, Jamaicans may switch from purchasing Trinidadian goods to Jamaican goods, causing the 'supply' of Jamaican dollars 'demanding' TT dollars to fall (i.e. the supply curve shifts to the left).

Note that the exchange rate is now TT$4.00 to JM$1.00.

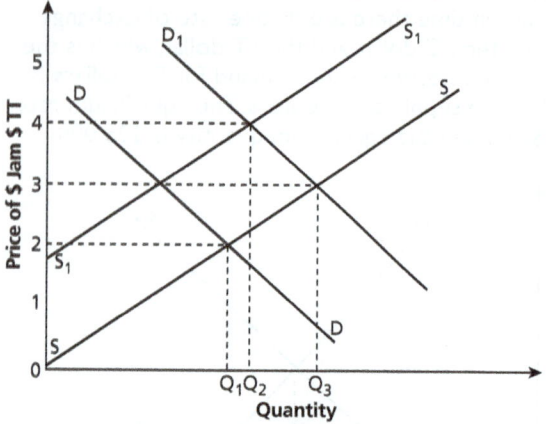

Figure 33.5 The effect of inflation on the equilibrium exchange rate

The Jamaican dollar has appreciated against the TT dollar. Correspondingly, the TT dollar has depreciated against the Jamaican dollar, due to a higher rate of inflation in Trinidad.

Changes in real income levels

Real income levels represent incomes adjusted for inflation. Apart from the issue of inflation itself, income levels adjusted for inflation may cause the demand curve for a foreign currency to shift.

Assume that real income levels in Antigua are higher than real income levels in Guyana. This would enable Antiguans to purchase Guyanese-made products and to vacation in Guyana, in much the same way that a rise in income would cause consumers to purchase more goods and services.

If, therefore, real income levels are higher in the developed countries of the North it is likely to boost Caribbean tourism. Caribbean currencies would therefore strengthen against the US dollar, sterling or euro, since the demand for Caribbean vacations would cause an increase in demand for Caribbean currencies, causing the demand curve to shift to the right.

Changes in real interest rates

Real interest rates are interest rates adjusted for inflation. For example, if the rate of interest is 10 percent and the rate of inflation is 5 per cent, the real rate of interest is 5 per cent. If the real interest rate in Trinidad is 10 per cent while in Guyana it is 6 per cent, investors will be encouraged to shift their investments from Guyanese dollars into TT dollars, effectively demanding more TT dollars. As a result, the TT dollar is likely to strengthen against the Guyanese dollar.

Other factors which may cause a shift in the demand curve for a currency are:

> **External shocks**, e.g., the World Trade Center disaster negatively affected the demand for travel and tourism and consequently for Caribbean currencies.
> **Political instability** may affect foreign investment decisions, hence the demand for currency.
> **Economic integration**, i.e., the formation of trading blocs can also impact negatively on the demand for goods and services from countries in other trading groups. Exchange rates are therefore affected.
> **Aggressive market development** may also have an impact on foreign currency demand, since a successful market promotion could increase the demand for exports and hence a rise in demand for domestic currency.
> **Confidence in a currency** may fall, leading to a movement into safe currencies.

Speculation in the world's foreign currency markets in recent times has affected exchange rates (negatively or positively) that are freely floating. In particular, volatile 'hot money' capital has been the cause of fluctuating exchange rates in the world's major financial centres.

Flexible or freely floating exchange rate

A flexible exchange rate is one determined by the free market forces of demand and supply. Previous knowledge of market forces indicates that demand and supply curves can shift to the right or left, thereby changing the equilibrium rate. The same applies to a flexible exchange rate. As with freely determined prices, if the demand curve for EC shifts to the right, for example, because of an advertisement for vacations in Grenada, the demand curve will shift to the right from DD to D_1D_1 and there will be a new equilibrium price of EC$1.00 = TT$5.00, as shown in figure 33.6. Similarly, if Grenadian exports are too costly, the demand curve for its currency will shift to the left, from DD to D_2D_2.

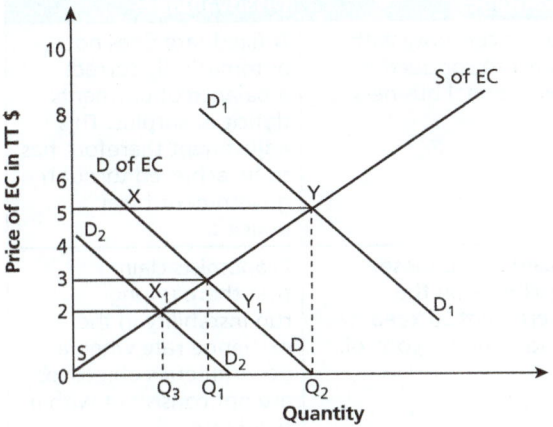

Figure 33.6 Effects on equilibrium from a shift in the demand of EC dollars

When the price of a freely floating currency increases, this is called an appreciation of the currency. If Trinidadians shift their vacation away from Grenada, the demand curve for EC will shift to the left from D_1D_1 to D_2D_2 to a new equilibrium price of EC$2.00, as in figure 33.6. This price fall in a freely determined currency price is called a depreciation of the currency.

Note that both appreciation and depreciation could also be caused by a shift of the supply curve.

EC dollars are supplied when a Grenadian demands TT dollars. If Trinidad and Tobago cement or oil products are in demand in Grenada, the supply of EC dollars to purchase TT dollars will shift the curve to the right from SS to S_1S_1, causing a depreciation of the EC dollar from EC$3.00 to EC$1.00. The strengthening of a currency is, in effect, the purchase of an increased quantity of another currency. For example, if EC$1.00 buys TT$2.00 in one month, but the rate of exchange moves to EC$1.00 = TT$4.00 in another month, this is a strengthening of the EC dollar and a weakening of the TT dollar. See figure 33.7.

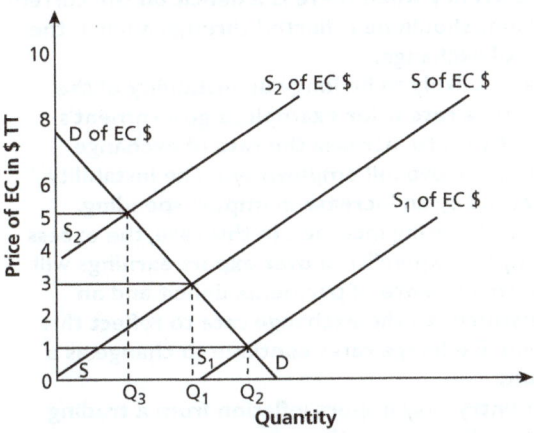

Figure 33.7 The effects on equilibrium from a shift in the supply of EC$

Note that if the prices of Trinidad and Tobago oil and cement rise, the supply curve may shift to the left to S_2S_2.

Advantages of a floating or flexible exchange rate

> The balance of payments is kept in equilibrium and facilitates automatic adjustment, i.e., resolves deficits and surpluses of the balance of payments.
> There is no need to keep reserves to support the exchange rate or to finance deficits.
> Governments are free to manage the domestic economy, rather than developing economic policies for coping with the external sector.

Disadvantages of a floating or flexible exchange rate

> The uncertainty of exchange rate movements affect the confidence of traders.
> The volume of trade is likely to be negatively affected.
> Speculation is encouraged when rates are flexible, leading to unstable rates of exchange.
> Depreciating exchange rates can exert inflationary pressure in the short-term if import demand is price inelastic.
> Since the external price of domestically produced goods is subject to unpredictable changes, demand patterns may accordingly change.
> The output plans of firms are also affected by changes in demand as a result of changing external prices.
> For flexible rates to be effective, much depends on the price elasticity of demand.
> When the price of a currency rises, 'Dutch disease' may occur when exports become uncompetitive and lead to a balance of payments deficit.

The floating exchange rates and the balance of payments

In theory there is a relationship between a flexible exchange rate and the balance of payments.

For example, a flexible exchange rate will cause a balance of payments deficit or surplus to correct itself through the flexible exchange rate mechanism. If high levels of imports result in a balance of payments deficit, the increased spending required to purchase foreign exchange will cause the supplied currency to depreciate. With this depreciation, import prices effectively rise and become very expensive, while exports effectively become cheap. Further, if imports are elastic in demand, the level of imports is likely to decline. However, the level of exports will rise, causing a demand for the depreciated currency.

The net effect of these two factors will cause exports to rise and imports to decline, eliminating the deficit. Once again, this will happen if the demand for exports is elastic.

Flexible exchange rate and inflation

Changes in flexible exchange rates are cited as a cause of inflation. For example, if St Lucia purchases goods and services from Trinidad and Tobago when the EC dollar has depreciated, this means that imports into St Lucia are more costly after the depreciation. If imports demanded in St Lucia are inelastic, then higher prices will not seriously affect demand and St Lucians will pay more for imported Trinidad and Tobago goods, creating cost-push inflationary pressure.

Fixed exchange rate

A fixed exchange rate is in operation when the price of a currency is tied or pegged to another currency. This rate is fixed and maintained by the central bank of a country on behalf of the government, by intervention buying and selling of the currency at the fixed rate.

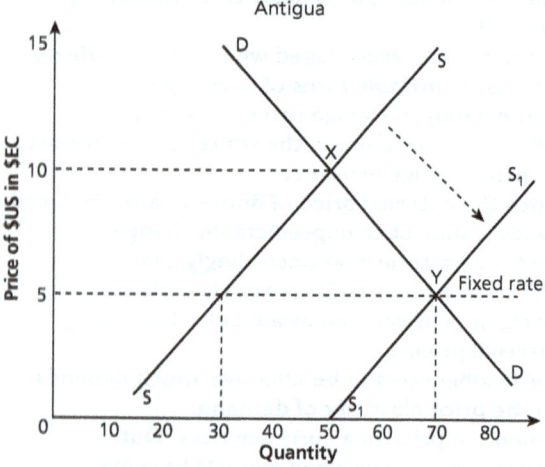

Figure 33.8 The fixed exchange rate

For example, in figure 33.8 Antigua decides to operate a fixed exchange rate and fixes the EC dollar rate to EC $5.00 = US$1.00. At that rate, there is an excess demand of US$40 m ($70 m − $30 m). Under a flexible rate the exchange rate would rise to EC$10.00 for US$1.00. But under a fixed exchange rate, the excess demand of $40 m is supplied by the central bank, the supply curve moves downward from S to S_1 and the fixed rated of EC$5.00 is maintained.

Under a fixed exchange rate the central bank sells from its reserves to meet this excess demand, which prevents the price from rising. This is called intervention selling of currency to support a fixed exchange rate.

Note that the central bank sells foreign currency to accommodate the excess demand. If there is an excess supply of foreign currency, the price of the currency will depreciate without government intervention. In such circumstances the central bank will enter the market and purchase the excess supply to 'preserve' the fixed rate of $5.00.

The advantages and disadvantages of a fixed rate of exchange

Table 33.2 Advantages and disadvantages of a fixed exchange rate

Advantages	Disadvantages
There is certainty with respect to conducting international business.	A fixed rate does not automatically correct a balance of payments deficit or surplus. This adjustment therefore has to be achieved through government fiscal policies.
A fixed rate imposes a discipline on the government to keep inflation under control.	Economists claim that there is long-run instability in the exchange rate when a government's objectives are not consistent with a fixed rate.
Speculation against rising or falling rates of exchange is removed.	Fixed exchange rates fail to prevent inflation from being transmitted to trading partners, as flexible rates do.

Although the summary in table 33.2 provides a brief summary of the advantages and disadvantages of a fixed rate of exchange, some points need further clarification, which are as follows.

Advantages

While uncertainty may be created by a flexible or freely floating rate of exchange, fixed rates of exchange reduce the risk of future changes in currency prices when fixed payments are made. Business confidence is therefore high under fixed rates of exchange.

Disadvantages

› Whereas a flexible exchange rate will automatically correct a balance of payments disequilibrium, all things being equal, this is not so under a fixed rate of exchange. A fall in demand for currency when there is a deficit on the current account should be reflected through a fall in the rate of exchange.
› There is likely to be long-run instability of the exchange rate if, for example, a government's objective is to increase the rate of exchange and to achieve full employment. The instability is caused by an increase in import spending, caused by rising incomes. In this case, the excess of import expenditure over export earnings will lead to a balance of payments deficit and an adjustment to the exchange rate to reflect this deficit. Exchange rates continue to change as a result.
› A country may import inflation from a trading partner if the exporting country operates a fixed exchange rate. For example, if Jamaica is

experiencing inflation of 15 per cent and the inflation rate in Barbados is 3 per cent, Barbados will purchase imported goods at high prices.

Fixed exchange rates: over- and undervalued currencies

A currency is overvalued when the central bank fixes the exchange rate above the rate that would exist according to the free market forces of demand and supply. A currency is undervalued when its price is fixed below that of the free market.

Overvalued currency

In many cases, overvaluation is a deliberate attempt to earn the currencies of trading partners with which to purchase critical imports. In figure 33.9 below, Barbados, for example, decides to overvalue its currency against the Trinidad and Tobago dollar.

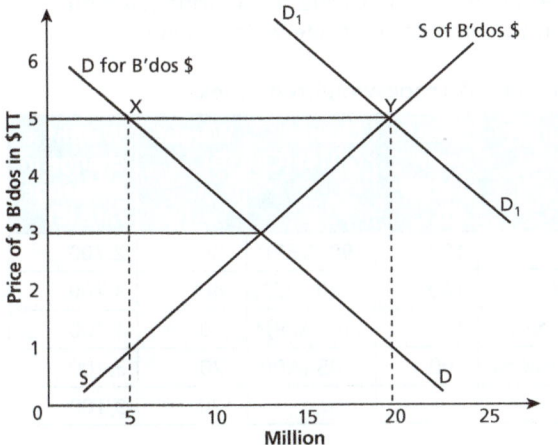

Figure 33.9 Overvaluation of currencies

Note that at first the price of Bds$1.00 = TT$3.00 is determined in a free market. Then the price is fixed at TT$5.00 for Bds$1.00. At this new price, the supply of Barbados dollars is greater than the demand by Bds$15 million ($20m − $5m). The central bank could then use its reserves of Barbados dollars to purchase this surplus $15 million, causing the demand curve for Barbados dollars to shift to the right to D_1D_1. Overvaluation makes a currency more expensive and will negatively affect exports earnings. On the other hand, imports become cheap. A currency may be overvalued to reduce a trade surplus.

Undervalued currency

A currency is undervalued when its price is fixed below that of the free market, in effect making the currency cheaper and creating a stimulus for exports. At the same time, imports will become more costly. If the Jamaican dollar is undervalued it would boost export revenue. Imports spending would decline because imports would become more expensive.

Apart from the effect on exports and imports, the terms of trade are also affected. Jamaica will have to export more goods and services in order to purchase a unit of food import from Barbados.

A balance of payments surplus on the current account is also a likely consequence of an undervalued currency, since export earnings will probably exceed import spending.

Managed or 'dirty' floating exchange rates

A managed exchange rate is a combination of fixed and flexible rates. The rate of exchange is allowed flexibility within a high and low rate. For example, if the Barbados exchange rate with Trinidad and Tobago is managed, then the rate of exchange will be allowed to rise or fall within a range, of say, a low TT$2.50 = Bds$1.00 to TT$3.50 = Bds$1 as illustrated in figure 33.10.

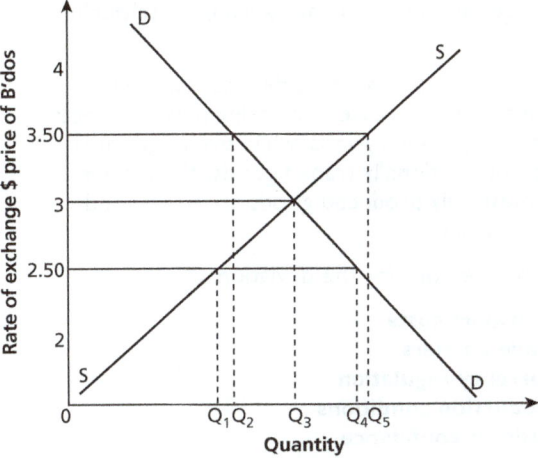

Figure 33.10 Managed exchange rates

However, if the rate is TT$3.50 = Bds$1 and there is a high demand for the Barbados dollar, which the banking system cannot accommodate, the price will move beyond TT$3.50 = Bds$1.00. When this happens the Central Bank of Trinidad and Tobago will intervene to sell Barbados dollars to commercial banks to satisfy this excess demand and prevent the rate from moving past the high rate of TT$3.50 = Bds$1.00.

Similarly, if the rate, for example, is TT$2.50 = Bds$1.00 and there is an excess supply of Barbados dollars, the exchange rate would fall below TT$2.50 = Bds$1.00, all things being equal. To prevent this from happening, the central bank will again intervene to purchase the excess supply of Barbados dollars, in order to maintain the low rate of TT$2.50 = Bds$1.00. Managed exchange rates combine the advantages of flexible and fixed rates of exchange. The advantages are:

- **Certainty and stability:** fixed rates of exchange
- **Automatic adjustment of the balance of payments and protection against inflation** that can happen under flexible rates of exchange.

To conclude, intervention to support a floating rate is designed to stabilise or influence the rate, according to monetary policy.

The purchasing power parity exchange rate theory

A purchasing power parity (PPP) exchange rate is one that is adjusted to reflect the purchasing power of a currency. For example, if EC$1.00 = TT$3.00 then, according to PPP, items that could be bought in Trinidad with $3.00 can also be bought in Antigua for EC$1.00 (EC$1.00 = TT$3.00). To further explain, if a can of orange juice costs $1.00, a pack of flour $1.50, and a bag of potatoes 50 cents in Trinidad, the total cost of this basket is $3.00.

If these three items cost $1.00 in Antigua, it would imply that the EC dollar is three times the value of the TT dollar and, therefore, this ratio should be reflected in its exchange rate. Note that this is not an actual exchange rate but what the exchange rate ought to be.

In reality, exchange rates deviate from PPP exchange rates because purchasing power reflects domestically traded goods, while exchange rates reflect internationally traded goods. Many types of domestically produced goods are not traded internationally.

Other reasons for the deviation are:

› Transport costs
› Trade barriers
› Currency regulation
› Production conditions
› Business confidence
› Speculation, interest rates, movements
› Non-price competitiveness.

Nominal and real exchange rates

A nominal exchange rate is the rate at which one currency exchanges for another in foreign currency markets. All exchange rates quoted in the newspapers or banks are therefore nominal rates.

Real exchange rates are adjusted for changes in the average prices of exports compared to average import prices, in domestic currency prices. In this sense, the exchange rate is adjusted for changes in terms of trade. The real exchange rate may be expressed as:

Real exchange rate – nominal exchange rate × Px/Pm,

Where:

Px is the domestic price of exports

Pm is the the foreign currency prices of imports.

Therefore, if export prices are rising faster than import prices, the real exchange rate will similarly rise relative to its nominal rate. In effect, when this happens an increased quantity of imports can be obtained for a given volume of exports. Real exchange rates are a better gauge of a country's competitiveness. The lower the real exchange rate, the more competitive will be the country's exports.

The effective exchange rate

The effective exchange rate is also called the trade-weighted index. As a country's currency may be expressed in different currencies at different rates, an effective rate measures the external value of the currency against a basket of other currencies in which it trades.

The effective exchange rate is, however, a weighted average that shows the importance of each country's trading activities. For example, if Jamaica conducts 50 per cent of its trade with Trinidad and Tobago, the weight is given a value of 50 or 0.5.

Assume that Guyana has four trading partners: Jamaica, Barbados, the UK and the USA. The assumed figures in table 33.3 provide the information with which to compute the trade-weighted index.

Table 33.3 A trade-weighted index

Country (A)	Base year (2007) (B)	Change (2014) (C)	Weight (D)	Weight × change in exchange rate (E)
UK	100	90 (DEP)*	30	2,700
USA	100	80 (DEP)	40	3,200
Jamaica	100	110 (APP)*	10	1,100
Barbados	100	105 (APP)	20	2,100
			100	9,100

(F) 9100/100 = 91.00

Notes to table 33.3

› *DEP: depreciation
› *APP: appreciation
  • Column A: these are selected trading partners.
  • Column B: changes in the exchange rate are measured from the year 2007, which is the base year.
  • Column C: this is the year 2014 and it shows what has happened to the change in value of the Guyanese dollar with respect to each trading partner.

For example, the Guyanese dollar depreciated by 10 per cent against the UK pound but appreciated against the Jamaican dollar by 10 per cent. The trade-weighted index is then computed as follows.

Step 1 Multiply column C by D, e.g., 90 × 30 = 2,700

Step 2 Place the value in column E

Step 3 Add up column E (9,100)

Step 4 Divide this total by sum of the weights (100) Therefore 9,100/100 = 91.00

This tells us that the Guyanese dollar declined (depreciated) in value by 9 per cent against the currencies of its four trading partners, measured from the year 2007 (the base year).

Key point
A trade-weighted indexed rate of exchange, or the effective exchange rate, gives the value of a country's currency with respect to a basket of currencies in which it trades.

Chapter summary

> - The exchange rate is the price at which one country's currency is exchanged for another.
> - Exchange rates facilitate international trade.
> - The exchange rate may be determined by: the free forces of demand and supply; fixed rates (by the government); or a combination of fixed and flexible rates, called a managed float.
> - The demand for a foreign currency is derived from the demand for imports.
> - Fixed exchange rates are noted for their ability to discourage speculation and increase confidence and currency stability, but a government needs reserves to support a fixed rate.
> - Governments' economic policies may be manipulated by their external position under fixed rates.
> - Flexible rates serve to bring the balance of payments and exchange rates into equilibrium through market forces.
> - Purchasing power parity is the oldest theory of exchange rates. It proposes that an exchange rate should reflect domestic purchasing power. If an exchange rate is EC$1.00 = TT$3.00 then, at this rate, the same quantity of goods can be bought in either country.
> - Nominal exchange rates are those quoted in the newspapers and by commercial banks.
> - Real exchange rates are adjusted for changes in the prices of exports compared to import prices, in domestic currency (in essence, the terms of trade).
> - The effective exchange rate is called the trade-weighted exchange rate and places a value of one currency against a basket of currencies of countries with which trade is carried out.

Practice questions

1. Explain how the exchange rate is determined in a fixed exchange rate system.
2. State three advantages and three disadvantages of a fixed exchange rate system.
3. Explain how the exchange rate is determined in a free-floating exchange rate system.
4. State three advantages and three disadvantages of a free-floating exchange rate system.

INTRODUCTORY ECONOMICS A TEXTBOOK FOR CAPE ECONOMICS STUDENTS

34 Balance of payments

Chapter 34 Balance of payments

LEARNING OBJECTIVES

- Explain the balance of payments.
- Describe balance of payments accounts.
- Explain the current account.
- Explain the capital account (net transactions in external assets and liabilities).
- Explain the calculation of the balance of payments.
- Explain balance of payments surplus and deficit.
- Analyse causes and consequences of balance of payments deficits and surpluses.
- Identify measures designed to cure a deficit or reduce a surplus.

REQUIRED KNOWLEDGE

- International trade
- Inflation
- Interest rates, elasticity of demand
- Productivity
- Fiscal monetary policy and exchange rates.

TOPIC VALUE

Most Caribbean economies suffer from the burden of foreign debt as a result of persistent balance of payment deficits. An overreliance on imported goods and services is the reason for this chronic problem.

Introduction

International trade consists of the sale of exports and the purchase of imports. This usually involves a vast number of transactions and flows of money between countries, so there is a need to keep an overall record of what has taken place.

It is for this purpose that all countries keep a balance of payments; this is a record of the financial inflows or outflows that take place between a country and the rest of the world, usually over a one-year period.

Financial flows are not only associated with the purchase and sale of goods and services, but also banking, investment, or any transfer of finance such as receiving or sending money gifts between residents of one country and another. These financial inflows are recorded in the same manner that one would record the financial inflows of a firm. Any financial inflow is entered as a credit or plus sign, while any outflow is entered as debit or negative sign.

The account is recorded in double entry format.

If total inflows for the year exceed outflows, the balance of payments is in surplus. Alternatively, if outflows exceed inflows the balance of payments is in deficit.

The different sections of the balance of payments will be discussed in detail in this chapter to further your understanding of what is recorded and the reason for recording it. The main categories of the balance of payments are outlined below. It is made up of four simple sections, as shown in figure 34.1, namely:

1. **Current account (A)**
2. **Capital account (B)**
3. **Financial accounts (C)**
4. **Balancing item (D).**

To summarise the balance of payments, simply add A + B + C + D = O. Each section will now be examined, followed by an explanation of how it would sum to zero.

Key point

To determine whether to enter a plus or minus sign in the balance of payments, remember this rule: an inflow of money is entered with a plus sign and a financial outflow is indicated with a negative sign.

The current account

The four simple sections in the current account (A) are shown in figure 34.1.

The merchandise account

The merchandise or visible balance consists of:

› **Visible exports + 100 m**
› **Visible imports – 120 m**
› **Visible balance = – 20**

The merchandise account shows exports and imports of physical goods and services. For example, exports may include bananas sent from St Lucia to Barbados, while imports may include sugar sent from Barbados to St Lucia. Note that exports carry a positive sign indicating an inflow of money, hence a receipt, while imports carry a negative sign indicating an outflow of money, or a payment. The merchandise balance is also called the balance of trade. The balance may be positive or negative, depending on whether export receipts are lesser or greater than import payments.

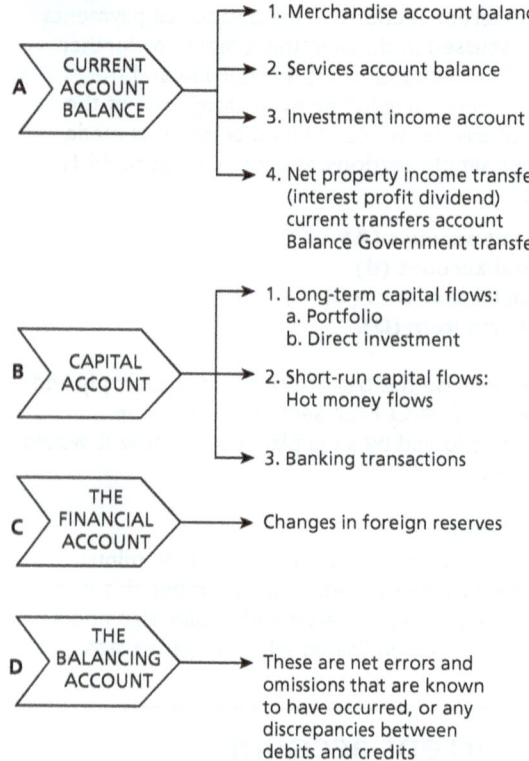

Figure 34.1 The balance of payments account

Key point
Note that investment income (interest, profits, and dividends) are recorded in the current account while the instruments that generate these incomes (capital flows, direct investment) are recorded in the capital account.

The current transfers balance
A transfer is a payment or receipt made without any equivalent exchange of goods or services; for example, money gifts, also called remittances, received by residents in the Caribbean from relatives living overseas.

Included in this category is government expenditure on embassies abroad, which is called government transfers. Subscriptions paid to the Caribbean Development Bank are also transfers. Aid received from foreign countries is also included in this account.

Current account balance
When the above four sections are added together, the current account balance is then determined. Except for the balance of trade or merchandise account, all other transactions in this group are called invisible trade.

Note, however, that expenditures recorded in the current account are referred to as autonomous expenditures because they represent independent decisions to spend by firms and individuals.

The capital account

Many countries have replaced the capital account with another all-inclusive account called the transactions in assets and liabilities account, because transactions recorded in this account result in a change of ownership of assets and liabilities between firms, individuals and organisations of one country and the rest of the world. These transactions also trace capital movements between countries, which may be short- or long-term in nature.

An outward capital flow from Guyana takes place when, for example, a Guyanese firm or resident purchases an asset in Barbados. If a Barbadian firm purchases a factory in Guyana, this would be an inward capital flow in favour of Guyana. These two transactions are an example of how assets and liabilities change ownership between Guyana's nationals and nationals living in other Caribbean territories. Since an asset is a productive resource, it may assume different forms. For this reason, we will distinguish between long-term and short-term capital flows.

Long-term flows
Long-term private investment may be placed in two categories:

1. Fixed or direct capital
2. Portfolio capital.

Services account
Services such as banking, tourism, insurance, transport, accounting and financial services are recorded in this account, e.g.

Exports + 150 m

Imports − 75 m

Invisible balance = +75

For example, when a Jamaican attends test match cricket in Kensington Oval, Barbados, this is an inflow or export in Barbados's favour. A Barbadian flying on Caribbean Airlines will earn revenue for Trinidad and Tobago, hence it is an export for Trinidad and Tobago but an import for Barbados. In the services account of Barbados, this will be a negative entry. This account may be in deficit or surplus.

Investment income account
The third section of the current account is the investment income account. Here, the income represents interest, profits, rents and dividend income, all of which are also called property income. Note that to earn dividend income or profit, one must first own shares of a company or own an interest-bearing asset. The purchase or sale of these investments are, however, recorded in the capital account.

Much of foreign direct investment in the Caribbean involves profits returning to main offices abroad. RBC Bank in St Lucia would remit their profits to their head office in Port of Spain, Trinidad and Tobago. Since there is much foreign direct investment in the Caribbean, profits returned abroad are significant.

Fixed or direct capital

Fixed capital involves the creation of physical assets such as factories, firms, mines or company buyouts. For example, if Trinidad Cement Ltd purchases the Arawak plant in Barbados, this is an example of a private long-term capital outward flow from Trinidad. By the same token, if Grace Kennedy of Jamaica purchases a company in Trinidad and Tobago, this would represent an inward long-term capital flow in Trinidad and Tobago's favour. Note that profits earned by such a firm and returned to Jamaica represent a negative sign in Trinidad and Tobago's current account, although the original sale is recorded in the capital account or the net transactions in assets and liabilities account.

Portfolio capital

Portfolio investment takes place when residents (firms, individuals, public corporations) purchase stocks, shares or foreign government securities. This type of capital expenditure therefore does not create physical assets. With globalisation firmly entrenched, this type of capital expenditure is expected to rise significantly. Long-term flows are very predictable and stable, since they tend to coincide with shifts in comparative advantages.

Short-term capital flows

Short-term capital flows arise through bank transactions. A typical example is St Lucia's RBC Bank lending to overseas firms or individuals or local residents. In particular, there are transactions that take place involving very liquid assets or hard currencies, which seek out profitable differences in interest and exchange rates of other countries. These are called 'hot money' flows.

Banks, companies and wealthy private investors move these funds, speculating in the expectation that interest and exchange rates may rise, earning them a sizeable profit or avoiding an anticipated loss. These 'hot money' flows are highly unpredictable and can destabilise the exchange rate of a small open economy.

Official capital flows

These flows refer to long-term lending and borrowing by the government itself. For example, if the government borrows from a foreign bank, such as, First Boston Credit Suisse of the USA, to finance a public works project, this will result initially in an inflow. The government may also make loan repayments, which is an outflow.

Official flows

Prior to 1998 the official financing segment of the balance of payments recorded the changes in the official reserves related to payments and receipts of an autonomous nature. For example, autonomous outflows may comprise visible and invisible imports from the current account and outflows of long-term capital in the capital account. If these outflows exceed exports and long-term capital inflows, then the deficit so created must be matched by corresponding financing of such expenditure.

For this reason, changes in foreign currency reserves are called accommodating transactions, since they finance autonomous transactions in the current and capital account. If the current account is summed with the capital account and outflows exceed inflows, the resulting balance of payments deficit will be 'accommodated' by changes in the official reserves. The reverse will take place if there is a balance of payments surplus, that is, inflows exceed outflows. Very importantly, changes in the official reserves denote whether there is, in fact, a balance of payments deficit or surplus. Included in official capital flows is debt forgiveness.

The balancing item

The balancing item is a figure that makes all debit items equal to credit items. Due to errors, non-recording or omissions, figures vary. For this purpose, the balancing item is given as the difference that represents transactions that have taken place, but for which there is no record.

The link between the current and capital account

The clearest link between these two major accounts is that investment in foreign countries, in any kind of asset, appears as a debit entry (−) in the capital account but as a credit entry (+) in the current account in the country of the investor when interest, profits or dividends are eventually paid. Similarly, investment by foreign residents is an inflow into the domestic economy and is a credit entry in the capital account. When profit or dividends are realised, they will be an outflow recorded as a debit in the current account. In other words, an autonomous debit in the current account will result in an autonomous credit in the capital account, hence a very direct relationship exists.

Expenditure recorded in the current account, particularly in the merchandise and services account, has a matching banking transaction in the capital account.

The overall balance of payments

After examining the different components of the balance of payments the question that needs to be addressed is, what is the ideal balance of payments for a country?

An overall surplus in the balance of payments may be interpreted positively or negatively. For example, if there is a current account surplus in the balance of payments, from a positive perspective this may mean:

› **Export competitiveness**
› **Economic strength externally in terms of trade and self-sufficiency**
› **Sufficient reserves to finance future imports, also called import cover**
› **Reserves to service external debt**

- A fairly strong and stable currency
- An injection into the economy with the potential to promote export-led growth.

On the negative side, a current account surplus may mean:

- An increase in the money supply with the potential to cause demand inflation if the economy is at full employment.
- A fall in the standard of living on the basis that a surplus infers reduced access to foreign goods and services and greater diversity and choice in consumption and trade. Explained another way, a surplus on the current account simply means an opportunity cost of using domestic resources.
- A current account surplus may mean a deficit with another trading partner, who may try to resolve the deficit with protectionist measures. The case of the USA, Japan and China in the recent past is a case in point, where the USA had a trade deficit in the region of billions of dollars.
- A surplus may also lead to a strong currency which may mean a rise in the cost of trade, also called 'Dutch disease'. This may impact negatively on future trade.

Measures to resolve a current account surplus

Having identified the positive and negative effects of a balance of payments surplus on the current account, it should be noted that a small surplus does not cause any negative consequences for a country.

Measures to reduce a current account surplus include:

- Removal of import restrictions to increase the demand for imports.
- A reflationary fiscal and monetary policy, which will cause an expansion in the economy and hence stimulate demand for imports. Since import demand is income elastic, with imports spending increasing at a faster rate than export revenue, a surplus is likely to be reduced in the short- to medium-term.
- Reducing the rate of interest and decreasing direct taxes to encourage import spending.
- Revaluation of the currency: this is another option that a government may adopt, since in this instance the currency's price can be set higher. This can lead to a dampening of demand for exports that are elastic in demand. A revaluation is also likely to cause a surplus to become larger in the short-term before subsequently becoming smaller.

Summary

A satisfactory balance may be an overall equality of autonomous credits and debits in the long-term without the need for policy measures that would affect the main objectives of the government. Some governments are prepared, for example, to allow a short-term deficit on the current account, such as the purchase of raw materials, which will create output for export in the future.

A current account deficit

A current account deficit is caused when financial outflows of this account exceed financial inflows.

Factors contributing to a current account deficit are:

- Lack of comparative advantage in goods and services
- High rates of domestic inflation, which make exports uncompetitive in the export markets
- High level of expenditure on imported goods and services when an economy enjoys boom conditions, or when interest rates are low
- Significant outflows of profit from multinational companies, along with dividend and interest income associated with foreign direct investment
- Low rates of domestic productivity due to outdated methods of production, poorly trained labour and outdated technology
- The inability to achieve low costs from scale economies due to limited market size
- A high exchange rate, at which imported goods are purchased that are inelastic in demand
- An expansionary monetary and fiscal policy that generates increases in domestic income and high import expenditure
- A lack of resources with which to manufacture exported goods, e.g., arable land, skilled labour and modern technology.

Reducing a current account deficit therefore is the long-term objective of Caribbean economies in pursuit of sustainable development.

Measures to resolve a persistent deficit in the current account of the balance of payments

Prescribing measures to resolve a balance of payments deficit on the current account will depend on:

- Size of the deficit: whether it is large or small
- Root causes of the deficit
- Exchange-rate mechanism in operation.

A small short-term deficit is no cause for concern if there are sufficient reserves to finance it. If the cause of the deficit is that exports are uncompetitive, then the government must seek to implement strategies designed to reverse this weakness.

The exchange rate mechanism is a significant factor with respect to the balance of payments, because a fixed exchange rate is similar in most cases to a price ceiling and market forces do not directly impact on fixed exchange rates. If a flexible rate of exchange is in force, a deficit on the balance of payments would imply a falling exchange rate, which would have the effect of improving export revenue.

Import spending would fall, eliminating the deficit or the need to use reserves to finance the deficit. Nevertheless, measures to reduce a deficit on the current account of the balance of payments will first require an expenditure-reducing strategy designed to reduce not only demand for imports, but also the other components of aggregate demand, that is, consumption, investment and government spending. When this happens and aggregate demand falls, aggregate supply will correspondingly fall and create spare capacity.

This spare capacity is what is needed when the government employs expenditure-switching strategies designed to shift spending away from imports to domestic substitutes. For example, a tariff may raise the price of an import and if price elasticity of demand for imports is elastic then import spending is likely to fall, creating opportunities for local substitutes. The demand for domestically produced goods and services increases as a result.

Expenditure reduction and import substitution are seen to be collaborative, rather than separate strategies. Note that a deflationary fiscal and monetary policy would also reduce the rate of inflation.

Summary

Identifying specific measures to reduce or resolve a persistent deficit may be summarised as:

> **Immediate measures to instantly reduce import demand, e.g., foreign exchange control or conservation. Foreign exchange may be rationed in favour of inputs to industry such as raw materials, or imports necessary to preserve life, e.g., medicines. This may be regarded as an expenditure-reducing method with some expenditure-switching effects.**
> **Short- to medium-term measures, deflationary in nature. Contractionary fiscal policy such as cuts in government spending and an increase in direct taxes, e.g., income tax, may be implemented. If used with an increase in interest rates, this will reduce national expenditure as a whole with the expected time lags.**

Short- to medium-term measures acting with reduced expenditure in the economy create spare capacity and pave the way for the government to institute expenditure-switching measures. Some examples of these expenditure-switching measures are tariffs, quotas, embargoes and other import restrictions, which serve to raise prices to domestic consumers. Consumers are likely to 'switch' away from imports if demand for these goods and services is elastic. There must be low-priced local substitutes as an alternative to imports, however.

Only if these substitutes are available will this switching policy succeed. Demand for imports must also be elastic.

Short- to medium-term measure: devaluation of the currency

Another short- to medium-term measure is a devaluation of the currency by the monetary authorities. This implies, for example, that if the US dollar exchanges for TT$6.30, a devaluation will cause the rate to be perhaps TT$10.00 to US$1.00, effectively reducing the price of a US dollar in terms of a TT dollar. For example, if US$1.00 = TT$10.00 then the price of a TT dollar is US$0.10. If, however, TT$6.30 is required to buy US$1.00, the TT dollar is approximately US$ 0.16.

A devaluation of the currency is an option some countries have adopted in recent times when faced with a persistent long-term deficit on the current account. However, a devaluation will only succeed after an initial deterioration of the balance of payments, as explained in figure 34.2.

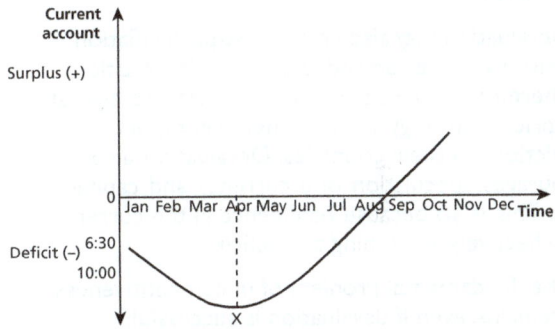

Figure 34.2 The 'J' curve effect

The 'J' curve in figure 34.2 seeks to illustrate how a devaluation may cause an initial deterioration of the current account before a recovery is achieved.

Note a devaluation in the month of January causes the balance of payments deficit to become worse, before recovering to go gradually into surplus in September. The balance of payments becomes worse because:

> **Imports become more expensive, so there is a greater outflow of foreign exchange for import orders already negotiated.**
> **Exports become cheaper, so the same volume of exports is now earning less foreign exchange (exports are cheaper because the TT dollar previously US$0.16 is now US$0.10).**

New orders for imports are likely to fall in April due to the rise in price, so a reduced volume of imports and hence reduced outflow of foreign exchange takes place. There will probably be a greater volume of exports and export revenue inflow because TT dollars, required to purchase exports, are now valued at US$0.10. The combined effect of increased exports and reduced imports is the reason for the improvement in the current account. An important condition for this recovery is that the sum of elasticities for exports and imports must be greater than unity. This is known as the Marshall–Lerner principle. For an example, refer to table 34.1.

Table 34.1 **The Marshall–Lerner principle**

Jamaica		Antigua	
Price elasticity of demand for		Price elasticity of demand for	
Exports	Imports	Exports	Imports
0.5	0.8	0.5	0.4

Table 34.1 shows the price elasticities for exports and imports for Jamaica and Antigua. Note that in Jamaica's case the sum of the elasticities is 1.3 and therefore elastic, indicating that a devaluation is likely to succeed in bringing the balance of payments into surplus. Antigua, however, has a combined elasticity of 0.9, an unfavourable condition for a devaluation to have the desired effect. In practice, a devaluation will only succeed for a short period, provided that spare capacity is available and supply is elastic in the short-term.

Devaluation may also create cost-push inflation, and more so if the demand for imports is inelastic. Furthermore, trading partners may retaliate against this pricing strategy by implementing import restrictions in their countries. Devaluation also encourages speculation of a currency and capital flight. This is so because confidence in the currency falls, effectively worsening the deficit.

The fundamental problem of uncompetitiveness still remains, even if devaluation is successful. Devaluation is an expenditure-switching measure.

Long-term measures

Long-term measures are employed at the same time as short- to medium-term measures, except that the achievement lag is longer. Examples of long-term measures are:

> Increased tourism drive in Caribbean economies, or countries dependent on tourism for foreign earnings. This would depend on the initiatives of a country's tourism authorities.
> Export subsidies designed to reduce the cost of exports, so making them more competitive.
> Subsidies for products that are intended as substitutes for foreign products, e.g., local orange juice.
> 'Buy local' campaigns designed to promote local products and promote awareness of supporting the local economy and jobs.
> Government-sponsored trade missions, to develop external markets.
> Government-promoted trade expositions that promote a country's products to foreign buyers.
> Development of export-processing zones exclusive to exporters, in effect making infrastructure available at reduced cost.
> Measures designed to improve the productivity of domestic factors of production.

Note that these measures are supply-side measures.

Included in these supply-side measures are tax concessions on replacing worn out capital and purchase of new technology, for example information technology. High interest rates, however, while a disincentive to import expenditure, may also encourage 'hot money' inflows into the capital account. Notwithstanding this fact, high interest rates are likely also to be inflationary since the cost of transacting business would increase.

Chapter summary

> The balance of payments is an accounting record of the international monetary flows between trading partners.
> The current account is one part of the balance of payments and is considered to be the object of governments' attention.
> The balance of payments sums to zero in the accounting sense.
> Both a large persistent surplus and deficit may have negative consequences for a country, particularly a Caribbean territory.
> Expenditure-reducing and switching-measures are included in short-, medium- and long- term remedies designed to cure a persistent balance of payments deficit.
> Revaluation, free trade and expansionary policy are the main remedies for a current account surplus.
> Extensive borrowing becomes necessary to finance an external deficit, particularly if it is growing.
> Borrowing from the International Monetary Fund may lead to harsh repayment conditions.
> An outflow of money decreases the money supply and is a leakage that may cause a small economy to contract, with negative effects on growth, development and employment.
> The objective of most governments is generally to achieve a balance of payments that can support six months of import cover. It must also be sustainable in the long-term without having to resort to measures that will negatively impact on the economy.

Practice questions

1. What is a balance of payments statement?
   a. Explain the difference between a current account transaction and a capital account transaction.
   b. Explain how foreign direct investment (FDI) is classified in the balance of payments.

2. Which of the following transactions will appear in the capital account of the Trinidad and Tobago's balance of payments?
   a. Purchase by a Grenadian investor of an oil refinery in Trinidad and Tobago
   b. Purchase of petroleum products from Trinidad and Tobago by foreigners
   c. Purchase of cement by a Trinidadian importer from a foreign country
   d. Money spent by foreign tourists in Trinidad and Tobago.

3. If a country has a deficit in its balance of payments, then, all else being equal, its money supply is likely to:
   a. Increase because the foreign currency received from exports will be exchanged for domestic currency
   b. Remain unchanged, because its imports were obtained at world prices
   c. Fall because the domestic currency will depreciate
   d. Remain unchanged, because its exports are bought with domestic currency.

4. Which of the following policies can be used to eliminate a current account surplus?
   a. Devaluation of the currency
   b. Introduction of deflationary fiscal policy
   c. Imposition of import controls
   d. Revaluation of the currency.

35 Foreign direct investment

Chapter 35 Foreign direct investment

LEARNING OBJECTIVES

- Explain multinational/transnational corporations.
- Explain foreign direct investment: benefits and cost.
- Explain foreign direct investment in the Caribbean: a historical and present dilemma.

REQUIRED KNOWLEDGE

- Investment
- Multinational corporations
- Economic development
- Net property income
- Comparative advantage.

TOPIC VALUE

For centuries, Caribbean states have played a pivotal role in enlarging the wealth of those countries in the North that visited Caribbean shores in search of wealth. Foreign direct investment (FDI) gave rise to the birth of the Caribbean states. It would also be accurate to point out that a boost to FDI was provided by the liberalisation of many socialist economies and the fall of the Berlin Wall. This initial energy is currently strengthening the globalisation process and is directly linked to FDI.

Introduction

FDI may be defined as the purchase, ownership and control of the assets of a country by a foreign, multinational company (MNC), or the establishment of a new enterprise by multinational corporations, which are long-term in nature.

The topic of FDI is linked to net property income, which was analysed in the discussion about measuring gross domestic product. FDI was also referred to in the analysis of the balance of payments, particularly the investment income flows in the current account.

In the short space of 5 years, FDI in China increased from US$3.5 billion to US$53.5 billion. In the Caribbean, FDI has been present for many years in alumina (Guyana and Jamaica), oil and natural gas (Trinidad and Tobago), and at the Point Lisas Industrial Estate (Trinidad and Tobago), where methanol, fertiliser, ethanol, and steel billets are manufactured.

Common error

Be careful not to confuse FDI with foreign portfolio investment, which is the purchase of company shares. Strictly speaking, this only becomes investment when the money from the sale of equity is used to set up a factory, plant or manufacturing enterprise.

Rationale for FDI: historical context

Sir Arthur Lewis, the eminent Caribbean economist and Nobel laureate, is credited with the FDI initiative as a strategy for the region's industrialisation. He advocated funding Caribbean industrialisation via FDI, and pointed out that Caribbean states had surplus labour, but low rates of savings, foreign exchange, technological capability, and managerial expertise, and, most crucially, limited access to foreign markets. These he saw as growth gaps and, therefore, envisioned the active invitation to multinational corporations to base themselves in the Caribbean as the solution to all of these problems. Hence, the popular phrase 'industrialisation by invitation' is attributed to him.

Point Lisas Industrial Estate in Trinidad and Tobago became the flagship of industrialisation, utilising the revenue from the petro-boom and FDI in the late 1970s.

As a consequence, Trinidad and Tobago is perhaps the most industrialised of the Caribbean states because of the large presence of multinational corporations in the energy sector. The fact that there are other multinational corporations in the Caribbean suggests that FDI is still regarded as a strategy of industrialisation and development.

Some Caribbean states find it difficult to reject FDI, having become dependent on this developmental model. In Trinidad and Tobago there is some effort to assert control over FDI by purchasing controlling interest in some of these enterprises. Other CARICOM states are hoping that the presence of multinational corporations can open a pathway to foreign markets, in order to benefit from globalised trade.

Benefits of FDI for small, open economies

Multinational corporations are a worldwide phenomenon and China has grown at an unprecedented rate, largely due to the presence of multinational corporations that manufacture high-end-value products. There are many arguments for and against FDI, with particular reference to small open economies.

Arguments in favour of FDI advanced by economists closely resemble those advanced by the Caribbean economist Sir Arthur Lewis.

Sir Arthur Lewis identified several growth deficiencies, or gaps, in the economic growth strategies of small Caribbean states. He advanced the theory that these gaps can industrialise a country and serve to provide the stimulus for growth and development.

Gaps in the economic growth strategies are set out below.

Savings and investment gap

The rate of savings in most CARICOM states is below that which normally sustains investment. It is a well-known fact that the rate of savings in a country affects the rate of investment or capital formation in most cases.

If you recall the accelerator theory and note the connection between the rate of growth of capital and the change in national income or output, you will appreciate the need for an increased rate of savings to finance the growth of capital formation. An increase in the rate of savings, however, also implies a fall in consumption, which is a key variable in aggregate demand. Such a fall in consumption may affect business optimism, slow down economic growth and contribute to a reverse accelerator effect. It is argued that too much saving may cause a paradox of thrift, where an increase in savings in one period causes national income to fall and savings to subsequently fall thereafter.

It is in this context that multinational corporations play a vital role, since small economies are not required to risk an increased rate of savings and investment when it can be provided by an external source. From this point of view, multinational corporations are regarded as an agent of growth.

Human capital gap

Although literacy levels in many small economies have improved in recent years, they still lag behind those of developed economies in the North. The transfer of skills to the local labour force is therefore seen as a noteworthy objective. This development of human capital would otherwise have taken a longer period of time to achieve. The long-term value of such transfer of skills, as with management skills in general, lies in the circulation of such skills from one firm to another. The extended benefits of this skill multiplier is also a source of external economies of scale.

Foreign exchange gap

Most small economies are faced from time to time with foreign exchange gaps created mainly by deficits stemming from lack of competitiveness and comparative advantage, plus low rates of productivity and high rates of inflation. Foreign investment flows therefore provide for this shortfall. Another perspective is that capital equipment may be brought into the country by FDI. This represents a saving in foreign exchange.

The enterprise gap

Enterprise is the lifeblood of any economy. Since many small economies in the Caribbean are tourism-based, the level of enterprise is concentrated in micro enterprises such as personal services and peasant farming.

Even in the larger economies like Trinidad and Tobago, Jamaica and Barbados, attitudes towards entrepreneurship, as elsewhere, is risk avoidance. Incentives to small businesses abound in these economies, yet their potential for employment opportunities cannot compare with medium to large companies.

The management gap

Developed countries in the North have evolved over a long period of time, dating back to many centuries ago. As a result, modern techniques of management and best practices have been the benefits of this long process.

The specialised expertise that such experience can bring to a small economy, and the transfer potential it offers, cannot be underestimated. Since multinational corporations have worldwide networks, management of large-scale enterprises is their strength. The transfer of these skills may assist a small economy to bridge the management gap.

The employment gap

It is argued that multinational corporations provide a boost to local employment. In the construction phase of any FDI project, many skilled workers are employed. The more sustainable form of employment, however, comes from the support services linked to the foreign multinational corporations. These are power, communication, transport, banking, shipping and packaging, all of which provide external scale economies for the multinational corporations.

Such an arrangement, therefore, is mutually beneficial. Multinational corporations are valued for their long-term employment potential. This fact is mainly responsible for the negotiating advantage they hold with a host country, since unemployment is a major concern of small open economies.

If such foreign exchange earnings are invested in growth industries with export potential, then the multinational corporations can be viewed as an engine of diversification for small economies.

The tax revenue gap

In many instances when host governments attempt to achieve infrastructural improvement, they borrow extensively to finance such development and increase the national debt. Tax revenue paid to governments by multinational corporations greatly reduces the debt burden of such governments.

Another perspective is that governments should increase the rate of taxes to raise revenue for the management of the economy. However, when taxes are received through multinational corporations, the need to raise taxes is reduced, which safeguards the negative effects of taxation. It is also a fact that multinational corporations negotiate tax holidays to avoid paying taxes immediately.

The technology gap

Technological transfer is one of the significant contributions made by multinational corporations to the development of small economies. Their use of modern equipment, tools and processes can boost productivity and brings small economies like those in the Caribbean into contact with cutting-edge technology.

Examples of the application of advanced technology are: using sea water to supply a population with potable water, employing a reverse osmosis process; solar panels in St Lucia; the use of robotics in auto assembly plants in Trinidad and Tobago; and computer aided design (CAD).

Networking and external market gap

Since multinational corporations operate beyond their national boundaries, and may have secure markets and financial networks overseas, their valuable networks are made available to local manufacturers. These markets and networks help to open doors and business opportunities for local entrepreneurs. Increased market size provides welcome opportunities to exploit scale economies and gives a competitive edge in export performance.

Disadvantages of FDI

While the developmental benefits of FDI to small economies cannot be disputed, economic commentators have raised a number of arguments against multinational corporations. These are as follows.

Property income gone abroad

Property income gone abroad includes interest, profit and dividends, which are remitted to head offices of the home country. This is valuable revenue that is lost to a host country and may be measured in terms of a drain in financial capital. Such financial capital is usually injected into the money and capital markets, with significant investment potential. Property income gone abroad is therefore a lost opportunity for development to the host country.

Preferential tax holidays

Multinational corporations hold a negotiating edge with governments of small economies. In the Caribbean this is most pronounced, particularly in the case of Trinidad and Tobago where tax holidays have in some instances been granted for a duration of 8 to 10 years.

Part of the reason for such generous terms stems from the fact that governments of small economies set out by competing with one another to attract FDI. It is this attempt to attract the favour of large multinational corporations that leads to such tax concessions.

High importation of capital and other inputs

Many multinational corporations import their capital equipment and raw material to manage their operations. The effect of this is that it excludes domestic suppliers.

Negative externalities

The case of an industrial accident by a Canadian firm operating in Guyana, and Amoco oil spills in Trinidad and Tobago, serve to highlight the pollution problems associated with multinational corporations. The proposed Alcoa and Alutrin aluminium smelter plants and Essar Corporation in steel in Trinidad and Tobago have caused environmentalists to express serious reservations about the threat to human life, with the siting of the plants near to rural communities.

Political manipulation

Multinational corporations are regarded as being very influential in governments' major decisions. In particular, their lobbying powers are considerable when they seek to gain an advantage for themselves. In some cases, as with the smelter plants, isolated communities and valuable mangrove resources are sacrificed.

Exploitation of non-renewable resources

It is perhaps due to protectionist barriers and transport costs that multinational corporations have opted to build plants in foreign countries near to their raw materials, markets and sources of energy. The building of such plants is, however, only part of the value chain of the products concerned.

Oil, alumina, methanol and ammonia are all transferred to processing plants located in the home country of the multinational corporations, where the full value of the investment is added. When, however, the full value has been added it is resold to residents in the host country who 'repurchase' their natural resources in the form of a finished product. These resources are non-renewable. The counter argument to this is that non-exploitation of natural resources incurs an opportunity cost to the host country.

Demonstration effect of high wages

Since multinational corporations tend to offer higher wages than the domestic average, the resulting wage pressures cause local industries to pay higher wages, which may lead to falling profit levels.

It is frequently argued that incomes rise due to this demonstration effect.

Economic dualism

Economic dualism points to two levels of income created over time by multinational corporations. Wages are high in a technology enriched industry, while those in peasant agriculture, for example, are low. The movement of labour from low-wage industries to high-wage industries is very much like that which took place during the Industrial Revolution in England in the 1800s.

Suppression of domestic entrepreneurship

Many multinational corporations command vast international networks in insurance, banking, communications, mining and hotels, to the extent that the value of such resources vastly outweigh those of the host country.

In negotiating preferential advantages for their operations, multinational corporations acquire monopoly power in addition to their superior management, technological, financial and network advantages. In the final analysis, their commercial might enables them to increase market share at the expense of small domestic producers, in effect crowding out domestic businesses.

Chapter summary

> FDI may be defined as the purchase, ownership and control of the assets of a country by a foreign, MNC, or the establishment of a new enterprise by multinational corporations, which are long-term in nature.
> The gaps in savings, investment, human capital, enterprise, management, employment, tax revenue and technology in the host country are the reasons advanced for FDI.
> Factors influencing FDI are favourable demand conditions, exchange rates, tax concessions, low transport costs and government policy.
> The main disadvantages of FDI are repatriation of profits, negative externalities, political manipulation and exploitation of non-renewable resources.

Practice questions

1. Explain how foreign direct investment is classified in the balance of payments.
2. Using the experience of any Caribbean country, discuss three negative aspects of foreign direct investment (by multinational companies).

36 Economic growth

274 INTRODUCTORY ECONOMICS A TEXTBOOK FOR CAPE ECONOMICS STUDENTS

LEARNING OBJECTIVES

- Define economic growth.
- Explain the types of growth in the short-run and long-run.
- Identify the determinants of growth.
- Explain endogenous growth.
- Explain the objectives of growth.
- Identify the costs and benefits of growth.
- Explain issues related to growth over time.

REQUIRED KNOWLEDGE

- Production possibility curves
- Short-term changes in national income
- AS/AD model of the economy
- Multiplier and accelerator theory
- Investment.

TOPIC VALUE

When an economy is growing, jobs are easy to find as incomes are rising, but so too is the level of prices. There is much economic activity, people can import many things that are not locally available and the standard of living improves. Not everyone becomes well off, however, because our wealth is not evenly distributed and the quality of life is not the same for everyone. This is essentially what economic growth and development tries to address.

Introduction

Economic growth is defined as the long-term growth in the productive capacity of a country measured over a period of time. Current practice calculates economic growth as the monetary increases of real national income on a yearly basis.

Economic growth is a high priority for the government, since it coincides with employment, structural development and opportunities for improved living standards. These analyses are all short-term in nature, and factors such as population, technology and new resources are all assumed to be fixed.

These factors are precisely those that contribute to an increase in the productive capacity of the economy over an extended period and which, therefore, determines the rate of economic growth in an economy. It is prudent to view economic growth in two ways:

› **Short-term actual growth**
› **Long-term actual growth.**

Short-term actual growth

Short-term or actual growth is taken to mean changes in real GDP on an annual basis. For example, if the real GDP of a small CARICOM territory is EC$40 billion in 2013 and EC$42 billion in 2014, there would be a short-term actual growth of 42b – 40b = 2b or 2b/40b × 100 = 5% growth.

This growth is possible perhaps through the employment of idle land, labour or capital and other spare capacity in the economy. Using the familiar Keynesian diagrams and production possibility frontier, we may easily observe how short-term actual economic growth takes place in figures 36.1a and b, and 36.1c representing long-term economic growth.

Although changes in real GDP may move the economy from Y_1 to Y_2 in figures 36.1a and 36.1b, the economy is in fact operating with a deflationary gap, or under its full capacity of Y_{FE} (full employment). Similarly, it may be operating at Y_4, beyond its productive capacity.

The trade cycle in figure 36.2 shows the difference in short-term or actual growth (AB) and long-term or potential growth. The output gaps shown as the shaded area are a result of changes in real GDP. At the same time the capacity of the economy is increasing, represented by potential or trend growth XY.

In other words, long-term growth is caused by changes in long-run aggregate supply. While changes in Keynesian aggregate demand lead to short-term growth, monetarist long-run changes in aggregate supply, however, lead to potential growth. In this

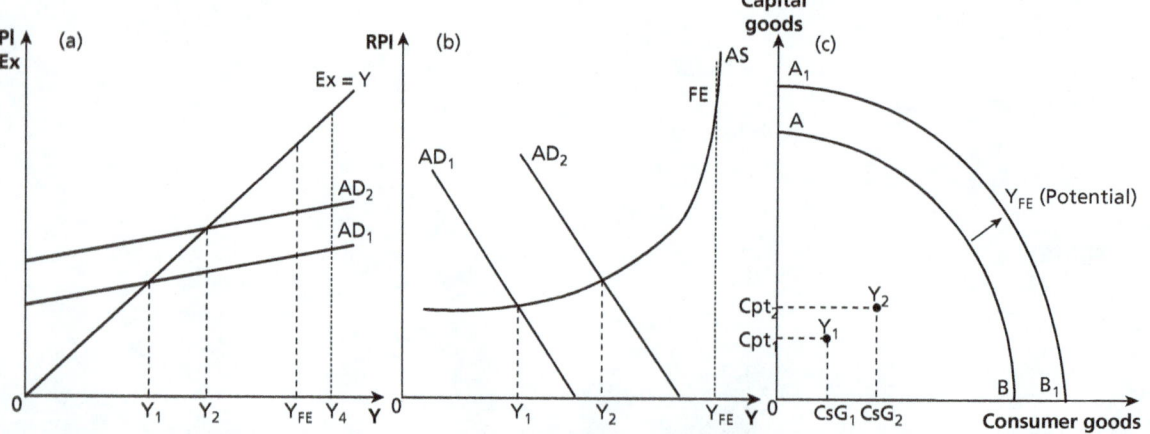

Figures 36.1 a and b Short-term actual growth using Keynesian cross and production possibility frontiers, and (c) long-term growth

model, trend or potential growth is rising throughout. The reason for this will be explored further in this chapter.

If you refer to figures 36.1a, b and c, you will also note that even though an economy can operate with a short-term growth of Y_1 to Y_2, no real growth or capacity can be achieved unless capacity creating investment is undertaken. Figure 36.1c shows that it is only if the production possibility frontier shifts to the right that long-term growth is possible. This can be achieved when there are accumulated increases in population, capital stock, technical and technological advances and newly discovered resources.

Sources of short-term actual growth

Short-term actual growth is created by changes in: consumption; investment; government spending; and exports.

Changes in consumption

Changes in consumption may result from increased consumer confidence, falling interest rates and a more even distribution of wealth. Consumer expenditure creates buoyant economic activity in the manufacturing and retail services sector.

Changes in investment

Changes in investment may be caused by changes in business confidence, falling interest rates or improved technology. The demand for capital goods will increase and there will be a positive impact on aggregate output.

Changes in government spending

Changes in government spending are necessary when there is a short-term growth in the population because there will be a rise in demand for public goods (roads) and merit goods (health and education).

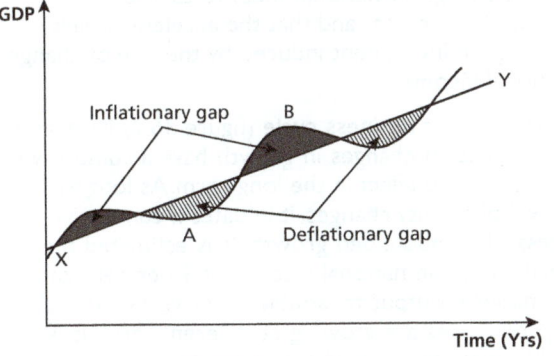

Figure 36.2 The trade cycle

Changes in exports

Changes in the level of exports in the short-run may be determined by the movements in exchange rates, competitiveness due to high productivity, or low domestic inflation relative to foreign inflation levels. Exports are an injection, which increase the money supply and may be a growth factor when domestic inflation is low.

Some short-term changes also have a long-term impact. For example, although investment is a short-term demand-side factor, it contributes to long-term capacity enhancement as a long-term supply factor.

Similarly, government expenditure may function as a short-term demand factor but also a long-term supply factor, due to the provision of drainage, ports, buildings, schools and hospitals, and so on. The tourism export sector's investment in hotel resorts and related facilities (water, sports, golf) also increases the capacity of the economy for this sector.

Reallocation of resources

The reallocation of resources from low-productive use and low-priced products, for example primary production in sugar, to highly productive output at a high value, for example finished aluminium, leads to automation, large-scale production and economies of scale.

A final important point that should be emphasised in discussing actual growth is that aggregate demand must be sufficient to absorb the level of output produced to avoid inflationary pressure. The rate of growth is a crucial factor in this respect because when aggregate supply falls behind aggregate demand, the price level will be pulled up.

Long-run potential growth

Long-run potential growth takes place over an extended period of time, by the cumulative process of a series of short-run growth and recession (deflationary gap), as illustrated in the upward trend in the trade cycle in figure 36.2 The main reasons for this type of growth stem from the fact that population growth increases the quantity of human resources. Net investment and technical progress also increase the quantity and quality of capital resources. Economic growth is assumed to be long-run potential growth, because the growth in capacity over this period enables increased production of more goods.

Sources of long-run growth

One of the main sources of long-term growth is a growth in the size and quality of the labour force. Specifically, this refers to the training, health and productivity of the workforce and the prevailing conditions of work. A highly trained workforce is productive. This makes the goods and services sector very competitive. The participation rate (percentage of population in the labour force) is also a crucial factor. This, however, is dependent on the composition of the population. The occupational and geographic mobility of labour underlines the need to be retrained and to adapt as the structure of the economy changes over time.

Reductions in participation rates and working hours are not necessarily impediments to economic growth, because of the demands for more leisure hours and short working weeks. More importantly, the improved quality of the workforce is a significant objective in modern economies.

Investment and capital accumulation

Net investment is a crucial element of long-term growth because of the increased productive capacity of investment in conjunction with labour. If labour is equipped with modern tools such as management information systems (MIS) and trained to use them, it will impact on long-term growth. It is insufficient to merely accumulate capital and expect that economic growth will take place. It is necessary to invest in growth-creating investment. Residential construction and military spending have little impact on increases in real output, compared to investment in modern plants in manufacturing industries and modernised agriculture. Modernisation of plant and retooling are therefore major elements of long-term growth.

Investment, however, requires a sacrifice. For investment to take place, resources are required to shift from the production of consumer goods to capital goods. Furthermore, investment funds must be made available through a dynamic capital and money market and targeted for future development. An increased rate of savings therefore is vital to investment.

The investment of funds into manufacturing products of high value is also an important issue related to long-term growth; for example, the contribution of the electronics and auto industries to the robust Japanese economy. Most developing countries concentrate on low-value unprocessed primary production typically found in Caribbean countries. The size of the accelerator is a determinant of the impact that investment may have on long-term growth.

Technical and technological progress

The very industrialised countries of the North have achieved long-term growth rates consistently, due to keeping pace with technology and making technical improvements in production. Invention and innovation, and high rates of employment of technology, have helped those countries to achieve long-term growth. Invention is the creation of new products, improving old ones, and innovation is simply putting such new ideas, tools or techniques into commercial use. Computerised production is a very good example of how information technology can play a vital role in long-term growth. It is for this reason that most modern companies have a research and development department.

Long-term growth will not take place if there is insufficient demand for output. The growth of the population and consumer confidence, therefore, provide a stimulus for growth to take place over the long-term. Moreover, the composition of the population may also be a determining factor. If the population is ageing, the expenditure pattern of this group offers limited potential for consumer goods and it will influence the type of output produced. Large populations enable firms to benefit from economies of scale, reduced costs and increased competitiveness at home and in foreign markets.

Discovery of new high-value resources and land

Since the discoveries of new fields of oil and gas in most oil-producing countries, new techniques of production and modern equipment have accelerated growth. Middle Eastern countries, as well as the Caribbean territories of Trinidad and Tobago and Barbados, have used these discoveries to advance the industrialisation of their respective countries.

Political stability

Long-term economic growth is achieved in countries that are not ravaged by civil unrest or war. War and unrest are a drain and diversion of resources, in addition to negatively affecting the business climate of a country. In war-torn economies or countries under terrorist threat, the investment climate is not conducive to potential growth, especially foreign direct investment (FDI).

Key point

Short-term economic growth is determined by the components of aggregate demand, while long-term growth is determined by supply-side measures including new technology, a skilled work force, innovation and invention, capital accumulation, population growth, the discovery of new resources and political stability.

The cumulative aspects of growth

Trend or potential growth is theoretically explained by the interaction of the multiplier and accelerator effects over the long-term. Recall that the multiplier links the change in national income to the expenditure increases and that the accelerator links the change in investment induced by the rate of change in national income.

The trade or business cycle (figure 36.2) illustrates how short-term changes in growth have a cumulative or compounded effect in the long-term. As long as the level of activity changes, it initiates a cumulative process of compounded growth. It is estimated that a small change in national income of 3 per cent can cause national output to double in 24 years. Indeed, if two countries are growing at different rates, it is possible through this cumulative process for one country to double the income of the other, provided that they both started at a similar level of income.

This is precisely the reason why the gap in growth rates between more industrialised countries and their developing counterparts has become larger over time. The rate of growth in Barbados, therefore, will not catch up with the USA, even if its growth rates were the same, simply because the USA is more developed.

Chapter 36 Economic growth

Desirability of growth

Economic growth is desirable for most societies, as long as the benefits of growth are greater than the costs. Economic growth encourages FDI. Foreign investors in the manufacturing sector will be encouraged to set up in a growing economy that is stable, especially if the country in question is viewed as a potential market.

Overall, economic growth is desirable for the following reasons:

1. It is linked to an improvement in the quality of life of most citizens.
2. Poverty is reduced when higher revenues from the increased taxation of a growing economy are spent on welfare, health, education, recreation and other social amenities.
3. The quality of life is improved for the average citizen. In the Caribbean, as elsewhere, the standard of living is dependent on an even distribution of income. A steadily growing economy may accumulate the financial resources to enable a reduction in taxes and a shortened working week.

From the viewpoint of trade, a country would need to achieve an economic growth rate similar to those in the international environment in a bid to become competitive. Growing economies also provide the economic conditions necessary to achieve a fully employed labour force.

But in spite of the benefits of growth there may be undesirable effects. These include:

› Inflationary pressure if the economy is close to full employment
› Rising incomes may stimulate high import spending, leading eventually to a balance of payments deficit and possible devaluation of the currency
› Over-consumption
› A rise in demand for demerit goods that have harmful external costs to society, e.g., alcoholism, gambling, drug addiction
› An opportunity cost with regard to the use of non-renewable resources
› A tendency for the gap between high and low-income earners to widen, and redistribution of incomes may not be successful
› Industrial unrest may result when rising profits induce demand for higher wages
› Rise in white-collar crime
› A growing debt problem for small island states such as the CARICOM. Vagrancy, social stress and suicide rates are also associated with growth
› Negative externalities are a by-product of economic growth, notwithstanding the best efforts of environmental protection agencies
› Automation, and mechanisation and modern tools may replace human labour. If such labour is occupationally immobile, unemployment may result.

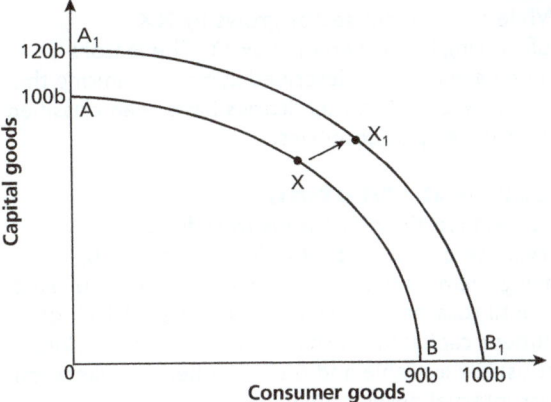

Figure 36.3 Production possibility frontier in the long-run, showing balanced growth

Key point

There are many benefits to be achieved through sustained growth rates, but these may be counterbalanced by the costs of growth. The benefits of growth include high employment, reduction of poverty, increased public and merit goods, social capital and increased leisure time. Costs associated with economic growth are pollution, over-consumption, opportunity costs of non-renewable resources, balance of payments deficits, inflation and the replacement of human labour by automation and mechanisation.

Unbalanced growth

Economic growth may be unbalanced or dualistic in nature, and this is most readily observable in Caribbean territories. For example, the Windward Islands are very dependent on banana production and Trinidad and Tobago is heavily dependent on oil and gas revenues. Despite the rents received from high oil prices by Trinidad and Tobago, the economy is still not diversified to produce even growth, despite growing continuously from 1992 to 2008.

A tourism- or agriculture-based economy may not have experienced even growth (figure 36.3), and typically their PPF may assume the profile of figure 36.4.

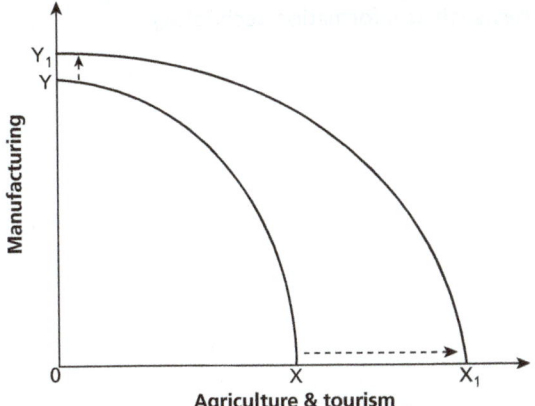

Figure 36.4 Production possibility frontier showing unbalanced growth

While the tourism sector grows by XX_1, manufacturing has grown only by YY_1. The factors affecting development described above are among the reasons why Caribbean territories have been classified as lesser developed countries.

Import substitution

In this instance, the objective is to reduce an overreliance on imported goods and services by replacing them with domestic production on a phased basis, until total self-sufficiency is achieved. A lack of investment capital for such an ambitious undertaking is not usually available and there is a heavy reliance on FDI for internal development.

Technological dualism

Technological dualism occurs when the structure of the economy is made up of two main sectors. The first is: an advanced industrial sector concentrated near to ports and specialising in primary production such as mining, large-scale agriculture, tourism and the indirect services; or the tertiary sector that supports industries such as banking, transportation, finance, insurance and information technology. The other sector is characterised by traditional activities such as peasant agriculture, small-plot farming and home-based small businesses, all of which are operated and owned by rural individuals employing outmoded techniques and methods.

One of the drawbacks of this dualism is urban drift, which is the movement of labour to urban regions where wages are higher. Many rural industries such as the coconut, cocoa, and sugar estates have collapsed as a result.

Endogenous growth

Endogenous growth is defined as economic growth achieved through factors within the economy, as opposed to external factors. Examples of these internal factors are: improvements in labour productivity such as training and equipping workers with modern technology; modern techniques in production and management; and educating the workforce by targeting labour shortages and growth industries such as information technology.

Exogenous growth

Exogenous growth is determined by external factors such as tourism, FDI, favourable movements in commodity prices in the world markets, and the importation of raw materials and technology. All of these factors relate to Caribbean economies. Guyana and Jamaica depend on revenue from alumina exports. Trinidad and Tobago continue to depend very heavily on tax rents from its oil and gas production, while all Caribbean economies invest heavily in tourism.

Chapter summary

› Economic growth is defined as the growth in the long-term productive capacity of a country.
› Growth may be actual short-term or potential long-term and is a cumulative process.
› Sources of short-term growth are increases in the levels of consumption, government spending, exports and investment. These changes also have supply-side long-term growth potential.
› Sources of long-term potential growth are the rate of capital formation, a reallocation of resources, increased productivity of the labour force, technical progress, the discovery of natural resources and political stability.
› The benefits of growth are higher living standards, poverty reduction, full employment, an increase in public and merit goods and other social amenities, increased prospects for wage increases and income redistribution.
› The costs of growth include: inflationary pressure, over-consumption, negative externalities, a rise in the consumption of demerit goods, balance of payments deficits, and the inability to replace non-renewable resources.

Practice question

What factors might be attributed to the low rates of economic growth in the Caribbean?

37 Economic development

LEARNING OBJECTIVES

- Define and explain economic development.
- Identify and analyse the difference between growth and development.
- Identify and evaluate indicators of development.
- Explain human development and its constraints.
- List the characteristics of lesser developed countries (LDCs).
- List the characteristics of Caribbean economies.

REQUIRED KNOWLEDGE

- Measures of standard of living
- Accelerator theory
- Production possibility frontier
- Economic growth
- Supply-side measures.

TOPIC VALUE

The focus of economic development for the government is the standard of living and quality of life of its citizens.

Introduction

A country's economic development is concerned with human development, derived from sustained long-term per capita growth and the physical transformation of the economy. When these objectives are achieved the overall standard of living of the average citizen is expected to improve.

In the words of economist Mahabub Ul Haq, economic development is concerned with the 'enlargement of choices'. He identified four important choices necessary to human development, which are as follows:

1. **Standard of living computed as GDP per capita income at purchasing power parities**
2. **Having gainful employment and a low rate of inflation**
3. **Longevity and good health measured by life expectancy and access to medical care**
4. **Education as measured by adult literacy rates and numbers enrolled in education.**

Many aspects of the quality of life of a Caribbean national, or an individual elsewhere in the world, could be added to these basic qualitative factors. Other factors may include access to water and hospital beds, infant mortality rates, income distribution, human rights, the level of pollution, crime and ethnic discrimination.

The Measure of Economic Welfare (MEW, developed by Nordhaus and Tobin) is another measure of welfare that relates directly to human development. The MEW is adjusted for positive and negative factors such as leisure time and pollution. Leisure time is referred to as 'desirables' and pollution as 'regrettables'. National income is then adjusted as regrettables + desirables = MEW, so that if national income is $100 billion and regrettables and desirables are $24 billion and $3 billion respectively, MEW is calculated as: $100b − $24b + $3b = $79b.

The Physical Quality of Life Index (PQLI) is another method of evaluating the welfare of a citizen. This index measures basic variables such as infant mortality rates, literacy levels, life expectancy and computes an average value, which indicates basic standard of living.

Classification of development

The world economies have historically been ranked as first, second, third or fourth world in terms of their economic development. In this instance, first world refers to the group of eight (G8) countries that are very developed economically and distinguished by their high level of industrialisation. These countries are also referred to as more developed countries (MDCs), as opposed to lesser developing countries (LDCs) that have a low level of industrialisation.

The World Bank classifies development into income groups; for example, high income (G8), upper-middle income (Malaysia), lower-middle income (South Africa) and low income (Caribbean territories). Barbados, the Bahamas and Trinidad and Tobago may be regarded as upper-middle income, based on the fact that the GDP purchasing power parity for each country is above US$8,000.

Characteristics of underdevelopment

Although economies differ in their size and level of development, most underdeveloped nations have features in common. Caribbean economies can also be thus classified and have the following characteristics.

Small open economies

This makes them vulnerable to shocks to the international sector.

High population growth rates

High population growth rates create the need for increasing amounts of goods and services that contribute to a reasonable standard of living. The economic dilemma presented in this case is simply that large amounts of capital investment require a sacrifice in consumption to facilitate the production of capital goods. As a result, consumer goods may not be produced in the required quantities.

In the Caribbean, foreign direct investment (FDI) has, in part, compensated for this investment deficit. In addition, high population growth rates increase the dependency ratio, in which a high ratio of the young who are not of working age become dependent on a small working population.

Unskilled labour force

An unskilled labour force is due in a large measure to low rates of adult literacy. It is necessary in the circumstances for a country to import skilled labour, such as doctors and engineers. Moreover, poor health reduces productivity levels in these countries.

Dependence on low-priced agricultural products

It is not uncommon in developing countries to have more than 60–70 per cent of the population engaged in agriculture, using outmoded techniques of production and over-cultivating arable land. In such cases, productivity is once again very low. National output is, therefore, less than optimal.

Lack of natural resources/limited resource base

While some countries are endowed with a rich reserve of fossil fuels or other resources such as nitrates, coal, nickel and copper, LDCs may only have land resources that are poorly irrigated. Crops are, therefore, unable to thrive in near-drought conditions.

Composition of exports

The majority of exports consist mainly of primary products that are subject to the vagaries of international prices.

High rates of employment and underemployment

High levels of unemployment are mainly due to a lack of employment opportunities, caused by a lack of physical capital such as factories, plants and refineries and a poorly trained labour force. Underemployment may also result from part-time or seasonal work.

Poor infrastructural development

Poor infrastructural development is a supply constraint, because growth in the economy depends on improvement in capacity provided by proper infrastructure such as water, roads, power, communications, ports and drainage. A lack of basic infrastructure reduces efficiency and increases costs, effectively reducing productive capacity and limiting the export potential of local output.

A one crop economy

Usually a lesser developing economy will be dependent on a single product for its foreign earnings. Much of the time it is agricultural produce that is the exported product. However, drought, over-supply and unstable prices result in low foreign earnings.

Lack of diversification

A lack of diversification makes LDCs dependent on one main source of earning foreign revenue. Most Caribbean economies depend on tourism and its linkages for foreign earnings. There is a need for a long-term diversification plan. This is also one of the reasons why many lesser developing economies are always in debt to larger, first world economies and have to seek debt relief from the international lending agencies.

Cycle of poverty

A cycle of poverty is a recurring theme in the majority of LDCs. Industrialisation is one of the preferred methods of development for LDCs. The benefits which may be derived from industrialisation are:

› **Permanent employment**
› **The employment of local resources**
› **Reliance on domestic substitutes in place of foreign imports as a means of reducing a food import bill**
› **Export revenue.**

One of the primary obstacles to industrialisation is the lack of capital, due in large measure to a low rate of savings. Since savings are a function of income, low incomes in lesser developing economies give rise to low savings. A lack of capital, therefore, reduces productivity. The eventual consequence is once again low incomes. The cycle illustrated in figure 37.1 explains the problem.

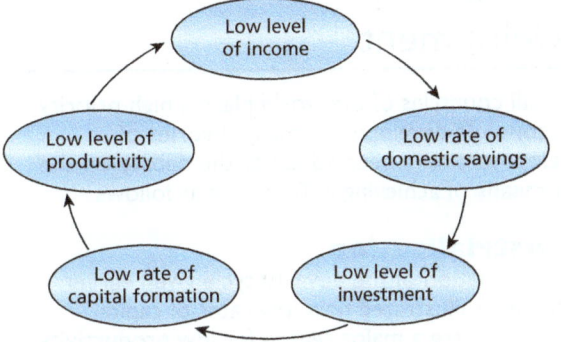

Figure 37.1 The cycle of poverty

Problems of development in the Caribbean

The factors affecting development that have been identified so far are also the reasons why Caribbean territories have been classified as LDCs. A few more factors can be added that are peculiar to the region, however. These include the following.

Migration

Most of the skilled nationals of Caribbean countries contribute to the problem of human capital flight or the 'Brain Drain'. As a result, even larger economies like Trinidad and Tobago are currently importing skilled professionals.

Technological dualism
Technological dualism is a feature of LDCs and it occurs when the structure of the economy is made up of two main sectors. (Refer to chapter 36 for a more detailed explanation.)

Natural disasters
Many Caribbean economies have the disadvantage of lying in the path of destructive hurricanes. Small island states like Grenada, St Kitts, St Lucia, Antigua and Montserrat have been devastated by powerful hurricanes and this fact is perhaps the main reason for the lack of economic development that exists in these territories.

The openness of Caribbean economies and the heavy reliance on the tourism sector are other reasons for the slow rate of development of these territories. The economies of these islands cannot match the technological capability of developed countries. As a result, there is a heavy reliance on the importation of goods and services without the requisite means of payment.

Strategies for economic development

Since all countries of the world place a high priority on economic development, many theories of development have been added to the debate on the best means of achieving it. These are as follows.

Industrialisation
The explanation of the poverty cycle given earlier in the book illustrated how low rates of capital formation were a major reason for low productivity. It is precisely for this reason that LDCs focus very heavily on attracting FDI as a means of solving development gaps. These gaps are the shortfalls in savings, investment, technology, enterprise, foreign exchange and management skills. This issue is discussed in detail in chapter 35 on foreign direct investment.

Diversification
Essentially diversification requires that countries target overall development, modifying the 'one crop' economy. For example, agriculture and agro-processing present many opportunities for linkages to the secondary and tertiary sectors in Caribbean countries. Permanent employment, food, self-sufficiency, export potential, and the building of the economy from within are the main benefits of such an approach.

Export-led growth is another preferred method made popular by Japan whose phenomenal rate of industrialisation took a mere 50 years (1944 to 1994). Much of Japan's success was attributed to the importation of raw material, together with the employment of a skilled and a productive workforce to successfully capture export markets. The linkages associated with this strategy also created well-established tertiary industries and opportunities for employment. Many South Asian economies have successfully followed this model of growth and it continues to be a commonly adopted strategy for most newly industrialised countries.

Tourism
Many LDCs, and indeed other middle income countries, have adopted tourism as a strategy for growth because of the many linkages it has to other sectors of the economy. It is particularly popular in Caribbean islands that are not endowed with mineral resources.

Economic aid
When the governments of LDCs do not possess the means to develop their countries, they often seek foreign assistance from first world industrialised nations such as Canada or the USA. Although the premise for foreign aid is based on first world generosity, much of the time political and other considerations also play a role.

Criticism of economic development theories

The main criticism of industrialisation as a strategy is first of all the debt liabilities created by borrowing to finance diversification. The initial stages of industrialisation and diversification require a need for protecting 'infant' industries in a globalised trade environment. It is argued that protection gives rise to inefficiency and loss of competitiveness.

A tourism-based industry on its own has merit because of the many linkages to indigenous resources, but development in this case is outwardly generated, rather than inward. In recent times, the World Trade Center disaster negatively impacted on foreign travel. In spite of this, Caribbean tourism is on the rebound since the terrorist threat is perceived to be greater in the North. Another criticism of a tourism-based strategy is the conservationist argument of harm to the natural environment from a tourism-based infrastructure. Another commonly cited criticism is the low levels of income at the bottom of the wage structure of the industry, which are almost exclusively earned by the local population.

Implications for Caribbean regional economies based on their characteristics
Based on the characteristics of the Caribbean region the implications are as follows:

> **Dependence on aid for social and economic development**
> **The need for preferential trade agreements in order to compete in international markets**

- The need for FDI as a strategy for development
- Vulnerability to natural and man-made changes
- Changes in world prices have a significant impact on such small open economies, especially if prices plummet.

Primary production

The main criticism of the primary production approach is the fact that as a revenue earner it is declining in importance to the knowledge-based industries. In addition, fluctuating world prices require countries to hedge against losses and to enlist government support for prices that will bring a reasonable profit for farmers. Further, large investors from the North have played a pivotal role in controlling the supply of primary agricultural commodities – as the banana dispute clearly demonstrated, and to the detriment of the banana-producing Caribbean states.

Export-led strategy

While this approach has invoked success stories about the newly industrialised countries, much of their success was attributed to increased levels of productivity using cheap but productive labour and a strategy of targeting domestic and foreign markets. The limitations associated with this approach have been the inability of LDCs to achieve the level of scale economies and advanced technological capability and developed external markets that MDCs have achieved in their long years of economic development. When added to the comparative advantages that MDCs hold, protectionist policies make MDCs dominant in world trade.

Foreign direct investment

The arguments for and against FDI are discussed in more detail in chapter 35. The main criticism of FDI as a developmental strategy is that development is based on external rather than internal resources and that there is little value added for domestic industries linked to these activities. The repatriation of profits and the opportunity cost of extracted non-renewable resources are other criticisms.

Chapter summary

- Economic development is concerned with human development, derived from sustained long-term per capita growth and the physical transformation of the economy; growth in GDP per capita income at purchasing power parities; having gainful employment; a low rate of inflation; longevity and good health measured by life expectancy and access to medical care. Education as measured by adult literacy rates and numbers enrolled in education are also factors.
- The Measure of Economic Welfare (MEW) by Nordhaus and Tobin is another measure of welfare that relates directly to human development (1972).
- Most underdeveloped nations have features in common. These are: high population growth rates; an unskilled labour force; dependence on low-priced agricultural products; a lack of natural resources; high rates of employment and underemployment; poor infrastructural development; and lack of diversification.
- Strategies for economic development include: industrialisation; diversification; export-led growth; tourism; economic aid; and investment in education and training and health.

Practice question

Differentiate between economic growth and development. In what ways are economic development linked to economic growth?

38 Globalisation

Chapter 38 Globalisation

LEARNING OBJECTIVES

- Explain the forces that shape globalisation.
- Identify the benefits of globalisation.
- Identify the costs of globalisation.
- Explain trade liberalisation.

REQUIRED KNOWLEDGE

- Multinational corporations (MNCs)
- Foreign direct investment (FDI)
- International trade
- Factor mobility
- The role of communications technology
- The International Monetary Fund (IMF) and the World Trade Organization (WTO).

TOPIC VALUE

The process of globalisation has dramatically changed the way the world interacts. Communication may now take place between countries almost instantly.

Introduction

Many have claimed that the invention of the printing press by Guttenburg was the catalyst for the advancement of human civilisation. The printing press enabled the spread of ideas and was the forerunner of the information technology that drives today's modern world.

The communications revolution has acted like a drawstring threaded through all nations, creating a world without boundaries. The internet, email, facsimile machines, satellite technology and a host of other sophisticated technologies have dramatically accelerated our interaction with firms, people, professional organisations and governments in the most distant economies. This acceleration in the ease of interaction has created a world economy, virtually without borders.

Globalisation, therefore, may be defined as an acceleration in the connectedness of the economies of the world to the extent that it has become one supranational economy, made possible through the following forces:

> Communications technology
> Removal of trade barriers
> Formation of trading blocs
> Operations of multinational corporations
> Efforts of the IMF
> WTO.

The colonisation of the West Indian islands by European interests provided the start of the long globalisation process. This momentum gathered speed during the transatlantic slave trade, but sailing ship travel was the only means of communication. Although trade continued for 500 years, the pace of globalisation was very slow.

It was the advent of the IMF and the WTO after the Second World War that provided a timely boost to the globalisation process, since the WTO was responsible for promoting international trade between countries by negotiating the removal of trade barriers. The IMF ensured that there was a sound global financial system that would facilitate payments and receipts connected to trade. This liberalisation of trade provided an accelerated thrust into foreign markets that were previously protected.

Perhaps the two most powerful forces that have impacted on globalisation were the fall of the Berlin Wall, with the movement towards free market economies in the USSR, and the information revolution that coincided with advances in computer technology.

The combined effect of all these events served to intensify the connectedness of the economies of the world to the extent that there were spillover effects that were both positive and negative. These effects influenced the following areas:

> International trade
> Finance
> Economic policy
> Political influence
> Culture
> The environment
> Foreign policy
> Foreign direct investment (FDI)
> Free movement of factors of production and financial capital across borders.

Positive effects of globalisation

The positive effects of globalisation are as follows:

> **The removal of trade barriers between countries has resulted in increased competition. Increased productivity of the factors of production has been a by-product of competition. The resulting benefit from such productivity has been low prices, increased global output of goods and services, enhanced quality of products, research and a greater diversity of products for the consumer market.**
> **Access to a wide range of high quality and low-priced goods and services has contributed to rising living standards across the world.**
> **Trading activities in foreign markets have created increased opportunities for and benefits from economies of scale and specialisation.**
> **Many benefits are attributed to FDI, particularly Caribbean states. FDI is associated with the activities of MNCs. Although the benefits of foreign investment have been fully explored in chapter 35, they may be summarised as resolving the deficits in technology, savings, foreign revenue, modern management, accounting practices, tax revenue and investment.**
> **There has been a revolution in air and sea transportation arising out of competition for air and sea routes. As a result, the costs of international transportation have been significantly reduced.**
> **Globalisation has also created economic opportunities for employment through the activities of MNCs and through the free**

movement of labour between international boundaries. Since there are also backward and forward linkages related to the activities of MNCs, permanent employment opportunities are created.
> Globalisation has been cited as creating opportunities for market access both through the removal of barriers and the external networks to which MNCs are connected.
> Perhaps one of the most significant positive aspects of globalisation has been the complementary relationship between communications technology and the movement of financial capital. The rapid transfer of financial capital between countries has been an accommodating factor in resolving the savings and investment gap.
> The emergence of trading blocs has also been another positive benefit arising out of the globalisation process. The North American Free Trade Area has a market of 360 million people. Apart from the marketing potential, such markets offer solidarity and cooperation between nations. These are key benefits.

The negative aspects of globalisation

Many of the benefits of globalisation have been challenged. Although it is claimed that globalisation, in general, and FDI, in particular, create employment in the host country, this claim is not wholly accepted. Since there is a high demand for skilled rather than unskilled labour, wages in the skilled sector increase relative to other sectors. This creates a dualistic wage structure, which further creates increased union activity and wage inflation pressure. It also contributes to income inequality.

The activities of MNCs in the globalisation process also create a phenomenon called 'Dutch disease', which is caused by a high demand for resources in a booming sector that leads to an appreciating exchange rate. Eventually, exports become uncompetitive and the export-oriented sector goes into decline, creating structural unemployment and the start of business contraction and de-industrialisation.

Although Caribbean economists have acknowledged the contribution of globalisation to the savings pool of small developing states, other economic commentators have noted such savings have not been available to domestic capital markets. In such cases, it is argued that these savings are repatriated to their home countries to create competition for domestic industries. For example, it has been argued that Tate and Lyle, the predecessor to the Sugar Manufacturing Company of Trinidad and Tobago, used repatriated savings to invest in beet sugar at a much reduced cost of production.

It is therefore not surprising that the Sugar Manufacturing Company of Trinidad and Tobago is being phased out. Companies in Chile and Brazil had similar experiences in natural rubber and nitrates respectively. With respect to the contribution of tax revenue to host countries by the process of globalisation, it is argued that tax holidays, sometimes extending to 8 years, have rendered such claims highly exaggerated. As globalisation intensifies the interconnectedness of the world, economic 'shocks' in one country or region may radiate to all countries very quickly and to the rest of the world, as the US recession has recently demonstrated.

Although the Asian financial crisis is the often quoted example of the negative consequences of globalisation shocks, the USA's 9/11 disaster as well as negative growth in major economies such as the USA, Japan, Germany and the UK sent shocks that set up negative chain reactions in other economies. The most recent, however, is the recession of the United States in 2008, the collapse of that country's financial markets and the start of a global recession.

Other negative consequences of globalisation are:

> Spread of international terrorism
> Undermining of small economies by drug transshipments
> Spread of fatal diseases, e.g., SARS, AIDS, Avian flu, H1N1 virus
> Money laundering activities
> Industrial espionage
> Subversion of culture, e.g., the decline in interest in the game of cricket in favour of American basketball or Halloween festivities instead of local Caribbean festivals
> Environment degradation
  • Competition for Caribbean firms from larger international firms.

Chapter summary

Globalisation is the acceleration of the interconnectedness of the world's economies through the removal of trade barriers, communications technology, the formation of trading blocs and the initiatives of the IMF, the World Bank and the WTO.

Practice questions

1. What do you understand by the term 'globalisation'?
2. Discuss whether globalisation is a help or a hindrance to the international trading process.

39 International financial institutions

LEARNING OBJECTIVES

- Describe the main international financial institutions.
- Describe the International Monetary Fund (IMF).
- Describe IBRD (World Bank and its two affiliate banks).
- Describe the World Trade Organization (WTO).

REQUIRED KNOWLEDGE

- Balance of payments
- International trade
- Exchange rates
- Trade agreements
- Protectionism
- Globalisation.

TOPIC VALUE

International financial institutions such as the International Monetary Fund (IMF), the World Trade Organization (WTO) and International Bank for Reconstruction and Development (IBRD) play a crucial role in Caribbean economic affairs.

The role of financial institutions

Chapter 38 on globalisation highlighted the accelerating inter-connectedness of countries around the world. But the world has large, small, developed and developing countries, all of which interact with each other and, to a large extent, depend on each other. It is for these reasons that it is necessary to have institutions in place to promote cooperation in economic relationships such as trade, exchange rates and balance of payments. These economic variables impact on employment, inflation, economic growth, global distribution of income and, eventually, standards of living.

Three main institutions were appointed to promote, oversee, regulate and supervise the smooth operations of trade, balance of payments and exchange rates.

These three main institutions are the International Monetary Fund (IMF), the International Bank for Reconstruction and Development (IBRD) (now The World Bank) and World Trade Organization (WTO).

Investment financial institutions came into existence to reduce friction and barriers and promote cooperation among countries with respect to trade, balance of payments, exchange rates and economic development.

The activities of these three main institutions are complementary to each other. Their overall objectives are poverty reduction and economic development of vulnerable states. The IMF concentrates on the stabilisation of macroeconomic fundamentals and maintaining confidence in the financial sector. The World Bank focuses its lending on infrastructural projects aimed at economic development and the WTO (formerly General Agreement on Tarriffs and Trade (GATT)) on the smooth conduct of trade.

It is easy to understand how the IBRD's economic development initiatives led to self-sufficiency, productivity and competitiveness. This competitiveness may be enhanced by the initiatives of the WTO. The entire exercise is also assisted by the IMF's financing of international trade and promotion of foreign exchange rate stability.

International Monetary Fund

J.M. Keynes was invited to the New Hampshire resort of Bretton Woods, USA in 1944, along with other economists to formulate a new post-war economic strategy. They were all mindful of the Great Depression, protectionist barriers, devaluations and the inability of poorer nations to access funding for infrastructural development. This Bretton Woods conference identified two main needs:

1. **Financial assistance to help countries with short-term balance of payments difficulties**
2. **Access to capital for long-term projects related to infrastructure development such as ports, drainage, roads and dams for water.**

The first need required the setting up of the IMF and the second required the intervention of a related institution called IBRD, also known as the World Bank.

The IMF came into existence in 1944–45 in Washington, USA, by international agreement and now includes 184 member countries. The original objectives of the IMF, written into its articles of agreement were:

- **Establish a system of exchange rates**
- **Monitor and supervise this system in order to promote confidence in international trade, remove exchange rate restrictions and promote exchange rate stability**
- **Increase international liquidity by designating financial instruments that are acceptable as payment in international trade**
- **Promote international cooperation.**

Since 1945, many events have brought these objectives into practice to ensure efficient global economic activity. From 1945 to 1972, fixed exchange rates were in effect, but, thereafter, floating exchange rates became the norm, both events requiring the supervision of the IMF. In the recent past, the IMF has concentrated on three main areas:

- **Financial assistance for countries with balance of payments deficits and financial strategies designed to prevent their recurrence**
- **Increasing the level of international liquidity**
- **Supervising the smooth management of exchange rates among member countries.**

How the IMF manages its operations

The financial resources of the IMF come from its members who must all pay a quota or subscription in its own currency. Developed countries pay a larger quota than small developing states.

This pool of resources therefore consists of many of the world's different currencies. The IMF also has a special currency called SDRs (special drawing rights).

How the IMF provides assistance to member countries

A country in foreign exchange crisis may seek the assistance of the IMF. The IMF provides loans by exchanging a country's quota contribution for foreign currencies, for example US dollars. These are called basic drawing rights and are lent in instalments, called tranches.

Early tranches carry no attached conditionalities. Later tranches carry conditionalities that are IMF-designed prescriptions, which must be followed and agreed to by the debtor country in a 'letter of intent'. The basic drawing rights can be drawn up to 125 per cent of a country's quota for approximately two years.

Additional borrowing

Additional lending by the IMF is granted in special circumstances. These are:

> **Extended fund facility** which is to assist countries with longer persistent deficits
> **Compensatory financing facility** that is granted if a country's exports have been affected by unforeseen circumstances, e.g., if hurricanes destroy Caribbean food crops that are main foreign exchange earners
> **Supplementary financing facility** is granted if a country is affected by rising oil prices
> **Buffer stock facility**, to stabilise the prices of primary products
> **Emergency facility**, for compensation for destabilising natural disasters.

International liquidity provisions of the IMF

International liquidity provisions are acceptable currencies necessary to finance trade. These are:

> IMF drawing rights
> SDRs
> Standby credit, which is provided by individual countries.

The IMF also gives approval for countries to borrow from commercial banks, provided they possess the ability to repay. It was in this manner that the euro (€) was created when wealthy Middle Eastern states deposited their 'petro' dollars in European banks.

IMF conditionalities

When debtor countries borrow from the IMF they are subject to conditionalities; these may simply be certain monetary and fiscal targets that must be met before tranches are loaned. In instances of persistent deficit, the IMF may impose austerity measures; for example, cutting subsidies, removing tariffs, or increasing direct taxation. These 'bitter pills' affect the poorer classes and in some instances lead to civil unrest, particularly when unsustainable state employment programmes are disbanded and the social safety nets are dismantled.

Devaluation is one of the options available to a country with a persistent deficit on its current account. The devaluation is advised with IMF approval.

Other IMF activities

Apart from its three main functions outlined earlier in this chapter, the IMF also provides:

> Financial advice to member countries
> Advice on macroeconomic policy such as monetary and fiscal policy as it relates to the country's fundamentals
> Advice on weakness in economic management to ensure sustainable growth and positive outcomes for the macroeconomic fundamentals.

Criticisms of IMF lending policies

Many small states have criticised the structural adjustment strategies imposed by harsh IMF conditionalities. Other criticisms include:

> Deflationary policies destabilised certain weakly performing economies, where per capita income was very low.
> The duration of loans was, on occasions, very short, e.g., 14 months in the case of Trinidad and Tobago during the recession of 1985–90, when the country was trying to turn around its balance of payments deficit.
> The duration and terms of lending were influenced by members of the IMF from the very developed countries who are insensitive to the needs of small developing countries.
> Devaluations prescribed by the IMF caused vital imports to rise in price and to create inflation and generally lower living standards.

Key point

The IMF was mandated in 1945 to assist member countries with balance of payments deficits and provide international liquidity with which to finance trade and to manage/supervise stable exchange rates of its members.

The International Bank for Reconstruction and Development (IBRD) or World Bank

The World Bank (IBRD) is the other major Bretton Woods Institution included in the international agreement. It came into existence on 27 December 1945, when 28 nations signed both the IMF and World Bank Charter.

The World Bank commenced operations on 25 June 1946. The role of this bank is to:

> Provide loans or guarantee them for productive reconstruction and development.
> Lend finance from its own members and mobilise additional sources of finance from private finance institutions in the world capital markets. The risk of lending is shared by the bank members, according to their economic strength.
> Provide technical advice and training to member countries.
> Promote economic development mainly through financing infrastructure such as road building, power and water capacity, schools, hospitals and drainage.

Organisation of the World Bank

Membership of the World Bank can only be achieved if a country is already a member of the IMF. There are currently 184 members whose shareholding is in proportion to their economic strength, the largest of which is the USA. The administration of the fund is undertaken by a board of governors, but the more developed countries of the world have a greater influence on decisions taken.

The World Bank includes two specialised lending agencies: the International Development Association (IDA), which was established in 1960 and the International Finance Corporation (IFC), which was established in 1956. These two institutions lend, in addition to the World Bank.

International Development Association

The role of IDA is as follows:

> To provides soft loans for a long-term period, 10-year grace periods and interest free. However, a 75 per cent service fee is charged on the paid-out portion of each credit in order to cover administration costs.
> IDA credits are designed to assist poorer nations that cannot afford to borrow under the World Bank's strict terms and conditions.
> The IDA finances projects such as agriculture, education, power stations, ports and urban development.

> IDA also provides technical assistance and occasionally makes available foreign exchange to purchase critical imports not related to specific projects.

International Finance Corporation

The IFC is a member of the World Bank group in a similar way to the IDA. IFC lending is geared towards the growth of productive enterprise in the private sector of developing countries.

The role of the IFC is mainly as a finance provider and facilitator and it may directly lend to private enterprise or assist in raising capital in the world capital markets in the manner of a private sector mentor.

In addition, the IFC may itself invest in projects as a partner, establish new businesses, or expand, diversify or modernise existing businesses. Apart from sourcing financial capital for private enterprise, it may also provide technical and managerial support for a project.

Investment proposals are considered by IFC in two main ways: as an investment bank and development institution. The three basic conditions necessary to IFC involvement are:

1. Project earning prospects
2. Benefit for a country
3. Local participation.

IFC also ensures the following:

1. Alternative funding at reasonable cost, if not available
2. That financial plans are achievable
3. There is a potential or existing market for the good or service
4. There is an experienced cadre of business professionals to oversee projects
5. They have substantial shareholding of the project sponsor.

The IFC is also supportive of joint venture partnerships between the state and private enterprise.

Key point

The IFC is that part of the World Bank that provides loans at generous terms and conditions to developing countries.

The World Trade Organization

The WTO was formerly known as GATT, which came into existence in 1941. The WTO succeeded GATT in 1995.

The main function of the WTO is to enable free trade among the world's exporting countries. Obstacles to trade date back to events following the Wall Street crash of 1929, which led to the Great Depression. The resulting fall in the level of exports led to balance of payments difficulties. Import restrictions came into existence, resulting in a dramatic decrease in world trade. In 1947, GATT started with 23 countries but has grown to 148 member countries, representing approximately 98 per cent of world trade.

The main functions of the WTO are to:

- **Administer trade agreements**
- **Provide a forum for trade negotiations**
- **Arbitrate in trade disputes between member countries.**

Other functions include:

- **Providing assistance to member countries with respect to the formulation of trade policy**
- **Promoting international cooperation.**

WTO rules

Unlike GATT the WTO has the power of sanction. They deliberate over the following:

- **Allow a country to erect tariff barriers, as in the case of the USA when protecting its steel industry from producers in EU countries**
- **The most favoured nation clause is also a concession to one trading partner to extend to other members, except where customs union or free trade areas exist**
- **Reciprocity: the mutual lowering of tariff barriers**
- **Banning of quotas as a form of protectionism**
- **Fair competition: sanctions are imposed on countries in breach of rules, e.g., illegal dumping**
- **Tariff cooperation: countries cannot raise tariff barriers without first negotiating with their trading partners.**

Trade negotiations

Since inception, there have been negotiations between members to resolve trading issues. The latest round is the Doha Round, currently taking place in Qatar and which commenced in 2001. Previous rounds have been the Uruguayan Round of 1986, the Tokyo Round of 1972 and the Kennedy Round of 1961.

The consensus among many economic commentators is that free trade favours developed countries with superior technology, productivity and economic power. It is argued that only countries with comparative advantages may really benefit from free trade.

From the Caribbean perspective, however, the multilateral approach to free trade, that is, single market economy is perhaps the best hope there is for Caribbean trade, since a regional approach offers a unified and a stronger bargaining position.

Key point

The WTO is the legal body responsible for liberalising trade and arbitrating trade disputes by legally committing all 148 members to a set of rules. Nevertheless, countries persist with measures to get around illegal barriers by the use of administrative barriers and voluntary restraints. These are the future challenges for the WTO.

Chapter summary

Three major international institutions are the IMF, the IBRD (the World Bank) and WTO (formerly GATT). In the recent past, the IMF has concentrated on three main areas: financial assistance for countries with balance of payments deficits and financial strategies designed to prevent their reoccurrence; increasing the level of international liquidity; and supervising the smooth management of exchange rates among member countries.

The World Bank includes two specialised lending agencies: the IDA, which was established in 1960, and the International Finance Corporation, which was established in 1956. These two institutions lend, in addition to the World Bank.

The IFC is that part of the World Bank that provides loans at generous terms and conditions to developing countries.

Practice questions

1. Discuss the major functions of each of the following international institutions:
   a. The International Monetary Fund (IMF)
   b. The World Bank (IBRD)
   c. The World Trade Organization (WTO).

2. Identify four measures that have been recommended by the International Monetary Fund (IMF) for the reform and stabilisation of developing countries.

3. Discuss the effects of one of the institutions identified in 1 above on the economies of developing countries.

INTRODUCTORY ECONOMICS A TEXTBOOK FOR CAPE ECONOMICS STUDENTS

40 Guidelines for internal assessment project

Chapter 40 Guidelines for internal assessment project

Your internal assessment project is similar in content and objective to the SBA project you submitted for your CXC Principles of Business Examination. It contributes 20 per cent of your final assessment and it is graded out of a total of 60 marks. You are required to choose specific objectives from the three modules in Unit One or Two and you will be graded out of a total of 20 marks for each module.

For example, if you are in Form 6 Lower or the 12th grade, you must select a research topic and select a Module 1 objective that you wish to investigate. You may choose from scarcity, demand, elasticity of demand, supply, short-run output, cost, profit, market type, market failure, externalities, efficiency, wages, asymmetrical information or distribution of income.

It may not be possible to include all of these topics, which cover your three modules, because you have a word limit and may be penalised with the reduction of your total mark by 10 per cent if you do not respect the word limit.

Many students are unsure about the way they should approach this task. You may be assisted by very simple guidelines. The objective of this exercise is simple. The understanding of economic principles is made complete when you observe first-hand how they apply to a real life situation, for example, a farm, a cement plant, or fiscal policy or international trade in your country. Students of science have a laboratory where they can observe scientific principles. In our case, we need this project to analyse economic principles operating in the real world and observe knowledge in action.

The benefits of project research

Perhaps you need to be reminded of the many benefits gained by doing research projects. Some benefits are listed below:

- Conducting research could provide you with insight when opening your own business so you may not be dependent on others to get a job.
- Your research skills teach you how to gather or source information and data, compile them, analyse and act on them.
- You would not be overly reliant on textbook learning by gaining valuable real world practice on your own.
- You will enter the examination room with marks already achieved. This gives you confidence to score a high grade.
- Complex aspects of running a business are made simple through this project.
- It is very likely that you will improve your technological and presentation abilities once the project is complete.
- This project will form part of your curriculum vitae and will be invaluable to you in a job interview.
- You should have a more certain idea of your career path.
- You will have the benefit of your teacher's assistance while preparing the project.

Step 1
Obtain a copy of the Economics syllabus and read it thoroughly. If you are doing a project on Unit 1 familiarise yourself with the three modules in Unit 1. If you are doing a project on Unit 2, then do likewise.

Step 2: Choosing the project
Unit 1: Suggestions
It will perhaps be more meaningful to research a particular economic issue that interests you. Consult your teacher if you are in doubt.

Remember to choose your project very early in consultation with your teacher. Obtain a letter of introduction from your school, which you may present to persons you are interviewing so that they will know the purpose of your visit. Keep a note book in which to record information when you visit the business site.

When do you start?
Many students wait until they are well advanced in the unit they are studying before they start their project. Again, consult your teacher for guidelines on this. Bear in mind that you may have to submit more than one project, which may put pressure on you during revision period nearer to your examinations. You should try to spread the project over a long period.

For example, discuss with your teacher the possibility of allocating time to project preparation immediately after a topic is completed. If you complete elasticity of demand, for example, ask your teacher to demonstrate how elasticity issues relate to the project. Then do a draft preparation for elasticty of demand as an assignment. You could do this for any other topic. By December, whatever objectives have been completed should be related to your topic. You may also find that your project will greatly assist your understanding of economic theory because the project is done close to the time that you learn the economic principles.

If you manage to do this every day, it will just be a matter of typing and fine-tuning your projects with minimal fuss and stress. You will also have more time for revision closer to the examination date.

Remember:
- Choose your topic in consultation with your teacher.
- As soon as a topic is completed, ask questions on how it relates to your project, e.g., cost, output, market structure, etc.
- Do a draft for homework that makes your project a work in progress.
- Choose which objectives you wish to include in your project and be mindful of the word limit.
- Do this for all your courses that require a project.

Skill requirements
You are required to demonstrate lower and higher order skills in your report. Lower order skills include knowledge and comprehension. Higher order skills include application, analysis, synthesis, evaluation and expression.

Knowledge
Knowledge skills simply test your ability to remember facts, e.g., list the factors that affect the demand for a good or define the term 'profit maximisation'.

Comprehension
You are required to demonstrate that you understand what you read. You may be familiar with the skills of comprehension because we are often given comprehension exercises in English Language classes. Comprehension skills ask the question, 'Do you understand what you have read?' For example, can you identify which of the following four factors are related to demand? Other question commands that require comprehension are classify, explain and describe.

Application
Generally speaking, application skills require you to transfer your understanding of a concept, for example, a formula, to a situation or event. In other words, how does this concept of the optimal purchase rule solve a person's indecision about dividing his pocket money between a snack or drink, given a limited income and prices of the two goods.

Another example is, 'Explain with the aid of a diagram how a bumper harvest may cause prices to fall'. Command words related to this thinking skill are: show, relate, predict and illustrate.

Analysis
Many different and small parts of a whole unit may be viewed through a microscope. In economics this is frequently done. Analysing involves breaking a whole into smaller parts to understand how they work together; for example, what factors are necessary to increase productivity in a firm? Question commands related to analysis are choose, assemble or arrange.

Synthesis
Synthesis means to bring together or integrate in the same way that a synthesiser joins musical notes together. In other words, how do the parts of a jigsaw puzzle become a picture. Words related to a synthesis are arrange, select, plan, organise or combine.

Evaluation
To evaluate is to make judgment of quality. In other words, an evaluation could be very poor, poor, fair, good, very good or excellent. For example, 'Assess the ways a government may control negative externalities' or 'Critically evaluate the measures the government may employ to control the rate of inflation'. Words related to evaluate are: appraise, assess, consider, to what extent, or judge.

Now that the skills that you are required to demonstrate have been described, we may now apply these skills to the different objectives we have selected. Before we attempt this exercise there are other points to consider.

Presentation
The project document should be presented in a soft folder. The cover page of the folder should have the candidate's number, name, name of subject, title of the project and the date submitted. Also include:

> Table of contents
> Aims and objectives
> Methodology employed
> Acknowledgments
> Word limit of 2,000 to 2,500 words
> Graphs, charts and tables where applicable
> Correct grammar and clarity of expression.

As a further guide, an imaginary company will be chosen for analysis so that you have a clear idea about how to proceed, particularly in demonstrating low and high order skills.

Step by step project guidelines for sample project

Unit 1 Research topic
An investigation into the operation of CARICOM Beverage Company Ltd

Specific objectives		Chapter numbers
Module 1	Topic 1: Scarcity	1, 2, 3, 4, 5, 6, 8
Module 1	Topic 2: Tools of analysis	5, 7
Module 1	Topic 3: Consumer demand	1, 2, 6, 7, 8, 9, 12, 14
Module 1	Topic 4: Theory of supply	1, 4, 7, 9
Module 2	Topic 1: Market structure	1, 4, 5
Module 2	Topic 2: Market failure	1, 2, 3, 4, 6
Module 3	Topic 1: Theory of income distribution	1, 3, 4, 5, 6, 13
Module 3	Topic 2: Decision making with incomplete info	2

The plan outlined above provides details of your internal assessment project. You may not be able to fit all of the specific objectives into your chosen research, since you are working with a word limit of 2,000–2,500. Choose specific objectives which fit your project in a relevant way.

Chapter 40 Guidelines for internal assessment project

Make sure you explain the theory underlying the objectives and then relate the theory to your project. Strive to be simple yet clear; watch out for assumptions you should make. Remember that for each module, you must demonstrate lower and higher order skills of learning.

A sample of specific objectives will be chosen to fit our soft drink company so you will have an idea how it fits into your project. The learning skills will also be identified.

The guidelines are not by any means a perfect plan, so you should at all times consult your teacher for advice on the way to proceed. Remember they are your examiners.

Topic	Suggestions
Scarcity	1 Define scarcity (knowledge) Wants satisfied (soft drink beverages) 2 The problem of opportunity cost 3 Demonstrate opportunity cost
PPF	For example, use a PPF to show that if the company is producing bottled water or soft drinks there would be an opportunity cost (comprehension and application).
Topic 2	Topic 2 requires you to explain the use of diagrams. For this topic it is suggested that you explain the difference between a variable and a constant. You could choose to describe the fixed cost of the beverage firm as a constant and the variable cost of production as variable factors. Use diagrams to do this.
Topic 3	Chapter numbers: 1, 2, 6, 7, 8 and 9, 11, 12, 14 are suggested for explanation. Since it is not possible to do both ordinal and cardinal theory you should choose one theory. If you choose utility: define then explain how more soft drinks will be demanded at lower prices due to the law of diminishing marginal utility. Derive a curve. In your explanation, mention consumer equilibrium MU = P and the optimal purchase rule $\frac{MU_x}{P_x} = \frac{MU_y}{P_y}$ If you choose indifference curve analysis: demonstrate the first law of demand using budget and indifference curves. Show income and substitution effects for the fall in price of soft drinks. Identify the good as a normal good. State factors that determine demand for soft drinks; for example, advertising, tastes, price of substitutes, etc.
Topic 8	Explain movement along and shifts of the curve. For a shift it must be caused by the change in non-price factors.
Topic 11	Explain the concept of consumer surplus with a diagram when the price of the soft drink falls.
Topic 12	Define all the elasticities and focus on price and cross elasticity, since soft drinks may not qualify as an income elastic good. Explain the availability of substitutes as a very significant factor in price elasticity of demand. You may also wish to point out that expenditure on a soft drink is not a major proportion of income. For cross elasticity, demonstrate what would happen if the price of a substitute increased or decreased. Explain how the beverage firm can use the elasticity concept to increase its profits. For example, pricing the soft drink competitively or heavy advertising to make demand more inelastic and create brand loyalty.
Topic 4	Chapter numbers 1, 4, 7, 9 1 Identify the factors of production in the firm, for example, fixed and variable factors. 2 Explain total, marginal and average product with diagrams and use the firm you select to explain these three concepts. Explain the law of diminishing returns. For example, 'the firm has expanded from the short-run to the long- because of an increase in demand for its product'. 3 Briefly describe the cost of the firm: FC + VC = TC and AFC + AVC = ATC and MC = DTC/DQ. 4 Identify these costs in the firm. Explain and demonstrate how the upward sloping marginal cost curve is a result of the short-run diminishing returns. 5 Provide details on internal and external economies and diseconomies of scale that occur in the firm, making sure to draw a LRAC. Remember LRAC could also be saucer shaped.
Elasticity of supply	Explain the four time periods and relate each to the firm, i.e., market or momentary period, short-, long- and very long-run. In the case of our beverage firm the use of IT or automation and mechanisation or opening a branch is an example of the long-run. Module 2 (1, 4, 6, 10, 11). Define market structure and say to what type of market structure the firm belongs. For a beverage company it is likely to be an oligopoly. What barriers to entry exist – high set-up costs and branding?

Topic	Suggestions
Profit concepts	Does the firm earn normal or supernormal profits? Does it profit maximise? Does it use cost-based pricing? Answer these questions based on answers from your questionnaire. Introduce the concept of the concentration ratio and HHI. Is the firm in a concentrated or non-concentrated market structure? Demonstrate how the HHI shows how market share is distributed among the firms. Do a revision of this topic first.
Topic 2	Market failure. You should: 1 Define market failure 2 Give a brief explanation of efficiency criterion 3 List four types of market failure, e.g., market structure, externalities, price discrimination and branding. Choose a market structure such as oligopoly and show how the failure to prevent externalities such as pollution causes market failure. Use a diagram to explain PMC, SMC, PMB and SMB. Module 3 (1, 3, 4, 6, 7) Topic 2 (1, 2, 3, 4) Identify the rewards to the input factors, e.g., wages, interest, profit and rent.
Topic 3	Give a brief outline of MRP theory and show that it is not likely to explain wages in the firm adequately. Explain that at best it may explain demand for labour. Explain also the supply factors of labour, e.g., skill, training, shift work. Emphasise that compensating differentials play a role in high wages, e.g., shift work or safety details on goods vehicles. Emphasise the role of unions. They play a major role in wage determination. Introduce the concept of a minimum wage as a price floor. Explain a price floor. Explain why differences in wages exist in the firm. Give reasons, e.g., seniority, productivity, training and education, ability and experience. Draw an elasticity diagram to illustrate this concept. Why do some workers decline work and extra pay on public holidays? Explain the backward bending supply curve.

Topic	Suggestions
Topic 2	Information asymmetry Explain that if the firm hires a mechanic to repair the company vehicle, this is a case of asymmetric information, but if it hires a tax consultant or an IT repair person, this is a market failure of information between agent and principal.
Moral hazard	This may occur if company-driven cars are carelessly managed by workers because they know the vehicles are insured.
Adverse selection	This is likely to happen with the company's health insurance plan. Revise this concept before you attempt it. Finally, I have only suggested what approach you may adopt if you are unsure of the way to proceed. Always consult your teacher and you will be given helpful suggestions. I have not included a lot of detail in my suggestions because you need to do your part as well. Good luck and Godspeed on your project. If done properly, it should earn between 50 and 55 marks at the very least.

Glossary

Above normal profit profit earned by a firm that is greater than normal profit or (AR > ATC)

Absolute advantage the ability of a country to produce more of a good than another country due to superior productivity

Absolute poverty when citizens of a country live below an accepted minimum level of subsistence

Accelerator principle a theory of investment that links the rate of net investment to the rate and magnitude of changes in national income

Active balances money held for everyday transactions and unplanned events

Adverse selection the lack of information by insurance companies about clients in good or poor health that causes the company to charge a high price to all

Aggregate demand the total planned expenditure in an economy at given levels of prices and incomes. Expressed in formula as C + I + G + X − M

Aggregate supply the total output all firms are willing to supply at a given price level

Allocative efficiency when marginal cost is equal to price or average revenue, indicating that the appropriate quantity of resources is being used in production. Expressed in formula as P = MC

Appreciation when an exchange increases in value against other currencies making exports prices relatively higher and imports relatively lower in price

Asymmetric information when one party has more knowledge and expertise than another in a transaction, e.g., a mechanic is more knowledgeable than his client

Automatic stabilisers specific government spending and taxation that automatically reduces the severity of fluctuations in economic activity and not caused by deliberate government action

Autonomous investment investment not related to changes in level of national income but other factors such as the rate of interest or an increase in business optimism

Average product total output divided by total input, e.g., total output/quantity of labour

Average propensity to consume the proportion of total disposal income that is spent on consumption

Average propensity to save the proportion of total disposal income that is saved

Average revenue total revenue divided by quantity sold also the same as price or demand

Average total cost the cost of producing one unit or when total cost is divided by total output

Balance of payments an annual record of a country's financial inflows and outflows with the rest of the world

Balance of trade the merchandise or visible balance of the balance of payments accounts

Balanced budget when government spending is equal to taxation receipts

Balanced budget multiplier when equal amounts of government spending and taxation increase national income by the exact amount of government spending

Barriers to entry and exit any restriction that prevents easy entry of new firms into a market or the exit of any firm from the market

Barter the exchange of goods among individuals in order to satisfy wants

Bilateral monopoly where a sole buyer interacts with a sole seller

Broad money a measure of the money supply that is not regarded as liquid and that earns interest

Budget the annual financial plan of the government for the management of the economy

Budget deficit when government spending is greater than revenue

Budget line line that shows the combination of two goods that a consumer can purchase with a given income and the prices of the two goods

Budget surplus when government spending is less than revenue

Capital account the section of the balance of payments showing the movement of financial assets between countries

Capital consumption loss of value of capital goods as they become older

Cartel a number of firms who collude in order to fix prices

Change in demand a change in the non-price factors of demand

Circular flow of income the flow of income between consumers and producers in a country

Comparative advantage related to trade when one country can produce at a lower opportunity cost than another

Complements goods that are demanded jointly, e.g., flashlights and batteries

Concentration ratio a measure of the fraction of the sales, output or market share by the largest firms in a market

Consumer surplus the difference between the market price of a good and the price a consumer is willing to pay as reflected by the demand curve

Consumption function the relationship between consumption and the level of income

Contestable market a market with no barriers to entry and entrants waiting to capitalise on profit opportunities

Cost push inflation an increase in the price level due to input cost factors such as increased wages

Credit creation an increase in the money supply when banks issue loans

Credit creation multiplier the number that links bank deposits to the change in the money supply

Cross elasticity of demand the change in demand for a good due to a change in the price of a related good

Current account an annual record of a country's trade in visible goods, services, income and transfers

Debt ratio the public debt as a percentage of GDP

Debt service ratio principal plus interest as a percentage of valued exports

Deflationary gap the amount by which expenditure should be increased to enable the economy to reach full employment through the multiplier effect

Demand pull inflation increases in the general price level due to increases in aggregate demand when the economy is at full employment

Demerit goods any good over consumed out of ignorance and which creates a negative externality

Derived demand when the demand for a factor of production is linked to what the factor can produce, e.g., the demand for a bus driver is linked to the demand for transport

Devaluation the deliberate reduction in the external value of a country's currency by the government

Diminishing marginal utility when satisfaction falls as each additional unit of a good or service is consumed

Diminishing returns when the rate of returns to the variable factors falls as additional variable factors are added to a fixed factor

Discretionary fiscal policy deliberate changes to government spending and taxation to regulate economic activity

Diseconomies of scale the increase in long-run average total costs as a firm increases the scale of production

Disequilibrium unemployment when aggregate supply of labour exceeds aggregate demand at the prevailing wage rate

Division of labour when a main task is broken up into several smaller tasks also known as specialisation

Economic development an improvement in standard of living and quality of life

Economic efficiency the maximum achievable output at the lowest cost

Economic growth an increase in the productive capacity of a country over time

Economic rent the difference in the market price of a good and the supply price of the producer

Economies of scale the reductions in costs due to increasing the scale of production

Effective demand the demand for a good or service supported by the ability to pay for it

Exchange rate the price at which one currency is exchanged for another

External benefits the positive spillover benefits provided to third parties from an economic transaction related to consumption or production

External costs the negative spillover costs imposed on third parties from a transaction between two parties

External debt the public debt owed to foreign creditors

Factor payments the rewards to the factors of production such as wages, interest, rent and profit

Fiscal policy the employment of government spending, transfers, taxation and borrowing to regulate economic activity

Fixed costs these costs are constant and do not change when production changes

Fixed exchange rate this is the rate of exchange set by the monetary authorities and remains unaltered

Fixed factors these are factors of production that are long lasting and that are not altered during production, e.g., a stove in a restaurant

Floating exchange rate this is the rate of exchange determined by changes in demand and supply for a currency

Free ride a benefit enjoyed by a third party without paying for the good or service

Functional distribution of income the distribution of national income among the factors of production

Giffen goods goods that are subject to an extreme negative income effect

Gini coefficient a measurement of income inequality expressed as a decimal or percentage with a range of zero (perfectly equal) to 1 (perfectly unequal)

Globalisation the increased connectivity of the economies of the world

Gross domestic product the annual value of a country's output that arises from economic activity within its land and maritime boundaries

Gross national product the annual value of output that arises from the nationally owned factors of production wherever they are located

Hirfindahl Hirchman Index an index that measures industrial concentration by the addition of market share that is squared

Human development index an index consisting of per capita income, life expectancy and literacy and school enrolment that measures standard of living

Income effect the positive or negative change in demand due to an increase in purchasing power caused by a fall in price

Increasing returns to scale when the percentage change in output exceeds the percentage change in inputs

Indifference curve this shows the combination of two goods with which a consumer is equally satisfied

Inferior good a good with negative income elasticity of demand

Inflation a sustained increase in the average price level over time in an economy

Inflationary gap this measures the amount by which expenditure must be reduced to enable the economy to return to the full employment level of national income

Injections spending in the economy such as investment, government spending and exports excluding household expenditure

Investment a flow of expenditure on capital goods that adds to the capital stock of a country

Keynesian theory a theory that advocates an active role for the government in regulating the demand side of the economy using fiscal policy initiatives

Leakages incomes received in the circular flow of income not returned to the flow in the year of measurement

Liquidity preference theory a Keynesian theory of interest rate determination

Lorenz curve a measure of income inequality

Managed float a rate of exchange that is flexible between a range of maximum and minimum values by intervention buying and selling

Marginal efficiency of capital the expected percentage returns from an investment

Glossary

Marginal propensity to consume the fraction of every increase in income that is spent on consumption

Marginal propensity to import the fraction of every increase in income that is spent on imports

Marginal propensity to save the fraction of every increase in income that is saved

Marginal propensity to tax the fraction of every increase in income that goes to taxes paid

Market failure a failure to achieve efficiency in the allocation of resources

Monetary policy the regulation of the growth of the money supply, the interest and exchange rates to manage the economy

Multiplier a number that links the change in national income to changes in expenditure

Negative externality the negative spillover effect imposed on third parties from an economic transaction between two parties

Non-excludable the inability to exclude others from consuming a good or service because it is collectively consumed, e.g., a public good such as streetlights

Normal good a good with positive income elasticity of demand

Open market operations the purchase of securities from or sales to commercial banks by the central bank to regulate the growth of the money supply

Opportunity cost the sacrifice of the second best alternative when choices are made

Poverty line the minimum requirements that sustain human life

Precautionary motive money demanded for unplanned events

Price ceiling the maximum legal price that a consumer is required to pay

Price discrimination the charging of a different price to different customers for the same good or service where the cost to all is the same

Price floor the minimum legally set price paid to a producer

Productive efficiency when a firm produces at its lowest cost at minimum average cost

Profit maximisation this is called the equilibrium level of output where marginal cost is equal to marginal revenue

Quantity theory $MV = PT$. The monetarist theory that asserts that changes in the money supply (M) cause the price level (P) to rise by the same proportion where V and T are constant

Quota a limit on the quantity of imports into a country that raises prices of the imports

Real effective exchange rate the inflation adjusted exchange rate compared to a basket of other currencies

Relative poverty where persons are living below an average or typical level of consumption

Social costs when external marginal costs are added to private marginal costs to achieve social marginal costs

Speculative motive the demand for money to capitalise on expected profits from the purchase of fixed return bonds

Substitution effect purchasing more of a good whose price has fallen and less of a substitute whose price has not changed

Sustainable growth economic growth achieved without negative consequences for future generations

Tariff a tax on imported goods

Time lag the time lapse between economic action and expected result

Trade creation when low cost domestic producers replace high cost domestic producers

Trade diversion when trade is diverted from low costs outside of a customs union to high costs within the union

Transfer earnings the minimum reward to a factor of production to prevent it from transferring to an alternative use

Unit of account a function of money as a measure of value

Velocity the number of times money changes hands in order to absorb the output of a country

Index

A
Absolute income hypothesis, 169
Absolute poverty, 150, 151
Accelerator principle, of investment, 178–179
  limitations of, 179
Activity rate, labour, 145
Adverse selection, 116, 119–120
  in banking, 117
Aggregate demand, 23
  discretionary fiscal policy, 191
Aggregate demand/aggregate supply (AS/AD) model, 227–228
Aggregate expenditure/aggregate monetary demand, 169
Allocative efficiency, 110–111
  and consumer surplus, 111
  and Pareto optimality, 112
APC. See Average propensity to consume (APC)
APP. See Average physical product (APP)
APS. See Average propensity to save (APS)
AR. See Average revenue (AR)
AS/AD model. See Aggregate demand/aggregate supply (AS/AD) model
Assets
  financial, 201
  physical, 201
Assumptions, 18
Asymmetric information, 116
ATC. See Average total cost (ATC)
Automatic fiscal policy, 190
Autonomous investment, 175
Average/midpoint price elasticity of demand, 38
Average physical product (APP), 47–48
Average propensity to consume (APC), 170
Average propensity to save (APS), 172
Average revenue (AR), 80, 81
Average total cost (ATC), 68–69

B
Backward bending supply curve, 130–131
Balanced budget multiplier, 184–185
Balance of payments, 191–192, 261–266
  capital account, 262–263
  current account, 261–262, 264–265
  flexible/freely floating exchange rate and, 255
  overall, 263–266
Balance sheet, of commercial banks, 201
Balancing item, 263
Banks/banking
  adverse selection in, 117
  commercial (See Commercial banks)
  deposits, 200
  multiplier, 200–201
Barometric price leader, 102

Benefits
  cash, 150–151
  in kind, 151
  means-tested, 151
  monetary values to, 180
  of trade diversion, 247–248
Budget line, 28–30
  shifts of, 28
Business optimism, 176

C
Capital, 6, 176. See also Investments
  fixed, 263
  official flows, 263
  physical/human, 175
  short-term flows, 263
Capital expenditure, 194
Cardinalist theory of demand, 23–25
  utility, 24–25
Caribbean
  problems of development in, 281–282
CARIFTA (Caribbean free trade area), 248
Cartel, 102
Cash benefits, 150–151
CED. See Cross elasticity of demand (CED)
Ceiling, prices, 63, 150
Central banks
  functions of, 204
Ceteris paribus assumptions, 18, 25, 26, 29, 34
Claimant count, 221
Classical economic ideas, 227
  long-run aggregate supply curve, 229
  supply-side measures, 230–233
Classical unemployment, 222
Closed economy, 6. See also Three-sector economy
Collectivist economy system. See Planned economy system
Collusion, as model behaviour, 101
Command economy system. See Planned economy system
Commercial banks
  balance sheet of, 201
  functions of, 204
  and money creation, 200
Commodity money, 200
Common market, 246
  costs and benefits of, 248
Company voluntary agreements (CVA), 124
Concentration ratio, 107
Conditions, of supply, 52
  change in, 60
  price and, 61
Constant, 19
Constant returns to scale, 49
constraint. See budget line
Consumer equilibrium, 26, 29
Consumer surplus, 26–27, 62–63
  allocative efficiency and, 111
Consumption, 169, 228
  factors influencing, 170

fixed/autonomous, 169, 170
induced, 169, 170
life-cycle hypothesis, 171
permanent income hypothesis, 171
relative income hypothesis, 171
Contestable markets, 103–104
characteristics, 103
evaluation of, 104
Corporate code conduct, 124
Corporate ethics, 124
Corporation taxes, 176, 177
Cost benefit analysis, 179
problems associated with, 180
Cost of capital, 177
Cost-push inflation, 214
measures to curb, 217–218
Costs
explicit, 67
fixed, 67
indirect, 67
marginal, 69–70
opportunity, 7, 67
of poverty, 150
production, 67–73
short-run, 69–73
sunk, 67
total, 68
of trade diversion, 247–248
Costs
of monopoly, 97
Counter-inflation policy, 216–217
Credit cards, money and, 200
Cross elasticity of demand (CED), 41–42
independent goods, 42
value, to firm, 42
Cuba, 14
Currency
devaluation, 265–266
foreign (See Foreign currency)
Current account, 261–262
balance, 262
deficit, 264
surplus, 264
Current expenditure, 194
Customs union, 246
costs and benefits of, 248
CVA. See Company voluntary agreements (CVA)
Cycle of poverty, 281

D

Deadweight loss, 111
Debt for equity swap, 194
Debt interest, 194
Debt ratio, 193
Debt refinancing, 194
Debt rescheduling, 194
Debt restructuring, 194
Debt retirement, 194
Debt trap, 193
Debt write-off, 194

Decision making
in economic system, 12
YED value and, 44
Deductive reasoning, 18
Deflationary fiscal policy, and inflation, 217
Deflationary gaps, 185–186, 222
Demand
aggregate, 23
cardinalist approach to, 24–25
change in, 33–34, 60–61
defined, 23
derived, 23, 126
elasticity (See Elasticity of demand)
for foreign currency, 252–253
international, shifts in, 242
joint, 23
for money, 201
non-price factors and, 23
optimal purchase rule/law of equi-marginal returns, 25–27
price factors and, 23
rate of interest and, 203–204
Demand curves
for Giffen goods, 32
individual, 34
for inferior goods, 32
market, 34
movement along, 32–33
Demand-pull inflation, 213–214
Demand theory
budget line/constraint, 28–30
cardinalist, 23–25
income/substitution effect (See Income/substitution effect)
optimal purchase rule/law of equi-marginal returns, 25–27
ordinalist, 27–28
Demerit goods, 113
Depreciation, 175
Deregulation, 122
Derived demand, 23, 126
Devaluation, currency, 265–266
Direct capital. See Fixed capital
Direct tax, 195, 196
Discretionary fiscal policy, 190
and aggregate demand, 191
and balance of payments, 191–192
and economic growth, 191
and inflation, 191
limitations of, 192
and unemployment, 191
Diseconomies of scale (DOS)
internal, 73
Disequilibrium, 165–166
Distribution, of income, 126–132, 148–151
size, 148
Diversification, and economic development, 282
Domestic prices, 242
Domestic production, 242
Dominant price leader, 102

DOS. *See* Diseconomies of scale (DOS)
Dynamic efficiency, 112

E

Economic aid, and development, 282
Economically active population, 145
Economic analysis, tools of, 17–21
   assumptions, 18
   constant, 19
   gradient/slope of functions, 19–20
   linear function, 18–19
   model, 18
   non-linear function, 19
   positive/normative statement, 21
   scatter diagram, 20
   variables (*See* Variables)
   vertical intercept, 20
Economic development, 280–283
   classification of, 280–281
   criticism of, 282–283
   strategies for, 282
Economic dualism, 271
Economic efficiency. *See also* specific types
   allocative efficiency (*See* Allocative efficiency)
   equity and, 120–121
   and Pareto optimality, 111–112
   and perfect competition, 112
   productive efficiency, 110
Economic growth, 274–278
   defined, 274
   desirability, 277
   endogenous, 278
   exogenous, 278
   long-run potential growth, 275–278
   short-term actual growth, 274–275
   unbalanced, 277–278
Economic integration, 246–248
Economic problem, 6. *See also* Scarcity, resources
   solution to, planned economic system and, 15
Economic rent, 137, 138
   and elasticity of supply, 138
Economic system
   decision making in, 12
   defined, 12
   evaluation of, 12
   free market system/market economy, 13–14
   issues addressed by, 12
   mixed economy, 15–16
   planned/collectivist/command economy system, 14–15
   selection of, 12
   success of, 12
Economic union, 246
   costs and benefits of, 248
Economies of scale, 72, 176
   external, 73
   internal, 73

Economy
   defined, 6
   market, 13–14
   subsistence, 12
Effective exchange rate, 258–259
Efficiency. *See* Economic efficiency
Elasticity of demand, 37–44
   cross, 41–42
   defined, 37
   income (*See* Income elasticity of demand (YED))
   price (*See* Price elasticity of demand (PED))
Elasticity of supply
   of labour, 132
   price, 138
   transfer earnings/economic rent and, 138
EMB. *See* External marginal benefit (EMB)
EMC. *See* External marginal cost (EMC)
Endogenous growth, 278
Endogenous variable, 19
Engel curve, 43
Enterprise, 6
Equilibrium, 166
   consumer, 26, 29
   defined, 24
   exchange rates, 253
   long-run, 94
   market, 59–65
   national income, 182–187
   short-run, 93–94
   three-sector, 166–167
Equity, and economic efficiency, 120–121
Exchange rates, 242, 252–259. *See also* Foreign exchange
   defined, 252
   determination, 252
   effective, 258–259
   equilibrium, 253
   fixed, 256–257
   flexible/freely floating, 254–256
   managed, 257–259
   nominal, 258
   purchasing power parity, 258
   real, 258
Exit conditions. *See* Shut-down/exit conditions
Exogenous growth, 278
Exogenous variable, 19
Expenditure method
   and national income calculation, 159
   notes on, 159
Explicit costs, 67
Exports, 208, 237
   revenue, 242
Externalities, and market failure, 114–117
   negative, 115–116
   positive, 116
External marginal benefit (EMB), 114
External marginal cost (EMC), 114
Extremes, in price elasticity of demand
   perfect elasticity, 39–40
   zero elasticity, 39

Index

F
Factors of production, 6. See also specific factors
FDI. See Foreign direct investment (FDI)
Fiat money, 200
Financial assets, 201
First degree price discrimination, 94
Fiscal policy, 189–197
    aims of, 190–191
    automatic, 190
    discretionary (See Discretionary fiscal policy)
    Keynesian, 189–193
    Monetarist, 189
    national debt, 193–194
    potency of, 192
    time lags, 192–193
Fisher theory of exchange, 215
Fixed capital, 263
Fixed costs, 67
Fixed exchange rate, 256–257
    advantages, 256
    disadvantages, 256–257
    overvalued currency, 257
    undervalued currency, 257
Fixed factor, of production, 46
Flexible/freely floating exchange rate, 254–256
    advantages of, 255
    and balance of payments, 255
    disadvantages of, 255
    and inflation, 256
Foreign currency
    demand for, 252–253
    factors affecting, 253–254
    investment in, 204
Foreign direct investment (FDI), 269–272, 283
    benefits of, 269–271
    defined, 269
    disadvantages of, 271
    historical context, 269
Foreign exchange. See also Exchange rates
    equilibrium, 253
    supply of, 253
Free market system, 13–14
    equilibrium in, 59
    evaluation of, 14
    features of, 13
    weaknesses in, 13
Free trade area, 246
Frictional unemployment, 223–224
Functions
    constant, 19
    gradient/slope of, 19–20
    linear, 18–19
    non-linear, 19
    production, 46

G
GATT. See General Agreement on Tariffs and Trade (GATT)
GDP. See Gross domestic product (GDP)
GDP deflator, 161
General Agreement on Tariffs and Trade (GATT), 246
Giffen goods
    demand curves for, 32
    income/substitution effect of price change/fall for, 31
Gini coefficient, 148, 149
Globalisation, 285–286
    defined, 285
    negative aspects of, 286
GNP. See Gross national product (GNP)
Goods
    demerit, 113
    direct provision of, 150
    Giffen, income/substitution effect of price change/fall for, 31
    independent, 42
    inferior, income/substitution effect for, 31
    merit, 113
    normal, income/substitution effect of price change/fall for, 30–31
    private, 113
    public, 113, 119
Government
    expenditure, 190, 194–195, 207 (See also specific expenditures)
    incentives, 176, 177
    intervention in free market, 119
    market failures and, 119–120
    regulation of monopoly, 119
    revenues, sources of, 197
Gradient, of function, 19–20
Gross domestic product (GDP), 157, 160
    gaps, 186–187
    nominal, 160–161
    real, 161
Gross investment, 175
Gross national product (GNP), 157

H
Herfindahl-Hirschman Index (HHI), 107
HHI. See Herfindahl-Hirschman Index (HHI)
High population growth rates, 280
Human capital, 175
Human Development Index (HDI), 151, 160

I
IDA. See International Development Association (IDA)
IFC. See International Finance Corporation (IFC)
IMF. See International Monetary Fund (IMF)
Imperfect competition, 77–78
Imports, 237
    gains and losses through, 241–242
Incentives, 61
    government, 176, 177
Income
    distribution of, 126–132, 148–151
    inequality, factors causing, 149
    inequality, measures to reduce, 150

international, level of, 243
national (See National income)
permanent, 171
real, 254
Income elasticity of demand (YED), 42–44
  factors affecting, 43
  formula for, 42
  value and decision making, 44
Income/substitution effect, 30–34
  for inferior goods, 31
  of price change/fall (for Giffen good), 31
  of price change/fall (for normal good), 30–31
Independent goods, 42
Independent variable. See Exogenous variable
Indifference curve theory, 27–28
  combinations of, 27
  defined, 27
  limitations of, 32
  and marginal rate of substitution, 27
Indifference map, 28
Indirect costs, 67
Indirect tax, 64, 195
Individual demand curve, 34
Individual supply curve, 130
Induced Investment, 175
Inductive reasoning, 18
Industrialisation, and economic development, 282
Inferior goods
  demand curves for, 32
  income/substitution effect for, 31
Inflation, 213–219
  consequences of, 215–218
  cost-push, 214
  counter-inflation policy, 216–217
  defined, 213
  deflationary fiscal policy, 217
  demand-pull, 213–214
  discretionary fiscal policy and, 191
  external effects of, 216
  flexible exchange rate, 256
  internal effects of, 215–216
  monetarist theories, 214–215
  rate of, 213, 254
  retail price index, 218–219
  runaway, 213
  stagflation, 219
  unemployment and, 224
Inflationary gaps, 185–186
Interdependence, as model behaviour, 101
Interest, determination of, 143
International activity, 242
International Bank for Reconstruction and Development (IBRD). See World Bank
International demand, shifts in, 242
International Development Association (IDA), 290
International Finance Corporation (IFC), 290
International financial institutions, 288–291
  IMF, 288–289
  World Bank, 290
  WTO, 290–291

International incomes, 243
International Monetary Fund (IMF), 288–289
  additional lending by, 289
  conditionalities, 289
  functions of, 289
  international liquidity provisions, 289
  lending policies, criticisms of, 289
  operations of, 289
International trade, 237–249, 261
  absolute advantage, 238–239
  comparative advantage, 238, 239–241
  defined, 237
  gains and loss from, 241
  gains from, 238
  protectionism, 243–246
  reason for, 237
  and small open economies, 237
  terms of, 243
International unemployment, 222–223
Investment income account, 261
Investments, 175–180, 207, 228. See also Capital
  accelerator principle, 178–179
  autonomous, 175
  and capital accumulation, 276
  categories of, 175–176
  defined, 175
  in foreign currency, 204
  gross, 175
  induced, 175
  levels of, factors determine, 176
  net, 175
  planned, 175
  public, 179
  unplanned, 175
  volatility of, 179

J
Joint demand, 23

K
Keynesian cross model, 164–165, 182–187
  deflationary gaps, 185–186
  inflationary gaps, 185–186
  multiplier (See Multiplier (k))
  three-sector, 182–183
Keynesian fiscal policy, 189–193
Keynesian transmission mechanisms, 208
Keynes's economic ideas, 227, 233–234
  long-run aggregate supply curve, 229–230

L
Labour, 6
  cheap, 244
  demand for (See Derived demand)
  elasticity of supply, 132
  immobility, 120
  imperfect market, MRP and, 129
  Keynes's explanation of, 233
  long-run demand curve, 128–129

participation rate of, 145
PED for, 129–130
supply curve of, 131–132
supply of, 130–132
unions (See Unions)
Labour force, 145–146
Land, 6, 144–145
Law of constant opportunity costs, 9
Law of diminishing returns (LDMR)
assumptions of, 48
Law of equi-marginal returns. See Optimal purchase rule
LDMR. See Law of diminishing returns (LDMR)
Life-cycle hypothesis, 171
Linear function, 18–19
Linear PPF, 9
Line of perfect equality (LOPE), 148
Liquidity, money and, 199
Liquidity assets ratio, 201
Liquidity preference theory, 202–203
Loanable funds, 143
market for, 233
Long-run average cost (LRAC), 71
returns to scale and, 72
Long-run equilibrium, 94
Long run law of returns to scale, 49
Long-run period of production, 46, 49
Long-run potential growth, 275–278
sources of, 275–276
Long-run supply curve (LRS), 90–91
LOPE. See Line of perfect equality (LOPE)
Lorenz curves, 148
Loss, 86
LRAC. See Long-run average cost (LRAC)
LRS. See Long-run supply curve (LRS)
Lump-sum tax, 96

M

Macroeconomics, 154
circular flow diagram, 154
long-run in, 187
objectives, 154–155
short-run in, 187
variables, 154, 155
Managed exchange rates, 257–259
Management by objectives, 105
Managerial utility, 105
Manufactured resources, 6
Marginal cost, 69–70
Marginal efficiency of capital (MEC), 143, 176–177
criticisms of, 177–178
Marginal efficiency of investment, 176–177
Marginalist approach
strengths and weaknesses of, 104–106
Marginal physical product (MPP), 47–48
Marginal physical product of labour (MPPL), 127
Marginal propensity to consume (MPC), 169, 170
Marginal propensity to save (MPS), 171, 172

Marginal rate of substitution (MRS)
defined, 27
indifference curve and, 27
Marginal revenue (MR), 80, 81
Marginal revenue product (MRP), 127–128
assumptions of, 127
and imperfect labour market, 129
Marginal utility (MU), 24–25
Market demand curve, 34
Market economy
evaluation of, 13
Market equilibrium, 59–65
consumer/producer surplus, 62–63
effects of taxes and subsidies on, 64
price control, 63–65
price mechanism, 61–62
Market failure
causes of, 113–117, 123
externalities, 114–117
and government measures, 119–120
private sector intervention in correction of, 124
state intervention to correct, 121–124
Market period of production. See Momentary period of production
Market structure
comaprison of, 103
factors to determine, 76
imperfect, 113
imperfect competition, 77–78
market concentration and, 107
monopoly, 77
oligopoly, 78
perfect/pure competition, 76–77
and revenue (See Revenue)
Market system
role in mixed economy, 16
Marshall–Lerner principle, 265, 266
Maximum value, variables, 20
Measure of Economic Welfare (MEW), 151, 160, 280
MEC. See Marginal efficiency of capital (MEC)
Medium of exchange, money as, 199
Merchandise account, 261
Merit goods, 113
MEW. See Measure of Economic Welfare (MEW)
Microeconomics, 154
short-run in, 187
Minimum value, variables, 20
Mixed economy, 15–16
role of market system/state system in, 16
MNC. See Multinational corporation (MNC)
Model
behaviour of, 101
defined, 18
Momentary period of production, 46
Monetarist fiscal policy, 189
aims of, 191
Monetarist transmission mechanism, 208
Monetary policy, 207–210
exports, 208
government expenditure, 207

instruments of, 208–210
investment, 207
Keynesian transmission mechanisms, 208
lags associated with, 209
monetarist transmission mechanism, 208
potency of, 209–210
targets of, 209
Monetary strategy, 209
Monetary validation, 215
Money
characteristics of, 199
creation, commercial banks and, 200
and credit cards, 200
demand for, 201
functions of, 199
Keynesian view of demand for, 202–204
and liquidity, 199
precautionary demand for, 202
supply, factors affecting, 201
transaction demand for, 202
types of, 199–200 (See also specific types)
Monopolistic competition, 77–78, 98–99
long-run equilibrium, 94
short-run equilibrium, 93–94
Monopoly
benefits and costs of, 97
characteristics, 77
evaluation, 97–98
forms of, 77
government regulation of, 119
marginal revenue in, 82
profit maximisation for, 85
regulation of, 96–97
total revenue in, 81–83
vs. perfect competition, 93, 97–98
Monopoly by merger, 77
Moral hazard, 116, 119–120
MPC. See Marginal propensity to consume (MPC)
MPP. See Marginal physical product (MPP)
MPPL. See Marginal physical product of labour (MPPL)
MPS. See Marginal propensity to save (MPS)
MR. See Marginal revenue (MR)
MRP. See Marginal revenue product (MRP)
MRS. See Marginal rate of substitution (MRS)
MU. See Marginal utility (MU)
Multinational corporation (MNC)
advantages of producing in foreign country, 106–107
effects on host countries, 107
features of, 106
Multiplier (k), 183–184
balanced budget, 184–185

N
National debt, 193–194
burden of, 193–194
government expenditure, 194–195
managing, 194
National income, 157–161
determination, 164–167
equilibrium, 182–187
expenditure method of calculating, 159
income method of calculating, 158
international comparisons, 160
measurement, notes on, 159–160
statistics, 160
Natural monopoly, 77, 96
Natural rate of unemployment (NRU), 224
Natural resources, 6
Net investment, 175
Nominal exchange rate, 258
Nominal GDP, 160–161
Non-linear function, 19
Non-price competition, as model behaviour, 101
Non-price factors
and demand, 23
and supply, 52
Normal goods
income/substitution effect of price change/fall for, 30–31
Normative statement, 21
NRU. See Natural rate of unemployment (NRU)

O
Oligopoly, 78, 101
advantages and disadvantages of, 102–103
barometric price leader, 102
cartel, 102
dominant price leader, 102
evaluation, 102–103
features of, 101
Sweezy model, 101–102
Open economy, 6
Opportunity cost, 7
Opportunity costs, 67
Optimal purchase rule, 25–27
Ordinalist theory of demand, 27–28
Output/GDP gaps, 186–187
Output method, 159
Overhead, 67
Overvalued currency, 257

P
Pareto optimality, 9
efficiency and, 111–112
Participation rate, labour, 145
PED. See Price elasticity of demand (PED)
Per capita income, 160
Perfect elasticity, 39–40
Perfect/pure competition, 76–77, 87–91
efficiency and, 112
long-run equilibrium of, 88–89
monopoly vs., 93, 97–98
Periods, of production, 46–47. See also specific periods
Permanent income, 171
Permanent income hypothesis, 171
PES. See Price elasticity of supply (PES)
Physical assets, 201
Physical capital, 175
Physical Quality of Life Index (PQLI), 280

Planned economy system, 14–15
    evaluation of, 15
    features of, 14
    positive and negative aspects of, 15
Planned investment, 175
    factors influencing, 177–178
PMB. See Private marginal benefit (PMB)
PMC. See Private marginal cost (PMC)
Point price elasticity of demand, 40–41
Poor infrastructural development, 281
Positive statement, 21
Poverty, 150
    absolute, 150, 151
    costs of, 150
    cycle of, 281
    measurement, 151
    relative, 150
PPF. See Production possibility frontier (PPF)
PQLI. See Physical Quality of Life Index (PQLI)
Precautionary demand, for money, 202
Price
    ceiling, 63, 150
    and conditions of supply, 61
    control, 63–65, 120
    equilibrium, rise in, 59
    fall in, 60
    stability/rigidity, as model behaviour, 101
    supply and, 52
Price consumption curve, 30
Price discrimination, 94–95
    advantages and disadvantages, 95
    first degree, 94
    second degree, 94–95
    third degree, 95
Price elasticity of demand (PED), 37–41, 82–83
    average/midpoint, 38
    cross (See Cross elasticity of demand (CED))
    extremes in, 39–40
    factors affecting, 40
    formula to measure, 37–38
    for labour, 129–130
    PES and, 54
    point, changing values of, 40–41
    total revenue method to estimate, 38–39, 40
    usefulness of, 41
Price elasticity of supply, 138
Price elasticity of supply (PES), 54–56
    determinants of, 55–56
    determining other than by formula, 54–55
    PED and, 54
    spare capacity, 55
    uses of, 56
Price equilibrium
    effect of subsidy on, 64
Price factors
    and demand, 23
    and supply, 52
Price floor, 63, 150
Price mechanism, 61–62
    functions of, 61
Price system, 7

Private efficiency, 112
Private goods, 113
Private marginal benefit (PMB), 114
Private marginal cost (PMC), 114
Private sector
    intervention in correction of market failure, 124
Privatisation, 121
Producer surplus. See Consumer surplus
Production
    cost of, 67–73
    defined, 46
    factors, comparison of, 145
    fixed factor of, 46
    function, 46
    periods of, 46–47
    stages of, 48
    unit of, 46
    variable factor of, 46
Production possibility curve. See Production possibility frontier (PPF)
Production possibility frontier (PPF)
    concave shape of, 8
    convex shape of, 8–9
    drawing, assumptions while, 7
    linear, 9
    and opportunity cost, 7–9
    points within and outside, 9
Productive efficiency, 110
Profit, 143–144. See also Revenue
    determination of, 76, 86
    functions of, 144
    level of, 176, 177
    normal, 86
    in short-run, 86–87, 88
Profit maximisation, 83–86, 104–105
    for monopoly, 85
    in perfectly competitive firm, 83–84
Progressive tax, 190, 196
Proportional tax, 196
Protectionism, 243–246
PSDR. See Public sector debt repayment (PSDR)
PSIP. See Public sector investment programme (PSIP)
PSNCR. See Public Sector Net Cash Requirement (PSNCR)
Public goods, 113, 119
Public investment, 179
Public sector debt repayment (PSDR), 193
Public sector investment programme (PSIP), 194
Public Sector Net Cash Requirement (PSNCR), 193
Purchasing power parity (PPP) exchange rates, 258
Pure competition. See Perfect/pure competition

Q
Quotas, 245

R
Rate of interest, 176, 203–204
Rationing, price mechanism and, 61
Real exchange rates, 258
Real GDP, 161

Real income, 254
Reasoning, 18. See also specific types
Regional trade, in Caribbean, 248–249
Regional unemployment, 222
Regressive tax, 196
Relative income hypothesis, 171
Relative poverty, 150
Research projects
    benefits, 293–294
    guidelines, 294–296
Resource allocation, 61
Retail price index, 213, 218–219
Revenue
    average, 80
    and elasticity, 82–83
    exports, 242
    government, sources of, 197
    marginal, 80, 81
    total, 80
Rewards, 61
Runaway inflation, 213

S

Sales maximisation, 105
Savings, 171–173
    defined, 171
    factors influencing, 173
Say's law of markets, 233
Scarcity, resources, 6–7
Scatter diagram, 20
Seasonal unemployment, 223
Second degree price discrimination, 94–95
Services account, 262
Short-run costs, 69–73
Short-run equilibrium, 93–94
Short-run period of production, 46, 47–48
    increasing returns in, 48
Short-run supply curve, 89–90
Shut-down/exit conditions, 89
Size distribution of income, 148
    Gini coefficient, 148, 149
    Lorenz curves, 148
Slope, of function. See Gradient, of function
Small open economies
    international trade and, 237
Social efficiency, 112
Social responsibility, 124
Stabilisation policy. See Automatic fiscal policy
Stagflation, 219
Standard of living, 160
State system
    role in mixed economy, 16
Static efficiency, 112
Structural unemployment, 222–223
Subsidies, 150, 245
    effects on monopoly, 96–97
    and market equilibrium, 64
    and price equilibrium, 64
Subsistence economy, 12

Substitution effect. See Income/substitution effect
Substitution effect of wages, 130
Sunk costs, 67
Supply
    change in, 53, 60–61
    conditions of, 52, 60, 61
    curve (See Supply curve)
    defined, 52
    factors affecting, 52
    of foreign exchange, 253
    of labour, 130–132
    money, factors affecting, 201
    and price, 52
    price elasticity (See Price elasticity of supply (PES))
Supply curve, 52
    backward bending, 130–131
    horizontal addition of, 54
    individual, 130
    of labour, 131–132
    movements along, 52–53
    shifting, 53
    short-run, 89–90
Supply-side measures, 230–233
Sweezy model, oligopolistic behaviour, 101–102

T

Tariffs, 245
Taxes, 195–197
    aims of, 195
    corporation, 176, 177
    defined, 195
    direct, 195, 196
    effects of, 196–197
    effects on market equilibrium, 64
    effects on monopoly, 96
    indirect, 64, 195
    lump-sum, 96
    progressive, 190, 196
    proportional, 196
    qualities of, 195–196
    regressive, 196
Technological dualism, 278
Technological unemployment, 222
TFC. See Total fixed cost curve (TFC)
Third degree price discrimination, 95
Three-sector economy, 166–167
Three-sector Keynesian cross model, 182–183
Time lags, 216–217
    fiscal policy, 192–193
    monetary policy, 209
Top-down reasoning, 18
Total costs, production, 68
    average, 68–69
Total fixed cost curve (TFC), 68
Total investment. See Gross investment
Total physical product (TPP), 47–48
Total revenue (TR), 80, 81
    in monopoly market structure, 81–83
    for price elasticity of demand estimation, 38–39, 40
Total utility (TU), 24–25

Total variable cost curve (TVC), 67, 68
Tourism, and economic development, 282
TPP. See Total physical product (TPP)
TR. See Total revenue (TR)
Trade diversion, 247
  costs and benefits of, 247–248
Trade liberalisation, 231, 238
Trade-weighted index, 258
Transaction demand, for money, 202
Transfer earnings
  and economic rent, 137–138
Transfer payments, 194
Transmission mechanisms, 207
TU. See Total utility (TU)
TVC. See Total variable cost curve (TVC)

U

Underemployment, 225
Undervalued currency, 257
Unemployment, 221–225
  claimant count, 221
  classical, 222
  consequences of, 224–225
  defined, 221
  discretionary fiscal policy and, 191
  frictional, 223–224
  and inflation, 224
  international, 222–223
  Keynesian/demand-deficit/cyclical, 221–222
  Keynes's explanation of, 233
  natural rate of, 224
  regional, 222
  seasonal, 223
  structural, 222–223
  technological, 222
  types of, 221
  underemployment, 225
Unions, 136–137
  customs, 246
  economic, 246
  in imperfect labour market, 137
Unitary elasticity, 39
Unit of account, 199
Unit of management, 46
Unit of production, 46
Unplanned investment, 175

Unskilled labour force, 281
Utility
  marginal, 24–25
  total, 24–25

V

Value of marginal product (VMP), 127
Variable factor, of pzroduction, 46
Variables
  defined, 18
  endogenous, 19
  exogenous, 19
  functional relationship, 18
  macroeconomics, 154, 155
  maximum/minimum value of, 20
VER. See Voluntary export restraint (VER)
Vertical intercept, 20
Very long-run period of production, 46
VMP. See Value of marginal product (VMP)
Voluntary export restraint (VER), 245

W

Wages
  determination of, 135–136
  differentials, 139–141
  minimum, 140–141
  substitution effect of, 130
  traditional economic theory, 127
Welfare equity, 151
Welfare maximisation, 106
World Bank
  IDA, 290
  IFC, 290
  organisation of, 290
World Trade Organization (WTO), 290–291
WTO. See World Trade Organization (WTO)

Y

YED. See Income elasticity of demand (YED)

Z

Zero elasticity, 39
Zero income-elastic response, 43